# Solutions Manual, Volume 2, Chapters 13-21

## to accompany

# Intermediate Accounting

### Fourth Edition

J. David Spiceland
*University of Memphis*

James F. Sepe
*Santa Clara University*

Lawrence A. Tomassini
*The Ohio State University*

Prepared by
J. David Spiceland
James F. Sepe

 **McGraw-Hill
Irwin**

Boston   Burr Ridge, IL   Dubuque, IA   Madison, WI   New York   San Francisco   St. Louis
Bangkok   Bogotá   Caracas   Kuala Lumpur   Lisbon   London   Madrid   Mexico City
Milan   Montreal   New Delhi   Santiago   Seoul   Singapore   Sydney   Taipei   Toronto

**McGraw-Hill Irwin**

Solutions Manual, Volume 2, Chapters 13-21 to accompany
INTERMEDIATE ACCOUNTING
J. David Spiceland, James F. Sepe, and Lawrence A. Tomassini

Published by McGraw-Hill/Irwin, an imprint of The McGraw-Hill Companies, Inc., 1221 Avenue of the Americas, New York, NY 10020. Copyright © 2007 by The McGraw-Hill Companies, Inc. All rights reserved.

1 2 3 4 5 6 7 8 9 0 QSR/QSR 0 9 8 7 6 5

10-ISBN 0-07-313046-X
13-ISBN 978-007-313046-0

www.mhhe.com

# Table of Contents

# Chapter 13  Current Liabilities and Contingencies

## QUESTIONS FOR REVIEW OF KEY TOPICS

### Question 13-1

A liability entails the present, the future, and the past.  It is a present responsibility, to sacrifice assets in the future, caused by a transaction or other event that already has happened.  Specifically, "Elements of Financial Statements," Statement of Financial Accounting Concepts No. 6, par. 36, describes three essential characteristics:  Liabilities–

1. are *probable, future* sacrifices of economic benefits
2. that arise from *present* obligations (to transfer goods or provide services) to other entities
3. that result from *past* transactions or events.

### Question 13-2

Liabilities traditionally are classified as either *current* liabilities or *long-term* liabilities in a classified balance sheet.  Current liabilities are those expected to be satisfied with *current assets* or by the creation of other *current liabilities* (Committee on Accounting Procedure, American Institute of CPAs, *Accounting Research and Terminology Bulletin, Final Edition*, p. 21).  Usually, but with exceptions, current liabilities are obligations payable within one year or within the firm's operating cycle, whichever is longer.

### Question 13-3

In concept, liabilities should be reported at their *present values*; that is, the valuation amount is the present value of all future cash payments resulting from the debt, usually principal and/or interest payments.  In this case, the amount would be determined as the present value of $100,000, discounted for three months at an appropriate rate of interest for a debt of this type.

This is proper because of the time value of money.  In practice, liabilities ordinarily are reported at their *maturity amounts if* payable within one year because the relatively short time period makes the interest or time value component immaterial. *Accounting Principles Board Opinion No 21*, "Interest on Receivables and Payables," specifically exempts from present value valuation all liabilities arising in connection with suppliers in the normal course of business and due within a year.

## Answers to Questions *(continued)*

## Question 13-4

Lines of credit permit a company to borrow cash from a bank up to a prearranged limit at a predetermined, usually floating, rate of interest. The interest rate often is based on current rates of the prime London interbank borrowing, certificates of deposit, bankers' acceptance, or other standard rates. Lines of credit usually must be available to support the issuance of commercial paper.

Lines of credit can be noncommitted or committed. A *noncommitted* line of credit allows the company to borrow without having to follow formal loan procedures and paperwork at the time of the loan and is less formal, usually without a commitment fee. Sometimes a compensating balance is required to be on deposit with the bank as compensation for the service. A *committed* line of credit is more formal. It usually requires a commitment fee in the neighborhood of $1/4$ of one percent of the unused balance during the availability period. Sometimes compensating balances also are required.

## Question 13-5

When interest is "discounted" from the face amount of a note at the time it is written, it usually is referred to as a "noninterest-bearing" note. They do, of course entail interest, but the interest is deducted (or discounted) from the face amount to determine the cash proceeds made available to the borrower at the outset and included in the amount paid at maturity. In fact, the effective interest rate is higher than the stated discount rate because the discount rate is applied to the face value, but the cash borrowed is less than the face value.

## Question 13-6

Commercial paper represents loans from other corporations. It refers to unsecured notes sold in minimum denominations of $25,000 with maturities ranging from 30 to 270 days. The firm would be required to file a registration statement with the SEC if the maturity is beyond 270 days. The name "commercial paper" implies that a paper certificate is issued to the lender to represent the obligation. But, increasingly, no paper is created because the entire transaction is computerized. Recording the issuance and payment of commercial paper is the same as for notes payable.

The interest rate usually is lower than in a bank loan because commercial paper (a) typically is issued by large, sound companies (b) directly to the lender, and (c) normally is backed by a line of credit with a bank.

## Question 13-7

This is an example of an *accrued expense* – an expense incurred during the current period, but not yet paid. The expense and related liability should be recorded as follows:

| | | |
|---|---|---|
| Salaries expense | 5,000 | |
| Salaries payable | | 5,000 |

This achieves a proper matching of this expense with the revenues it helps generate.

# Question 13-8

An employer should accrue an expense and the related liability for employees' compensation for future absences, like vacation pay, if the obligation meets each of four conditions: (1) the obligation is attributable to employees' services *already performed*, (2) the paid absence can be taken in a later year – the benefit vests (will be compensated even if employment is terminated) or the benefit can be accumulated over time, (3) the payment is *probable*, and (4) the amount can be reasonably *estimated*.

Customary practice should be considered when deciding whether an obligation exists. For instance, whether the rights to paid absences have been earned by services already rendered sometimes depends on customary policy for the absence in question. An example is whether compensation for upcoming sabbatical leave should be accrued. Is it granted only to perform research beneficial to the employer? Or, is it customary that sabbatical leave is intended to provide unrestrained compensation for past service.

Similar concerns also influence whether unused rights to the paid absences can be carried forward or expire. Although holiday time, military leave, maternity leave, and jury time typically do not accumulate if unused, if it is customary practice that one can be carried forward, a liability is accrued if it's probable employees will be compensated in a future year. Similarly, *sick pay* is specifically excluded by SFAS 43 from mandatory accrual because future absence depends on future illness, which usually is not a certainty. But, if company policy or custom is that employees are paid "sick pay" even when their absence is not due to illness, a liability for unused sick pay should be recorded.

# Question 13-9

When a company collects cash from a customer as a refundable deposit or as an advance payment for products or services, a liability is created obligating the firm to return the deposit or to supply the products or services. When the amount is to be returned to the customer in cash, it is a refundable deposit. When the amount will be applied to the purchase price when goods are delivered or services provided (gift certificates, magazine subscriptions, layaway deposits, special order deposits, and airline tickets) it is a customer advance.

# Question 13-10

Examples of amounts collected for third parties that represent liabilities until remitted are sales taxes, and payroll-related deductions such as federal and state income taxes, social security taxes, employee insurance, employee contributions to retirement plans, and union dues.

## Answers to Questions (continued)

## Question 13-11

1. **Current liability** — The requirement to classify currently maturing debt as a current liability includes debt that is *callable*, or due on demand, *by the creditor* in the upcoming year even if the debt is not expected to be called.

2. **Long-term liability** — The current liability classification includes (a) situations in which the creditor has the right to demand payment because an existing violation of a provision of the debt agreement makes it callable and (b) situations in which debt is not yet callable, but will be callable within the year if an existing violation is not corrected within a specified grace period – unless it's *probable* the violation will be corrected within the grace period. In this case, the existing violation is expected to be corrected within 6 months.

## Question 13-12
Short-term obligations can be reported as noncurrent liabilities if the company (a) *intends* to refinance on a long-term basis and (b) demonstrates the *ability* to do so by a refinancing agreement or by actual financing.

## Question 13-13
A loss contingency is an existing situation, or set of circumstances involving potential loss that will be resolved when some future event occurs or doesn't occur. Examples: (1) an unsettled tax deficiency assessed by the IRS, (2) a possible uncollectible receivable, (3) being the defendant in a lawsuit.

## Question 13-14
The likelihood that the future event(s) will confirm the incurrence of the liability must be categorized as:

**PROBABLE** – the confirming event is likely to occur.

**REASONABLY POSSIBLE**– the chance the confirming event will occur is more than remote but less than likely.

**REMOTE**– the chance the confirming event will occur is slight.

## Question 13-15
A liability should be *accrued* if it is both *probable* that the confirming event will occur and the amount can be at least *reasonably estimated*.

## Question 13-16
If one or both of the accrual criteria is not met, but there is at least a *reasonable possibility* that an obligation exists (the loss will occur), a *disclosure note* should describe the contingency. The note also should provide an estimate of the possible loss or range of loss, if possible. If an estimate cannot be made, a statement to that effect should be included.

## Answers to Questions (continued)

## Question 13-17

1. Manufacturers' product warranties — these inevitably involve expenditures, and reasonably accurate estimates of the *total* liability for a period usually are possible, based on prior experience.

2. Cash rebates and other premium offers — these inevitably involve expenditures, and reasonably accurate estimates of the *total* liability for a period usually are possible, based on prior experience.

## Question 13-18

The contingent liability for warranties and guarantees usually is accrued. The estimated warranty (guarantee) liability is credited and warranty (guarantee) expense is debited in the reporting period in which the product under warranty is sold. An extended warranty provides warranty protection beyond the manufacturer's original warranty. A manufacturer's warranty is offered as an integral part of the product package. By contrast, an extended warranty is priced and sold separately from the warranted product. It essentially constitutes a separate sales transaction and is recorded as such.

## Question 13-19

Several weeks usually pass between the end of a company's fiscal year and the date the financial statements for that year actually are issued. Any enlightening events occurring during this period should be used to assess the nature of a loss contingency existing at the report date. Since a liability should be accrued if it is both probable that the confirming event will occur and the amount can be at least reasonably estimated, the contingency should be accrued.

## Question 13-20

When a contingency comes into existence only after the year-end, a liability cannot be accrued because none existed at the end of the year. Yet, if the loss is probable and can be reasonably estimated, the contingency should be described in a disclosure note. The note should include the effect of the loss on key accounting numbers affected. Furthermore, even events other than contingencies that occur after the year-end but before the financial statements are issued must be disclosed in a "subsequent events" disclosure note if they have a material effect on the company's financial position. (i.e., an issuance of debt or equity securities, a business combination, or discontinued operations).

## Answers to Questions (concluded)

### Question 13-21

When an assessment is probable, reporting the possible obligation would be warranted if an unfavorable settlement is at least reasonably possible. This means an estimated loss and contingent liability would be accrued if (a) an unfavorable outcome is probable and (b) the amount can be reasonably estimated. Otherwise footnote disclosure would be appropriate. So, when the assessment is unasserted as yet, a two-step process is involved in deciding how it should be reported:

1.  Is the assessment *probable*? If it is not, no disclosure is warranted.
2.  If the assessment is *probable*, evaluate (a) the likelihood of an unfavorable outcome and (b) whether the dollar amount can be estimated to determine whether it should be accrued, disclosed only, or neither.

### Question 13-22

You should not accrue your gain. A gain contingency should not be accrued. This conservative treatment is consistent with the general inclination of accounting practice to anticipate losses, but to recognize gains only at their realization. Though gain contingencies are not recorded in the accounts, they should be disclosed in notes to the financial statements. Attention should be paid that the disclosure note not give "misleading implications as to the likelihood of realization."

# BRIEF EXERCISES

## Brief Exercise 13-1

| | | |
|---|---|---|
| Cash ....................................................... | 60,000,000 | |
| Notes payable ............................................. | | 60,000,000 |
| | | |
| Interest expense ($60,000,000 x 12% x $3/12$)....... | 1,800,000 | |
| Interest payable ......................................... | | 1,800,,000 |

## Brief Exercise 13-2

| | | |
|---|---|---|
| Cash (difference)......................................... | 54,600,000 | |
| Discount on notes payable ($60,000,000 x 12% x $9/12$). | 5,400,000 | |
| Notes payable (face amount)................................... | | 60,000,000 |
| | | |
| Interest expense ($60,000,000 x 12% x $3/12$)................. | 1,800,000 | |
| Discount on notes payable ................................. | | 1,800,000 |

## Brief Exercise 13-3

**a.**

### December 31
$$\$100,000 \times 12\% \times 6/12 = \$6,000$$

**b.**

### September 30
$$\$100,000 \times 12\% \times 3/12 = \$3,000$$

# Brief Exercise 13-4

| | | |
|---|---|---|
| Cash (difference) ................................................... | 11,190,000 | |
| Discount on notes payable ($12,000,000 x 9% x $9/12$)... | 810,000 | |
|    Notes payable (face amount) ................................. | | 12,000,000 |

| | | |
|---|---|---|
| Interest expense ...................................................... | 810,000 | |
|    Discount on notes payable......................................... | | 810,000 |

| | | |
|---|---|---|
| Notes payable (face amount) ................................... | 12,000,000 | |
|    Cash ........................................................................ | | 12,000,000 |

# Brief Exercise 13-5

| | | |
|---|---|---|
| Cash (difference) .................................................... | 9,550,000 | |
| Discount on notes payable ($10,000,000 x 6% x $9/12$)... | 450,000 | |
|    Notes payable (face amount) ................................. | | 10,000,000 |

**Effective interest rate:**

| | |
|---|---|
| Discount ($10,000,000 x 6% x $9/12$) | $ 450,000 |
| Cash proceeds | ÷ $9,550,000 |
| Interest rate for 9 months | 4.712% |
| | x 12/9 |
| Annual effective rate | 6.3% |

# Brief Exercise 13-6

**December 12**

| | | |
|---|---|---|
| Cash............................................................. | 24,000 | |
|     Liability – customer advance ........................... | | 24,000 |

**January 16**

| | | |
|---|---|---|
| Cash............................................................. | 216,000 | |
| Liability – customer advance ............................... | 24,000 | |
|     Sales revenue ................................................. | | 240,000 |

# Brief Exercise 13-7

| | | |
|---|---|---|
| Accounts receivable.............................................. | 645,000 | |
|     Sales revenue .................................................... | | 600,000 |
|     Sales taxes payable ([6% + 1.5%] x $600,000)....... | | 45,000 |

# Brief Exercise 13-8

This is a loss contingency and the estimated warranty liability is credited and warranty expense is debited in the period in which the products under warranty are sold.  Right will report a liability of $130,000:

### Warranty Liability

| Actual expenditures 20,000 | 150,000 Warranty expense (1% x $15,000,000) |
|---|---|
| | 130,000 Balance |

# Brief Exercise 13-9

This is a loss contingency and should be accrued because it is both probable that the confirming event will occur and the amount can be at least reasonably estimated.  Goo Goo should report a $5.5 million loss in its income statement and a $5.5 million liability in its balance sheet

Loss – product recall ......................................................... 5,500,000
      Liability - product recall ........................................... 5,500,000

A disclosure note also is appropriate.

# Brief Exercise 13-10

This is a gain contingency. Gain contingencies are not accrued even if the gain is probable and reasonably estimable. The gain should be recognized only when realized. A carefully worded disclosure note is appropriate.


# Brief Exercise 13-11

This is a loss contingency. A liability should be *accrued* if it is both *probable* that the confirming event will occur and the amount can be at least *reasonably estimated*. If one or both of these criteria is not met (as in this case), but there is at least a reasonable possibility that the loss will occur, a *disclosure note* should describe the contingency. That's what Bell should do here.


# Brief Exercise 13-12

Only the third situation's costs should be accrued. A liability should be *accrued* for a loss contingency if it is both *probable* that the confirming event will occur and the amount can be at least *reasonably estimated*. If one or both of these criteria is not met, but there is at least a reasonable possibility that the loss will occur, a *disclosure note* should describe the contingency. Both criteria are met only for the warranty costs.

# Brief Exercise 13-13

No disclosure is required because an EPS claim is not yet asserted, and an assessment is *not probable*. Even if an unfavorable outcome is thought to be probable in the event of an assessment and the amount is estimable, disclosure is not required unless an unasserted claim is probable.

# EXERCISES

## Exercise 13-1

### Requirement 1

| | | |
|---|---|---|
| Cash ............................................................. | 8,000,000 | |
| Notes payable.............................................. | | 8,000,000 |

### Requirement 2

| | | |
|---|---|---|
| Interest expense ($8,000,000 x 12% x $2/12$)........ | 160,000 | |
| Interest payable........................................... | | 160,000 |

### Requirement 3

| | | |
|---|---|---|
| Interest expense ($8,000,000 x 12% x $7/12$)........ | 560,000 | |
| Interest payable (from adjusting entry) .............. | 160,000 | |
| Notes payable (face amount) ............................. | 8,000,000 | |
| Cash (total) ................................................. | | 8,720,000 |

## Exercise 13-2

1.

| Interest rate | Fiscal year-end |
|---|---|
| 12% | December 31 |

$200 million x 12% x $6/12$ = $12 million

2.

| Interest rate | Fiscal year-end |
|---|---|
| 10% | September 30 |

$200 million x 10% x $3/12$ = $5 million

3.

| Interest rate | Fiscal year-end |
|---|---|
| 9% | October 31 |

$200 million x 9% x $4/12$ = $6 million

4.

| Interest rate | Fiscal year-end |
|---|---|
| 6% | January 31 |

$200 million x 6% x $7/12$ = $7 million

## Exercise 13-3
1. b
2. a

# Exercise 13-4

**2006**

**Jan. 13** No entry is made for a line of credit until a loan actually is made. It would be described in a disclosure note.

**Feb. 1**

| | | |
|---|---|---|
| Cash .................................................................... | 5,000,000 | |
|    Notes payable............................................ | | 5,000,000 |

**May 1**

| | | |
|---|---|---|
| Interest expense ($5,000,000 x 10% x $3/12$) .................. | 125,000 | |
| Notes payable (face amount)..................................... | 5,000,000 | |
|    Cash ($5,000,000 + 125,000) ..................................... | | 5,125,000 |

**Dec. 1**

| | | |
|---|---|---|
| Cash (difference)...................................................... | 9,325,000 | |
| Discount on notes payable ($10,000,000 x 9% x $9/12$) ... | 675,000 | |
|    Notes payable (face amount)..................................... | | 10,000,000 |

**Dec. 31**

The effective interest rate is 9.6515% ($675,000 ÷ $9,325,000) x $12/9$. So, properly, interest should be recorded at that rate times the outstanding balance times one-twelfth of a year:

| | | |
|---|---|---|
| Interest expense ($9,325,000 x 9.6515% x $1/12$) ............. | 75,000 | |
|    Discount on notes payable ................................... | | 75,000 |

However the same results are achieved if interest is recorded at the discount rate times the maturity amount times one-twelfth of a year:

| | | |
|---|---|---|
| Interest expense ($10,000,000 x 9% x $1/12$) ................... | 75,000 | |
|    Discount on notes payable ................................... | | 75,000 |

*Exercise 13-4 (concluded)*

**2007**

**Sept. 1**

| | | |
|---|---|---|
| Interest expense ($10,000,000 x 9% x $8/12$)*................ | 600,000 | |
| Discount on notes payable ................................... | | 600,000 |
| | | |
| Notes payable (balance)............................................ | 10,000,000 | |
| Cash (maturity amount) ............................................ | | 10,000,000 |

\* or, ($9,325,000 x 9.6515% x $8/12$) = $600,000

# Exercise 13-5

Wages expense (increases wages expense to $410,000)............  6,000
    Liability – compensated future absences ...................        6,000*

    * ($404,000 - 4,000] = $400,000   non-vacation wages
             x $1/40$ =  $10,000   vacation pay earned
                 (4,000)   vacation pay taken
          = $ 6,000   vacation pay carried over

# Exercise 13-6

## Requirement 1

Wages expense (700 x $900).............................................   630,000
    Liability – compensated future absences ...........          630,000

## Requirement 2

Liability – compensated future absences .................   630,000
Wages expense ($31 million + [5% x $630,000])..............  31,031,500
    Cash (or wages payable) (total).............................          31,661,500

# Exercise 13-7

## Requirement 1

| | | |
|---|--:|--:|
| Cash............................................................................ | 5,200 | |
| Liability – gift certificates ...................................... | | 5,200 |
| | | |
| Cash ($2,100 + 84 - 1,300)...................................... | 884 | |
| Liability – gift certificates ........................................ | 1,300 | |
| Sales revenue.......................................................... | | 2,100 |
| Sales taxes payable (4% x $2,100)............................ | | 84 |

## Requirement 2

| | |
|---|--:|
| Gift certificates sold | $5,200 |
| Gift certificates redeemed | 1,300 |
| Liability to be reported at December 31 | $3,900 |

## Requirement 3

The sales tax liability is a current liability because it is payable in January.

The liability for gift certificates is part current and part noncurrent:

| | |
|---|--:|
| Gift certificates sold | $5,200 |
| | x 80% |
| Estimated current liability | $4,160 |
| Gift certificates redeemed | (1,300) |
| Current liability at December 31 | $2,860 |
| Noncurrent liability at December 31 ($5,200 x 20%) | 1,040 |
| Total | $3,900 |

# Exercise 13-8

## Requirement 1

**Deposits Collected**

| | | |
|---|---:|---:|
| Cash .................................................................... | 850,000 | |
|    Liability – refundable deposits ..................... | | 850,000 |

**Containers Returned**

| | | |
|---|---:|---:|
| Liability – refundable deposits ......................... | 790,000 | |
|    Cash ................................................................ | | 790,000 |

**Deposits Forfeited**

| | | |
|---|---:|---:|
| Liability – refundable deposits ......................... | 35,000 | |
|    Revenue – sale of containers........................ | | 35,000 |
| | | |
| Cost of goods sold............................................ | 35,000 | |
|    Inventory of containers ............................... | | 35,000 |

## Requirement 2

| | |
|---|---:|
| Balance on January 1 | $530,000 |
|    Deposits received | 850,000 |
|    Deposits returned | (790,000) |
|    Deposits forfeited | (35,000) |
| Balance on December 31 | $555,000 |

# Exercise 13-9

**Requirement 1**

| | | |
|---|---|---|
| Cash......................................................................... | 7,500 | |
| Liability – customer advance ........................... | | 7,500 |

**Requirement 2**

| | | |
|---|---|---|
| Cash......................................................................... | 25,500 | |
| Liability – refundable deposits ......................... | | 25,500 |

**Requirement 3**

| | | |
|---|---|---|
| Accounts receivable ............................................ | 856,000 | |
| Sales revenue ..................................................... | | 800,000 |
| Sales taxes payable ([5% + 2%] x $800,000)......... | | 56,000 |

# Exercise 13-10

Normally, short-term debt (payable within a year) is classified as current liabilities. However, when such debt is to be refinanced on a long-term basis, it may be included with long-term liabilities. The narrative indicates that Sprint has both (1) the intent and (2) the ability ("existing long-term credit facilities") to refinance on a long-term basis. Thus, Sprint reported the debt as long-term liabilities.

# Exercise 13-11

1. **Current liability: $10 million**

   The requirement to classify currently maturing debt as a current liability includes debt that is callable by the creditor in the upcoming year – even if the debt is not expected to be called.

2. **Noncurrent liability: $14 million**

   The current liability classification includes (a) situations in which the creditor has the right to demand payment because an existing violation of a provision of the debt agreement makes it callable and (b) situations in which debt is not yet callable, but will be callable within the year if an existing violation is not corrected within a specified grace period – unless it's *probable* the violation will be corrected within the grace period. In this case, the existing violation is expected to be corrected within 6 months.

3. **Current liability: $7 million**

   The debt should be reported as a current liability because it is payable in the upcoming year, will not be refinanced with long-term obligations, and will not be paid with a bond sinking fund.

# Exercise 13-12

## Requirement 1

This is a loss contingency. There may be a future sacrifice of economic benefits (cost of satisfying the warranty) due to an existing circumstance (the warranted awnings have been sold) that depends on an uncertain future event (customer claims).

The liability is probable because product warranties inevitably entail costs. A reasonably accurate estimate of the total liability for a period is possible based on prior experience. So, the contingent liability for the warranty is accrued. The estimated warranty liability is credited and warranty expense is debited in 2006, the period in which the products under warranty are sold.

## Requirement 2

**2006 Sales**

| | | |
|---|---|---|
| Accounts receivable ........................................... | 5,000,000 | |
| Sales ............................................................... | | 5,000,000 |

**Accrued liability and expense**

| | | |
|---|---|---|
| Warranty expense (3% x $5,000,000) ........................ | 150,000 | |
| Estimated warranty liability ........................... | | 150,000 |

**Actual expenditures**

| | | |
|---|---|---|
| Estimated warranty liability ............................. | 37,500 | |
| Cash, wages payable, parts and supplies, etc. | | 37,500 |

## Requirement 3

### Warranty Liability

| Actual expenditures 37,500 | 150,000 Estimated liability |
|---|---|
| | 112,500 Balance |

# Exercise 13-13

## Requirement 1

This is not a loss contingency. An extended warranty is priced and sold separately from the warranted product and therefore essentially constitutes a separate sales transaction. Since the earning process for an extended warranty continues during the contract period, revenue should be recognized over the same period. Revenue from separately priced extended warranty contracts are deferred as a liability at the time of sale, and recognized over the contract period on a straight-line basis.

## Requirement 2

**During 2006**

| | | |
|---|---|---|
| Accounts receivable............................................. | 412,000 | |
| Unearned revenue – extended warranties ....... | | 412,000 |

**December 31, 2006 (adjusting entry)**

| | | |
|---|---|---|
| Unearned revenue – extended warranties............ | 103,000 | |
| Revenue – extended warranties | | |
| ([\$412,000 ÷ 2 years] x 1/2 year*) ...................... | | 103,000 |

\* Since sales of warranties were made evenly throughout the year, one-half of one year's revenue is considered earned.

# Exercise 13-14

## Requirement 1

This is a loss contingency. A liability is *accrued* if it is both *probable* that the confirming event will occur and the amount can be at least *reasonably estimated*. If one or both of these criteria is not met, but there is at least a reasonable possibility that the loss will occur, a *disclosure note* should describe the contingency. In this case, a liability is *accrued* since both of these criteria are met.

## Requirement 2

*Loss:*

$2 million

## Requirement 3

*Liability:*

$2 million

## Requirement 4

| | | |
|---|---|---|
| Loss – product recall................................................................ | 2,000,000 | |
|        Liability - product recall .......................................... | | 2,000,000 |

A disclosure note also is appropriate.

# Exercise 13-15

## Requirement 1

This is a loss contingency. Some loss contingencies don't involve liabilities at all. Some contingencies when resolved cause a noncash asset to be impaired, so accruing it means reducing the related asset rather than recording a liability. The most common loss contingency of this type is an uncollectible receivable, as described in this situation.

## Requirement 2

Bad debt expense:  3% x $2,400,000 = $72,000

## Requirement 3

| | | |
|---|---|---|
| Bad debt expense (3% x $2,400,000)................................ | 72,000 | |
|     Allowance for uncollectible accounts ................. | | 72,000 |

## Requirement 4

*Allowance for uncollectible accounts:*

| | |
|---|---|
| Beginning of 2006 | $75,000 |
| Write off of bad debts* | 73,000 |
| | $ 2,000 |
| Year-end accrual (Req. 3) | 72,000 |
| End of 2006 | $74,000 |

| | | |
|---|---|---|
| * Allowance for uncollectible accounts....................... | 73,000 | |
|     Accounts receivable ........................................... | | 73,000 |

*Net realizable value:*

| | |
|---|---|
| Accounts receivable | $490,000 |
| Less: Allowance for uncollectible accounts | (74,000) |
| Net realizable value | $416,000 |

# Exercise 13-16

## Requirement 1

Promotional expense:

    70% x $5 x 20,000 = $70,000

## Requirement 2

Premium liability:

    $70,000 – 22,000 = $48,000

## Requirement 3

| | | |
|---|---|---|
| Promotional expense ([70% x $5 x 20,000] – $22,000)....... | 48,000 | |
| Estimated premium liability ..................................... | | 48,000 |

# Exercise 13-17

## Scenario 1

No disclosure is required because an IRS claim is as yet unasserted, and an assessment is *not probable.*

## Scenario 2

No disclosure is required because an IRS claim is as yet unasserted, and an assessment is *not probable.* Even if an unfavorable outcome is thought to be probable in the event of an assessment and the amount is estimable, disclosure is not required unless an unasserted claim is probable.

## Scenario 3

A disclosure note is required because an IRS claim is as yet unasserted, but an assessment is *probable.* Since an unfavorable outcome is not thought to be probable in the event of an assessment, no accrual is needed, but since an unfavorable outcome is thought to be *reasonably possible* in the event of an assessment, disclosure in a footnote is required. Keep in mind, though, that in practice, disclosure of an unasserted claim is rare. Such disclosure would alert the other party, the IRS in this case, of a potential point of contention that may otherwise not surface. The outcome of litigation and any resulting loss are highly uncertain, making difficult the determination of their possibility of occurrence.

## Scenario 4

Accrual of the loss is required because an IRS claim is as yet unasserted, but an assessment is *probable.* Since an unfavorable outcome also is thought to be *probable* in the event of an assessment, accrual is needed. Keep in mind, though, that in practice, accrual of an unasserted claim is rare. Such disclosure would alert the other party, the IRS in this case, of a potential point of contention that may otherwise not surface. Accrual could be offered in court as an admission of responsibility. A loss usually is not recorded until after the ultimate settlement has been reached or negotiations for settlement are substantially completed.

# Exercise 13-18

## Requirement 1

| | | |
|---|---|---|
| Warranty expense ([4% x $2,000,000] - $30,800)............. | 49,200 | |
|     Estimated warranty liability .................................. | | 49,200 |

## Requirement 2

| | | |
|---|---|---|
| Bad debt expense (2% x $2,000,000)............................... | 40,000 | |
|     Allowance for uncollectible accounts .................. | | 40,000 |

## Requirement 3

This is a loss contingency. Classical can use the information occurring after the end of the year and before the financial statements are issued to determine appropriate disclosure.

| | | |
|---|---|---|
| Loss – litigation......................................................... | 1,500,000 | |
|     Liability - litigation ............................................... | | 1,500,000 |

A disclosure note also is appropriate.

## Requirement 4

This is a gain contingency. Gain contingencies are not accrued even if the gain is probable and reasonably estimable. The gain should be recognized only when realized. A disclosure note is appropriate.

## Requirement 5

| | | |
|---|---|---|
| Loss – product recall ..................................................... | 500,000 | |
|     Liability - product recall .......................................... | | 500,000 |

A disclosure note also is appropriate.

## Requirement 6

| | | |
|---|---|---|
| Promotional expense ([60% x $25 x 10,000] – $105,000)... | 45,000 | |
|     Estimated premium liability ...................................... | | 45,000 |

# Exercise 13-19

1. d
2. d
3. a
4. a

# Exercise 13-20

| | | Item | | Reporting Method |
|---|---|---|---|---|
| C | 1. | Commercial paper. | N. | Not reported |
| D | 2. | Noncommitted line of credit. | C. | Current liability |
| C | 3. | Customer advances. | L. | Long-term liability |
| C | 4. | Estimated warranty cost. | D. | Disclosure note only |
| C | 5. | Accounts payable. | A. | Asset |
| C | 6. | Long-term bonds that will be callable by the creditor in the upcoming year unless an existing violation is not corrected (there is a reasonable possibility the violation will be corrected within the grace period). | | |
| C | 7. | Note due March 3, 2007. | | |
| C | 8. | Interest accrued on note, Dec. 31, 2006. | | |
| L | 9. | Short-term bank loan to be paid with proceeds of sale of common stock. | | |
| D | 10. | A determinable gain that is contingent on a future event that appears extremely likely to occur in three months. | | |
| C | 11. | Unasserted assessment of back taxes that probably will be asserted, in which case there would probably be a loss in six months. | | |
| N | 12. | Unasserted assessment of back taxes with a reasonable possibility of being asserted, in which case there would probably be a loss in 13 months. | | |
| C | 13. | A determinable loss from a past event that is contingent on a future event that appears extremely likely to occur in three months. | | |
| A | 14. | Bond sinking fund. | | |
| C | 15. | Long-term bonds callable by the creditor in the upcoming year that are not expected to be called. | | |

# Exercise 13-21

## Requirement 1

**Accrued liability and expense**

Warranty expense (3% x $3,600,000) ............................................ 108,000

    Estimated warranty liability ............................................... 108,000

**Actual expenditures (summary entry)**

Estimated warranty liability ................................................... 88,000

    Cash, wages payable, parts and supplies, etc. ................... 88,000

## Requirement 2

**Actual expenditures (summary entry)**

Estimated warranty liability ($50,000 – $23,000) ..................... 27,000

Loss on product warranty (3% – 2%] x $2,500,000)................... 25,000

    Cash, wages payable, parts and supplies, etc. ................... 52,000*

      *(3% x $2,500,000) – $23,000 = $52,000

# Exercise 13-22

1. This is a change in estimate.

**To revise the liability on the basis of the new estimate:**
Liability - litigation ($1,000,000 – 600,000) ................... 400,000
    Gain – litigation ...................................................... 400,000

2. A disclosure note should describe the effect of a change in estimate on income before extraordinary items, net income, and related per-share amounts for the current period.

# Exercise 13-23

The note describes a loss contingency. Dow anticipates a future sacrifice of economic benefits (cost of remediation and restoration) due to an existing circumstance (environmental violations) that depends on an uncertain future event (requirement to pay claim).

Dow considers the liability probable and the amount is reasonably estimable. As a result, the company accrued the liability:

($ in millions)

Loss provision from environmental claims ................... 381
    Liability for settlement of environmental claims ... 381

# Exercise 13-24

1. **d.** SFAS 43 lists four requirements that must be met before a liability is accrued for future compensated absences. These requirements are that the obligation must arise for past services, the employee rights must vest or accumulate, payment is probable, and the amount can be reasonably estimated. If the amount cannot be reasonably estimated, no liability should be recorded. However, the obligation should be disclosed.

2. **c.** SFAS 5 requires a contingent liability to be recorded, along with the related loss, when it is probable that an asset has been impaired or a liability has been incurred, and the amount of the loss can be reasonably estimated. The key words are "probable" and "reasonably estimated."

3. **c.** SFAS 5 prescribes accounting for contingencies. The likelihood of contingencies is divided into three categories: probable (likely to occur), reasonably possible, and remote. When contingent losses are probable and the amount can be reasonably estimated, the amount of the loss should be charged against income. If the amount cannot be reasonably estimated but the loss is at least reasonably possible, full disclosure should be made, including a statement that an estimate cannot be made.

4. **b.** If an enterprise intends to refinance short-term obligations on a long-term basis and demonstrates an ability to consummate the refinancing, the obligations should be excluded from current liabilities and classified as noncurrent (SFAS 6, *Classification of Short-Term Obligations Expected to Be Refinanced*). The ability to consummate the refinancing may be demonstrated by a post-balance-sheet-date issuance of a long-term obligation or equity securities, or by entering into a financing agreement.

# Exercise 13-25

| | | |
|---|---:|---:|
| Salaries and wages expense (total amount earned)..... | 500,000 | |
| Withholding taxes payable (federal income tax)... | | 100,000 |
| Social security taxes payable ($500,000 x 6.2%) . | | 31,000 |
| Medicare taxes payable ($500,000 x 1.45%) ........ | | 7,250 |
| Salaries and wages payable (net pay) ................. | | 361,750 |
| | | |
| Payroll tax expense (total)..................................... | 69,250 | |
| Social security payable (employer's matching amount) | | 31,000 |
| Medicare taxes payable (employer's matching amount) | | 7,250 |
| Federal unemployment tax payable ($500,000 x 0.8%) | | 4,000 |
| State unemployment tax payable ($500,000 x 5.4%) | | 27,000 |

# PROBLEMS

## Problem 13-1

### Requirement 1

**Blanton Plastics**

| | | |
|---|---|---|
| Cash ............................................................ | 14,000,000 | |
|     Notes payable............................................ | | 14,000,000 |

**N,C&I Bank**

| | | |
|---|---|---|
| Notes receivable ........................................... | 14,000,000 | |
|     Cash ....................................................... | | 14,000,000 |

### Requirement 2

#### Adjusting entries (December 31, 2006)

**Blanton Plastics**

| | | |
|---|---|---|
| Interest expense ($14,000,000 x 12% x $3/12$) ............... | 420,000 | |
|     Interest payable........................................ | | 420,000 |

**N,C&I Bank**

| | | |
|---|---|---|
| Interest receivable ....................................... | 420,000 | |
|     Interest revenue ($14,000,000 x 12% x $3/12$)............ | | 420,000 |

#### Maturity (January 31, 2007)

**Blanton Plastics**

| | | |
|---|---|---|
| Interest expense ($14,000,000 x 12% x $1/12$) ............... | 140,000 | |
| Interest payable (from adjusting entry) ...................... | 420,000 | |
| Notes payable (face amount) ...................................... | 14,000,000 | |
|     Cash (total) ............................................... | | 14,560,000 |

**N,C&I Bank**

| | | |
|---|---|---|
| Cash (total)................................................... | 14,560,000 | |
|     Interest revenue ($14,000,000 x 12% x $1/12$)............... | | 140,000 |
|     Interest receivable (from adjusting entry) ................. | | 420,000 |
|     Notes receivable (face amount) ............................. | | 14,000,000 |

## Problem 13-1 (concluded)

### Requirement 3

#### Issuance of note (October 1, 2006)

| | | |
|---|---|---|
| Cash (difference)...................................................... | 13,440,000 | |
| Discount on notes payable ($14,000,000 x 12% x $^4/_{12}$) | 560,000 | |
| Notes payable (face amount)........................................ | | 14,000,000 |

#### Adjusting entry (December 31, 2006)

| | | |
|---|---|---|
| Interest expense ($14,000,000 x 12% x $^3/_{12}$)................ | 420,000 | |
| Discount on notes payable ................................... | | 420,000 |

#### Maturity (January 31, 2007)

| | | |
|---|---|---|
| Interest expense ($14,000,000 x 12% x $^1/_{12}$)................ | 140,000 | |
| Discount on notes payable ................................... | | 140,000 |
| Notes payable (face amount)........................................ | 14,000,000 | |
| Cash ................................................................. | | 14,000,000 |

### Effective interest rate:

| | | |
|---|---|---|
| Discount ($14,000,000 x 12% x $^4/_{12}$) | $ | 560,000 |
| Cash proceeds | ÷ | $13,440,000 |
| Interest rate for 4 months | | 4.1666% |
| | x | $12/_4$ |
| Annual effective rate | | 12.5% |

# Problem 13-2

## Requirement 1

### 2006

a. No entry is made for a line of credit until a loan actually is made. It would be described in a disclosure note.

b.
| | | |
|---|---|---|
| Cash ................................................................. | 12,000,000 | |
|     Notes payable ........................................... | | 12,000,000 |

c.
| | | |
|---|---|---|
| Cash ................................................................. | 2,600 | |
|     Liability – refundable deposits ..................... | | 2,600 |

d.
| | | |
|---|---|---|
| Accounts receivable (total) .................................. | 4,346,000 | |
|     Sales revenue (given) ......................................... | | 4,100,000 |
|     Sales taxes payable ([3% + 3%] x $4,100,000) ... | | 246,000 |

e.
| | | |
|---|---|---|
| Interest expense ($12,000,000 x 10% x $3/12$) ........... | 300,000 | |
|     Interest payable ............................................. | | 300,000 |

### 2007

f.
| | | |
|---|---|---|
| Cash ................................................................. | 10,000,000 | |
|     Bonds payable ............................................... | | 10,000,000 |

| | | |
|---|---|---|
| Interest expense ($12,000,000 x 10% x $2/12$) ........... | 200,000 | |
| Interest payable (from adjusting entry) ................... | 300,000 | |
| Notes payable (face amount) ................................ | 12,000,000 | |
|     Cash ($12,000,000 + 500,000) ............................ | | 12,500,000 |

g.
| | | |
|---|---|---|
| Liability – refundable deposits .......................... | 1,300 | |
|     Cash .............................................................. | | 1,300 |

# Problem 13-2 (concluded)

## Requirement 2

**CURRENT LIABILITIES:**

| | |
|---|---|
| Accounts payable | $  252,000 |
| Current portion of bank loan | 2,000,000* |
| Liability – refundable deposits | 2,600 |
| Sales taxes payable | 246,000 |
| Accrued interest payable | 300,000 |
| *Total current liabilities* | $2,800,600 |

**LONG-TERM LIABILITIES:**

| | |
|---|---|
| Bank loan to be refinanced on a long-term basis | $10,000,000* |

\* The intent of management is to refinance all $12,000,000 of the bank loan, but the actual refinancing demonstrates the ability only for $10,000,000.

# Problem 13-3

## Requirement 1

a. The requirement to classify currently maturing debt as a current liability includes debt that is callable by the creditor in the upcoming year – even if the debt is not expected to be called. So, the entire $40 million debt is a current liability.

b. $5 million can be reported as long term, but $1 million must be reported as a current liability. Short-term obligations that are expected to be refinanced with long-term obligations can be reported as noncurrent liabilities only if the firm (a) *intends* to refinance on a long-term basis and (b) actually has *demonstrated the ability* to do so. Ability to refinance on a long-term basis can be demonstrated by either an existing *refinancing agreement* or by *actual financing* prior to the issuance of the financial statements. The refinancing agreement in this case limits the ability to refinance to $5 million of the notes. In the absence of other evidence of ability to refinance, the remaining $1 million cannot be reported as long term.

c. The entire $20 million maturity amount should be reported as a current liability because that amount is payable in the upcoming year and it will not be refinanced with long-term obligations nor paid with a bond sinking fund.

d. The entire $12 million loan should be reported as a long-term liability because that amount is payable in 2012 and it will not be refinanced with long-term obligations nor paid with a bond sinking fund. The current liability classification includes (a) situations in which the creditor has the right to demand payment because an existing violation of a provision of the debt agreement makes it callable and (b) situations in which debt is not yet callable, but will be callable within the year if an existing violation is not corrected within a specified grace period – unless it's *probable* the violation will be corrected within the grace period. Here, the existing violation is expected to be corrected within 6 months (actually 3 months in this case).

*Problem 13-3 (concluded)*
**Requirement 2**

## December 31, 2006

|  | ($ in millions) |
|---|---|

**Current Liabilities**

|  |  |  |
|---|---|---|
| Accounts payable and accruals | | $ 22 |
| 10% notes payable due May 2007 | | 1 |
| Currently maturing portion of long-term debt: | | |
|    11% bonds due October 31, 2017, | | |
|       redeemable on October 31, 2007 | $40 | |
|    12% bonds due September 30, 2007 | 20 | 60 |
|   *Total Current Liabilities* | | 83 |

**Long-Term Debt**

|  |  |
|---|---|
| Currently maturing debt classified as long-term: | |
|    10% notes payable due May 2007 (Note X) | 5 |
| 9% bank loan due October 2009 | 12 |
|   *Total Long-Term Liabilities* | 17 |
| **Total Liabilities** | $100 |

---

NOTE X: *CURRENTLY MATURING DEBT CLASSIFIED AS LONG-TERM*

The Company intends to refinance $6 million of 10% notes that mature in May of 2007. In March, 2007, the Company negotiated a line of credit with a commercial bank for up to $5 million any time during 2007. Any borrowings will mature two years from the date of borrowing. Accordingly, $5 million was reclassified to long-term liabilities.

---

# Problem 13-4

## Requirement 1

a. Interest expense ($600,000 x 10% x $5/12$)..................... 25,000
      Interest payable............................................... 25,000

b. No adjusting entry since interest has been paid up to December 31. $950,000 can be reported as a noncurrent liability, because (a) intent and (b) ability to refinance has been demonstrated for that amount.

c. Accounts receivable (to eliminate the credit balance)... 18,000
      Advances from customers ................................ 18,000

d. Rent revenue ($10/12$ x $30,000) .............................. 25,000
      Unearned rent revenue ................................... 25,000

## Requirement 2

| CURRENT LIABILITIES: | |
|---|---|
| Accounts payable | $ 35,000 |
| Current portion of long-term debt | 250,000 |
| Accrued interest payable | 25,000 |
| Advances from customers | 18,000 |
| Unearned rent revenue | 25,000 |
| Bank notes payable | 600,000 |
| *Total current liabilities* | $953,000 |

| LONG-TERM LIABILITIES: | |
|---|---|
| Mortgage note payable | $950,000 |

# Problem 13-5

## Requirement 1

B = .10 ($150,000 - B - T), where     B = the bonus

                                                              T = income tax

T = .30 ($150,000 - B),

## Requirement 2

Since income tax (T) is a component of both equations, we can combine the two and then solve for the remaining unknown amount (B):

**Substitute value of T for T:**

B = .10 [ $150,000 - B - .30 ($150,000 - B)]

**Reduce the right-hand side of the equation to one known and one unknown value:**

B = .10 ( $150,000 - B - $45,000 + .30B)

B = .10 ( $105,000 - .70B)

B = $10,500 - .07B

**Add .07B to both sides**

1.07B = $10,500

**Divide both sides by 1.07**

B = $9,813

## Requirement 3

| | | |
|---|---|---|
| Bonus compensation expense............................ | 9,813 | |
|     Accrued bonus compensation payable ........... | | 9,813 |

## Requirement 4

The approach is the same in any case: (1) express the bonus formula as one or more algebraic equation(s), (2) use algebra to solve for the amount of the bonus. For example, the bonus might specify that the bonus is 10% of the division's income *before tax,* but after the bonus itself:

B = .10 ($150,000 - B)

B = $15,000 - .10B

1.10B = $15,000

B = $13,636

# Problem 13-6

a. This is a loss contingency. Eastern can use the information occurring after the end of the year in determining appropriate disclosure. It is unlikely that Eastern would choose to accrue the $122 million loss because the judgment will be appealed and that outcome is uncertain. A disclosure note is appropriate:

---

**Note X: Contingency**

In a lawsuit resulting from a dispute with a supplier, a judgment was rendered against Eastern Corporation in the amount of $107 million plus interest, a total of $122 million at February 3, 2007. Eastern plans to appeal the judgment. While management and legal counsel are presently unable to predict the outcome or to estimate the amount of any liability the company may have with respect to this lawsuit, it is not expected that this matter will have a material adverse effect on the company.

---

b. This is a loss contingency. Eastern can use the information occurring after the end of the year in determining appropriate disclosure. Eastern should accrue the $140 million loss because the ultimate outcome appears settled and the loss is probable.

| | | |
|---|---|---|
| Loss – litigation............................................. | 140,000,000 | |
|     Liability - litigation.................................... | | 140,000,000 |

A disclosure note also is appropriate:

---

**Notes: Litigation**

In November 2005, the State of Nevada filed suit against the Company, seeking civil penalties and injunctive relief for violations of environmental laws regulating hazardous waste. On January 12, 2007, the Company announced that it had reached a settlement with state authorities on this matter. Based upon discussions with legal counsel, the Company, has accrued and charged to operations in 2006, $140 million to cover the anticipated cost of all violations. The Company believes that the ultimate settlement of this claim will not have a material adverse effect on the Company's financial position.

---

## Problem 13-6 (concluded)

c. This is a gain contingency. Gain contingencies are not accrued even if the gain is probable and reasonably estimable. The gain should be recognized only when realized.

Though gain contingencies are not recorded in the accounts, they should be disclosed in notes to the financial statements.

---

**Note X: Contingency**
Eastern is the plaintiff in a pending lawsuit filed against United Steel for damages due to lost profits from rejected contracts and for unpaid receivables. The case is in final appeal. No amount has been accrued in the financial statements for possible collection of any claims in this litigation.

---

d. No disclosure is required because an IRS claim is as yet unasserted, and an assessment is not *probable*. Even if an unfavorable outcome is thought to be probable in the event of an assessment and the amount is estimable, disclosure is not required unless an unasserted claim is probable.

# Problem 13-7

## Requirement 1

Yes, Northeast's frequent flyer program is offered in order to enhance revenues. Under the matching principle the cost is properly recognized as an operating expense in the year sales are made (travel miles are earned).

## Requirement 2

*Expense:*

25% x $40 million = $10 million

## Requirement 3

*Liability:*

| | |
|---|---|
| Beginning of 2006 | $25,000 |
| Redemption | (8,000) |
| | $17,000 |
| Year-end accrual (Req. 2) | 10,000 |
| End of 2006 | $27,000 |

## Requirement 4

|  | $ in millions |
|---|---|
| Operating expense ............................................ | 10 |
| Air traffic liability (25% x $40 million) ............. | 10 |

# Problem 13-8

## Requirement 1

Heinrich would record a contingent liability (and loss) of $27,619,020, calculated as follows:

$$
\begin{array}{rcl}
\$40{,}000{,}000 \times 20\% &=& \$\ 8{,}000{,}000 \\
30{,}000{,}000 \times 50\% &=& 15{,}000{,}000 \\
20{,}000{,}000 \times 30\% &=& \underline{6{,}000{,}000} \\
&& \$29{,}000{,}000 \\
&& \underline{\times\ .95238^*} \\
&& \$27{,}619{,}020
\end{array}
$$

*Present value of $1, $n = 1$, $i = 5\%$ (from Table 6A-2)

## Requirement 2

| | | |
|---|---|---|
| Loss – product recall | 27,619,020 | |
| Liability – product recall | | 27,619,020 |

## Requirement 3

The difference between $29,000,000 and the initial value of the liability of $27,619,020 represents interest expense, which Heinrich will accrue during 2007 as follows:

| | | |
|---|---|---|
| Interest expense | 1,380,980 | |
| Liability – product recall | | 1,380,980 |

## Requirement 4

Interest increases the liability to $29 million at the end of 2007. Since there is a difference between the actual costs, $30 million, and the $29 million liability, Heinrich will record an additional loss.

| | | |
|---|---|---|
| Liability – product recall | 29,000,000 | |
| Loss – product recall | 1,000,000 | |
| Cash | | 30,000,000 |

# Problem 13-9

### Case 1

**Note Only.** When a contingency comes into existence after the year-end, a liability cannot be accrued because it didn't exist at the end of the year. However, if the loss is probable and can be estimated, the situation should be described in a disclosure note.

### Case 2

**Note Only.** Since an unasserted claim or assessment is probable, the likelihood of an unfavorable outcome and the feasibility of estimating a dollar amount should be considered in deciding whether and how to report the possible loss. An estimated loss and contingent liability cannot be accrued since an unfavorable outcome is only reasonably possible even though the amount can be reasonably estimated.

### Case 3

**Accrual and Disclosure Note.** When the cause of a loss contingency occurs before the year-end, a clarifying event before financial statements are issued can be used to determine how the contingency is reported. Even though the loss was not probable at year-end, it becomes so before financial statements are issued. The situation also should be described in a disclosure note.

### Case 4

**No Disclosure.** Even though the cause of the contingency occurred before year-end, Lincoln is unaware of the loss contingency when the financial statements are issued.

# Problem 13-10

| | List A | | List B |
|---|---|---|---|
| _i_ | 1. Face amount x Interest rate x Time | a. | Informal agreement |
| _g_ | 2. Payable with current assets | b. | Secured loan |
| _h_ | 3. Short-term debt to be refinanced with common stock | c. | Refinancing prior to the issuance of the financial statements |
| _i_ | 4. Present value of interest plus present value of principal | d. | Accounts payable |
| _d_ | 5. Noninterest-bearing | e. | Accrued liabilities |
| _a_ | 6. Noncommitted line of credit | f. | Commercial paper |
| _b_ | 7. Pledged accounts receivable | g. | Current liabilities |
| _c_ | 8. Reclassification of debt | h. | Long-term liability |
| _f_ | 9. Purchased by other corporations | i. | Usual valuation of liabilities |
| _e_ | 10. Expenses not yet paid | j. | Interest on debt |
| _l_ | 11. Liability until refunded | k. | Customer advances |
| _k_ | 12. Applied against purchase price | l. | Customer deposits |

# Problem 13-11

| | | |
|---|---:|---:|
| Salaries and wages expense (total amount earned)........... | 2,000,000 | |
| Withholding taxes payable (federal income tax) .......... | | 400,000 |
| Withholding taxes payable (local income tax) ............. | | 53,000 |
| Social security taxes payable ($2,000,000 x 6.2%) ...... | | 124,000 |
| Medicare taxes payable ($2,000,000 x 1.45%) ............. | | 29,000 |
| Medical insurance payable ($42,000 x 20%)............... | | 8,400 |
| Life insurance payable ($9,000 x 20%)........................... | | 1,800 |
| Retirement plan payable (employees' investment) ......... | | 84,000 |
| Salaries and wages payable (net pay) ........................ | | 1,299,800 |
| | | |
| Payroll tax expense (total) ........................................... | 277,000 | |
| Social security taxes payable (employer's matching amount) | | 124,000 |
| Medicare taxes payable (employer's matching amount). | | 29,000 |
| FUTA payable ($2,000,000 x 0.8%) ............................. | | 16,000 |
| State unemployment tax payable ($2,000,000 x 5.4%) | | 108,000 |
| | | |
| Salaries and wages expense (fringe benefits) ................. | 124,800 | |
| Medical insurance payable ($42,000 x 80%)............... | | 33,600 |
| Life insurance payable ($9,000 x 80%)........................... | | 7,200 |
| Retirement plan payable (matching amount) ................. | | 84,000 |

# CASES

## Research Case 13-1

**[Note: This case encourages the student to reference authoritative pronouncements.]**

The $2,000,000 of commercial paper liquidated in November 2006 would be classified as a current liability in Cheshire's balance sheet at September 30, 2006. The essence of a current liability is that its payment requires the use of current assets or the creation of other current liabilities. If a liability is liquidated after the year-end with current assets, it is reported as a current liability as of the end of the reporting period – even if the current assets are later replenished by proceeds of a long-term obligation before the issuance of the financial statements.

The $3,000,000 of commercial paper liquidated in January 2007 but refinanced by the long-term debt offering in December 2006 would be excluded from current liabilities in the balance sheet at the end of September 2006. It should be noted that the existence of a financing agreement at the date of issuance of the financial statements rather than a completed financing at that date would not change these classifications.

# Real World Case 13-2

Collecting cash from a customer as a refundable deposit normally creates a liability to return the deposit if the deposit is expected to be refunded. In this case, the deposit is not returnable to the customer, but payment still will be made – to the zoo – if the pails are returned. The possible future payment represents a loss contingency to Zoo Doo. A liability is *accrued* if it is both (a) *probable* that the pails will be returned and (b) the amount of payment can be *reasonably estimated*. In that case a liability should be credited (say "Liability – donations for returnable containers"). Since the cost of the containers and the amount of the donation differ, it may be desirable also to employ a receivable account for the cost of containers expected to be returned. To illustrate, assume the sale of 1,000 containers of fertilizer and the expectation that 40% will be returned:

---

### When Containers Purchased

| | | |
|---|---|---|
| Inventory (1,000 x $1.76)............................................. | 1,760 | |
| Cash ..................................................................... | | 1,760 |

### When Product Sold

| | | |
|---|---|---|
| Cash ..................................................................... | 12,500 | |
| Sales (1,000 x $12.50)............................................. | | 12,500 |

| | | |
|---|---|---|
| Cost of goods sold ($1,760 - [400 x $.76])) ...................... | 1,456 | |
| Containers receivable ([1,000 x $1.76] x 40%)................. | 704 | |
| Inventory (1,000 x $1.76) ......................................... | | 1,760 |
| Liability – donations for returnable containers ([1,000 x $1.00] x 40%) ................................................ | | 400 |

### When Containers Returned

| | | |
|---|---|---|
| Inventory (1,000 x 40% x $1.76)...................................... | 704 | |
| Liability – donations for returnable containers ............ | 400 | |
| Containers receivable................................................. | | 704 |
| Cash (1,000 x 40% x $1.00) ......................................... | | 400 |

### When Unreturned Containers Replaced

| | | |
|---|---|---|
| Inventory (600 x $1.76) ................................................. | 1,056 | |
| Cash ....................................................................... | | 1,056 |

---

*Case 13-2 (concluded)*

It is probable that at least some pails will be returned. But this is a start-up company without past experience and there are no other firms with similar operations. So, it is likely that a reasonable estimate cannot be made. [The company president stated this was the case.]

If one or both of the accrual criteria is not met, but there is at least a reasonable possibility that the cost will be incurred, a *disclosure note* should describe the contingency. It also should provide an estimate of the possible loss or range of loss, if possible. If an estimate cannot be made, a statement to that effect is needed.

# Research Case 13-3

**[Note: This case encourages the student to reference authoritative pronouncements.]**

Paragraph 54 of SFAC No. 6 explains:

"Assets are probable future economic benefits owned or controlled by the entity. Its liabilities are claims to the entity's assets by other entities and, once incurred, involve nondiscretionary future sacrifices of assets that must be satisfied on demand, at a specified or determinable date, or on occurrence of a specified event. In contrast, equity is a residual interest – what remains after liabilities are deducted from assets – and depends significantly on the profitability of a business enterprise."

Briefly stated, creditors and owners have claims to a single set of probable future economic benefits owned or controlled by the company.

# Judgment Case 13-4

## Requirement 1

The conditions, all of which must be met for accrual, are:
1. The obligation is attributable to employees' services *already performed.*
2. The paid absence can be taken in a later year – the benefit vests (will be compensated even if employment is terminated) or the benefit can be accumulated over time
3. Payment is *probable.*
4. The amount can be reasonably *estimated.*

## Requirement 2

### a. Military leave, maternity leave, and jury time

Custom and practice also influence whether unused rights to paid absences expire or can be carried forward. Obviously, if rights vest (payable even if employment is terminated) they haven't expired. But typically, absence periods for these types of potential absences do not accumulate if unused, so a liability for those benefits usually is not accrued. Company policy and custom may dictate otherwise, however. An example would be a company policy that permits, say, two weeks paid absence each year for such activities as military leave and jury time, where employees not called to such duty can use the time for leisure activities. If the four accrual conditions are otherwise met, a liability for those benefits should be accrued.

### b. Paid sabbatical leave

An expense and related liability should not be accrued if the sabbatical leave is granted for the benefit of the employer, say for the purpose of new product research. However, if the sabbatical leave is intended to provide unrestricted compensated absence for the last four years' service and other conditions are met, accrual is appropriate. Company policy, custom, and actual practice should determine proper treatment.

### c. Sick days

If payment of sick pay benefits depends on future illness, an employer does not have to accrue a liability for benefits, even if the four accrual conditions are met. However, the decision of whether to accrue nonvesting sick pay should be based on actual custom and practice. If the employer routinely pays "sick pay" even when absence is not due to illness, a liability for unused sick pay should be recorded.

# Ethics Case 13-5

Discussion should include these elements.

**Liabilities had been recorded previously.**
When a high degree of uncertainty exists concerning the collection of receivables, revenue should not be recorded at the time of sale. Instead, unearned revenue - a liability - should be recorded. With the high degree of uncertainty surrounding "sales" of Outdoors R Us, it would be very hard to justify recording sales revenue when memberships are signed.

**Ethical Dilemma:**

How does a doubtful justification for a change in reporting methods compare with the perceived need to maintain profits?

**Who is affected ?**
Rice
Sun
Other managers?
The company's auditor
Shareholders
Potential shareholders
The employees
The creditors

# Trueblood Accounting Case 13-6

A solution and extensive discussion materials accompany each case in the Deloitte & Touche Trueblood Case Study Series. These are available to instructors at: https://secure.deloitte.com/rmtbcs00/casesolutions.asp.

# Communication Case 13-7

Assumptions students make will determine the correct answer to some classifications. Depending on the assumptions made, different views can be convincingly defended. The process of developing and synthesizing the arguments will likely be more beneficial than any single solution. Each student should benefit from participating in the process, interacting first with his or her partner, then with the class as a whole. It is important that each student actively participate in the process. Domination by one or two individuals should be discouraged.

A significant benefit of this case is forcing students' consideration of why liabilities currently due are sometimes classified as long-term. It also requires them to carefully consider the profession's definition of current liabilities. Arguments likely will include the following:

a. **Commercial paper**

If it's assumed that early April is prior to the actual issuance of the financial statements, then $12 million can be reported as long-term, but $3 million must be reported as a current liability. Short-term obligations that are expected to be refinanced with long-term obligations can be reported as noncurrent liabilities only if the firm (a) *intends* to refinance on a long-term basis and (b) actually has *demonstrated the ability* to do so. Ability to refinance on a long-term basis can be demonstrated by either an existing *refinancing agreement* or by *actual financing* prior to the issuance of the financial statements. The refinancing agreement in this case limits the ability to refinance to $12 million of the notes. In the absence of other evidence of ability to refinance, the remaining $3 million cannot be reported as long term.

If it's assumed that early April is after the actual issuance of the financial statements, the ability to refinance has not been demonstrated, and all would be reported as short-term.

b. **11% notes**

Unless it's assumed that the investments are noncurrent assets, earmarked as a sinking fund for the notes, the debt should be reported as a current liability because it is payable in the upcoming year, will not be refinanced with long-term obligations, and will not be paid with a noncurrent asset.

## Case 13-7 (concluded)

### c.  10% notes

Short-term obligations that are expected to be refinanced with long-term obligations can be reported as noncurrent liabilities only if the firm (a) *intends* to refinance on a long-term basis and (b) actually has *demonstrated the ability* to do so. Ability to refinance on a long-term basis can be demonstrated by either an existing *refinancing agreement* or by *actual financing* prior to the issuance of the financial statements.  Management's ability to refinance at least some of the notes on a long-term basis was demonstrated by the issuance of new bonds prior to the issuance of the financial statements.  No mention is made of the proceeds of the new bonds or whether they were used to pay off the maturing notes.  If it's assumed the intent was to refinance the notes, then notes would be classified as noncurrent to the extent of the proceeds of the bonds.

### d.  Bonds

If it's assumed that March 15 is prior to the actual issuance of the financial statements, the bonds can be reported as noncurrent liabilities.  The firm (a) *intends* to refinance on a long-term basis with common stock, and (b) actually has *demonstrated the ability* to do so by a *refinancing agreement* prior to the issuance of the financial statements. Refinancing with *either debt or equity* serves this purpose.

# Communication Case 13-8

**Memorandum:**

**To:**   Mitch Riley
**From:** Your Name
**Re:**   Accounting for contingencies

Below is a brief overview of my initial thoughts on how Western should account for the four contingencies in question.

1. The labor disputes constitute a loss contingency. Though a loss is probable, the amount of loss is not reasonably estimable. A disclosure note is appropriate:

> ***Note X: Contingency***
> During 2006, the Company experienced labor disputes at three of its plants. The Company hopes an agreement will soon be reached. However negotiations between the Company and the unions have not produced an acceptable settlement and, as a result, strikes are ongoing at these facilities.

2. The A. J. Conner matter is a gain contingency. Gain contingencies are not accrued even if the gain is probable and reasonably estimable. The gain should be recognized only when realized.

   Though gain contingencies are not recorded in the accounts, they should be disclosed in notes to the financial statements.

> ***Note X: Contingency***
> In accordance with a 2004 contractual agreement with A.J. Conner Company, the Company is entitled to $37 million for certain fees and expense reimbursements. The bankruptcy court has ordered A.J. Conner to pay the Company $23 million immediately upon consummation of a proposed merger with Garner Holding Group.

## Case 13-8 (concluded)

3. The contingency for warranties should be accrued:

Warranty expense ([2% x $2,100 million] – $1 million)   41,000,000
   Estimated warranty liability                              41,000,000

The liability at December 31, 2006, is reported as $41 million.

4. The Crump Holdings lawsuit is a loss contingency. Even though the lawsuit occurred in 2007, the cause for the action occurred in 2006. Only a disclosure note is needed because an unfavorable outcome is reasonably possible, but not probable. Also, the amount is not reasonably estimable.

---

**Note X: Contingency**
Crump Holdings filed suit in January 2007 against the Company seeking $88 million, as an adjustment to the purchase price in connection with the Company's sale of its textile business in 2006. Crump alleges that the Company misstated the assets and liabilities used to calculate the purchase price for the division. The Company has answered the complaint and intends to vigorously defend the lawsuit. Management believes that the final resolution of the case will not have a material adverse effect on the Company's financial position.

---

We can discuss these further in our meeting later today.

# Judgment Case 13-9

This is a loss contingency. Valleck can use the information from the Februar negotiations (occurring after the end of the year) in determining appropriat disclosure. The cause for the suit existed at the end of the year. Valleck shoul accrue both the $190,000 compliance cost and the $205,000 penalty because a agreement has been reached making the loss probable and the amount at leas reasonably estimable. These are the two conditions that require accrual of a los contingency.

The disclosure note should also indicate that accrual was made. This can b accomplished by adding the following sentence to the end of the note:

> ....... Both of the above amounts have been fully accrued as of December 31, 2006.

# Communication Case 13-10

## Suggested Grading Concepts and Grading Scheme:

**Content** (80% )

_____  20   Identifies the situation as a change in estimate.

_____ The liability was originally (appropriately) estimated as $750,000.

_____ The final settlement indicates the estimate should be revised.

_____  40   Describes the journal entry related to the change in amounts.

_____ The liability must be reduced (a debit).

_____ A gain should be recorded (a credit).

_____ The amount of the gain should be $275,000 ($750,000 – $475,000).

_____  20   Indicates that additional disclosure is necessary.

_____  **Bonus (4)** Provides detail regarding the disclosure note.

_____ A disclosure note should describe the effect of a change in estimate on key items.

_____ The effect on income before extraordinary items, net income, and related per share amounts for the current period should be indicated.

_____  80-84 points

**Writing** (20%)

_____  5   Terminology and tone appropriate to the audience of a Vice President.

_____  6   Organization permits ease of understanding.

_____ Introduction that states purpose.

_____ Paragraphs separate main points.

_____  9   English.

_____ Word selection.

_____ Spelling.

_____ Grammar.

_____  20 points

# Research Case 13-11

A liability is accrued if it is both probable that a loss will occur and the amount can be at least reasonably estimated. If one or both of these criteria is not met, but there is at least a reasonable possibility that the loss will occur, a *disclosure note* should describe the nature of the contingency. It also should provide an estimate of the possible loss or range of loss, if possible. If an estimate cannot be made, a statement to that effect is needed.

Often such disclosure notes provide only a very general description of contingencies for losses that were not accrued in the financial statements, reducing the usefulness of the information to investors and creditors.

# Communication Case 13-12
## Suggested Grading Concepts and Grading Scheme:

**Content** (80%)

_____   30   Warranty for awnings (5 each; maximum of 30 for this part)
- _____ change in estimate
- _____ change is effected prospectively only
- _____ no prior financial statements are adjusted
- _____ will affect the adjusting entry for warranty expense in 2006 [Warranty expense and Estimated warranty liability (2% x $4,000,000)]

_____   30   Clean air lawsuit (5 each; maximum of 30 for this part)
- _____ change in estimate
- _____ change is effected prospectively only
- _____ no prior financial statements are adjusted
- _____ will require a revision of the previously recorded liability [Loss – litigation and Liability - litigation increased by $150,000 ($350,000 – 200,000)]

_____   20   Indicates that additional disclosure is necessary for both

_____   **Bonus (4)** Provides detail regarding the disclosure note
- _____ a disclosure note should describe the effect of a change in estimate on key items
- _____ the effect on income before extraordinary items, net income, and related per-share amounts for the current period should be indicated

_____   80-84 points

**Writing** (20%)

_____   5   Terminology and tone appropriate to the audience of division managers

_____   6   Organization permits ease of understanding
- _____ introduction that states purpose
- _____ paragraphs separate main points

_____   9   English
- _____ word selection
- _____ spelling
- _____ grammar

# Real World Case 13-13

## Requirement 1

The frequent flyer program is offered in order to enhance revenues and under the matching principle is properly recognized as an operating expense in the year sales are made (travel miles are earned).

## Requirement 2

Incremental cost refers to the additional cost of providing the free travel that otherwise would not be incurred. This is the conceptually appropriate measure of the operating expense.

## Requirement 3

Theoretically, the cost of the portion of the travel to be provided in the coming year should be considered current. Because the awards earned do not expire for several years, presumably, at least a portion of the cost should theoretically be considered long term.

## Requirement 4

|  | $ in millions |
|---|---|
| Operating expense (given in note)............................ | 215 |
| Air traffic liability ............................................. | 215 |

# Real World Case 13-14

## Requirement 1

The litigation represents a loss contingency. A loss contingency should be accrued if payment is both probable and reasonably estimable. Both criteria were met in this case, necessitating the accrual.

## Requirement 2

The liability is different for two reasons. First, $30.3 million of the costs were paid in 2004. Second, "estimates were refined and accruals were adjusted accordingly."

## Requirement 3

|  | ($ in millions) |  |
| --- | --- | --- |
| Remediation liability ($158.1 – 127.5) ............. | 30.6 |  |
| Cash ........................................................ |  | 30.3 |
| Gain - accrual adjustment (to balance)......... |  | .3 |

# Ethics Case 13-15

Discussion should include these elements.

**Warranty estimate**

The cost of product warranties (or product guarantees) cannot be predicted with certainty. However, to match expenses and revenues, we estimate the cost. The estimated warranty liability is credited and warranty expense is debited in the reporting period in which the product under warranty is sold. In this case, the estimate is probably "softer" than normal because the company is new and has little experience in these estimates. However, Craig presumably made the estimates on the basis of the best information available. The current effort to change the estimate clearly is motivated by the desire to "window dress" performance.

**Ethical Dilemma:**

Is Craig's obligation to challenge the questionable change in estimates greater than the obligation to the financial interests of his employer and bosses?

**Who is affected?**

Craig

President, controller, and other managers

Shareholders

Potential shareholders

The employees

The creditors

The company's auditors

# International Case 13-16

The analysis should indicate similarities and differences between the United States and the chosen country focusing on the following issues:

a. Depending on the country chosen, the financial statement differences may be minimal. In most countries, current liabilities are reported as a separate classification of liabilities as in the U.S. In other countries, Great Britain, for example, they often are netted against current assets.

b. In most countries, like the United States, loss contingencies must be accrued if estimable and probable. Precise meaning of those criteria varies. In a few countries, China, for example, no treatment is specified. In Argentina, gain contingencies are accrued if highly probable, but in most countries they are disclosed only. In several countries, Germany, Italy, and Spain, for instance, they are not disclosed.

The analysis might also comment whether cultural differences are likely contributors to the differences observed.

# Analysis Case 13-17

## Requirement 1

Current ratio      $=$     $\dfrac{\text{Current assets}}{\text{Current liabilities}}$

                $=$     $\dfrac{\$1,879}{\$1,473}$

                $=$     <u>1.28</u>

*Industry average* $= 1.5$

The current ratio is one of the most widely used ratios. It is intended as a measure of short-term solvency and is determined by dividing current assets by current liabilities. Comparing assets that either are cash or will be converted to cash in the near term, with those liabilities that must be satisfied in the near term, provides a useful measure of a company's liquidity. A ratio of 1 to 1 or higher often is considered a rule-of-thumb standard, but like other ratios, acceptability should be evaluated in the context of the industry in which the company operates and other specific circumstances. IGF's current ratio is slightly less than the industry average which, on the surface, might indicate a liquidity problem. Keep in mind, though, that industry averages are only one indication of adequacy and that the current ratio is but one indication of liquidity.

## Case 13-17 (concluded)

## Requirement 2

| | | |
|---|---|---|
| **Acid-test ratio** | = | Quick assets |
| **(or quick ratio)** | | Current liabilities |

$$\text{Acid-test ratio} = \frac{\$48 + 347 + 358}{\$1,473}$$

$$= \underline{0.51}$$

*Industry average* = 0.80

The acid-test or quick ratio attempts to adjust for the implicit assumption of the current ratio that all current assets are equally liquid. This ratio is similar to the current ratio, but is based on a more conservative measure of assets available to pay current liabilities. Specifically, the numerator, quick assets, includes only cash and cash equivalents, short-term investments, and accounts receivable. By eliminating current assets such as inventories and prepaid expenses that are less readily convertible into cash, the acid-test ratio provides a more rigorous indication of a company's short-term solvency than does the current ratio.

Once again, IGF's ratio is less than that of the industry as a whole. Is this confirmation that liquidity is an issue for IGF? Perhaps; perhaps not. It does, though, raise a red flag that suggests caution when assessing other areas. It's important to remember that each ratio is but one piece of the puzzle. For example, profitability is probably the best long run indication of liquidity. Also, management may be very efficient in managing current assets so that some current assets – receivables or inventory – are more liquid than they otherwise would be and more readily available to satisfy liabilities.

# Analysis Case 13-18

1.  The four components of current liabilities are:

| ($ in millions) | 2004 | 2003 |
|---|---|---|
| **Current Liabilities:** | | |
| Current portion of long-term debt | $ 750 | $ 308 |
| Accrued salaries and employee benefits | 1,062 | 724 |
| Accounts payable | 1,615 | 1,168 |
| Accrued expenses | 1,305 | 1,135 |
| Total current liabilities | $4,732 | $3,335 |

2.  Current assets are sufficient to cover current liabilities in both 2004 and 2003:

Total current assets:     2004: $4,970     2003: $3,941

The current ratio for 2004 is: $4,970 \div 4,732 = 1.05$
The current ratio for 2003 is: $3,941 \div 3,335 = 1.18$,
   which is slightly higher.

Comparing liabilities that must be satisfied soon with assets that either are cash or will be converted to cash soon provides a useful measure of a company's liquidity. A current ratio of 1 to 1 or higher sometimes is considered a rule-of-thumb standard. However, the current ratio is but one indication of liquidity. Each ratio is but one piece of the puzzle.

3.  From Note 3 we see that the two largest accrued expenses for FedEx in 2004 were employee benefits and insurance expense. An accrued expense is an expense incurred during the current period, but not yet paid. FedEx recorded these as adjusting entries at the end of the reporting period with debits to the appropriate expenses and credits to related liabilities. This helps achieve a proper matching of expenses with the revenues they help generate.

# Chapter 14 Bonds and Long-Term Notes

## QUESTIONS FOR REVIEW OF KEY TOPICS

### Question 14-1

Periodic interest is calculated as the *effective interest rate times the amount of the debt outstanding during the period*. This same principle applies to the flip side of the transaction, i.e., the creditor's receivable or investment. The approach also is the same regardless of the specific form of the debt – that is, whether in the form of notes, bonds, leases, pensions, or other debt instruments.

### Question 14-2

Long-term liabilities are appropriately reported at their *present values*. The present value of a liability is the present value of its related cash flows – specifically the present value of the face amount of the debt instrument, if any, plus the present value of stated interest payments, if any. Both should be discounted to present value at the effective (market) rate of interest at issuance.

### Question 14-3

Bonds and notes are very similar. Both typically obligate the issuing corporation to repay a stated amount (e.g., the *principal, par value, face amount*, or *maturity value*) at a specified *maturity date*. In return for the use of the money borrowed, the company also agrees to pay *interest* to the lender between the issue date and maturity. The periodic interest is a stated percentage of face amount. In concept, bonds and notes are accounted for in precisely the same way.

Normally a company will borrow cash from a bank or other financial institution by signing a promissory note. Corporations, especially medium- and large- sized firms, often choose to borrow cash by issuing bonds instead. A bond issue, in effect, breaks down a large debt into manageable parts ($1,000 units). Also, bonds typically have longer maturities than notes. The most common form of corporate debt is bonds.

### Question 14-4

All of the specific promises made to bondholders are described in a bond indenture. This formal agreement will specify the bond issue's face amount, the stated interest rate, the method of paying interest (whether the bonds are registered bonds or coupon bonds), whether the bonds are backed by a lien on specified assets, and whether they are subordinated to other debt. The bond indenture also might provide for their redemption through a call feature, by serial payments, through sinking fund provisions, or by conversion. It also will specify the trustee (usually a commercial bank or other financial institution) appointed by the issuing firm to represent the rights of the bondholders. The bond indenture serves as a contract between the company and the bondholder(s). If the company fails to live up to the terms of the bond indenture, the trustee may bring legal action against the company on behalf of the bondholders.

*Answers to Questions (continued)*

## Question 14-5
All bonds sell at their price plus any interest that has accrued since the last interest date to simplify the process of paying and recording interest. The buyer is asked to pay the seller accrued interest for any time that has elapsed since the last interest date in addition to the price of the bonds so that when a full six months' interest is paid at the next interest date, the net interest paid/received will be correct for the time the bonds have been held by the investor.

## Question 14-6
In order for Brandon to sell its bonds that pay only 11.5% stated interest in a 12.25% market the bonds would have to be priced at a discount from face amount. The discount would be the amount that causes the bond issue to be *priced to yield the market rate.* In other words, an investor paying that price would earn an effective rate of return on the investment equal to the 12.25% market rate.

## Question 14-7
The price will be the present value of the periodic cash *interest* payments (face amount x stated rate) plus the present value of the *principal* payable at maturity. Both interest and principal are discounted to present value at the market rate of interest for securities of similar risk and maturity.

## Question 14-8
In a strict sense, it's true that zero-coupon bonds pay no interest. "Zeros" offer a return in the form of a "deep discount" from the face amount. Still, interest accrues at the effective rate times the outstanding balance, but no interest is paid periodically. So, interest on zero-coupon bonds is determined and reported in precisely the same manner as on interest-paying bonds. Under the concept of *accrual accounting*, the periodic effective interest is unaffected by when the cash actually is paid. Corporations can deduct for tax purposes the annual interest expense, but without cash outflow until the bonds mature.

## Question 14-9
When bonds are issued at a premium the debt *declines* each period because the effective interest each period is *less than* the cash interest paid. The "overpayments" each period reduce the balance owed. This is precisely the opposite of when debt is sold at a discount. In that case, the effective interest each period is more than the cash paid, and the "underpayment" of interest adds to the amount owed.

## Question 14-10

By the **effective interest method,** interest is recorded each period as the *effective market rate of interest multiplied by the outstanding balance of the debt* (during the interest period). This simply is n application of the accrual concept, consistent with accruing all expenses as they are incurred. The unpaid" (or "overpaid") portion of the effective interest increases (or decreases) the existing liability nd is reflected as "amortization" of the discount (or premium).

An exception to the conceptually appropriate method of determining interest for bond issues is he **straight-line method.** Companies are allowed to determine interest indirectly by allocating a iscount or a premium *equally* to each period over the term to maturity if doing so produces results aat are not materially different from the interest method. The firm's decision should be guided by vhether the straight-line method would tend to mislead investors and creditors in the particular ircumstance.

The straight-line method results in a *constant dollar amount* of interest each period. By the traight-line method, the amount of the discount to be reduced periodically is calculated, and the ffective interest is the "plug" figure. By the effective interest method, the dollar amounts of interest ary over the term to maturity because the *percentage rate* of interest remains constant, but is pplied to a changing debt balance. The "straight-line method," is not an alternative method of etermining interest in a conceptual sense, but is an application of the *materiality concept.*

## Question 14-11

The prescribed treatment requires a debit to an asset account – "debt issue costs" which is then llocated to expense, usually on a straight-line basis. An appealing alternative would be to reduce he recorded amount of the debt by the debt issue costs. This approach has the appeal of reflecting he effect debt issue costs have on the effective interest rate.

Debt issue costs reduce the net cash the company receives from the sale of the financial nstrument. A lower net amount is borrowed at the same cost, increasing the effective interest rate. he actual increase in the effective interest rate is reflected in the interest expense if the issue cost is llowed to reduce the premium (or increase the discount) on the debt.

This approach also is consistent with the treatment of issue costs when shares of stock are sold. hare issue costs are recorded as a reduction in the amount credited to stock accounts (Chapter 19).

## Question 14-12

When the *stated* interest rate is not indicative of the *market* rate at the time a note is negotiated, he value of the asset (cash or noncash) or service exchanged for the note establishes the market rate. his rate is the *implicit rate of interest.*

If the value of the asset (or service) is not readily determinable, the implicit rate may not be pparent. In that case an appropriate rate should be "imputed" as the rate that would be expected in a imilar transaction, under similar circumstances.

The economic essence of a transaction should prevail over its outward appearance. The ccountant should look beyond the *form* of this transaction and record its *substance.* The amount ctually paid for the asset is the present value of the cash flows called for by the loan agreement, liscounted at the "imputed" market rate. Both the asset acquired and the liability used to purchase it hould be recorded at the *real* cost.

# Answers to Questions (continued)

## Question 14-13

In accordance with FAS 150, mandatorily redeemable shares, which the issuing company i obligated to buy back in exchange for cash or other assets, must be reported as liabilities.

## Question 14-14

When notes are paid in installments, rather than a single amount at maturity, installmen payments typically are equal amounts each period. Each payment will include both an amoun representing interest and an amount representing a reduction of principal. At maturity, the principa is completely paid. The installment amount is calculated by dividing the amount of the loan by th appropriate discount factor for the present value of an annuity.

Determining periodic interest is the same as for a note whose principal is paid at maturity - effective interest rate times the outstanding principal. But the periodic cash payments are larger an there is no lump-sum payment at maturity.

## Question 14-15

For all long-term borrowings, disclosure should include (a) the fair values, (b) the aggregat amounts maturing, and (c) sinking fund requirements (if any) for *each of the next five years*.

## Question 14-16

Regardless of the method used to retire debt prior to its scheduled maturity date, the gain or los on the transaction is simply the difference between the carrying amount of the debt at that time an the cash paid to retire it. To record the extinguishment the account balances pertinent to the debt ar removed from the books. Cash is credited for the amount paid (the call price or market price). Th difference between the carrying amount and the reacquisition price is the gain or loss.

## Question 14-17

Gains and losses are reported as extraordinary items when they are considered to be both unusua and infrequent. In that case they are reported separate from ordinary operations and net of thei related income tax effects.

## Question 14-18

GAAP requires that the entire issue price of convertible bonds be recorded as debt, precisely th same way, in fact, as for nonconvertible bonds. On the other hand, the issue price of bonds witl detachable warrants is allocated between the two different securities on the basis of their marke values.

The difference is based on the relative separability of the debt and equity features of the tw securities. In the case of convertible bonds, the two features of the security, the debt and th conversion option, are physically inseparable — the option cannot be exercised without surrenderin the debt. But the debt and equity features of bonds with detachable warrants *can* be separated Unlike a conversion feature, warrants can be separated from the bonds and can be exercise independently or traded in the market separately from bonds. In substance, two different securities - the bonds and the warrants – are sold as a "package" for a single issue price.

## Answers to Questions (concluded)

### Question 14-19

Additional consideration a company provides to induce conversion of convertible debt should be recorded as an expense of the period. It is measured at the fair value of that consideration. This might be cash paid, the market price of stock warrants given, or the market value of additional shares issued due to modifying the conversion ratio.

### Question 14-20

By definition, a troubled debt restructuring involves some *concessions* on the part of the creditor (lender). A creditor may feel it can minimize losses by *restructuring* a debt agreement, rather than forcing liquidation. A troubled debt restructuring takes one of two forms, with the second further categorized for accounting purposes:

1. The debt may be *settled* at the time of the restructuring, or
2. The debt may be *continued*, but with *modified terms*.
    a. Under the modified terms, total cash to be paid *is less than* the carrying amount of the debt.
    b. Under the modified terms, total cash to be paid *exceeds* the carrying amount of the debt.

### Question 14-21

Pratt has a *gain* of $2 million (the difference between the carrying amount of the debt and the fair value of the property transferred). Pratt also must adjust the carrying amount of the land to its fair value prior to recording its exchange for the debt. Pratt would need to change the recorded amount for the property specified in the exchange agreement from $2 million to the $3 million fair market value. This produces a "gain on disposition of assets" of $1 million. So, Pratt would report two items on its income statement in connection with the troubled debt restructuring: (1) a $2 million gain on troubled debt restructuring and (2) a "gain on disposition of assets" of $1 million.

### Question 14-22

(a) When the total future cash payments are less than the carrying amount of the debt, the difference is recorded as a *gain* to the *debtor* at the date of restructure. *No interest* is recorded thereafter. All subsequent cash payments produce reductions of principal.

(b) When the total future cash payments exceed the carrying amount of the debt, no reduction of the existing debt is necessary and no entry is required at the time of the debt restructuring. The accounting objective is to determine the new (lower) effective interest and to record interest expense for the remaining term of the loan at that new, lower rate.

# BRIEF EXERCISES

## Brief Exercise 14-1

$$\underset{\substack{\text{face} \\ \text{amount}}}{\$30,000,000} \times \underset{\substack{\text{annual} \\ \text{rate}}}{6\%} \times \underset{\substack{\text{fraction of the} \\ \text{annual period}}}{3/12} = \underset{\substack{\text{accrued} \\ \text{interest}}}{\$450,000}$$

## Brief Exercise 14-2

| | | | | |
|---|---|---|---|---|
| Interest | $ 2,000,000 ¥ | x | 23.11477* = | $46,229,540 |
| Principal | $80,000,000 | x | 0.30656** = | 24,524,800 |
| *Present value (price) of the bonds* | | | | $70,754,340 |

¥  [5÷2] % x $80,000,000
*   present value of an ordinary annuity of $1: n=40, i=3%
**  present value of $1: n=40, i=3%

## Brief Exercise 14-3

The price will be the present value of the periodic cash *interest* payments (face amount x stated rate) plus the present value of the *principal* payable at maturity. Both interest and principal are discounted to present value at the market rate of interest for securities of similar risk and maturity. When the stated rate and the market rate are the same, the bonds will sell at face value, $75 million in this instance.

## Brief Exercise 14-4

| | | | | |
|---|---|---|---|---|
| Interest | $ 2,500,000 ¥ | x | 27.35548* = | $ 68,388,700 |
| Principal | $100,000,000 | x | 0.45289** = | 45,289,000 |
| *Present value (price) of the bonds* | | | | $113,677,700 |

¥  [5÷2] % x $100,000,000
*   present value of an ordinary annuity of $1: n=40, i=2%
**  present value of $1: n=40, i=2%

# Brief Exercise 14-5

Interest will be the effective rate times the outstanding balance:

4% x $82,218,585 = $3,288,743

# Brief Exercise 14-6

Interest will be the effective rate times the outstanding balance:

### June 30
| | | |
|---|---|---|
| Interest expense (2% x $69,033,776).............................. | 1,380,676 | |
| Discount on bonds payable (difference)................. | | 180,676 |
| Cash (1.5% x $80,000,000)....................................... | | 1,200,000 |

### December 31
| | | |
|---|---|---|
| Interest expense (2% x [$69,033,776 + 180,676]).......... | 1,384,289 | |
| Discount on bonds payable (difference)................. | | 184,289 |
| Cash (1.5% x $80,000,000)....................................... | | 1,200,000 |

$1,380,676 + 1,384,289 = $2,764,965

# Brief Exercise 14-7

Interest will be a plug figure:

$80,000,000 - 69,033,776 = $10,966,224 discount

$10,966,224 / 40 semiannual periods = $274,156 reduction each period

### June 30
| | | |
|---|---|---|
| Interest expense (to balance)......................................... | 1,474,156 | |
| Discount on bonds payable (difference)................. | | 274,156 |
| Cash (1.5% x $80,000,000)....................................... | | 1,200,000 |

### December 31
| | | |
|---|---|---|
| Interest expense (to balance)......................................... | 1,474,156 | |
| Discount on bonds payable (difference)................. | | 274,156 |
| Cash (1.5% x $80,000,000)....................................... | | 1,200,000 |

$1,474,156 + 1,474,156 = $2,948,312

# Brief Exercise 14-8

Interest will be the effective rate times the outstanding balance:

**June 30**

| | | |
|---|---|---|
| Cash (1.5% x $80,000,000) ........................................... | 1,200,000 | |
| Discount on investment in bonds (difference)............ | 180,676 | |
|    Interest revenue (2% x $69,033,776) ........................... | | 1,380,676 |

**December 31**

| | | |
|---|---|---|
| Cash (1.5% x $80,000,000) ........................................... | 1,200,000 | |
| Discount on investment in bonds (difference)............ | 184,289 | |
|    Interest revenue (2% x [$69,033,776 + 180,676]) ....... | | 1,384,289 |

# Brief Exercise 14-9

| | | | | | |
|---|---|---|---|---|---|
| Interest | $6,000¥ | x | 2.72325 * | = | $ 16,340 |
| Principal | $300,000 | x | 0.86384 ** | = | 259,152 |
| *Present value (price) of the note* | | | | | $275,492 |

¥  2% x $300,000

\*  present value of an ordinary annuity of $1: n=3, i=5%

\*\* present value of $1: n=3, i=5%

| | | |
|---|---|---|
| Equipment (price determined above) ................................ | 275,492 | |
| Discount on notes payable (difference) .......................... | 24,508 | |
|    Notes payable (face amount) ......................................... | | 300,000 |

# Brief Exercise 14-10

$$\$300,000 \div 2.72325 = \$110,163$$

| amount of loan | (from Table 4) n=3, i=5% | installment payment |
|---|---|---|

Helpful, but not required:

| Dec.31 | Cash Payment | Effective Interest 5% x Outstanding Balance | Decrease in Balance Balance Reduction | Outstanding Balance |
|---|---|---|---|---|
| | | | | 300,000 |
| 1 | 110,163 | .05 (300,000) = 15,000 | 95,163 | 204,837 |
| 2 | 110,163 | .05 (204,837) = 10,242 | 99,921 | 104,917 |
| 3 | 110,163 | .05(104,917) = 5,246 | 104,917 | 0 |

| | | |
|---|---|---|
| Interest expense (5% x ($300,000 – [$110,163 – 5% x $300,000])) | 10,242 | |
| Note payable (difference) ................................................. | 99,921 | |
| Cash (payment determined above) ................................. | | 110,163 |

# Brief Exercise 14-11

| | ($ in millions) |
|---|---|
| Bonds payable (face amount)...................................... | 60.0 |
| Loss on early extinguishment (to balance)................. | 3.2 |
| Discount on bonds (given)...................................... | 2.0 |
| Cash ($60,000,000 x 102%) ...................................... | 61.2 |

# Brief Exercise 14-12

The issue price of bonds with detachable warrants is allocated between the two different securities on the basis of their market values.

|  | ($ in millions) | |
|---|---|---|
| Cash (102% x $60 million) ................................................. | 61.2 | |
| Discount on bonds payable (difference) ............................... | 1.8 | |
|     Bonds payable (face amount)............................................ | | 60.0 |
|     Paid-in capital – stock warrants outstanding | | |
|       ($5 x 10 warrants x 60,000 bonds) ...................................... | | 3.0 |

# Brief Exercise 14-13

GAAP requires that the entire issue price of convertible bonds be recorded as debt, precisely the same way, in fact, as for nonconvertible bonds.

|  | ($ in millions) | |
|---|---|---|
| Cash (102% x $60 million) ...................................................... | 61.2 | |
|     Premium on bonds payable (difference) ........................... | | 1.2 |
|     Bonds payable (face amount)............................................. | | 60.0 |

# EXERCISES

## Exercise 14-1

### Requirement 1

$100 million  x    12%     x     ²/₁₂      =      $2 million
   face         annual     fraction of the     accrued
  amount      rate     annual period      interest

### Requirement 2

|                                                                              | ($ in millions) |     |
| ---------------------------------------------------------------------------- | :-------------: | :-: |
| Cash ($99 million plus accrued interest) .....................................  |       101       |     |
| Discount on bonds ($100 million – $99 million).....................            |        1        |     |
|   Bonds payable (face amount)..............................................    |                 | 100 |
|   Interest payable (accrued interest determined above)............         |                 |  2  |

# Exercise 14-2

The DD Corp. bonds are appropriately priced to yield the market rate of interest. The GG Corp. bonds are slightly underpriced at the stated price and therefore are the most attractive. The BB Corp. bonds are slightly overpriced at the stated price and therefore are the least attractive. Bonds should be priced to yield the market rate, 10% in this case. When this rate is used to price the bonds, we get the prices shown below. Presumably, the market rate changed since the underwriters priced two of the bond issues.

**BB Corp. bonds:**

| | | | | | |
|---|---|---|---|---|---|
| Interest | $ 5,500,000 ¥ | x | 17.15909 * | = | $ 94,374,995 |
| Principal | $100,000,000 | x | 0.14205 ** | = | 14,205,000 |
| *Present value (price) of the bonds* | | | | | $108,579,995 |

¥   [11÷2] % x $100,000,000
\*   present value of an ordinary annuity of $1: n=40, i=5%
\*\*   present value of $1: n=40, i=5%

**DD Corp. bonds:**

| | | | | | |
|---|---|---|---|---|---|
| Interest | $ 5,000,000 ¥ | x | 17.15909 * | = | $ 85,795,450 |
| Principal | $100,000,000 | x | 0.14205 ** | = | 14,205,000 |
| *Present value (price) of the bonds* | | | | | $100,000,450 |

Note: The result differs from $100,000,000 only because the present value factors in any present value table are rounded. Because the stated rate and the market rate are the same, the true present value is $100,000,000.

¥   [10÷2] % x $100,000,000
\*   present value of an ordinary annuity of $1: n=40, i=5%
\*\*   present value of $1: n=40, i=5%

**GG Corp. bonds:**

| | | | | | |
|---|---|---|---|---|---|
| Interest | $ 4,500,000 ¥ | x | 17.15909 * | = | $77,215,905 |
| Principal | $100,000,000 | x | 0.14205 ** | = | 14,205,000 |
| *Present value (price) of the bonds* | | | | | $91,420,905 |

¥   [9÷2] % x $100,000,000
\*   present value of an ordinary annuity of $1: n=40, i=5%
\*\*   present value of $1: n=40, i=5%

# Exercise 14-3

**1.**

| Maturity | Interest paid | Stated rate | | Effective (market) rate | |
|---|---|---|---|---|---|
| 10 years | annually | 10% | | 12% | |
| Interest | $100,000 ¥ | x | 5.65022 * = | | $565,022 |
| Principal | $1,000,000 | x | 0.32197 ** = | | 321,970 |
| *Present value (price) of the bonds* | | | | | $886,992 |

¥   10% x $1,000,000
*   present value of an ordinary annuity of $1: n=10, i=12%
**   present value of $1: n=10, i=12%

**2.**

| Maturity | Interest paid | Stated rate | | Effective (market) rate | |
|---|---|---|---|---|---|
| 10 years | semiannually | 10% | | 12% | |
| Interest | $50,000 ¥ | x | 11.46992 * = | | $573,496 |
| Principal | $1,000,000 | x | 0.31180 ** = | | 311,800 |
| *Present value (price) of the bonds* | | | | | $885,296 |

¥   5% x $1,000,000
*   present value of an ordinary annuity of $1: n=20, i=6%
**   present value of $1: n=20, i=6%

**3.**

| Maturity | Interest paid | Stated rate | | Effective (market) rate | |
|---|---|---|---|---|---|
| 10 years | semiannually | 12% | | 10% | |
| Interest | $60,000 ¥ | x | 12.46221 * = | $ 747,733 | |
| Principal | $1,000,000 | x | 0.37689 ** = | | 376,890 |
| *Present value (price) of the bonds* | | | | | $1,124,623 |

¥   6% x $1,000,000
*   present value of an ordinary annuity of $1: n=20, i=5%
**   present value of $1: n=20, i=5%

**4.**

| Maturity | Interest paid | Stated rate | | Effective (market) rate | |
|---|---|---|---|---|---|
| 20 years | semiannually | 12% | | 10% | |
| Interest | $60,000 ¥ | x | 17.15909 * = | | $1,029,545 |
| Principal | $1,000,000 | x | 0.14205 ** = | | 142,050 |
| *Present value (price) of the bonds* | | | | | $1,171,595 |

¥   6% x $1,000,000
*   present value of an ordinary annuity of $1: n=40, i=5%
**   present value of $1: n=40, i=5%

# Exercise 14-3 (concluded)

**5. Maturity**     **Interest paid**     **Stated rate**     **Effective (market) rate**

| 20 years | semiannually | 12% | | | 12% |
|---|---|---|---|---|---|
| Interest | $60,000 ¥ | x | 15.04630 * | = | $902,778 |
| Principal | $1,000,000 | x | 0.09722 ** | = | 97,220 |
| *Present value (price) of the bonds* | | | | | $999,998 |

actually, **$1,000,000** if PV table factors were not rounded

¥   6% x $1,000,000

*   present value of an ordinary annuity of $1: n=40, i=6%

**   present value of $1: n=40, i=6%

# Exercise 14-4

## 1. Price of the bonds at January 1, 2006

| | | | | | |
|---|---|---|---|---|---|
| Interest | $4,000,000¥ | x | 11.46992 * | = | $45,879,680 |
| Principal | $80,000,000 | x | 0.31180 ** | = | 24,944,000 |
| *Present value (price) of the bonds* | | | | | $70,823,680 |

¥   5% x $80,000,000
*   present value of an ordinary annuity of $1: n=20, i=6%
** present value of $1: n=20, i=6%

## 2. January 1, 2006

| | | |
|---|---|---|
| Cash (price determined above) ...................................... | 70,823,680 | |
| Discount on bonds (difference) .................................. | 9,176,320 | |
| Bonds payable (face amount)................................ | | 80,000,000 |

## 3. June 30, 2006

| | | |
|---|---|---|
| Interest expense (6% x $70,823,680).............................. | 4,249,421 | |
| Discount on bonds payable (difference)................. | | 249,421 |
| Cash (5% x $80,000,000) ........................................ | | 4,000,000 |

## 4. December 31, 2006

| | | |
|---|---|---|
| Interest expense (6% x [$70,823,680 + 249,421])............ | 4,264,386 | |
| Discount on bonds payable (difference)................. | | 264,386 |
| Cash (5% x $80,000,000) ........................................ | | 4,000,000 |

# Exercise 14-5

## 1. January 1, 2006

| | | | | |
|---|---|---|---|---|
| Interest | $4,000,000¥ | x 11.46992 * | = | $45,879,680 |
| Principal | $80,000,000 | x 0.31180 ** | = | 24,944,000 |
| *Present value (price) of the bonds* | | | | $70,823,680 |

¥ 5% x $80,000,000
* present value of an ordinary annuity of $1: n=20, i=6%
** present value of $1: n=20, i=6%

| | | |
|---|---|---|
| Bond investment (face amount).................................. | 80,000,000 | |
| Discount on bond investment (difference).............. | | 9,176,320 |
| Cash (price determined above) .................................. | | 70,823,680 |

## 2. June 30, 2006

| | | |
|---|---|---|
| Cash (5% x $80,000,000).............................................. | 4,000,000 | |
| Discount on bond investment (difference) .................... | 249,421 | |
| Interest revenue (6% x $70,823,680)............................ | | 4,249,421 |

## 3. December 31, 2006

| | | |
|---|---|---|
| Cash (5% x $80,000,000).............................................. | 4,000,000 | |
| Discount on bond investment (difference) ................. | 264,386 | |
| Interest revenue (6% x [$70,823,680 + 249,421])........ | | 4,264,386 |

# Exercise 14-6

## 1. Price of the bonds at January 1, 2006

| | | | | |
|---|---|---|---|---|
| Interest | $16,000,000¥ | X | 11.46992 * = | $183,518,720 |
| Principal | $320,000,000 | X | 0.31180 ** = | 99,776,000 |
| *Present value (price) of the bonds* | | | | $283,294,720 |

¥  5% x $320,000,000

*  present value of an ordinary annuity of $1: n=20, i=6%

** present value of $1: n=20, i=6%

## 2. Liability at December 31, 2006

| | |
|---|---|
| Bonds payable (face amount)........................................ | $320,000,000 |
| Less: discount .......................................................... | 36,705,280 |
| Initial balance, January 1, 2006.................................. | $283,294,720 |
| June 30, 2006 discount amortization........................... | 997,683* |
| Dec. 31, 2006 discount amortization........................... | 1,057,544** |
| December 31, 2006 net liability ................................. | $285,349,947 |

## 3. Interest expense for year ended December 31, 2006

| | |
|---|---|
| June 30, 2006 interest expense .................................. | $16,997,683* |
| Dec. 31, 2006 interest expense .................................. | 17,057,544** |
| Interest expense for 2006........................................... | $34,055,227 |

## 4. Statement of cash flows for year ended December 31, 2006

Myriad would report the cash inflow of $283,294,720*** from the sale of the bonds as a cash inflow from financing activities in its statement of cash flows.

The $32,000,000 cash interest paid *, ** is cash outflow from operating activities because interest is an income statement (operating) item.

## *Exercise 14-6 (concluded)*

### Calculations:

#### January 1, 2006***
Cash (price determined above)......................................283,294,720
Discount on bonds (difference)................................... 36,705,280
   Bonds payable (face amount) ...............................      320,000,000

#### June 30, 2006*
Interest expense (6% x $283,294,720) ........................... 16,997,683
   Discount on bonds payable (difference) ................      997,683
   Cash (5% x $320,000,000) ......................................    16,000,000

#### December 31, 2006**
Interest expense (6% x [$283,294,720 + 997,683]) .......... 17,057,544
   Discount on bonds payable (difference) ................    1,057,544
   Cash (5% x $320,000,000) ......................................    16,000,000

# Exercise 14-7

## 1. Price of the bonds at June 30, 2006

| | | | | | |
|---|---|---|---|---|---|
| Interest | $58,500¥ | x | 15.04630 * | = | $880,209 |
| Principal | $900,000 | x | 0.09722 ** | = | 87,498 |
| *Present value (price) of the bonds* | | | | | $967,707 |

¥   6.5% x $900,000

*   present value of an ordinary annuity of $1: n=40, i=6%

**   present value of $1: n=40, i=6%

## 2. June 30, 2006

| | | |
|---|---|---|
| Cash (price determined above) ....................................... | 967,707 | |
| Bonds payable (face amount)................................... | | 900,000 |
| Premium on bonds (difference) ............................. | | 67,707 |

## 3. December 31, 2006

| | | |
|---|---|---|
| Interest expense (6% x $967,707)................................... | 58,062 | |
| Premium on bonds payable (difference)...................... | 438 | |
| Cash (6.5% x $900,000) ......................................... | | 58,500 |

## 4. June 30, 2007

| | | |
|---|---|---|
| Interest expense (6% x [$967,707 – 438]) ...................... | 58,036 | |
| Premium on bonds payable (difference)...................... | 464 | |
| Cash (6.5% x $900,000) ......................................... | | 58,500 |

# Exercise 14-8

### 1. Price of the bonds at January 1, 2006

| | | | | | |
|---|---|---|---|---|---|
| Interest | $7,500,000¥ | x | 13.76483 * | = | $103,236,225 |
| Principal | $150,000,000 | x | 0.17411 ** | = | 26,116,500 |
| *Present value (price) of the bonds* | | | | | $129,352,725 |

¥  5% x $150,000,000
*  present value of an ordinary annuity of $1: n=30, i=6%
** present value of $1: n=30, i=6%

### 2. January 1, 2006

| | | |
|---|---|---|
| Cash (price determined above)................................ | 129,352,725 | |
| Discount on bonds (difference)............................ | 20,647,275 | |
| Bonds payable (face amount) ........................... | | 150,000,000 |

### 3. June 30, 2006

| | | |
|---|---|---|
| Interest expense ($7,500,000 + $688,243) ........................ | 8,188,243 | |
| Discount on bonds payable ($20,647,275 ÷ 30) ........ | | 688,243 |
| Cash (5% x $150,000,000) ........................................ | | 7,500,000 |

### 4. December 31, 2013

| | | |
|---|---|---|
| Interest expense ($7,500,000 + $688,243) ........................ | 8,188,243 | |
| Discount on bonds payable ($20,647,275 ÷ 30) ........ | | 688,243 |
| Cash (5% x $150,000,000) ........................................ | | 7,500,000 |

*[Using the straight-line method, each interest entry is the same.]*

# Exercise 14-9

### 1. January 1, 2006

| | | | | | |
|---|---|---|---|---|---|
| Interest | $7,500,000¥ | x | 13.76483 * | = | $103,236,225 |
| Principal | $150,000,000 | x | 0.17411 ** | = | 26,116,500 |
| | *Present value (price) of the bonds* | | | | $129,352,725 |

¥   5% x $150,000,000
*    present value of an ordinary annuity of $1: n=30, i=6%
**  present value of $1: n=30, i=6%

| | | |
|---|---|---|
| Bond investment (face amount) .............................. | 150,000,000 | |
| Discount on bond investment (difference) ......... | | 20,647,275 |
| Cash (price determined above)............................... | | 129,352,725 |

### 2. June 30, 2006

| | | |
|---|---|---|
| Cash (5% x $150,000,000) ........................................ | 7,500,000 | |
| Discount on bond investment ($20,647,275 ÷ 30) ........ | 688,243 | |
| Interest revenue ($7,500,000 + $688,243) ................... | | 8,188,243 |

### 3. December 31, 2013

| | | |
|---|---|---|
| Cash (5% x $150,000,000) ........................................ | 7,500,000 | |
| Discount on bond investment ($20,647,275 ÷ 30) ........ | 688,243 | |
| Interest revenue ($7,500,000 + $688,243) ................... | | 8,188,243 |

*[Using the straight-line method, each interest entry is the same.]*

# Exercise 14-10

## 1. January 1, 2006

| | | |
|---|---|---|
| Cash (price given)..................................................... | 739,814,813 | |
| Discount on bonds (difference)............................. | 60,185,187 | |
| Bonds payable (face amount) ............................ | | 800,000,000 |

## 2. June 30, 2006

| | | |
|---|---|---|
| Interest expense (6% x $739,814,813)....................... | 44,388,889 | |
| Discount on bonds payable (difference) ........... | | 388,889 |
| Cash (5.5% x $800,000,000)................................ | | 44,000,000 |

## 3. December 31, 2006

| | | |
|---|---|---|
| Interest expense (6% x [$739,814,813 + 388,889]) .... | 44,412,222 | |
| Discount on bonds payable (difference) ........... | | 412,222 |
| Cash (5.5% x $800,000,000)................................ | | 44,000,000 |

# Exercise 14-11

## 1. Price of the bonds at January 1, 2006

| | | | | | | |
|---|---|---|---|---|---|---|
| Interest | $22,500¥ | x | 6.46321 * | = | $145,422 |
| Principal | $500,000 | x | 0.67684 ** | = | 338,420 |
| *Present value (price) of the bonds* | | | | | $483,842 |

¥  4.5% x $500,000

*  present value of an ordinary annuity of $1: n=8, i=5%

**  present value of $1: n=8, i=5%

## 2. January 1, 2006

| | | |
|---|---|---|
| Cash (price determined above) ......................... | 483,842 | |
| Discount on bonds (difference) ...................... | 16,158 | |
| Bonds payable (face amount)...................... | | 500,000 |

## 3. Amortization schedule

| | Cash Interest 4.5% x Face Amount | Effective Interest 5% x Outstanding Balance | | | Increase in Balance Discount Reduction | Outstanding Balance |
|---|---|---|---|---|---|---|
| | | | | | | 483,842 |
| 1 | 22,500 | .05 (483,842) | = | 24,192 | 1,692 | 485,534 |
| 2 | 22,500 | .05 (485,534) | = | 24,277 | 1,777 | 487,311 |
| 3 | 22,500 | .05 (487,311) | = | 24,366 | 1,866 | 489,177 |
| 4 | 22,500 | .05 (489,177) | = | 24,459 | 1,959 | 491,136 |
| 5 | 22,500 | .05 (491,136) | = | 24,557 | 2,057 | 493,193 |
| 6 | 22,500 | .05 (493,193) | = | 24,660 | 2,160 | 495,353 |
| 7 | 22,500 | .05 (495,353) | = | 24,768 | 2,268 | 497,621 |
| 8 | 22,500 | .05 (497,621) | = | 24,879* | 2,379 | 500,000 |
| | 180,000 | | | 196,158 | 16,158 | |

* rounded.

*Exercise 14-11 (concluded)*

**4. June 30, 2006**

| | | |
|---|---|---|
| Interest expense (5% x $483,842) ...................... | 24,192 | |
| Discount on bonds payable (difference) ..... | | 1,692 |
| Cash (4.5% x $500,000)................................ | | 22,500 |

**5. December 31, 2009**

| | | |
|---|---|---|
| Interest expense (5% x $497,621) ...................... | 24,879* | |
| Discount on bonds payable (difference) ..... | | 2,379 |
| Cash (4.5% x $500,000)................................ | | 22,500 |
| | | |
| Bonds payable ..................................................... | 500,000 | |
| Cash ............................................................. | | 500,000 |

\* rounded value from table

# Exercise 14-12

## 1. February 1, 2006

| | | |
|---|---|---|
| Cash (price given) ............................................. | 731,364 | |
| Discount on bonds (difference) ...................... | 68,636 | |
|    Bonds payable (face amount) ...................... | | 800,000 |

## 2. July 31, 2006

| | | |
|---|---|---|
| Interest expense (5% x $731,364 ) ...................... | 36,568 | |
|    Discount on bonds payable (difference) ..... | | 568 |
|    Cash (4.5% x $800,000) ............................... | | 36,000 |

## 3. December 31, 2006

| | | |
|---|---|---|
| Interest expense ($5/6$ x 5% x [$731,364 + 568]). | 30,497 | |
|    Discount on bonds payable (difference) ..... | | 497 |
|    Interest payable ($5/6$ x 4.5% x $800,000) ...... | | 30,000 |

## 4. January 31, 2007

| | | |
|---|---|---|
| Interest expense ($1/6$ x 5% x [$731,364 + 568]) | 6,100* | |
| Interest payable (from adjusting entry) ............. | 30,000 | |
|    Discount on bonds payable (difference) ..... | | 100 |
|    Cash (4.5% x $800,000) ............................... | | 36,000 |

\* rounded

# Exercise 14-13

### 1. March 1, 2006

| | | |
|---|---|---|
| Cash (price given)............................................ | 294,000 | |
| Discount on bonds (difference)........................ | 6,000 | |
| Bonds payable (face amount) ...................... | | 300,000 |

### 2. August 31, 2006

| | | |
|---|---|---|
| Interest expense ($21,000 + 150) ........................ | 21,150 | |
| Discount on bonds payable ($6,000 ÷ 40)... | | 150 |
| Cash (7% x $300,000) .................................. | | 21,000 |

### 3. December 31, 2006

| | | |
|---|---|---|
| Interest expense ($4/6$ x $21,150) ........................ | 14,100 | |
| Discount on bonds payable ($4/6$ x $150) .... | | 100 |
| Interest payable ($4/6$ x $21,000)................... | | 14,000 |

### 4. February 28, 2007

| | | |
|---|---|---|
| Interest expense ($2/6$ x $21,150) ........................ | 7,050 | |
| Interest payable ($4/6$ x $21,000) ..................... | 14,000 | |
| Discount on bonds payable ($2/6$ x $150) .... | | 50 |
| Cash (7% x $300,000) ................................... | | 21,000 |

# Exercise 14-14

1. b
2. c
3. d

# Exercise 14-15

## Requirement 1

| | | | | | | |
|---|---|---|---|---|---|---|
| Interest | $24,000¥ | x | 2.40183 * | = | $ 57,644 | |
| Principal | $600,000 | x | 0.71178 ** | = | 427,068 | |
| | Present value (price) of the bonds | | | | $484,712 | |

¥  4% x $600,000

*  present value of an ordinary annuity of $1: n=3, i=12%

**  present value of $1: n=3, i=12%

| | |
|---|---|
| Operational assets (price determined above)........................... | 484,712 |
| Discount on notes payable (difference)............................... | 115,288 |
|    Notes payable (face amount)............................................ | 600,000 |

## Requirement 2

| | Cash Interest 4% x Face Amount | Effective Interest 12% x Outstanding Balance | | | Increase in Balance Discount Reduction | Outstanding Balance |
|---|---|---|---|---|---|---|
| | | | | | | 484,712 |
| 1 | 24,000 | .12 (484,712) | = | 58,165 | 34,165 | 518,877 |
| 2 | 24,000 | .12 (518,877) | = | 62,265 | 38,265 | 557,142 |
| 3 | 24,000 | .12 (557,142) | = | 66,858* | 42,858 | 600,000 |
| | 72,000 | | | 187,288 | 115,288 | |

* rounded.

## Requirement 3

| | | |
|---|---|---|
| Interest expense (market rate x outstanding balance)................ | 58,165 | |
|    Discount on notes payable (difference)............................ | | 34,165 |
|    Cash (stated rate x face amount) ..................................... | | 24,000 |
| | | |
| Interest expense (market rate x outstanding balance)................ | 62,265 | |
|    Discount on notes payable (difference)............................ | | 38,265 |
|    Cash (stated rate x face amount) ..................................... | | 24,000 |
| | | |
| Interest expense (market rate x outstanding balance)................... | 66,858 | |
|    Discount on notes payable (difference)............................ | | 42,858 |
|    Cash (stated rate x face amount) ..................................... | | 24,000 |
| | | |
| Notes payable................................................................ | 600,000 | |
|    Cash (stated rate x face amount) ..................................... | | 600,000 |

# Exercise 14-16

## 1. January 1, 2006

| | | |
|---|---|---|
| Operational assets ............................................................. | 4,000,000 | |
| Notes payable................................................................. | | 4,000,000 |

## 2. Amortization schedule

| $4,000,000 | ÷ | 3.16987 | = | $1,261,881 |
|---|---|---|---|---|
| amount | | (from Table 4) | | installment |
| of loan | | n=4, i=10% | | payment |

| Dec.31 | Cash Payment | Effective Interest 10% x Outstanding Balance | Decrease in Balance Balance Reduction | Outstanding Balance |
|---|---|---|---|---|
| | | | | 4,000,000 |
| 2006 | 1,261,881 | .10 (4,000,000) = 400,000 | 861,881 | 3,138,119 |
| 2007 | 1,261,881 | .10 (3,138,119) = 313,812 | 948,069 | 2,190,050 |
| 2008 | 1,261,881 | .10 (2,190,050) = 219,005 | 1,042,876 | 1,147,174 |
| 2009 | 1,261,881 | .10 (1,147,174) = 114,707* | 1,147,174 | 0 |
| | **5,047,524** | **1,047,524** | **4,000,000** | |

\* rounded.

## 3. December 31, 2006

| | | |
|---|---|---|
| Interest expense (10% x outstanding balance) ............................. | 400,000 | |
| Note payable (difference)........................................................ | 861,881 | |
| Cash (payment determined above) ........................................ | | 1,261,881 |

## 4. December 31, 2008

| | | |
|---|---|---|
| Interest expense (10% x outstanding balance) ............................. | 219,005 | |
| Note payable (difference)........................................................ | 1,042,876 | |
| Cash (payment determined above) ........................................ | | 1,261,881 |

# Exercise 14-17

| | | |
|---|---:|---:|
| Bonds payable (face amount)........................................ | 90,000,000 | |
| Loss on early extinguishment (to balance)................. | 4,800,000 | |
|    Discount on bonds (given)...................................... | | 3,000,000 |
|    Cash ($90,000,000 x 102%)..................................... | | 91,800,000 |

# Exercise 14-18

## Requirement 1

**Gless (Issuer)**

| | | |
|---|---|---|
| Cash (101% x $12 million) ............................................ | 12,120,000 | |
|     Convertible bonds payable (face amount)............... | | 12,000,000 |
|     Premium on bonds payable (difference) ................ | | 120,000 |

**Century (Investor)**

| | | |
|---|---|---|
| Investment in convertible bonds (10% x $12 million) . | 1,200,000 | |
| Premium on bond investment (difference) ................... | 12,000 | |
|     Cash (101% x $1.2 million)...................................... | | 1,212,000 |

## Requirement 2

**Gless (Issuer)**

| | | |
|---|---|---|
| Interest expense ($540,000 - $6,000) ............................ | 534,000 | |
| Premium on bonds payable ($120,000 ÷ 20) ............... | 6,000 | |
|     Cash (4.5% x $12,000,000) ..................................... | | 540,000 |

**Century (Investor)**

| | | |
|---|---|---|
| Cash (4.5% x $1,200,000)............................................ | 54,000 | |
|     Premium on bond investment ($12,000 ÷ 20) ......... | | 600 |
|     Interest revenue ($54,000 - $600) ............................... | | 53,400 |

*[Using the straight-line method, each interest entry is the same.]*

## Requirement 3

**Gless (Issuer)**

| | | |
|---|---|---|
| Convertible bonds payable (10% of the account balance) | 1,200,000 | |
| Premium on bonds payable | | |
|     (($120,000 - [$6,000 x 11]) x 10%) ........................... | 5,400 | |
|     Common stock ([1,200 x 40 shares] x $1 par) ............ | | 48,000 |
|     Paid-in capital – excess of par (to balance)............. | | 1,157,400 |

**Century (Investor)**

| | | |
|---|---|---|
| Investment in common stock ....................................... | 1,205,400 | |
|     Investment in convertible bonds (account balance) . | | 1,200,000 |
|     Premium on bond investment  ($12,000 - [$600 x 11]) | | 5,400 |

# Exercise 14-19

### Requirement 1

|  | ($ in millions) | |
|---|---|---|
| **Limbaugh (Issuer)** | | |
| Cash (104% x $30 million)...................................................... | 31.2 | |
| Discount on bonds payable (difference).............................. | 3.6 | |
|   Bonds payable (face amount) ............................................ | | 30.0 |
|   Paid-in capital – stock warrants outstanding | | |
|     ($8 x 20 warrants x [$30,000,000 ÷ $1,000] bonds) .............. | | 4.8 |
| | | |
| **Interstate (Investor)** | | |
| Investment in stock warrants ($4.8 million x 20%) ............... | 0.96 | |
| Investment in bonds (20% x $30 million)............................. | 6.00 | |
|   Discount on bonds (difference) ........................................ | | 0.72 |
|   Cash (104% x $30 million x 20%) ...................................... | | 6.24 |

### Requirement 2

|  | ($ in millions) | |
|---|---|---|
| **Limbaugh (Issuer)** | | |
| Cash (20% x 30,000 bonds x 20 warrants x $60)........................ | 7.20 | |
| Paid-in capital – stock warrants outstanding | | |
|     ($4.8 million x 20%) ....................................................... | 0.96 | |
|   Common stock (20% x 30,000 x 20 shares x $10 par)........... | | 1.20 |
|   Paid-in capital – excess of par (to balance)...................... | | 6.96 |
| | | |
| **Interstate (Investor)** | | |
| Investment in common stock (to balance)............................. | 8.16 | |
|   Investment in stock warrants ($4.8 million x 20%) ........... | | .96 |
|   Cash (20% x 30,000 x 20 warrants x $60) ............................. | | 7.20 |

# Exercise 14-20

## 1. National Equipment Transfer Corporation

| | | |
|---|---|---|
| Cash (priced at par)............................................ | 200,000,000 | |
| Bonds payable (face amount) ....................... | | 200,000,000 |

### IgWig

| | | |
|---|---|---|
| Cash (99% x $350 million) .............................. | 346,500,000 | |
| Discount on notes (difference)........................ | 3,500,000 | |
| Notes payable (face amount) ....................... | | 350,000,000 |

## 2. National Equipment Transfer Corporation

| | | |
|---|---|---|
| Interest expense .................................................. | 7,460,000 | |
| Cash ([7.46% ÷ 2] x $200 million ) ................ | | 7,460,000 |

### IgWig

| | | |
|---|---|---|
| Interest expense ([6.56% ÷ 2] x $346,500,000). | 11,365,200 | |
| Discount on bonds payable (difference) ..... | | 60,200 |
| Cash ([6.46% ÷ 2] x $350 million )................ | | 11,305,000 |

# Exercise 14-21

## Requirement 1

The error caused both 2004 net income and 2005 net income to be *overstated*, so retained earnings is overstated by a total of $85,000. Also, the note payable would be *understated* by the same amount. Remember, the entry to record interest is:

| | | |
|---|---|---|
| Interest expense ................................................................................ | xxx | |
| Note payable (difference) ........................................................ | xxx | |
|    Cash................................................................................. | | xxx |

So, if interest expense is understated, the reduction in the note will be too much, causing the balance in that account to be understated.

## Requirement 2

| | | |
|---|---|---|
| Retained earnings (overstatement of 2004-05 income) ................. | 85,000 | |
|    Note payable (understatement determined above).................... | | 85,000 |

## Requirement 3

The financial statements that were incorrect as a result of the error would be *retrospectively restated* to report the correct interest amounts, income, and retained earnings when those statements are reported again for comparative purposes in the current annual report. A *"prior period adjustment"* to retained earnings would be reported, and a *disclosure note* should describe the nature of the error and the impact of its correction on each year's net income, income before extraordinary items, and earnings per share.

# Exercise 14-22

The 2006 interest expense is overstated by the extra interest recorded in February. Similarly, retained earnings is overstated the same amount because 2005 interest expense was understated when the accrued interest was not recorded.

### To correct the error:

| | | |
|---|---:|---:|
| Retained earnings ................................................. | 61,000 | |
|    Interest expense ($73,200 – $12,200*)...................... | | 61,000 |

*$73,000 x $^1/_6$

### 2006 adjusting entry:

| | | |
|---|---:|---:|
| Interest expense ($^5/_6$ x $73,200)................................. | 61,000 | |
|    Discount on bonds payable ($^5/_6$ x $1,200) .............. | | 1,000 |
|    Interest payable ($^5/_6$ x $72,000)............................... | | 60,000 |

#### *ENTRIES THAT SHOULD HAVE BEEN RECORDED:*
#### 2005 adjusting entry:

| | | |
|---|---:|---:|
| Interest expense ($^5/_6$ x $73,200)............................................. | 61,000 | |
|    Discount on bonds payable ($^5/_6$ x $1,200) ........................ | | 1,000 |
|    Interest payable ($^5/_6$ x $72,000) ......................................... | | 60,000 |

#### February 1, 2006:

| | | |
|---|---:|---:|
| Interest expense ($^1/_6$ x $73,200)............................................. | 12,200 | |
| Interest payable ($^5/_6$ x $72,000)............................................. | 60,000 | |
|    Discount on bonds payable ($^1/_6$ x $1,200) ........................ | | 200 |
|    Cash ( given)....................................................................... | | 72,000 |

# Exercise 14-23

1.  **a.** Because the bonds sold for more than their face value, they were sold at a premium. The premium adjusted the yield of the bonds to the effective rate (presumably, the market rate).

2.  **d.** The annual interest cash outlay is $70,000 (7% nominal rate x $1,000,000), or $35,000 each semiannual period. Interest expense is less than $35,000, however, because the bonds were originally issued at a premium. That premium should be amortized over the life of the bond. Thus, interest expense for the first 6 months is $31,884 [$1,062,809 x 6% x (6 months / 12 months)], and premium amortization is $3,116 ($35,000 - $31,884).

3.  **b.** A bond liability is shown at its face value (maturity value), minus any related discount, or plus any related premium. Thus, a bond issued at a premium is shown at its maturity value plus the unamortized portion of the premium. The premium account is sometimes called an adjunct account because it is shown as an addition to another account.

# Exercise 14-24

| | | |
|---|---|---|
| Land  ($450,000 – $325,000) ........................................ | 125,000 | |
| Gain on disposition of assets .............................. | | 125,000 |
| | | |
| Note payable (face amount) ......................................... | 600,000 | |
| Accrued interest payable (11% x $600,000)............... | 66,000 | |
| Gain on troubled debt restructuring (difference).... | | 216,000 |
| Land  (fair market value) ......................................... | | 450,000 |

# Exercise 14-25

**Analysis:** *Carrying amount*:   $12 million + $1.2 million =    $13,200,000
          *Future payments*:   ($1 million x 2) + $11 million =    13,000,000
          Gain to debtor                                $    200,000

## 1. January 1, 2006

| | | |
|---|---|---|
| Accrued interest payable (10% x $12,000,000)............ | 1,200,000 | |
|   Note payable ($13 million – $12 million)* ................ | | 1,000,000 |
|   Gain on troubled debt restructuring .................... | | 200,000 |

  * Establishes a balance in the note account equal to the total cash payments under the new agreement.

## 2. December 31, 2007

| | | |
|---|---|---|
| Note payable............................................................ | 1,000,000 | |
|   Cash (revised "interest" amount) ............................... | | 1,000,000 |

*Note*:   No interest should be recorded after the restructuring. All subsequent cash payments result in reductions of principal.

## 3. December 31, 2008

| | | |
|---|---|---|
| Note payable............................................................ | 1,000,000 | |
|   Cash (revised "interest" amount) ............................... | | 1,000,000 |
| | | |
| Note payable............................................................ | 11,000,000 | |
|   Cash (revised principal amount) ............................... | | 11,000,000 |

# Exercise 14-26

**Analysis:**  *Carrying amount*: $240,000 + (10% \times \$240,000) =$  $\qquad$ $264,000

*Future payments*: ($11,555 x 3) + $240,000 =  $\qquad$ (274,665)

Interest  $\qquad$ $ 10,665

The discount rate that "equates" the present value of the debt ($264,000) and its future value ($274,665) is the effective rate of interest:

$264,000 ÷ $274,665 = .961 – the Table 2 value for *n* = 2, *i* = ?

In row 2 of Table 2, the value .961 is in the 2% column. So, this is the **new** effective interest rate. A financial calculator will produce the same rate.

To simplify the record keeping, it may be desirable to combine the two debt accounts – the note and the accrued interest – into a single account:

## 1. January 1, 2006

Accrued interest payable (10% x $240,000)............... 24,000
Note payable (original debt)........................................ 240,000
  Note payable (present carrying amount) .................... 264,000

## 2. December 31, 2006

Interest expense (2% x $264,000) ............................. 5,280
  Note payable........................................................ 5,280

*[Unpaid interest is accrued at the effective rate times the carrying amount of the debt.]*

## 3. December 31, 2007

Interest expense (2% x [$264,000 + 5,280]) ................. 5,385*
  Note payable........................................................ 5,385

*rounded

After adding accrued interest for each year, the balance of the note account is equal to the amount scheduled to be paid at maturity.

Note payable ($264,000 + 5,280 + 5,385) .................... 274,665
  Cash ([$11,555 x 3] + $240,000) ............................. 274,665

# PROBLEMS

## Problem 14-1

### Requirement 1

| | | | | | | |
|---|---|---|---|---|---|---|
| Interest | $2,500,000¥ | x | 15.04630 * | = | $37,615,750 |
| Principal | $50,000,000 | x | 0.09722 ** | = | 4,861,000 |
| | *Present value (price) of the bonds* | | | | $42,476,750 |

¥  5% x $50,000,000
*  present value of an ordinary annuity of $1: n=40, i=6%
** present value of $1: n=40, i=6%

| | | |
|---|---|---|
| Cash (price determined above)........................................ | 42,476,750 | |
| Discount on bonds (difference).................................... | 7,523,250 | |
| Bonds payable (face amount) ................................ | | 50,000,000 |

### Requirement 2

| | | | | | | |
|---|---|---|---|---|---|---|
| Interest | $ 2,500,000 | x | 18.40158 * | = | $46,003,950 |
| Principal | $50,000,000 | x | 0.17193 ** | = | 8,596,500 |
| | *Present value (price) of the bonds* | | | | $54,600,450 |

*  present value of an ordinary annuity of $1: n=40, i=4.5%
** present value of $1: n=40, i=4.5%

| | | |
|---|---|---|
| Cash (price determined above)........................................ | 54,600,450 | |
| Premium on bonds (difference).............................. | | 4,600,450 |
| Bonds payable (face amount) ................................ | | 50,000,000 |

### Requirement 3

| | | |
|---|---|---|
| Investment in bonds (face amount)............................... | 50,000,000 | |
| Premium on bond investment ................................ | 4,600,450 | |
| Cash (price calculated above)..................................... | | 54,600,450 |

# Problem 14-2

### 1. Liabilities at September 30, 2006

| | |
|---|---|
| Bonds payable (face amount)...................................... | $160,000,000 |
| Less: discount .......................................................... | 20,000,000 |
| Initial balance, March 1, 2006............................... | $140,000,000 |
| June 30, 2006 discount amortization....................... | 266,667* |
| Sept. 30, 2006 discount amortization ...................... | 208,000** |
| Sept. 30, 2006 net bonds payable ........................... | $140,474,667 |
| | |
| Interest payable ** .................................................. | $4,000,000 |

### 2. Interest expense for year ended September 30, 2006

| | |
|---|---|
| June 30, 2006 interest expense ............................... | $5,600,000* |
| September 30, 2006 interest expense ...................... | 4,208,000** |
| Interest expense for fiscal 2006.............................. | $9,808,000 |

### 3. Statement of cash flows for year ended September 30, 2006

Baddour would report the cash inflow of $140,000,000*** from the sale of the bonds as a cash flow from financing activities in its statement of cash flows. The accrued interest portion of the cash receipt was paid on June 30 and is part of the cash outflow from operating activities (below).

The $8,000,000 cash interest paid * is a cash outflow from operating activities because interest is an income statement (operating) item.

## Problem 14-2 (concluded)

### Calculations:

#### March 1, 2006***
Cash ($140 million plus accrued interest) ........................ 142,666,667
Discount on bonds (difference).................................. 20,000,000
    Bonds payable (face amount) ................................. 160,000,000
    Interest payable ($160 million x 10% x 2/12) ........... 2,666,667

#### June 30, 2006*
Interest expense (6% x $140,000,000 x 4/6).................... 5,600,000
Interest payable (balance)........................................... 2,666,667
    Discount on bonds payable (difference) ................. 266,667
    Cash (5% x $160,000,000) ....................................... 8,000,000

#### September 30, 2006**
Interest expense (6% x [$140,000,000 + 266,667] x 3/6 )   4,208,000
    Discount on bonds payable (difference) ................. 208,000
    Interest payable (5% x $160,000,000 x 3/6).............. 4,000,000

# Problem 14-3

## Requirement 1

| | Cash Interest 4.5% x Face Amount | Effective Interest 5% x Outstanding Balance | | Increase in Balance | Outstanding Balance |
|---|---|---|---|---|---|
| | | | | | 96,768 |
| 1 | 4,500 | .05 (96,768) | = 4,838 | 338 | 97,106 |
| 2 | 4,500 | .05 (97,106) | = 4,855 | 355 | 97,461 |
| 3 | 4,500 | .05 (97,461) | = 4,873 | 373 | 97,834 |
| 4 | 4,500 | .05 (97,834) | = 4,892 | 392 | 98,226 |
| 5 | 4,500 | .05 (98,226) | = 4,911 | 411 | 98,637 |
| 6 | 4,500 | .05 (98,637) | = 4,932 | 432 | 99,069 |
| 7 | 4,500 | .05 (99,069) | = 4,953 | 453 | 99,522 |
| 8 | 4,500 | .05 (99,522) | = 4,978* | 478 | 100,000 |
| | 36,000 | | 39,232 | 3,232 | |

* rounded.

## Requirement 2

| | Cash Interest 4.5% x Face Amount | Recorded Interest Cash plus Discount Reduction | | Increase in Balance $3,232 ÷ 8 | Outstanding Balance |
|---|---|---|---|---|---|
| | | | | | 96,768 |
| 1 | 4,500 | (4,500 + 404) | = 4,904 | 404 | 97,172 |
| 2 | 4,500 | (4,500 + 404) | = 4,904 | 404 | 97,576 |
| 3 | 4,500 | (4,500 + 404) | = 4,904 | 404 | 97,980 |
| 4 | 4,500 | (4,500 + 404) | = 4,904 | 404 | 98,384 |
| 5 | 4,500 | (4,500 + 404) | = 4,904 | 404 | 98,788 |
| 6 | 4,500 | (4,500 + 404) | = 4,904 | 404 | 99,192 |
| 7 | 4,500 | (4,500 + 404) | = 4,904 | 404 | 99,596 |
| 8 | 4,500 | (4,500 + 404) | = 4,904 | 404 | 100,000 |
| | 36,000 | | 39,232 | 3,232 | |

## Problem 14-3 (continued)

### Requirement 3

> (effective interest)
> Interest expense (5% x $98,226) .....................................     4,911
>     Discount on bonds payable (difference) .................            411
>     Cash (4.5% x $100,000).............................................            4,500

> (straight-line)
> Interest expense ($4,500 + 404) .....................................     4,904
>     Discount on bonds payable ($3,232 ÷ 8) ...............            404
>     Cash (4.5% x $100,000).............................................            4,500

### Requirement 4

By the straight-line method, a company determines interest indirectly by allocating a discount or a premium *equally* to each period over the term to maturity. This is allowed if doing so produces results that are not materially different from the interest method. The decision should be guided by whether the straight-line method would tend to mislead investors and creditors in the particular circumstance.

Allocating the discount or premium equally over the life of the bonds by the straight-line method results in an **unchanging dollar amount** of interest each period. By the straight-line method, the amount of the discount to be reduced periodically is calculated, and the effective interest is the "plug" figure.

Unchanging dollar amounts like these are not produced when the effective interest approach is used. By that approach, the dollar amounts of interest vary over the term to maturity because the **percentage rate** of interest remains constant, but is applied to a changing debt balance.

Remember that the "straight-line method," is not an alternative method of determining interest in a conceptual sense, but is an application of the **materiality concept**. The appropriate application of GAAP, the effective interest method, is by-passed as a practical expediency in situations when doing so has no "material" effect on the results.

## Problem 14-3 (concluded)

### Requirement 5

The amortization schedule in requirement 1 gives us the answer: $9,864. The outstanding debt balance after the June 30, 2008, interest payment (line 5) is the present value at that time ($98,637) of the remaining payments. Since $10,000 face amount of the bonds is 10% of the entire issue, we take 10% of the table amount.

This can be confirmed by calculating the present value:

| | | | | | |
|---|---|---|---|---|---|
| Interest | $450¥ | x | 2.72325 * | = | $1,225 |
| Principal | $10,000 | x | 0.86384 ** | = | 8,638 |
| *Present value (price) of the bonds* | | | | | $9,864 (rounded) |

¥    4.5% x $10,000

\*   present value of an ordinary annuity of $1: n=3, i=5%

\*\*  present value of $1: n=3, i=5%

# Problem 14-4

**Requirement 1**

$8,000,000 (outstanding balance at maturity)

**Requirement 2**

$6,627,273 (outstanding balance at sale date)

**Requirement 3**

20 years (40 semiannual periods)

**Requirement 4**

At the effective interest rate (By the alternative straight-line approach, interest would be the same amount each period)

**Requirement 5**

8%   [($320,000 ÷ $8,000,000) x 2]

**Requirement 6**

10%   [($331,364 ÷ $6,627,273) x 2]

**Requirement 7**

$12,800,000   ($320,000 x 40)

**Requirement 8**

$14,172,727 ($12,800,000 + [$8,000,000 – $6,627,273])
                    (Total cash interest plus the discount)

# Problem 14-5

## Requirement 1

| | | | | | |
|---|---|---|---|---|---|
| Interest | $3,600,000¥ | x | 6.46321 * | = | $23,267,556 |
| Principal | $80,000,000 | x | 0.67684 ** | = | 54,147,200 |
| | Present value (price) of the bonds | | | | $77,414,756 |

¥    4.5% x $80,000,000
*    present value of an ordinary annuity of $1: n=8, i=5%
**    present value of $1: n=8, i=5%

## Requirement 2

### (a) Cromley

| | Cash Interest 4.5% x Face Amount | Effective Interest 5% x Outstanding Balance | | | Increase in Balance Discount Reduction | Outstanding Balance |
|---|---|---|---|---|---|---|
| | | | | | | 77,414,756 |
| 1 | 3,600,000 | .05 (77,414,756) | = | 3,870,738 | 270,738 | 77,685,494 |
| 2 | 3,600,000 | .05 (77,685,494) | = | 3,884,275 | 284,275 | 77,969,769 |
| 3 | 3,600,000 | .05 (77,969,769) | = | 3,898,488 | 298,488 | 78,268,257 |
| 4 | 3,600,000 | .05 (78,268,257) | = | 3,913,413 | 313,413 | 78,581,670 |
| 5 | 3,600,000 | .05 (78,581,670) | = | 3,929,084 | 329,084 | 78,910,754 |
| 6 | 3,600,000 | .05 (78,910,754) | = | 3,945,538 | 345,538 | 79,256,292 |
| 7 | 3,600,000 | .05 (79,256,292) | = | 3,962,815 | 362,815 | 79,619,107 |
| 8 | 3,600,000 | .05 (79,619,107) | = | 3,980,893* | 380,893 | 80,000,000 |
| | 28,800,000 | | | 31,385,244 | 2,585,244 | |

* rounded.

## Problem 14-5 (continued)

### (b) Barnwell

| | Cash Interest 4.5% x Face Amount | Effective Interest 5% x Outstanding Balance | Increase in Balance Discount Reduction | Outstanding Balance |
|---|---|---|---|---|
| | | | | 77,415 |
| 1 | 3,600 | .05 (77,415) = 3,871 | 271 | 77,686 |
| 2 | 3,600 | .05 (77,686) = 3,884 | 284 | 77,970 |
| 3 | 3,600 | .05 (77,970) = 3,899 | 299 | 78,269 |
| 4 | 3,600 | .05 (78,269) = 3,913 | 313 | 78,582 |
| 5 | 3,600 | .05 (78,582) = 3,929 | 329 | 78,911 |
| 6 | 3,600 | .05 (78,911) = 3,946 | 346 | 79,257 |
| 7 | 3,600 | .05 (79,257) = 3,963 | 363 | 79,620 |
| 8 | 3,600 | .05 (79,620) = 3,980 * | 380 | 80,000 |
| | 28,800 | 31,385 | 2,585 | |

*rounded

## Requirement 3

**February 1, 2006 (Cromley)**

| | | |
|---|---|---|
| Cash (price determined above).............................. | 77,414,756 | |
| Discount on bonds (difference)............................ | 2,585,244 | |
| Bonds payable (face amount) ............................ | | 80,000,000 |

**February 1, 2006 (Barnwell)**

| | | |
|---|---|---|
| Bond investment (face amount)............................ | 80,000 | |
| Discount on bond investment (difference)........ | | 2,585 |
| Cash (price paid)............................................... | | 77,415 |

*Problem 14-5 (continued)*

**Requirement 4**

**July 31, 2006 (Cromley)**

| | | |
|---|---|---|
| Interest expense (from schedule) .............................. | 3,870,738 | |
| Discount on bonds payable (from schedule) ..... | | 270,738 |
| Cash (from schedule) ........................................... | | 3,600,000 |

**July 31, 2006 (Barnwell)**

| | | |
|---|---|---|
| Cash (from schedule) ............................................ | 3,600 | |
| Discount on investment (from schedule)................... | 271 | |
| Interest revenue (from schedule)............................ | | 3,871 |

**December 31, 2006 (Cromley)**

| | | |
|---|---|---|
| Interest expense ($5/6$ x $3,884,275) ........................... | 3,236,896 | |
| Discount on bonds payable ($5/6$ x $284,275)..... | | 236,896 |
| Interest payable ($5/6$ x $3,600,000)...................... | | 3,000,000 |

**December 31, 2006 (Barnwell)**

| | | |
|---|---|---|
| Interest receivable ($5/6$ x $3,600) .......................... | 3,000 | |
| Discount on investment ($5/6$ x $284) ..................... | 237 | |
| Interest revenue ($5/6$ x $3,884) .............................. | | 3,237 |

**January 31, 2007 (Cromley)**

| | | |
|---|---|---|
| Interest expense ($1/6$ x $3,884,275) ........................... | 647,379 | |
| Interest payable (from adjusting entry above)............. | 3,000,000 | |
| Discount on bonds payable ($1/6$ x $284,275)..... | | 47,379 |
| Cash (stated rate x face amount) .......................... | | 3,600,000 |

**January 31, 2007 (Barnwell)**

| | | |
|---|---|---|
| Cash (stated rate x face amount) .............................. | 3,600 | |
| Discount on bond investment ($1/6$ x $284)........... | 47 | |
| Interest receivable (from adjusting entry above) ... | | 3,000 |
| Interest revenue ($1/6$ x $3,884) .............................. | | 647 |

## Problem 14-5 *(concluded)*

**July 31, 2007 (Cromley)**

| | | |
|---|---|---|
| Interest expense (from schedule) .............................. | 3,898,488 | |
|     Discount on bonds payable (from schedule) ..... | | 298,488 |
|     Cash (from schedule) ....................................... | | 3,600,000 |

**July 31, 2007 (Barnwell)**

| | | |
|---|---|---|
| Cash (from schedule) ............................................. | 3,600 | |
| Discount on investment (from schedule)................... | 299 | |
|     Interest revenue (from schedule)............................ | | 3,899 |

**December 31, 2007 (Cromley)**

| | | |
|---|---|---|
| Interest expense ($5/6$ x $3,913,413) .......................... | 3,261,177 | |
|     Discount on bonds payable ($5/6$ x $313,413) .... | | 261,177 |
|     Interest payable ($5/6$ x $3,600,000) ..................... | | 3,000,000 |

**December 31, 2007 (Barnwell)**

| | | |
|---|---|---|
| Interest receivable ($5/6$ x $3,600)......................... | 3,000 | |
| Discount on investment ($5/6$ x $313)..................... | 261 | |
|     Interest revenue ($5/6$ x $3,913)............................. | | 3,261 |

**January 31, 2008 (Cromley)**

| | | |
|---|---|---|
| Interest expense ($1/6$ x $3,913,413) .......................... | 652,236* | |
| Interest payable (from adjusting entry above)............. | 3,000,000 | |
|     Discount on bonds payable ($1/6$ x $313,413) .... | | 52,236* |
|     Cash (stated rate x face amount).......................... | | 3,600,000 |

**January 31, 2008 (Barnwell)**

| | | |
|---|---|---|
| Cash (stated rate x face amount).............................. | 3,600 | |
| Discount on bond investment ($1/6$ x $313)........... | 52 | |
|     Interest receivable (from adjusting entry above)... | | 3,000 |
|     Interest revenue ($1/6$ x $3,913) ............................. | | 652 |

    *rounded

# Problem 14-6

**Requirement 1**

### April 1, 2006 (Western)

| | | |
|---|---|---|
| Cash ($29,300,000 + [$1/12$ x 12% x $30,000,000])....... | 29,600,000 | |
| Discount on bonds ($30 million - $29.3 million)....... | 700,000 | |
|    Bonds payable (face amount)............................ | | 30,000,000 |
|    Interest payable ($1/12$ x 12% x $30,000,000) ....... | | 300,000 |

### April 1, 2006 (Stillworth)

| | | |
|---|---|---|
| Bond investment (face amount)............................ | 30,000 | |
| Interest receivable ($1/12$ x 12% x $30,000) ............. | 300 | |
|    Discount on bond investment ($30,000 - $29,300) | | 700 |
|    Cash ($29,300 + [$1/12$ x 12% x $30,000]) .............. | | 29,600 |

*Alternative: Some accountants prefer to credit (debit) interest expense (revenue), rather than interest payable (receivable), when bonds are sold (purchased).*

### April 1, 2006 (Western)

| | | |
|---|---|---|
| Cash ($29,300,000 + [$1/12$ x 12% x $30,000,000])...... | 29,600,000 | |
| Discount on bonds ($30 million - $29.3 million)....... | 700,000 | |
|    Bonds payable (face amount)............................ | | 30,000,000 |
|    Interest expense ($1/12$ x 12% x $30,000,000)....... | | 300,000 |

### April 1, 2006 (Stillworth)

| | | |
|---|---|---|
| Bond investment (face amount)............................ | 30,000 | |
| Interest revenue ($1/12$ x 12% x $30,000) ................... | 300 | |
|    Discount on bond investment ($30,000 - $29,300) | | 700 |
|    Cash ($29,300 + [$1/12$ x 12% x $30,000]) .............. | | 29,600 |

If the alternate entries are used, entries at the next interest date would require simply a debit (credit) to interest expense (revenue) for the full interest. The interest accounts would then reflect the same *net* debit of five months' interest.

## Problem 14-6 (continued)

### Requirement 2

The original maturity of the bonds was 3 years, or 36 months. But since the bonds weren't sold until one month after they were dated, they are outstanding for only 35 months. Straight-line amortization, then, is $700,000 ÷ 35 months = $20,000 per month for Western (and $700 ÷ 35 months = $20 per month for Stillworth's investment).

**August 31, 2006 (Western)**

| | | |
|---|---|---|
| Interest expense ($1,800,000 + $100,000 – $300,000) | 1,600,000 | |
| Interest payable (accrued interest from above) ........... | 300,000 | |
|    Discount on bonds payable ($20,000 x 5 months) | | 100,000 |
|    Cash ($30,000,000 x 12% x $6/12$) ........................ | | 1,800,000 |

**August 31, 2006 (Stillworth)**

| | | |
|---|---|---|
| Cash ($30,000 x 12% x $6/12$) ................................. | 1,800 | |
| Discount on investment ($20 x 5 months) ............... | 100 | |
|    Interest receivable (accrued interest from above). | | 300 |
|    Interest revenue ($1,800 + $100 – $300) ................ | | 1,600 |

### *If alternate method of recording accrued interest is used:*

**August 31, 2006 (Western)**

| | | |
|---|---|---|
| Interest expense ($1,800,000 + $100,000) ................ | 1,900,000 | |
|    Discount on bonds payable ($20,000 x 5 months) | | 100,000 |
|    Cash ($30,000,000 x 12% x $6/12$) ........................ | | 1,800,000 |

**August 31, 2006 (Stillworth)**

| | | |
|---|---|---|
| Cash ($30,000 x 12% x $6/12$) ................................. | 1,800 | |
| Discount on investment ($20 x 5 months) ............... | 100 | |
|    Interest revenue ($1,800 + $100) ........................... | | 1,900 |

*Problem 14-6 (continued)*

**December 31, 2006 (Western)**

| | | |
|---|---|---|
| Interest expense ($1,200,000 + $80,000) ................... | 1,280,000 | |
|    Discount on bonds payable ($20,000 x 4 months) | | 80,000 |
|    Interest payable ($30,000,000 x 12% x $4/12$)........ | | 1,200,000 |

**December 31, 2006 (Stillworth)**

| | | |
|---|---|---|
| Interest receivable ($30,000 x 12% x $4/12$) .............. | 1,200 | |
| Discount on investment ($20 x 4 months)............. | 80 | |
|    Interest revenue ($1,200 + $80)............................ | | 1,280 |

**February 28, 2007 (Western)**

| | | |
|---|---|---|
| Interest expense ($1,800,000 + $40,000 – $1,200,000) | 640,000 | |
| Interest payable (from adjusting entry)..................... | 1,200,000 | |
|    Discount on bonds payable ($20,000 x 2 months) | | 40,000 |
|    Cash ($30,000,000 x 12% x $6/12$) ........................ | | 1,800,000 |

**February 28, 2007 (Stillworth)**

| | | |
|---|---|---|
| Cash ($30,000 x 12% x $6/12$).................................... | 1,800 | |
| Discount on bond investment ($20 x 2 months) .... | 40 | |
|    Interest receivable (from adjusting entry) ............ | | 1,200 |
|    Interest revenue ($1,800 + $40 – $1,200) .............. | | 640 |

**August 31, 2007 (Western)**

| | | |
|---|---|---|
| Interest expense ($1,800,000 + $120,000) ................. | 1,920,000 | |
|    Discount on bonds payable ($20,000 x 6 months) | | 120,000 |
|    Cash ($30,000,000 x 12% x $6/12$) ........................ | | 1,800,000 |

**August 31, 2007 (Stillworth)**

| | | |
|---|---|---|
| Cash ($30,000 x 12% x $6/12$) .................................... | 1,800 | |
| Discount on investment ($20 x 6 months) ............... | 120 | |
|    Interest revenue ($1,800 + $120)........................... | | 1,920 |

**December 31, 2007 (Western)**

| | | |
|---|---|---|
| Interest expense ($1,200,000 + $80,000) ................... | 1,280,000 | |
|    Discount on bonds payable ($20,000 x 4 months) | | 80,000 |
|    Interest payable ($30,000,000 x 12% x $4/12$)........ | | 1,200,000 |

**Problem 14-6 (continued)**

### December 31, 2007 (Stillworth)

| | | |
|---|---|---|
| Interest receivable ($30,000 x 12% x $4/12$)............. | 1,200 | |
| Discount on investment ($20 x 4 months) ............. | 80 | |
|    Interest revenue ($1,200 + $80) ............................ | | 1,280 |

### February 28, 2008 (Western)

| | | |
|---|---|---|
| Interest expense ($1,800,000 + $40,000 – $1,200,000) | 640,000 | |
| Interest payable (from adjusting entry) ................... | 1,200,000 | |
|    Discount on bonds payable ($20,000 x 2 months) | | 40,000 |
|    Cash ($30,000,000 x 12% x $6/12$) ........................ | | 1,800,000 |

### February 28, 2008 (Stillworth)

| | | |
|---|---|---|
| Cash ($30,000 x 12% x $6/12$) .................................. | 1,800 | |
| Discount on bond investment ($20 x 2 months).... | 40 | |
|    Interest receivable (from adjusting entry)............ | | 1,200 |
|    Interest revenue ($1,800 + $40 – $1,200) ............. | | 640 |

### August 31, 2008 (Western)

| | | |
|---|---|---|
| Interest expense ($1,800,000 + $120,000) ................. | 1,920,000 | |
|    Discount on bonds payable ($20,000 x 6 months) | | 120,000 |
|    Cash ($30,000,000 x 12% x $6/12$) ........................ | | 1,800,000 |

### August 31, 2008 (Stillworth)

| | | |
|---|---|---|
| Cash ($30,000 x 12% x $6/12$) .................................. | 1,800 | |
| Discount on investment ($20 x 6 months) ............... | 120 | |
|    Interest revenue ($1,800 + $120)............................ | | 1,920 |

### December 31, 2008 (Western)

| | | |
|---|---|---|
| Interest expense ($1,200,000 + $80,000) ................... | 1,280,000 | |
|    Discount on bonds payable ($20,000 x 4 months) | | 80,000 |
|    Interest payable ($30,000,000 x 12% x $4/12$) ....... | | 1,200,000 |

### December 31, 2008 (Stillworth)

| | | |
|---|---|---|
| Interest receivable ($30,000 x 12% x $4/12$)............. | 1,200 | |
| Discount on investment ($20 x 4 months) ............. | 80 | |
|    Interest revenue ($1,200 + $80)............................ | | 1,280 |

# Problem 14-6 (concluded)

## February 28, 2009 (Western)

| | | |
|---|---|---|
| Interest expense ($1,800,000 + $40,000 − $1,200,000) | 640,000 | |
| Interest payable (from adjusting entry)..................... | 1,200,000 | |
| Discount on bonds payable ($20,000 x 2 months) | | 40,000 |
| Cash ($30,000,000 x 12% x $^6/_{12}$) ........................ | | 1,800,000 |
| | | |
| Bonds payable ..................................................... | 30,000,000 | |
| Cash ................................................................ | | 30,000,000 |

## February 28, 2009 (Stillworth)

| | | |
|---|---|---|
| Cash ($30,000 x 12% x $^6/_{12}$).................................. | 1,800 | |
| Discount on bond investment ($20 x 2 months)...... | 40 | |
| Interest receivable (from adjusting entry) ............ | | 1,200 |
| Interest revenue ($1,800 + $40 − $1,200) .............. | | 640 |
| | | |
| Cash ................................................................... | 30,000 | |
| Investment in bonds ....................................... | | 30,000 |

# Problem 14-7

**Requirement 1**

| | | | | | | |
|---|---|---|---|---|---|---|
| Interest | $16,000,000¥ | x | 17.15909 * | = | $274,545,440 |
| Principal | $400,000,000 | x | 0.14205 ** | = | 56,820,000 |
| | *Present value (price) of the bonds* | | | | $331,365,440 |

¥ 4% x $400,000,000

* present value of an ordinary annuity of $1: n=40, i=5%

** present value of $1: n=40, i=5%

**Requirement 2**

(a)

| | | |
|---|---|---|
| Cash (price determined above)................................ | 331,365,440 | |
| Discount on bonds (difference)............................ | 68,634,560 | |
| Bonds payable (face amount) ............................ | | 400,000,000 |

(b)

| | | |
|---|---|---|
| Bond investment (face amount)............................ | 400,000 | |
| Discount on bond investment (difference)........ | | 68,635 |
| Cash (0.1% x $331,365,440)................................ | | 331,365 |

**Requirement 3**

(a)

| | | |
|---|---|---|
| Interest expense (5% x $331,365,440) ......................... | 16,568,272 | |
| Discount on bonds payable (difference) ........... | | 568,272 |
| Cash (4% x $400,000,000) ................................... | | 16,000,000 |

(b)

| | | |
|---|---|---|
| Cash (4% x $400,000) ............................................. | 16,000 | |
| Discount on bond investment (difference) ........... | 568 | |
| Interest revenue (5% x $331,365)........................... | | 16,568 |

**Requirement 4**

(a)

| | | |
|---|---|---|
| Interest expense (5% x [$331,365,440 + $568,272]).. | 16,596,686 | |
| Discount on bonds payable (difference) ........... | | 596,686 |
| Cash (4% x $400,000,000) ................................... | | 16,000,000 |

(b)

| | | |
|---|---|---|
| Cash (4% x $400,000) ............................................. | 16,000 | |
| Discount on bond investment (difference) ........... | 597 | |
| Interest revenue (5% x [$331,365 + $568])............. | | 16,597 |

# Problem 14-8

## Requirement 1

| | | |
|---|---|---|
| Cash (price given) ..................................................... | 5,795,518 | |
| Discount on bonds (difference) ............................ | 12,204,482 | |
| Bonds payable (face amount) ............................. | | 18,000,000 |

## Requirement 2

The discount rate that "equates" the present value of the debt ($5,795,518) and its future value ($18,000,000) is the effective rate of interest:

$5,795,518 ÷ $18,000,000 = .32197 – the Table 2 value for $n = 10$, $i = $ ?

In row 10 of Table 2, the value .32197 is in the 12% column. So, this is the effective interest rate. A financial calculator will produce the same rate.

## Requirement 3

| | | |
|---|---|---|
| Interest expense (12% x $5,795,518) ......................... | 695,462 | |
| Discount on bonds payable ............................ | | 695,462 |

## Requirement 4

| | | |
|---|---|---|
| Interest expense (12% x [$5,795,518 + $695,462]) .... | 778,918 | |
| Discount on bonds payable ............................ | | 778,918 |

## Requirement 5

| | | |
|---|---|---|
| Bonds payable ....................................................... | 18,000,000 | |
| Cash ............................................................. | | 18,000,000 |

# Problem 14-9

## Requirement 1

| | | |
|---|---|---|
| Land .................................................................................... | 600,000 | |
|    Notes payable (face amount) .......................................... | | 600,000 |

| | | |
|---|---|---|
| Interest expense (12% x $600,000) ..................................... | 72,000 | |
|    Cash (12% x $600,000) .................................................. | | 72,000 |

## Requirement 2

| | | |
|---|---|---|
| Office equipment (price given) ........................................... | 94,643 | |
| Discount on notes payable (difference) ........................... | 5,357 | |
|    Notes payable (face amount) .......................................... | | 100,000 |

The discount rate that "equates" the present value of the debt ($94,643) and its future value ($100,000 + $6,000) is the effective rate of interest:

$94,643 ÷ $106,000 = .8929 – the Table 2 value for $n = 1$, $i = ?$

In row 1 of Table 2, the value .8929 is in the 12% column. So, this is the effective interest rate. A financial calculator will produce the same rate.

***PROOF:***

| | | | | |
|---|---|---|---|---|
| Interest | $6,000¥ | x | 0.89286 * = | $ 5,357 |
| Principal | $100,000 | x | 0.89286 ** = | 89,286 |
| *Present value (price) of the bonds* | | | | $94,643 |

¥   6% x $100,000
*   present value of an ordinary annuity of $1: n=1, i=12%
**  present value of $1: n=1, i=12%

| | | |
|---|---|---|
| Interest expense (12% x $94,643) ..................................... | 11,357 | |
|    Discount on note payable (determined above) ............. | | 5,357 |
|    Cash (6% x $100,000) ..................................................... | | 6,000 |

## Problem 14-9 (concluded)

*Not required, but recorded at the same date (may be combined with interest entry):*

| | | |
|---|---|---|
| Note payable (face amount) ............................................ | 100,000 | |
| Cash...................................................................... | | 100,000 |

## Requirement 3

| $1,000,000 | x | 2.40183 | = | $2,401,830 |
|---|---|---|---|---|
| installment | | (from Table 4) | | present |
| payments | | n=3, i=12% | | value |

| | | |
|---|---|---|
| Building (implicit price)................................................. | 2,401,830 | |
| Note payable (present value determined above) ............. | | 2,401,830 |
| | | |
| Interest expense (12% x $2,401,830) .............................. | 288,220 | |
| Note payable (difference) .............................................. | 711,780 | |
| Cash (given)............................................................... | | 1,000,000 |

# Problem 14-10

### Requirement 1

| | | | | | |
|---|---|---|---|---|---|
| Interest | $ 6,000 | x | 3.79079 * | = | $ 22,745 |
| Principal | $150,000 | x | 0.62092 ** | = | 93,138 |
| | Present value (price) of the note | | | | $115,883 |

\* present value of an ordinary annuity of $1: n=5, i=10%

\*\* present value of $1: n=5, i=10%

| | | |
|---|---|---|
| Equipment (fair market value ).......................................... | 115,883 | |
| Discount on notes payable (difference) .......................... | 34,117 | |
| Note payable (face amount)........................................... | | 150,000 |

### Requirement 2

**December 31, 2006**

| | | |
|---|---|---|
| Interest expense (10% x $115,883)...................................... | 11,588 | |
| Discount on notes payable (difference) ...................... | | 5,588 |
| Cash (given) ................................................................. | | 6,000 |

### Requirement 3

**December 31, 2007**

| | | |
|---|---|---|
| Interest expense (10% x [$115,883 + 5,588])....................... | 12,147 | |
| Discount on notes payable (difference) ...................... | | 6,147 |
| Cash (given) ................................................................. | | 6,000 |

# Problem 14-11

## Requirement 1

$6,074,700 ÷ $2,000,000 = 3.03735
present  installment  present value
value   payment   table amount

This is the Table 4 value for $n = 4$, $i = ?$  In row 4 of Table 4, the number 3.03735 is in the 12% column.  So, 12% is the implicit interest rate.

## Requirement 2

| | | |
|---|---|---|
| Machine (fair market value )............................................ | 6,074,700 | |
|  Notes payable (present value ) .................................... | | 6,074,700 |

## Requirement 3

| | | |
|---|---|---|
| Interest expense (12% x outstanding balance)....................... | 728,964 | |
| Notes payable (difference)............................................... | 1,271,036 | |
|  Cash (given)................................................................ | | 2,000,000 |

## Requirement 4

| | | |
|---|---|---|
| Interest expense (12% x [$6,074,700 – 1,271,036]).............. | 576,440 | |
| Note payable (difference) .............................................. | 1,423,560 | |
|  Cash (given)................................................................ | | 2,000,000 |

## Requirement 5

$2,000,000 x 3.10245 =  $6,204,900
installment (from Table 4)  present
payment  n=4, i=11%   value

| | | |
|---|---|---|
| Machine............................................................... | 6,204,900 | |
|  Notes payable............................................................ | | 6,204,900 |

# Problem 14-12

## Requirement 1

| | | | | | | |
|---|---|---|---|---|---|---|
| Interest | $5,000¥ | x | 3.16987 * | = | $15,849 | |
| Principal | $100,000 | x | 0.68301 ** | = | 68,301 | |
| *Present value (price) of the note* | | | | | $84,150 | |

¥  5% x $100,000

\*  present value of an ordinary annuity of $1: n=4, i=10%

\*\*  present value of $1: n=4, i=10%

| | | |
|---|---|---|
| Operational assets (price determined above) ..................... | 84,150 | |
| Discount on notes payable (difference) ......................... | 15,850 | |
| Notes payable (face amount) ....................................... | | 100,000 |

## Requirement 2

| Dec.31 | Cash Interest | Effective Interest | | | Increase in Balance | Outstanding Balance |
|---|---|---|---|---|---|---|
| | | | | | | 84,150 |
| 2006 | 5,000 | .10 (84,150) | = | 8,415 | 3,415 | 87,565 |
| 2007 | 5,000 | .10 (87,565) | = | 8,757 | 3,757 | 91,322 |
| 2008 | 5,000 | .10 (91,322) | = | 9,132 | 4,132 | 95,454 |
| 2009 | 5,000 | .10 (95,454) | = | 9,546* | 4,546 | 100,000 |
| | 20,000 | | | 35,850 | 15,850 | |

\* rounded

## Requirement 3

| | | |
|---|---|---|
| Interest expense (market rate x outstanding balance) .......... | 9,132 | |
| Discount on notes payable (difference) ...................... | | 4,132 |
| Cash (stated rate x face amount)........................................ | | 5,000 |

# Problem 14-12 (concluded)

## Requirement 4

$$\$84{,}150 \;\div\; 3.16987 \;=\; \$26{,}547$$

| amount of loan | (from Table 4) n=4, i=10% | installment payment |
|---|---|---|

## Requirement 5

| Dec.31 | Cash Payment | Effective Interest 10% x Outstanding Balance | | Decrease in Balance Balance Reduction | Outstanding Balance |
|---|---|---|---|---|---|
| | | | | | 84,150 |
| 2006 | 26,547 | .10 (84,150) = | 8,415 | 18,132 | 66,018 |
| 2007 | 26,547 | .10 (66,018) = | 6,602 | 19,945 | 46,073 |
| 2008 | 26,547 | .10 (46,073) = | 4,607 | 21,940 | 24,133 |
| 2009 | 26,547 | .10 (24,133) = | 2,414* | 24,133 | 0 |
| | 106,188 | | 22,038 | 84,150 | |

* rounded

## Requirement 6

| | | |
|---|---|---|
| Interest expense (market rate x outstanding balance).......... | 4,607 | |
| Note payable (difference) ............................................... | 21,940 | |
|     Cash (payment determined above) ................................ | | 26,547 |

# Problem 14-13

| | | |
|---|---|---|
| Bonds payable (face amount) ............................................ | 800,000 | |
| Loss on early extinguishment (to balance) ..................... | 13,100 | |
| Debt issue costs ($^7/_{10}$ x $3,000)..................................... | | 2,100 |
| Discount on bonds ($^7/_{10}$ x [$800,000 – $770,000]) ....... | | 21,000 |
| Cash (given) ................................................................. | | 790,000 |

# Problem 14-14

## Requirement 1

| | | |
|---|---|---|
| Interest expense (7% x $19,000,000)..................................... | 1,330,000 | |
| Discount on bonds payable (difference) ..................... | | 130,000 |
| Cash (6% x $20,000,000)................................................. | | 1,200,000 |

## Requirement 2

| | | |
|---|---|---|
| Bonds payable (face amount) ......................................... | 20,000,000 | |
| Loss on early extinguishment (to balance) ..................... | 1,270,000 | |
| Discount on bonds ($1,000,000 – 130,000) .................. | | 870,000 |
| Cash (redemption price)................................................. | | 20,400,000 |

# Problem 14-15

**2006**

**July 1**

| | | |
|---|---|---|
| Bond investment (face amount) ...................................... | 16,000,000 | |
|    Discount on bond investment (difference) ................. | | 300,000 |
|    Cash (price paid) ................................................ | | 15,700,000 |

**Oct. 1**

| | | |
|---|---|---|
| Bond investment (face amount) ...................................... | 30,000,000 | |
| Premium on bond investment ...................................... | 1,160,000 | |
| Interest receivable ($30,000,000 x 12% x $^4/_{12}$) ................ | 1,200,000 | |
|    Cash ($31,160,000 + $1,200,000) ............................. | | 32,360,000 |

**Dec. 1**

| | | |
|---|---|---|
| Cash (6% x $30,000,000) ................................................ | 1,800,000 | |
|    Premium on investment* ............................................. | | 20,000 |
|    Interest receivable (from October entry) ........................ | | 1,200,000 |
|    Interest revenue (to balance) ........................................... | | 580,000 |

  \* 10 years – (June-September) = 116 months
    $1,160,000 ÷ 116 months = $10,000 / month
    $10,000 x 2 months = $20,000

**Dec. 31   Accrued interest**

**Bracecourt**

| | | |
|---|---|---|
| Interest receivable ($16,000,000 x 10% x $^6/_{12}$) ................ | 800,000 | |
| Discount on bond investment * ................................... | 7,500 | |
|    Interest revenue (to balance) ........................................... | | 807,500 |

  \* 20 years = 240 months
    $300,000 ÷ 240 months = $1,250 / month
    $1,250 x 6 months = $7,500

**Framm**

| | | |
|---|---|---|
| Interest receivable ($30,000,000 x 12% x $^1/_{12}$) ................ | 300,000 | |
|    Premium on investment ($10,000 x 1 month) ................ | | 10,000 |
|    Interest revenue (to balance) ........................................... | | 290,000 |

## Problem 14-15 (continued)

**2007**

**Jan. 1**

| | | |
|---|---|---|
| Cash (10% x $16,000,000 x $^6/_{12}$) ............................................... | 800,000 | |
| Interest receivable (from adjusting entry) ..................... | | 800,000 |

**June 1**

| | | |
|---|---|---|
| Cash (12% x $30,000,000 x $^6/_{12}$) ........................................... | 1,800,000 | |
| Premium on investment ($10,000 x 5 months) ............... | | 50,000 |
| Interest receivable (from adjusting entry)....................... | | 300,000 |
| Interest revenue (to balance) ......................................... | | 1,450,000 |

**July 1**

| | | |
|---|---|---|
| Cash (10% x $16,000,000 x $^6/_{12}$) ....................................... | 800,000 | |
| Discount on bond investment ($1,250 x 6 months) ........... | 7,500 | |
| Interest revenue (to balance) ......................................... | | 807,500 |

**Sept. 1**

| | | |
|---|---|---|
| Interest receivable (12% x $15,000,000 x $^3/_{12}$)................. | 450,000 | |
| Premium on investment ($10,000 x 3 months x $^{15}/_{30}$).. | | 15,000 |
| Interest revenue (difference)........................................... | | 435,000 |

| | | |
|---|---|---|
| Cash ([101% x $15,000,000] + $450,000) .......................... | 15,600,000 | |
| Loss on sale of investment ** ...................................... | 375,000 | |
| Bond investment (face amount)...................................... | | 15,000,000 |
| Premium on bond investment * ............................... | | 525,000 |
| Interest receivable (12% x $15,000,000 x $^3/_{12}$)............. | | 450,000 |

* ([$1,160,000 − 20,000 − 10,000 − 50,000 ] x $^{15}/_{30}$ ) − $15,000 =  $525,000, or
[$1,160,000 x $^{105}/_{116}$ x $^{15}/_{30}$] = $525,000

** [$15,000,000 + 525,000] − [101% x $15,000,000]) = $375,000

## Problem 14-15 *(continued)*

### Dec. 1

| | | |
|---|---|---|
| Cash (12% x $15,000,000 x $^6/_{12}$) ............................................ | 900,000 | |
|    Premium on investment* ................................................ | | 30,000 |
|    Interest revenue (to balance) ......................................... | | 870,000 |

\* ($10,000 x 6 months x $^{15}/_{30}$)

### Dec. 31 Accrued interest

**Bracecourt**

| | | |
|---|---|---|
| Interest receivable (10% x $16,000,000 x $^6/_{12}$)................. | 800,000 | |
| Discount on bond investment ($1,250 x 6 months) ........... | 7,500 | |
|    Interest revenue (to balance) ......................................... | | 807,500 |

**Framm**

| | | |
|---|---|---|
| Interest receivable ($15,000,000 x 12% x $^1/_{12}$) ................ | 150,000 | |
|    Premium on investment ($10,000 x 1 month x $^{15}/_{30}$).... | | 5,000 |
|    Interest revenue (to balance) ......................................... | | 145,000 |

### 2008

### Jan. 1

| | | |
|---|---|---|
| Cash (10% x $16,000,000 x $^6/_{12}$) ...................................... | 800,000 | |
|    Interest receivable (from adjusting entry).................... | | 800,000 |

*Problem 14-15 (concluded)*

**Feb. 28**

| | | |
|---|---|---|
| Interest receivable (12% x $15,000,000 x $2/12$)................ | 300,000 | |
|   Premium on investment ($10,000 x 2 months x $15/30$).. | | 10,000 |
|   Interest revenue (difference)............................................. | | 290,000 |
| | | |
| Cash ([102% x $15,000,000] + $150,000 + $300,000)........... | 15,750,000 | |
| Loss on sale of investment ** ....................................... | 195,000 | |
|   Bond investment (face amount).................................... | | 15,000,000 |
|   Premium on bond investment * .............................. | | 495,000 |
|   Interest receivable (12% x $15,000,000 x $3/12$)............. | | 450,000 |

   * $1,160,000 – 20,000 – 10,000 – 50,000 – 15,000 – 525,000 – 30,000 – 5,000 –
      10,000 = $495,000, or  [$1,160,000 x $99/116$ x $15/30$] = $495,000

   ** [$15,000,000 + 495,000] – [102% x $15,000,000]) = $195,000


**Dec. 31   Accrued interest**

| | | |
|---|---|---|
| Interest receivable (10% x $16,000,000 x $6/12$)................ | 800,000 | |
| Discount on bond investment ($1,250 x 6 months) ........... | 7,500 | |
|   Interest revenue (to balance) ............................................. | | 807,500 |

# Problem 14-16

## 1. Issuance of the bonds.

| | | |
|---|---|---|
| Cash ($385,000 – 1,500) ............................................ | 383,500 | |
| Debt issue costs (given)............................................. | 1,500 | |
| Discount on bonds payable ($400,000 – 385,000) ............. | 15,000 | |
|    Bonds payable (face amount)...................................... | | 400,000 |

## 2. December 31, 2006

| | | |
|---|---|---|
| Interest expense ($20,000 + 750 )................................... | 20,750 | |
|    Discount on bonds payable ($15,000 ÷ 20) ............... | | 750 |
|    Cash (5% x $400,000)............................................... | | 20,000 |
| | | |
| Debt issue expense ($1,500 ÷ 20)................................... | 75 | |
|    Debt issue costs ...................................................... | | 75 |

## 3. June 30, 2007

| | | |
|---|---|---|
| Interest expense ($20,000 + 750 )................................... | 20,750 | |
|    Discount on bonds payable ($15,000 ÷ 20) ............... | | 750 |
|    Cash (5% x $400,000)............................................... | | 20,000 |
| | | |
| Debt issue expense ($1,500 ÷ 20)................................... | 75 | |
|    Debt issue costs ...................................................... | | 75 |

## 4. Call of the bonds

| | | |
|---|---|---|
| Bonds payable (face amount)......................................... | 400,000 | |
| Loss on early extinguishment (to balance)...................... | 9,850 | |
|    Debt issue costs ($9/10$ x $1,500) ............................... | | 1,350 |
|    Discount on bonds ($9/10$ x [$400,000 – $385,000])....... | | 13,500 |
|    Cash (given)........................................................... | | 395,000 |

# Problem 14-17

| | List A | | List B |
|---|---|---|---|
| j | 1. Effective rate times balance | a. | Straight-line method |
| h | 2. Promises made to bondholders | b. | Discount |
| o | 3. Present value of interest plus present value of principal | c. | Liquidation payments after other claims satisfied |
| m | 4. Call feature | d. | Name of owner not registered |
| l | 5. Debt issue costs | e. | Premium |
| b | 6. Market rate higher than stated rate | f. | Checks are mailed directly |
| d | 7. Coupon bonds | g. | No specific assets pledged |
| k | 8. Convertible bonds | h. | Bond indenture |
| e | 9. Market rate less than stated rate | i. | Backed by a lien |
| n | 10. Stated rate times face amount | j. | Interest expense |
| f | 11. Registered bonds | k. | May become stock |
| g | 12. Debenture bond | l. | Legal, accounting, printing |
| i | 13. Mortgage bond | m. | Protection against falling rates |
| a | 14. Materiality concept | n. | Periodic cash payments |
| c | 15. Subordinated debenture | o. | Bond price |

# Problem 14-18

## Requirement 1

| | | |
|---|---|---|
| Bonds payable (face amount)............................................ | 20,000,000 | |
| Premium on bonds ($20/40$ x $6,000,000) ......................... | 3,000,000 | |
| Gain on early extinguishment (to balance) ................ | | 2,600,000 |
| Cash ($20,000,000 x 102%)............................................. | | 20,400,000 |

## Requirement 2

| | | |
|---|---|---|
| Bonds payable (face amount)............................................ | 10,000,000 | |
| Premium on bonds ($10/40$ x $6,000,000) ......................... | 1,500,000 | |
| Gain on early extinguishment (to balance) ................ | | 1,000,000 |
| Cash (given)................................................................... | | 10,500,000 |

# Problem 14-19

## Requirement 1

|  | ($ in millions) |
|---|---|

**Convertible Bonds – 1993 issue**

| | | |
|---|---|---|
| Cash (97.5% x $200 million)............................................................ | 195 | |
| Discount on bonds (difference)........................................................ | 5 | |
|   Convertible bonds payable (face amount)............................. | | 200 |

**Bonds With Warrants – 1997 issue**

| | | |
|---|---|---|
| Cash (102% x $50 million) ............................................................. | 51 | |
| Discount on bonds payable (difference) ......................................... | 3 | |
|   Bonds payable (face amount)................................................... | | 50 |
|   Paid-in capital – stock warrants outstanding (given)............ | | 4 |

## Requirement 2

|  | ($ in millions) |
|---|---|

| | | |
|---|---|---|
| Convertible bonds payable (90% x  $200 million) ....................... | 180 | |
|   Discount on bonds payable (90% x  $2 million) ...................... | | 1.8 |
|   Common stock (90% x [200,000 x 40 shares] x $1 par).............. | | 7.2 |
|   Paid-in capital – excess of par (to balance)............................ | | 171.0 |

| | | |
|---|---|---|
| Convertible bonds payable (10% x  $200 million) ....................... | 20.0 | |
| Loss on early extinguishment (to balance) ................................. | .4 | |
|   Discount on bonds payable (10% x  $2 million) ...................... | | .2 |
|   Cash (101% x 10% x $200 million) ........................................... | | 20.2 |

## Requirement 3

|  | ($ in millions) |
|---|---|

| | | |
|---|---|---|
| Convertible bonds payable (90% x  $200 million) ....................... | 180 | |
| Conversion expense (90% x 200,000 bonds x $150)...................... | 27 | |
|   Discount on bonds payable (90% x  $2 million) ...................... | | 1.8 |
|   Common stock (90% x [200,000 x 40 shares] x $1 par)............. | | 7.2 |
|   Paid-in capital – excess of par (to balance)............................ | | 171.0 |
|   Cash (90% x 200,000 bonds x $150)............................................. | | 27.0 |

## Problem 14-19 (concluded)

### Requirement 4

|  | ($ in millions) |
|---|---|
| Convertible bonds payable (90% x  $200 million)....................... | 180.0 |
| Conversion expense |  |
| (90% x [200,000 x (45 – 40) shares] x $32)................................. | 28.8 |
| Discount on bonds payable (90% x  $2 million)....................... | 1.8 |
| Common stock (90% x [200,000 x 45 shares] x $1 par) .............. | 8.1 |
| Paid-in capital – excess of par (to balance)........................... | 198.9 |

### Requirement 5

|  | ($ in millions) |
|---|---|
| Cash (40% x 50,000 x 40 warrants x $25) ...................................... | 20.0 |
| Paid-in capital – stock warrants outstanding (40% x $4 million) | 1.6 |
| Common stock (40% x 50,000 x 40 shares x $1 par)................... | .8 |
| Paid-in capital – excess of par (to balance)........................... | 20.8 |

# Problem 14-20

## Requirement 1

|  | ($ in millions) |  |
|---|---|---|
| Land............................................................ | 3 | |
|    Gain on disposal ........................................... | | 3 |
| | | |
| Note payable................................................ | 20 | |
| Accrued interest payable .................................. | 2 | |
|    Land .......................................................... | | 16 |
|    Gain on debt restructuring............................... | | 6 |

## Requirement 2

**Analysis:**

| | | | |
|---|---|---|---|
| *Carrying amount*: | $20 million + $2 million = | $22,000,000 |
| *Future payments*: | ($1 million x 4) + $15 million = | 19,000,000 |
| Gain to debtor | | $ 3,000,000 |

($ in millions)

**(a) January 1, 2006**

| | | |
|---|---|---|
| Accrued interest payable ............................... | 2 | |
| Note payable *.............................................. | 1 | |
|    Gain on debt restructuring............................... | | 3 |

   \* establishes a balance in the note account equal to the total cash payments under the new agreement ($20 million – 1 million = $19 million)

**(b) December 31, 2006, 2007, 2008, and 2009 revised "interest" payments**

| | | |
|---|---|---|
| Note payable.............................................. | 1 | |
|    Cash ....................................................... | | 1 |

*Note*: No interest expense should be recorded after the restructuring. All subsequent cash payments result in reductions of principal.

**(c) December 31, 2009 revised principal payment**

| | | |
|---|---|---|
| Note payable.............................................. | 15 | |
|    Cash ....................................................... | | 15 |

*Problem 14-20 (continued)*

**Requirement 3**

**Analysis:**   *Carrying amount:*   $20,000,000 + $2,000,000 =   $22,000,000
                     *Future payments:*                                 27,775,000
                          Interest                                    $ 5,775,000

**Calculation of the new effective interest rate:**

- $22,000,000 ÷ $27,775,000 = .79208 – the Table 2 value for $n = 4$, $i = $ **?**

- In row 4 of Table 2, the number .79209 is in the 6% column. So, this is the **new** effective interest rate.

**(a) January 1, 2006**

*[Since the total future cash payments are not less than the carrying amount of the debt, no reduction of the existing debt is necessary and no entry is required at the time of the debt restructuring.]*

*Amortization Schedule (not required)*

| Dec.31 | Cash Interest | Effective Interest 6% x Outstanding Balance | Increase in Balance | Outstanding Balance |
|--------|---------------|---------------------------------------------|---------------------|---------------------|
|        |               |                                             |                     | 22,000,000          |
| 2006   | 0             | .06 (22,000,000) = 1,320,000                | 1,320,000           | 23,320,000          |
| 2007   | 0             | .06 (23,320,000) = 1,399,200                | 1,399,200           | 24,719,200          |
| 2008   | 0             | .06 (24,719,200) = 1,483,152                | 1,483,152           | 26,202,352          |
| 2009   | 0             | .06 (26,202,352) = 1,572,648*               | 1,572,648           | 27,775,000          |
|        | 0             | 5,775,000                                   | 5,775,000           |                     |

* rounded

*Problem 14-20 (concluded)*

**(b) December 31, 2006**

| | | |
|---|---|---|
| Interest expense ................................................. | 1,320,000 | |
|    Interest payable................................................. | | 1,320,000 |

**December 31, 2007**

| | | |
|---|---|---|
| Interest expense ................................................. | 1,399,200 | |
|    Interest payable................................................. | | 1,399,200 |

**December 31, 2008**

| | | |
|---|---|---|
| Interest expense ................................................. | 1,483,152 | |
|    Interest payable................................................. | | 1,483,152 |

**December 31, 2009**

| | | |
|---|---|---|
| Interest expense ................................................. | 1,572,648 | |
|    Interest payable................................................. | | 1,572,648 |

**(c) December 31, 2009  revised payment**

| | | |
|---|---|---|
| Interest payable................................................. | 7,775,000 | |
| Note payable....................................................... | 20,000,000 | |
|    Cash ................................................................ | | 27,775,000 |

# CASES
## Communication Case 14-1
### Suggested Grading Concepts and Grading Scheme:

**Content** (80% )

_____ 20 Convertible bonds

_____ Entire proceeds of the bond issue should be allocated to the debt and the related premium or discount accounts.

_____ 20 Bonds with detachable warrants

_____ Proceeds of their sale should be allocated between the debt and the warrants.

_____ Basis of allocation is their relative fair values.

_____ Relative values are usually determined by the price at which the respective instruments are traded in the open market.

_____ Portion of the proceeds assigned to the warrants should be accounted for as paid-in capital.

_____ 20 Reasons why all the proceeds of convertible bonds should be allocated to the debt

_____ The option is inseparable from the debt: no way to retain one right while selling the other.

_____ The valuation presents practical problems: would be subjective.

_____ 20 Arguments that accounting for convertible debt should be the same as for debt issued with detachable stock purchase warrants

_____ Convertible debt has features of both debt and shareholders' equity, and separate recognition should be given to the fundamental elements at the time of issuance.

_____ Difficulties in separating the relative values of the features are not insurmountable.

_____ **Bonus (5)** Other relevant arguments not mentioned above

_____ 80-85 points

**Writing** (20%)

_____ 5 Terminology and tone appropriate to the audience (CFO).

_____ 6 Organization permits ease of understanding.

_____ Introduction that states purpose.

_____ Paragraphs separate main points.

_____ 9 English.

_____ Word selection.

_____ Spelling.

_____ Grammar.

# Real World Case 14-2

## Requirement 1

|  | ($ in millions) |
|---|---|
| Cash (price given)............................................................ | 968 |
| Discount on notes (difference).................................... | 832 |
| Notes payable (face amount) .................................... | 1,800 |

## Requirement 2

| Fiscal Year-end | Cash | Interest Expense | | | | Decrease in Balance | Outstanding Balance |
|---|---|---|---|---|---|---|---|
| 1997 |  |  |  |  |  |  | 968 |
| 1998 | 0 | 0.03149 | (968) | = | 30 | 30 | 998 |
| 1999 | 0 | 0.03149 | (998) | = | 31 | 31 | 1,030 |
| 2000 | 0 | 0.03149 | (1,030) | = | 32 | 32 | 1,062 |
| 2001 | 0 | 0.03149 | (1,062) | = | 33 | 33 | 1,096 |
| 2002 | 0 | 0.03149 | (1,096) | = | 35 | 35 | 1,130 |
| 2003 | 0 | 0.03149 | (1,130) | = | 36 | 36 | 1,166 |
| 2004 | 0 | 0.03149 | (1,166) | = | 37 | 37 | 1,203 |
| 2005 | 0 | 0.03149 | (1,203) | = | 38 | 38 | 1,240 |
| 2006 | 0 | 0.03149 | (1,240) | = | 39 | 39 | 1,280 |
| 2007 | 0 | 0.03149 | (1,280) | = | 40 | 40 | 1,320 |
| 2008 | 0 | 0.03149 | (1,320) | = | 42 | 42 | 1,361 |
| 2009 | 0 | 0.03149 | (1,361) | = | 43 | 43 | 1,404 |
| 2010 | 0 | 0.03149 | (1,404) | = | 44 | 44 | 1,449 |
| 2011 | 0 | 0.03149 | (1,449) | = | 46 | 46 | 1,494 |
| 2012 | 0 | 0.03149 | (1,494) | = | 47 | 47 | 1,541 |
| 2013 | 0 | 0.03149 | (1,541) | = | 49 | 49 | 1,590 |
| 2014 | 0 | 0.03149 | (1,590) | = | 50 | 50 | 1,640 |
| 2015 | 0 | 0.03149 | (1,640) | = | 52 | 52 | 1,691 |
| 2016 | 0 | 0.03149 | (1,691) | = | 53 | 53 | 1,745 |
| 2017 | 0 | 0.03149 | (1,745) | = | 55 | 55 | 1,800 |

## Case 14-2 (concluded)

### Requirement 3

In a strict sense, zero-coupon debt pays no interest. "Zeros" offer a return in the form of a "deep discount" from the face amount. In fact, though, interest accrues at the effective rate (3.149% in this case) times the outstanding balance ($968 million during 1998), even though no interest is paid periodically. Interest on zero-coupon debt is determined and reported in precisely the same manner as on interest-paying debt. Under the concept of *accrual accounting*, the periodic effective interest is unaffected by when the cash actually is paid. Corporations can even deduct for tax purposes the annual interest expense. So, for 1998, HP's earnings were reduced by $30 million (.03149 x $968) and increased by the tax savings from being able to deduct the $30 million. If the tax rate was 35%, that savings would have been 35% x $30, or $10.5 million, and the net decrease in earnings would have been $19.5 million ($30 – 10.5).

### Requirement 4

From the amortization schedule, we can see that the book value of the debt at the end of 2002 was $1,130 million.

### Requirement 5

The journal entry Hewlett-Packard used to record the early extinguishment of debt in 2002, assuming the purchase was made at the end of the year was:

| | | |
|---|---|---|
| Notes payable (given)............................................. | 257 | |
|     Discount (calculated below)................................. | | 96 |
|     Gain on the early extinguishment of debt (to balance) | | 34 |
|     Cash (given) ........................................................ | | 127 |

**Calculations:**

$257 / $1,800 = 14.28% of notes were repurchased

14.28% x $1,130 = $161 million book value of notes repurchased

$257 – 161 = **$96** million discount on notes repurchased

# Communication Case 14-3

You may wish to suggest to your students that they consult the FASB 1990 Discussion Memorandum, "Distinguishing between Liability and Equity Instruments and Accounting for Instruments with Characteristics of Both," which sets forth the most common arguments on the issues in this case. Or, you may prefer that they think for themselves and approach the issue from scratch.

There is no right or wrong answer. Both views can and often are convincingly defended. The process of developing and synthesizing the arguments will likely be more beneficial than any single solution. Each student should benefit from participating in the process, interacting first with his or her partner, then with the class as a whole. It is important that each student actively participate in the process. Domination by one or two individuals should be discouraged.

Arguments brought out in the FASB DM include the following:

*Case 14-3 (continued)*

**Arguments Supporting View 1:**

1. Those who favor accounting for convertible debt as entirely a liability until it is either converted or repaid argue that a convertible bond offers the holder two mutually exclusive choices. The holder cannot both redeem the bond for cash at maturity and convert it into common stock. They contend that the accounting before conversion or other settlement should reflect only the issuer's current position as a borrower and the holder's current position as a creditor. Until the conversion option is exercised, the bondholder is entitled to receive, and the enterprise is obligated to pay, only the periodic interest payments. If the option has not been exercised at the date the bonds mature, the issuer is obligated to pay the face amount, not to issue stock to the holder. Advocates of accounting for convertible debt according to its governing characteristics argue that a convertible bond is a single instrument, not two. To account for it as two instruments would not be representationally faithful. (par. 295)

2. Supporters of the first alternative generally also are concerned about the ability to measure reliably the components of convertible debt because neither is separately traded. They conclude that because the market does not determine a separate value for the conversion option, any value attributed to it would be subjective. Opinion 14 cited "the uncertain duration of the right to obtain the stock and the uncertainty as to the future value of the stock obtainable upon conversion" as factors further complicating valuation of the conversion option. (par. 296)

3. Supporters of that view argue that factors other than the conversion feature typically affect the pricing of convertible debt and therefore may complicate an attempt to allocate the proceeds from issuance between the straight debt and the conversion feature. For example, convertible bonds generally have covenants that are less restrictive than those for nonconvertible bonds on matters such as issuing more debt, maintaining specified financial ratios, paying large dividends on common stock, and establishing sinking funds. Less restrictive covenants may result in some reduction in market value and a corresponding increase in yield, which would complicate valuing the debt component of a convertible bond by comparing it with nonconvertible bonds with similar terms issued by enterprises with comparable credit ratings (par. 297).

## Case 14-3 (continued)

4. Moreover, no cash payment from holder to issuer is required when a convertible bond is converted; the bond itself represents the consideration received by the issuing enterprise for the stock into which the bond is converted. Thus, the price paid by the holder upon conversion effectively depends on the market price of the bond at the time of conversion. Those who would account for convertible debt as entirely a liability argue that the absence of a fixed cash price for which a bondholder obtains an equity interest complicates an attempt to value the straight debt and conversion feature components (par. 298).

**Arguments Supporting View 2:**

1. Those who favor separate recognition of the liability and equity components of convertible debt argue that to ignore the existence of the conversion feature in recognizing the issuance of the bond results in overstating the liability and understating the interest expense. The effect of the conversion feature is to lower the rate for otherwise comparable straight debt (par. 333).

2. The higher interest expense recognized if the components are separately recognized than if all of the proceeds of issuance are recorded as a liability reflects the fact that an enterprise that issues debt at less than its face amount pays an effective interest rate that is higher than the coupon rate. The lower reported interest expense that results if the convertible debt is accounted for as entirely a liability leads those who support separate accounting to argue that failure to attribute a portion of the proceeds to the conversion option, thereby overstating the amount of the enterprise's liability, does not faithfully represent the economics of the transaction between the enterprise and the bondholder (par. 334).

3. Supporters of separate accounting contend that accounting for convertible debt as entirely a liability impairs comparability between enterprises. If convertible debt is reported as entirely a liability, an enterprise with a relatively high credit rating that issues nonconvertible debt appears to have a higher cost of borrowing than a company with a lower credit rating that issues convertible debt because inclusion of the conversion feature lowers the nominal interest rate significantly (par. 335).

*Case 14-3 (concluded)*

4. Those who support separate recognition of the liability and equity components of convertible debt point to the different values assigned by the market to convertible and nonconvertible debt with like terms as evidence of the inherent value of the conversion feature. They argue that accounting for a convertible bond as if it were entirely a debt instrument fails to recognize and display appropriately the obligation to issue stock, that is, the option embedded in convertible debt. The conversion feature has essentially the same economic value as the call on stock represented by a separately traded call option or warrant. The fact that the conversion feature cannot be sold separately does not justify ignoring its existence (par. 336).

5. In the 21 years since Opinion 14 was issued, the idea that many financial instruments may be broken down into more fundamental components, which then may be traded separately, has been embraced by the Wall Street community. The cash flows from instruments that have generally not been thought of as containing different components, such as government bonds, have been unbundled and recombined. Those who support separate accounting for the fundamental components of convertible debt argue that separate accounting would be consistent with the current economic environment. They contend that it is neither necessary nor appropriate to wait until the components of a financial instrument like convertible debt, which so obviously has both liability and equity characteristics, are physically separated to give accounting recognition to the existence of the separate components (par. 337).

# Analysis Case 14-4

## Requirement 1

The notice is being placed by the four underwriters listed at the bottom of the notice. The purpose is to announce the sale of the bonds described. Actually, the sale by Craft Foods already has occurred at this point. The underwriters resell the securities to the investing public. These are ten-year bonds. The stated rate of interest is 7.75%, but the bonds are priced to yield a higher rate, which accounts for the fact they are offered at a discount, 99.57% of face value.

## Requirement 2

In practice, debt securities rarely are priced at a premium in their initial offering. The reason is primarily a marketing consideration. It's psychologically more palatable for a security salesperson to approach a customer with an issue that is offered at a *discount* off its face value and that provides a return *greater* than its stated rate than one which is priced *above* its face value and provides a return *less* than its stated rate.

## Requirement 3

The accounting considerations for Craft Foods are to recognize the liability and related debt issue costs, as well as to record interest expense semiannually over the ten-year term to maturity at the effective rate of interest. The bonds were recorded at their selling price: $750,000,000 x 99.57 = $746,775,000 (Bonds payable at face, discount of $3,225,000). Craft Foods also recorded debt issue costs in a separate account to be amortized over the term to maturity (probably straight-line). We do not know the amount of those costs. It also is not apparent exactly when the sale by Craft Foods was made to the underwriters and therefore the amount of any accrued interest. Any accrued interest would be recorded as interest payable to be paid at the first interest date as part of the first semiannual interest payment.

# Judgment Case 14-5

Obviously, no rational lender will lend money without interest. The zero interest loan described actually does implicitly bear interest. The amount and rate of interest can be inferred from either the market rate of interest at the time for this type of transaction or from the fair value of the asset being sold. The case information provides no information about either, other than that the stated price of the asset is higher than prices for this model Mr. Wilde had seen elsewhere.

If we knew, for instance, that the market rate of interest at the time for this type of transaction is 8%, we would assume that's the effective interest rate and could calculate the price of the equipment as follows:

$$\underset{\substack{\text{installment} \\ \text{payment}}}{\$17,000} \quad \times \quad \underset{\substack{\text{(from Table 4)} \\ n=12, \, i=2.0\%}}{10.57534} \quad = \quad \underset{\substack{\text{actual} \\ \text{price}}}{\$179,781}$$

Both the asset acquired and the liability used to purchase it should be recorded at the *real* cost, $179,781. Similarly, if we knew the cash price of the equipment is $185,430, then we could calculate the effective rate of interest as follows:

The discount rate that "equates" the present value of the debt ($185,430) and the installment payments ($17,000) is the effective rate of interest:

$185,430 \div \$17,000 = 10.9076$: the Table 4 value for $n = 12$, $i = $ ?

In row 12 of Table 4, the value 10.90751 is in the 1.5% column. Since payments are quarterly, this equates to a 1.5 x 4 = 6% annual rate. So, 6% is the effective interest rate. A financial calculator will produce the same rate.

In any case, Mr. Wilde will not avoid interest charges with this offer. Interest expense must be recorded at the effective rate, 8% in our first scenario, and 6% in the second.

# Judgment Case 14-6

Although not specifically discussed in the chapter, concepts studied in this and other chapters provide the logic for addressing the situation described. (APB 21 also addresses this type of situation.)

The company's accountant is incorrect in valuing the note at $200,000. The note should be valued at the present value of the receivable using the prevailing market rate and the difference between the present value and the cash given is regarded as an addition to the cost of products purchased during the contract term.

In this case, the note would be valued at $136,602, computed as follows:

$$PV = \$200,000 \text{ x } .68301$$
$$\text{PV of } \$1:$$
$$n=4, i=10\% \text{ (from Table 2)}$$

$$PV = \$136,602$$

The journal entry to record the initial transaction is as follows

| | | |
|---|---|---|
| Note receivable (above) ................................. | 136,602 | |
| Prepaid inventory (difference) ........................ | 63,398 | |
| Cash ............................................................. | | 200,000 |

Interest revenue is recognized over the 4-year life of the note using the effective interest rate of 10%. Accrued interest will increase the receivable valuation to $200,000.

Prepaid inventory is credited and inventory is debited as inventory is purchased, thus increasing the cost of inventory from the prices paid to market value.

# Communication Case 14-7

The critical question that student groups should address is the valuation of the note receivable. In this case, there is a correct answer. The note should be valued at the present value of $300,000 using the appropriate market rate of interest. The difference between present value and the $300,000 should be accounted for by Pastel as *prepaid advertising*. Interest revenue over the life of the note will be recognized using the effective rate. As advertising services are provided by the radio station, advertising expense is debited and prepaid advertising credited.

It is important that each student actively participate in the process of arriving at a solution. Domination by one or two individuals should be discouraged. Students should be encouraged to contribute to the group discussion by (a) offering information on relevant issues, and (b) clarifying or modifying ideas already expressed, or (c) suggesting alternative direction.

# Analysis Case 14-8

1.a. The 11% bonds were issued at a premium (more than face amount). Although the bonds provide for the payment of interest of 11% of face amount, this rate was more than the prevailing or market rate for bonds of similar quality at the time the bonds were issued. Thus, the bonds must sell at a premium to yield 9%.

  b. The amount of interest expense would be higher in the first year of the life of the bond issue than in the second year of the life of the bond issue. According to the effective interest method of amortization, the 9% effective interest rate is applied to a declining bond carrying amount, and results in a lower interest expense in each successive year.

2. a. Gain or loss on early extinguishment of debt should be determined by comparing the net carrying amount of the bonds at the date of extinguishment with the reacquisition price. If the net carrying amount exceeds the reacquisition price, a gain results. If the net carrying amount is less than the reacquisition price, a loss results. In this case, a gain results. The bonds were issued at a premium; therefore, the carrying amount of the bonds at the date of extinguishment must exceed face amount. Thus, the net carrying amount exceeds the reacquisition price.

  b. Brewster should report a gain on the early extinguishment in net income for 2006.

*Case 14-8 (concluded)*

3. a. Net income is not affected by conversion under the book value method. The book value method views the convertible bonds as possessing substantial characteristics of equity capital. The conversion represents the completion of a prior transaction (the issuance of the convertible debt), not the culmination of an earning process.

   b. A gain or loss results, and thus net income is affected by conversion under the market value method when market value differs from the carrying amount of the convertible bonds. The market value method views the convertible bonds primarily as debt whose conversion was a significant economic transaction. The conversion represents the culmination of an earning process. The market value method views the market value of the common stock at the date of the conversion to be the proper measurement at which to carry the common stock.

# Ethics Case 14-9

Discussion should include these elements.

**Facts:**

Inducing a bond conversion is a common method of indirectly issuing stock, though typically not for the purpose of enhancing profits.

*Reported* performance will increase.

Company managers stand to benefit from the change.

**Ethical Dilemma:**

Should Hunt Manufacturing enter into these transactions primarily for "window dressing" rather than for economic reasons?

**Who is affected?**

Meyer

Barr

Other managers

Bondholders

Hunt's auditors

Shareholders

Potential shareholders

The employees

Other creditors

# Judgment Case 14-10

## Requirement 1

The debt to equity ratio is computed by dividing total liabilities by total shareholders' equity. The ratio summarizes the capital structure of the company as a mix between the resources provided by creditors and those provided by owners. For example, a ratio of 2.0 means that twice as many resources (assets) have been provided by creditors as those provided by owners.

$$\text{Debt to equity ratio} = \frac{\text{Total liabilities}}{\text{Shareholders' equity}}$$

$$= \frac{\$2,414}{\$2,931}$$

$$= \underline{0.82}$$

*Industry average* = 1.0

In general, debt increases risk. Debt places owners in a subordinate position relative to creditors because the claims of creditors must be satisfied first in case of liquidation. In addition, debt requires payment, usually on specific dates. Failure to pay debt interest and principal on a timely basis may result in default and perhaps even bankruptcy. Other things being equal, the higher the debt to equity ratio, the higher the risk. The type of risk this ratio measures is called default risk because it presumably indicates the likelihood a company will default on its obligations. IGF's debt to equity ratio is not particularly high – in fact it's less than the industry average.

## Requirement 2

Debt also can be used to enhance the return to shareholders. This concept is known as leverage. If a company earns a return on borrowed funds in excess of the cost of borrowing the funds, shareholders are provided with a total return greater than what could have been earned with equity funds alone. This desirable situation is called "favorable financial leverage." Unfortunately, leverage is not always favorable. Sometimes the cost of borrowing the funds exceeds the returns they generate. This illustrates the typical risk-return tradeoff faced by shareholders.

## Case 14-10 (continued)

IGF has experienced favorable leverage, as demonstrated by calculating and comparing the return on assets and the return on shareholders' equity for 2006:

$$\text{Rate of return on assets} = \frac{\text{Net income}}{\text{Average total assets}}$$

$$= \frac{\$487}{[\$5,345 + 4,684] / 2}$$

$$= \underline{9.7\%}$$

$$\text{Rate of return on shareholders' equity} = \frac{\text{Net income}}{\text{Average shareholders' equity}}$$

$$= \frac{\$487}{[\$2,931 + 2,671] / 2}$$

$$= \underline{17.4\%}$$

The debt to equity ratio is not particularly high, but the debt the company does have has been used to shareholders' advantage. The return on equity is greater than the return on assets. In fact, it may be that debt is being under-utilized by IGF. More debt might increase the potential for return, but the price would be higher risk. This is a fundamental tradeoff faced by virtually all firms when trying to settle on the optimal capital structure.

## Requirement 3

Creditors generally demand interest payments as compensation for the use of their capital. Failure to pay interest as scheduled may cause several adverse consequences including bankruptcy. Therefore, another way to measure a company's ability to pay its obligations is by comparing interest payments with cash flow generated from operations. The times interest earned ratio does this by dividing income before subtracting interest expense or income tax expense by interest expense.

*Case 14-10 (concluded)*

**Times interest earned** $=$ $\dfrac{\text{Net income} + \text{interest} + \text{taxes}}{\text{Interest}}$

$= \dfrac{\$487 + 54 + 316}{\$54}$

$= \underline{15.9 \text{ times}}$

*Industry average* $= 5.1$ times

Two points about this ratio are important. First, because interest is deductible for income tax purposes, income before interest and taxes is a better indication of a company's ability to pay interest than is income after interest and taxes (i.e., net income). Second, income before interest and taxes is a rough approximation for cash flow generated from operations. The primary concern of decision-makers is, of course, the cash available to make interest payments. In fact, this ratio often is computed by dividing cash flow generated from operations by interest payments.

IGF's fixed charges are covered over 15 times, far exceeding the industry norm. The interest coverage ratio seems to indicate an ample safety cushion for creditors, particularly when considered in conjunction with their debt-equity ratio. There seems also to be considerable room for additional borrowing in the event the firm wanted to increase its leverage in an attempt to further enhance the return to shareholders.

# Real World Case 14-11

The following is from Procter and Gamble's annual report. The responses to the questions will vary depending on the date of the 10-K accessed.

|  | 2004 | 2003 |
|---|---|---|
| **Requirement 3** | ($ in millions) | |
| Total Current Liabilities | $22,147 | $12,358 |
| Long-term Debt | 12,554 | 11,475 |
| Deferred Income Taxes | 2,261 | 1,396 |
| Other Noncurrent Liabilities | 2,808 | 2,291 |
| Total | $39,770 | $27,520 |

Total debt has increased by 45%.

| **Requirement 4** | | |
|---|---|---|
| Total debt | $39,770 | $27,520 |
| Shareholders' Equity | $17,278 | $16,186 |
| | | |
| Total debt | 39,770 | 27,520 |
| Shareholders' Equity | 17,278 | 16,186 |
| | | |
| Ratio | 2.30 | 1.70 |

The debt to equity ratio has increased by 35% since last year.

**Requirement 5**

The vast majority is in the form of notes.

Aggregate required payments of maturities of long-term debt for the next five fiscal years (generally increasing) are as follows:

| Dollars in Millions | 2005 | 2006 | 2007 | 2008 | 2009 |
|---|---|---|---|---|---|
| Required payments | $1,518 | $2,625 | $1,433 | $972 | $1,150 |

The current portion of long-term debt is $1,518 million and $1,093 in 2004 and 2003, respectively. No short-term debt is classified as long-term in 2004. It would be classified as long-term if the company intended to refinance any currently maturing debt on a long-term basis and could demonstrate the ability to do so.

# Chapter 15 Leases

## QUESTIONS FOR REVIEW OF KEY TOPICS

### Question 15-1
Regardless of the legal form of the agreement, a lease is accounted for as either a rental agreement or a purchase/sale accompanied by debt financing depending on the substance of the leasing arrangement. Capital leases are agreements that are formulated outwardly as leases, but that are in reality installment purchases. Professional judgment is needed to differentiate between leases that represent "rental agreements" and those that in reality are "installment purchases/sales." The FASB provides guidance for distinguishing between the two fundamental types of leases.

### Question 15-2
Periodic interest expense is calculated by the lessee as the effective interest rate times the amount of the outstanding lease liability during the period. This same principle applies to the flip side of the transaction, i.e., the lessor's lease receivable (net investment). The approach is the same regardless of the specific form of the debt – that is, whether in the form of notes, bonds, leases, pensions, or other debt instruments.

### Question 15-3
Leases and installment notes are very similar. The fundamental nature of the transaction remains the same regardless of whether it is negotiated as an installment purchase or as a lease. In return for providing financing, the borrower (lessee) pays *interest* over the maturity (lease term). Conceptually, leases and installment notes are accounted for in precisely the same way.

### Question 15-4
The criteria are: (1) the agreement specifies that ownership of the asset transfers to the lessee, (2) the agreement contains a bargain purchase option, (3) the lease term is equal to *75% or more* of the expected economic life of the asset, or (4) the present value of the minimum lease payments is equal to or greater than *90% of the fair value* of the leased asset.

### Question 15-5
A bargain purchase option is a provision in the lease contract that gives the lessee the option of purchasing the leased property at a "bargain" price – defined as price sufficiently lower than the expected fair value of the property when the option becomes exercisable that the exercise of the option appears reasonably assured at the inception of the lease. Because exercise of the option appears reasonably assured, transfer of ownership is expected.

## *Answers to Questions (continued)*

## Question 15-6

The lease is a capital lease to Seminole because the present value of the minimum lease payments ($5.2 million) is greater than 90% of the fair value of the asset (90% x $5.6 million = $5.04 million). Since the additional lessor conditions also are met, it is a nonoperating lease to Lukawitz. Furthermore it is a sales-type lease because the present value of the minimum lease payments exceeds the lessor's cost.

## Question 15-7

Yes. The minimum lease payments for the lessee exclude any residual value not guaranteed by the lessee. On the other hand, the lessor includes any residual value not guaranteed by the lessee but guaranteed by a third-party guarantor. Even when minimum lease payments are the same, their present values will differ if the lessee uses a discount rate different from the lessor's implicit rate. This would occur if the lessee is unaware of the implicit rate or if the implicit rate exceeds the lessee's incremental borrowing rate.

## Question 15-8

The way a BPO is included in determining minimum lease payments is precisely the same way that a lessee-guaranteed residual value is included. The expectation that the option price will be paid effectively adds an additional cash flow to the lease. That additional payment is included as a component of minimum lease payments. It therefore is included in the computation of the amount to be capitalized (as an asset and liability) by the *lessee*. But, a residual value not guaranteed by the lessee is ignored.

## Question 15-9

Executory costs are costs usually associated with ownership of an asset such as maintenance, insurance, and taxes. These are responsibilities of ownership that we assume are transferred to the lessee in a capital lease. When paid by the lessee, these expenditures are expensed by the lessee as incurred. When paid by the lessor, rental payments usually are inflated for this reason. These executory costs, including any lessor profit thereon, are excluded in determining the minimum lease payments and still are expensed by the lessee, even though paid by the lessor.

## Question 15-10

The *lessor's* discount rate is the effective interest rate the lease payments provide the lessor over and above the "price" at which the asset is "sold" under the lease. It is the desired rate of return the lessor has in mind when deciding the size of the rental payments. When the lessor's implicit rate is unknown, the lessee should use its own incremental borrowing rate. When the lessor's implicit rate is known, the *lessee* should use the lower of the two rates. This is the rate the lessee would be expected to pay a bank if funds were borrowed to buy the asset.

*Answers to Questions (continued)*

# Question 15-11

Contingent rentals are *not* included in minimum lease payments but are reported in disclosure notes by both the lessor and lessee. This is because they are not determinable at the inception of the lease. They are included as components of income when (and if) the payments occur. However, increases or decreases in rental payments that are dependent only upon the passage of time are *not* contingent rentals; these are part of minimum lease payments.

# Question 15-12

The costs of negotiating and consummating a completed lease transaction incurred by the lessor that are associated directly with originating a lease and are essential to acquire that lease are referred to as initial direct costs. They include legal fees, evaluating the prospective lessee's financial condition, commissions, and preparing and processing lease documents.

# Question 15-13

In an operating lease initial direct costs are recorded as prepaid expenses (assets) and amortized as an operating expense (usually straight-line) over the lease term. This approach is due to the nature of operating leases in which rental revenue is earned over the lease term. Initial direct costs are matched, along with depreciation and other associated costs, with the rent revenues they help generate.

In a *direct financing lease* initial direct costs are amortized over the lease term. This is accomplished by offsetting *unearned revenue* by the initial direct costs. This recognizes the initial direct costs at the same rate (that is, proportionally), as the interest revenue to which it is related. The nature of the lease motivates this treatment. The only revenue a direct financing lease generates for the lessor is interest revenue, which is earned over the lease term. So initial direct costs are matched proportionally over the term of the lease.

In a sales-type lease, GAAP requires that initial direct costs be expensed in the period of "sale" – that is, at the inception of the lease. This treatment implicitly assumes that in a sales-type lease the primary reason for incurring these costs is to facilitate the sale of the leased asset.

# Question 15-14

On the surface there are two separate transactions. But the seller/lessee still retains the use of the asset that it had prior to the sale-leaseback. In reality the seller/lessee has cash from the sale and a noncancelable obligation to repay a debt. In substance, the seller/lessee simply has borrowed cash to be repaid with interest over the lease term. So "substance over form" dictates that the gain on the sale of the asset not be immediately recognized, but deferred and recognized over the term of the lease. There typically is an interdependency between the lease terms and the price at which the asset is sold. So the earnings process is not complete at the time of sale but is completed over the term of the lease. Viewing the sale and the leaseback as a single transaction is consistent with the revenue realization principle.

# Answers to Questions (concluded)

## Question 15-15
The FASB specified exceptions to the general classification criteria for leases that involve land because of the unlimited useful life of land and the inexhaustibility of its inherent value through use. When title passes to the lessee – through automatic title passage or bargain purchase – these leases are clearly *capital* in nature and should be classified as such by the lessee. However, the Board felt that there would be difficulty in applying the other two criteria. Because land has essentially an infinite life, no lease term could possibly exceed 75 percent of its useful life, and the criterion was not applicable. The fourth criterion calls for comparing the present value of the lease payments with 90 percent of the property's fair value to determine if the lessor will recover its investment through the payments. When land is involved, the Board felt that the lease was not intended to recover the lessor's investment. Further, the lessor would have the land at the end of the lease term in essentially the same condition. Accordingly, the FASB concluded that leases involving material amounts of land should be classified as operating leases unless title passes automatically or as the result of a bargain purchase option.

## Question 15-16
The guidelines for determining when a material amount of land is involved in a lease indicate that leases involving property where land constitutes 25 percent or more of the total value should be treated as if they are *two* leases. The portion of the lease attributable to the land should be treated as an operating lease while the portion attributable to the other property should be judged on its own characteristics and accounted for accordingly. If the land value is less than 25 percent of the total value of the property, no allocation needs to be made.

## Question 15-17
A **leveraged lease** involves significant long-term, nonrecourse financing by a third-party creditor. The lessor serves the role of a mortgage broker and earns income by serving as an agent between a company needing to acquire property and a lender looking for an investment. The lender provides enough cash to the lessor to acquire the property. The leased property is then leased to the lessee under a capital lease with lease payments applied to the note held by the lender.

A lessee accounts for a leveraged lease the same way as a nonleveraged lease. A lessor records its investment (receivable) *net* of the nonrecourse debt and reports income from the lease only in those years when the receivable exceeds the liability.

# BRIEF EXERCISES

## Brief Exercise 15-1

Because none of the four classification criteria is met, this is an operating lease. Accordingly, LTT will record rent expense for each of the four $25,000 payments, reducing its earnings by $100,000 each year.

## Brief Exercise 15-2

Because none of the four classification criteria is met, this is an operating lease. Accordingly, Lakeside will record rent revenue for each of the four $25,000 payments, increasing its earnings by $100,000 each year. In addition Lakeside, as owner of the asset, will record depreciation. Assuming straight-line depreciation of the $2 million cost over the 25-year life, that's $80,000 depreciation expense each year. So, earnings are increased by a net $20,000 ($100,000 – 80,000).

## Brief Exercise 15-3

Because this is an operating lease, Ward will record rent expense for each of the $5,000 payments. The advance payment also represents rent, recorded initially as prepaid rent and allocated equally over the ten years of the lease. As a result, Ward's rent expense for the year reduces its earnings by $70,000 each year.

$5,000 x 12 =    $60,000
$100,000 / 10 =    10,000
                 $70,000

## Brief Exercise 15-4

The lease is a capital lease to Athens because the present value of the minimum lease payments ($20.4 million) is greater than 90% of the fair value of the asset (90% x $22.4 million = $20.16 million). None of the other three classification criteria is met.

## Brief Exercise 15-5

The present value of the minimum lease payments ($20.4 million) is greater than 90% of the fair value of the asset (90% x $22.4 million = $20.16 million). Since the additional lessor conditions also are met, it is a nonoperating lease to Corinth. Furthermore it is a sales-type lease because the present value of the minimum lease payments exceeds the lessor's cost ($16 million).

## Brief Exercise 15-6

In direct financing leases, the lessor records a receivable for the total payments to be received ($10,313,000 for Sonic). The difference between the total of the lease payments and the present value of the lease payments to be received over the term of the lease ($7,161,000 for Sonic) represents unearned interest revenue. Over the term of the leases, Sonic will report this amount ($10,313,000 minus $7,161,000 = $3,152,000) as interest revenue, determined as the effective interest rate times the outstanding balance (net investment) each period.

# Brief Exercise 15-7

The amount of interest expense the lessee would record in conjunction with the second quarterly payment at October 1 is $2,892:

| | |
|---|---|
| Initial balance, July 1 (given) ................................... | $150,000 |
| Reduction for first payment, January 1 .................... | (5,376) |
| Balance................................................................. | $144,624 |

Interest expense October 1: 2% x $144,624 = **$2,892**

*Journal entries (not required):*
**July 1**

| | | |
|---|---|---|
| Leased asset (given)............................................... | 150,000 | |
|    Lease payable................................................... | | 150,000 |
| | | |
| Lease payable .................................................... | 5,376 | |
|    Cash (rental payment)......................................... | | 5,376 |

**Oct. 1**

| | | |
|---|---|---|
| Interest expense (2% x [$150,000 – 5,376])............... | 2,892 | |
| Lease payable (difference)...................................... | 2,484 | |
|    Cash (lease payment)......................................... | | 5,376 |

The amount of interest revenue the lessor would record in conjunction with the second quarterly payment at October 1 also is **$2,892**, determined in the same manner.

# Brief Exercise 15-8

The lease liability in the balance sheet will be **$113,731**:

| | |
|---|---:|
| Initial balance, January 1 (calculated below)............... | $140,000 |
| Reduction for first payment, January 1 ..................... | (26,269) |
| December 31, net liability ..................................... | $113,731 |

$$\$26{,}269 \times 5.32948^{\Phi} \quad = \quad \$140{,}000$$
(rounded)

$^{\Phi}$ present value of an annuity due of $1: n=6, i=5%

The liability for interest on the lease liability in the balance sheet will be **$5,687**:

| | | |
|---|---:|---:|
| Interest expense (5% x [$140,000 – 26,269]) ............... | 5,687 | |
| Interest payable ..................................... | | 5,687 |

# Brief Exercise 15-9

Pretax earnings will be reduced by $29,020 as calculated below:

| | |
|---|---:|
| January 1 interest expense........................................ | $  0 |
| Dec. 31, interest expense (5% x [$140,000* – 26,269]) | 5,687 |
| Interest expense for the year ................................... | $ 5,687 |
| | |
| Depreciation expense ($140,000* / 6 years)............... | 23,333 |
| Total expenses ...................................... | $29,020 |

$$*\$26{,}269 \times 5.32948^{\Phi} \quad = \quad \$140{,}000$$
(rounded)

$^{\Phi}$ present value of an annuity due of $1: n=6, i=5%

# Brief Exercise 15-10

The price at which the lessor is "selling" the asset being leased is the present value of the lease payments:

$$*\$26{,}269 \times 5.32948\,\Phi \quad = \quad \$140{,}000$$

(rounded)

$\Phi$ present value of an annuity due of $1: n=6, i=5\%

Pretax earnings will be increased by $20,687 as calculated below:

| | |
|---|---:|
| January 1 interest revenue ...................................... | $ 0 |
| Dec. 31, interest revenue (5% x [$140,000* – 26,269]) | 5,687 |
| Interest revenue for the year .................................... | $ 5,687 |
| | |
| Sales revenue* .................................................... | 140,000 |
| Cost of goods sold ............................................... | (125,000) |
| Income effect ...................................................... | $ 20,687 |

*Journal entry (not required):*

| | | |
|---|---:|---:|
| Lease receivable ($26,269 x 6)........................................ | 157,614 | |
| Cost of goods sold (lessor's cost)................................. | 125,000 | |
| Sales revenue (present value) ............................. | | 140,000 |
| Unearned interest revenue ($157,614 – 140,000)....... | | 17,614 |
| Inventory of equipment (lessor's cost)....................... | | 125,000 |

# Brief Exercise 15-11

$$\$100{,}000 \quad \div \quad 16.67846** \quad = \quad \$5{,}996$$

| fair market value | lease payments |
|---|---|

** present value of an annuity due of $1: n=20, i=2%

# Brief Exercise 15-12

| | |
|---|---|
| Amount to be recovered (fair market value) | $700,000 |
| *Less:* Present value of the residual value ($100,000 x .82270*) | (82,270) |
| Amount to be recovered through periodic rental payments | $617,730 |

Rental payments at the beginning
of each of the next 4 years:    ($617,730 ÷ 3.54595**)    $174,207

\* present value of $1: n=4, i=5%

\*\* present value of an ordinary annuity of $1: n=4, i=5%


# Brief Exercise 15-13

| | |
|---|---|
| Amount to be recovered (fair market value) | $600,000 |
| *Less:* Present value of the BPO price ($100,000 x .74726*) | (74,726) |
| Amount to be recovered through periodic rental payments | $525,274 |

Rental payments at the beginning
of each of the next 5 years:    ($525,274 ÷ 4.46511**)    $117,640

\* present value of $1: n=5, i=6%

\*\* present value of an annuity due of $1: n=5, i=6%

# EXERCISES

## Exercise 15-1

### (a) Nath-Langstrom Services, Inc. (Lessee)

**June 30, 2006**

| | | |
|---|---|---|
| Rent expense...................................... | 10,000 | |
| Cash ............................................ | | 10,000 |

**December 31, 2006**

| | | |
|---|---|---|
| Rent expense...................................... | 10,000 | |
| Cash ............................................ | | 10,000 |

### (b) ComputerWorld Corporation (Lessor)

**June 30, 2006**

| | | |
|---|---|---|
| Cash................................................ | 10,000 | |
| Rent revenue................................ | | 10,000 |

**December 31, 2006**

| | | |
|---|---|---|
| Cash................................................ | 10,000 | |
| Rent revenue................................ | | 10,000 |
| | | |
| Depreciation expense ($90,000 ÷ 6 years) | 15,000 | |
| Accumulated depreciation ......... | | 15,000 |

# Exercise 15-2

### January 1, 2006

| | | |
|---|---|---|
| Prepaid rent (advance payment) ........................ | 96,000 | |
|     Cash ........................................................ | | 96,000 |
| | | |
| Prepaid rent (annual rent payment) .................... | 80,000 | |
|     Cash ........................................................ | | 80,000 |
| | | |
| Leasehold improvements............................. | 180,000 | |
|     Cash ........................................................ | | 180,000 |

### December 31, 2006

| | | |
|---|---|---|
| Rent expense (annual rent)............................. | 80,000 | |
|     Prepaid rent .............................................. | | 80,000 |
| | | |
| Rent expense (advance payment allocation)....... | 32,000 | |
|     Prepaid rent ($96,000 ÷ 3)........................... | | 32,000 |
| | | |
| Depreciation expense ($180,000 ÷ 3 years)....... | 60,000 | |
|     Accumulated depreciation......................... | | 60,000 |

# Exercise 15-3
1.   d
2.   d

# Exercise 15-4

## Present Value of Minimum Lease Payments:

$$(\$15,000 \times 7.47199^*) = \$112,080$$

rental            present

payments          value

\* present value of an annuity due of $1: n=8, i=2%

[i = 2% (8% ÷ 4) because the lease
calls for quarterly payments]

## Lease Amortization Schedule

| | Rental Payments | Effective Interest<br>2% x Outstanding Balance | Decrease in Balance | Outstanding Balance |
|---|---|---|---|---|
| | | | | 112,080 |
| 1 | 15,000 | | 15,000 | 97,080 |
| 2 | 15,000 | .02 (97,080) = 1,942 | 13,058 | 84,022 |
| 3 | 15,000 | .02 (84,022) = 1,680 | 13,320 | 70,702 |
| 4 | 15,000 | .02 (70,702) = 1,414 | 13,586 | 57,116 |
| 5 | 15,000 | .02 (57,116) = 1,142 | 13,858 | 43,258 |
| 6 | 15,000 | .02 (43,258) = 865 | 14,135 | 29,123 |
| 7 | 15,000 | .02 (29,123) = 582 | 14,418 | 14,705 |
| 8 | 15,000 | .02 (14,705) = 295* | 14,705 | 0 |
| | 120,000 | 7,920 | 112,080 | |

\* adjusted for rounding of other numbers in the schedule

**January 1, 2006**

| | | |
|---|---|---|
| Leased equipment (calculated above) ..................... | 112,080 | |
|    Lease payable (calculated above)........................ | | 112,080 |
| | | |
| Lease payable ..................................................... | 15,000 | |
|    Cash (rental payment) ......................................... | | 15,000 |

## Exercise 15-4 (concluded)

**April 1, 2006**

| | | |
|---|---|---|
| Interest expense (2% x [$112,080 – 15,000]) ............. | 1,942 | |
| Lease payable (difference) .................................... | 13,058 | |
|    Cash (rental payment)......................................... | | 15,000 |

**July 1, 2006**

| | | |
|---|---|---|
| Interest expense (2% x $84,022: from schedule)........ | 1,680 | |
| Lease payable (difference) .................................... | 13,320 | |
|    Cash (rental payment)......................................... | | 15,000 |

**October 1, 2006**

| | | |
|---|---|---|
| Interest expense (2% x $70,702: from schedule)........ | 1,414 | |
| Lease payable (difference) .................................... | 13,586 | |
|    Cash (rental payment)......................................... | | 15,000 |

**December 31, 2006**

| | | |
|---|---|---|
| Interest expense (2% x $57,116: from schedule)........ | 1,142 | |
|    Interest payable ............................................. | | 1,142 |
| | | |
| Depreciation expense ($112,080 ÷ 2 years) .............. | 56,040 | |
|    Accumulated depreciation.............................. | | 56,040 |

**January 1, 2007**

| | | |
|---|---|---|
| Interest payable (from adjusting entry)...................... | 1,142 | |
| Lease payable (difference) .................................... | 13,858 | |
|    Cash (rental payment)......................................... | | 15,000 |

# Exercise 15-5

## Lease Amortization Schedule

| | Rental Payments | Effective Interest 2% x Outstanding Balance | | | Decrease in Balance | Outstanding Balance |
|---|---|---|---|---|---|---|
| | | | | | | 112,080 |
| 1 | 15,000 | | | | 15,000 | 97,080 |
| 2 | 15,000 | .02 (97,080) | = | 1,942 | 13,058 | 84,022 |
| 3 | 15,000 | .02 (84,022) | = | 1,680 | 13,320 | 70,702 |
| 4 | 15,000 | .02 (70,702) | = | 1,414 | 13,586 | 57,116 |
| 5 | 15,000 | .02 (57,116) | = | 1,142 | 13,858 | 43,258 |
| 6 | 15,000 | .02 (43,258) | = | 865 | 14,135 | 29,123 |
| 7 | 15,000 | .02 (29,123) | = | 582 | 14,418 | 14,705 |
| 8 | 15,000 | .02 (14,705) | = | 295* | 14,705 | 0 |
| | 120,000 | | | 7,920 | 112,080 | |

\* adjusted for rounding of other numbers in the schedule

**January 1, 2006**

| | | |
|---|---|---|
| Lease receivable ($15,000 x 8) ............................. | 120,000 | |
| Unearned interest revenue ($120,000 - 112,080) | | 7,920 |
| Inventory of equipment (lessor's cost) .............. | | 112,080 |

| | | |
|---|---|---|
| Cash (rental payment) ............................................. | 15,000 | |
| Lease receivable ............................................. | | 15,000 |

**April 1, 2006**

| | | |
|---|---|---|
| Cash (rental payment) ............................................. | 15,000 | |
| Lease receivable ............................................. | | 15,000 |

| | | |
|---|---|---|
| Unearned interest revenue ................................ | 1,942 | |
| Interest revenue (2% x [$112,080 – 15,000])........ | | 1,942 |

**July 1, 2006**

| | | |
|---|---|---|
| Cash (rental payment) ............................................. | 15,000 | |
| Lease receivable ............................................. | | 15,000 |

| | | |
|---|---|---|
| Unearned interest revenue ................................ | 1,680 | |
| Interest revenue (2% x $84,022: from schedule)... | | 1,680 |

*Exercise 15-5 (concluded)*

**October 1, 2006**

| | | |
|---|---|---|
| Cash (rental payment)................................................ | 15,000 | |
| Lease receivable ............................................. | | 15,000 |
| | | |
| Unearned interest revenue ................................ | 1,414 | |
| Interest revenue  (2% x $70,702: from schedule)... | | 1,414 |

**December 31, 2006**

| | | |
|---|---|---|
| Unearned interest revenue ................................ | 1,142 | |
| Interest revenue  (2% x $57,116: from schedule)... | | 1,142 |

**January 1, 2007**

| | | |
|---|---|---|
| Cash (rental payment)................................................ | 15,000 | |
| Lease receivable ............................................. | | 15,000 |

# Exercise 15-6

## Requirement 1

### Lessor's Calculation of Rental Payments

Amount to be recovered (fair market value)      $112,080

Rent payments at the beginning
  of each of eight quarters:      ($112,080 ÷ 7.47199**)    $15,000

** present value of an annuity due of $1: n=8, i=2%

## Requirement 2

**January 1, 2006**

| | | |
|---|---|---|
| Lease receivable ($15,000 x 8) ............................ | 120,000 | |
| Cost of goods sold (lessor's cost) ......................... | 85,000 | |
|    Sales revenue (fair market value)....................... | | 112,080 |
|    Unearned interest revenue ($120,000 - 112,080) | | 7,920 |
|    Inventory of equipment (lessor's cost) .............. | | 85,000 |
| | | |
| Cash (rental payment) ......................................... | 15,000 | |
|    Lease receivable .............................................. | | 15,000 |

**April 1, 2006**

| | | |
|---|---|---|
| Cash (rental payment) ......................................... | 15,000 | |
|    Lease receivable .............................................. | | 15,000 |
| | | |
| Unearned interest revenue ................................ | 1,942 | |
|    Interest revenue (2% x [$112,080 – 15,000])........ | | 1,942 |

# Exercise 15-7

## Requirement 1     January 1, 2006

| | | |
|---|---|---|
| Leased assets ....................................................... | 4,000,000 | |
|     Lease payable ................................................ | | 4,000,000 |

## Requirement 2

$$\$4,000,000 \;\div\; 3.16987^{**} \;=\; \$1,261,881$$

<table>
<tr><td>present<br>value</td><td></td><td>lease<br>payment</td></tr>
</table>

$^{**}$ present value of an ordinary annuity of $1: n=4, i=10%

---

### Lease Amortization Schedule

| | Rental Payments | Effective Interest 10% x Outstanding Balance | Decrease in Balance | Outstanding Balance |
|---|---|---|---|---|
| | | | | 4,000,000 |
| 2006 | 1,261,881 | .10 (4,000,000) = 400,000 | 861,881 | 3,138,119 |
| 2007 | 1,261,881 | .10 (3,138,119) = 313,812 | 948,069 | 2,190,050 |
| 2008 | 1,261,881 | .10 (2,190,050) = 219,005 | 1,042,876 | 1,147,174 |
| 2009 | 1,261,881 | .10 (1,147,174) = 114,707* | 1,147,174 | 0 |
| | 5,047,524 | 1,047,524 | 4,000,000 | |

\* adjusted for rounding of other numbers in the schedule

---

## Requirement 3     December 31, 2006

| | | |
|---|---|---|
| Interest expense (10% x outstanding balance).......... | 400,000 | |
| Lease payable (difference) ..................................... | 861,881 | |
|     Cash (payment determined above)........................ | | 1,261,881 |

## Requirement 4     December 31, 2008

| | | |
|---|---|---|
| Interest expense (10% x outstanding balance).......... | 219,005 | |
| Lease payable (difference) ..................................... | 1,042,876 | |
|     Cash (payment determined above)........................ | | 1,261,881 |

# Exercise 15-8

## 1. Calculation of the present value of lease payments

$$\$562{,}907 \times 5.32948^{\Phi} \quad = \quad \$3{,}000{,}000$$
$$\text{(rounded)}$$

$\Phi$ present value of an annuity due of $1: n=6, i=5%

## 2. Liability at December 31, 2006

| | |
|---|---:|
| Initial balance, June 30, 2006 | $3,000,000 |
| June 30, 2006 reduction | (562,907)* |
| Dec. 31, 2006 reduction | (441,052)** |
| December 31, 2006 net liability | $1,996,041 |

### Asset at December 31, 2006

| | |
|---|---:|
| Initial balance, June 30, 2006 | $3,000,000 |
| Accumulated depreciation at Dec. 31, 2006 | (500,000)** |
| December 31, 2006 | $2,500,000 |

## 3. Expenses for year ended December 31, 2006

| | |
|---|---:|
| June 30, 2006 interest expense | $ 0* |
| Dec. 31, 2006 interest expense | 121,855** |
| Interest expense for 2006 | $121,855 |
| | |
| Depreciation expense for 2006 | 500,000 |
| Total expenses | $621,855 |

### Calculations:

**June 30, 2006***

| | | |
|---|---:|---:|
| Leased equipment (calculated in req. 1) | 3,000,000 | |
| Lease payable (calculated in req. 1) | | 3,000,000 |
| | | |
| Lease payable | 562,907 | |
| Cash (rental payment) | | 562,907 |

**December 31, 2006****

| | | |
|---|---:|---:|
| Interest expense (5% x [$3 million – 562,907]) | 121,855 | |
| Lease payable (difference) | 441,052 | |
| Cash (rental payment) | | 562,907 |
| | | |
| Depreciation expense ($3 million / 3 years x ½ year) | 500,000 | |
| Accumulated depreciation | | 500,000 |

# Exercise 15-9

### 1. Receivable at December 31, 2006

|  | Receivable | – Unearned Interest | = Net Rec. |
|---|---|---|---|
| Initial balance, June 30, 2006.............. | $3,377,442 | 377,442 | $3,000,000 |
| June 30, 2006 reduction ..................... | (562,907)* | 0 | (562,907) |
| Dec. 31, 2006 reduction ..................... | (562,907)** | (121,855) | (441,052) |
| December 31, 2006 net receivable..... | $2,251,628 | 255,587 | $1,996,041 |

The receivable is reported as:

| Lease receivable ................................. | $2,251,628 |
|---|---|
| Less: unearned interest revenue......... | (255,587) |
|  | $1,996,041 |

The receivable replaces the $3,000,000 machine on the balance sheet.

### 2. Interest revenue for year ended December 31, 2006

| June 30, 2006 interest revenue................................... | $       0* |
|---|---|
| Dec. 31, 2006 interest revenue................................... | 121,855** |
| Interest revenue for 2006 ......................................... | $121,855 |

**Calculations:**
**June 30, 2006***

| Lease receivable ($562,907 x 6) ..................................... | 3,377,442 |  |
|---|---|---|
| Unearned interest revenue ($3,377,442 – 3,000,000)... |  | 377,442 |
| Inventory of equipment (lessor's cost) ........................ |  | 3,000,000 |
| Cash (rental payment) ...................................................... | 562,907 |  |
| Lease receivable ............................................................ |  | 562,907 |

**December 31, 2006****

| Cash (rental payment)...................................................... | 562,907 |  |
|---|---|---|
| Lease receivable ............................................................ |  | 562,907 |
| Unearned interest revenue ............................................ | 121,855 |  |
| Interest revenue  (5% x [$3,000,000 – 562,907]).......... |  | 121,855 |

# Exercise 15-10

## 1. Calculation of the present value of lease payments ("selling price")

$$\$562,907 \times 5.32948 \, \Phi \quad = \quad \$3,000,000$$
(rounded)

$\Phi$ present value of an annuity due of $1: n=6, i=5\%

## 2. Receivable at December 31, 2006

|  | Receivable | − Unearned Interest | = Net Rec. |
|---|---|---|---|
| Initial balance, June 30, 2006............. | $3,377,442 | 377,442 | $3,000,000 |
| June 30, 2006 reduction...................... | (562,907)* | 0 | (562,907) |
| Dec. 31, 2006 reduction..................... | (562,907)** | (121,855) | (441,052) |
| December 31, 2006 net receivable .... | $2,251,628 | 255,587 | $1,996,041 |

The receivable is reported as:

| | |
|---|---|
| Lease receivable.................................. | $2,251,628 |
| Less: unearned interest revenue......... | (255,587) |
| | $1,996,041 |

The receivable replaces the $2,500,000 machine on the balance sheet.

## 3. Income effect for year ended December 31, 2006

| | |
|---|---|
| June 30, 2006 interest revenue ............................... | $ 0* |
| Dec. 31, 2006 interest revenue ............................... | 121,855** |
| Interest revenue for 2006......................................... | $ 121,855 |
| | |
| Sales revenue* ......................................................... | 3,000,000 |
| Cost of goods sold* .................................................. | (2,500,000) |
| Income effect .......................................................... | $ 621,855 |

*Exercise 15-10 (concluded)*

**Calculations:**

**June 30, 2006\***

| | | |
|---|---:|---:|
| Lease receivable ($562,907 x 6) ...................................... | 3,377,442 | |
| Cost of goods sold (lessor's cost) ................................. | 2,500,000 | |
|    Sales revenue (present value)...................................... | | 3,000,000 |
|    Unearned interest revenue ($3,377,442 – 3,000,000) ... | | 377,442 |
|    Inventory of equipment (lessor's cost) ...................... | | 2,500,000 |
| | | |
| Cash (rental payment) ..................................................... | 562,907 | |
|    Lease receivable ......................................................... | | 562,907 |

**December 31, 2006\*\***

| | | |
|---|---:|---:|
| Cash (rental payment)...................................................... | 562,907 | |
|    Lease receivable ......................................................... | | 562,907 |
| | | |
| Unearned interest revenue .............................................. | 121,855 | |
|    Interest revenue  (5% x [$3,000,000 – 562,907]).......... | | 121,855 |

# Exercise 15-11
## Situation 1

    **(a)**    $600,000  ÷  6.53705\*\*  =      $91,785

                  fair market                                  lease

                    value                                   payments

  \*\* present value of an annuity due of $1: n=10, i=11%

    **(b)**    $91,785  x  6.53705\*\*  =      $600,000   (rounded)

                  lease                              leased asset/

                payments                            lease liability

  \*\* present value of an annuity due of $1: n=10, i=11%

## Situation 2

    **(a)**    $980,000  ÷  9.95011\*\*  =      $98,491

                  fair market                                  lease

                    value                                   payments

  \*\* present value of an annuity due of $1: n=20, i=9%

    **(b)**    $98,491  x  9.95011\*\*  =      $980,000   (rounded)

                  lease                              leased asset/

                payments                            lease liability

  \*\* present value of an annuity due of $1: n=20, i=9%

## Situation 3

    **(a)**    $185,000  ÷  3.40183\*\*  =      $54,382

                  fair market                                  lease

                    value                                   payments

  \*\* present value of an annuity due of $1: n=4, i=12%

    **(b)**    $54,382  x  3.44371\*\*  =      $187,276

                  lease                              leased asset/

                payments                            lease liability

  \*\* present value of an annuity due of $1: n=4, i=11%

But since this amount exceeds the asset's fair value, the lessee must capitalize the **$185,000** fair value instead.

# Exercise 15-12
## Situation 1

  **(a)**  $600,000 ÷ 5.88923**  =   $101,881
       fair market            lease
        value             payments

 ** present value of an ordinary annuity of $1: n=10, i=11%

  **(b)**  $101,881 x 5.88923**  =   $600,000*
       lease            leased asset/
       payments           lease liability

 * rounded

 ** present value of an ordinary annuity of $1: n=10, i=11%


## Situation 2

  **(a)**  $980,000 ÷ 9.12855**  =   $107,355
       fair market            lease
        value             payments

 ** present value of an ordinary annuity of $1: n=20, i=9%

  **(b)**  $107,355 x 9.12855**  =   $980,000‡
       lease            leased asset/
       payments           lease liability

 ** present value of an ordinary annuity of $1: n=20, i=9%
 ‡ rounded for convenience


## Situation 3

  **(a)**  $185,000 ÷ 3.03735**  =   $60,908
       fair market            lease
        value             payments

 ** present value of an ordinary annuity of $1: n=4, i=12%

  **(b)**  $60,908 x 3.10245**  =   $188,964
       lease            leased asset/
       payments           lease liability

 ** present value of an ordinary annuity of $1: n=4, i=11%


But since this amount exceeds the asset's fair value, the lessee must capitalize the **$185,000** fair value instead.

# Exercise 15-13

## Situation 1

Amount to be recovered (fair market value)          $50,000

Rental payments at the beginning    $\downarrow$
    of each of the next 4 years:     ($50,000 ÷ 3.48685$^{**}$)    <u>$ 14,340</u>

           $^{**}$ present value of an annuity due of $1: n=4, i=10%

## Situation 2

Amount to be recovered (fair market value)         $350,000

*Less:* Present value of the residual value ($50,000 x .48166$^{*}$)    <u>(24,083)</u>

Amount to be recovered through periodic rental payments    <u>$325,917</u>

Rental payments at the beginning    $\downarrow$
    of each of the next 7 years:     ($325,917 ÷ 5.23054$^{**}$)      <u>$ 62,310</u>
         $^{*}$ present value of $1: n=7, i=11%
       $^{**}$ present value of an annuity due of $1: n=7, i=11%

## Exercise 15-13 (concluded)

### Situation 3

| | |
|---|---|
| Amount to be recovered (fair market value) | $75,000 |
| *Less:* Present value of the residual value ($7,000 x .64993*) | (4,550) |
| Amount to be recovered through periodic rental payments | $70,450 |

Rental payments at the beginning
of each of the next 5 years:     ($70,450 ÷ 4.23972**)     $ 16,617

     \* present value of $1: n=5, i=9%
    \*\* present value of an annuity due of $1: n=5, i=9%

### Situation 4

| | |
|---|---|
| Amount to be recovered (fair market value) | $465,000 |
| *Less:* Present value of the residual value ($45,000 x .40388*) | (18,175) |
| Amount to be recovered through periodic rental payments | $446,825 |

Rental payments at the beginning
of each of the next 8 years:     ($446,825 ÷ 5.56376**)     $ 80,310

     \* present value of $1: n=8, i=12%
    \*\* present value of an annuity due of $1: n=8, i=12%

# Exercise 15-14

| | Situation | | | |
|---|---|---|---|---|
| | **1** | **2** | **3** | **4** |
| **A. The lessor's:** | | | | |
| 1. Minimum lease payments[1] | $700,000 | $750,000 | $800,000 | $840,000 |
| 2. Gross investment in the lease[2] | 700,000 | 750,000 | 850,000 | 900,000 |
| 3. Net investment in the lease[3] | 548,592 | 547,137 | 610,168 | 596,764 |
| 4. Unearned interest revenue[4] | 151,408 | 202,863 | 239,832 | 303,236 |
| **B. The lessee's:** | | | | |
| 5. Minimum lease payments[5] | 700,000 | 750,000 | 800,000 | 840,000 |
| 6. Leased asset[6] | 548,592 | 547,137 | 586,842 | 572,531 |
| 7. Lease liability[7] | 548,592 | 547,137 | 586,842 | 572,531 |

[1] ($100,000 x number of payments) + residual value guaranteed by lessee and/or by third party; for situation 4: ($100,000 x 8) + ($40,000).

[2] Minimum lease payments plus unguaranteed residual value; for situation 4: ($840,000 + $60,000).

[3] Present value of gross investment (discounted at lessor's rate); for situation 4: ($100,000 x 5.56376) + ($100,000 x .40388).

[4] Gross investment - net investment; for situation 4: ($900,000 - 596,764).

[5] ($100,000 x number of payments) + residual value guaranteed by *lessee*; for situation 4: ($100,000 x 8) + $40,000.

[6] Present value of minimum lease payments (discounted at lower of lessor's rate and lessee's incremental borrowing rate); should not exceed fair market value; for situation 4: ($100,000 x 5.56376) + ($40,000 x .40388).

[7] Present value of minimum lease payments (discounted at lower of lessor's rate and lessee's incremental borrowing rate); should not exceed fair market value; for situation 4: ($100,000 x 5.56376) + ($40,000 x .40388).

# Exercise 15-15

---

**Situation 1**

| | |
|---|---|
| Amount to be recovered (fair market value) | $60,000 |
| *Less:* Present value of the BPO price ($10,000 x .56743*) | (5,674) |
| Amount to be recovered through periodic rental payments | $54,326 |
| Rental payments at the beginning of each of the next 5 years: ($54,326 ÷ 4.03735**) | $13,456 |

       * present value of $1: n=5, i=12%

    ** present value of an annuity due of $1: n=5, i=12%

---

**Situation 2**

| | |
|---|---|
| Amount to be recovered (fair market value) | $420,000 |
| *Less:* Present value of the BPO price ($50,000 x .59345*) | (29,673) |
| Amount to be recovered through periodic rental payments | $390,327 |
| Rental payments at the beginning of each of the next 5 years: ($390,327 ÷ 4.10245**) | $95,145 |

       * present value of $1: n=5, i=11%

    ** present value of an annuity due of $1: n=5, i=11%

**Note:** Since a BPO is expected to be exercised, the lease term ends for accounting purposes when the option becomes exercisable.

*Exercise 15-15 (concluded)*

| Situation 3 | |
|---|---|
| Amount to be recovered (fair market value) | $185,000 |
| | |
| *Less:* Present value of the BPO price ($22,000 x .77218[*]) | (16,988) |
| | |
| Amount to be recovered through periodic rental payments | $168,012 |
| | ↓ |
| | |
| Rental payments at the beginning      ↓ | |
|   of each of the next 3 years:     ($168,012 ÷ 2.75911[**]) | $60,894 |

      [*] present value of $1: n=3, i=9%

    [**] present value of an annuity due of $1: n=3, i=9%

**Note:** Since a BPO is expected to be exercised, the lease term ends for accounting purposes when the option becomes exercisable.

# Exercise 15-16

## Requirement 1

**Note:**
Because exercise of the option appears at the inception of the lease to be reasonably assured, payment of the option price ($45,000) is expected to occur when the option becomes exercisable (at the *end* of the third year).

| | |
|---|---|
| Present value of annual rental payments ($36,000 x 2.69005**) | $ 96,842 |
| *Plus:* Present value of the BPO price ($45,000 x .71178*) | 32,030 |
| Present value of minimum lease payments | $128,872 |

* present value of $1: n=3, i=12%<br>** present value of an annuity due of $1: n=3, i=12%

## Requirement 2

### Lease Amortization Schedule

| Dec. 31 | Payments | Effective Interest 12% x Outstanding Balance | Decrease in Balance | Outstanding Balance |
|---|---|---|---|---|
| | | | | 128,872 |
| 2005 | 36,000 | | 36,000 | 92,872 |
| 2006 | 36,000 | .12 (92,872) = 11,145 | 24,855 | 68,017 |
| 2007 | 36,000 | .12 (68,017) = 8,162 | 27,838 | 40,179 |
| 2008 | 45,000 | .12 (40,179) = 4,821 | 40,179 | 0 |
| | 153,000 | 24,128 | 128,872 | |

## *Exercise 15-16 (concluded)*

**Requirement 3**
### December 31, 2005
| | | |
|---|---:|---:|
| Leased equipment (calculated above)...................... | 128,872 | |
|    Lease payable (calculated above)......................... | | 128,872 |

| | | |
|---|---:|---:|
| Lease payable ...................................................... | 36,000 | |
|    Cash (annual payment)......................................... | | 36,000 |

### December 31, 2006
| | | |
|---|---:|---:|
| Depreciation expense ($128,872 ÷ 6 years*) .............. | 21,479 | |
|    Accumulated depreciation .............................. | | 21,479 |

| | | |
|---|---:|---:|
| Interest expense (12% x [$128,872 - 36,000]).............. | 11,145 | |
| Lease payable (difference : from schedule) ............... | 24,855 | |
|    Cash (annual payment)......................................... | | 36,000 |

### December 31, 2007
| | | |
|---|---:|---:|
| Depreciation expense ($128,872 ÷ 6 years*) .............. | 21,479 | |
|    Accumulated depreciation .............................. | | 21,479 |

| | | |
|---|---:|---:|
| Interest expense (12% x $68,017 : from schedule)....... | 8,162 | |
| Lease payable (difference : from schedule) ............... | 27,838 | |
|    Cash (annual payment)......................................... | | 36,000 |

### December 31, 2008
| | | |
|---|---:|---:|
| Depreciation expense ($128,872 ÷ 6 years*) .............. | 21,479 | |
|    Accumulated depreciation .............................. | | 21,479 |

| | | |
|---|---:|---:|
| Interest expense (12% x $40,179: from schedule)........ | 4,821 | |
| Lease payable (difference : from schedule) ............... | 40,179 | |
|    Cash (BPO price) ................................................. | | 45,000 |

\* Because title passes with the expected exercise of the BPO, depreciation is for the entire six-year useful life of the asset. The depreciation entry will be recorded for three years after the completion of the lease term.

# Exercise 15-17

## Requirement 1

| | |
|---|---:|
| Amount to be recovered (fair market value) | $30,900 |
| *Less:* Present value of the BPO price ($12,000 x .75131*) | (9,016) |
| Amount to be recovered through periodic rental payments | $21,884 |
| Rental payments at the beginning each of three years: ($21,884 ÷ 2.73554**) | $8,000 |

    * present value of $1: n=3, i=10%

    ** present value of an annuity due of $1: n=3, i=10%

## Requirement 2

### Lease Amortization Schedule

| Dec. 31 | Payments | Effective Interest 10% x Outstanding Balance | Decrease in Balance | Outstanding Balance |
|---|---|---|---|---|
| | | | | 30,900 |
| 2005 | 8,000 | | 8,000 | 22,900 |
| 2006 | 8,000 | .10 (22,900) = 2,290 | 5,710 | 17,190 |
| 2007 | 8,000 | .10 (17,190) = 1,719 | 6,281 | 10,909 |
| 2008 | 12,000 | .10 (10,909) = 1,091 | 10,909 | 0 |
| | 36,000 | 5,100 | 30,900 | |

## Exercise 15-17 (concluded)

### Requirement 3
**December 31, 2005**

| | | |
|---|---|---|
| Lease receivable ([$8,000 x 3] + $12,000)............................ | 36,000 | |
|    Unearned interest revenue ($36,000 - 30,900) ............... | | 5,100 |
|    Inventory of equipment (lessor's cost) ......................... | | 30,900 |
| | | |
| Cash (lease payment) ......................................................... | 8,000 | |
|    Lease receivable................................................................ | | 8,000 |

**December 31, 2006**

| | | |
|---|---|---|
| Cash (lease payment) ......................................................... | 8,000 | |
|    Lease receivable................................................................ | | 8,000 |
| | | |
| Unearned interest revenue ............................................... | 2,290 | |
|    Interest revenue (10% x [$30,900 - 8,000]) ...................... | | 2,290 |

**December 31, 2007**

| | | |
|---|---|---|
| Cash (lease payment) ......................................................... | 8,000 | |
|    Lease receivable................................................................ | | 8,000 |
| | | |
| Unearned interest revenue ............................................... | 1,719 | |
|    Interest revenue (10% x $17,190 : from schedule)............... | | 1,719 |

**December 30, 2008**

| | | |
|---|---|---|
| Unearned interest revenue (account balance)........................ | 1,091 | |
|    Interest revenue (10% x $10,909 : from schedule)............... | | 1,091 |
| | | |
| Cash (BPO price) ................................................................ | 12,000 | |
|    Lease receivable (account balance) ................................. | | 12,000 |

# Exercise 15-18

**December 31, 2005**
**Brand Services (Lessee)**

| | | |
|---|---:|---:|
| Leased equipment (present value of lease payments) ............ | 316,412 | |
|     Lease payable (present value of lease payments) .............. | | 316,412 |
| | | |
| Lease payable (payment less executory costs) ...................... | 50,000 | |
| Prepaid maintenance (2006 fee) ............................................ | 5,000 | |
|     Cash (annual payment) ...................................................... | | 55,000 |

**NRC Credit (Lessor)**

| | | |
|---|---:|---:|
| Lease receivable ($50,000 x 10)............................................ | 500,000 | |
|     Unearned interest revenue ($500,000 - 316,412) ........... | | 183,588 |
|     Inventory of equipment (lessor's cost)........................... | | 316,412 |
| | | |
| Cash (annual payment) ........................................................ | 55,000 | |
|     Maintenance fee payable [or cash]............................. | | 5,000 |
|     Lease receivable ............................................................. | | 50,000 |

**December 31, 2006**
**Brand Services (Lessee)**

| | | |
|---|---:|---:|
| Maintenance expense (2006 fee)............................................ | 5,000 | |
|     Prepaid maintenance (paid in 2005)................................. | | 5,000 |
| | | |
| Interest expense (12% x [$316,412 – 50,000]) ......................... | 31,969 | |
| Lease payable (difference) .................................................... | 18,031 | |
| Prepaid maintenance (2007 fee) ............................................ | 5,000 | |
|     Cash (lease payment)........................................................ | | 55,000 |
| | | |
| Depreciation expense ($316,412 ÷ 10 years) ......................... | 31,641 | |
|     Accumulated depreciation........................................... | | 31,641 |

**NRC Credit (Lessor)**

| | | |
|---|---:|---:|
| Cash (lease payment)........................................................... | 55,000 | |
|     Lease receivable (payment less executory costs) .............. | | 50,000 |
|     Maintenance fee payable [or cash]............................. | | 5,000 |
| | | |
| Unearned interest revenue ................................................. | 31,969 | |
|     Interest revenue (12% x [$316,412 – 50,000]).................... | | 31,969 |

# Exercise 15-19

**December 31, 2006**
**Brand Services (Lessee)**

| | | |
|---|---|---|
| Maintenance expense (2006 fees plus lessor profit).............. | 5,950 | |
|    Prepaid maintenance (paid in 2005).................................. | | 5,950 |

| | | |
|---|---|---|
| Interest expense (12% x [$316,412 – 50,000]) ....................... | 31,969 | |
| Lease payable (difference).................................................. | 18,031 | |
| Prepaid maintenance (2007 fees plus lessor profit)................ | 5,950 | |
|    Cash (lease payment) ....................................................... | | 55,950 |

| | | |
|---|---|---|
| Depreciation expense ($316,412 ÷ 10 years) ........................ | 31,641 | |
|    Accumulated depreciation ............................................. | | 31,641 |

**NRC Credit (Lessor)**

| | | |
|---|---|---|
| Unearned miscellaneous revenue (received in 2005).......... | 250 | |
|    Miscellaneous revenue (2006 fee) ................................. | | 250 |

| | | |
|---|---|---|
| Cash (lease payment) ......................................................... | 55,950 | |
|    Lease receivable (payment less executory costs).............. | | 50,000 |
|    Maintenance fee payable ............................................. | | 5,000 |
|    Insurance premium payable .......................................... | | 700 |
|    Unearned miscellaneous revenue (2007 fee)................ | | 250 |

| | | |
|---|---|---|
| Unearned interest revenue .............................................. | 31,969 | |
|    Interest revenue (12% x [$316,412 – 50,000]).................... | | 31,969 |

# Exercise 15-20

1.   d
2.   a
3.   a

# Exercise 15-21

## Requirement 1

### January 1

| | | |
|---|---|---|
| Cash ........................................................................... | 20,873 | |
|    Unearned rent revenue* ........................................... | | 20,873 |

| | | |
|---|---|---|
| Deferred initial direct cost ........................................... | 2,062 | |
|    Cash ........................................................................ | | 2,062 |

### December 31

| | | |
|---|---|---|
| Unearned rent revenue ................................................ | 20,873 | |
|    Rent revenue* ........................................................... | | 20,873 |

| | | |
|---|---|---|
| Lease expense ($2,062 ÷ 3 years) .................................... | 687 | |
|    Deferred initial direct cost ........................................ | | 687 |

| | | |
|---|---|---|
| Depreciation expense ($100,000 ÷ 6 years) ....................... | 16,667 | |
|    Accumulated depreciation ........................................... | | 16,667 |

\* Alternatively, Rent revenue. Either way, an adjusting entry is needed at the end of the reporting period to assure that the earned portion of the payment is recorded in Rent revenue and the unearned portion in Unearned rent revenue

## Requirement 2

### January 1

**Proof that new effective rate is 9% (not required):**

$$\underset{\substack{\text{lessor's}\\\text{net investment}}}{\$102,062} \div 4.88965^{**} = \underset{\substack{\text{lease}\\\text{payments}}}{\$20,873}$$

\*\* present value of an annuity due of $1: n=6, i=**9%**

# Exercise 15-21 (concluded)

### January 1

| | | |
|---|---|---|
| Lease receivable ($20,873 x 6) .......................................... | 125,238 | |
|    Unearned interest revenue ($125,238 - 100,000) ............ | | 25,238 |
|    Inventory of equipment (lessor's cost) .......................... | | 100,000 |
| | | |
| Unearned interest revenue ............................................. | 2,062 | |
|    Cash (initial direct costs) ................................................ | | 2,062 |
| | | |
| Cash (lease payment) ......................................................... | 20,873 | |
|    Lease receivable ................................................................ | | 20,873 |

### December 31

| | | |
|---|---|---|
| Unearned interest revenue ............................................. | 7,307 | |
|    Interest revenue (9% x [$100,000 + 2,062 - 20,873]) ........ | | 7,307 |

## Requirement 3
### January 1

| | | |
|---|---|---|
| Lease receivable ($20,873 x 6) .......................................... | 125,238 | |
| Cost of goods sold (lessor's cost) ..................................... | 85,000 | |
|    Sales revenue (fair market value)...................................... | | 100,000 |
|    Unearned interest revenue ($125,238 - 100,000) ............ | | 25,238 |
|    Inventory of equipment (lessor's cost) .......................... | | 85,000 |
| | | |
| Selling expense ................................................................. | 2,062 | |
|    Cash (initial direct costs) ................................................ | | 2,062 |
| | | |
| Cash (lease payment) ......................................................... | 20,873 | |
|    Lease receivable ................................................................ | | 20,873 |

### December 31

| | | |
|---|---|---|
| Unearned interest revenue ............................................. | 7,913 | |
|    Interest revenue (10% x [$100,000 - 20,873]) .................. | | 7,913 |

# Exercise 15-22

**January 1, 2006, 2007, 2008**

| | | |
|---|---|---|
| Cash............................................................... | 137,000 | |
|    Rent revenue*.......................................... | | 137,000 |
| | | |
| Deferred initial direct cost............................. | 2,400 | |
|    Cash................................................. | | 2,400 |

**December 31, 2006, 2007, 2008**

| | | |
|---|---|---|
| Lease expense ($2,400 ÷ 3 years)..................... | 800 | |
|    Deferred initial direct cost......................... | | 800 |
| | | |
| Depreciation expense ($800,000 ÷ 8 years)........ | 100,000 | |
|    Accumulated depreciation............................ | | 100,000 |

\*   Alternatively, Unearned rent revenue. If so, an adjusting entry is needed at the end of the reporting period to transfer the $137,000, now earned, from Unearned rent revenue to Rent revenue.

# Exercise 15-23

## 1. January 1, 2006

| | | |
|---|---|---|
| Lease receivable ($184,330 x 3) ......................................... | 552,990 | |
|    Unearned interest revenue ($552,990 - 500,000) ............ | | 52,990 |
|    Inventory of equipment (lessor's cost) ......................... | | 500,000 |
| | | |
| Unearned interest revenue ............................................. | 4,242 | |
|    Cash (initial direct costs) ................................................ | | 4,242 |
| | | |
| Cash (lease payment) ......................................................... | 184,330 | |
|    Lease receivable........................................................ | | 184,330 |

## 2. Effective rate of interest revenue:

Since the unearned interest is reduced by the initial direct costs, the net investment is higher: $500,000 + $4,242. The new effective rate is the discount rate that equates the net investment and the future lease payments:

$$\$504,242 \div \text{?}^{**} = \$184,330$$

lessor's           lease

net investment        payments

$^{**}$ present value of an annuity due of $1: n=3, i=?%

Rearranging algebraically: $504,242 ÷ $184,330= 2.73554.

When you consult the present value table for an annuity due, you search row 3 (n=3) for this value and find it in the 10% column. So the effective interest rate is 10%. The net investment is amortized at the new rate.

## 3. December 31, 2006

| | | |
|---|---|---|
| Unearned interest revenue ............................................. | 31,991 | |
|    Interest revenue (10% x [$500,000 + 4,242 - 184,330]) ..... | | 31,991 |

# Exercise 15-24

**Inception of the Lease**

| | | |
|---|---:|---:|
| Lease receivable ($69,571 x 5)............................................ | 347,855 | |
| Cost of goods sold (lessor's cost).................................... | 265,000 | |
|    Sales revenue (fair market value) .................................... | | 300,000 |
|    Unearned interest revenue ($347,855 - 300,000) ........... | | 47,855 |
|    Inventory of equipment (lessor's cost)......................... | | 265,000 |
| | | |
| Selling expense............................................................. | 7,500 | |
|    Cash (initial direct costs) ................................................ | | 7,500 |
| | | |
| Cash (lease payment)........................................................ | 69,571 | |
|    Lease receivable ...................................................... | | 69,571 |

**December 31**

| | | |
|---|---:|---:|
| Unearned interest revenue.............................................. | 18,434 | |
|    Interest revenue (8% x [$300,000 - 69,571) .................... | | 18,434 |

# Exercise 15-25

Present value of periodic rental payments*
    ($102,771 x 7.49236**)    $\underline{\$770,000}$*

  * rounded

  ** present value of an annuity due of $1: n=13, i=11%

The lease meets at least one (actually 3 of 4 in this case) criteria for classification as a capital lease.

**January 1, 2006**

| | | |
|---|---|---|
| Cash (given).................................................................... | 770,000 | |
|  Airplanes (carrying value) ............................................... | | 620,000 |
|  Deferred gain on sale-leaseback (difference)................ | | 150,000 |
| | | |
| Leased airplane (present value of lease payments) ................... | 770,000 | |
|  Lease payable (present value of lease payments)............... | | 770,000 |
| | | |
| Lease payable ................................................................. | 102,771 | |
|  Cash.......................................................................... | | 102,771 |

**December 31, 2006**

| | | |
|---|---|---|
| Interest expense (11% x [$770,000 - 102,771])....................... | 73,395 | |
|  Interest payable ............................................................ | | 73,395 |
| | | |
| Depreciation expense ($770,000 ÷ 15 years*)..................... | 51,333 | |
|  Accumulated depreciation ........................................... | | 51,333 |
| | | |
| Deferred gain on sale-leaseback ($150,000 ÷ 15 years)....... | 10,000 | |
|  Depreciation expense ................................................. | | 10,000 |

* The airplane is depreciated over its remaining useful life rather than the lease term because title transfers to the lessee.

# Exercise 15-26

**January 1, 2006**

| | | |
|---|---|---|
| Cash (given) .................................................................. | 800,000 | |
| Accumulated depreciation (cost - carrying amount)............ | 350,000 | |
|    Building (original cost)...................................................... | | 1,000,000 |
|    Deferred gain on sale-leaseback (difference) ............... | | 150,000 |

**December 31, 2006**

| | | |
|---|---|---|
| Rent expense......................................................................... | 100,000 | |
|    Cash (rental payment)............................................................ | | 100,000 |
| | | |
| Deferred gain on sale-leaseback ($150,000 ÷ 12 years)....... | 12,500 | |
|    Rent expense ..................................................................... | | 12,500 |

# Exercise 15-27

1. d
2. a

# Exercise 15-28

| | List A | | List B |
|---|---|---|---|
| _j_ | 1. Effective rate times balance. | a. | PV of BPO price. |
| _k_ | 2. Realization principle. | b. | Lessor's net investment. |
| _c_ | 3. Minimum lease payments plus unguaranteed residual value. | c. | Lessor's gross investment. |
| | | d. | Operating lease. |
| _l_ | 4. Periodic rent payments plus lessee-guaranteed residual value. | e. | Depreciable assets. |
| | | f. | Loss to lessee. |
| _b_ | 5. PV of minimum lease payments plus PV of unguaranteed residual value. | g. | Executory costs. |
| | | h. | Depreciation longer than lease term. |
| _n_ | 6. Initial direct costs. | i. | Disclosure only. |
| _d_ | 7. Rent revenue. | j. | Interest expense. |
| _m_ | 8. Bargain purchase option. | k. | Additional lessor conditions. |
| _e_ | 9. Leasehold improvements. | l. | Lessee's minimum lease payments |
| _f_ | 10. Cash to satisfy residual value guarantee. | m. | Purchase price less than fair market value. |
| _g_ | 11. Capital lease expense. | n. | Sales-type lease selling expense. |
| _a_ | 12. Deducted in lessor's computation of rental payments. | o. | Lessor's minimum lease payments. |
| _h_ | 13. Title transfers to lessee. | | |
| _i_ | 14. Contingent rentals. | | |
| _o_ | 15. Rent payments plus lessee-guaranteed and 3rd-party-guaranteed residual value. | | |

# Exercise 15-29

**Note:**
Because exercise of the option appears at the inception of the lease to be reasonably assured, payment of the option price ($100,000) is expected to occur when the option becomes exercisable (at the *end* of the 10th year). When the leased property includes both land and a building and the lease is expected to transfer ownership by exercise of a BPO, the lessee should record each leased asset separately. The present value of the minimum lease payments is allocated between the leased land and leased building accounts on the basis of their relative market values.

| | |
|---|---:|
| Present value of lease payments ($200,000 x 6.75902[**]) | $1,351,804 |
| *Plus:* Present value of the BPO price ($100,000 x .38554[*]) | 38,554 |
| Present value of minimum lease payments | $1,390,358 |

[*]   present value of $1: n=10, i=10%
[**] present value of an annuity due of $1: n=10, i=10%

### January 1, 2006

| | | |
|---|---:|---:|
| Leased land (fair value)................................................... | 400,000 | |
| Leased building ($1,390,358 - 400,000) ............................ | 990,358 | |
|    Lease liability (calculated above)..................................... | | 1,390,358 |
| | | |
| Lease liability ............................................................. | 200,000 | |
|    Cash (annual rental) ........................................................ | | 200,000 |

### December 31, 2006

| | | |
|---|---:|---:|
| Depreciation expense ([$990,358 - 150,000] ÷ 20 years) ....... | 42,018 | |
|    Accumulated depreciation – leased building.............. | | 42,018 |
| | | |
| Interest expense ([$1,390,358 - 200,000] x 10%)..................... | 119,036 | |
|    Interest payable ......................................................... | | 119,036 |

# Exercise 15-30

1. **d.** For both sales-type and direct-financing leases, the lessor should record as the gross investment in the lease the amount of the minimum lease payments (which include periodic payments plus guaranteed residual value) plus any amounts of unguaranteed residual value. The net investment in the lease is equal to the gross investment, plus any unamortized initial direct costs, minus unearned income. The unguaranteed residual value is the expected value of the leased asset in excess of the guaranteed residual value at the end of the lease term (SFAS 13).

2. **b.** SFAS 91 defines initial direct costs as having two components: (1) the lessor's external costs to originate a lease incurred in dealings with independent third parties and (2) the internal costs directly related to specified activities performed by the lessor for that lease. According to SFAS 13, in a sales-type lease, the cost, or carrying amount if different, plus any initial direct costs, minus the present value of any unguaranteed residual value, is charged against income in the same period that the present value of the minimum lease payments is credited to sales. The result is the recognition of a net profit or loss on the sales-type lease.

3. **d.** A lessee records a lease as a capital lease if it meets any one of four criteria. Existence of a bargain purchase option is one of these criteria. If a lease involving land and a building contains a bargain purchase option or if the lease transfers ownership to the lessee at the end of its term, the lessee separately capitalizes the land and the building.

# PROBLEMS

## Problem 15-1

**December 31, 2010**

| | | |
|---|---|---|
| Rent expense ($10,000 + [$500 x 20 ÷ 2])*...................... | 15,000 | |
| Deferred rent expense payable (difference)................. | | 3,000 |
| Cash ($10,000 + [$500 x 4]) .......................................... | | 12,000 |

**December 31, 2020**

| | | |
|---|---|---|
| Rent expense ($10,000 + [$500 x 20 ÷ 2])*...................... | 15,000 | |
| Deferred rent expense payable (difference)..................... | 2,000 | |
| Cash ($10,000 + [$500 x 14]) ......................................... | | 17,000 |

\* This is the average rent over the 20-year period.

Also:   ($10,000  +  $20,000)    ÷   2
         Beg. Rent    Ending Rent

# Problem 15-2

### 1. NIC's lease liability at the inception of the lease

$172,501:   [$192,501 – 20,000] (present value of minimum lease payments or initial lease balance minus first payment)

### 2. Leased asset

$192,501 (present value of minimum lease payments; initial lease balance)

### 3. Lease term in years

20 years

### 4. Asset's residual value expected at the end of the lease term

$35,000

### 5. Residual value guaranteed by the lessee

$35,000 (would not be part of lessee's minimum lease payments unless lessee-guaranteed)

### 6. Effective annual interest rate

10%:   ($17,250 ÷ $172,501)

### 7. Total of minimum lease payments

$435,000:  [$20,000 x 20 years] + $35,000

### 8. Total effective interest expense over the term of the lease

$242,499:  [$435,000 - 192,501]

# Problem 15-3

## Requirement 1

**Capital lease to lessee;      Direct financing lease to lessor.**

Since the present value of minimum lease payments (same for both the lessor and the lessee) is equal to (>90%) the fair value of the asset, the 90% recovery criterion is met.

---

### Calculation of the Present Value of Minimum Lease Payments

Present value of periodic rental payments
$$\$130,516 \times 15.32380^{**} \quad = \quad \$2,000,000$$
(rounded)

** present value of an annuity due of \$1: n=20, i=3%

---

The 75% of useful life criterion is met also.  Both additional lessor conditions are met for a nonoperating lease.  There is no dealer's profit because the fair value equals the lessor's cost.

## Requirement 2

**Mid-South Urologists Group (Lessee)**
**January 1, 2006**

| | | |
|---|---|---|
| Leased equipment (calculated above)................................ | 2,000,000 | |
|     Lease payable (calculated above)..................................... | | 2,000,000 |
| | | |
| Lease payable ............................................................... | 130,516 | |
|     Cash (rental payment)......................................................... | | 130,516 |

**April 1, 2006**

| | | |
|---|---|---|
| Interest expense (3% x [\$2 million – 130,516]) ...................... | 56,085 | |
| Lease payable (difference) ................................................. | 74,431 | |
|     Cash (rental payment)......................................................... | | 130,516 |

## Problem 15-3 (concluded)

### Physicians' Leasing (Lessor)
**January 1, 2006**

| | | |
|---|---|---|
| Lease receivable ($130,516 x 20) ..................................... | 2,610,320 | |
|    Unearned interest revenue ($2,610,320 - 2,000,000)....... | | 610,320 |
|    Inventory of equipment (lessor's cost) .......................... | | 2,000,000 |
| | | |
| Cash (rental payment)............................................... | 130,516 | |
|    Lease receivable ............................................... | | 130,516 |

**April 1, 2006**

| | | |
|---|---|---|
| Cash (rental payment)............................................... | 130,516 | |
|    Lease receivable ............................................... | | 130,516 |
| | | |
| Unearned interest revenue ........................................ | 56,085 | |
|    Interest revenue (3% x [$2 million – 130,516]).................. | | 56,085 |

## Requirement 3

### Rand Medical (Lessor)
**January 1, 2006**

| | | |
|---|---|---|
| Lease receivable ($130,516 x 20) ..................................... | 2,610,320 | |
| Cost of goods sold (lessor's cost) ..................................... | 1,700,000 | |
|    Sales revenue (fair market value)................................... | | 2,000,000 |
|    Unearned interest revenue ($2,610,320 - 2,000,000)....... | | 610,320 |
|    Inventory of equipment (lessor's cost) .......................... | | 1,700,000 |
| | | |
| Cash (rental payment)............................................... | 130,516 | |
|    Lease receivable ............................................... | | 130,516 |

**April 1, 2006**

| | | |
|---|---|---|
| Cash (rental payment)............................................... | 130,516 | |
|    Lease receivable ............................................... | | 130,516 |
| | | |
| Unearned interest revenue ........................................ | 56,085 | |
|    Interest revenue (3% x [$2 million – 130,516]).................. | | 56,085 |

# Problem 15-4

*[Note: This problem is the lease equivalent of Problem 14-11, which deals with a parallel situation in which the machine was acquired with an installment note.*

## 1. Effective rate of interest implicit in the agreement

$$\underset{\substack{\text{present} \\ \text{value}}}{\$6{,}074{,}700} \div \underset{\substack{\text{lease} \\ \text{payment}}}{\$2{,}000{,}000} = \underset{\substack{\text{present value} \\ \text{table amount}}}{3.03735}$$

This is the ordinary annuity present value table amount for $n = 4$, $i = $ **?** In row 4 of the present value table, the number 3.03735 is in the 12% column. So, 12% is the implicit interest rate.

## 2. Inception of the lease

| | | |
|---|---|---|
| Leased asset (fair market value ) .......................................... | 6,074,700 | |
| Leases payable (present value ) ...................................... | | 6,074,700 |

## 3. December 31, 2006

| | | |
|---|---|---|
| Interest expense (12% x $6,074,700)........................................ | 728,964 | |
| Leases payable (difference)................................................. | 1,271,036 | |
| Cash (rental payment)....................................................... | | 2,000,000 |

## 4. December 31, 2007

| | | |
|---|---|---|
| Interest expense (12% x [$6,074,700 – 1,271,036]).................. | 576,440 | |
| Lease payable (difference) ................................................. | 1,423,560 | |
| Cash (rental payment)....................................................... | | 2,000,000 |

## 5. Inception of the lease

$$\underset{\substack{\text{rental} \\ \text{payment}}}{\$2{,}000{,}000} \times 3.10245^{**} = \underset{\substack{\text{present} \\ \text{value}}}{\$6{,}204{,}900}$$

** present value of an ordinary annuity of $1: n=4, i=11%

| | | |
|---|---|---|
| Leased asset ................................................................. | 6,204,900 | |
| Lease payable ............................................................... | | 6,204,900 |

# Problem 15-5

## 1. Calculation of the present value of lease payments

$$\$391,548 \times 15.32380^{\Phi} = \$6,000,000$$
(rounded)

$\Phi$ present value of an annuity due of $1: n=20, i=3%

## 2. Liability at December 31, 2006

| | |
|---|---|
| Initial balance, September 30, 2006 ........................ | $6,000,000 |
| Sept. 30, 2006 reduction.......................................... | (391,548)* |
| Dec. 31, 2006 reduction........................................... | (223,294)** |
| December 31, 2006 net liability .............................. | $5,385,158 |

The current and noncurrent portions of the liability would be reported separately.

### Asset at December 31, 2006

| | |
|---|---|
| Initial balance, September 30, 2006 ........................ | $6,000,000 |
| Accumulated depreciation at Dec. 31, 2006............ | (300,000)** |
| December 31, 2006 ............................................ | $5,700,000 |

## 3. Expenses for year ended December 31, 2006

| | |
|---|---|
| Sept. 30, 2006 interest expense .............................. | $        0* |
| Dec. 31, 2006 interest expense................................ | 168,254** |
| Interest expense for 2006......................................... | $168,254 |
| | |
| Depreciation expense for 2006................................ | 300,000 |
| Total expenses......................................................... | $468,254 |

## Problem 15-5 (concluded)

### 4. Statement of cash flows for year ended December 31, 2006

Werner would report the $6,000,000* investment in the protein analyzer and its financing with a capital lease as a significant noncash investing and financing activity in the disclosure notes to the financial statements.

The $783,096 ($391,548 x 2) cash lease payments *, ** are divided into the interest portion and the principal portion. The interest portion, $168,254, is reported as cash outflows from operating activities. The principal portion, $391,548 + $223,294, is reported as cash outflows from financing activities.

Note: By the indirect method of reporting cash flows from operating activities, we would add back to net income the $300,000 depreciation expense since it didn't actually reduce cash. The $168,254 interest expense that reduced net income actually did reduce cash [the interest portion of the $783,096 ($391,548 x 2) cash lease payments], so for it, no adjustment to net income is necessary.

### Calculations:
**September 30, 2006***

| | | |
|---|---|---|
| Leased equipment (calculated in req. 1)............................ | 6,000,000 | |
| Lease payable (calculated in req. 1) ............................. | | 6,000,000 |
| | | |
| Lease payable ................................................................ | 391,548 | |
| Cash (rental payment)......................................................... | | 391,548 |

**December 31, 2006****

| | | |
|---|---|---|
| Interest expense (3% x [$6 million − 391,548]) ................ | 168,254 | |
| Lease payable (difference)................................................. | 223,294 | |
| Cash (rental payment)......................................................... | | 391,548 |
| | | |
| Depreciation expense ($6 million / 5 years x ¼ year) ....... | 300,000 | |
| Accumulated depreciation............................................. | | 300,000 |

# Problem 15-6

## 1. Receivable at December 31, 2006

| | Receivable | – Unearned Interest | = Net Rec. |
|---|---|---|---|
| Initial balance, September 30, 2006 .. | $7,830,960 | 1,830,960 | $6,000,000 |
| Sept. 30, 2006 reduction .................... | (391,548)* | 0 | (391,548) |
| Dec. 31, 2006 reduction..................... | (391,548)** | (168,254) | (223,294) |
| December 31, 2006 net receivable .... | $7,047,864 | 1,662,706 | $5,385,158 |

The receivable is reported as:

| | |
|---|---|
| Lease receivable................................. | $7,047,864 |
| Less: unearned interest revenue......... | (1,662,706) |
| | $5,385,158 |

The receivable replaces the $6,000,000 machine on the balance sheet.

## 2. Interest revenue for year ended December 31, 2006

| | |
|---|---|
| Sept. 30, 2006 interest revenue............................... | $ 0* |
| Dec. 31, 2006 interest revenue ............................... | 168,254** |
| Interest revenue for 2006....................................... | $168,254 |

## 3. Statement of cash flows for year ended December 31, 2006

Abbott would report the $6,000,000* direct financing lease of the protein analyzer as a significant noncash investing activity (acquiring one asset and disposing of another) in the disclosure notes to the financial statements.

The $783,096 ($391,548 x 2) cash lease payments *, ** are divided into the interest portion and the principal portion. The interest portion, $168,254, is reported as cash inflows from operating activities. The principal portion, $391,548 + $223,294, is reported as cash inflows from investing activities.

Note: By the indirect method of reporting cash flows from operating activities, the $168,254 interest revenue that increased net income actually did increase cash [the interest portion of the $783,096 ($391,548 x 2) cash lease payments], so no adjustment to net income is necessary.

# Problem 15-6 (concluded)

**Calculations:**

**September 30, 2006\***

| | | |
|---|---|---|
| Lease receivable ($391,548 x 20) ................................... | 7,830,960 | |
|    Unearned interest revenue ($7,830,960 – 6,000,000)... | | 1,830,960 |
|    Inventory of equipment (lessor's cost) ........................ | | 6,000,000 |
| | | |
| Cash (rental payment)....................................................... | 391,548 | |
|    Lease receivable ................................................................ | | 391,548 |

**December 31, 2006\*\***

| | | |
|---|---|---|
| Cash (rental payment)....................................................... | 391,548 | |
|    Lease receivable ................................................................ | | 391,548 |
| | | |
| Unearned interest revenue ............................................. | 168,254 | |
|    Interest revenue (3% x [$6,000,000 – 391,548])........... | | 168,254 |

# Problem 15-7

## 1. Calculation of the present value of lease payments ("selling price")

$$\$391,548 \times 15.32380^\Phi = \$6,000,000$$
(rounded)

$^\Phi$ present value of an annuity due of \$1: n=20, i=3%

## 2. Receivable at December 31, 2006

| | Receivable | – Unearned Interest | = Net Rec. |
|---|---|---|---|
| Initial balance, September 30, 2006 .. | \$7,830,960 | 1,830,960 | \$6,000,000 |
| Sept. 30, 2006 reduction..................... | (391,548)* | 0 | (391,548) |
| Dec. 31, 2006 reduction...................... | (391,548)** | (168,254) | (223,294) |
| December 31, 2006 net liability ......... | \$7,047,864 | 1,662,706 | \$5,385,158 |

The receivable is reported as:

| | |
|---|---|
| Lease receivable................................. | \$7,047,864 |
| Less: unearned interest revenue.......... | (1,662,706) |
| | \$5,385,158 |

The receivable replaces the \$5,000,000 machine in inventory in the balance sheet.

## 3. Income effect for year ended December 31, 2006

| | |
|---|---|
| Sept. 30, 2006 interest revenue............................... | \$ 0* |
| Dec. 31, 2006 interest revenue ............................... | 168,254** |
| Interest revenue for 2006........................................ | \$ 168,254 |
| | |
| Sales revenue* ...................................................... | 6,000,000 |
| Cost of goods sold* ................................................ | (5,000,000) |
| Income effect ..................................................... | \$1,168,254 |

## Problem 15-7 (continued)

### 4. Statement of cash flows for year ended December 31, 2006

NutraLabs would report the $6,000,000* sales-type lease of the protein analyzer as a significant noncash activity in the disclosure notes to the financial statements.

The $783,096 ($391,548 x 2) cash lease payments *, ** are considered to be cash flows from operating activities. A sales-type lease differs from a direct financing lease in that we assume the lessor is actually selling its product, an operating activity. Thus, both the interest portion, $168,254, and the principal portion, $391,548 + $223,294, are reported as cash inflows from operating activities.

Note: By the indirect method of reporting cash flows from operating activities, the $1,000,000 (Sales revenue: $6,000,000 – Cost of goods sold: $5,000,000) dealer's profit must be deducted from net income because it is included in net income but won't increase cash flows until the lease payments are collected over the next five years. This addition, however, occurs automatically as we make the usual adjustments for the change in receivables (to adjust sales to cash received from customers) and for the change in inventory (to adjust cost of goods sold to cash paid to suppliers).

The $168,254 interest revenue that increased net income actually did increase cash [the interest portion of the $783,096 ($391,548 x 2) cash lease payments], so for it, no adjustment to net income is necessary. The principal portion, $391,548 + $223,294, must be added because it is not otherwise included in net income. This, too, though, occurs automatically as we make the usual adjustments for the change in receivables (to adjust sales to cash received from customers).

*Noncash adjustments to convert net income to cash flows from operating activities:*

| | |
|---|---:|
| Increase in lease receivable......................................... | ($7,830,960) |
| Increase in unearned interest (contra lease receivable) | 1,830,960 |
| Decrease in inventory of equipment .......................... | 5,000,000 |
| Decrease in lease receivable, Sept. 30 ...................... | 391,548 |
| Decrease in lease receivable, Dec. 31 ....................... | 391,548 |
| Decrease in unearned interest (contra lease receivable), Dec. 31 | (168,254) |

# Problem 15-7 (concluded)

### Calculations:

**September 30, 2006***

| | | |
|---|---:|---:|
| Lease receivable ($391,548 x 20)..................................... | 7,830,960 | |
| Cost of goods sold (lessor's cost)................................... | 5,000,000 | |
|    Sales revenue (present value)........................................ | | 6,000,000 |
|    Unearned interest revenue ($7,830,960 – 6,000,000) ... | | 1,830,960 |
|    Inventory of equipment (lessor's cost)......................... | | 5,000,000 |
| | | |
| Cash (rental payment)........................................................ | 391,548 | |
|    Lease receivable........................................................... | | 391,548 |

**December 31, 2006****

| | | |
|---|---:|---:|
| Cash (rental payment)........................................................ | 391,548 | |
|    Lease receivable........................................................... | | 391,548 |
| | | |
| Unearned interest revenue ............................................... | 168,254 | |
|    Interest revenue (3% x [$6,000,000 – 391,548]) ........... | | 168,254 |

# Problem 15-8

## Requirement 1

| **Lessor's Calculation of Rental Payments** | |
| --- | --- |
| Amount to be recovered (fair market value) | $365,760 |
| | |
| *Less:* Present value of the guaranteed residual value ($25,000 x .68301*) | (17,075) |
| | |
| Amount to be recovered through periodic rental payments | $348,685 |
| | |
| Rental payments at the beginning of each of four years: ($348,685 ÷ 3.48685**) | $100,000 |

    * present value of $1: n=4, i=10%

    ** present value of an annuity due of $1: n=4, i=10%

## Requirement 2

The lessee's incremental borrowing rate (12%) is more than the lessor's implicit rate (10%). So, both parties' calculations should be made using a 10% discount rate:

## Application of Classification Criteria

**1** Does the agreement specify that
ownership of the asset transfers
to the lessee?                                    NO

**2** Does the agreement contain a
bargain purchase option?                          NO

**3** Is the lease term equal to 75%
or more of the expected                           NO
economic life of the asset?              {4 yrs < 75% of 6 yrs}

**4** Is the present value of the
minimum lease payments equal
to or greater than 90% of the                     YES
fair value of the asset?          {$365,760[b] > 90% of $365,760}

b See calculation below.

## Present Value of Minimum Lease Payments

Present value of periodic rental payments
      ($100,000 x 3.48685[**])                     $348,685

*Plus:* Present value of the lessee-guaranteed
     residual value ($25,000 x .68301[*])            17,075

Present value of minimum lease payments                $365,760

       \*   present value of $1: n=4, i=10%

    \*\* present value of an annuity due of $1: n=4, i=10%

## Problem 15-8 (continued)

### (a) By Western Soya Co. (the lessee)

Since at least one criterion is met, this is a **capital lease** to the lessee. Western Soya records the present value of minimum lease payments as a leased asset and a lease liability.

### (b) By Rhone-Metro (the lessor)

Since the fair market value equals the lessor's carrying value, there is no dealer's profit, making this a **direct financing lease**.

## Requirement 3

**December 31, 2006**

**Western Soya Co. (Lessee)**

| | | |
|---|---|---|
| Leased equipment (calculated above)................................ | 365,760 | |
| Lease payable (calculated above) ................................... | | 365,760 |
| | | |
| Lease payable ................................................................ | 100,000 | |
| Cash (rental payment).................................................... | | 100,000 |

**Rhone-Metro (Lessor)**

| | | |
|---|---|---|
| Lease receivable ([$100,000 x 4] + $25,000)...................... | 425,000 | |
| Unearned interest revenue ($425,000 - 365,760) ........... | | 59,240 |
| Inventory of equipment (lessor's cost)......................... | | 365,760 |
| | | |
| Cash (rental payment)......................................................... | 100,000 | |
| Lease receivable ......................................................... | | 100,000 |

## Problem 15-8 (continued)

### Requirement 4

Since both use the same discount rate and since the residual value is lessee-guaranteed, the same amortization schedule applies to both the lessee and lessor:

| Dec. 31 | Payments | Effective Interest 10% x Outstanding Balance | Decrease in Balance | Outstanding Balance |
|---|---|---|---|---|
| 2006 | | | | 365,760 |
| 2006 | 100,000 | | 100,000 | 265,760 |
| 2007 | 100,000 | .10 (265,760) = 26,576 | 73,424 | 192,336 |
| 2008 | 100,000 | .10 (192,336) = 19,234 | 80,766 | 111,570 |
| 2009 | 100,000 | .10 (111,570) = 11,157 | 88,843 | 22,727 |
| 2010 | 25,000 | .10 (22,727) = 2,273 | 22,727 | 0 |
| | 425,000 | 59,240 | 365,760 | |

**Lease Amortization Schedule**

### Requirement 5
**December 31, 2007**

**Western Soya Co. (Lessee)**

| | | |
|---|---|---|
| Interest expense (10% x [$365,760 - 100,000]) | 26,576 | |
| Lease payable (difference) | 73,424 | |
| Cash (rental payment) | | 100,000 |

| | | |
|---|---|---|
| Depreciation expense ([$365,760 - 25,000] ÷ 4 years) | 85,190 | |
| Accumulated depreciation | | 85,190 |

**Rhone-Metro (Lessor)**

| | | |
|---|---|---|
| Cash (rental payment) | 100,000 | |
| Lease receivable | | 100,000 |

| | | |
|---|---|---|
| Unearned interest revenue | 26,576 | |
| Interest revenue (10% x [$365,760 - 100,000]) | | 26,576 |

*Problem 15-8 (concluded)*

**Requirement 6**

**December 31, 2010**
**Western Soya Club (Lessee)**

| | | |
|---|---|---|
| Depreciation expense ([$365,760 - 25,000] ÷ 4 years) ......... | 85,190 | |
| Accumulated depreciation........................................... | | 85,190 |

| | | |
|---|---|---|
| Interest expense (10% x 22,727: from schedule)..................... | 2,273 | |
| Lease payable (difference : from schedule)......................... | 22,727 | |
| Accumulated depreciation ($365,760 - 25,000) ................. | 340,760 | |
| Loss on residual value guarantee ($25,000 - 1,500)............. | 23,500 | |
| Leased equipment (account balance)............................. | | 365,760 |
| Cash ($25,000 - 1,500) ......................................... | | 23,500 |

**Rhone-Metro (Lessor)**

| | | |
|---|---|---|
| Inventory of equipment (actual residual value)................... | 1,500 | |
| Cash ($25,000 - 1,500) ......................................... | 23,500 | |
| Lease receivable (account balance).............................. | | 25,000 |

| | | |
|---|---|---|
| Unearned interest revenue (account balance) .................... | 2,273 | |
| Interest revenue (10% x 22,727: from schedule)................. | | 2,273 |

# Problem 15-9

## Requirement 1

| Lessor's Calculation of Rental Payments | | |
|---|---|---|
| Amount to be recovered (fair market value) | | $365,760 |
| *Less:* Present value of the unguaranteed residual value ($25,000 x .68301*) | | (17,075) |
| Amount to be recovered through periodic rental payments | | $348,685 |
| Rental payments at the beginning of each of four years: | ($348,685 ÷ 3.48685**) | $100,000 |
| *Plus:* Executory costs | | 4,000 |
| Rental payments including executory costs | | $104,000 |

        * present value of $1: n=4, i=10%

       ** present value of an annuity due of $1: n=4, i=10%

## Problem 15-9 *(continued)*

### Requirement 2

The lessee's incremental borrowing rate (12%) is more than the lessor's implicit rate (10%). So, both parties' calculations should be made using a 10% discount rate:

---

### Application of Classification Criteria

**1** Does the agreement specify that ownership of the asset transfers to the lessee?      NO

**2** Does the agreement contain a bargain purchase option?      NO

**3** Is the lease term equal to 75% or more of the expected economic life of the asset?

NO

{4 yrs < 75% of 6 yrs}

**4** Is the present value of the minimum lease payments equal to or greater than 90% of the fair value of the asset?

YES

{$348,685[a] > 90% of $365,760}

[a] See calculation below.

---

### Present Value of Minimum Lease Payments

Present value of periodic rental payments excluding
    executory costs of $4,000      ($100,000[*] x 3.48685[**])      $348,685

        [**] present value of an annuity due of $1: n=4, i=10%

[*] Since the residual value is not guaranteed, it is excluded from both the lessor's and the lessee's minimum lease payments and therefore does not affect the 90% of fair value test.

---

### (a) by Western Soya Co. (the lessee)

Since at least one criterion is met, this is a **capital lease** to the lessee. Western Soya records the present value of minimum lease payments as a leased asset and a lease liability.

### (b) by Rhone-Metro (the lessor)

Since the fair market value exceeds the lessor's carrying value, the equipment is being "sold" at a profit, making this a **sales-type lease:**

| | |
|---|---|
| Fair market value | $365,760 |
| *minus* | |
| Carrying value | (300,000) |
| *equals* | |
| Dealer's profit | $ 65,760 |

## Requirement 3
### December 31, 2006

**Western Soya Co. (Lessee)**

| | | |
|---|---|---|
| Leased equipment (calculated above) | 348,685 | |
|    Lease payable (calculated above) | | 348,685 |
| | | |
| Lease payable | 100,000 | |
| Prepaid operating expense (2007 expenses) | 4,000 | |
|    Cash (rental payment) | | 104,000 |

**Rhone-Metro (Lessor)**

| | | |
|---|---|---|
| Lease receivable ([$100,000 x 4] + $25,000) | 425,000 | |
| Cost of goods sold ($300,000 - [$25,000 x .68301]) | 282,925 | |
|    Sales revenue ($365,760 - [$25,000 x .68301]) | | 348,685 |
|    Unearned interest revenue ($425,000 - 365,760) | | 59,240 |
|    Inventory of equipment (lessor's cost) | | 300,000 |
| | | |
| Cash (rental payment) | 104,000 | |
|    Payable (maintenance, insurance, etc.) | | 4,000 |
|    Lease receivable | | 100,000 |

## Problem 15-9 (continued)

### Requirement 4

#### Lessee (unguaranteed residual value excluded):

### Lease Amortization Schedule

| Dec. 31 | Payments | Effective Interest 10% x Outstanding Balance | Decrease in Balance | Outstanding Balance |
|---|---|---|---|---|
| 2006 | | | | 348,685 |
| 2006 | 100,000 | | 100,000 | 248,685 |
| 2007 | 100,000 | .10 (248,685) = 24,869 | 75,131 | 173,554 |
| 2008 | 100,000 | .10 (173,554) = 17,355 | 82,645 | 90,909 |
| 2009 | 100,000 | .10 (90,909) = 9,091 | 90,909 | 0 |
| | 400,000 | 51,315 | 348,685 | |

#### Lessor (unguaranteed residual value included):

### Lease Amortization Schedule

| Dec. 31 | Payments | Effective Interest 10% x Outstanding Balance | Decrease in Balance | Outstanding Balance |
|---|---|---|---|---|
| 2006 | | | | 365,760 |
| 2006 | 100,000 | | 100,000 | 265,760 |
| 2007 | 100,000 | .10 (265,760) = 26,576 | 73,424 | 192,336 |
| 2008 | 100,000 | .10 (192,336) = 19,234 | 80,766 | 111,570 |
| 2009 | 100,000 | .10 (111,570) = 11,157 | 88,843 | 22,727 |
| 2010 | 25,000 | .10 (22,727) = 2,273 | 22,727 | 0 |
| | 425,000 | 59,240 | 365,760 | |

# Problem 15-9 (continued)

## Requirement 5

**December 31, 2007**

**Western Soya Co. (Lessee)**

| | | |
|---|---|---|
| Depreciation expense ([$348,685] ÷ 4 years)......................... | 87,171 | |
|     Accumulated depreciation ........................................... | | 87,171 |
| | | |
| Operating expense (2007 expenses) .................................... | 4,000 | |
|     Prepaid operating expense (paid in 2006)....................... | | 4,000 |
| | | |
| Interest expense (10% x [$348,685– 100,000]) ........................ | 24,869 | |
| Lease payable (difference)................................................ | 75,131 | |
| Prepaid operating expense (2008 expenses)....................... | 4,000 | |
|     Cash (rental payment) ................................................ | | 104,000 |

**Rhone-Metro (Lessor)**

| | | |
|---|---|---|
| Cash (rental payment) ......................................................... | 104,000 | |
|     Payable (maintenance, insurance, etc.)....................... | | 4,000 |
|     Lease receivable............................................................. | | 100,000 |
| | | |
| Unearned interest revenue ............................................. | 26,576 | |
|     Interest revenue  (10% x [$365,760– 100,000])................... | | 26,576 |

*Problem 15-9 (concluded)*

## Requirement 6

**December 31, 2010**
**Western Soya Co. (Lessee)**

| | | |
|---|---|---|
| Operating expense (2010 expenses)................................ | 4,000 | |
|     Prepaid operating expense (paid in 2009) .................... | | 4,000 |
| | | |
| Depreciation expense ([$348,685] ÷ 4 years)....................... | 87,171 | |
|     Accumulated depreciation......................................... | | 87,171 |
| | | |
| Accumulated depreciation (account balance) ................... | 348,685 | |
|     Leased equipment (account balance)............................. | | 348,685 |

**Rhone-Metro (Lessor)**

| | | |
|---|---|---|
| Inventory of equipment (actual residual value)................... | 1,500 | |
| Loss on leased assets ($25,000 - 1,500)............................ | 23,500 | |
|     Lease receivable (account balance).............................. | | 25,000 |
| | | |
| Unearned interest revenue (account balance) ................... | 2,273 | |
|     Interest revenue (10% x 22,727: from schedule)................. | | 2,273 |

# Problem 15-10

## Requirement 1

| Lessor's Calculation of Rental Payments | |
|---|---|
| Amount to be recovered (fair market value) | $365,760 |
| | |
| *Less:* Present value of the BPO price ($10,000 x .75131[*]) | (7,513) |
| Amount to be recovered through periodic rental payments | $358,247 |
| | |
| Rental payments at the beginning | |
|   of each of three years:     ($358,247 ÷ 2.73554[**]) | $130,960 |
| *Plus:* Executory costs | 4,000 |
| Rental payments including executory costs | $134,960 |

[*]   present value of $1: n=3, i=10%
[**] present value of an annuity due of $1: n=3, i=10%

## Requirement 2

The lessee's incremental borrowing rate (12%) is more than the lessor's implicit rate (10%).  So, both parties' calculations should be made using a 10% discount rate:

*Problem 15-10 (continued)*

---

### Application of Classification Criteria

**1** Does the agreement specify that
ownership of the asset transfers
to the lessee?                                                    NO

**2** Does the agreement contain a
bargain purchase option?                                          YES

**3** Is the lease term equal to 75%
or more of the expected                                          NO
economic life of the asset?                          {3 yrs[a] < 75% of 6 yrs}

**4** Is the present value of the
minimum lease payments equal
to or greater than 90% of the                                    YES
fair value of the asset?                        {$365,760[b] > 90% of $365,760}

[a] The lease term is considered to end at the date a BPO becomes exercisable.
[b] See calculation below.

---

### Present Value of Minimum Lease Payments

Present value of periodic rental payments excluding
  executory costs of $4,000      ($130,960 x 2.73554[**])          $358,247[***]

*Plus:* Present value of the BPO price ($10,000 x .75131[*])            7,513

Present value of minimum lease payments                             $365,760

  [*]   present value of $1: n=3, i=10%
  [**]  present value of an annuity due of $1: n=3, i=10%
  [***] rounded

Note: The BPO price is included in both the lessor's and the lessee's minimum lease payments.
  Also the lease term ends for accounting purposes after 3 years, when the BPO becomes
  exercisable.

---

***Problem 15-10 (continued)***

### (a) by Western Soya Co. (the lessee)

Since at least one (two in this case) classification criterion is met, this is a **capital lease** to the lessee. Western Soya records the present value of minimum lease payments as a leased asset and a lease liability.

### (b) by Rhone-Metro (the lessor)

Since the fair market value exceeds the lessor's carrying value, the equipment is being "sold" at a profit, making this a **sales-type lease**:

| | |
|---|---|
| Fair market value | $365,760 |
| *minus* | |
| Carrying value | (300,000) |
| *equals* | |
| Dealer's profit | $ 65,760 |

## Requirement 3

**December 31, 2006**

**Western Soya Co. (Lessee)**

| | | |
|---|---|---|
| Leased equipment (calculated above) ................................ | 365,760 | |
|    Lease payable (calculated above) ...................................... | | 365,760 |
| | | |
| Lease payable ......................................................................... | 130,960 | |
| Prepaid operating expense (2007 executory costs) .............. | 4,000 | |
|    Cash (rental payment) ......................................................... | | 134,960 |

**Rhone-Metro (Lessor)**

| | | |
|---|---|---|
| Lease receivable ([$130,960 x 3] + $10,000) ....................... | 402,880 | |
| Cost of goods sold (lessor's cost) ........................................ | 300,000 | |
|    Sales revenue (present value of minimum lease payments) . | | 365,760 |
|    Unearned interest revenue ($402,880 - 365,760) ............ | | 37,120 |
|    Inventory of equipment (lessor's cost) .......................... | | 300,000 |
| | | |
| Cash (rental payment) .......................................................... | 134,960 | |
|    Payable (maintenance, insurance, etc.) ......................... | | 4,000 |
|    Lease receivable .......................................................... | | 130,960 |

## Problem 15-10 *(continued)*

## Requirement 4

### Lessee and lessor (BPO included):

Since both use the same discount rate and since the bargain purchase option is included as an additional payment for both, the same amortization schedule applies to both the lessee and lessor. The lease term ends for accounting purposes after 3 rental payments, because the BPO becomes exercisable before the fourth:

| Dec. 31 | Payments | Effective Interest 10% x Outstanding Balance | Decrease in Balance | Outstanding Balance |
|---------|----------|-----------------------------------------------|---------------------|---------------------|
| 2006 | | | | 365,760 |
| 2006 | 130,960 | | 130,960 | 234,800 |
| 2007 | 130,960 | .10 (234,800) = 23,480 | 107,480 | 127,320 |
| 2008 | 130,960 | .10 (127,320) = 12,732 | 118,228 | 9,092 |
| 2009 | 10,000 | .10  (9,092) =  908* | 9,092 | 0 |
| | 402,880 | 37,120 | 365,760 | |

**Lease Amortization Schedule**

\* adjusted for rounding of other numbers in the schedule

## Problem 15-10 (continued)

## Requirement 5

### December 31, 2007

#### Western Soya Co. (Lessee)

| | | |
|---|---|---|
| Depreciation expense ($365,760 ÷ 6 years*) ........................ | 60,960 | |
|    Accumulated depreciation ......................................... | | 60,960 |
| | | |
| Operating expense (2007 executory costs) ........................ | 4,000 | |
|    Prepaid operating expense (paid in 2006) .................... | | 4,000 |
| | | |
| Interest expense (10% x [$365,760 – 130,960]) ..................... | 23,480 | |
| Lease payable (difference)................................................ | 107,480 | |
| Prepaid operating expense (2008 executory costs).............. | 4,000 | |
|    Cash (rental payment) ...................................................... | | 134,960 |

#### Rhone-Metro (Lessor)

| | | |
|---|---|---|
| Cash (rental payment) ....................................................... | 134,960 | |
|    Payable (maintenance, insurance, etc.)....................... | | 4,000 |
|    Lease receivable......................................................... | | 130,960 |
| | | |
| Unearned interest revenue ............................................ | 23,480 | |
|    Interest revenue  (10% x [$365,760 – 130,960])................. | | 23,480 |

* If ownership transfers (a) by contract or (b) by the expected exercise of a bargain purchase option, the asset should be depreciated over the asset's useful life. This reflects the fact that the lessee anticipates using the leased asset for its full useful life. In this case, the equipment is expected to be useful for 6 years.

## Problem 15-10 (concluded)

### Requirement 6

**December 31, 2009**
**Western Soya Club (Lessee)**

| | | |
|---|---:|---:|
| Depreciation expense ($365,760 ÷ 6 years) ........................... | 60,960 | |
|    Accumulated depreciation........................................... | | 60,960 |
| | | |
| Interest expense (10% x $9,092: from schedule[rounded])..... | 908 | |
| Lease payable (from schedule) ........................................... | 9,092 | |
|    Cash (BPO price)................................................................ | | 10,000 |
| | | |
| Operating expense (2009 executory costs)......................... | 4,000 | |
|    Prepaid operating expense (paid in 2008)..................... | | 4,000 |
| | | |
| Prepaid operating expense (2010 executory costs)*............ | 4,000 | |
|    Cash (paid to lessor or supplier of services) ....................... | | 4,000 |
| | | |
| Equipment ........................................................................ | 365,760 | |
|    Leased equipment ....................................................... | | 365,760 |

**Rhone-Metro (Lessor)**

| | | |
|---|---:|---:|
| Cash (BPO price)................................................................ | 10,000 | |
|    Lease receivable ......................................................... | | 10,000 |
| | | |
| Unearned interest revenue ................................................ | 908 | |
|    Interest revenue (10% x $9,092: from schedule[rounded]). | | 908 |
| | | |
| Cash (if executory costs continue to be paid by lessor)............. | 4,000 | |
|    Payable (maintenance, insurance, etc.) ...................... | | 4,000 |

\* If paid to suppliers of services, the payments and this entry may occur in 2010.

# Problem 15-11

## Requirement 1

| Lessor's Calculation of Rental Payments | |
|---|---|
| Amount to be recovered (fair market value) | $659,805 |
| | |
| *Less:* Present value of the third-party-guaranteed | |
| residual value* ($150,000 x .75131*) | (112,697) |
| Amount to be recovered through periodic rental payments | $547,108 |
| | ↓ |
| Rental payments at the beginning ↓ | |
| of each of three years:    ($547,108 ÷ 2.73554**) | $200,000 |
| *  present value of $1: n=3, i=10% | |
| ** present value of an annuity due of $1: n=3, i=10% | |

Note: Since the residual value is guaranteed to the lessor, it is included in the lessor's minimum lease payments and therefore affects the 90% of fair value test.

## Requirement 2

Since [1] title to the conveyer does not transfer to the lessee, [2] there is no BPO, and [3] the lease term (3 years) is less than 75% of the estimated useful life (6 years), the critical classification criterion is [4] whether the present value of minimum lease payments exceeds 90% of the fair value of the conveyer ($659,805). The present value is influenced by the fact that the residual value is (a) relatively large and (b) guaranteed, but by a third-party, not the lessee. The residual value, if guaranteed (by the lessee or by a third party guarantor), is included in the minimum lease payments by the lessor when applying the 90% of fair value criterion and thus increases the likelihood that it is met. However, when the residual value is guaranteed by a third-party guarantor and not by the lessee, it is **not** included in the lessee's minimum lease payments. So, if a residual value is sufficiently large and guaranteed by a third-party guarantor, it may cause the 90% of fair value criterion to be met by the lessor, but not by the lessee.

### Problem 15-11 (continued)

For the lessor, the criterion is met: The present value of minimum lease payments ($659,805) is more than 90% of the fair value ($659,805 x 90% = $593,825). Also, since the fair market value exceeds the lessor's carrying value, the conveyer is being "sold" at a profit, making this a **sales-type lease:**

| | |
|---|---|
| Fair market value | $659,805 |
| *minus* | |
| Carrying value | (450,000) |
| *equals* | |
| Dealer's profit | $209,805 |

---

**Lessee's Calculation of the
Present Value of Minimum Lease Payments**

Present value of periodic rental payments[*]
($200,000 x 2.73554[**])                                    $547,108

[**] present value of an annuity due of $1: n=3, i=10%

[*] Since the residual value is not guaranteed *by the lessee*, it is excluded from the lessee's minimum lease payments and therefore does not affect the 90% of fair value test.

---

For the lessee, the criterion is not met: The present value of minimum lease payments ($547,108) is less than 90% of the fair value ($659,805 x 90% = $593,825). So, this is an **operating lease** to the lessee.

*Problem 15-11 (continued)*

## Requirement 3

### December 31, 2006

#### Poole (Lessee)

| | | |
|---|---|---|
| Prepaid rent (2006 payment; 2007 expense)......................... | 200,000 | |
| Cash (rental payment) ...................................................... | | 200,000 |

#### Allied (Lessor)

| | | |
|---|---|---|
| Lease receivable ([$200,000 x 3] + $150,000) ..................... | 750,000 | |
| Cost of goods sold (lessor's cost) ..................................... | 450,000 | |
| Sales revenue (present value of minimum lease payments). | | 659,805 |
| Unearned interest revenue ($750,000 - 659,805 ) ........... | | 90,195 |
| Inventory of equipment (lessor's cost) ......................... | | 450,000 |
| | | |
| Cash (rental payment) ....................................................... | 200,000 | |
| Lease receivable................................................................. | | 200,000 |

## Requirement 4

Since the lessee records the lease as an operating lease, interest expense is not recorded and an amortization schedule is not applicable.

**Lessor (third-party-guaranteed residual value included):**

|  | | Lease Amortization Schedule | | |
|---|---|---|---|---|
| Dec. 31 | Payments | Effective Interest 10% x Outstanding Balance | Decrease in Balance | Outstanding Balance |
| 2006 | | | | 659,805 |
| 2006 | 200,000 | | 200,000 | 459,805 |
| 2007 | 200,000 | .10 (459,805) = 45,981 | 154,019 | 305,786 |
| 2008 | 200,000 | .10 (305,786) = 30,579 | 169,421 | 136,365 |
| 2009 | 150,000 | .10 (136,365) = 13,635* | 136,365 | 0 |
| | 750,000 | 90,195 | 659,805 | |

\* rounded

**Requirement 5**

**December 31, 2007**

**Poole (Lessee)**

| | | |
|---|---|---|
| Rent expense.............................................................. | 200,000 | |
|     Prepaid rent (2006 payment; 2007 expense) ..................... | | 200,000 |

| | | |
|---|---|---|
| Prepaid rent................................................................. | 200,000 | |
|     Cash (2007 payment; 2008 expense)............................... | | 200,000 |

**Allied (Lessor)**

| | | |
|---|---|---|
| Cash (rental payment)...................................................... | 200,000 | |
|     Lease receivable ...................................................... | | 200,000 |

| | | |
|---|---|---|
| Unearned interest revenue ............................................. | 45,981 | |
|     Interest revenue  (10% x [$659,805 – 200,000]).................. | | 45,981 |

**December 31, 2008**

**Poole (Lessee)**

| | | |
|---|---|---|
| Rent expense.............................................................. | 200,000 | |
|     Prepaid rent (2007 payment; 2008 expense) ..................... | | 200,000 |

| | | |
|---|---|---|
| Prepaid rent................................................................. | 200,000 | |
|     Cash (2008 payment; 2009 expense)............................... | | 200,000 |

**Allied (Lessor)**

| | | |
|---|---|---|
| Cash (rental payment)...................................................... | 200,000 | |
|     Lease receivable ...................................................... | | 200,000 |

| | | |
|---|---|---|
| Unearned interest revenue................................................ | 30,579 | |
|     Interest revenue (10% x 305,786: from schedule)................ | | 30,579 |

*Problem 15-11 (concluded)*

**December 31, 2009**
**Poole (Lessee)**

| | | |
|---|---|---|
| Rent expense ................................................................ | 200,000 | |
| Prepaid rent (2008 payment; 2009 expense)...................... | | 200,000 |

**Allied (Lessor)**

| | | |
|---|---|---|
| Inventory of equipment (actual residual value) ................... | 105,000 | |
| Cash ($150,000 - 105,000: from 3rd party guarantor)............... | 45,000 | |
| Lease receivable (account balance) ............................... | | 150,000 |
| | | |
| Unearned interest revenue (account balance)..................... | 13,635 | |
| Interest revenue (10% x 136,365: from schedule)............... | | 13,635 |

# Problem 15-12

| | | Situation | | |
|---|---|---|---|---|
| | **1** | **2** | **3** | **4** |
| A.  The lessor's: | | | | |
| 1.  Minimum lease payments[1] | $40,000 | $44,000 | $44,000 | $40,000 |
| 2.  Gross investment in the lease[2] | 40,000 | 44,000 | 44,000 | 44,000 |
| 3.  Net investment in the lease[3] | 34,437 | 37,072 | 37,072 | 37,072 |
| 4.  Unearned interest revenue[4] | 5,563 | 6,928 | 6,928 | 6,928 |
| B.  The lessee's: | | | | |
| 5.  Minimum lease payments[5] | 40,000 | 44,000 | 40,000 | 40,000 |
| 6.  Leased asset[6] | 34,437 | 37,072 | 34,437 | 34,437 |
| 7.  Lease liability[7] | 34,437 | 37,072 | 34,437 | 34,437 |

[1] ($10,000 x number of payments) + Residual value guaranteed by lessee and/or by third party.

[2] Minimum lease payments plus unguaranteed residual value.

[3] Present value of gross investment.

[4] Gross investment - Net investment.

[5] ($10,000 x number of payments) + Residual value guaranteed by lessee.

[6] Present value of minimum lease payments; should not exceed fair market value.

[7] Present value of minimum lease payments; should not exceed fair market value.

# Problem 15-13

| | Situation | | | |
|---|---|---|---|---|
| | **1** | **2** | **3** | **4** |
| **A. The lessor's:** | | | | |
| 1. Minimum lease payments[1] | $400,000 | $553,000 | $640,000 | $510,000 |
| 2. Gross investment in the lease[2] | $430,000 | 553,000 | 675,000 | 550,000 |
| 3. Net investment in the lease[3] | 369,175 | 433,809 | 533,685 | 451,137 |
| 4. Unearned interest revenue[4] | 60,825 | 119,191 | 141,315 | 98,863 |
| 5. Sales revenue[5] | N/A | N/A | 512,816 | 423,817 |
| 6. Cost of goods sold[6] | N/A | N/A | 479,131 | 372,680 |
| 7. Dealer's profit[7] | N/A | N/A | 33,685 | 51,137 |
| **B. The lessee's:** | | | | |
| 8. Minimum lease payments[8] | $400,000 | 553,000 | 640,000 | 460,000 |
| 9. Leased asset[9] | 353,129 | 449,896 | 512,816 | 389,666 |
| 10. Lease liability[10] | 353,129 | 449,896 | 512,816 | 389,666 |

**Note:** Since executory costs are excluded from minimum lease payments, they have no effect on any of the calculated amounts.

1. ($100,000 x Number of payments) + Residual value guaranteed by lessee and/or by third party; for situation 4: ($100,000 x 4) + ($60,000 + 50,000)

2. Minimum lease payments plus unguaranteed residual value; for situation 4: ($510,000 + $40,000)

3. Present value of gross investment (discounted at lessor's rate); for situation 4: ($100,000 x 3.48685) + ($150,000 x .68301)

4. Gross investment - Net investment; for situation 4: ($550,000 - 451,137)

5. Present value of minimum lease payments; also, Net investment - Present value of unguaranteed residual value; for situation 4: ($100,000 x 3.48685) + ($110,000 x .68301); also, $451,137 - 27,320 ($40,000 x .68301)

6. Lessor's cost - Present value of unguaranteed residual value; for situation 4: ($400,000 - ($40,000 x .68301)

7. Sales revenue - cost of goods sold; also, Net investment - Lessor's cost ; for situation 4: ($423,817 - 372,680); also, ($451,137 - 400,000)

8. ($100,000 x number of payments) + Residual value guaranteed by *lessee*; for situation 4: ($100,000 x 4) + $60,000

9. Present value of minimum lease payments (discounted at lower of lessor's rate and lessee's incremental borrowing rate); should not exceed fair market value; for situation 4: ($100,000 x 3.48685) + ($60,000 x .68301)

10. Present value of minimum lease payments (discounted at lower of lessor's rate and lessee's incremental borrowing rate); should not exceed fair market value; for situation 4: ($100,000 x 3.48685) + ($60,000 x .68301)

# Problem 15-14

## Requirement 1

### Branson Construction (Lessee)

| | | |
|---|---|---|
| Interest expense (10% x [$936,500 – 100,000]) ...................... | 83,650 | |
| Lease payable (difference)................................................ | 16,350 | |
|    Cash (lease payment) ............................................... | | 100,000 |

| | | |
|---|---|---|
| Maintenance expense............................................... | 3,000 | |
|    Cash (2006 expenses as incurred) ...................................... | | 3,000 |

| | | |
|---|---|---|
| Depreciation expense ($936,500 ÷ 20 years) ......................... | 46,825 | |
|    Accumulated depreciation ......................................... | | 46,825 |

### Branif Leasing (Lessor)

| | | |
|---|---|---|
| Cash (lease payment) ............................................... | 100,000 | |
|    Lease receivable................................................... | | 100,000 |

| | | |
|---|---|---|
| Unearned interest revenue .................................... | 83,650 | |
|    Interest revenue (10% x [$936,500 – 100,000]).................... | | 83,650 |

## Requirement 2

### Branson Construction (Lessee)

| | | |
|---|---|---|
| Interest expense (10% x [$936,500 – 100,000]) ...................... | 83,650 | |
| Lease payable (difference)................................................ | 16,350 | |
| Maintenance expense (annual fee)* ...................................... | 3,000 | |
|    Cash (lease payment) ............................................... | | 103,000 |

| | | |
|---|---|---|
| Depreciation expense ($936,500 ÷ 20 years) ......................... | 46,825 | |
|    Accumulated depreciation ......................................... | | 46,825 |

* This debit to maintenance expense is the net effect of (a) expensing the current year's costs that were prepaid with the first lease payment the last day of 2005 and (b) prepaying next year's expense with the 2006 payment:

| | | |
|---|---|---|
| Maintenance expense (2006 costs) ................................................ | 3,000 | |
|    Prepaid maintenance expense (paid in 2005)........................... | | 3,000 |

| | | |
|---|---|---|
| Interest expense (10% x [$936,500 – 100,000])........................... | 83,650 | |
| Lease payable (difference).............................................. | 16,350 | |
| Prepaid maintenance expense (2007 costs) ............................... | 3,000 | |
|    Cash (lease payment) .............................................. | | 103,000 |

## Problem 15-14 (concluded)

**Branif Leasing (Lessor)**

| | | |
|---|---|---|
| Cash (lease payment).......................................................... | 103,000 | |
| Lease receivable (payment less executory costs) .............. | | 100,000 |
| Maintenance fee payable [or cash]................................ | | 3,000 |
| | | |
| Unearned interest revenue ............................................ | 83,650 | |
| Interest revenue (10% x [$936,500 – 100,000])................... | | 83,650 |

### Requirement 3

**Branson Construction (Lessee)**

| | | |
|---|---|---|
| Interest expense (10% x [$936,500 – 100,000])...................... | 83,650 | |
| Lease payable (difference) ................................................ | 16,350 | |
| Maintenance expense (annual fee)* ........................................ | 3,300 | |
| Cash (lease payment)........................................................ | | 103,300 |
| | | |
| Depreciation expense ($936,500 ÷ 20 years) ........................ | 46,825 | |
| Accumulated depreciation....................................... | | 46,825 |

* This debit to maintenance expense is the net effect of (a) expensing the current year's costs that were prepaid with the first lease payment the last day of 2005 and (b) prepaying next year's expense with the 2006 payment:

| | | |
|---|---|---|
| Maintenance expense (2006 costs) ....................................... | 3,300 | |
| Prepaid maintenance expense (paid in 2005)........................... | | 3,300 |
| | | |
| Interest expense (10% x [$936,500 – 100,000])........................... | 83,650 | |
| Lease payable (difference)................................................ | 16,350 | |
| Prepaid maintenance expense (2007 costs) ............................... | 3,300 | |
| Cash (lease payment) ................................................ | | 103,300 |

**Branif Leasing (Lessor)**

| | | |
|---|---|---|
| Cash (lease payment)........................................................ | 103,300 | |
| Maintenance fee payable [or cash]........................... | | 3,000 |
| Miscellaneous revenue................................................. | | 300 |
| Lease receivable (payment less executory costs) .............. | | 100,000 |
| | | |
| Unearned interest revenue ............................................ | 83,650 | |
| Interest revenue (10% x [$936,500 – 100,000]).................. | | 83,650 |

# Problem 15-15

## Requirement 1

**Note:**
Because exercise of the option appears at the inception of the lease to be reasonably assured, payment of the option price ($6,000) is expected to occur when the option becomes exercisable (at the end of the eighth quarter). Also, the lease contract specifies that the BPO becomes exercisable before the designated lease term ends. Since a BPO is expected to be exercised, the lease term ends for accounting purposes when the option becomes exercisable (after two years of the three-year lease term).

| | |
|---|---|
| Present value of quarterly rental payments ($3,000 x 7.23028**) | $21,691 |
| *Plus:* Present value of the BPO price ($6,000 x .78941*) | 4,736 |
| Present value of minimum lease payments | $26,427 |

> \* present value of $1: n=8, i=3%
>
> \*\* present value of an annuity due of $1: n=8, i=3%

| | |
|---|---|
| "Selling price" | $26,427 |
| *minus* | |
| Truck's cost | (25,000) |
| *equals* | |
| Dealer's profit | $ 1,427 |

## Problem 15-15 (continued)

> **Not required in the problem, but helpful to see that the present value calculation is precisely the reverse of the lessor's calculation of quarterly payments:**
>
> Amount to be recovered (fair market value)                   $26,427
>
> *Less:* Present value of the BPO price ($6,000 x .78941[*])       (4,736)
>
> Amount to be recovered through quarterly rental payments     $21,691
>
> Rental payments at the beginning
>     each of the next eight quarters:     ($21,691 ÷ 7.23028[**])     $3,000
>
>         [*]   present value of $1: n=8, i=3%
>       [**] present value of an annuity due of $1: n=8, i=3%

## Requirement 2
### September 30, 2006

#### Anything Grows (Lessee)

| | | |
|---|---|---|
| Leased equipment ........................................................ | 26,427 | |
|    Lease payable (present value of minimum lease payments) | | 26,427 |
| | | |
| Lease payable ............................................................ | 3,000 | |
|    Cash (lease payment)................................................. | | 3,000 |

#### Mid-South Auto Leasing (Lessor)

| | | |
|---|---|---|
| Lease receivable ([$3,000 x 8] + $6,000)........................... | 30,000 | |
| Cost of goods sold (lessor's cost)..................................... | 25,000 | |
|    Sales revenue (calculated above)................................... | | 26,427 |
|    Unearned interest revenue ($30,000 - 26,427)............... | | 3,573 |
|    Inventory of equipment (lessor's cost)......................... | | 25,000 |
| | | |
| Cash (lease payment)....................................................... | 3,000 | |
|    Lease receivable ....................................................... | | 3,000 |

# Problem 15-15 *(continued)*

## Requirement 3

Since both use the same discount rate, the amortization schedule for the lessee and lessor is the same:

### Lease Amortization Schedule

| Date | Payments | Effective Interest 3% x Outstanding Balance | | Decrease in Balance | Outstanding Balance |
|------|----------|------------|------|------------|------------|
| 9/30/06 | | | | | 26,427 |
| 9/30/06 | 3,000 | | | 3,000 | 23,427 |
| 12/31/06 | 3,000 | .03 (23,427) = | 703 | 2,297 | 21,130 |
| 3/31/07 | 3,000 | .03 (21,130) = | 634 | 2,366 | 18,764 |
| 6/30/07 | 3,000 | .03 (18,764) = | 563 | 2,437 | 16,327 |
| 9/30/07 | 3,000 | .03 (16,327) = | 490 | 2,510 | 13,817 |
| 12/31/07 | 3,000 | .03 (13,817) = | 415 | 2,585 | 11,232 |
| 3/31/08 | 3,000 | .03 (11,232) = | 337 | 2,663 | 8,569 |
| 6/30/08 | 3,000 | .03 (8,569) = | 257 | 2,743 | 5,826 |
| 9/29/08 | 6,000 | .03 (5,826) = | 174* | 5,826 | 0 |
| | **30,000** | | **3,573** | **26,427** | |

* adjusted for rounding of other numbers in the schedule

# Problem 15-15 (concluded)

## Requirement 4
### Anything Grows (Lessee)

| | | |
|---|---|---|
| Depreciation expense ([$26,427 ÷ 4 years*] x $\frac{1}{4}$ year).......... | 1,652 | |
|     Accumulated depreciation............................................ | | 1,652 |
| | | |
| Interest expense (3% x [$26,427 - 3,000]: from schedule) ..... | 703 | |
| Lease payable (difference : from schedule).......................... | 2,297 | |
|     Cash (lease payment)................................................ | | 3,000 |

### Mid-South Auto Leasing (Lessor)

| | | |
|---|---|---|
| Cash (lease payment)................................................ | 3,000 | |
|     Lease receivable ................................................ | | 3,000 |
| | | |
| Unearned interest revenue ............................................. | 703 | |
|     Interest revenue (3% x [$26,427 - 3,000]) .......................... | | 703 |

* Because title passes with the expected exercise of the BPO, depreciation is over the full 4-year useful life.

## Requirement 5
### Anything Grows (Lessee)

| | | |
|---|---|---|
| Depreciation expense ([$26,427 ÷ 4 years*] x $\frac{3}{4}$ year)......... | 4,955 | |
|     Accumulated depreciation............................................ | | 4,955 |
| | | |
| Interest expense (3% x $5,826 : from schedule)........................ | 174 | |
| Lease payable (difference : from schedule).......................... | 5,826 | |
|     Cash (BPO price)................................................. | | 6,000 |

### Mid-South Auto Leasing (Lessor)

| | | |
|---|---|---|
| Cash (BPO price)................................................. | 6,000 | |
|     Lease receivable (account balance)................................ | | 6,000 |
| | | |
| Unearned interest revenue (account balance) .................... | 174 | |
|     Interest revenue (3% x $5,826 : from schedule)................... | | 174 |

* Because title passes with the expected exercise of the BPO, depreciation is over the full 4-year useful life.

# Problem 15-16

## Requirement 1

Since at least one (exactly one in this case) criterion is met, this is a **capital lease** to the lessee:

---

**Lessee's Application of Classification Criteria**

**1** Does the agreement specify that ownership of the asset transfers to the lessee?                    NO

**2** Does the agreement contain a bargain purchase option?                    NO

**3** Is the lease term equal to 75% or more of the expected economic life of the asset?

YES
{4 yrs > 75% of 5 yrs}

**4** Is the present value of the minimum lease payments equal to or greater than 90% of the fair value of the asset?

NO
{$39,564[a] < 90% of $45,114 = $40,603}

[a] See schedule 1 below.

---

The lessee's incremental borrowing rate (9%) is less than the lessor's implicit rate (10%). So, calculations should be made using a 9% discount rate.

*Problem 15-16 (continued)*

**Schedule 1: Lessee's Calculation of the**
**Present Value of Minimum Lease Payments**

Present value of periodic rental payments
excluding executory costs of $1,000   ($10,000 x 3.53129[**])        $35,313

*Plus:* Present value of the lessee-guaranteed
residual value ($6,000 x .70843[*])                                     4,251

Present value of lessee's minimum lease payments                     $39,564

[*]   present value of $1: n=4, i=9%
[**]  present value of an annuity due of $1: n=4, i=9%

### Requirement 2

Present value of lessee's minimum lease payments, calculated in Schedule 1 above:      $39,564

The leased asset should not be recorded at more than its fair market value (not a factor in this case).

### Requirement 3

Since at least one (two in this case) classification criterion and both additional lessor conditions are met, this is a **nonoperating lease** to the lessor:

*Problem 15-16 (continued)*

---

### Application of Classification Criteria

**1** Does the agreement specify that
ownership of the asset transfers
to the lessee?                                           NO

**2** Does the agreement contain a
bargain purchase option?                                 NO

**3** Is the lease term equal to 75%
or more of the expected                                  YES
economic life of the asset?                   {4 yrs > 75% of 5 yrs}

**4** Is the present value of the
minimum lease payments equal
to or greater than 90% of the                            YES
fair value of the asset?         {$42,382[a] > 90% of $45,114=$40,603}

[a] See schedule 2 below.

---

### Schedule 2: Lessor's Calculation of the Present Value of Minimum Lease Payments

Present value of periodic rent payments ($10,000 x 3.48685[**])      $34,869
*Plus:* Present value of the guaranteed
    residual value ($11,000[***] x .68301[*])              7,513

Present value of lessor's minimum lease payments                     $42,382

[*]   present value of $1: n=4, i=10%
[**]  present value of an annuity due of $1: n=4, i=10%
[***] includes $6,000 guaranteed by the lessee and $5,000 guaranteed by a third-party
    guarantor

## Problem 15-16 (continued)

Since the fair market value exceeds the lessor's carrying value, the asset is being "sold" at a profit, making this a **sales-type lease**:

| | |
|---|---|
| Fair market value | $45,114 |
| *minus* | |
| Carrying value | (40,000) |
| *equals* | |
| Dealer's profit | $ 5,114 |

also:

| | |
|---|---|
| Sales revenue | $42,382 (Lessor's PV of minimum lease |
| *Minus* | payments per sch.2) |
| Cost of goods sold | (37,268) ($40,000 – [$4,000* x .68301]) |
| *equals* | |
| Dealer's profit | $ 5,114 |

\* This is the unguaranteed residual value: $15,000 – 11,000.

## Requirement 4

| **Lessor's Calculation of Lease Payments** | |
|---|---|
| Amount to be recovered (fair market value) | $45,114 |
| | |
| *Less:* Present value of the residual value ($15,000 x .68301*) | (10,245) |
| | |
| Amount to be recovered through periodic rental payments | $34,869 |
| | |
| Rent payments at the beginning | |
| of each of the next four years: ($34,869 ÷ 3.48685**) | $10,000 |
| *Plus*: Executory costs | 1,000 |
| Rental payments including executory costs | $ 11,000 |

     \* present value of $1: n=4, i=10%
   \*\* present value of an annuity due of $1: n=4, i=10%

## Problem 15-16 (continued)

### Requirement 5

Present value of lessor's minimum lease payments, calculated in Schedule 2 above:  $42,382

### Requirement 6
### December 31, 2005

**Yard Art Landscaping (Lessee)**

| | | |
|---|---|---|
| Leased equipment (calculated in requirement 1) ................. | 39,564 | |
| Lease payable (calculated requirement 1)......................... | | 39,564 |

| | | |
|---|---|---|
| Lease payable (payment less executory costs)....................... | 10,000 | |
| Prepaid maintenance expense (2006 fee)........................... | 1,000 | |
| Cash (lease payment) ....................................................... | | 11,000 |

**Branch Motors (Lessor)**

| | | |
|---|---|---|
| Lease receivable ([$10,000 x 4] + $15,000)......................... | 55,000 | |
| Cost of goods sold ($40,000 - [$4,000[a] x .68301])............... | 37,268 | |
| Sales revenue (calculated in Schedule 2)......................... | | 42,382 |
| Unearned interest revenue ($55,000 - 45,114) .............. | | 9,886 |
| Inventory of equipment (lessor's cost) ........................ | | 40,000 |

| | | |
|---|---|---|
| Cash (lease payment) ......................................................... | 11,000 | |
| Maintenance fee payable [or prepaid maintenance*]. | | 1,000 |
| Lease receivable (payment less executory costs).............. | | 10,000 |

[a] This is the unguaranteed residual value: $15,000 - 11,000.
\* If paid previously.

## Problem 15-16 *(continued)*

### Requirement 7

#### Lessee's Amortization Schedule

| Dec. 31 | Payments | Effective Interest 9% x Outstanding Balance | Decrease in Balance | Outstanding Balance |
|---|---|---|---|---|
| | | | | 39,564 |
| 2005 | 10,000 | | 10,000 | 29,564 |
| 2006 | 10,000 | .09 (29,564) = 2,661 | 7,339 | 22,225 |
| 2007 | 10,000 | .09 (22,225) = 2,000 | 8,000 | 14,225 |
| 2008 | 10,000 | .09 (14,225) = 1,280 | 8,720 | 5,505 |
| 2009 | 6,000 | .09 (5,505) = 495 | 5,505 | 0 |
| | **46,000** | **6,436** | **39,564** | |

### Requirement 8

#### Lessor's Amortization Schedule

| Dec. 31 | Payments | Effective Interest 10% x Outstanding Balance | Decrease in Balance | Outstanding Balance |
|---|---|---|---|---|
| | | | | 45,114 |
| 2005 | 10,000 | | 10,000 | 35,114 |
| 2006 | 10,000 | .10 (35,114) = 3,511 | 6,489 | 28,625 |
| 2007 | 10,000 | .10 (28,625) = 2,863 | 7,137 | 21,488 |
| 2008 | 10,000 | .10 (21,488) = 2,149 | 7,851 | 13,637 |
| 2009 | 15,000 | .10 (13,637) = 1,363* | 13,637 | 0 |
| | **55,000** | **9,886** | **45,114** | |

\* adjusted for rounding of other numbers in the schedule

*Problem 15-16 (continued)*

**Requirement 9**

**December 31, 2006**
**Yard Art Landscaping (Lessee)**

| | | |
|---|---|---|
| Maintenance expense (2006 fee)............................................ | 1,000 | |
|    Prepaid maintenance expense (paid in 2005) ................... | | 1,000 |
| | | |
| Interest expense (9% x [$39,564 – 10,000])............................ | 2,661 | |
| Lease payable (difference)...................................................... | 7,339 | |
| Prepaid maintenance expense (2007 fee)............................. | 1,000 | |
|    Cash (lease payment)................................................... | | 11,000 |
| | | |
| Depreciation expense ([$39,564 - 6,000] ÷ 4 years)............. | 8,391 | |
|    Accumulated depreciation ........................................... | | 8,391 |

**Branch Motors (Lessor)**

| | | |
|---|---|---|
| Cash (lease payment) ............................................................. | 11,000 | |
|    Maintenance fee payable [or prepaid maintenance*]. | | 1,000 |
|    Lease receivable (payment less executory costs).............. | | 10,000 |
| | | |
| Unearned interest revenue ................................................. | 3,511 | |
|    Interest revenue (10% x [$45,114 - 10,000]) ...................... | | 3,511 |

* If paid previously.

*Problem 15-16 (continued)*

**Requirement 10**

**December 31, 2008**
**Yard Art Landscaping (Lessee)**

| | | |
|---|---|---|
| Maintenance expense (2008 fee)............................................. | 1,000 | |
|     Prepaid maintenance expense (paid in 2007) ................... | | 1,000 |
| | | |
| Interest expense (9% x $14,225 – from schedule).................... | 1,280 | |
| Lease payable (difference – from schedule) .......................... | 8,720 | |
| Prepaid maintenance expense (2009 fee)............................. | 1,000 | |
|     Cash (lease payment)....................................................... | | 11,000 |
| | | |
| Depreciation expense ([$39,564 - 6,000] ÷ 4 years).............. | 8,391 | |
|     Accumulated depreciation............................................. | | 8,391 |

**Branch Motors (Lessor)**

| | | |
|---|---|---|
| Cash (lease payment)............................................................ | 11,000 | |
|     Maintenance fee payable [or prepaid maintenance*] | | 1,000 |
|     Lease receivable (payment less executory costs) .............. | | 10,000 |
| | | |
| Unearned interest revenue ................................................ | 2,149 | |
|     Interest revenue (10% x $21,488 – from schedule).............. | | 2,149 |

* If paid previously.

*Problem 15-16 (concluded)*

**Requirement 11**

**December 31, 2009**
**Yard Art Landscaping (Lessee)**

| | | |
|---|---:|---:|
| Maintenance expense (2009 fee)............................................... | 1,000 | |
|    Prepaid maintenance expense (paid in 2008) ................... | | 1,000 |
| | | |
| Depreciation expense ([$39,564 - 6,000] ÷ 4 years) .............. | 8,391 | |
|    Accumulated depreciation ............................................ | | 8,391 |
| | | |
| Interest expense (9% x $5,505 : from schedule)........................ | 495 | |
| Lease payable (difference : from schedule) .......................... | 5,505 | |
| Accumulated depreciation (account balance)....................... | 33,564 | |
| Loss on residual value guarantee ($6,000 - 4,000) ............ | 2,000 | |
|    Leased equipment (account balance) .............................. | | 39,564 |
|    Cash ($6,000 - 4,000) ...................................................... | | 2,000 |

**Branch Motors (Lessor)**

| | | |
|---|---:|---:|
| Inventory of equipment (actual residual value) ................... | 4,000 | |
| Cash ($11,000 - $4,000)............................................................ | 7,000* | |
| Loss on leased assets ($15,000 - $11,000)........................... | 4,000 | |
|    Lease receivable (account balance) ............................... | | 15,000 |
| | | |
| Unearned interest revenue (account balance)...................... | 1,363 | |
|    Interest revenue (10% x $13,637 : from schedule)............... | | 1,363 |

\* $2,000 from lessee and $5,000 from third-party guarantor

# Problem 15-17

## Requirement 1

### Application of Classification Criteria

**1** Does the agreement specify that ownership of the asset transfers to the lessee?  NO

**2** Does the agreement contain a bargain purchase option?  NO

**3** Is the lease term equal to 75% or more of the expected economic life of the asset?  YES
{8 yrs > 75% of 8 yrs}

**4** Is the present value of the minimum lease payments equal to or greater than 90% of the fair value of the asset?  YES
{$645,526[a] > 90% of $645,526}

[a] See calculation below.

The lessee's incremental borrowing rate (11%) is more than the lessor's implicit rate (10%). So, both parties' calculations should be made using a 10% discount rate:

Present value of minimum lease payments ($110,000 x 5.86842[**])   $645,526

[**] present value of an annuity due of $1: n=8, i=10%

## Problem 15-17 (continued)

**(a)** Since at least one (two in this case) classification criterion and both additional lessor conditions are met, this is a **nonoperating lease** to the lessor (Bidwell Leasing). Since the fair market value is the lessor's cost, there is no dealer's profit, making this a **direct financing lease**:

**(b)** Since at least one (two in this case) criterion is met, this is a **capital lease** to the lessee. Red Baron records the present value of minimum lease payments as a leased asset and a lease liability.


## Requirement 2

### December 31, 2005

**Red Baron Flying Club (Lessee)**

| | | |
|---|---|---|
| Leased equipment (calculated above)................................. | 645,526 | |
| Lease payable (calculated above)................................... | | 645,526 |
| | | |
| Lease payable................................................................ | 110,000 | |
| Cash (lease payment) .................................................... | | 110,000 |

**Bidwell Leasing (Lessor)**

| | | |
|---|---|---|
| Lease receivable ($110,000 x 8) ...................................... | 880,000 | |
| Unearned interest revenue ($880,000 - 645,526)............ | | 234,474 |
| Inventory of equipment (lessor's cost) .......................... | | 645,526 |
| | | |
| Unearned interest revenue ............................................. | 18,099 | |
| Cash (initial direct costs)............................................... | | 18,099 |
| | | |
| Cash (lease payment) ..................................................... | 110,000 | |
| Lease receivable............................................................ | | 110,000 |

# Problem 15-17 (continued)

## Requirement 3

### Lease Amortization Schedule

| Dec. 31 | Payments | Effective Interest 10% x Outstanding Balance | Decrease in Balance | Outstanding Balance |
|---|---|---|---|---|
| | | | | 645,526 |
| 2005 | 110,000 | | 110,000 | 535,526 |
| 2006 | 110,000 | .10 (535,526) = 53,553 | 56,447 | 479,079 |
| 2007 | 110,000 | .10 (479,079) = 47,908 | 62,092 | 416,987 |
| 2008 | 110,000 | .10 (416,987) = 41,699 | 68,301 | 348,686 |
| 2009 | 110,000 | .10 (348,686) = 34,869 | 75,131 | 273,555 |
| 2010 | 110,000 | .10 (273,555 = 27,356 | 82,644 | 190,911 |
| 2011 | 110,000 | .10 (190,911) = 19,089* | 90,911 | 100,000 |
| 2012 | 110,000 | .10 (100,000) = 10,000 | 100,000 | 0 |
| | **880,000** | | 234,474 | 645,526 |

\* adjusted for rounding of other numbers in the schedule

## Requirement 4

With the initial direct costs, the rental payments are the same, but the net investment is higher: $645,526 + 18,099 = $663,625. The new effective rate is the discount rate that equates the net investment and the future lease payments:

$$\$663,625 \div \mathbf{?}^{**} = \$110,000$$

lessor's investment          lease payments

** present value of an annuity due of $1: n=8, i=**?**

Rearranging algebraically we find that the present value table value is $663,625 ÷ $110,000 = 6.03295. When you consult the present value table, you search row 8 (n=8) for this value and find it in the 9% column. So the effective interest rate has declined from 10% to 9%.

The net investment is amortized at the 9% rate.

# Problem 15-17 (continued)

## Requirement 5

### Lease Amortization Schedule

| Dec. 31 | Payments | Effective Interest 9% x Outstanding Balance | Decrease in Balance | Outstanding Balance |
|---|---|---|---|---|
| | | | | 663,625 |
| 2005 | 110,000 | | 110,000 | 553,625 |
| 2006 | 110,000 | .09 (553,625) = 49,826 | 60,174 | 493,451 |
| 2007 | 110,000 | .09 (493,451) = 44,411 | 65,589 | 427,862 |
| 2008 | 110,000 | .09 (427,862) = 38,508 | 71,492 | 356,370 |
| 2009 | 110,000 | .09 (356,370) = 32,073 | 77,927 | 278,443 |
| 2010 | 110,000 | .09 (278,443) = 25,060 | 84,940 | 193,503 |
| 2011 | 110,000 | .09 (193,503) = 17,415 | 92,585 | 100,918 |
| 2012 | 110,000 | .09 (100,918) = 9,082* | 100,918 | 0 |
| | **880,000** | **216,375** | **663,625** | |

\* adjusted for rounding of other numbers in the schedule

*Problem 15-17 (concluded)*

## Requirement 6

### December 31, 2006
### Red Baron Flying Club (Lessee)

| | | |
|---|---|---|
| Interest expense (10% x [$645,526 – 110,000]) | 53,553 | |
| Lease payable (difference) | 56,447 | |
|    Cash (lease payment) | | 110,000 |
| | | |
| Depreciation expense ($645,526 ÷ 8 years) | 80,691 | |
|    Accumulated depreciation | | 80,691 |

### Bidwell Leasing (Lessor)

| | | |
|---|---|---|
| Cash (lease payment) | 110,000 | |
|    Lease receivable | | 110,000 |
| | | |
| Unearned interest revenue | 49,826 | |
|    Interest revenue (9% x [$663,625 - 110,000]) | | 49,826 |

## Requirement 7

### December 31, 2012
### Red Baron Flying Club (Lessee)

| | | |
|---|---|---|
| Interest expense (10% x $100,000 : from schedule) | 10,000 | |
| Lease payable (difference) | 100,000 | |
|    Cash (lease payment) | | 110,000 |
| | | |
| Depreciation expense ($645,526 ÷ 8 years) | 80,691 | |
|    Accumulated depreciation | | 80,691 |

### Bidwell Leasing (Lessor)

| | | |
|---|---|---|
| Cash (lease payment) | 110,000 | |
|    Lease receivable | | 110,000 |
| | | |
| Unearned interest revenue | 9,082 | |
|    Interest revenue (9% x $100,918 : from schedule) | | 9,082 |

# Problem 15-18

**Requirement 1**

---

## Application of Classification Criteria

**1** Does the agreement specify that ownership of the asset transfers to the lessee?                    NO

**2** Does the agreement contain a bargain purchase option?                    NO

**3** Is the lease term equal to 75% or more of the expected economic life of the asset?
                    YES
                    {8 yrs > 75% of 8 yrs}

**4** Is the present value of the minimum lease payments equal to or greater than 90% of the fair value of the asset?
                    YES
                    {$645,526[a] > 90% of $645,526}

[a] See calculation below.

---

The lessee's incremental borrowing rate (11%) is more than the lessor's implicit rate (10%). So, both parties' calculations should be made using a 10% discount rate:

---

Present value of minimum lease
payments ($110,000 x 5.86842[**])                    $645,526

[**] present value of an annuity due of $1: n=8, i=10%

---

## Problem 15-18 (continued)

**(a)** Since at least one (two in this case) classification criterion and both additional lessor conditions are met, this is a **nonoperating lease** to the lessor (Bidwell Leasing).

Since the fair market value exceeds the lessor's carrying value, the plane was "sold" at a profit, making this a **sales-type lease**:

| | |
|---|---|
| Fair market value | $645,526 |
| *minus* | |
| Carrying value | (400,000) |
| *equals* | |
| Dealer's profit | $ 245,526 |

**(b)** Since at least one (two in this case) criterion is met, this is a **capital lease** to the lessee. Red Baron records the present value of minimum lease payments as a leased asset and a lease liability.

### Requirement 2

**December 31, 2005**

**Red Baron Flying Club (Lessee)**

| | | |
|---|---|---|
| Leased equipment (calculated above)................................ | 645,526 | |
|     Lease payable (calculated above) .................................... | | 645,526 |
| | | |
| Lease payable ................................................................... | 110,000 | |
|     Cash (lease payment)........................................................ | | 110,000 |

**Bidwell Leasing (Lessor)**

| | | |
|---|---|---|
| Lease receivable ($110,000 x 8)....................................... | 880,000 | |
| Cost of goods sold............................................................ | 400,000 | |
|     Sales revenue (calculated above)..................................... | | 645,526 |
|     Unearned interest revenue ($880,000 - 645,526) ........... | | 234,474 |
|     Inventory of equipment (lessor's cost).......................... | | 400,000 |
| | | |
| Selling expense................................................................. | 18,099 | |
|     Cash (initial direct costs) ................................................ | | 18,099 |
| | | |
| Cash (lease payment)......................................................... | 110,000 | |
|     Lease receivable ............................................................. | | 110,000 |

**Lease Amortization Schedule**

| Dec. 31 | Payments | Effective Interest 10% x Outstanding Balance | Decrease in Balance | Outstanding Balance |
|---|---|---|---|---|
| | | | | 645,526 |
| 2005 | 110,000 | | 110,000 | 535,526 |
| 2006 | 110,000 | .10 (535,526) = 53,553 | 56,447 | 479,079 |
| 2007 | 110,000 | .10 (479,079) = 47,908 | 62,092 | 416,987 |
| 2008 | 110,000 | .10 (416,987) = 41,699 | 68,301 | 348,686 |
| 2009 | 110,000 | .10 (348,686) = 34,869 | 75,131 | 273,555 |
| 2010 | 110,000 | .10 (273,555) = 27,356 | 82,644 | 190,911 |
| 2011 | 110,000 | .10 (190,911) = 19,089* | 90,911 | 100,000 |
| 2012 | 110,000 | .10 (100,000) = 10,000 | 100,000 | 0 |
| | **880,000** | **234,474** | **645,526** | |

\* adjusted for rounding of other numbers in the schedule

**Requirement 4**

**December 31, 2006**
**Red Baron Flying Club (Lessee)**

| | | |
|---|---|---|
| Interest expense (10% x [$645,526 – 110,000]) | 53,553 | |
| Lease payable (difference) | 56,447 | |
| Cash (lease payment) | | 110,000 |

| | | |
|---|---|---|
| Depreciation expense ($645,526 ÷ 8 years) | 80,691 | |
| Accumulated depreciation | | 80,691 |

**Bidwell Leasing (Lessor)**

| | | |
|---|---|---|
| Cash (lease payment) | 110,000 | |
| Lease receivable | | 110,000 |

| | | |
|---|---|---|
| Unearned interest revenue | 53,553 | |
| Interest revenue (10% x [$645,526 – 110,000]) | | 53,553 |

*Problem 15-18 (concluded)*

**Requirement 5**

**December 31, 2012**
**Red Baron Flying Club (Lessee)**

| | | |
|---|---:|---:|
| Interest expense (10% x $100,000 : from schedule)................. | 10,000 | |
| Lease payable (difference) ................................................. | 100,000 | |
|    Cash (lease payment)......................................................... | | 110,000 |
| | | |
| Depreciation expense ($645,526 ÷ 8 years)........................ | 80,691 | |
|    Accumulated depreciation........................................... | | 80,691 |

**Bidwell Leasing (Lessor)**

| | | |
|---|---:|---:|
| Cash (lease payment)......................................................... | 110,000 | |
|    Lease receivable ........................................................ | | 110,000 |
| | | |
| Unearned interest revenue ............................................... | 10,000 | |
|    Interest revenue (10% x $100,000 : from schedule)............. | | 10,000 |

# Problem 15-19

## Requirement 1

Present value of periodic rental payments
        ($88,492 x 5.65022**)             $\underline{500,000}$*

    *  rounded

    ** present value of an ordinary annuity of $1: n=10, i=12%

### January 1, 2006

| | | |
|---|---:|---:|
| Cash ................................................................... | 500,000 | |
| Accumulated depreciation (cost - carrying amount) ............ | 600,000 | |
|    Buildings (original cost)................................................ | | 1,000,000 |
|    Deferred gain on sale-leaseback (difference)................ | | 100,000 |
| | | |
| Leased building (present value of lease payments)................... | 500,000 | |
|    Lease payable (present value of lease payments)............... | | 500,000 |

Note: Because the title transfers to the lessee, this is a capital lease.

### December 31, 2006

| | | |
|---|---:|---:|
| Interest expense (12% x $500,000)......................................... | 60,000 | |
| Lease payable (difference).................................................. | 28,492 | |
|    Cash (rental payment) ........................................................ | | 88,492 |
| | | |
| Depreciation expense ($500,000 ÷ 12 years*)..................... | 41,667 | |
|    Accumulated depreciation ............................................. | | 41,667 |
| | | |
| Deferred gain on sale-leaseback ($100,000 ÷ 12 years*)..... | 8,333 | |
|    Depreciation expense ................................................... | | 8,333 |

* The building is depreciated over its remaining useful life rather than the lease term because title transfers to the lessee. The remaining useful life can be calculated as:

total life x $^{carrying\ amount}/_{cost}$ = 30 years x $^{\$400,000}/_{\$1,000,000}$ = 12 years

## Problem 15-19 (continued)

### Requirement 2

**BALANCE SHEET**

**Assets:**

| | |
|---|---|
| Leased asset............................................................. | $500,000 |
| *less*: accumulated depreciation............................ | (41,667) |
| *less*: deferred gain ($100,000 - 8,333).................... | (91,667) |
| | $366,666 |

**Liabilities:**
*Current:*

| | |
|---|---|
| Lease payable ($88,492 - {12% x [$500,000 - 28,492]}) | $31,911 |

*Noncurrent:*

| | |
|---|---|
| Lease payable ($500,000 - 28,492 - 31,911) .............. | $439,597 |

**INCOME STATEMENT**

| | |
|---|---|
| Interest expense.................................................... | $60,000 |
| Depreciation expense ($41,667 - 8,333) .................. | 33,334 |
| | $93,334 |

**Portion of Amortization Schedule – not required, but verifies several amounts:**

### Lease Amortization Schedule

| Date | Payments | Effective Interest 12% x Outstanding Balance | Decrease in Balance | Outstanding Balance |
|---|---|---|---|---|
| 1/1/06 | | | | 500,000 |
| 12/31/06 | 88,492 | .12 (500,000) = 60,000 | 28,492 | 471,508 |
| 12/31/07 | 88,492 | .12 (471,508) = 56,581 | **31,911** | **439,597** |
| | ~ | ~  ~ | ~ | ~ |
| | ~ | ~  ~ | ~ | ~ |

# Problem 15-20

## Requirement 1

Since the fair value of the land ($400,000) is more than 25% of the combined fair value ($1,450,000), both the lessee and the lessor treat the land and building as two separate leases. The land lease is an operating lease, and the building lease is, in this case, a capital lease. Since land could be rented without the building for $59,000, the portion of the annual rental attributable to the building is $200,000 - 59,000 = $141,000.

---

Present value of lease payments ($141,000 x 6.75902[**])     $953,022

      [**] present value of an annuity due of $1: n=10, i=10%

---

**January 1, 2006**

| | | |
|---|---:|---:|
| Leased building (calculated above) ................................... | 953,022 | |
|    Lease liability (calculated above) ................................... | | 953,022 |
| | | |
| Rent expense (given) ........................................................ | 59,000 | |
| Lease liability (difference)............................................... | 141,000 | |
|    Cash (annual rental)........................................................ | | 200,000 |

**December 31, 2006**

| | | |
|---|---:|---:|
| Depreciation expense ($953,022 ÷ 10 years) ......................... | 95,302 | |
|    Accumulated depreciation – leased building ............. | | 95,302 |
| | | |
| Interest expense ([$953,022 - 141,000] x 10%)....................... | 81,202 | |
|    Interest payable ............................................................ | | 81,202 |

## Problem 15-20 (continued)

### Requirement 2

Since the fair value of the land ($200,000) is less than 25% of the combined fair value ($1,450,000), it is in effect ignored and the land and building are treated as a single unit. The "single" leased asset is depreciated as if land were not involved.

---

Present value of lease payments ($200,000 x 6.75902**)   $1,351,804

** present value of an annuity due of $1: n=10, i=10%

---

**January 1, 2006**

| | | |
|---|---|---|
| Leased property (calculated above) | 1,351,804 | |
|     Lease liability (calculated above) | | 1,351,804 |
| | | |
| Lease liability | 200,000 | |
|     Cash (annual rental) | | 200,000 |

**December 31, 2006**

| | | |
|---|---|---|
| Depreciation expense ($1,351,804 ÷ 10 years) | 135,180 | |
|     Accumulated depreciation – leased property | | 135,180 |
| | | |
| Interest expense ([$1,351,804 - 200,000] x 10%) | 115,180 | |
|     Interest payable | | 115,180 |

# CASES
## Analysis Case 15-1

1. When FedEx's management says some leases "qualify as off-balance-sheet" financing, it is referring to the fact that when assets are acquired under operating leases, accounting standards do not require the lessee to record a liability as would be the case under a capital lease. Thus the financing escapes the balance sheet. Most of FedEx's leases do not meet any of the four classification criteria that would cause the lease to be capitalized.

2. Note 7: "Lease Commitments" indicates that:

   At May 31, 2004, the present value of net minimum lease payments for capital lease obligations was $534,000,000.

3. If the operating leases were capitalized, the capital lease liability would increase by approximately a multiple of 23. Note 7 below indicates that future minimum lease payments under non-cancelable operating leases are about 23 times higher than for capital leases (15,016 / 639). Assuming comparable discount rates and timing of payments, the present value of future minimum lease payments for operating leases would be about: $534,000,000 x 23 = $12,282 million. Of course, we could also make some reasonable assumptions about discount rates and the timing of payments and estimate the present value of all future payments to be made on the operating leases as we did in the "Decision-Makers' Perspective" section at the end of the chapter. Results should be comparable. In either case, we have a rough estimate.

---

**Note 7: Lease Commitments (in part)**

A summary of future minimum lease payments under capital leases and non- cancelable operating leases (principally aircraft, retail locations, and facilities) with an initial or remaining term in excess of one year at May 31, 2004, is as follows ($ in millions):

|  | Capital Leases | Operating Leases |
|---|---|---|
| 2005 | $ 160 | $1,707 |
| 2006 | 122 | 1,555 |
| 2007 | 22 | 1,436 |
| 2008 | 99 | 1,329 |
| 2009 | 11 | 1,169 |
| Thereafter | 225 | 7,820 |
|  | $639 | $15,016 |
| Less amount representing interest | 105 |  |
| Present value of net minimum lease payments | $534 |  |

---

## Case 15-1 (concluded)

4. In general, debt increases risk. Debt places owners in a subordinate position relative to creditors because the claims of creditors must be satisfied first in case of liquidation. Also, debt requires payment, usually on specific dates, and failure to pay interest and principal may result in default and perhaps even bankruptcy. The debt-to-equity ratio, total liabilities/shareholders' equity, frequently is calculated to measure the degree of risk. Other things being equal, the higher the ratio, the higher the risk. The debt-equity ratio for FedEx is:

$$[\$19,134 - 8,036] \div \$8,036 = \underline{1.38}$$

If debt is increased by $12,282 million from capitalizing operating leases, the debt to equity ratio more than doubles:

$$([\$19,134 - 8,036] + 12,282) \div \$8,036 = \underline{2.91}$$

As shown in the chapter, adding the assets from capitalizing operating leases also causes the return on assets to decline. Analysts and management should be alert to the off-balance-sheet effect of operating leases. Remember, though, debt also can be an advantage. Debt can be used to enhance the return to shareholders. If a company earns a return on borrowed funds in excess of the cost of borrowing the funds, shareholders are provided with a total return greater than what could have been earned with equity funds alone. This desirable situation is called "favorable financial leverage."

# Research Case 15-2

## Requirement 1

After the first full year under the warehouse lease, the balance in Dowell's lease liability is $30,816,422. This is the balance after reductions from the first five quarterly lease payments as shown in this amortization schedule. (The first payment was at December 31 of the previous year, the inception of the lease.)

### Lease Amortization Schedule

| Payments | Effective Interest 10% x Outstanding Balance | | | Decrease in Balance | Outstanding Balance |
|---|---|---|---|---|---|
| | | | | | 40,000,000 |
| 2,398,303 | | | | 2,398,303 | 37,601,697 |
| 2,398,303 | .02 (37,601,697) | = | 752,034 | 1,646,269 | 35,955,428 |
| 2,398,303 | .02 (35,955,428) | = | 719,109 | 1,679,194 | 34,276,234 |
| 2,398,303 | .02 (34,276,234) | = | 685,525 | 1,712,778 | 32,563,456 |
| 2,398,303 | .02 (32,563,456) | = | 651,269 | 1,747,034 | **30,816,422** |
| 2,398,303 | .02 (30,816,422) | = | 616,328 | 1,781,975 | 29,034,448 |
| 2,398,303 | .02 (29,034,448) | = | 580,689 | 1,817,614 | 27,216,835 |
| 2,398,303 | .02 (27,216,835) | = | 544,337 | 1,853,966 | 25,362,869 |
| 2,398,303 | .02 (25,362,869) | = | 507,257 | 1,891,046 | 23,471,823 |
| 2,398,303 | .02 (23,471,823) | = | 469,436 | 1,928,867 | 21,542,957 |
| 2,398,303 | .02 (21,542,957) | = | 430,859 | 1,967,444 | 19,575,514 |
| 2,398,303 | .02 (19,575,514) | = | 391,510 | 2,006,793 | 17,568,722 |
| 2,398,303 | .02 (17,568,722) | = | 351,374 | 2,046,929 | 15,521,794 |
| 2,398,303 | .02 (15,521,794) | = | 310,436 | 2,087,867 | 13,433,927 |
| 2,398,303 | .02 (13,433,927) | = | 268,679 | 2,129,624 | 11,304,303 |
| 2,398,303 | .02 (11,304,303) | = | 226,086 | 2,172,217 | 9,132,086 |
| 2,398,303 | .02 (9,132,086) | = | 182,642 | 2,215,661 | 6,916,425 |
| 2,398,303 | .02 (6,916,425) | = | 138,328 | 2,259,975 | 4,656,450 |
| 2,398,303 | .02 (4,656,450) | = | 93,129 | 2,305,174 | 2,351,276 |
| 2,398,303 | .02 (2,351,276) | = | 47,027* | 2,351,276 | 0 |

* rounded

## Case 15-2 (continued)

### Requirement 2

After the first full year under the warehouse lease, the carrying amount (after accumulated depreciation) of Dowell's leased warehouses is 32,000,000:

| | |
|---|---|
| $40,000,000 | Leased warehouses, PV of lease payments |
| ÷     5 years | Life of lease |
| $ 8,000,000 | Accumulated depreciation after one year |

| | |
|---|---|
| $40,000,000 | Leased warehouses, PV of lease payments |
| (8,000,000) | Accumulated depreciation after one year |
| $32,000,000 | Carrying amount after one year |

### Requirement 3

The appropriate accounting treatment for the proposed sublease is specified in SFAS 13 "Accounting for Leases." Accounting and Reporting for Subleases and Similar Transactions is described in paragraphs 35-40. Dowell's proposed sublease fits the description of Par. 35(b):

35.  This section deals with the following types of leasing transactions:

    a.  The leased property is re-leased by the original lessee to a third party, and the lease agreement between the two original parties remains in effect (a sublease).

    b.  A new lessee is substituted under the original lease agreement. The new lessee becomes the primary obligor under the agreement, and the original lessee may or may not be secondarily liable.

    c.  A new lessee is substituted through a new agreement, with cancellation of the original lease agreement.

## Case 15-2 (continued)

Because Dowell's proposed sublease fits the description of 35.b, accounting for it is described in Par. 38(a):

38. If the nature of the transaction is such that the original lessee is relieved of the primary obligation under the original lease, as would be the case in transactions of the type described in paragraphs 35(b) and 35(c), the termination of the original lease agreement shall be accounted for as follows:

a. If the original lease was a capital lease, the asset and obligation representing the original lease shall be removed from the accounts, gain or loss shall be recognized for the difference, and, if the original lessee is secondarily liable, the loss contingency shall be treated as provided by FASB Statement No. 5, "Accounting for Contingencies." Any consideration paid or received upon termination shall be included in the determination of gain or loss to be recognized.

b. If the original lease was an operating lease and the original lessee is secondarily liable, the loss contingency shall be treated as provided by FASB Statement No. 5.

## Requirement 4

In accordance with 38(a), the asset and obligation representing the original lease would be removed from the accounts and a loss would be recognized for the difference. The journal entry would Dowell record in connection with the sublease is:

| | | |
|---|---|---|
| Lease payable (balance after 4 quarters; from req. 1) .. | 30,816,422 | |
| Loss on sublease (to balance) ................................ | 1,183,578 | |
| Accumulated depreciation (balance: from req. 2) .... | 8,000,000 | |
|     Leased warehouses (balance: PV of lease payments) | | 40,000,000 |

*Case 15-2 (concluded)*

**Requirement 5**

In accordance with 38(a), because Dowell, the original lessee, is secondarily liable, the loss contingency would be treated as provided by FASB Statement No. 5, "Accounting for Contingencies." Recall from Chapter 13 that a loss contingency is accrued as a liability only if (a) it is probable a loss will occur and (b) the amount can be reasonably estimated. Because it would not be probable, no accrual is required, but because it would be reasonably possible that American Tankers would default and Dowell would be required to fulfill those obligations, disclosure of the contingency would be required in the notes to the financial statements throughout the term of the sublease.

# Communication Case 15-3

First, this case has no single right answer. The process of developing the proposed solutions will likely be more beneficial than the solutions themselves. Students should benefit from participating in the process, interacting first with other group members, then with the class as a whole.

It is important that each student actively participate in the process. Domination by one or two individuals should be discouraged. Discussion likely will include the following:

a. **Possible advantages of leasing include:**
1. Leasing can preserve the ability to borrow under lines of credit.
2. Leasing can provide an interest rate lower than the incremental borrowing rate.
3. Leasing may avoid violating restrictive loan agreements that prohibit the issuance of additional debt securities.
4. Leasing can lessen the risk of obsolescence.
5. Leasing allows 100% financing at fixed interest rates as compared with 70% to 90% financing when assets are purchased.

b. **The lessee views a noncancelable lease as a capital lease if it meets at least one of the following criteria.**
1. The lease transfers ownership of the property to the lessee at the end of the lease term.
2. The lease contains a bargain purchase option.
3. The lease term is equal to 75% or more of the estimated economic life of the leased property.
4. The present value of the minimum lease payments, excluding executory costs, equals or exceeds 90% of the fair value of the leased property.

1. and 3. are not met. 2. and 4. are met – if the purchase option is viewed as a *bargain* purchase option. Is $290,000 enough less than $300,000 that exercise of the option is expected to occur? If so:

2. The right to purchase the vans at the end of the lease term for $290,000, when the estimated fair market value is $300,000, is a bargain purchase option.

4. The present value of the minimum lease payments, not including the executory costs, is greater than 90% of the fair market value of the vans, calculated as follows:

**Present value of minimum lease payments, assuming a BPO:**

| | |
|---|---|
| Lease payments ($300,000 x 3.48685) | $1,046,055 |
| Bargain purchase price ($290,000 x 0.68301) | 198,073 |
| Total | $1,244,128 |

In this case, it is a *capital lease.*

Otherwise:

**Present value of minimum lease payments, assuming the purchase option is not a BPO:**

Lease payments ($300,000 x 3.48685)     $1,046,055

| | |
|---|---|
| Fair value of vans | $1,240,000 |
| | x 90% |
| 90% of the fair value of the vans | $1,116,000 |

In this case, it is an *operating lease* to the **lessee.**
Either way, it is a *nonoperating lease* to the **lessor:**

**Present value of minimum lease payments, assuming a BPO:**

| | |
|---|---|
| Lease payments ($300,000 x 3.48685) | $1,046,055 |
| Bargain purchase price ($290,000 x 0.68301) | 198,073 |
| Total | $1,244,128 |

**Present value of minimum lease payments, assuming the purchase option is not a BPO:**

| | |
|---|---|
| Lease payments ($300,000 x 3.48685) | $1,046,055 |
| Residual value ($300,000 x 0.68301) | 204,903 |
| Total | $1,250,958 |

Since Interstate's cost, $1,050,000, was less than its "selling price," this is a sales-type lease to Interstate.

## Case 15-3 (concluded)

**c. VIP would record the following at December 31, 2006:**

| | | |
|---|---:|---:|
| Interest expense ([$1,100,000 - 300,000] x 10%)..................... | 80,000 | |
| Lease liability................................................................ | 220,000 | |
| Cash.......................................................................... | | 300,000 |
| | | |
| Operating expenses........................................................ | 1,000 | |
| Cash.......................................................................... | | 1,000 |

*If a BPO is assumed, VIP would have the vans for 7 years:*

| | | |
|---|---:|---:|
| Depreciation expense ([$1,100,000 - 50,000]÷ 7 yrs.) | 150,000 | |
| Accumulated depreciation ......................................... | | 150,000 |

*If a BPO is not assumed, VIP would have the vans for 4 years:*

| | | |
|---|---:|---:|
| Depreciation expense ([$1,100,000 - 300,000]÷ 4 yrs.) | 200,000 | |
| Accumulated depreciation ......................................... | | 200,000 |

# International Case 15-4

The basic objective of accounting for leases is the same in both countries. Leases that transfer to the lessee substantially all risks and rewards of ownership are distinguished from operating leases. In the U.K. these are referred to as finance leases; in the U.S.A., these are termed capital leases. By either name, the present value of underlying lease payments is recorded as both an asset and a liability. Rental expense under operating leases is charged against income as incurred.

Although the fundamental accounting approach is the same, disclosures differ, particularly the extensiveness of disclosures. In the U.S.A., virtually all aspects of leases must be disclosed. Required disclosures are specific to the type of lease and include:

**FOR CAPITAL LEASES:**
A. Gross amount of leased **property under capital leases** as of the date of each balance sheet (by major classes according to nature or function).
B. Future **minimum lease payments** as of the date of the latest balance sheet presented – in the *aggregate* and for each of the *5 succeeding fiscal years*, with separate deductions for the:
   1. amount representing *executory costs* (including any profit),
   2. amount representing *interest* (called finance charges by BP).
C. **Minimum sublease rentals** to be received under noncancelable subleases.
D. **Contingent rentals** actually incurred.

**FOR OPERATING LEASES**
A. **Rental expense** with separate amounts for minimum rentals, contingent rentals, and sublease rentals.
B. Future **minimum rental payments** as of the date of the latest balance sheet presented – in the *aggregate* and for each of the *5 succeeding fiscal years*.
C. **Minimum sublease rentals** to be received under noncancelable subleases.

Some of this information is provided by BP's disclosures, but a U.S. company's disclosures typically would be more extensive.

# Judgment Case 15-5

## Requirement 1

($ in millions)

| Fiscal years | Operating leases | PV factor 12% | Present value |
|---|---|---|---|
| 2005 | $ 1,066 | .893 | $   952 |
| 2006 | 999 | .797 | 796 |
| 2007 | 982 | .712 | 699 |
| 2008 | 931 | .636 | 592 |
| 2009 | 838 | .567 | 475 |
| 2010 and subsequent | 7,525 | .322* | 2,423 |
| Total minimum rentals | $12,341 | | $5,937 |

*   This is the PV factor for i=12%, n=10, which treats payments after 2009 as occurring in 2014, 5 years after 2009, the midpoint of the 9 years after 2009.

      or:

An alternative (more accurate, but more difficult) way to estimate the present value of the payments *beyond 2009* is: to view them as a deferred annuity:

    $836 ($7,525/9)    x   5.328**  =    $4,454

    $4,454            x   .567*** =   $2,525

**   present value of an ordinary annuity of $1, i=12%, n=9

***  present value of $1, i=12%, n=5 (2005-2009)

## Requirement 2

If capitalized, these operating lease commitments would add $5,937 million to American's liabilities.   The impact this on the percentage of the company's debt comprising lease liabilities would be to increase the percentage from 4.6% to 22.5%:

**Without capitalization:**    $1,165 / $25,567 = 4.6%

**With capitalization:**       ($1,165 + $5,937) / ($25,567 + $5,937) = 22.5%

# Real World Case 15-6

## Requirement 1

Leasing can allow a firm to conserve assets, to avoid some risks of owning assets, and obtain favorable tax benefits. Also, leasing sometimes is used as a means of "off-balance-sheet financing." When funds are borrowed to purchase an asset, the liability has a detrimental effect on the company's debt-equity ratio and other mechanical indicators of riskiness. Also, the purchased asset increases total assets and thus reduces calculations of the rate of return on assets. In spite of research that indicates the market is not fooled, managers continue to avoid reporting of assets and liabilities by leasing rather than buying and by constructing lease agreements in such a way that capitalizing the assets and liabilities is not required. Whether or not there is any real effect on security prices, off-balance-sheet financing can help a firm avoid exceeding contractual limits on designated financial ratios (like the debt to equity ratio, for instance). In fact, in its annual report, Safeway indicates that they have several restrictive covenants, one of which relates to the debt to equity ratio.

## Requirement 2

When capital leases are first recorded, both assets and liabilities increase by the present value of minimum lease payments. In later years, though, the amounts differ. Leased assets are reduced by depreciation. Lease liabilities are reduced by the principal portion of lease payments.

## Requirement 3

|  | ($ in millions) |
|---|---|
| Interest expense (difference)........................ | 69.2 |
| Lease payable (current obligation - given).. | 42.8 |
| Cash (rental payment - given)................. | 112.0 |

## Requirement 4

| $758.1 | Property under capital lease, beg. of 2004 |
|---|---|
| ÷ $ 49.3 | 2004 amortization (230.9 – 181.6) |
| 15.4 | |

Approximate average life of capital leases = <u>15.4 years</u>

*Case 15-6 (concluded)*

**Requirement 5**

| | |
|---|---|
| $ 69.2 | 2005 interest (from requirement 3) |
| ÷  718.8 | Beginning balance in lease liability – given: $50.5 + 668.3 |
| 9.6 % | |

Approximate average interest rate = <u>9.6%</u>

# Ethics Case 15-7

Discussion should include these elements:

## Leasehold improvement depreciation period
There may be some degree of latitude associated with uncertainty concerning the life of the leasehold improvements. However, trade publications indicate 25 years probably is out of range. The suggestion to use 25 years clearly is motivated by the desire to "window dress" performance.

## Ethical Dilemma:

How does a doubtful justification for the estimated life of leasehold improvements compare with the perceived need to increase reported profits?

## Who is affected?:
Person
Keene
Other managers
Shareholders
Potential shareholders
Employees
Creditors
The company's auditors

# Research Case 15-8

Results will vary depending on companies chosen. Kroger provided the following disclosures in its annual report for the year ending December 31, 2003:

## LIABILITIES
### Current liabilities

| | | |
|---|---:|---:|
| Current portion of long-term debt including obligations under capital leases | $   248 | $   352 |
| Accounts payable | 3,058 | 3,269 |
| Accrued salaries and wages | 547 | 571 |
| Deferred income taxes | 138 | 39 |
| Other current liabilities | 1,595 | 1,377 |
| Total current liabilities | 5,586 | 5,608 |

### Long-term debt

| | | |
|---|---:|---:|
| Face value long-term debt including obligations under capital leases | 8,116 | 8,222 |
| Deferred income taxes | 990 | 709 |
| Other long-term liabilities | 1,481 | 1,713 |
| Total Liabilities | 16,173 | 16,252 |

## 11. LEASES

The Company operates primarily in leased facilities. Lease terms generally range from 10 to 20 years with options to renew for varying terms. Terms of certain leases include escalation clauses, percentage rents based on sales, or payment of executory costs such as property taxes, utilities, or insurance and maintenance. Rent expense for leases with escalation clauses, capital improvement funding and other lease concessions is accounted for on a straight-line basis over the minimum lease term. Portions of certain properties are subleased to others for periods generally ranging from one to 20 years.

Rent expense (under operating leases) consists of:

| | 2003 | 2002 | 2001 |
|---|---|---|---|
| Minimum rentals | $ 740 | $ 739 | $ 718 |
| Contingent payments | 9 | 10 | 14 |
| Sublease income | (96) | (93) | (82) |
| | $ 653 | $ 656 | $ 650 |

## Case 15-8 (concluded)

Minimum annual rentals for the five years subsequent to 2003 and in the aggregate are:

| | Capital Leases | Operating Leases |
|---|---|---|
| 2004 | $ 66 | $ 784 |
| 2005 | 64 | 746 |
| 2006 | 61 | 691 |
| 2007 | 57 | 644 |
| 2008 | 54 | 595 |
| Thereafter | 439 | 4,201 |
| | 741 | $ 7,661 |
| Less estimated executory costs included in capital leases | (6) | |
| Net minimum lease payments under capital leases | 735 | |
| Less amount representing interest | (348) | |
| Present value of net minimum lease payments | $ 387 | |

Total future minimum rentals under noncancellable subleases at January 31, 2004, were $354.

## Requirements 3 & 4

The $387 million capital lease liability represents 2.4 % of the $16,173 million total liabilities. However, the obligations under operating leases are roughly 10 times those for capital leases, so the lease liability also would be roughly ten times higher if the operating leases were capitalized (treated as capital leases).

# Real World Case 15-9

## Requirement 1

In a sale-leaseback transaction the owner of an asset sells the asset and immediately leases it back from the new owner. We view the sale and simultaneous leaseback of the asset as a single borrowing transaction. On the surface there appear to be two separate transactions, but the substance of the agreement indicates otherwise. The seller-lessee (FedEx in our case) still retains the use of the asset owned prior to the sale-leaseback, but in the process acquires (a) cash from the sale and (b) an obligation to make lease payments over the term of the lease. In substance, the seller-lessee has borrowed cash to be repaid over the lease term (along with interest). So, from this perspective of "substance over form," we do not immediately recognize any gains that result from sale-leaseback transactions, but defer the gains to be recognized over the term of the lease. There typically is an interdependency between the lease terms and the price at which the asset is sold. As a result, the earnings process is not complete at the time of sale but is completed over the term of the lease. So, viewing the sale and the leaseback as a single transaction is consistent with the realization principle.

## Requirement 2

When amortizing the deferred gain over the lease term, if the lease meets the criteria to be viewed as a capital lease, we reduce depreciation expense each period by the amortized portion of the gain.

If the leaseback portion of a sale-leaseback transaction is classified as an operating lease, the gain still is deferred, but is recognized as a reduction of rent expense rather than depreciation. Because FedEx amortizes its deferred gains "ratably over the life of the lease as a reduction of rent expense" it apparently considers the leases to be operating leases.

# Communication Case 15-10

## Suggested Grading Concepts and Grading Scheme:

**Content (80%)**

_____     30     Sale portion of the sale-leaseback (10 each).

         _____ Record cash for the sale price.

         _____ Decrease equipment at its undepreciated cost.

         _____ Establish a deferred gain for the excess of the sale price of the equipment over its undepreciated cost.

_____     15     Gain on the sale portion (5 each; maximum 15).

         _____ Amortized over the lease term.

         _____ As a reduction of depreciation expense.

         _____ Results in essentially same depreciation and interest as if the asset were not sold and leased back, but a note issued for cash instead.

         _____ Because the sale and the leaseback are two components of a single transaction rather than two independent transactions.

         _____ Consistent with the realization principle.

_____     15     Leaseback portion of the sale-leaseback transaction (5 each; maximum 15).

         _____ Both an asset.

         _____ And a liability.

         _____ At the present value of minimum lease payments.

         _____ Excluding any executory costs.

         _____ Asset amount cannot exceed fair value.

_____     20     Conceptual basis (10 each).

         _____ Economic effect of a long-term capital lease on the lessee is similar to that of an installment purchase.

         _____ Transfers substantially all of the benefits and risks incident to the ownership of property to the lessee.

_____     80 points

**Writing**     (20%)

_____     5     Terminology and tone appropriate to the audience (CFO).

_____     6     Organization permits ease of understanding.

         _____ Introduction that states purpose.

         _____ Paragraphs separate main points.

_____     9     English

         _____ Word selection.

         _____ Spelling.

         _____ Grammar.

_____     20 points

# Trueblood Accounting Case 15-11

A solution and extensive discussion materials accompany each case in the Deloitte & Touche Trueblood Case Study Series. These are available to instructors at: https://secure.deloitte.com/rmtbcs00/casesolutions.asp

# Chapter 16 Accounting for Income Taxes

## QUESTIONS FOR REVIEW OF KEY TOPICS

### Question 16-1

Income tax expense is comprised of both the *current* and the *deferred* tax consequences of events and transactions already recognized. Specifically, it includes (a) the income tax that is payable currently and (b) the change in the deferred tax liability (or asset). Apparently, in the situation described, temporary differences required a $4.4 million increase in the deferred tax liability, a $4.4 million decrease in the deferred tax asset, or some combination of the two.

### Question 16-2

Temporary differences between the reported amount of an asset or liability in the financial statements and its tax basis are primarily caused by revenues, expenses, gains, and losses being included in taxable income in a year earlier or later than the year in which they are recognized for financial reporting purpose, although there are other, less common, events that can cause these temporary differences. Some temporary differences create *deferred tax liabilities* because they result in *taxable* amounts in some future year(s) when the related assets are recovered or the related liabilities are settled (when the temporary differences reverse). An example is the receivable created when installment sale gross profit is recognized for financial reporting purposes. When this asset is recovered, taxable amounts are produced because the installment sale gross profit is then recognized for tax purposes. Some temporary differences create *deferred tax assets* because they result in *deductible* amounts in some future year(s) when the related assets are recovered or the related liabilities are settled (when the temporary differences reverse). An example is the liability created when estimated warranty expense is recognized for financial reporting purposes. When this liability is settled, deductible amounts are produced because the warranty cost is then deducted for tax purposes. The deferred tax liability or asset each year is the tax rate times the temporary difference between the *financial statement carrying amount* of the receivable or liability and its *tax basis*.

### Question 16-3

Future deductible amounts mean that taxable income will be *decreased* relative to accounting income in one or more future years. Two examples are (a) estimated expenses that are recognized on income statements when incurred, but deducted on tax returns in later years when actually paid and (b) revenues that are taxed when collected, but are recognized on income statements in later years when actually earned. These situations have favorable tax consequences that are recognized as deferred tax assets.

### Question 16-4

Deferred tax assets are recognized for all deductible temporary differences and operating loss carryforwards. However, a deferred tax asset is then reduced by a valuation allowance if it is "more likely that not" that some portion or all of the deferred tax asset will not be realized. The decision as to whether a valuation allowance is needed should be based on the weight of all available evidence.

# Answers to Questions (continued)

## Question 16-5
Nontemporary or "permanent" differences are caused by transactions and events that under existing tax law will never affect taxable income or taxes payable. Some provisions of the tax laws exempt certain revenues from taxation and prohibit the deduction of certain expenses. Provisions of the tax laws, in some other instances, dictate that the amount of a revenue that is taxable or expense that is deductible permanently differs from the amount reported in the income statement. Nontemporary or "permanent" differences are disregarded when determining both the tax payable currently and the deferred tax effect.

## Question 16-6
Examples of nontemporary or "permanent" differences are:

- Interest received from investments in bonds issued by state and municipal governments (not taxable)

- Investment expenses incurred to obtain tax-exempt income (not tax deductible)

- Life insurance proceeds upon the death of an insured executive (not taxable)

- Premiums paid for life insurance policies (not tax deductible)

- Compensation expense pertaining to some employee stock option plans (not tax deductible)

- Expenses due to violations of the law (not tax deductible)

- Portion of dividends received from U.S. corporations that is not taxable due to the "dividends received deduction"

- Tax deduction for depletion of natural resources (percentage depletion) that permanently exceeds the income statement depletion expense (cost depletion)

## Question 16-7
A deferred tax liability (or asset) is based on enacted tax rates and laws. Hudson should use the 35% rate, the currently *enacted* tax rate that will be effective in the year(s) the temporary difference reverses. Calculations are not based on anticipated legislation that would alter the company's tax rate.

## Question 16-8
When a change in a tax law or rate occurs, a deferred tax liability or asset must be adjusted to reflect the amount to be paid or recovered in the future. If a deferred tax liability was established with the expectation that the future taxable amount would be taxed at 34%, it would now be adjusted to reflect taxation at 36% instead. The usual practice of recalculating the desired balance in a deferred tax liability each period and comparing that amount with any previously existing balance automatically takes into account tax rate changes. The effect is reflected in operating income (adjustment to income tax expense) in the year of the enactment of the change in the tax law or rate.

## Question 16-9

The income tax benefit of either an operating loss carryback or an operating loss carryforward is recognized for accounting purposes in the year the operating loss occurs. The net *after-tax* operating loss reflects the reduction of past taxes from the loss carryback or future tax savings that the loss carryforward is expected to create.

An operating loss carryforward creates future deductible amounts, so a deferred tax asset is recognized for an operating loss carryforward. The deferred tax asset is then reduced by a valuation allowance if it is "more likely that not" that some portion or all of the deferred tax asset will not be realized due to insufficient taxable income expected in the carryforward years.

## Question 16-10

Deferred tax assets and deferred tax liabilities are not reported individually, but combined instead into a *net current* amount and a *net noncurrent* amount. Each is reported as either an asset – if deferred tax assets exceed deferred tax liabilities, or as a liability – if deferred tax liabilities exceed deferred tax assets.

Deferred tax assets and deferred tax liabilities are classified as either *current* or *noncurrent* according to how the related assets or liabilities are classified for financial reporting. For instance, a deferred tax liability arising from estimated warranty expenses would be classified as *current* if the warranty liability is classified as *current*. A deferred tax asset or liability that is not related to a specific asset or liability should be classified according to when the underlying temporary difference is expected to reverse.

## Question 16-11

Regarding deferred tax amounts reported in the balance sheet, disclosure notes should indicate (a) the total of all deferred tax liabilities, (b) the total of all deferred tax assets, (c) the total valuation allowance recognized for deferred tax assets, (d) the net change in the valuation allowance, and (e) the approximate tax effect of each type of temporary difference (and carryforward).

## Question 16-12

Pertaining to the income tax expense reported in the income statement, disclosure notes should indicate (a) the *current* portion of the tax expense (or tax benefit), (b) the *deferred* portion of the tax expense (or tax benefit), with separate disclosure of amounts attributable to (c) the portion that does not include the effect of the following separately disclosed amounts, (d) operating loss carryforwards, (e) adjustments due to changes in tax laws or rates, (f) adjustments to the beginning-of-the-year valuation allowance due to revised estimates, (g) investment tax credits.

## Question 16-13

Intraperiod tax allocation means the total income tax obligation for a reporting period is *allocated* among the income statement items that gave rise to the income tax. The following items should be reported *net* of their respective income tax effects:
- Income (or loss) from continuing operations
- Discontinued operations
- Extraordinary items

## Answers to Questions (concluded)

### Question 16-14

Some accountants contend that the tax liability for certain recurring events will never be paid because such temporary differences recur frequently and new originating differences more than offset reversing differences. This causes the balance in the deferred tax liability account to continually get larger and never require payment. Therefore temporary differences for recurring items like temporary differences due to depreciation do not represent liabilities. Since no future tax payment will be required, no liability should be recorded.

The counter argument that supports the FASB's view is that, although the aggregate amount of a deferred tax liability (such as that for depreciation differences) may get larger, the deferred tax liability for a specific temporary difference (such as for a particular depreciable asset) usually does require payment. This situation is similar to the total balance of accounts payable growing larger each year, but specific accounts payable requiring payment as they come due.

# BRIEF EXERCISES

## Brief Exercise 16-1

Since taxable income is less than accounting income, a future taxable amount will occur when the temporary difference reverses. This means a deferred tax liability should be recorded to reflect the future tax consequences of the temporary difference:

|  | ($ in millions) |  |
| --- | --- | --- |
| Income tax expense (to balance) | 4.0 |  |
|     Deferred tax liability ([$10 - 7] x 40%) |  | 1.2 |
|     Income tax payable ($7 x 40%) |  | 2.8 |

## Brief Exercise 16-2

Since taxable income is more than accounting income, a future deductible amount will occur when the temporary difference reverses. This means a deferred tax asset should be recorded to reflect the future tax savings from the temporary difference:

|  | ($ in millions) |  |
| --- | --- | --- |
| Income tax expense (to balance) | 4.0 |  |
| Deferred tax asset ([$12 - 10] x 40%) | .8 |  |
|     Income tax payable ($12 x 40%) |  | 4.8 |

## Brief Exercise 16-3

|  | ($ in millions) |  |
| --- | --- | --- |
| Income tax expense (to balance) | 52 |  |
| Deferred tax asset ($50 x 40%) | 20 |  |
|     Income tax payable ($180 x 40%) |  | 72 |

# Brief Exercise 16-4

|  | ($ in millions) | |
|---|---|---|
| Income tax expense (to balance) | 84 | |
| Deferred tax asset ([$20 – [$40 x 40%]) | | 4 |
| Income tax payable ($200 x 40%) | | 80 |

# Brief Exercise 16-5

|  | ($ in millions) | |
|---|---|---|
| Income tax expense (to balance) | 2 | |
| Deferred tax asset ($30 x 40%) | 12 | |
| Income tax payable ($35 x 40%) | | 14 |
| | | |
| Income tax expense | 3 | |
| Valuation allowance – deferred tax asset ($1/4$ x $12) | | 3 |

# Brief Exercise 16-6

Deferred tax assets are recognized for all deductible temporary differences and operating loss carryforwards. Deferred tax assets are then reduced by a valuation allowance if it is "more likely that not" that some portion or all of the deferred tax assets will not be realized. That would be the case if management feels taxable income will not be sufficient in future years to permit gaining the benefit of reducing taxable income by the future deductible amounts. This apparently is the case with Hypercom, which reported large losses in 2003 and prior years, perhaps indicative of insufficient taxable income in coming years to benefit from the tax savings.

# Brief Exercise 16-7

Since tax depreciation to date has been $100,000 more than depreciation for financial reporting purposes, a future taxable amount will occur when the temporary difference reverses. This means a deferred tax liability should be reported to reflect the future tax consequences of the temporary difference. At this point, that amount is $100,000 times 40%, or $40,000.

If the balance was $32,000 last year, we need an increase of $8,000. The entry to record income taxes is:

| | | |
|---|---|---|
| Income tax expense (to balance) | 1,608,000 | |
|     Deferred tax liability ($40,000 – 32,000) | | 8,000 |
|     Income tax payable ($4,000,000 x 40%) | | 1,600,000 |

# Brief Exercise 16-8

Since taxable income to date has been $40 million less than pretax accounting income because of the temporary difference, a future taxable amount of $40 million will occur when the temporary difference reverses. This means a deferred tax liability should be reported to reflect the future tax consequences of the temporary difference. That amount is $40 million times 40%, or $16 million.

# Brief Exercise 16-9

|  | Current year | Future taxable amount |
|---|---|---|
| **Accounting income** | $ 900,000 | |
| *Non-temporary difference:* | | |
| Municipal bond interest | (20,000) | |
| *Temporary difference:* | | |
| Depreciation | (120,000)* | $120,000 |
| **Taxable income** | $ 760,000 | |
| Enacted tax rate | 40% | 40% |
| Tax payable currently | $ 304,000 | |
| Deferred tax liability | | $ 48,000 |

**Journal entry**

| | | |
|---|---|---|
| Income tax expense (to balance) | 352,000 | |
|    Deferred tax liability ($120,000 x 40%) | | 48,000 |
|    Income tax payable (determined above) | | 304,000 |

| | |
|---|---|
| * tax depreciation: $800,000 x 40% | $320,000 |
| straight-line depreciation: $800,000 / 4 years | 200,000 |
| difference the first year | $120,000 |

# Brief Exercise 16-10

($ in 000s)

| | Current Year 2006 | Future Deductible Amounts | | | Total |
|---|---|---|---|---|---|
| | | 2007 | 2008 | 2009 | |
| **Accounting income** | 291 | | | | |
| *Temporary difference:* | | | | | |
| Warranty expense | 9 | (3) | (3) | (3) | |
| | | | | | |
| **Taxable income** | 300 | | | | |
| Enacted tax rate | 40% | 40% | 30% | 30% | |
| Tax payable currently | 120 | | | | |
| Deferred tax asset | | (1.2) | (.9) | (.9) | (3) |

### Journal entry at the end of 2006

| | | |
|---|---|---|
| Income tax expense (to balance) | 117 | |
| Deferred tax asset (determined above) | 3 | |
| Income tax payable ($300 x 40%) | | 120 |

# Brief Exercise 16-11

Superior should reduce its deferred tax liability this year by $4.5 million:

| | ($ in millions) | |
|---|---|---|
| Deferred tax liability last year | $8.0 | ($20 future taxable amount x 40%) |
| Deferred tax liability this year | 3.5 | ($10 future taxable amount x 35%) |
| Reduction needed to achieve desired balance | $4.5 | |

# Brief Exercise 16-12

Because the loss year is the Nile.com's first year of operations, the carryback option is unavailable. The loss is carried forward.

**Journal entry**

| | | |
|---|---|---|
| Deferred tax asset ($15 million x 40%) | 6,000,000 | |
| Income tax benefit – operating loss | | 6,000,000 |

# Brief Exercise 16-13

Because the operating loss is less than the previous two years taxable income, AirParts cannot get back all taxes paid those two years. It can reduce taxable income from two years ago by $15 million (to zero) and last year's taxable income by $10 million and get a refund of $10 million of the taxes paid those years.

**Journal entry**

| | | |
|---|---|---|
| Receivable – income tax refund ($25 million x 40%) | 10,000,000 | |
| Income tax benefit – operating loss | | 10,000,000 |

# Brief Exercise 16-14

Intraperiod tax allocation means the total income tax obligation for a reporting period is allocated among the income statement items that gave rise to the income tax. The following items should be reported net of their respective income tax effects:

- Income (or loss) from ordinary, continuing operations
- Discontinued operations
- Extraordinary items

Southeast Airlines had pre-tax earnings of $55 million before the extraordinary gain of $10 million. Since the company's tax rate is 40%, the amount of income tax expense that Southeast should report is $55 million x 40%, or $22 million. The extraordinary gain should be reported net of the tax on the gain: $10 million less 40% of $10 million, or $6 million. So, the total income tax obligation of $26 million ($65 million x 40%) is allocated between the income statement items that gave rise to the income tax:

| $ in millions | |
|---|---|
| Income from ordinary operations | $22 |
| Extraordinary gain | 4 |
| Total | $26 |

# EXERCISES

## Exercise 16-1

Since taxable income is less than accounting income, a future taxable amount will occur when the temporary difference reverses. This means a deferred tax liability should be recorded to reflect the future tax consequences of the temporary difference.

| | | |
|---|---|---|
| Income tax expense (to balance) | 140,000 | |
| Deferred tax liability ([$400,000 - 250,000] x 35%) | | 52,500 |
| Income tax payable ($250,000 x 35%) | | 87,500 |

## Exercise 16-2

| | | |
|---|---|---|
| Income tax expense (to balance) | 830,000 | |
| Deferred tax asset ($300,000 x 40%) | 120,000 | |
| Income tax payable (given) | | 950,000 |

## Exercise 16-3

| | | |
|---|---|---|
| Income tax expense (to balance) | 30,035,000 | |
| Deferred tax asset ([$1 million x 40%] - $435,000) | | 35,000 |
| Income tax payable ($75 million x 40%) | | 30,000,000 |

# Exercise 16-4

## Requirement 1

|  | ($ in millions) | |
| --- | :---: | :---: |
|  | **Current Year 2006** | **Future Deductible Amounts** |
| *Temporary difference:* |  | (70) |
|  |  |  |
| **Taxable income** | 180 |  |
| Enacted tax rate | 40% | 40% |
| Tax payable currently | 72 |  |
| Deferred tax asset |  | (28) |
|  |  | ↓ |
| **Deferred tax asset:** |  |  |
| Ending balance (balance currently needed) |  | $ 28 |
| Less: beginning balance ($75 x 40%) |  | (30) |
| *Change needed to achieve desired balance* |  | $( 2) |

| **Journal entry at the end of 2006** | | |
| --- | :---: | :---: |
| Income tax expense (to balance) | 74 | |
|   Deferred tax asset (determined above) | | 2 |
|   Income tax payable (determined above) | | 72 |

## Requirement 2

|  | ($ in millions) | |
| --- | :---: | :---: |
| Income tax expense (to balance) | 74 | |
|   Deferred tax asset (determined above) | | 2 |
|   Income tax payable (determined above) | | 72 |
|  |  |  |
| Income tax expense | 14 | |
|   Valuation allowance – deferred tax asset ($1/2$ x $28) | | 14 |

Of course, these two entries can be combined.

# Exercise 16-5

## Requirement 1

| | Current Year 2006 | Future Deductible Amounts |
|---|---|---|
| | | ($ in millions) |
| *Temporary difference:* | | (70) |
| | | |
| **Taxable income** | 180 | |
| Enacted tax rate | 40% | 40% |
|   Tax payable currently | 72 | |
|   Deferred tax asset | | (28) |
| | | ↓ |
| | | |
| **Deferred tax asset:** | | |
| Ending balance (balance currently needed) | | $ 28 |
| Less: beginning balance ($75 x 40%) | | (30) |
| *Change needed to achieve desired balance* | | $( 2) |

| | | |
|---|---|---|
| **Journal entries at the end of 2006** | | |
| Income tax expense (to balance) | 74 | |
|     Deferred tax asset (determined above) | | 2 |
|     Income tax payable (determined above) | | 72 |
| | | |
| Valuation allowance – deferred tax asset | 10 | |
|     Income tax expense | | 10 |
| Of course, these two entries can be combined. | | |

## Exercise 16-5 (concluded)

### Requirement 2

|  | ($ in millions) | |
|---|---|---|
| Income tax expense (to balance) | 74 | |
|     Deferred tax asset (determined above) | | 2 |
|     Income tax payable (determined above) | | 72 |
| | | |
| Income tax expense | 4 | |
|     Valuation allowance – deferred tax asset ([$^1/_2$ x $28]– $10) | | 4 |

Of course, these two entries can be combined.

© The McGraw-Hill Companies, Inc., 2007

# Exercise 16-6
**Requirement 1**

|  | ($ in millions) | |
|---|---|---|
|  | **Current Year 2006** | **Future Taxable Amount [total]** |
| **Accounting income** | 20 | |
| *Temporary difference:* | | |
| Depreciation   ($30 - 20) - ($28 - 13) = | (5) | 15   ($28 - 13) |
| **Taxable income** | 15 | |
| Enacted tax rate | 40% | 40% |
| Tax payable currently | 6 | |
| Deferred tax liability | | 6 ↓ |

| **Deferred tax liability:** | |
|---|---|
| Ending balance (balance currently needed) | $ 6 |
| Less: beginning balance ($30 - 20) x 40% | (4) |
| *Change needed to achieve desired balance* | $ 2 |

**Journal entry at the end of 2006**

| | | |
|---|---|---|
| Income tax expense (to balance) | 8 | |
| Deferred tax liability (determined above) | | 2 |
| Income tax payable (determined above) | | 6 |

**Requirement 2**

|  | ($ in millions) |
|---|---|
| Pretax accounting income | $20 |
| Income tax expense | (8) |
| Net income | $12 |

# Exercise 16-7
1.  d
2.  d
3.  a
4.  c

# Exercise 16-8

($ in millions)

|  | | December 31 | | | | | | | |
|---|---|---|---|---|---|---|---|---|---|
|  | **2006** | | **2007** | | **2008** | | **2009** | | |
| *Depreciable asset (net):* | | | | | | | | | |
| **Accounting basis** | $80 | (20) | $60 | (20) | $40 | (20) | $20 | (20) | $0 |
| **Tax basis** | 80 | (25) | 55 | (33) | 22 | (15) | 7 | (7) | 0 |
| TEMPORARY DIFFERENCE | | 5 | $ 5 | 13 | $18 | (5) | $13 | (13) | $0 |
| | | | | | | | | | |
| Tax rate | | | 40% | | 40% | | 40% | | 40% |
| DEFERRED TAX LIABILITY | | | $ 2 | | $7.2 | | $ 5.2 | | $0 |

↑       ↑       ↑       ↑

originating           reversing
differences        differences

# Exercise 16-9

  D    1. Accrual of loss contingency, tax-deductible when paid.

  D    2. Newspaper subscriptions; taxable when received, recognized for financial reporting when earned.

  T    3. Prepaid rent, tax-deductible when paid.

  D    4. Accrued bond interest expense; tax-deductible when paid.

  T    5. Prepaid insurance, tax-deductible when paid.

  D    6. Unrealized loss from recording investments available for sale at fair market (tax-deductible when investments are sold).

  D    7. Bad debt expense; allowance method for financial reporting; direct write-off for tax purposes.

  D    8. Advance rent receipts on an operating lease (as the lessor), taxable when received.

  T    9. Straight-line depreciation for financial reporting; accelerated depreciation for tax purposes.

  D  10. Accrued expense for employee postretirement benefits; tax-deductible when subsequent payments are made.

# Exercise 16-10

1. Liability – loss contingency

2. Liability – subscriptions

3. Prepaid rent

4. Accrued bond interest payable

5. Prepaid insurance

6. Unrealized loss on investments (shareholders' equity account)

7. Allowance for uncollectible accounts; and thus accounts receivable (net)

8. Liability – unearned rent

9. Accumulated depreciation; and thus depreciable assets (net)

10. Liability – postretirement benefits

# Exercise 16-11

## Requirement 1

| | Current Year 2006 | ($ in thousands) Future Taxable Amounts 2007 2008 2009 | Future Taxable Amounts |
|---|---|---|---|
| **Accounting income** | 300 | | |
| *Non-temporary difference:* | | | |
| Municipal bond interest | (40) | | |
| *Temporary difference:* | | | |
| Depreciation | (10) | (2)  2  10 | 10 |
| **Taxable income** | 250 | | |
| Enacted tax rate | 40% | | 40% |
| Tax payable currently | 100 | | |
| Deferred tax liability | | | 4 |
| | | | ↓ |
| **Deferred tax liability:** | | | |
| Ending balance (balance currently needed) | | | $ 4 |
| Less: beginning balance | | | 0 |
| *Change needed to achieve desired balance* | | | $ 4 |

| **Journal entry at the end of 2006** | | |
|---|---|---|
| Income tax expense (to balance) | 104 | |
| Deferred tax liability (determined above) | | 4 |
| Income tax payable (determined above) | | 100 |

## Requirement 2

| | ($ in thousands) |
|---|---|
| Pretax accounting income | $300 |
| Income tax expense | (104) |
| Net income | $196 |

# Exercise 16-12

## Requirement 1

| ($ in millions) | Current Year 2006 | Future Taxable Amounts 2007 2008 | Future Taxable Amounts [total] |
|---|---|---|---|
| **Accounting income** | 63 | | |
| *Non-temporary difference:* | | | |
| Goodwill amortization | (3) | | |
| *Temporary difference:* | | | |
| Plot sales | (40) | 24    16 | 40 |
| | | | |
| **Taxable income** | 20 | | |
| Enacted tax rate | 40% | | 40% |
| Tax payable currently | 8 | | |
| Deferred tax liability | | | 16 |
| | | | ↓ |

**Deferred tax liability:**

| | |
|---|---|
| Ending balance (balance currently needed) | $ 16 |
| Less: beginning balance | (0) |
| *Change needed to achieve desired balance* | $16 |

| **Journal entry at the end of 2006** | | |
|---|---|---|
| Income tax expense (to balance) | 24 | |
| Deferred tax liability (determined above) | | 16 |
| Income tax payable (determined above) | | 8 |

## Requirement 2

| | ($ in millions) |
|---|---|
| Pretax accounting income | $63 |
| Income tax expense | (24) |
| Net income | $39 |

# Exercise 16-13

## Requirement 1

| ($ in millions) | Current Year 2006 | Future Deductible Amounts | | | | Total |
|---|---|---|---|---|---|---|
| | | 2007 | 2008 | 2009 | 2010 | |
| **Accounting income** | 14 | | | | | |
| *Temporary difference:* | | | | | | |
| Warranty expense | 6 | (2) | (1) | (1) | (2) | |
| | | | | | | |
| **Taxable income** | 20 | | | | | |
| Enacted tax rate | 35% | 30% | 30% | 30% | 25% | |
| Tax payable currently | 7 | | | | | |
| Deferred tax asset | | (0.6) | (0.3) | (0.3) | (0.5) | (1.7) |

$\downarrow$

| **Deferred tax asset:** | |
|---|---|
| Ending balance (balance currently needed) | $ 1.7 |
| Less: beginning balance | (0.0) |
| *Change needed to achieve desired balance* | $1.7 |

| **Journal entry at the end of 2006** | | |
|---|---|---|
| Income tax expense (to balance) | 5.3 | |
| Deferred tax asset (determined above) | 1.7 | |
| Income tax payable (determined above) | | 7.0 |

## Requirement 2

| | ($ in millions) |
|---|---|
| Pretax accounting income | $14.0 |
| Income tax expense | (5.3) |
| Net income | $ 8.7 |

# Exercise 16-14

## Requirement 1

| | ($ in millions) Current Year 2006 | | Future Taxable Amounts | | | Future Taxable Amounts [total] |
|---|---|---|---|---|---|---|
| | | 2007 | 2008 | 2009 | 2010 | |
| **Accounting income** | 33 | | | | | |
| *Temporary difference:* | | | | | | |
| Advance rent payment | (8) | 2 | 2 | 2 | 2 | 8 |
| | | | | | | |
| **Taxable income** | 25 | | | | | |
| Enacted tax rate | 40% | | | | | 40% |
| Tax payable currently | 10 | | | | | |
| Deferred tax liability | | | | | | 3.2 |
| | | | | | | ↓ |

| **Deferred tax liability:** | |
|---|---|
| Ending balance (balance currently needed) | $3.2 |
| Less: beginning balance | 0.0 |
| *Change needed to achieve desired balance* | $3.2 |

| **Journal entry at the end of 2006** | | |
|---|---|---|
| Income tax expense (to balance) | 13.2 | |
| Deferred tax liability (determined above) | | 3.2 |
| Income tax payable (determined above) | | 10.0 |

## Exercise 16-14 (continued)

### Requirement 2

| ($ in millions) | Current Year 2007 | Future Taxable Amounts | | | Future Taxable Amounts |
|---|---|---|---|---|---|
| | | 2008 | 2009 | 2010 | [total] |
| **Accounting income** | 50 | | | | |
| *Temporary difference:* | | | | | |
| Advance rent payment | 2 | 2 | 2 | 2 | 6 |
| | | | | | |
| **Taxable income** | 52 | | | | |
| Enacted tax rate | 40% | | | | 40% |
| Tax payable currently | 20.8 | | | | |
| Deferred tax liability | | | | | 2.4 |
| | | | | | ↓ |
| **Deferred tax liability:** | | | | | |
| Ending balance (balance currently needed) | | | | | $ 2.4 |
| Less: beginning balance | | | | | (3.2) |
| *Change needed to achieve desired balance* | | | | | $(0.8) |

| **Journal entry at the end of 2007** | | |
|---|---|---|
| Income tax expense (to balance) | 20.0 | |
| Deferred tax liability (determined above) | 0.8 | |
| Income tax payable (determined above) | | 20.8 |

# Exercise 16-14 (concluded)

## Requirement 3

| ($ in millions) | Current Year 2007 | Future Taxable Amounts | | | Future Taxable Amounts |
|---|---|---|---|---|---|
| | | 2008 | 2009 | 2010 | [total] |
| **Accounting income** | 50 | | | | |
| *Temporary difference:* | | | | | |
| Advance rent payment | 2 | 2 | 2 | 2 | 6 |
| | | | | | |
| **Taxable income** | 52 | | | | |
| Enacted tax rate | 40% | | | | 30% |
| Tax payable currently | 20.8 | | | | |
| Deferred tax liability | | | | | 1.8 |
| | | | | | ↓ |
| **Deferred tax liability:** | | | | | |
| Ending balance (balance currently needed) | | | | | $ 1.8 |
| Less: beginning balance | | | | | (3.2) |
| *Change needed to achieve desired balance* | | | | | $(1.4) |

| Journal entry at the end of 2007 | | |
|---|---|---|
| Income tax expense (to balance) | 19.4 | |
| Deferred tax liability (determined above) | 1.4 | |
| Income tax payable (determined above) | | 20.8 |

## Requirement 4

*Without* the change income tax expense in 2007 [requirement 2] is $20 million. However, when the tax rate changes to 30%, the deferred tax liability must be reduced to reflect the fact that future taxable amounts will be taxed at a lower rate than the rate assumed when the liability was recorded in 2006. The adjustment is the future taxable amount, $6 million, times the rate change, 40% – 30%, or $0.6 million. SFAS 109 requires that the adjustment be reflected in operating income in the year of the change. Application of the asset/liability approach automatically accomplishes that goal. The income tax expense *with* the change in 2007 [requirement 3] is $19.4 million ($20 – 0.6 million).

# Exercise 16-15

A deferred tax liability is established using the currently enacted tax rate for the year(s) a temporary difference is expected to reverse. In this case that rate was 40%. The change in the tax law in 2007 constitutes a change in estimate. The deferred tax liability is simply revised to reflect the new rate.

|  | ($ in millions) |  |
| --- | --- | --- |
| Income tax expense (to balance)................................................ | 10 | |
| Deferred tax liability ($20 million x [40% – 30%]) ...................... | 2 | |
| Income tax payable ($30 million x 40%)................................. | | 12 |

When a company revises a previous estimate, prior financial statements are *not* revised. No adjustment is made to existing accounts. A disclosure note should describe the effect of a change in estimate on income before extraordinary items, net income, and related per-share amounts for the current period.

# Exercise 16-16

|  |  |  |
| --- | --- | --- |
| Income tax expense (to balance)................................................ | 32,000 | |
| Deferred tax asset ($12,000 x 40%)............................................ | 4,800 | |
| Deferred tax liability ($77,000 x 40%).................................. | | 30,800 |
| Income tax payable ($15,000 x 40%) ..................................... | | 6,000 |

# Exercise 16-17

## Requirement 1

|  | ($ in millions) | |
| --- | --- | --- |
| Income tax expense (to balance) ................................................ | 80 | |
| Deferred tax asset ($25 million x 40%) ...................................... | 10 | |
| Deferred tax liability ($80 million x 40%).............................. | | 32 |
| Income tax payable ($145 million x 40%) .............................. | | 58 |

## Requirement 2

|  | ($ in millions) |
| --- | --- |
| Pretax accounting income | $200 |
| Income tax expense | (80) |
| Net income | $120 |

# Exercise 16-18

($ in thousands)

| | Situation | | | |
|---|---|---|---|---|
| | **1** | **2** | **3** | **4** |
| a. Taxable income | $ 85 | $215 | $195 | $260 |
| Tax rate | 40% | 40% | 40% | 40% |
| **Income tax payable** | $ 34 | $ 86 | $ 78 | $104 |
| | | | | |
| b. Future deductible amounts | $(15) | | $(20) | $(20) |
| Tax rate | 40% | 40% | 40% | 40% |
| **Deferred tax asset** - bal. | $ (6) | 0 | $ (8) | $ (8) |
| *Beginning of the year:* | 2 | 0 | 9 | 4 |
| c. Deferred tax asset: **(dr) cr** | $ (4) | 0 | $ 1 | $ (4) |
| | | | | |
| d. Future taxable amounts | | $15 | $15 | $30 |
| Tax rate | 40% | 40% | 40% | 40% |
| **Deferred tax liability** - bal. | $ 0 | $ 6 | $ 6 | $12 |
| *Beginning of the year:* | 0 | 2 | 2 | 0 |
| e. Deferred tax liability: **(dr) cr** | $ 0 | $ 4 | $ 4 | $12 |
| | | | | |
| f. Income tax payable currently | $34 | $ 86 | $78 | $104 |
| Deferred tax asset: (dr) cr | (4) | 0 | 1 | (4) |
| Deferred tax liability: (dr) cr | 0 | 4 | 4 | 12 |
| **Income tax expense** | $30 | $90 | $83 | $112 |

# Exercise 16-19

|  | 1 | 2 | 3 | 4 | 5 | 6 | 7 | 8 |
|---|---|---|---|---|---|---|---|---|
| ACCOUNTING INCOME | $100 | $100 | $100 | $100 | $100 | $100 | $100 | $100 |

*Temporary differences:*
Income statement first:

|  | 1 | 2 | 3 | 4 | 5 | 6 | 7 | 8 |
|---|---|---|---|---|---|---|---|---|
| Revenue |  | (20) |  |  | (15) |  | (15) | (15) |
| Expense | 20 |  |  |  | 20 | 20 | 20 | 20 |

Tax return first:

|  | 1 | 2 | 3 | 4 | 5 | 6 | 7 | 8 |
|---|---|---|---|---|---|---|---|---|
| Revenue |  |  | 20 |  |  | 15 |  | 5 |
| Expense | ___ | ___ | ___ | (20) | ___ | ___ | (10) | (10) |
| TAXABLE INCOME | $120 | $80 | $120 | $80 | $105 | $135 | $95 | $100 |

# Exercise 16-20

## Requirement 1

| ($ in thousands) | Current Year 2006 | Future Taxable Amounts | Future Deductible Amounts |
|---|---|---|---|
| **Accounting income** | 977 | | |
| *Non-temporary difference:* | | | |
| Municipal bond interest | (32) | | |
| *Temporary differences:* | | | |
| Depreciation | (55) | 85 | |
| Warranty expense | 10 | | (10) |
| **Taxable income** | 900 | | |
| Enacted tax rate | 40% | 40% | 40% |
| Tax payable currently | 360 | | |
| Deferred tax liability | | 34 | |
| Deferred tax asset | | | (4) |
| | | ↓ | ↓ |
| | | **Deferred tax liability** | **Deferred tax asset** |
| Ending balances (balances currently needed): | | $34 | $ 4 |
| Less: beginning balances: | | (12) | (0) |
| *Change needed to achieve desired balances* | | $22 | $ 4 |

| **Journal entry at the end of 2006** | | |
|---|---|---|
| Income tax expense (to balance) | 378 | |
| Deferred tax asset (determined above) | 4 | |
| Deferred tax liability (determined above) | | 22 |
| Income tax payable (determined above) | | 360 |

## Requirement 2

| | ($ in thousands) |
|---|---|
| Pretax accounting income | $ 977 |
| Income tax expense | (378) |
| Net income | $599 |

# Exercise 16-21

### Requirement 1

Because the loss year is the company's first year of operations, the carryback option is unavailable. The loss is carried forward.

| ($ in thousands) | Current Year 2006 | Future Deductible Amounts [total] |
|---|---|---|
| **Operating loss** | (375) | |
| Loss carryforward | <u>375</u> | (375) |
| | 0 | |
| Enacted tax rate | <u>40%</u> | <u>40%</u> |
| Tax payable | <u>0</u> | |
| Deferred tax asset | | (150) |
| | | ↓ |
| **Deferred tax asset:** | | |
| Ending balance (balance currently needed) | | $ 150 |
| Less: beginning balance | | <u>(0)</u> |
| *Change needed to achieve desired balance* | | <u>$150</u> |

| **Journal entry at the end of 2006** | | |
|---|---|---|
| Deferred tax asset (determined above) | 150 | |
|     Income tax benefit – operating loss (to balance) | | 150 |

Since the weight of available evidence suggests future taxable income sufficient to benefit from future deductible amounts from the operating loss carryforward, no valuation allowance is needed.

### Requirement 2

| ($ in thousands) | |
|---|---|
| Operating loss before income taxes | $375 |
|   Less: Income tax benefit – operating loss | <u>(150)</u> |
| Net operating loss | $225 |

# Exercise 16-22

## Requirement 1

| ($ in thousands) | Prior Years | | Current Year |
|---|---|---|---|
| | 2004 | 2005 | 2006 |
| **Operating loss** | | | (100) |
| Loss carryback | (80) | (20) | 100 |
| | | | 0 |
| Enacted tax rate | 40% | 45% | 40% |
| Tax payable (refundable) | (32) | (9) | 0 |

| **Journal entry at the end of 2006** | | |
|---|---|---|
| Receivable – income tax refund ($32 + 9) | 41 | |
| Income tax benefit – operating loss | | 41 |

## Requirement 2

| ($ in thousands) | |
|---|---|
| Operating loss before income taxes | $100 |
| *Less:* Income tax benefit from loss carryback | (41) |
| Net operating loss | $ 59 |

# Exercise 16-23

## Requirement 1

| ($ in thousands) | Prior Years | | Current Year | Future Deductible Amounts |
|---|---|---|---|---|
| | 2004 | 2005 | 2006 | [total] |
| **Operating loss** | | | (160) | |
| Loss carryback | (80) | (60) | 140 | |
| Loss carryforward | | | 20 | (20) |
| | | | 0 | |
| Enacted tax rate | 40% | 45% | 40% | 40% |
| Tax payable (refundable) | (32) | (27) | 0 | |
| Deferred tax asset | | | | (8) |
| | | | | ↓ |

|  | |
|---|---|
| **Deferred tax asset:** | |
| Ending balance (balance currently needed) | $ 8 |
| Less: beginning balance | (0) |
| *Change needed to achieve desired balance* | $8 |

**Journal entry at the end of 2006**

| | | |
|---|---|---|
| Receivable – income tax refund ($32 + 27) | 59 | |
| Deferred tax asset (determined above) | 8 | |
|    Income tax benefit – operating loss (to balance) | | 67 |

## Requirement 2

| ($ in thousands) | | |
|---|---|---|
| Operating loss before income taxes | | $160 |
| *Less:* Income tax benefit: | | |
|   Tax refund from loss carryback | $59 | |
|   Future tax savings from loss carryforward | 8 | (67) |
| Net operating loss | | $ 93 |

# Exercise 16-24

| ($ in millions)  Related Balance Sheet Account | Classification current-C noncurrent-N | Future Taxable (Deductible) Amounts | Tax Rate | Deferred Tax (Asset) Liability C | N |
|---|---|---|---|---|---|
| Liability – warranty expense | C | (15) | x 40% | (6) | |
| Depreciable assets | N | 120 | x 40% | | 48 |
| Receivable – installment sales | C | 10 | x 40% | 4 | |
| Receivable – installment sales | N | 40 | x 40% | | 16 |
| Allowance – uncollectible accounts | C | (25) | x 40% | (10) | |
| | | | | — | |
| Net **current** liability (asset) | | | | (12) | |
| Net **noncurrent** liability (asset) | | | | | 64 |

> **Current Assets:**
> Deferred tax asset          $12
>
> **Long-Term Liabilities:**
> Deferred tax liability      $64

Note: Before offsetting assets and liabilities within the current and noncurrent categories, the **total** deferred tax assets is $16 ($6+10) and the **total** deferred tax liabilities is $68 ($4+48+16).

# Exercise 16-25

## Requirement 1

| ($ in thousands) | Current Year 2006 | Future Taxable Amounts | | |
|---|---|---|---|---|
| | | 2007 | 2008 | 2009 |
| **Accounting income** | 810 | | | |
| *Non-temporary difference* | (10) | | | |
| *Temporary difference:* | | | | |
| Installment sales | (600) | 150 | 250 | 200 |
| **Taxable income** | 200 | | | |
| Enacted tax rate | 30% | 30% | 40% | 40% |
| Tax payable currently | 60 | | | |
| Deferred tax liability | | 45 | 100 | 80 | 225 |

225 ↓

**Deferred tax liability:**

| | |
|---|---|
| Ending balance (balance currently needed) | $225 |
| Less: beginning balance | (0) |
| *Change needed to achieve desired balance* | $225 |

**Journal entry at the end of 2006**

| | | |
|---|---|---|
| Income tax expense (to balance) | 285 | |
| Deferred tax liability (determined above) | | 225 |
| Income tax payable (determined above) | | 60 |

## Requirement 2

| | ($ in thousands) |
|---|---|
| Pretax accounting income | $ 810 |
| Income tax expense | (285) |
| Net income | $525 |

## Exercise 16-25 (concluded)

### Requirement 3

In a classified balance sheet, deferred tax assets and deferred tax liabilities are classified as either *current* or *noncurrent* according to how the related assets or liabilities are classified for financial reporting. The deferred tax liability arising from installment sales would be classified as part *current* and part *noncurrent* because the related installment receivable would properly be classified as part *current* and part *noncurrent*. Since there are no other temporary differences, this is the only deferred tax liability:

| | | |
|---|---|---|
| ***Current Liabilities:*** | | |
| Deferred tax liability | $45,000 | |
| | | |
| ***Long-Term Liabilities:*** | | |
| Deferred tax liability | $180,000 | ($100,000 + 80,000) |

# Exercise 16-26

## Requirement 1

| ($ in thousands) | Current Year 2006 | Future Taxable (Deductible) Amounts | | | Deferred Tax Liab. | Deferred Tax Asset |
|---|---|---|---|---|---|---|
| | | 2007 | 2008 | 2009 | | |
| **Accounting income** | 810 | | | | | |
| *Non-temporary difference* | (10) | | | | | |
| *Temporary differences:* | | | | | | |
| Installment sales | (600) | 150 | 250 | 200 | | |
| | | 30% | 40% | 40% | | |
| Deferred tax liability | | 45 | 100 | 80 | 225 | |
| Warranty expense | 60 | (20) | (25) | (15) | | |
| | | 30% | 40% | 40% | | |
| Deferred tax asset | | (6) | (10) | (6) | | (22) |
| **Taxable income** | 260 | | | | | |
| Enacted tax rate | 30% | | | | | |
| Tax payable currently | 78 | | | | | |

| | Deferred Tax Liab. | Deferred Tax Asset |
|---|---|---|
| Ending balances (balances currently needed): | $225 | $22 |
| Less: beginning balances: | 0 | 0 |
| *Change needed to achieve desired balances* | $225 | $22 |

**Journal entry at the end of 2006**

| | | |
|---|---|---|
| Income tax expense (to balance) | 281 | |
| Deferred tax asset (determined above) | 22 | |
| Deferred tax liability (determined above) | | 225 |
| Income tax payable (determined above) | | 78 |

*Exercise 16-26 (concluded)*

## Requirement 2

   ($ in thousands)

| | |
|---|---|
| Pretax accounting income | $810 |
| Income tax expense | (281) |
| Net income | $529 |

## Requirement 3

In a classified balance sheet, deferred tax assets and deferred tax liabilities are classified as either *current* or *noncurrent* according to how the related assets or liabilities are classified for financial reporting. Both the deferred tax liability arising from installment sales and deferred tax asset arising from warranties would be classified as part *current* and part *noncurrent* because the related installment receivable and estimated warranty liability would properly be classified as part *current* and part *noncurrent*. The deferred tax liabilities and deferred tax assets are offset to get the net current and the net noncurrent amounts:

| | |
|---|---|
| *Current Liabilities:* | |
| Deferred tax liability | $39,000 |
| ($45,000 - 6,000) | |
| | |
| *Long-Term Liabilities:* | |
| Deferred tax liability | $164,000 |
| ([$100,000 + 80,000] − [10,000 + 6,000]) | |

# Exercise 16-27

__L__ 1.  Advance payments on an operating lease deductible when paid.

__A__ 2.  Estimated warranty costs, tax deductible when paid.

__A__ 3.  Rent revenue collected in advance; cash basis for tax purposes.

__N__ 4.  Interest received from investments in municipal bonds.

__L__ 5.  Prepaid expenses tax deductible when paid.

__A__ 6.  Operating loss carryforward.

__N__ 7.  Operating loss carryback.

__A__ 8.  Bad debt expense; allowance method for accounting; direct write-off for tax.

__A__ 9.  Organization costs expensed when incurred; tax deductible over 15 years.

__N__ 10.  Life insurance proceeds received upon the death of the company president.

# Exercise 16-28

| List A | List B |
|---|---|
| __g__ 1. No tax consequences | a. Deferred tax liability |
| __e__ 2. Originates, then reverses | b. Deferred tax asset |
| __h__ 3. Revise deferred tax amounts | c. 2 years |
| __l__ 4. Operating loss | d. Current and deferred tax consequence combined |
| __a__ 5. Future tax effect of prepaid expenses tax deductible when paid | e. Temporary difference |
| __c__ 6. Loss carryback | f. Specific tax rates times amounts reversing each year |
| __b__ 7. Future tax effect of estimated warranty expense | g. Non temporary differences |
| __j__ 8. Valuation allowance | h. When enacted tax rate changes |
| __f__ 9. Phased-in change in rates | i. Same as related asset or liability |
| __i__ 10. Balance sheet classifications | j. "More likely than not" test |
| __k__ 11. Individual tax consequences of financial statement components | k. Intraperiod tax allocation |
| __d__ 12. Income tax expense | l. Negative taxable income |

# Exercise 16-29

## Income Statement
## For the fiscal year ended March 31, 2006

|  | ($ in millions) |
|---|---:|
| Revenues | $830 |
| Cost of goods sold | (350) |
| Gross profit | $480 |
| Operating expenses | (180) |
| Income from continuing operations before income taxes | $300 |
| Income tax expense | (120) |
| Income before discontinued operations and extraordinary item | $180 |
| Loss from discontinued operations, less applicable income taxes of $30 | (45) |
| Extraordinary casualty loss, less applicable income taxes of $4 | (6) |
| Net income | $129 |

# Exercise 16-30

1. **c.** A deferred tax asset records the deferred tax consequences attributable to deductible temporary differences and carryforwards. Advance rental receipts accounted for on the accrual basis for financial statement purposes and on a cash basis for tax purposes would give rise to a deferred tax asset. The financial statements would report no income and no related tax expense because the rental payments apply to future periods. The tax return, however, would treat the rent as income when the cash was received, and a tax would be due in the year of receipt. Because the tax is paid prior to recording the income for financial statement purposes, it represents an asset that will be recognized as an expense when income is finally recorded.

2. **d.** For financial reporting purposes, the reported amount (cost – accumulated depreciation of the machine at year-end, assuming straight-line depreciation and no salvage value, will be $80,000 [$100,000 cost – ($100,000 / 5 years)]. The tax basis of this asset will be $66,670 [$100,000 (33.33% x $100,000)]. A taxable temporary difference has arisen because the excess of the reported amount over the tax basis will result in a net future taxable amount over the recovery period. A taxable temporary difference requires recognition of a deferred tax liability. Assuming the 35% rate applies during the asset's entire life, the deferred tax liability equals the applicable enacted tax rate times the temporary difference, or $4,666 [35% x ($80,000 - $66,670)].

3. **d.** When one tax rate does not apply to all relevant years, a more complex calculation is necessary. In this question, different rates apply during the recovery period. During the years 2008-2010, book depreciation will equal $60,000 [3 x ($100,000 / 5)], and tax depreciation will equal $66,670 (the tax basis at December 31, 2007, will be recovered in full by December 31, 2010). Based on the applicable enacted 40% tax rate, the net deferred tax liability for 2008-2010 will be $2,668 [40% x ($66,670 - $60,000)]. However, the excess of book over tax depreciation in 2004 will be $20,000 ($20,000 - $0). Based on the applicable enacted 45% tax rate, the deferred tax liability for 2011 will be $9,000 (45% x $20,000). Accordingly, the net deferred tax liability at December 31, 2007, is $6,332 ($9,000 - $2,668).

# PROBLEMS

## Problem 16-1

### Requirement 1

|  | ($ in millions) | |
| --- | --- | --- |
| **Temporary Differences** | **Future Taxable Amounts** | **Future Deductible Amounts** |
| Accounts receivable (net of allowance) |  | $ (2) |
| Prepaid insurance | $ 20 |  |
| Prepaid rent expense (operating lease) | 6 |  |
| Buildings and equipment (net) | 80 |  |
| Liability – subscriptions received |  | (14) |
| Liability – postretirement benefits |  | (594) |
| Unrealized gain | 4 |  |
| Totals | $110 | $(610) |
| Tax rate | 40% | 40% |
| Deferred tax liability | $ 44 |  |
| Deferred tax asset |  | $(244) |

### Requirement 2

|  | Deferred tax liability | Deferred tax asset |
| --- | --- | --- |
| Ending balances (balances currently needed): | $ 44 | $244 |
| Less: beginning balances: | (40) | (250) |
| *Change needed to achieve desired balances* | $ 4 | $ (6) |

### Requirement 3

Taxable income *times* tax rate *equals* income tax payable
$120 million     x     40%     =     $48 million

## Problem 16-1 (concluded)

### Requirement 4

| | | |
|---|---|---|
| Income tax expense (to balance) | 58 | |
| Deferred tax asset (determined above) | | 6 |
| Deferred tax liability (determined above) | | 4 |
| Income tax payable (determined above) | | 48 |

### Requirement 5

($ in millions)

| Related Balance Sheet Account | Classification current-C noncurrent-N | Future Taxable (Deductible) Amounts | Tax Rate | Deferred Tax (Asset) Liability C | N |
|---|---|---|---|---|---|
| Allowance–uncollectible accounts | C | (2) | x 40% | (0.8) | |
| Prepaid insurance | C | 20 | x 40% | 8.0 | |
| Prepaid rent | C | 6 | x 40% | 2.4 | |
| Buildings and equipment | N | 80 | x 40% | | 32.0 |
| Liability–subscriptions received | C | (14) | x 40% | (5.6) | |
| Liability–postretirement benefits | N | (594) | x 40% | | (237.6) |
| Unrealized gain on investments | N | 4 | x 40% | | 1.6 |
| Net **current** liability (asset) | | | | 4.0 | |
| Net **noncurrent** liability (asset) | | | | | (204.0) |

**Current Liabilities:**
Deferred tax liability     $ 4

**Other assets:**
Deferred tax asset     $204

**RECONCILIATION [NOT REQUIRED]:**

| | |
|---|---|
| Deferred tax liability | $ (4) |
| Deferred tax asset | 204 |
| | $200 |

**Total amounts from requirement 1:**

| | |
|---|---|
| Deferred tax liability | $ (44) |
| Deferred tax asset | 244 |
| | $200 |

# Problem 16-2

**Requirement 1**

A liability for unearned subscription revenue is created when subscriptions are received (debit: cash, credit: liability - subscriptions).   For *tax purposes*, no such liability is recorded.   This causes a temporary difference between the *financial statement carrying amount* of the subscription liability and its *tax basis*.

**Requirement 2**

|  | | ($ in millions) | |
| --- | --- | --- | --- |
|  | | **December 31** | |
|  | **2006** | **2007** | **2008** |
| *Liability – subscriptions:* | | | |
|  | $ 0 | $ 40 | $ 20 |
|  | (250) | (240) | (230) |
|  | 290 | 220 | 260 |
| **Accounting basis** | $40 | $20 | $50 |
| **Tax basis** | 0 | 0 | 0 |
| TEMPORARY DIFFERENCE | $40 | $ 20 | $ 50 |

**Requirement 3**

| TEMPORARY DIFFERENCE | $40 | $ 20 | $ 50 |
| --- | --- | --- | --- |
| Tax rate | x 40% | x 40% | x 40% |
| DEFERRED TAX ASSET | $ 16 | $ 8 | $ 20 |

**Requirement 4**

Because these are one-year subscriptions, the liability for unearned subscriptions would be classified as a current liability.  Accordingly, the related deferred tax asset should be classified as current also.  It would be reported in a classified balance sheet as a current asset.

# Problem 16-3

## Requirement 1

| ($ in millions) | Current Year 2006 | Future Taxable Amounts | | | Future Taxable Amounts [total] |
|---|---|---|---|---|---|
| | | 2007 | 2008 | 2009 | |
| **Accounting income** | 16 | | | | |
| *Temporary difference:* | | | | | |
| Lot sales | (12) | 4 | 5 | 3 | 12 |
| | | | | | |
| **Taxable income** | 4 | | | | |
| Enacted tax rate | 40% | | | | 40% |
| Tax payable currently | 1.6 | | | | |
| Deferred tax liability | | | | | 4.8 |
| | | | | | ↓ |
| **Deferred tax liability:** | | | | | |
| Ending balance (balance currently needed) | | | | | $ 4.8 |
| Less: beginning balance | | | | | (0.0) |
| *Change needed to achieve desired balance* | | | | | $4.8 |

| **Journal entry at the end of 2006** | | |
|---|---|---|
| Income tax expense (to balance) | 6.4 | |
|     Deferred tax liability (determined above) | | 4.8 |
|     Income tax payable (determined above) | | 1.6 |

## Problem 16-3 (concluded)
## Requirement 2

| ($ in millions) | Current Year 2007 | Future Taxable Amounts 2008 | Future Taxable Amounts 2009 | Future Taxable Amounts [total] |
|---|---|---|---|---|
| **Accounting income** | 15 | | | |
| *Temporary difference:* | | | | |
| Lot sales | 4 | 5 | 3 | 8 |
| | | | | |
| **Taxable income** | 19 | | | |
| Enacted tax rate | 40% | | | 35% |
| Tax payable currently | 7.6 | | | |
| Deferred tax liability | | | | 2.8 |
| | | | | ↓ |

**Deferred tax liability:**

| | |
|---|---|
| Ending balance (balance currently needed) | $ 2.8 |
| Less: beginning balance | (4.8) |
| *Change needed to achieve desired balance* | $(2.0) |

**Journal entry at the end of 2007**

| | | |
|---|---|---|
| Income tax expense (to balance) | 5.6 | |
| Deferred tax liability (determined above) | 2.0 | |
| Income tax payable (determined above) | | 7.6 |

## Requirement 3

The balance in the deferred tax liability account at the end of 2007 would have been $3.2 million if the new tax rate had not been enacted:

| | |
|---|---|
| Future taxable amounts | $ 8 million |
| Previous tax rate | 40% |
| Deferred tax liability | $3.2 million |

The effect of the change is included in income tax expense, because income tax expense is less than it would have been if the rate had not changed.

# Problem 16-4

|                            | 2006       | 2007       | 2008       | 2009      |
|----------------------------|------------|------------|------------|-----------|
| Pretax accounting income   | $60,000    | $80,000    | $70,000    | $70,000   |
| Depreciation for tax       | (39,600)   | (52,800)   | (18,000)   | (9,600)   |
| Taxable Income             | $20,400    | $27,200    | $52,000    | $60,400   |
| Tax rate                   | 30%        | 30%        | 40%        | 40%       |
| Tax payable                | $ 6,120    | $ 8,160    | $20,800    | $24,160   |

|                        | 2006     | 2007     | 2008     | 2009     | Cumulative Temporary Difference |
|------------------------|----------|----------|----------|----------|---------------------------------|
| Straight-line          | 30,000   | 30,000   | 30,000   | 30,000   |                                 |
| Tax depreciation       | (39,600) | (52,800) | (18,000) | (9,600)  |                                 |
| **Temporary differences:** | (9,600)  | (22,800) | 12,000   | 20,400   | 0                               |
| 2006                   |          | (22,800) | 12,000   | 20,400   | $ 9,600                         |
| 2007                   |          |          | 12,000   | 20,400   | $32,400                         |
| 2008                   |          |          |          | 20,400   | $20,400                         |
| 2009                   |          |          |          |          | 0                               |

|                        | 2006     | 2007     | 2008      | 2009      |
|------------------------|----------|----------|-----------|-----------|
| Cumulative difference  | $ 9,600  | $32,400  | $20,400   | $    0    |
| Tax rate               | 30%      | 40%      | 40%       | 40%       |
| Year-end balance       | $ 2,880  | $12,960  | $ 8,160   | $    0    |
| Previous balance       | 0        | (2,880)  | (12,960)  | (8,160)   |
| Credit / (debit)       | $ 2,880  | $10,080  | $ (4,800) | $(8,160)  |

## Problem 16-4 (concluded)

**Journal entry at the end of 2006**

| | | |
|---|---|---|
| Income tax expense (to balance) | 9,000 | |
|     Deferred tax liability (determined above) | | 2,880 |
|     Income tax payable (determined above) | | 6,120 |

**Journal entry at the end of 2007**

| | | |
|---|---|---|
| Income tax expense (to balance) | 18,240 | |
|     Deferred tax liability (determined above) | | 10,080 |
|     Income tax payable (determined above) | | 8,160 |

**Journal entry at the end of 2008**

| | | |
|---|---|---|
| Income tax expense (to balance) | 16,000 | |
| Deferred tax liability (determined above) | 4,800 | |
|     Income tax payable (determined above) | | 20,800 |

**Journal entry at the end of 2009**

| | | |
|---|---|---|
| Income tax expense (to balance) | 16,000 | |
| Deferred tax liability (determined above) | 8,160 | |
|     Income tax payable (determined above) | | 24,160 |

# Problem 16-5

|  | 2006 | 2007 | 2008 | 2009 |
|---|---|---|---|---|
| Pretax accounting income | $350,000 | $270,000 | $340,000 | $380,000 |
| Installment sale | (50,000) | 20,000 | 25,000 | 5,000 |
| Municipal bond interest |  |  | (15,000) |  |
| Taxable Income | $300,000 | $290,000 | $350,000 | $385,000 |
| Tax rate | 30% | 30% | 25% | 25% |
| Income tax payable | $ 90,000 | $ 87,000 | $ 87,500 | $ 96,250 |

| | 2006 | 2007 | 2008 | 2009 | Cumulative Temporary Difference |
|---|---|---|---|---|---|
| **Temporary difference:** | (50,000) | 20,000 | 25,000 | 5,000 = | 0 |
| **2006** |  | 20,000 | 25,000 | 5,000 = | $50,000 |
| **2007** |  |  | 25,000 | 5,000 = | $30,000 |
| **2008** |  |  |  | 5,000 = | $ 5,000 |
| **2009** |  |  |  |  | 0 |

| | 2006 | 2007 | 2008 | 2009 |
|---|---|---|---|---|
| Cumulative difference | $50,000 | $30,000 | $ 5,000 | $    0 |
| Tax rate | 30% | 25% | 25% | 25% |
| Year-end balance | $15,000 | $ 7,500 | $ 1,250 | 0 |
| Previous balance | 0 | (15,000) | (7,500) | (1,250) |
| Credit / (debit) | $15,000 | $ (7,500) | $(6,250) | $(1,250) |

## Problem 16-5 (concluded)

### Journal entry at the end of 2006

| | | |
|---|---|---|
| Income tax expense (to balance) | 105,000 | |
| Deferred tax liability (determined above) | | 15,000 |
| Income tax payable (determined above) | | 90,000 |

### Journal entry at the end of 2007

| | | |
|---|---|---|
| Income tax expense (to balance) | 79,500 | |
| Deferred tax liability (determined above) | 7,500 | |
| Income tax payable (determined above) | | 87,000 |

### Journal entry at the end of 2008

| | | |
|---|---|---|
| Income tax expense (to balance) | 81,250 | |
| Deferred tax liability (determined above) | 6,250 | |
| Income tax payable (determined above) | | 87,500 |

### Journal entry at the end of 2009

| | | |
|---|---|---|
| Income tax expense (to balance) | 95,000 | |
| Deferred tax liability (determined above) | 1,250 | |
| Income tax payable (determined above) | | 96,250 |

# Problem 16-6

## Requirement 1

| ($ in millions) | | |
|---|---|---|
| Income tax expense (to balance) | 16.4 | |
| Deferred tax asset ($6 million x 40%) | 2.4 | |
|     Deferred tax liability ($39 million x 40%) | | 15.6 |
|     Income tax payable ($8 million x 40%) | | 3.2 |

## Requirement 2

In a classified balance sheet, deferred tax assets and deferred tax liabilities are classified as either *current* or *noncurrent* according to how the related assets or liabilities are classified for financial reporting. The deferred tax liabilities and deferred tax assets are offset to get the net current and the net noncurrent amounts:

| ($ in millions) Related Balance Sheet Account | Classification current-C noncurrent-N | Future Taxable (Deductible) Amounts | Tax Rate | Deferred Tax (Asset) Liability C | N |
|---|---|---|---|---|---|
| Liability – loss contingency | N | (6) | x 40% | | (2.4) |
| Depreciable assets | N | 30 | x 40% | | 12.0 |
| Prepaid insurance | C | 9 | x 40% | 3.6 | |
| | | | | | |
| Net **current** liability (asset) | | | | 3.6 | |
| Net **noncurrent** liability (asset) | | | | | 9.6 |
| | | | | | |
| ***Current Liabilities:*** | | | | | |
|     Deferred tax liability | $3.6 | | | | |
| | | | | | |
| ***Long-Term Liabilities:*** | | | | | |
|     Deferred tax liability | $9.6 | | | | |

## Problem 16-6 (concluded)

### Requirement 3

| ($ in millions) | Current Year 2006 | Future Taxable (Deductible) Amounts | | | Deferred Tax Liab. Asset | |
|---|---|---|---|---|---|---|
| | | 2007 | 2008 | 2009 | | |
| **Accounting income** | 41 | | | | | |
| *Temporary differences:* | | | | | | |
| Depreciation | (30) | (60) | 50 | 40 | | |
| Prepaid insurance | (9) | 9 | ___ | ___ | | |
| | | (51) | 50 | 40 | | |
| | | 40% | 35% | 35% | | |
| *Deferred tax liability* | | (20.4) | 17.5 | 14 | 11.1 | |
| | | | | | | |
| Loss contingency | 6 | | (6) | | | |
| | | | 35% | | | |
| *Deferred tax asset* | | | (2.1) | | | (2.1) |
| | | | | | | |
| **Taxable income** | 8 | | | | | |
| Enacted tax rate | 40% | | | | | |
| Tax payable currently | 3.2 | | | | | |

| | | Deferred Tax Liab. Asset | |
|---|---|---|---|
| | | ↓ | ↓ |
| Ending balances (balances currently needed): | | $11.1 | $2.1 |
| Less: beginning balances: | | (0.0) | (0.0) |
| *Change needed to achieve desired balances* | | $11.1 | $2.1 |

---

**Journal entry at the end of 2006**

| | | |
|---|---|---|
| Income tax expense (to balance) | 12.2 | |
| Deferred tax asset (determined above) | 2.1 | |
| Deferred tax liability (determined above) | | 11.1 |
| Income tax payable (determined above) | | 3.2 |

# Problem 16-7
## Requirement 1

| ($ in millions) | Current Year 2006 | Future Taxable (Deductible) Amounts | | Future Taxable Amounts [total] | Future Deductible Amounts [total] |
|---|---|---|---|---|---|
| | | 2007 | 2008 | | |
| **Accounting income** | 76 | | | | |
| *Non-temporary difference:* | | | | | |
| Fine paid | 2 | | | | |
| *Temporary differences:* | | | | | |
| Installment sales | (3) | 2 | 2 | 4 | |
| Depreciation | (15) | 8 | 13 | 21 | |
| Bad debts | 1 | (2) | | | (2) |
| Paid future absences | 7 | (4) | (3) | | (7) |
| Loss contingency | (2) | | | | |
| **Taxable income** | 66 | | | | |
| | | | | 25 | (9) |
| Enacted tax rate | 40% | | | 40% | 40% |
| Tax payable currently | 26.4 | | | | |
| Deferred tax liability | | | | 10.0 | |
| Deferred tax asset | | | | | (3.6) |
| | | | | ↓ | ↓ |

|  | Deferred Tax | |
|---|---|---|
| | Liab. | Asset |
| Ending balances (balances currently needed): | $10.0 | $3.6 |
| Less: beginning balances: | (2.8) | (1.2) |
| *Changes needed to achieve desired balances* | $7.2 | $2.4 |

| **Journal entry at the end of 2006** | | |
|---|---|---|
| Income tax expense (to balance) | 31.2 | |
| Deferred tax asset (determined above) | 2.4 | |
| Deferred tax liability (determined above) | | 7.2 |
| Income tax payable (determined above) | | 26.4 |

## Problem 16-7 *(concluded)*
## Requirement 2

|  | ($ in millions) |
|---|---|
| Pretax accounting income | $76.0 |
| Income tax expense | (31.2) |
| Net income | $44.8 |

# Requirement 3

| ($ in millions)<br><br>Related Balance<br>Sheet Account | Classification<br>current-C<br>noncurrent-N | Future<br>Taxable<br>(Deductible)<br>Amounts | Tax<br>Rate | Deferred<br>Tax (Asset)<br>Liability<br>C | N |
|---|---|---|---|---|---|
| Receivable – installment sales | C | 2 | x 40% | .8 | |
| Receivable – installment sales | N | 2 | x 40% | | .8 |
| Depreciable assets | N | 21 | x 40% | | 8.4 |
| Allowance – uncollectible accounts | C | (2) | x 40% | (.8) | |
| Liability – paid future absences | C | (4) | x 40% | (1.6) | |
| Liability – paid future absences | N | (3) | x 40% | | (1.2) |
| | | | | ___ | ___ |
| Net **current** liability (asset) | | | | (1.6) | |
| Net **noncurrent** liability (asset) | | | | | 8.0 |

**Current Assets:**
    Deferred tax asset      $1.6

**Long-Term Liabilities:**
    Deferred tax liability      $8.0

**RECONCILIATION [NOT REQUIRED]:**
    Net current asset      $ (1.6)
    Net noncurrent liability      8.0
         $6.4

**Total amounts from requirement 1:**
    Deferred tax asset      $ (3.6)
    Deferred tax liability      10.0
         $6.4

# Problem 16-8

## Requirement 1

The expense for life insurance premiums is a non-temporary difference each year because it's recognized as an income statement expense, but is not tax-deductible in any year. The others are temporary differences. The temporary differences for casualty insurance expense and the unrealized loss originate in 2005 and reverse in 2006. The temporary difference for subscriptions originates each year and reverses the following year. The temporary difference for the loss contingency originated in 2004 and reverses in 2005.

## Problem 16-8 *(continued)*
### Requirement 2

| ($ in millions) | Current Year 2005 | Future Taxable Amounts [2006] | Future Deductible Amounts [2006] |
|---|---|---|---|
| **Accounting income** | 128 | | |
| *Non-temporary difference:* | | | |
| Life insurance premiums | 2 | | |
| *Temporary differences:* | | | |
| Casualty insurance expense | (30) | 30 | |
| Subscriptions-2004 (reversing)* | (10) | | |
| Subscriptions-2005 ($33- [$25-10])* | 18 | | (18) |
| Unrealized loss | 17 | | (17) |
| Loss contingency (reversing) | (5) | | |
| **Taxable income** | 120 | | |
| | | 30 | (35) |
| Enacted tax rate | 40% | 40% | 40% |
| Tax payable currently | 48 | | |
| Deferred tax liability | | 12 | |
| Deferred tax asset | | | 14 |
| | | ↓ | ↓ |
| | | Deferred tax liability | Deferred tax asset |
| Ending balances (balances currently needed): | | $12 | $14 |
| Less: beginning balances: | | 0 | (6) |
| *Changes needed to achieve desired balances* | | $12 | $ 8 |

| Journal entry at the end of 2005 | | |
|---|---|---|
| Income tax expense (to balance) | 52 | |
| Deferred tax asset (determined above) | 8 | |
| Deferred tax liability (determined above) | | 12 |
| Income tax payable (determined above) | | 48 |

### * Temporary difference for subscriptions:

| | 2004 | 2005 | 2006 |
|---|---|---|---|
| **Earned in current yr. (reported on income statement)** | | $25 | $33 |
| Collected in prior yr., earned in current yr. (reversing difference) | | (10) | (18) |
| Collected in current yr., earned in following yr. (originating difference) | $10 | 18 | 20 |
| **Collected in current yr. (reported on tax return)** | | $33 | $35 |

## Problem 16-8 *(continued)*

### Requirement 3

Because all accounts related to the temporary differences (prepaid insurance, unearned revenues, and short-term investments) are classified as current, the deferred tax amounts will be classified as current also. The net current amount is $2 million [$14 asset − $12 liability]. Since this is a debit difference, it is reported as a current asset.

| ($ in millions) | Current Year 2006 | Future Taxable Amounts [2007] | Future Deductible Amounts [2007] |
|---|---|---|---|
| **Accounting income** | 183 | | |
| *Non-temporary difference:* | | | |
| Life insurance premiums | 2 | | |
| *Temporary differences:* | | | |
| Casualty insurance (reversing) | 30 | | |
| Subscriptions-2005 (reversing)* | (18) | | |
| Subscriptions-2006 ($35- [33-18])* | 20 | | (20) |
| Unrealized loss (reversing) | (17) | | |
| **Taxable income** | 200 | | |
| | | 0 | (20) |
| Enacted tax rate | 40% | 40% | 40% |
| Tax payable currently | 80 | | |
| Deferred tax liability | | 0 | |
| Deferred tax asset | | | (8) |
| | | ↓ | ↓ |
| | | Deferred tax liability | Deferred tax asset |
| Ending balances (balances currently needed): | | $ 0 | $ 8 |
| Less: beginning balances: | | (12) | (14) |
| *Changes needed to achieve desired balances* | | ($12) | ($ 6) |

| **Journal entry at the end of 2006** | | | |
|---|---|---|---|
| Income tax expense (to balance) | 74 | | |
| Deferred tax liability (determined above) | 12 | | |
| Deferred tax asset (determined above) | | 6 | |
| Income tax payable (determined above) | | 80 | |

| * **Temporary difference for subscriptions:** | 2004 | 2005 | 2006 |
|---|---|---|---|
| **Earned in current yr. (reported on income statement)** | | $25 | $33 |
| Collected in prior yr., earned in current yr. (reversing difference) | | (10) | (18) |
| Collected in current yr., earned in following yr. (originating difference) | $10 | 18 | 20 |
| **Collected in current yr. (reported on tax return)** | | $33 | $35 |

## Problem 16-8 (concluded)

### Requirement 5

Because the liability for subscriptions received in advance, related to the only temporary difference, is classified as current, the deferred tax asset will be classified as current also. The deferred tax asset is $8 million and is reported as a current asset.

# Problem 16-9

## Requirement 1

RELATED ASSET – CUMULATIVE BALANCE (NOT REQUIRED)

($ in thousands)

|  | Service Revenue | Collections previous year | Collections current year | Service Revenue Receivable *Balance* |
|---|---|---|---|---|
| 2005 |  |  |  | $30 |
| 2006 | $750 | 30 | 740 | 10 |
| 2007 | 715 | 10 | 690 | 25 |
| 2008 | 700 | 25 | 695 | 5 |

## Problem 16-9 (continued)

| ($ in thousands) | | Current Year 2006 | Future Taxable Amount |
|---|---|---|---|
| **Accounting income** | | 250 | |
| *Temporary difference:* | | | |
| 2005 services | (30) | 30 | |
| 2006 services | | (10) | 10 |
| **Taxable income** | | 270 | |
| Enacted tax rate | | 40% | 40% |
| Tax payable currently | | 108 | |
| Deferred tax liability | | | 4 |
| | | | ↓ |

**Deferred tax liability:**

| | |
|---|---|
| Ending balance (balance currently needed) | $ 4 |
| Less: beginning balance: ([$650 - 620] x 40%) | (12) |
| *Change needed to achieve desired balance* | $ (8) |

| **Journal entry at the end of 2006** | | |
|---|---|---|
| Income tax expense (to balance) | 100 | |
| Deferred tax liability (determined above) | 8 | |
| Income tax payable (determined above) | | 108 |

## Problem 16-9 (continued)

## Requirement 2

| ($ in thousands) | | Current Year 2007 | Future Taxable Amount |
|---|---|---|---|
| **Accounting income** | | 220 | |
| *Temporary difference:* | | | |
| 2006 services | (10) | 10 | |
| 2007 services | | (25) | 25 |
| **Taxable income** | | 205 | |
| Enacted tax rate | | 40% | 40% |
| Tax payable currently | | 82 | |
| Deferred tax liability | | | 10 ↓ |

| **Deferred tax liability:** | |
|---|---|
| Ending balance (balance currently needed) | $10 |
| Less: beginning balance: (from 2006 calculation) | (4) |
| *Change needed to achieve desired balance* | $ 6 |

| **Journal entry at the end of 2007** | | |
|---|---|---|
| Income tax expense (to balance) | 88 | |
| Deferred tax liability (determined above) | | 6 |
| Income tax payable (determined above) | | 82 |

## Problem 16-9 *(concluded)*

## Requirement 3

| ($ in thousands) | | Current Year 2008 | Future Taxable Amount |
|---|---|---|---|
| **Accounting income** | | 200 | |
| *Temporary difference:* | | | |
| 2007 services | (25) | 25 | |
| 2008 services | | (5) | 5 |
| **Taxable income** | | 220 | |
| | | | |
| Enacted tax rate | | 40% | 40% |
| Tax payable currently | | 88 | |
| Deferred tax liability | | | 2 |
| | | | ↓ |
| **Deferred tax liability:** | | | |
| Ending balance (balance currently needed) | | | $ 2 |
| Less: beginning balance: (from 2007 calculation) | | | (10) |
| *Change needed to achieve desired balance* | | | $ (8) |

| **Journal entry at the end of 2008** | | |
|---|---|---|
| Income tax expense (to balance) | 80 | |
| Deferred tax liability (determined above) | 8 | |
| Income tax payable (determined above) | | 88 |

# Problem 16-10

**Requirement 1**

| ($ in millions) | Prior Years | | Current Year | Future Deductible |
|---|---|---|---|---|
| | 2004 | 2005 | 2006 | Amounts [total] |
| **Accounting loss** | | | (135) | |
| *Non-temporary difference:* | | | | |
| Fine paid | | | 5 | |
| *Temporary differences:* | | | | |
| Loss contingency | | | 10 | (10) |
| **Taxable loss** | | | (120) | |
| Loss carryback | (75) | (30) | 105 | |
| Loss carryforward | | | 15 | (15) |
| | | | 0 | (25) |
| Enacted tax rate | 40% | 40% | 40% | 40% |
| Tax payable (refundable) | (30) | (12) | 0 | |
| Deferred tax asset | | | | (10) ↓ |

| **Deferred tax asset:** | |
|---|---|
| Ending balance (balance currently needed) | $ 10 |
| Less: beginning balance | (0) |
| *Change needed to achieve desired balance* | $10 |

| **Journal entry at the end of 2006** | | |
|---|---|---|
| Receivable – income tax refund ($30 + 12) | 42 | |
| Deferred tax asset (determined above) | 10 | |
| Income tax benefit (to balance) | | 52 |

**Requirement 2**

| ($ in millions) | | |
|---|---|---|
| Operating loss before income taxes | | $135 |
| *Less:* Income tax benefit: | | |
| Tax refund from loss carryback | $42 | |
| Future tax benefits | 10 | 52 |
| Net operating loss | | $ 83 |

## Problem 16-10 (concluded)

## Requirement 3

| ($ in millions) | Current Year 2007 | Future Deductible Amounts |
|---|---|---|
| **Accounting income** | 60 | |
| *Temporary differences:* | | |
| Loss contingency | (10) | |
| Operating loss carryforward | (15) | |
| **Taxable income** | 35 | 0 |
| Enacted tax rate | 40% | 40% |
| Tax payable | 14 | |
| Deferred tax asset | | 0 |
| | | ↓ |
| **Deferred tax asset:** | | |
| Ending balance (balance currently needed) | | $ 0 |
| Less: beginning balance | | (10) |
| *Change needed to achieve desired balance* | | $(10) |
| **Journal entry at the end of 2007** | | |
| Income tax expense (to balance) | 24 | |
| Deferred tax asset (determined above) | | 10 |
| Income tax payable (determined above) | | 14 |

# Problem 16-11

## Tempo Co.
## INCOME TAX EXPENSE AND NET INCOME
## For the Year Ended December 31, 2006

**1.**

| | | |
|---|---:|---:|
| Income before income taxes | | $430,000 |
| Income tax expense: | | |
| Current (30% x [430,000 - 30,000]) | $120,000 | |
| Deferred (see computation below) | 9,000 | 129,000 |
| Net income | | $301,000 |

Computation:
Deferred income tax expense
Temporary difference-depreciation

| | | |
|---|---:|---:|
| 2007 | $10,000 | |
| 2008 | 15,000 | |
| 2009 | 20,000 | $45,000 |
| | | |
| Effective tax rate for years 2007 through 2009 | | 35% |
| | | |
| Deferred tax liability, 12/31/06 | | $15,750 |
| | | |
| Less: | | |
| 12/31/05 deferred tax asset | 9,000 | |
| 12/31/05 deferred tax liability | (15,750) | (6,750) |
| | | $9,000 |

**2.**

## Tempo Co.
## CALCULATION OF INTEREST EXPENSE
## For the Year Ended December 31, 2006

| | | |
|---|---:|---:|
| Note payable - bank | | |
| 1/1/06 to 9/30/06  -  $75,000 x 10% x 9/12 | $5,625 | |
| 10/1/06 to 12/31/06 - $70,000 x 10% x 3/12 | 1,750 | $7,375 |
| | | |
| Capital lease obligation | | |
| 1/1/06/to12/31/06 | | 7,526 |
| | | |
| Bonds payable | | |
| 7/1/06 to 12/31/06 | | 27,584 |
| | | $42,485 |

*Problem 16-11 (concluded)*

**3.**

## Temp Co.
## LONG-TERM LIABILITIES SECTION OF BALANCE SHEET
### December 31, 2006

*Long-term liabilities:*

| | | |
|---|---:|---:|
| Note payable-bank; 14 principal payments of $5,000 | | |
| plus 10% interest due annually on September 30 | $70,000 | |
| Less current portion | 5,000 | $ 65,000 |
| Capital lease obligation - 15 payments of $9,000 | | |
| due annually on January 1 | $75,260 | |
| Less current portion | 1,474 | 73,786 |
| | | |
| 11% bonds payable due June 30, 2033, | | |
| less unamortized discount of $40,191 | | 459,809 |
| | | |
| Deferred income tax liability | | 15,750 |
| Total long-term liabilities | | $614,345 |

# CASES
## Analysis Case 16-1
### Requirement 1

Temporary differences originate in one or more years and reverse in one or more future years. Differing depreciation methods are a common example of a temporary difference. On the other hand, permanent differences are not offset by corresponding reversals in future periods. Interest on municipal bonds is a common example of a permanent difference.

### Requirement 2

*Intra*period tax allocation allocates the total income tax expense for a reporting period among the financial statement items that gave rise to the income tax expense. As a result, certain items should be reported *net* of their respective income tax effects:

- Income (or loss) from continuing operations
- Discontinued operations
- Extraordinary items

*Inter*period tax allocation recognizes the tax consequences of events in the year in which the events are recognized for financial reporting purposes. It results in matching income tax expense with the related revenues. An example is warranty expense. The expense is estimated and reported in the income statement when the warranted product is sold, but not deducted on the tax return until actually paid. The future tax benefit of that deduction is a deferred tax asset in the meantime.

### Requirement 3

Deferred tax liabilities are not reported individually, but instead combined with deferred tax assets into a *net current* amount and a *net noncurrent* amount. Each is reported as either an asset – if deferred tax assets exceed deferred tax liabilities, or as a liability – if deferred tax liabilities exceed deferred tax assets. Deferred tax assets and deferred tax liabilities are classified as either *current* or *noncurrent* according to how the related assets or liabilities are classified for financial reporting. For instance, a deferred tax liability arising from estimated warranty expenses would be classified as *current* if the warranty liability is classified as *current*. A deferred tax asset or liability that is not related to a specific asset or liability should be classified according to when the underlying temporary difference is expected to reverse.

# Integrating Case 16-2

## Requirement 1

Because postretirement costs aren't tax deductible until paid to, or on behalf of, employees, accruing compensation expense produces temporary differences that create *future deductible amounts*. These have favorable tax consequences that are recognized as deferred tax assets. The deferred tax assets represent the future tax benefit from the reversal of the temporary difference between the *financial statement carrying amount* of the postretirement benefit liability and its *tax basis*.

## Requirement 2

Unlike most temporary differences, the temporary difference for postretirement benefits is related to an estimated liability – postretirement benefit liability – that already is a discounted amount. The postretirement benefit liability is the discounted present value of estimated future postretirement benefits. Perhaps the appropriate objection to SFAS 109 regarding discounting is inconsistency; some amounts are discounted, some are not.

# Judgment Case 16-3

## Requirement 1

($ in millions, except per share amounts)

### Russell-James Corporation
### Income Statement
### For the year ended December 31, 2009

| | | |
|---|---:|---:|
| Revenues | | $300 |
| Cost of goods sold | | 90 |
| Gross profit | | $210 |
| Selling and administrative expenses | | (60) |
| Income from continuing operations before income taxes | | $150 |
| Income taxes | | 60 |
| Income from continuing operations | | $ 90 |
| Discontinued operations: | | |
| Loss from operations of cosmetics division, | | |
| less applicable income taxes of $40 | $(60) | |
| Gain from disposal of cosmetics division, | | |
| less applicable income taxes of $6 | 9 | (51) |
| Income before extraordinary item | | $ 39 |
| Extraordinary loss from earthquake, | | |
| less applicable income taxes of $4 | | (6) |
| Net income | | $ 33 |

**Per share of common stock (100 million shares):**

| | |
|---|---:|
| Income from continuing operations | $.90 |
| Loss from operations of cosmetics division, net of tax | (.60) |
| Gain from disposal of cosmetics division, net of tax | .09 |
| Income before extraordinary item | $.39 |
| Extraordinary loss from earthquake, net of tax | (.06) |
| Net income | $.33 |

*Case 16-3 (concluded)*

**Requirement 2**

| | |
|---|---|
| Income taxes on income from continuing operations | $60 |
| Tax savings on loss from cosmetics division | (40) |
| Tax on gain from disposal of cosmetics division | 6 |
| Tax savings on loss from earthquake | (4) |
| Income taxes (total, unallocated) | $22 |

# International Case 16-4

The report should indicate similarities and differences between the United States and the chosen country focusing on the following issues:

a. Variations between accounting income and taxable income are common in the United States, whereas in some countries no differences exist – accounting income and taxable income are the same.

b. In the United States, these differences, when temporary, create deferred taxes. In some countries, income taxes are not deferred. Tax expense is simply the actual tax paid.

c. A deferred tax liability or deferred tax asset is recognized in the United States for the tax consequences of all amounts that will become taxable or deductible in future years as a result of transactions or events that already have occurred. Under standards of the International Accounting Standards Committee (IASC) and many countries, income taxes are deferred, but if differences are not expected to reverse for at least three years, these amounts can be excluded from tax expense.

Optionally, the report might compare (a) the degree of conservatism in the approaches taken by the two countries or (b) whether cultural differences are likely contributors to the differences observed.

# Judgment Case 16-5
## Requirement 1

Increasing debt increases risk. Financial risk often is measured by the debt-to-equity ratio: total liabilities/shareholders' equity. The higher the debt-to-equity ratio, other things being equal, the higher the risk. Analysts sometimes maintain that deferred taxes should be excluded, arguing that in many cases the deferred tax liability account remains the same (or continually grows larger). The reasoning is that no future tax payment will be required.

## Requirement 2

If we follow the argument above, we would reduce the numerator by the deferred tax: $5,813 – 1,610. Reducing liabilities would necessitate also increasing equity to keep everything in balance: $5,524 + 1,610. (The reasoning behind adjusting both amounts is that we are in effect *reversing* the effect of recording the deferred tax liability over time which was:

Income tax expense (reduces income and therefore equity [retained earnings])  1,610
    Deferred tax liability (increases liabilities)                               1,610

So, the revised ratio would be:

$$(\$5,813 - 1,610) \div (\$5,524 + 1,610) = .59$$

This is a 44% reduction in the ratio.

## Requirement 3

The counterargument to this approach, though, is similar to other situations in which long-term borrowings tend to remain the same or continually grow larger. Academic research suggests that investors view deferred tax liabilities as real liabilities and they appear to discount them according to the timing and likelihood of the liability's settlement. So, omitting deferred tax liabilities might distort the real debt-equity position.

# Integrating Case 16-6

## Requirement 1

When an investment is acquired to be held for an *unspecified period of time*, it is reported at the *fair value* of the investment securities on the reporting date. Reporting investments at their fair values means adjusting their carrying amounts for changes in fair value after their acquisition (or since the last reporting date if they were held at that time.) These changes are called "unrealized holding gains and losses" because they haven't yet been realized through the sale of the securities. Investments in securities *available for sale* are reported at fair value.

Holding gains and losses from retaining securities during periods of price change are *not* included in the determination of income for the period. Instead, they are accumulated and reported as a separate *component of shareholders' equity*. That is, an unrealized holding gain would increase shareholders' equity; an unrealized holding loss would decrease shareholders' equity.

## Requirement 2

| ($ in 000s) | | |
|---|---|---|
| Investment in marketable equity securities (given).............. | 15,351 | |
| Unrealized holding gain on investments (given).............. | | 9,979 |
| Deferred income tax liability (difference) ........................ | | 5,372 |

Temporary differences between the reported amount of an asset (Investment in marketable equity securities in this case) in the financial statements and its tax basis result in deferred taxes (Deferred income tax liability in this case). This temporary difference creates a *deferred tax liability* because it results in *taxable* amounts in some future year(s) when the investment is sold (when the temporary difference reverses).

# Communication Case 16-7

Rayne Co.

**SCHEDULE OF INTEREST EXPENSE**

*For the Year Ended December 31, 2009*

**1. Schedule of interest expense for the year ended December 31, 2009**

| | | |
|---|---:|---|
| Note payable | $6,600 | [1] |
| Capital lease obligation | 4,750 | [2] |
| Bonds payable | 26,900 | [3] |
| Total interest expense | $38,250 | |

[1] 1,800 (90,000 x 8% x $3/12$) + 4,800 (80,000 x 8% x $9/12$)
[2] 10% x 47,500 (62,500 - 15,000)
[3] 538,000 x 10% x $1/2$

**2. Memo to Dunn from Green:**

**To:** Dunn
**From:** Green
**Re:** Accounting for income taxes

Below is a brief overview of accounting for income taxes in accordance with SFAS 109.

The objectives of accounting for income taxes are to recognize (a) the amount of taxes payable or refundable for the current year, and (b) deferred tax liabilities and assets for the estimated future tax consequences of temporary differences and carryforwards. Temporary differences are differences between the tax basis of assets or liabilities and their reported amounts in the financial statements that will result in taxable or deductible amounts in future years.

Deferred tax assets and liabilities are measured based on the provisions of enacted tax law; the effects of future changes in the tax laws or rates are not anticipated. The measurement of deferred tax assets is reduced if necessary, by a valuation allowance to reflect the net asset amount that is more likely than not to be realized. Deferred income tax expense or benefit is measured as the change during the year in an enterprise's deferred tax liabilities and assets.

# Integrating Case 16-8

a. This is a correction of an error.

> **To correct the error:**
> Prepaid insurance ($35,000 ÷ 5 yrs x 3 yrs: 2006-2008) ........... 21,000
>     Income tax payable  ($21,000 x 40%) .............................     8,400
>     Retained earnings* ..................................................   12,600
>       *($35,000 – [$35,000 ÷ 5 years x 2 years: 2004-05]) less $8,400 tax
>
> **2006 adjusting entry:**
> Insurance expense ($35,000 ÷ 5 years) ..................................... 7,000
>     Prepaid insurance ............................................................   7,000

The financial statements that were incorrect as a result of the error would be *retrospectively restated* to report the prepaid insurance acquired and reflect the correct amount of insurance expense when those statements are reported again for comparative purposes in the current annual report. A *"prior period adjustment"* to retained earnings would be reported, and a *disclosure note* should describe the nature of the error and the impact of its correction on each year's net income, income before extraordinary items, and earnings per share.

b. This is a correction of an error.

> **To correct the error:**
> Retained earnings  (net effect) ................................................. 15,000
> Refund - income tax  ($25,000 x 40%) ............................. 10,000
>     Inventory .................................................................   25,000

The financial statements that were incorrect as a result of the error would be *retrospectively restated* to report the correct inventory amounts, cost of goods sold, and retained earnings when those statements are reported again for comparative purposes in the current annual report. A *"prior period adjustment"* to retained earnings would be reported, and a *disclosure note* should describe the nature of the error and the impact of its correction on each year's net income, income before extraordinary items, and earnings per share.

# Case 16-8 (continued)

c. This is a change in accounting principle and is reported retrospectively.

| | | |
|---|---|---|
| **To record the change:** | | |
| Inventory (given) ............................................................... | 960,000 | |
| Deferred tax liability ($960,000 x 40%) ........................... | | 384,000 |
| Retained earnings (net effect) ................................................. | | 576,000 |

Most changes in accounting principle are accounted for retrospectively. Prior years' financial statements are recast to reflect the use of the new accounting method. The company should increases retained earnings to the balance it would have had if the FIFO method had been used previously; that is, by the cumulative net income difference between the LIFO and FIFO methods. Simultaneously, inventory is increased to the balance it would have had if the FIFO method had always been used. A disclosure note should justify that the change is preferable and describe the effect of the change on any financial statement line items and per share amounts affected for all periods reported.

For financial reporting purposes, but not for tax, the company is retrospectively *increasing* accounting income, but not taxable income. This creates a temporary difference between the two that will reverse over time as the unsold inventory becomes cost of goods sold. When that happens, taxable income will be higher than accounting income. When taxable income will be higher than accounting income as a temporary difference reverses, we have a "future taxable amount" and record a deferred tax liability.

## Case 16-8 (continued)

d.  This is a correction of an error.

> **To correct the error:**
> Retained earnings (net effect) ................................................. 9,300
> Refund - income tax ($15,500 x 40%) ................................... 6,200
>    Compensation expense ....................................................... 15,500

The 2005 financial statements that were incorrect as a result of the error would be *retrospectively restated* to report the correct compensation expense, net income, and retained earnings when those statements are reported again for comparative purposes in the current annual report.   A *"prior period adjustment"* to retained earnings would be reported, and a *disclosure note* should describe the nature of the error and the impact of its correction on each year's net income, income before extraordinary items, and earnings per share.

e.  This is a change in estimate resulting from a change in accounting principle and is accounted for prospectively.

> No entry is needed to record the change
>
> **2006 adjusting entry:**
> Depreciation expense calculated below) ................................... 57,600
>    Accumulated depreciation ............................................. 57,600

A change in depreciation method is considered a change in accounting estimate resulting from a change in accounting principle. Accordingly, Williams-Santana reports the change prospectively; previous financial statements are not revised. Instead, the company simply employs the straight-line method from now on.  The undepreciated cost remaining at the time of the change is depreciated straight-line over the remaining useful life.

| | |
|---|---|
| Undepreciated cost, Jan. 1, 2006 (given) | $460,800 |
| Estimated residual value | (0) |
| To be depreciated over remaining 8 years | $460,800 |
| | 8   years |
| Annual straight-line depreciation 2006-13 | $ 57,600 |

# Case 16-8 (concluded)

f.  This is a correction of an error.

---

**To correct the error:**

| | | |
|---|---:|---:|
| Equipment (cost) ................................................................ | 1,000,000 | |
|     Accumulated depreciation ([$1,000,000 ÷ 10] x 3 years).... | | 300,000 |
|     Deferred tax liability ([$1,000,000 - $300,000] x 40%) ...... | | 280,000 |
|     Retained earnings | | |
|       ($1,000,000 – [$100,000 x 3 years]) less $280,000 tax ........... | | 420,000 |

**2006 adjusting entry:**

| | | |
|---|---:|---:|
| Depreciation expense ($1,000,000 ÷ 10) ............................. | 100,000 | |
|     Accumulated depreciation ............................................. | | 100,000 |

---

The financial statements that were incorrect as a result of the error would be *retrospectively restated* to report the correct depreciation, assets, and retained earnings when those statements are reported again for comparative purposes in the current annual report.  A *"prior period adjustment"* to retained earnings would be reported, and a *disclosure note* should describe the nature of the error and the impact of its correction on each year's net income, income before extraordinary items, and earnings per share.

# Real World Case 16-9

Deferred tax assets and deferred tax liabilities are classified as either *current* or *noncurrent* according to how the related assets or liabilities are classified for financial reporting. A deferred tax asset or deferred tax liability is considered to be related to an asset or liability if reduction (including amortization) of that asset or liability will cause the temporary difference to reverse. Deferred tax assets and deferred tax liabilities are not reported separately. Instead, they are offset, and a net current amount and a net noncurrent amount are reported as either an asset or a liability.

Because it reports a *noncurrent* liability, "Deferred income taxes" of $327.6 million, while the "net deferred tax liability" reported in the disclosure note is only $270.3 million, Walgreen apparently has a net *current* asset – i.e., *current* deferred tax assets in excess of *current* deferred tax liabilities. The apparent amount of the net current asset is $327.6 million - $270.3 million, or $57.3 million. This is reported as a *current* asset in the balance sheet. The company reports noncurrent deferred tax liabilities in excess of noncurrent deferred tax assets, a $327.6 million net *noncurrent* liability as a long-term liability in the balance sheet.

The journal entry that summarizes the entries Walgreen used to record 2004 income taxes can be reconstructed from the information provided in the note:

| | ($ in millions) | |
|---|---|---|
| Income tax expense (given) | 816.1 | |
| Deferred tax asset ($484.9 – 419.4) | 65.5 | |
| Deferred tax liability ($755.2 – 617.5) | | 137.7 |
| Income tax payable (to balance*) | | 9.8 |
| Cash (given) | | 734.1 |

\* The income tax payable differs from the $734.1 million cash actually paid in 2007 because corporations make estimated tax payments throughout the year that often do not match exactly the eventual tax liability.

# Research Case 16-10

An objective of this case is to acquaint the student with information provided by the Treasury Department and the IRS on the Internet, and in particular the ability to download forms. Another goal is to provide perspective on various topics (e.g., deductions, temporary differences, net operating loss) discussed in the chapter.

Specific deductions are listed that are deductible from "total income" to arrive at "taxable income." On the 2004 Form 1120 these are items 12 (compensation of officers) through 29 (net operating loss deduction). Each of these items is a deduction that might not also be included among expenses in the income statement. In addition, the amounts for the items might be different on the two statements.

A "net operating loss deduction" would be reported if a company reported a net operating loss in a previous period that was not "carried back" to a prior period and hasn't yet been deducted as an operating loss carryforward. The deduction reduces taxable income and therefore taxes payable.

Temporary differences between taxable income and pretax income in the income statement are created when the amounts for various deductions differ from corresponding expenses in the income statement – if the differences will eventually be in the opposite direction, that is, if the differences will "reverse." Differences in revenue items on the two reports might also create temporary differences.

# Analysis Case 16-11

1. Deferred tax assets and deferred tax liabilities are classified as either *current* or *noncurrent* depending on how the related assets or liabilities are classified for financial reporting. The several deferred tax assets and liabilities should be combined into two summary amounts. Current deferred tax assets and liabilities should be netted together, with the *net current* amount reported as either a current asset, if deferred tax assets exceed deferred tax liabilities, or current liability, if deferred tax liabilities exceed deferred tax assets. A single *net noncurrent* amount, too, should be reported as a net noncurrent asset or a net noncurrent liability. FedEx reports deferred income taxes as both an asset and a liability because, apparently, the net current amount is a current asset and the net noncurrent amount is a liability.

2. Note 11 in the disclosure notes indicates that deferred tax assets are $1,265 million in 2004 and deferred tax liabilities are $1,957 million. The reason these amounts differ from the two amounts reported in the balance sheet relates to the answer to requirement 1. Both the $1,265 million deferred tax assets and the $1,957 million of deferred tax liabilities are separated into current and long-term classifications. The current portions of each are combined to produce a $489 million current asset and the noncurrent portions of each are combined to produce a long-term liability of $1,181 million. Note that $1,957 – 1,265 = **$692** and $1,181 – 489 = **$692.**

3. A valuation allowance is needed if it is "more likely than not" that some portion or all of a deferred tax asset will not be realized. FedEx recorded a valuation allowance of $37 million for its deferred tax assets as reported in Note 11.

# Real World Case 16-12

1. Kroger's Feb., 2005 (fiscal 2004) income statement reports the income tax expense for the year as $390 million. The current portion is $96 + 36 = $132 million. The deferred portion of the expense is $258 million.

2. Deferred tax assets and deferred tax liabilities are classified as either current or noncurrent according to how the related assets or liabilities are classified for financial reporting. A deferred tax asset or deferred tax liability is considered to be related to an asset or liability if reduction (including amortization) of that asset or liability will cause the temporary difference to reverse. Deferred tax assets and deferred tax liabilities are not necessarily reported separately. Instead, they are offset, and a net current amount and a net noncurrent amount are reported as either an asset or a liability.

In fiscal 2004, Kroger reports current deferred tax liabilities ($286 million) in excess of current deferred tax assets ($19 million), a $267 million net current liability. This is reported as part of "other current liabilities" in the balance sheet. The company reports noncurrent deferred tax liabilities ($1,705 million) in excess of net noncurrent deferred tax assets ($766 million), a $939 million net noncurrent liability. This is reported separately as a long-term liability (in "other liabilities") in the balance sheet.

# Chapter 17  Pensions and Other Postretirement Benefits

## QUESTIONS FOR REVIEW OF KEY TOPICS

### Question 17-1
Pension plans are arrangements designed to provide income to individuals during their retirement years. Funds are set aside during an employee's working years so that the accumulated funds plus earnings from investing those funds are available to replace wages at retirement. An individual has a pension fund when she or he periodically invests in stocks, bonds, CDs, or other securities for the purpose of saving for retirement. When an employer establishes a pension plan, the employer provides some or all of the periodic contributions to the retirement fund.

The motivation for corporations to establish pension plans comes from several sources. Pension plans provide employees with a degree of retirement security. They may fulfill a moral obligation many employers feel toward employees. Pension plans often enhance productivity, reduce turnover, satisfy union demands, and allow employers to compete in the labor market.

### Question 17-2
A qualified pension plan gains important tax advantages. The employer is permitted an immediate tax deduction for amounts paid into the pension fund. Conversely, the benefits to employees are not taxed until retirement benefits are received. Also, earnings on the funds set aside by the employer accumulate tax-free. For a pension plan to be qualified for special tax treatment, these general requirements must be met:
1. It must cover at least 70% of employees.
2. It cannot discriminate in favor of highly compensated employees.
3. It must be funded in advance of retirement through contributions to an irrevocable trust fund.
4. Benefits must "vest" after a specified period of service, commonly five years.
5. It complies with specific restrictions on the timing and amount of contributions and benefits.

### Question 17-3
This is a noncontributory plan because the corporation makes all contributions. When employees make contributions to the plan in addition to employer contributions, it's called a "contributory" plan. This is a *defined contribution* plan because it promises fixed annual contributions to a pension fund, without further commitment regarding benefit amounts at retirement.

### Question 17-4
The vested benefit obligation is the pension benefit obligation that is *not* contingent upon an employee's continuing service.

### Question 17-5
The *accumulated benefit obligation* is the discounted present value of retirement benefits calculated by applying the pension formula with no attempt to forecast what salaries will be when the formula actually is applied. The *projected benefit obligation* is the present value of those benefits when the actuary includes projected salaries in the pension formula.

*Answers to Questions (continued)*

## Question 17-6
The projected benefit obligation can change due to periodic service cost, accrued interest, revised estimates, plan amendments, and the payment of benefits.

## Question 17-7
The balance of the plan assets can change due to investment returns, employer contributions, and the payment of benefits.

## Question 17-8
The pension expense reported on the income statement is a composite of periodic changes that occur in both the pension obligation and the plan assets. These include service cost, interest cost, return on the plan assets, and the amortization of prior service cost and of net gains or losses.

## Question 17-9
The service cost in connection with a pension plan is the present value of benefits attributed by the pension formula to employee service during the period, projecting future salary levels (i.e., the projected benefits approach).

## Question 17-10
The interest cost is the projected benefit obligation outstanding at the beginning of the period multiplied by the actuary's interest (discount) rate. This is the "interest expense" that accrues on the PBO and is included as a component of pension expense rather than being separately reported.

## Question 17-11
SFAS 87 specifies that the *actual* return be included in the determination of pension expense. However, the actual return is adjusted for any difference between actual and expected return, meaning that the *expected* return is really the amount reflected in the calculation of pension expense. This "investment revenue" is deducted as a component of pension expense rather than being separately reported.

The difference between actual and expected return on plan assets is combined with gains and losses from other sources for possible future amortization to pension expense.

## Question 17-12
Prior service cost is the obligation (present value of benefits) due to giving credit to employees for years of service provided before either the date of an amendment to (or initiation of) a pension plan. Prior service cost is not formally recognized as a separate account in the company's records. The cost is allocated to pension expense over the service period of affected employees. The straight-line method allocates an equal amount of the prior service cost to each year. The service method recognizes the cost each year in proportion to the fraction of the total remaining "service years" worked in each of these years.

## Answers to Questions (continued)

### Question 17-13
Gains or losses related to pension plan assets represent the difference between the return on investments and what the return had been expected to be. They should be deferred until total net gains or losses exceed a defined threshold. Specifically, a *portion* of the excess is included in pension expense only if it exceeds an amount equal to 10% of the PBO, or 10% of plan assets, whichever is higher. The minimum amount that should be included is the excess divided by the average remaining service period of active employees expected to receive benefits under the plan. Gains or losses related to the pension obligation are treated the same way. In fact, gains and losses from both sources are combined to determine the net gains or net losses referred to above.

### Question 17-14
The PBO, plan assets, unrecognized prior service cost, and the unrecognized net loss (or gain) represent "memorandum" accounts not formally recognized as separate accounts in the company's records. Their balances are monitored in the informal records, though, because they are reported in disclosure notes, and changes in their balances affect amounts that are formally recognized.

### Question 17-15
The two components of pension expense that may reduce pension expense are the return on plan assets (always) and the amortization of a net gain (amortizing a net loss increases the expense).

### Question 17-16
The components of pension expense that involve delayed recognition are the prior service cost and gains and losses.

### Question 17-17
The excess of the *actual* return on plan assets over the *expected* return is considered a gain. It may, in fact, decrease the employer's pension cost, but not immediately. It is grouped with other gains and losses and is amortized as a component of pension expense only if the net gain or net loss exceeds an amount equal to 10% of the PBO, or 10% of plan assets, whichever is higher.

### Question 17-18
The difference between the pension expense and the cash contribution is debited or credited, depending on the situation, to a single account: prepaid (accrued) pension cost. Consistent with other situations when an expense is overpaid, the excess payment represents an asset – prepaid pension cost. Quite often, the cash payment is less than the expense. In those instances, the underpayment represents a liability.

## Question 17-19

Conceptually, the pension liability is best measured by the PBO. This apparently was the majority view of the FASB. The PBO also is specified for determining the service cost and interest cost components of the pension expense. However, the balance sheet reports either an *accrued* pension cost as a liability or a *prepaid* pension cost as an asset, depending on whether the prepaid (accrued) pension cost account has a credit or a debit balance. This amount is supplemented to provide a minimum reported liability equal to excess of the accumulated benefit obligation over the plan assets when the ABO is underfunded. Also, SFAS 87 requires offsetting despite a theoretical preference by the Board for recognizing the pension liability and plan assets as separate elements of the balance sheet. In fact, the FASB acknowledged that this requirement is made "even though the liability has not been settled, the assets may still be largely controlled, and substantial risks and rewards associated with both of those amounts are clearly borne by the employer."

## Question 17-20

The difference between the employer's obligation (PBO) and the resources available to satisfy that obligation (plan assets) is the funded status of the pension plan. If all the changes in the PBO and plan assets were immediately recognized in pension expense, the balance in the prepaid (accrued) pension cost would report the funded status. This is because that balance would be the cumulative difference between the cash contributions and what's been expensed. However, not all the changes in the PBO and plan assets are immediately recognized in pension expense (recognition is delayed for both gains and losses and the prior service cost). Therefore, the unrecognized portions of each of these are reflected in the funded status, but *not yet in the prepaid (accrued) pension cost.* This means the difference between the funded status and the balance in prepaid (accrued) pension cost can be reconciled by the unrecognized prior service cost and the unrecognized net loss. In fact, this reconciliation must be disclosed in the financial statements.

## Question 17-21

A minimum liability must be reported to the extent that the accumulated benefit obligation exceeds the fair value of plan assets. So, if there is a zero balance in the prepaid (accrued) pension cost account, an "additional liability" account must be established for the entire excess. If the account has a *credit* balance of more than the minimum liability, no additional liability would be required. Reporting the balance as a pension liability would be sufficient. If the account has a credit balance of less than the minimum liability, an additional liability would be required for the difference. If the account has a *debit* balance, an "additional liability" account must be established to combine with the prepaid (accrued) pension cost account balance to reflect the minimum liability.

## Answers to Questions (concluded)

### Question 17-22

Usually the "substantive plan" is the written plan. However, sometimes a company's consistent practice of providing benefits a certain way is a better indication of the employer's real plan for postretirement benefits than the written plan. In those cases, the "substantive plan" should override the written plan in determining the basis for accounting for postretirement benefits.

Anticipated *changes* in cost-sharing arrangements (before the plan actually is amended) should be considered when measuring the obligation and expense when the company (a) can demonstrate the intent and ability to make the change and (b) has communicated the intended change to plan participants.

### Question 17-23

The expected postretirement benefit obligation (EPBO) is the actuary's estimate of the total postretirement benefits (at their discounted present value) expected to be received by plan participants. When a plan is pay-related, future compensation levels are implicitly assumed. The accumulated postretirement benefit obligation (APBO) measures the obligation existing at a particular date, rather than the total amount expected to be earned by plan participants. The APBO is conceptually similar to a pension plan's *projected benefit obligation*. The EPBO has no counterpart in pension accounting.

### Question 17-24

The cost of benefits is "attributed" to the years during which those benefits are assumed to be earned by employees. The attribution period spans each year of service from the employee's date of hire to the employee's "full eligibility date," which is the date the employee has performed all the service necessary to have earned all the retiree benefits estimated to be received by that employee. The approach assigns an equal fraction of the EPBO to each of those years. The attribution period does not include any years of service beyond the full eligibility date, even if the employee is expected to work after that date.

### Question 17-25

The transition obligation could be recognized as part of the compensation expense by either of two methods. An employer could choose to recognize the entire transition obligation immediately or on a straight-line basis over the plan participants' future service periods (or optionally over a 20-year period if that's longer.)

### Question 17-26

The service cost for *pensions* reflects additional benefits employees earn from an additional year's service, whereas the service cost for *retiree health care* plans is simply an allocation to the current year of a portion of a fixed total cost.

### Question 17-27

The attribution period spans each year of service from the employee's date of hire to the employee's "full eligibility date," 30 years in this case. The APBO is $10,000 which represents the portion of the EPBO earned after 15 years of the 30-year attribution period: $20,000 x $15/30$ = $10,000.

© The McGraw-Hill Companies, Inc., 2007

# BRIEF EXERCISES

## Brief Exercise 17-1

|  | ($ in millions) |  |
|---|---|---|
| *Beginning* of the year | $80 | |
| Service cost | 10 | |
| Interest cost | 4 | → (5% x $80) |
| Loss (gain) on PBO | 0 | |
| Less: Retiree benefits | (6) | |
| *End* of the year | $88 | |

## Brief Exercise 17-2

|  | ($ in millions) |  |
|---|---|---|
| *Beginning* of the year | $80 | |
| Service cost | ? | |
| Interest cost | 4 | → (5% x $80) |
| Loss (gain) on PBO | 0 | |
| Less: Retiree benefits | (6) | |
| *End* of the year | $85 | |

**Service cost** = $85 – 80 – 4 + 6 = <u>$7 million</u>

## Brief Exercise 17-3

|  | ($ in millions) |  |
|---|---|---|
| *Beginning* of the year | $80 | |
| Service cost | 10 | |
| Interest cost | 4 | → (5% x $80) |
| Loss (gain) on PBO | 0 | |
| Less: Retiree benefits | (?) | |
| *End* of the year | $85 | |

**Retiree benefits** = $85 – 80 – 4 – 10 = – <u>$9 million</u>

# Brief Exercise 17-4

|  | ($ in millions) |
|---|---|
| *Beginning* of the year | $80 |
| Service cost | 10 |
| Interest cost | 4 → (5% x $80) |
| Loss (gain) on PBO | ? |
| Less: Retiree benefits | (6) |
| *End* of the year | $85 |

**Gain** = $85 – 80 – 10 – 4 + 6 = – <u>$3 million</u>

# Brief Exercise 17-5

|  | ($ in millions) |
|---|---|
| **Plan assets** |  |
| *Beginning* of the year | $80 |
| Actual return | 4 → (5% x $80) |
| Cash contributions | 7 |
| Less: Retiree benefits | (6) |
| *End* of the year | $85 |

# Brief Exercise 17-6

|  | ($ in millions) |
|---|---|
| **Plan assets** |  |
| *Beginning* of the year | $80 |
| Actual return | 4 → (5% x $80) |
| Cash contributions | 7 |
| Less: Retiree benefits | (?) |
| *End* of the year | $83 |

**Retiree benefits** = $83 – 80 – 4 – 7 = – <u>$8 million</u>

# Brief Exercise 17-7

($ in millions)

**Plan assets**

| | |
|---|---|
| *Beginning* of the year | $100 |
| Actual return | ?    → (? % x $100) |
| Cash contributions | 7 |
| Less: Retiree benefits | (6) |
| *End* of the year | $104 |

**Return on assets** = $104 − 100 − 7 + 6 =   $3 million

**Rate of return on assets** = $3 million ÷ $100 million = <u>3%</u>


# Brief Exercise 17-8

| | ($ in millions) |
|---|---|
| Service cost | $10 |
| Interest cost (5% x $80) | 4 |
| Actual return on the plan assets ($5) adjusted for: $1 gain* on the plan assets | (4) |
| Amortization of prior service cost | 0 |
| Amortization of net loss (gain) | 0 |
| **Pension expense** | <u>$10</u> |

\* $5 - 4


# Brief Exercise 17-9

| | ($ in millions) |
|---|---|
| Service cost | $10 |
| Interest cost | 4 |
| Actual return on the plan assets ($4) adjusted for: $2 loss* on the plan assets | (6) |
| Amortization of prior service cost | 2** |
| Amortization of net loss (gain) | 0 |
| **Pension expense** | <u>$10</u> |

\* $6 - 4

\*\* $20 ÷ 10 years = $2

# Brief Exercise 17-10

Gains or losses should be deferred until total net gains or losses exceed a defined threshold. Specifically, a *portion* of the excess is included in pension expense only if it exceeds an amount equal to 10% of the PBO, or 10% of plan assets, whichever is higher. The minimum amount that should be included is the excess divided by the average remaining service period of active employees expected to receive benefits under the plan. Amortization of net gains is deducted from pension expense; amortization of net losses is added to pension expense. Pension expense in this instance is decreased by a $2 million amortization of the net gain:

|  | ($ in millions) |
|---|---|
| Unamortized net gain | $30 |
| Less: 10% corridor (threshold)* | (10) |
| Excess | $20 |
| Service period | ÷ 10 |
| **Amortization** | $ 2 |

* 10% times either the PBO ($80) or plan assets ($100), whichever is larger


# Brief Exercise 17-11

|  | ($ in millions) |
|---|---|
| ABO | $30 |
| Plan assets | 25 |
| Minimum liability | $ 5 |

The accrued pension cost ($2 million) is insufficient to meet the minimum liability requirement, so an additional liability of $3 million is needed.

# Brief Exercise 17-12

| | **APBO** | **Service Cost** |
|---|---|---|
| **2006** | $50,000 \times 6/30 = \underline{\$10,000}$ | $50,000 \times 1/30 = \underline{\$1,667}$ |
| **2007** | $54,000 \times 7/30 = \underline{\$12,600}$ | $54,000 \times 1/30 = \underline{\$1,800}$ |

30 year attribution period (age 26-55)

# Brief Exercise 17-13

| | ($ in millions) |
|---|---|
| *Beginning* of 2006 | $25 |
| Service cost | 7 |
| Interest cost | 2 ← (8% x $25) |
| Gain on APBO | (1) |
| Less: Retiree benefits | (3) |
| *End* of 2006 | $30 |

# EXERCISES

## Exercise 17-1

**Events**

| | | |
|---|---|---|
| **I** | 1. | Interest cost. |
| **N** | 2. | Amortization of prior service cost. |
| **D** | 3. | A decrease in the average life expectancy of employees. |
| **I** | 4. | An increase in the average life expectancy of employees. |
| **I** | 5. | A plan amendment that increases benefits is made retroactive to prior years. |
| **D** | 6. | An increase in the actuary's assumed discount rate. |
| **N** | 7. | Cash contributions to the pension fund by the employer. |
| **D** | 8. | Benefits are paid to retired employees. |
| **I** | 9. | Service cost. |
| **N** | 10. | Return on plan assets during the year lower than expected. |
| **N** | 11. | Return on plan assets during the year higher than expected. |

## Exercise 17-2

|  | ($ in millions) | |
|---|---|---|
| *Beginning* of 2006 | $30 | |
| Service cost | 12 | |
| Interest cost | 3 | → (10% x $30) |
| Loss (gain) on PBO | 0 | |
| Less: Retiree benefits | (4) | |
| *End* of 2006 | $41 | |

# Exercise 17-3

### Events

| | | |
|---|---|---|
| **I** | 1. | Interest cost. |
| **I** | 2. | Amortization of prior service cost. |
| **N** | 3. | Excess of the expected return on plan assets over the actual return. |
| **D** | 4. | Expected return on plan assets. |
| **N** | 5. | A plan amendment that increases benefits is made retroactive to prior years. |
| **N** | 6. | Actuary's estimate of the PBO is increased. |
| **N** | 7. | Cash contributions to the pension fund by the employer. |
| **N** | 8. | Benefits are paid to retired employees. |
| **I** | 9. | Service cost. |
| **N** | 10. | Excess of the actual return on plan assets over the expected return. |
| **I** | 11. | Amortization of unrecognized net loss. |
| **D** | 12. | Amortization of unrecognized net gain. |

# Exercise 17-4

**Requirement 1**

|  | ($ in millions) |  |
|---|---|---|
| Pension expense | 14 |  |
| Cash |  | 14 |

**Requirement 2**

| Pension expense (given) | 14 |  |
|---|---|---|
| Prepaid (accrued) pension cost (difference) |  | 3 |
| Cash (given) |  | 11 |

**Requirement 3**

| Pension expense (given) | 14 |  |
|---|---|---|
| Prepaid (accrued) pension cost (difference) | 2 |  |
| Cash (given) |  | 16 |

# Exercise 17-5

|  | ($ in millions) |
|---|---|
| **Plan assets** |  |
| *Beginning* of 2006 | $600 |
| Actual return | 48 |
| Cash contributions | 100 |
| Less: Retiree benefits | (11) |
| *End* of 2006 | $737 |

# Exercise 17-6

PBO: ($ in millions)

| | |
|---|---|
| *Beginning* of 2006 | $360 |
| Service cost | ? |
| Interest cost | 36 → (10% x $360) |
| Loss (gain) on PBO | 0 |
| Less: Retiree benefits | (54) |
| *End* of 2006 | $465 |

**Service cost** = $465 - 360 - 36 + 54 = $123 million

# Exercise 17-7

**Plan assets** ($ in millions)

| | |
|---|---|
| *Beginning* of 2006 | $700 |
| Actual return | 77 → (11% x $700) |
| Cash contributions | ? |
| Less: Retiree benefits | (66) |
| *End* of 2006 | $750 |

**Cash contributions** = $750 - 700 - 77 + 66 = $39 million

# Exercise 17-8

| | ($ in 000s) |
|---|---|
| Service cost | $112 |
| Interest cost (6% x $850) | 51 |
| Actual return on the plan assets (11% x $900 = $99) adjusted for: $9 gain* on the plan assets | (90) |
| Amortization of prior service cost | 8 |
| Amortization of net loss | 1 |
| **Pension expense** | $82 |

\* (11% x $900) – (10% x $900)

# Exercise 17-9

## Requirement 1

|  | ($ in millions) |
|---|---|
| Service cost | $20 |
| Interest cost | 12 |
| Actual return on the plan assets, $9 million adjusted for $1 million gain on the plan assets | (8) |
| **Pension expense** | **$24** |

## Requirement 2

| | | |
|---|---|---|
| Pension expense (calculated above) | 24 | |
| Prepaid (accrued) pension cost (difference) | | 4 |
| Cash (given) | | 20 |

# Exercise 17-10

## Requirement 1

|  | ($ in 000s) |
|---|---|
| Service cost | $310 |
| Interest cost (7% x $2,300) | 161 |
| Actual return on the plan assets (9% x $2,400 = $216) adjusted for: $24 loss* on the plan assets | (240) |
| Amortization of prior service cost | 25 |
| Amortization of net gain | (6) |
| **Pension expense** | **$250** |

  * (10% x $2,400) – (9% x $2,400)

## Requirement 2

| | | |
|---|---|---|
| Pension expense (calculated above) | 250 | |
| Prepaid (accrued) pension cost (difference) | | 5 |
| Cash (given) | | 245 |

# Exercise 17-11

## Requirement 1

$$1.2\% \times \text{ service years } \times \text{ final year's salary} =$$
$$1.2\% \times 20 \times \$270,000 =$$

**$64,800**

## Requirement 2

The present value of the retirement annuity at the end of 2031 is
$64,800 x 9.10791* = **$590,193**

* present value of an ordinary annuity of $1: n=15, i=7%

## Requirement 3

The PBO is the present value of the retirement benefits at the end of 2006:
$590,193 x .18425* = **$108,743**

* present value of $1: n=25, i=7%

## Requirement 4

1.2% x 20 x **$80,000** = $19,200
$19,200 x 9.10791* = $174,872
$174,872 x .18425** = **$32,220**

* present value of an ordinary annuity of $1: n=15, i=7%
** present value of $1: n=25, i=7%

## Requirement 5

1.2% x **21** x $270,000 = $68,040
$68,040 x 9.10791* = $619,702
$619,702 x .19715** = **$122,174**

* present value of an ordinary annuity of $1: n=15, i=7%
** present value of $1: **n=24**, i=7%

*Exercise 17-11 (concluded)*

**Requirement 6**

| | |
|---|---|
| PBO at the *end* of 2007 | $122,174 |
| PBO at the end of 2006 | (108,743) |
| Change in PBO | $ 13,431 |
| Less: **Interest cost:** $108,743 x 7% | (7,612) |
| **Service cost:** | $ 5,819 |

The change due to service cost can be verified as follows ($1 difference due to rounding):

(1.2% x 1yr. x $270,000)   x   9.10791   x   .19715   =   $5,818
annual retirement benefits      to discount     to discount
from 2007 service          to 2031 *      to 2007 **

\*    present value of an ordinary annuity of $1: n=15, i=7%
\*\*   present value of $1: n=24, i=7%

# Exercise 17-12

## Requirement 1

| ($ in 000s) | Case 1 | Case 2 | Case 3 |
|---|---|---|---|
| Unamortized net loss or gain | $320 | $330 | $260 |
| Less: 10% corridor (threshold)* | (331) | (270) | (170) |
| Excess | none | $ 60 | $ 90 |
| Service period | ÷ 12 | 15 | 10 |
| **Amortization** | none | $  4 | $  9 |

\* 10% times either the PBO or plan assets (beginning of the year), whichever is larger

## Requirement 2

| ($ in 000s) | Case 1 | Case 2 | Case 3 |
|---|---|---|---|
| January 1, 2006 | $320 | $(330) | $260 |
| 2006 loss (gain) on plan assets | (11) | (8) | 2 |
| 2006 amortization | 0 | 4 | (9) |
| 2006 loss (gain) on PBO | (23) | 16 | (265) |
| January 1, 2007 | $286 | $(318) | $ (12) |

**Note:** Remember, the balance in this memorandum "account" is not recognized in the financial statements.

# Exercise 17-13

| ( )s indicate credits; debits otherwise ($ in thousands) | Informal Records | | | | Formal Records | | |
|---|---|---|---|---|---|---|---|
| | PBO | Plan Assets | Prior Service Cost | Net (gain) loss | Pension Expense | Cash | Prepaid (Accrued) Cost |
| Balance, Jan. 1, 2006 | (800) | 600 | 114 | 80 | | | (6) |
| Service cost | (84) | | | | 84 | | |
| Interest cost, 5% | (40) | | | | 40 | | |
| Actual return on assets | | 42 | | | (42) | | |
| Loss on assets | | | | 6 | (6) | | |
| Amortization of: | | | | | | | |
| Prior service cost | | | (6) | | 6 | | |
| Net loss | | | | | | | |
| Gain on PBO | 12 | | | (12) | | | |
| Contributions to fund | | 48 | | | | (48) | |
| Retiree benefits paid | 50 | (50) | | | | | |
| 2006 journal entry | | | | | 82 | (48) | (34) |
| Balance, Dec. 31, 2006 | (862) | 640 | 108 | 74 | | | (40) |

# Exercise 17-14

## Requirement 1

|  | ($ in millions) |
|---|---|
| ABO | $(22) |
| Plan assets | 20 |
| Minimum liability | $ (2) |

Because the accrued pension cost ($3 million) is sufficient, no additional liability is needed.

## Requirement 2

|  | ($ in millions) |
|---|---|
| Intangible pension asset | 5 |
| Additional liability ($3 million + 2 million) | 5 |

This adjustment achieves the objective of providing for a minimum liability of $2 million:

| | |
|---|---|
| Additional liability – credit balance | $(5) |
| Prepaid pension cost – debit balance | 3 |
| Pension liability (reported as a single amount on the balance sheet) | $(2) |

# Exercise 17-15

|  | ($ in millions) |
|---|---|
| ABO | $(117) |
| Plan assets | 105 |
|   Minimum liability | $ (12) |
| Less: prepaid pension cost – debit balance | 6* |
|   Additional liability needed | $ (18) |

| | | |
|---|---|---|
| * Pension expense (given) ..................................... | 40 | |
|   Prepaid (accrued) pension cost (difference)...... | | 2 |
|   Cash (given) ...................................................... | | 38 |

**Prepaid (accrued) pension cost:**

| | |
|---|---|
| Beginning of the year ........................................... | $8 |
|   Reduction from entry above............................. | 2 |
| End of year........................................................... | $6 |

| | ($ in millions) |
|---|---|
| Intangible pension asset | 18* |
|   Additional liability (calculated above) | 18** |

\*   The entire $18 million can be added to the intangible asset because its balance will not exceed the unrecognized prior service cost ($30 million)

\**   Data indicates no previous balance in the "additional liability" account

This adjustment achieves the objective of providing for a minimum liability of $12 million:

| | |
|---|---|
| Additional liability – credit balance | $(18) |
| Prepaid (accrued) pension cost – debit balance | 6 |
| Pension liability (reported as a single amount on the balance sheet) | $(12) |

# Exercise 17-16

| | List A | List B |
|---|---|---|
| d | 1. Future compensation levels estimated. | a. Additional minimum liability |
| f | 2. All funding provided by the employer. | b. Prepaid pension cost |
| b | 3. Cumulative employer's contributions in excess of recognized pension. | c. Vested benefit obligation |
| l | 4. Retirement benefits specified by formula. | d. Projected benefit obligation |
| e | 5. Trade-off between relevance and reliability. | e. Choice between PBO and ABO |
| | | f. Noncontributory pension plan |
| a | 6. Causes a debit to an intangible asset. | g. Accumulated benefit obligation |
| g | 7. Current pay levels implicitly assumed. | h. Plan assets |
| i | 8. Created by the passage of time. | i. Interest cost |
| c | 9. Not contingent on future employment. | j. Delayed recognition |
| k | 10. Risk borne by employee. | k. Defined contribution plan |
| h | 11. Increased by employer contributions. | l. Defined benefit plan |
| m | 12. Caused by plan amendment. | m. Prior service cost |
| j | 13. Gain on plan assets. | n. Amortize unrecognized net loss |
| n | 14. Excess over 10% of plan assets or PBO. | |

# Exercise 17-17

## Requirement 1

|  | ($ in millions) |
|---|---|
| Pension expense (calculated below) | 67* |
| Prepaid (accrued) pension cost (difference) | 3 |
|     Cash (given) | 70 |

| * | Service cost | $ 82 |
|---|---|---|
|  | Interest cost | 24 |
|  | Actual return on the plan assets ($40) | |
|  |    *Adjusted for: $5 loss on the plan assets* | (45) |
|  | Amortization of prior service cost | 8 |
|  | Amortization of net gain | (2) |
|  | *Pension expense* | $ 67 |

**Computation of net gain amortization:**

| | |
|---|---|
| Net gain ( previous gains exceeded previous losses) | $ 80 |
| 10% of $500 plan assets (greater than $480 PBO) | (50) |
|    *Amount to be amortized* | $ 30 |
| | ÷ 15 years |
| Amortization | $ 2 |

## Requirement 2

none required because the ABO ($490) does not exceed plan assets ($570)

## Requirement 3

| | |
|---|---|
| Minimum liability | $ (15) |
|   Less: accrued pension cost ($12 – 3) | (9) |
| Additional liability needed | $ (6) |

| | ($ in millions) |
|---|---|
| Intangible pension asset | 6* |
|   Additional liability (calculated above) | 6 |

\* The entire $6 million can be added to the intangible asset because its balance will not exceed the unrecognized prior service cost ($48 million - 8 million = $40 million)

# Exercise 17-18

## Requirement 1

($ in 000)

|  | 2006 | 2007 | 2008 |
|---|---|---|---|
| ABO | $900 | $1,050 | $1,200 |
| Plan Assets | (800) | (975) | (1,100) |
| Minimum liability | $100 | $ 75 | $ 100 |
| (Accrued) prepaid pension cost | (30) | (25) | 5 |
| Additional liability | $ 70 | $ 50 | $ 105 |

## Requirement 2

### 2006
($ in 000)

| | | |
|---|---|---|
| Intangible pension asset * ................................................ | 40 | |
| Unrealized pension cost (to balance) ............................... | 30 | |
|     Additional liability (calculated above)............................ | | 70 |

### 2007

| | | |
|---|---|---|
| Additional liability ($50 - 70)...................................... | 20 | |
|     Intangible pension asset ($32* - 40) ............................. | | 8 |
|     Unrealized pension cost (to balance).............................. | | 12 |

### 2008

| | | |
|---|---|---|
| Unrealized pension cost (to balance) ................................... | 63 | |
|     Intangible pension asset ($24* - 32) ............................. | | 8 |
|     Additional liability ($105 - 50)..................................... | | 55 |

*Intangible pension asset limited to unamortized prior service cost:
2006    $40
2007    $40 - 8 = $32
2008    $40 - 8 - 8 = $24

# Exercise 17-19

  1. d
  2. c
  3. d
  4. b


# Exercise 17-20

**_B_** 1. Change in actuarial assumptions for a defined benefit pension plan.

**_C_** 2. Determination that the accumulated benefits obligation under a pension plan exceeded the fair value of plan assets at the end of the previous year by $17,000. The only pension-related amount on the balance sheet was prepaid pension costs of $30,000.

**_B_** 3. Pension plan assets for a defined benefit pension plan achieving a rate of return in excess of the amount anticipated.

**_D_** 4. Instituting a pension plan for the first time and adopting Statement of Financial Accounting Standards No. 87, Employers' Accounting for Pensions.

# Exercise 17-21

**Requirement 1**                    $\underline{\textbf{\$72,000}}$
                                        EPBO
                                        2006

**Requirement 2**

$\$72,000$ x $^2/_{[2+28]}$ = $\underline{\textbf{\$4,800}}$
  EPBO          fraction              APBO
  2006          earned               2006

**Requirement 3**

$\$72,000$ x $1.06$ = $\$\underline{\textbf{76,320}}$
  EPBO      to accrue      EPBO
  2006      interest       2007

**Requirement 4**

$\$76,320$ x $^3/_{30}$ = $\underline{\textbf{\$7,632}}$
  EPBO        fraction         APBO
  2007        earned          2007

# Exercise 17-22

**Requirement 1**

$$\$50{,}000 \times \tfrac{3}{25} = \underline{\mathbf{\$6{,}000}}$$

EPBO      fraction      APBO
          earned

**Requirement 2**

$6,000 (beginning APBO) x 6% = $\underline{\mathbf{\$360}}$

**Requirement 3**

$$\$53{,}000 \times \tfrac{1}{25} = \underline{\mathbf{\$2{,}120}}$$

EPBO      attributed      service
2006      to 2006         cost

**Requirement 4**

| | | |
|---|---|---|
| Postretirement benefit expense ($360 + 2,120)....... | 2,480 | |
| Accrued postretirement benefit cost .............. | | 2,480 |

# Exercise 17-23

**Requirement 1**     22 years

**Requirement 2**     $44,000

**Requirement 3**

$$\underset{\text{EPBO}}{\$44{,}000} \quad \times \quad \underset{\substack{\text{fraction}\\\text{earned}}}{?/22} \quad = \quad \underset{\text{APBO}}{\$20{,}000}$$

$$\underset{\text{EPBO}}{\$44{,}000} \quad \times \quad \underset{\substack{\text{fraction}\\\text{earned}}}{10/22} \quad = \quad \underset{\text{APBO}}{\$20{,}000}$$

10 years before 2006:  beginning of 1997 (or end of 1996)

**Requirement 4**

$$\underset{\substack{\text{EPBO}\\\text{beg.}}}{\$?} \quad \times \quad \underset{\substack{\text{interest}\\\text{multiple}}}{1.10} \quad = \quad \underset{\substack{\text{EPBO}\\\text{end}}}{\$44{,}000}$$

$$\underset{\substack{\text{EPBO}\\\text{beg.}}}{\mathbf{\underline{\$40{,}000}}} \quad \times \quad \underset{\substack{\text{interest}\\\text{multiple}}}{1.10} \quad = \quad \underset{\substack{\text{EPBO}\\\text{end}}}{\$44{,}000}$$

*or, alternatively:*

$$\underset{\text{EPBO}}{\$?} \quad \times \quad \underset{\substack{\text{fraction}\\\text{earned}}}{9/22} \quad = \quad \underset{\text{APBO}}{\$16{,}364}$$

$$\underset{\text{EPBO}}{\mathbf{\underline{\$40{,}000}}} \quad \times \quad \underset{\substack{\text{fraction}\\\text{earned}}}{9/22} \quad = \quad \underset{\text{APBO}}{\$16{,}364}$$

# Exercise 17-24

## Requirement 1

|  | ($ in 000s) |
|---|---|
| Service cost | $124 |
| Interest cost (7% x $700) | 49 |
| Return on the plan assets (10% x $50) | (5) |
| Amortization of prior service cost | 0 |
| Amortization of net gain | (1) |
| Amortization of transition obligation | 2 |
| **Postretirement benefit expense** | **$169** |

## Requirement 2

|  | ($ in 000s) |
|---|---|
| Postretirement benefit expense (calculated above) .......................... | 169 |
| Prepaid (accrued) postretirement benefit cost (difference) .......... | 16 |
| Cash (contributions to fund)........................................................ | 185 |

# Exercise 17-25

## Requirement 1

|  | ($ in 000s) |
|---|---|
| Net loss (previous losses exceeded previous gains) | $336 |
| 10% of $2,800 ($2,800 is greater than $500) | 280 |
| Excess at the beginning of the year | $ 56 |
| Average remaining service years | ÷ 14 |
| **Amount amortized to 2006 expense** | $ 4 |

## Requirement 2

|  | ($ in 000s) |
|---|---|
| Postretirement benefit expense exclusive of net loss amortization | $212 |
| Amortization of net loss | 4 |
| **Postretirement benefit expense** | $216 |

## Requirement 3

|  | ($ in 000s) |
|---|---|
| Unamortized net loss, *beginning* of 2006 | $336 |
| 2006 gain on plan assets ([10% - 9%] x $500) | (5) |
| 2006 amortization | (4) |
| 2006 loss on PBO | 39 |
| Unamortized net loss, *end* of 2006 | $366 |

# Exercise 17-26

|  | ($ in millions) | |
|---|---|---|
| Service cost | $34 | |
| Interest cost | 12 | ← (8% x [$130 + 20]) |
| Return on plan assets | (0) | |
| Amortization of: | | |
|   transition obligation | 2 | ←($50 ÷ 25 yrs) |
|   prior service cost | 1 | ←($20 ÷ 20 yrs) |
| Postretirement benefit expense | $49 | |

# Exercise 17-27

## Requirement 1

The "negative" prior service cost must be offset against any existing prior service cost before it can be amortized.

|  | ($ in 000s) |
|---|---|
| Unrecognized prior service cost | $ 50 |
| Reduction for amendment | (80) |
| Negative prior service cost | $(30) |
| Service period to full eligibility | ÷ 15 years |
|    Amortization | $ 2 |

## Requirement 2

| | | |
|---|---|---|
| Service cost | $114 | |
| Interest cost | 36 | ← (8% x [$530 – 80]) |
| Return on plan assets | (0) | |
| Amortization of prior service cost | (2) | ←([$50 - 80] ÷ 15 yrs) |
| Postretirement benefit expense | $148 | |

## Requirement 3

If unrecognized transition obligation exists, any "negative" prior service cost remaining after being offset against existing prior service cost must be offset against the transition obligation before it can be amortized.

| | |
|---|---|
| Unrecognized prior service cost | $ 50 |
| Reduction for amendment | (80) |
|   Excess | $(30) |
| Unrecognized transition obligation | 120 |
| Unrecognized transition obligation after amendment | $ 90 |
| Amortization of prior service cost | none |

# Exercise 17-28

  a

# Exercise 17-29

1. **a.** SFAS 87 defines the PBO as the actuarial present value of all future benefits attributable to past employee service at a moment in time. It is based on assumptions as to future compensation if the pension plan formula is based on future compensation.

2. **c.** Under SFAS 87, a minimum liability must be recognized when the ABO exceeds the fair value of plan assets. Because the ABO exceeds the fair value of plan assets, the minimum liability to be recognized is $517,500 ($825,000 ABO - $307,500 FVPA).

3. **b.** Unrecognized prior service cost arises from the awarding of retroactive benefits resulting from plan initiation or amendments. Prior service cost is assigned to the future service periods of active employees using either a straight-line or another acceptable method of allocation. Given that the average remaining service life of the firm's employees is 10 years, the annual charge is $19,000 ($190,000 / 10).

# Exercise 17-30

## Requirement 1

| ($ in 000s) Year | Number of Employees Still Employed | Fraction of Total Service Years | Prior Service Cost | Amount Amortized |
|---|---|---|---|---|
| 2007 | 100 | 100/550 | x $110 | = $ 20 |
| 2008 | 90 | 90/550 | x 110 | = 18 |
| 2009 | 80 | 80/550 | x 110 | = 16 |
| 2010 | 70 | 70/550 | x 110 | = 14 |
| 2011 | 60 | 60/550 | x 110 | = 12 |
| 2012 | 50 | 50/550 | x 110 | = 10 |
| 2013 | 40 | 40/550 | x 110 | = 8 |
| 2014 | 30 | 30/550 | x 110 | = 6 |
| 2015 | 20 | 20/550 | x 110 | = 4 |
| 2016 | 10 | 10/550 | x 110 | = 2 |
| Totals | 550* | 550/550 | | $110 |
| | Total Number of Service Years | | | Total Amount Amortized |

## Requirement 2

$$\$110{,}000 \div 5.5 \text{ years*} = \$20{,}000/\text{year}$$

\* The average service life is the total estimated service years divided by the total number of employees in the group:

| 550 years | ÷ | 100 | = | 5.5 years |
|---|---|---|---|---|
| total number of service years | | total number of employees | | average service years |

# PROBLEMS

## Problem 17-1

### Requirement 1

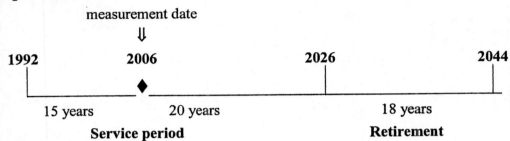

measurement date

| 1992 | 2006 | 2026 | 2044 |

15 years | 20 years | 18 years

**Service period** | **Retirement**

### Requirement 2

$$1.6\% \ \times 15 \ \times \$90,000 \ = \mathbf{\$21,600}$$

### Requirement 3

The present value of the retirement annuity as of the retirement date (end of 2026) is:

$$\$21,600 \times 10.05909^* = \mathbf{\$217,276}$$

\* present value of an ordinary annuity of \$1: n=18, i=7%

The ABO is the present value of the retirement benefits at the end of 2006:

$$\$217,276 \times .25842^* = \mathbf{\$56,148}$$

\* present value of \$1: n=20, i=7%

### Requirement 4

$$1.6\% \times \mathbf{18} \times \$100,000 = \$28,800$$
$$\$28,800 \times 10.05909^* = \$289,702$$
$$\$289,702 \times .31657^{**} = \mathbf{\$91,711}$$

\* present value of an ordinary annuity of \$1: n=18, i=7%

\*\* present value of \$1: **n=17**, i=7%

# Problem 17-2

## Requirement 1

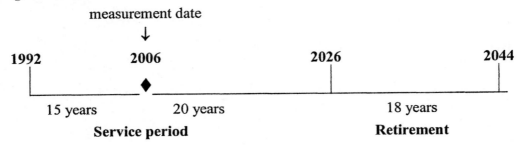

measurement date

↓

| 1992 | 2006 | | 2026 | | 2044 |

15 years      20 years        18 years

**Service period**       **Retirement**

## Requirement 2

$$1.6\% \ \times \ 15 \ \times \ \$240{,}000 \ = \ \textbf{\$57{,}600}$$

## Requirement 3

The present value of the retirement annuity as of the retirement date (end of 2026) is:

$$\$57{,}600 \times 10.05909^* = \$579{,}404$$

[This is the lump-sum equivalent of the retirement
annuity as of the retirement date]

\* present value of an ordinary annuity of $1: n=18, i=7%

The PBO is the present value of the retirement benefits at the end of 2006:

$$\$579{,}404 \times .25842^* = \textbf{\$149{,}730}$$

\* present value of $1: n=20, i=7%

## Requirement 4

$$1.6\% \times \textbf{18} \times \$240{,}000 = \$69{,}120$$
$$\$69{,}120 \times 10.05909^* = \$695{,}284$$
$$\$695{,}284 \times .31657^{**} = \textbf{\$220{,}106}$$

\*    present value of an ordinary annuity of $1: n=18, i=7%

\*\*   present value of $1: **n=17**, i=7%

# Problem 17-3

**Requirement 1**

$$1.6\% \times 14 \times \$240,000 = \$53,760$$
$$\$53,760 \times 10.05909^* = \$540,777$$
$$\$540,777 \times .24151^{**} = \mathbf{\$130,603}$$

\* present value of an ordinary annuity of $1: n=18, i=7%

\*\* present value of $1: **n=21**, i=7%

**Requirement 2**

$$1.6\% \times 1 \times \$240,000 = \mathbf{\$3,840}$$

**Requirement 3**

$$\$3,840 \times 10.05909^* = \$38,627$$
$$\$38,627 \times .25842^{**} = \mathbf{\$9,982}$$

\* present value of an ordinary annuity of $1: n=18, i=7%

\*\* present value of $1: n=20, i=7%

**Requirement 4**

$$\$130,603 \times 7\% = \mathbf{\$9,142}$$

**Requirement 5**

| | |
|---|---|
| PBO at the *beginning* of 2006 (end of 2005) | $130,603 |
| **Service cost:** | 9,982 |
| **Interest cost:** $130,603 × 7% | 9,142 |
| PBO at the *end* of 2006 | $149,727 |

**Note:** In requirement 3 of the previous problem this same amount is calculated without separately determining the service cost and interest elements (allowing for a $3 rounding adjustment)

# Problem 17-4

**Requirement 1**

<table>
<tr><th colspan="2" align="center">PBO Without Amendment</th><th colspan="2" align="center">PBO With Amendment</th></tr>
<tr><td>1.6% x 15 yrs. x $240,000 = $57,600</td><td></td><td>**1.75%** x 15 yrs. x $240,000 = $63,000</td><td></td></tr>
<tr><td>$57,600 x 10.05909* = $579,404</td><td></td><td>$63,000 x 10.05909* = $633,723</td><td></td></tr>
<tr><td>$579,404 x .25842** = <u>$149,730</u></td><td>↘</td><td>$633,723 x .25842** = <u>$163,767</u></td><td>↙</td></tr>
</table>

**$14,037**
*Prior service cost*

\* present value of an ordinary annuity of $1: n=18, i=7%

\*\* present value of $1: n=20, i=7%

*Alternative calculation: 1.75 - 1.6 =*　　　　**0.15%** x 15 yrs x $240,000 = $5,400

　　　　　　　　　　　　　　　　　　　$5,400 x 10.05909* = $54,319

　　　　　　　　　　　　　　　　　　　$54,319 x .25842** = <u>$14,037</u>

**Requirement 2**

$14,037 ÷ 20 years (expected remaining service) = <u>**$702**</u>

**Requirement 3**

　　　**1.75%** x 1 x $240,000 = 　$4,200
　　　$4,200 x 10.05909* = 　$42,248
　　　$42,248 x .27651** = <u>**$11,682**</u>

\* present value of an ordinary annuity of $1: n=18, i=7%

\*\* present value of $1: **n=19**, i=7%

**Requirement 4**

$163,767 x 7% = <u>**$11,464**</u>

**Requirement 5**

| | |
|---|---:|
| Service cost (from req. 3) | $11,682 |
| Interest cost (from req. 4) | 11,464 |
| Return on the plan assets (10% x $150,000 ) | (15,000) |
| Amortization of prior service cost (from req. 2) | 702 |
| Pension expense | **$8,848** |

# Problem 17-5

**PBO With Previous Rate**

1.6% x 15 yrs x $240,000 = $57,600

$57,600 x 10.05909[1] = $579,404

$579,404 x .25842[2] = <u>$149,730</u>

↘

**PBO With Revised Rate**

1.6% x 15 yrs x $240,000 = $57,600

$57,600 x 9.37189[3] = $539,821

$539,821 x .21455[4] = <u>$115,819</u>

↙

**$33,911**
*Gain on PBO*

[1] present value of an ordinary annuity of $1: n=18, i=7%
[2] present value of $1: n=20, i=7%
[3] present value of an ordinary annuity of $1: n=18, i=8%
[4] present value of $1: n=20, i=8%

# Problem 17-6

1. **Projected Benefit Obligation**  ($ in 000s)

|   |   |
|---|---|
| Balance, January 1, 2006 | $ 0 |
| Service cost | 150 |
| Interest cost (6% x $0) | 0 |
| Benefits paid | (0) |
| Balance, December 31, 2006 | $150 |
| Service cost | 200 |
| Interest cost (6% x $150) | 9 |
| Benefits paid | (0) |
| Balance, December 31, 2007 | $359 |

2. **Plan Assets**

|   |   |
|---|---|
| Balance, January 1, 2006 | $ 0 |
| Actual return on plan assets (10% x $0) | 0 |
| Contributions, 2006 | 160 |
| Benefits paid | (0) |
| Balance, December 31, 2006 | $160 |
| Actual return on plan assets (10% x $160) | 16 |
| Contributions, 2007 | 170 |
| Benefits paid | (0) |
| Balance, December 31, 2007 | $346 |

3. **Pension expense – 2006**

|   |   |
|---|---|
| Service cost | $150 |
| Interest cost (6% x $0) | 0 |
| Return on the plan assets (10% x $0) | 0 |
| Pension expense | $150 |

**Pension expense – 2007**

|   |   |
|---|---|
| Service cost | $200 |
| Interest cost (6% x $150) | 9 |
| Return on the plan assets (10% x $160) | (16) |
| Pension expense | $193 |

4. **Prepaid (accrued) pension cost**

|   |   |
|---|---|
| Balance, January 1, 2006 | $ 0 |
| 2006 debit ($150,000 – 160,000) | 10 |
| Balance, December 31, 2006 | $ 10 |
| 2007 credit ($193,000 – 170,000) | (23) |
| Balance, December 31, 2007 - credit | $(13) |

# Problem 17-7

## Requirement 1

|  | ($ in 000s) |
|---|---|
| Net gain (previous gains exceeded previous losses) | $170 |
| 10% of $1,400 ($1,400 is greater than $1,100) | 140 |
| Excess at the beginning of the year | $ 30 |
| Average remaining service period years | ÷ 15 |
| **Amount amortized to 2006 pension expense** | $ 2 |

## Requirement 2

| | |
|---|---|
| Pension expense exclusive of net gain amortization | $325 |
| Amortization of net gain | (2) |
| **Pension expense** | $323 |

## Requirement 3

| | |
|---|---|
| Unamortized net gain, *beginning* of 2006 | $(170) |
| 2006 loss on plan assets ([10% – 9%] x $1,100) | 11 |
| 2006 amortization | 2 |
| 2006 gain on PBO | (23) |
| Unamortized net gain, *end* of 2006 (beg. of 2007) | $(180) |

**Note:** Remember, the balance in this memorandum "account" is not recognized in the financial statements.

# Problem 17-8

## Requirement 1

| ( )s indicate credits; debits otherwise ($ in millions) | Informal Records | | | | Formal Records | | |
|---|---|---|---|---|---|---|---|
| | PBO | Plan Assets | Prior Service Cost | Net gain | Pension Expense | Cash | Prepaid (Accrued) Cost |
| *Jan. 1, 2006* | (600) | 800 | 26 | (95) | | | 131 |
| Service cost | (65) | | | | 65 | | |
| Interest cost, 7% | (42) | | | | 42 | | |
| Actual return on assets | | 72 | | | (72) | | |
| Gain on assets | | | | (8) | 8 | | |
| *Amortization of:* | | | | | | | |
| Prior service cost | | | (2) | | 2 | | |
| Net gain | | | | 1 | (1) | | |
| Loss on PBO | (4) | | | 4 | | | |
| Contributions to fund | | 30 | | | | (30) | |
| Retiree benefits paid | 52 | (52) | | | | | |
| 2006 journal entry | | | | | 44 | (30) | (14) |
| *Dec. 31, 2006* | (659) | 850 | 24 | (98) | | | 117 |

## Problem 17-8 (concluded)

### Requirement 2

|  | ($ in millions) |
|---|---|
| Pension expense (calculated above)............................................ | 44 |
|    Prepaid (accrued) pension cost (difference)........................ | 14 |
|    Cash (contribution to fund)...................................................... | 30 |

### Requirement 3

|  | ($ in millions) |
|---|---|
| Projected benefit obligation | $(659) |
| Plan assets | 850 |
|   Funded status | $ 191 |
| Unamortized prior service cost | 24 |
| Unamortized net gain | (98) |
|   Prepaid pension cost | $ 117 |

# Problem 17-9

**Note:** It's important to realize that the relationship given: plan assets - PBO = prepaid (accrued) pension cost, exists only when there are no unrecognized pension costs (prior service cost, net loss or gain). This also means pension expense contains no components for the amortization of such amounts.

1. **Pension expense**            ($ in 000s)

| | |
|---|---:|
| Service cost | $60 |
| Interest cost (5% x $320) | 16 |
| Return on the plan assets (9% x $400 ) | (36) |
| Amortization of prior service cost | 0 |
| Amortization of net loss or gain | 0 |
| **Pension expense** | **$40** |

2. **Prepaid (accrued) pension cost**

| | |
|---|---:|
| Balance, January 1 | $ 80 |
| 2006 debit ($120,000 – 40,000) | 80 |
| Balance, December 31 | $160 |

3. **Projected Benefit Obligation**

| | |
|---|---:|
| Balance, January 1 | $320 |
| Service cost | 60 |
| Interest cost | 16 |
| Benefits paid | (44) |
| Balance, December 31 | $352 |

4. **Plan Assets**

| | |
|---|---:|
| Balance, January 1 | $400 |
| Actual return on plan assets | 36 |
| Contributions 2006 | 120 |
| Benefits paid | (44) |
| Balance, December 31 | $512 |

# Problem 17-10
## Requirement 1

($ in millions)

| | 2006 | 2007 |
|---|---|---|
| Service cost (given) | $520 | $570 |
| Interest on PBO (2006: 10% x $2,200*; 2007: 10% x $2,540*) | 220 | 254 |
| Expected return (2006: 12% x $1,600; 2007: 12% x $1,920**) | (192) | (230.4) |
| Amortization of prior service costs ($400 ÷ 10 years) | 40 | 40 |
| Amortization of unrecognized net gain*** | (5) | none |
| Pension expense | $583 | $633.6 |

| *PBO | | | **Plan Assets | |
|---|---|---|---|---|
| Balance, 1-1-06 | $1,800 | | Balance, 1-1-06 | $1,600 |
| Prior service cost | 400 | | | |
| Balance, 1-2-06 | $2,200 | | | |
| Interest 10% | 220 | | 2006 contribution | 540 |
| Service cost | 520 | | 2006 actual return | 180 |
| Payments | (400) | | Payments | (400) |
| Balance, 12-31-06 | $2,540 | | Balance, 12-31-06 | $1,920 |
| Interest 10% | 254 | | 2007 contribution | 590 |
| Service cost | 570 | | 2007 actual return | 210 |
| Payments | (450) | | Payments | (450) |
| Balance, 12-31-07 | $2,914 | | Balance, 12-31-07 | $2,270 |

### ***Unrecognized Net Gain
#### 2006

| | |
|---|---|
| Net gain at 1-1-06 | $230 |
| 10% of $1,800 ($1,800 is greater than $1,600): | (180) |
| Excess at the beginning of the year | $ 50 |
| Average remaining service period | ÷ 10 years |
| **Amount amortized to 2006 pension expense** | **$ 5** |

#### 2007

| | |
|---|---|
| Net gain at 1-1-06 | $230 |
| Loss in 2006 (actual return: $180 - expected return: $192) | (12) |
| Amortization in 2006 (calculated above) | (5) |
| Net gain at 1-1-07 | $213 |
| 10% of $2,540 ($2,540 is greater than $1,920): | (254) |
| No excess at the beginning of the year | none |

### No amortization for 2007

## Problem 17-10 (concluded)

### Requirement 2

**2006**

| | | |
|---|---|---|
| Pension expense (calculated above)................................ | 583 | |
| Accrued (prepaid) pension cost (to balance).............. | | 43 |
| Cash (given) ................................................................ | | 540 |

**2007**

| | | |
|---|---|---|
| Pension expense (calculated above)................................ | 633.6 | |
| Accrued (prepaid) pension cost (to balance).............. | | 43.6 |
| Cash (given) ................................................................ | | 590.0 |

# Problem 17-11

| | Projected Benefit Obligation | Plan Assets | Pension Expense |
|---|---|---|---|
| Balance at Jan. 1 | $ 0 | $ 0 | |
| Prior service cost | 2,000,000 | 2,000,000 | |
| Amortization of prior service cost | | | |
| ($2,000,000 ÷ 10 years) | | | $200,000 |
| Service cost | 250,000 | | 250,000 |
| Interest cost | | | |
| ($2,000,000* x 9%) | 180,000 | | 180,000 |
| Return on plan assets | | | |
| Actual ($2,000,000** x 11%) | | 220,000 | |
| Expected ($2,000,000** x 9%) | | | (180,000) |
| Retirement payments | (16,000) | (16,000) | |
| Cash contribution | | 250,000 | |
| Balance at Dec. 31 | $2,414,000 | $2,454,000 | $450,000 |

**Note:** The $40,000 gain ($220,000 - 180,000) is not recognized yet; it is carried forward to be combined with future gains and losses, which will be recognized only if the net gain or net loss exceeds 10% of the higher of the PBO or plan assets.

\*   Since the plan was adopted at the beginning of the year, the prior service cost increased the PBO at that time.

\*\*  Since the prior service cost was funded at the beginning of the year, the plan assets were increased at that time.

# Problem 17-12

### 1. Actual return on plan assets

|  | ($ in 000s) |
|---|---|
| **Plan assets** | |
| *Beginning* of 2006 | $2,400 |
| Actual return | **?** |
| Cash contributions | 245 |
| Less: Retiree benefits | (270) |
| *End* of 2006 | $2,591 |

**Actual return** = $2,591 - 2,400 - 245 + 270 = $216

### 2. Loss or gain on plan assets

| | | |
|---|---|---|
| Expected return | $240 ➜ | (10% x $2,400) |
| Actual return | (216) | |
| **Loss on plan assets** | $24 | |

### 3. Service cost

| **PBO:** | | |
|---|---|---|
| *Beginning* of 2006 | $2,300 | |
| Service cost | **?** | |
| Interest cost | 161 ➜ | (7% x $2,300) |
| Loss (gain) on PBO | 0 | |
| Less: Retiree benefits | (270) | |
| *End* of 2006 | $2,501 | |

**Service cost** = $2,501 - 2,300 - 161 + 270 = $310

*Problem 17-12 (concluded)*

## 4. Pension expense

|  | | ($ in 000s) | |
|---|---|---|---|
| Service cost | | $310 | |
| Interest cost | | 161 | ➜ (7% x $2,300) |
| Actual return | $216 | | |
| Plus: loss | 24 | (240) | |
| Amortization of: | | | |
| prior service cost | | 25 | ➜ ($325 - 300) |
| net gain | | (6) | ➜ (330 - 300 - 24*) |
| **Pension expense** | | $250 | |

\* 2006 loss on plan assets

or, alternatively:

| | | |
|---|---|---|
| Pension expense (to balance) ............................... | **250** | |
| Prepaid (accrued) pension cost ($90 - 95)....... | | 5 |
| Cash (given)....................................................... | | 245 |

## 5. Average remaining service life of active employees

| | |
|---|---|
| Net gain, Jan. 1 | $330 |
| 10% of $2,400 | 240 |
| Excess | $ 90 |
| Amount amortized | ÷ 6 |
| *Average service period* | 15 years |

# Problem 17-13

## Requirement 1

|  | ($ in 000's) |  |  |
|---|---|---|---|
| Pension expense (calculated below) |  | 517* |  |
| Prepaid (accrued) pension cost (difference) |  |  | 17 |
| Cash (given) |  |  | 500 |

| | | |
|---|---|---|
| * Service cost | $410 |
| Interest cost | 200 |
| Actual return on the plan assets, $150 |  |
| *Adjusted for: $15 gain on the plan assets* | (135) |
| Amortization of prior service cost | 40 |
| Amortization of net loss (calculated below) | 2 |
| *Pension expense* | $517 |

**Computation of net loss amortization:**

| | |
|---|---|
| Net loss ( previous losses exceeded previous gains) | $230 |
| 10% of $2,000 (greater than $1,500) | (200) |
| *Amount to be amortized* | $ 30 |
| | ÷ 15 |
| Amortization | $ 2 |

## Requirement 2

| | | |
|---|---|---|
| Intangible pension asset | 113* | |
| Additional liability (calculated below) | | 113 |

\* The entire $113,000 can be added to the intangible asset because its balance will not exceed the unrecognized prior service cost ($240,000 - 40,000 = $200,000)

**Computation of additional liability:**

| | |
|---|---|
| ABO | $(2,100) |
| Plan assets | 1,940 |
| Minimum liability | $ (160) |
| Less: accrued pension cost ($30 + 17) | (47) |
| Additional liability needed | $ (113) |

## Problem 17-13 (concluded)

### Requirement 3

|  | ($ in 000's) |
|---|---|
| Minimum liability | $ (170) |
| Less: prepaid pension cost (debit balance) | 10 |
| Additional liability needed | $ (180) |
| Less: additional liability balance (from 2006) | (113) |
| To be added | $ (67) |

| | |
|---|---|
| Intangible pension asset ($67,000 - [180,000 - 160,000]) | 47* |
| Unrealized pension cost ($180,000 - 160,000) | 20 |
| Additional liability (calculated above) | 67 |

\*    The entire $67,000 cannot be added to the intangible asset because its balance ($113,000 + 67,000 = $180,000) would exceed the unrecognized prior service cost ($200,000 - 40,000 = $160,000).

# Problem 17-14

| ( )s indicate credits; debits otherwise ($ in 000s) | Informal Records | | | | Formal Records | | |
|---|---|---|---|---|---|---|---|
| | PBO | Plan Assets | Prior Service Cost | Net loss | Pen. Exp. | Cash | Prepaid Pension Cost |
| *Jan. 1, 2006* | (4,100) | 4,530 | 840 | 477 | | | 1,747 |
| Service cost[2] | (332) | | | | 332 | | |
| Interest cost, 7%[1] | (287) | | | | 287 | | |
| Actual return [3] | | 400 | | | (400) | | |
| Loss on assets[4] | | | | 53 | (53) | | |
| *Amortization of:* | | | | | | | |
| Prior service cost[5] | | | (70) | | 70 | | |
| Net loss[6] | | | | (2) | 2 | | |
| Gain on PBO | 44 | | | (44) | | | |
| Contributions to fund | | 340 | | | | (340) | |
| Retiree benefits paid | 295 | (295) | | | | | |
| 2006 journal entry | | | | | 238 | (340) | 102 |
| *Dec. 31, 2006* | (4,380) | 4,975 | 770 | 484 | | | 1,849 |

[1] 7% x $4,100 = $287
[2] $4,380 - 4,100 - 287 + 44 + 295 = $332
[3] $4,975 - 4,530 - 340 + 295 = $400
[4] 10% x $4,530 = $453 (expected) - 400 = $53
[5] $840 ÷ 12 = $70
[6] ($477 - 453) ÷ 12 = $2

# Problem 17-15

## Requirement 1

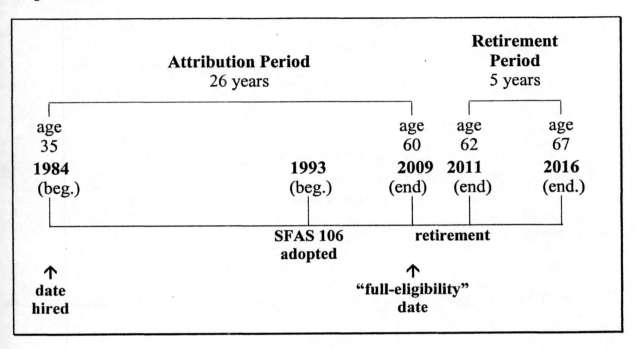

## Requirement 2

| Year End | Expected Net Cost | PV of $1 n=1-5, i=6% | Present Value at Jan. 1, 2012 |
|----------|-------------------|----------------------|-------------------------------|
| 2012 | $4,000 | x .94340 | $ 3,774 |
| 2013 | 4,400 | x .89000 | 3,916 |
| 2014 | 2,300 | x .83962 | 1,931 |
| 2015 | 2,500 | x .79209 | 1,980 |
| 2016 | 2,800 | x .74726 | 2,092 |
| | | | $13,693 |

## Problem 17-15 (concluded)

### Requirement 3

$$\$13{,}693 \times .33051^* = \underline{\underline{\$4{,}526}}$$

\* present value of \$1: **n=19**, i=6%
Beg. of 1993
to end of 2011

### Requirement 4

$$\$4{,}526 \times {}^{9 \text{ yrs}*}/_{26 \text{ yrs}**} = \underline{\underline{\$1{,}567}}$$

\*  1984-1992
\*\* attribution period (1984-2009)

### Requirement 5

$$\underline{\underline{\$1{,}567}}$$

The APBO existing when SFAS 106 was adopted is the transition obligation.

### Requirement 6

a. Immediate recognition?

$$\underline{\underline{\$1{,}567}}$$

b. Recognition over future service periods?

$$\$1{,}567 \div 19^* = \underline{\underline{\$82}}$$

\* 1993-2011

c. Optional recognition over a 20-year period?

$$\$1{,}567 \div 20^* = \underline{\underline{\$78}}$$

\* optional since longer than 16 years

# Problem 17-16

## Requirement 1

| Year End | Expected Net Cost | PV of $1 n=1-5, i=6% | Present Value at Jan. 1, 2012 |
|---|---|---|---|
| 2012 | $4,000 | x .94340 | $ 3,774 |
| 2013 | 4,400 | x .89000 | 3,916 |
| 2014 | 2,300 | x .83962 | 1,931 |
| 2015 | 2,500 | x .79209 | 1,980 |
| 2016 | 2,800 | x .74726 | 2,092 |
| | | | **$13,693** |

## Requirement 2

$$\$13,693 \text{ x } .74726^* = \underline{\mathbf{\$10,232}}$$

$^*$present value of $1: n=5, i=6%

## Requirement 3

$$\$10,232 \text{ x } {}^{23 \text{ yrs}^*}/_{26 \text{ yrs}^{**}} = \underline{\mathbf{\$9,051}}$$

\*    1984-2006

\*\* attribution period (1984-2009)

## Requirement 4

$$\$13,693 \text{ x } .79209^* = \underline{\mathbf{\$10,846}} \text{ (EPBO)}$$

\* present value of $1: n=4, i=6%

$$\$10,846 \text{ x } {}^{24 \text{ yrs}^*}/_{26 \text{ yrs}^{**}} = \underline{\mathbf{\$10,012}}$$

\*    1984-2007

\*\* attribution period (1984-2009)

## Problem 17-16 (concluded)

### Requirement 5

$$\$13,693 \times .79209^* = \underline{\mathbf{\$10,846}} \text{ (EPBO)}$$
$$^* \text{ present value of \$1: } n=4, i=6\%$$

$$\$10,846 \times {}^1\,yr/_{26}\,yrs = \underline{\mathbf{\$417}}$$

### Requirement 6

$$\$9,051 \text{ (beginning APBO)} \times 6\% = \underline{\mathbf{\$543}}$$

### Requirement 7

| | |
|---|---:|
| APBO at the *beginning* of 2007 (from req. 3) | $9,051 |
| Service cost: (from req. 5) | 417 |
| Interest cost: (from req. 6) | 543 |
| APBO at the *end* of 2007 (agrees with req. 4*) | $10,011 |

* $1 difference due to rounding

# Problem 17-17

| | EPBO | fraction earned | APBO | Service Cost | Interest Cost | Expense |
|---|---|---|---|---|---|---|
| | | | | | 10% | |
| 2006 | $18,000 | 1/8 | $ 2,250 | $ 2,250 | $ 0 | $ 2,250 |
| 2007 | 19,800 [1] | 2/8 | 4,950 [2] | 2,475 [3] | 225 [4] | 2,700 [5] |
| 2008 | 21,780 | 3/8 | 8,168 | 2,723 | 495 | 3,218 |
| 2009 | 23,958 | 4/8 | 11,979 | 2,995 | 817 | 3,812 |
| 2010 | 26,354 | 5/8 | 16,471 | 3,294 | 1,198 | 4,492 |
| 2011 | 28,989 | 6/8 | 21,742 | 3,624 | 1,647 | 5,271 |
| 2012 | 31,888 | 7/8 | 27,902 | 3,986 | 2,174 | 6,160 |
| 2013 | 35,077 | 8/8 | 35,077 | 4,385 | 2,790 | 7,175 |
| | | | | | | |
| | Totals | | | $25,732 | $9,346 | $35,078 |

[1] $18,000 x 1.10 = $19,800
[2] $19,800 x 2/8 = $4,950
[3] $19,800 x 1/8 = $2,475
[4] $2,250 (APBO) x 10% = $225
[5] $2,475 + 225 = $2,700

# Problem 17-18

## Requirement 1

|  | ($ in 000s) |  |
|---|---|---|
| **APBO:** |  |  |
| *Beginning* of 2006 | $460 |  |
| Service cost | **?** |  |
| Interest cost | 23 | → (5% x $460) |
| Loss (gain) on APBO | 0 |  |
| Less: Retiree benefits | (52) |  |
| *End* of 2006 | $485 |  |

**Service cost** = $485 - 460 - 23 + 52 = $54

## Requirement 2

|  | ($ in 000s) |  |
|---|---|---|
| Service cost | $54 |  |
| Interest cost | 23 | → (5% x $460) |
| Return on plan assets | (0) |  |
| Amortization of: |  |  |
| transition obligation | 10 | → ($120 - 110) |
| net gain | (1) | → ($50 - 49) |
| **Postretirement benefit expense** | $86 |  |

# Problem 17-19

## Requirement 1

|  | ($ in millions) |
|---|---|
| **APBO:** | |
| Beginning | $375 |
|   Service cost | 23 |
|   Interest cost (8% x $375) | 30 |
|   Loss on APBO | 92 |
|   Benefit payments | (20) |
| Ending | $500 |

## Requirement 2

|  | ($ in millions) |
|---|---|
| Service cost | $23 |
| Interest cost | 30 |
| Amortization of transition obligation ($375/15) | 25 |
|   Postretirement benefit expense | $78 |

## Requirement 3

|  | ($ in millions) |
|---|---|
| Postretirement benefit expense (determined above) | 78 |
|   Accrued postretirement benefit cost (difference) | 18 |
|   Cash (given) | 60 |

## Requirement 4

|  | ($ in millions) |
|---|---|
| APBO | $500 |
| Plan assets ($60 - 20) | (40) |
| Funded status | $460 |
| Unrecognized net loss | (92) |
| Unrecognized transition obligation ($375 - 25) | (350) |
|   Accrued postretirement benefit cost | $ 18 |

*Problem 17-19 (continued)*

**Requirement 5**

|  | APBO | Plan Assets |
|---|---|---|
| Balance, Jan. 1 | $500 | $40 |
| Service cost | 32 | |
| Interest cost ($500 x 8%) | 40 | |
| Return on plan assets | | 5 |
| Contributions | | 90 |
| Benefit payments | (55) | (55) |
| Balance, Dec. 31 | $517 | $80 |

**Requirement 6**

|  | ($ in millions) |
|---|---|
| Net loss (previous losses exceeded previous gains) | $92 |
| 10% of $500 ($500 is greater than $40) | (50) |
| Excess at the beginning of the year | $42 |
| Average remaining service period | $\div$ 14 years |
| Amount amortized to 1995 pension expense | $ 3 |

**Requirement 7**

|  |  | ($ in millions) |
|---|---|---|
| Service cost | | $32 |
| Interest cost | | 40 |
| Return on plan assets | $(5) | |
| Less: gain (12.5% x $40 – 10% x $40) | 1* | (4) |
| Amortization of transition obligation ($375/15) | | 25 |
| Amortization of net loss (determined above) | | 3 |
| Postretirement benefit expense | | $96 |

## Problem 17-19 (concluded)

### Requirement 8

|  | ($ in millions) |  |
|---|---|---|
| Postretirement benefit expense (determined above) | 96 |  |
| Accrued postretirement benefit cost (difference) |  | 6 |
| Cash (given) |  | 90 |

### Requirement 9

| | |
|---|---|
| APBO (req. 5) | $517 |
| Plan assets (req. 5) | (80) |
| Funded status | $437 |
| Unrecognized net loss  ($92 - 3 amortization -1 gain) | (88) |
| Unrecognized transition obligation ($375 - 25 - 25) | (325) |
| Accrued postretirement benefit cost | $ 24* |

* Note: $18 [req.4] + 6 [req. 8] = $24

# CASES

## Judgment Case 17-1

### Requirement 1

Here is a graphical depiction of your estimated service and retirement periods:

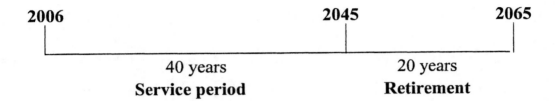

**2006**                      **2045**              **2065**

                40 years                20 years

              **Service period**             **Retirement**

Salary at retirement:
$100,000 x 3.26204, or
$100,000 x $(1.03)^{40}$ = $326,204

1.5%  x  40  x  $326,204 =  **$195,722**

The present value of the retirement annuity as of the retirement date (end of 2045) is:

$195,722 x 11.46992* = **$2,244,916**
[This is the lump-sum equivalent of the retirement
annuity as of the retirement date]

\* present value of an ordinary annuity of $1: n=20, i=6%

## Case 17-1 (continued)
## Requirement 2
The value of your plan assets as of the anticipated retirement date is **$1,985,360**:

| A | B | C | D |
|---|---|---|---|
| Years to Retirement | Salary | Contribution | Future Value at Retirement |
| 40 | 100,000 | 8,000 | 82,286 |
| 39 | 103,000 | 8,240 | 79,957 |
| 38 | 106,090 | 8,487 | 77,694 |
| 37 | 109,273 | 8,742 | 75,495 |
| 36 | 112,551 | 9,004 | 73,358 |
| 35 | 115,927 | 9,274 | 71,282 |
| 34 | 119,405 | 9,552 | 69,265 |
| 33 | 122,987 | 9,839 | 67,305 |
| 32 | 126,677 | 10,134 | 65,400 |
| 31 | 130,477 | 10,438 | 63,549 |
| 30 | 134,392 | 10,751 | 61,750 |
| 29 | 138,423 | 11,074 | 60,003 |
| 28 | 142,576 | 11,406 | 58,304 |
| 27 | 146,853 | 11,748 | 56,654 |
| 26 | 151,259 | 12,101 | 55,051 |
| 25 | 155,797 | 12,464 | 53,493 |
| 24 | 160,471 | 12,838 | 51,979 |
| 23 | 165,285 | 13,223 | 50,508 |
| 22 | 170,243 | 13,619 | 49,078 |
| 21 | 175,351 | 14,028 | 47,689 |
| 20 | 180,611 | 14,449 | 46,340 |
| 19 | 186,029 | 14,882 | 45,028 |
| 18 | 191,610 | 15,329 | 43,754 |
| 17 | 197,359 | 15,789 | 42,515 |
| 16 | 203,279 | 16,262 | 41,312 |
| 15 | 209,378 | 16,750 | 40,143 |
| 14 | 215,659 | 17,253 | 39,007 |
| 13 | 222,129 | 17,770 | 37,903 |
| 12 | 228,793 | 18,303 | 36,830 |
| 11 | 235,657 | 18,853 | 35,788 |
| 10 | 242,726 | 19,418 | 34,775 |
| 9 | 250,008 | 20,001 | 33,791 |
| 8 | 257,508 | 20,601 | 32,834 |
| 7 | 265,234 | 21,219 | 31,905 |
| 6 | 273,191 | 21,855 | 31,002 |
| 5 | 281,386 | 22,511 | 30,125 |
| 4 | 289,828 | 23,186 | 29,272 |
| 3 | 298,523 | 23,882 | 28,444 |
| 2 | 307,478 | 24,598 | 27,639 |
| 1 | 316,703 | 25,336 | 26,856 |
| Lump-sum equivalent of the retirement annuity as of the retirement date | | | 1,985,360 |

© The McGraw-Hill Companies, Inc., 2007

## Case 17-1 (concluded)

Your annual retirement pay assuming continuing investment of assets at 6% will be:

$1,985,360 ÷ 11.46992 = **$173,093**

$^{*}$ present value of an ordinary annuity of $1: n=20, i=6%

## Requirement 3

Based on the calculations alone, the State's defined benefit plan offers the larger retirement annuity and, therefore, lump-sum equivalent of the retirement annuity. Be aware though that many other factors need to be considered. Plans vary in terms of the flexibility regarding how you can choose to receive distributions of your retirement assets. Very often defined benefit plans provide benefits only until you and/or your spouse dies with no benefits to other beneficiaries; whereas, assets accumulated under defined contribution plans can be bequeathed to other beneficiaries.

Also, greater uncertainty is associated with defined contribution plans, in general. The employee bears the risk of uncertain investment returns and, potentially, might settle for far less at retirement than at first expected. On the other hand, results may exceed expectations as well. Risk is reversed in a defined benefit plan. Because specific benefits are promised at retirement, the employer is responsible for making up the difference when investment performance is less than expected.

Relatedly, uncertainty regarding mortality significantly affects the equation. Defined benefit plans pay benefits from retirement to death. Assets accumulated under defined contribution plans, however, are a fixed amount. How well that amount provides for retirement income depends on how many years you live after retirement.

# Communication Case 17-2
## Suggested Grading Concepts and Grading Scheme:

**Content** (80%)

_____ 25   The net periodic pension expense measures this compensation and consists of the following five elements which can vary differently from changes in employment.(5 each; maximum of 25 for this part)

     _____ The service cost component is the present value of the benefits earned by the employees during the current period.

     _____ The interest cost component is the increase in the projected benefit obligation due to the passage of time.

     _____ The return on plan assets reduces the pension expense. The actual return on plan assets component is the difference between the fair value of the plan assets at the beginning and the end of the period, adjusted for contributions and benefit payments. This amount is adjusted for any gain or loss, so it is the expected return that actually affects the calculation.

     _____ Prior service cost is created when a pension plan is amended and credit is given for employee service rendered in prior years. This retroactive credit is not recognized as pension expense entirely in the year the plan is amended, but is recognized in pension expense over the time that the employees who benefited from this credit work for the company.

     _____ Gains and losses arise from changes in estimates concerning the amount of the projected benefit obligation or the return on the plan assets being different from expected. These are not recognized as they occur.

_____ 20   Gains and losses occur when the PBO or the return on plan assets turns out to be different than expected. (10 each; maximum of 20 for this part)

     _____ A _net_ gain or a _net_ loss affects pension expense only if it exceeds an amount equal to 10% of the PBO, or 10% of plan assets, whichever is higher.

     _____ When the corridor is exceeded, the excess is not charged to pension expense all at once. Instead, the amount that should be included is the excess divided by the average remaining service period of active employees expected to receive benefits under the plan.

## Case 17-2 (concluded)

_____    20    PBO and ABO compared (10 each; maximum of 20 for this part)

     _____ Both the accumulated benefit obligation and the projected benefit obligation represent the present value of the benefits attributed by the pension benefit formula to employee service rendered prior to a specific date.

     _____ The accumulated benefit obligation is based on present salary levels and the projected benefit obligation is based on estimated future salary levels.

_____    15    An additional minimum liability must be recognized when:

     _____ the accumulated benefit obligation exceeds the fair value of the plan assets (10 points) and

     _____ there is not already a credit balance in the accrued pension cost account at least equal to the excess. (5 points)

_____    80 points

## Writing (20%)

_____    5    Terminology and tone appropriate to the audience of assistant controllers.

_____    6    Organization permits ease of understanding.

     ____ introduction that states purpose.

     ____ paragraphs separate main points.

_____    9    English

     ____ word selection.

     ____ spelling.

     ____ grammar.

_____    20 points

# Judgment Case 17-3

## Requirement 1

Yes, it's true that the pension expense is calculated *as if* the balance sheet contained certain amounts it doesn't report, specifically the projected benefit obligation, the pension assets, and other unrecognized amounts. The balance sheet reflects only the extent to which the pension expense has been higher or lower than cash contributions to the pension fund plus a so-called "minimum liability" to the extent the ABO exceeds the pension assets.

Actually, even the pension expense falls short of reflecting all changes in the PBO and plan assets due to methods invented by the FASB to defer the effect of gains, losses, prior service cost, and effects of changing to the new standard.

## Requirement 2

A small liability would be reported under GAAP. This is the accrued pension cost: $171,000 in 2006 and $149,000 in 2005. (The account has a credit balance; a debit balance would be an asset.) Also, no minimum liability is required if the ABO does not exceed the pension assets. This appears to be the case because no minimum liability is explicitly reported and, although the ABO is not separately reported, it would be considerably less than the PBO, and the PBO is only slightly more than plan assets.

## Case 17-3 (concluded)

### Requirement 3

No asset would be reported in the balance sheet. If the accrued pension cost had shown a debit balance, it would be an asset (prepaid pension cost).

### Requirement 4

None of the other amounts reported in the disclosure note are reported on the balance sheet. The plan assets, projected benefit obligation, unrecognized gain, and prior service cost each has a balance that is maintained informally only.

### Requirement 5

Gains and losses occur when either the PBO or the return on plan assets turns out to be different than expected. LGD's unrecognized net gain indicates that cumulative previous gains of either type have exceeded cumulative previous losses of either type. The loss in 2006 indicates the PBO is higher than previously expected due to some unspecified change in an actuarial assumption.

A *net* gain or a *net* loss affects pension expense only if it exceeds an amount equal to 10% of the PBO, or 10% of plan assets, whichever is higher. That appears to be the case with LGD and the amortized portion of the net gain is one component of the pension expense.

### Requirement 6

As mentioned in the previous part, the amortized portion of the net gain is one component of the pension expense. A second component is an amortized portion of the prior service cost. A company is required to report separately the components of pension expense.

# Communication Case 17-4

First, this case has no right or wrong answer. The process of developing the proposed solutions will likely be more beneficial than the solutions themselves. Students should benefit from participating in the process, interacting first with other group members, then with the class as a whole.

Solutions should take into account the facts brought out in the solution to the previous case on which this one is based. Also, it is likely that some of the suggestions will be variations of the following alternatives:

1. The FASB compromise approach as described in the text.

2. Full recognition of the projected benefit obligation and the plan assets with no "smoothing" – deferral of gains, losses, or prior service cost.

3. Recognition of the accumulated benefit obligation rather than the projected benefit obligation.

4. Alternatives 2 or 3, but with netting of the obligation and plan assets.

It is important that each student actively participate in the process. Domination by one or two individuals should be discouraged. Students should be encouraged to contribute to the group discussion by (a) offering information on relevant issues, (b) clarifying or modifying ideas already expressed, or (c) suggesting an alternative direction.

# International Case 17-5

The report should indicate similarities and differences between the United States and the chosen country focusing on the following issues:

a. Depending on the country chosen, the financial statement effect may be minimal. In many countries, including many South American and West European countries, pension benefits are uncommon.

b. In the United States, accrual of these benefits in the service periods is required. This is the objective also in many other countries such as Canada and the United Kingdom; however, significant variations exist in how that objective is accomplished. In other countries where pension benefits are commonly provided, little official guidance is offered. For instance, pension costs are not covered by accounting standards in Australia, Belgium, Denmark, and Switzerland, to name a few.

The report might also comment whether cultural differences are likely contributors to the differences observed.


# Ethics Case 17-6

Mr. Maxwell's apparent motivation for the change in the way contributions are handled is to have the company benefit from the earning power of the contributed funds for up to three months, prior to the funds being deposited for the benefit of the employees. Temporarily diverting 401(k) funds this way benefits the company at the expense of the employee.

There is some question as to whether the practice described is illegal. In practice, such cases are rarely prosecuted. Regardless of the legality, though, there is the ethical question of whether the employer should earn dividends, interest, etc. on funds deducted from employees' paychecks, prior to the funds being deposited to the employees' accounts.

# Research Case 17-7

Results will vary depending on companies chosen.

**Wal-Mart** provided the following disclosures in its annual report for the year ending January 31, 2004:

## 10 Retirement-Related Benefits (in part)

The Company maintains profit sharing plans under which most full-time and many part-time associates become participants following one year of employment and 401(k) plans to which associates may elect to contribute a percentage of their earnings. During fiscal 2004 participants could contribute up to 15% of their pretax earnings, but not more than statutory limits.

Annual Company contributions are made at the sole discretion of the Company, and were $662 million, $574 million and $479 million in 2004, 2003 and 2002, respectively.

## Case 17-7 (continued)

**United Airlines** reported the following information about its benefit plans:

### (12) Retirement and Postretirement Plans (in part)

We have various retirement plans, both defined benefit (qualified and non-qualified) and defined contribution, which cover substantially all employees.

The following table sets forth the reconciliation of the beginning and ending balances of the benefit obligation and plan assets, the funded status and the amounts recognized in the Statements of Consolidated Financial Position for the defined benefit and other postretirement plans as of December 31 (utilizing a measurement date of December 31):

(In millions)

| **Change in Benefit Obligation** | **Pension Benefits** | | **Other Benefits** | |
|---|---|---|---|---|
| | 2003 | 2002 | 2003 | 2002 |
| Benefit obligation at beginning of year | $ 12,673 | $10,095 | $ 3,965 | $ 2,359 |
| Service cost | 295 | 399 | 86 | 100 |
| Interest cost | 815 | 809 | 225 | 211 |
| Plan participants' contributions | 2 | 2 | 23 | 11 |
| Amendments | (66) | 544 | (1,382) | 217 |
| Actuarial (gain) loss | 279 | 1,442 | 583 | 1,218 |
| Curtailments | (81) | - | (113) | - |
| Foreign currency exchange rate changes | 19 | 17 | - | - |
| Special termination benefits | 10 | - | 4 | - |
| Benefits paid | (829) | (635) | (205) | (151) |
| Benefit obligation at end of year | $13,117 | $12,673 | $ 3,186 | $ 3,965 |

| **Change in Plan Assets** | | | | |
|---|---|---|---|---|
| | 2003 | 2002 | 2003 | 2002 |
| Fair value of plan assets at beginning of year | $ 6,298 | $ 7,575 | $ 119 | $ 118 |
| Actual return on plan assets | 1,400 | (704) | 6 | 6 |
| Employer contributions | 86 | 53 | 175 | 135 |
| Plan participants' contributions | 2 | 2 | 23 | 11 |
| Foreign currency exchange rate changes | 4 | 7 | - | - |
| Benefits paid | (829) | (635) | (205) | (151) |
| Fair value of plan assets at end of year | $ 6,961 | $ 6,298 | $ 118 | $ 119 |

## Case 17-7 (continued)

|  | 2003 | 2002 | 2003 | 2002 |
|---|---|---|---|---|
| Funded status | $ (6,156) | $ (6,377) | $(3,069) | $(3,846) |
| Unrecognized actuarial (gains) losses | 3,903 | 4,456 | 2,048 | 1,677 |
| Unrecognized prior service costs | 870 | 1,150 | (1,128) | 209 |
| Unrecognized net transition obligation | 11 | 13 | - | - |
| Net amount recognized | $ (1,372) | $ (758) | $(2,149) | $(1,960) |

| Amounts recognized in the statement of financial position consist of: | 2003 | 2002 | 2003 | 2002 |
|---|---|---|---|---|
| Prepaid (accrued) benefit cost | $ (1,372) | $ (758) | $(2,149) | $(1,960) |
| Accrued benefit liability | (4,327) | (3,956) | - | - |
| Intangible asset | 904 | 1,162 | - | - |
| Accumulated other comprehensive income | 3,423 | 2,794 | - | - |
| Net amount recognized | $ (1,372) | $ (758) | $(2,149) | $(1,960) |
| Increase in minimum liability included in other comprehensive income | $ 630 | $2,364 | na | na |

The following information relates to all pension plans with an accumulated benefit obligation in excess of plan assets:

| | December 31 | |
|---|---|---|
| (In millions) | 2003 | 2002 |
| Projected benefit obligation | $ 13,117 | $ 12,673 |
| Accumulated benefit obligation | 12,653 | 11,009 |
| Fair value of plan assets | 6,961 | 6,298 |

# Case 17-7 *(continued)*

The net periodic benefit [pension] cost included the following components:

| (In millions) | Pension Benefits | | |
| --- | --- | --- | --- |
| | **2003** | **2002** | **2001** |
| Service cost | $ 295 | $ 399 | $ 352 |
| Interest cost | 815 | 809 | 722 |
| Expected return on plan assets | (718) | (822) | (805) |
| Amortization of prior service cost including transition obligation/(asset) | 93 | 89 | 73 |
| Curtailment charge | 125 | - | 74 |
| Special termination benefit | 10 | - | - |
| Recognized actuarial (gain)/loss | 73 | 26 | 16 |
| Net periodic benefit costs | $ 693 | $ 501 | $ 432 |

The weighted-average assumptions used for the [pension] plans were as follows:

| | Pension Benefits | |
| --- | --- | --- |
| | **2003** | **2002** |
| Weighted-average assumptions used to determine benefit obligations at December 31 | | |
| | | |
| Discount rate | 6.25% | 6.75% |
| Rate of compensation increase | 3.44% | 4.30% |
| | | |
| Weighted-average assumptions used to determine net periodic benefit cost for years ended December 31 | | |
| | | |
| Discount rate | 6.51% | 7.50% |
| Expected long-term rate of return on plan assets | 9.00% | 9.75% |
| Rate of compensation increase | 3.24% | 4.20% |

The expected return on plan assets is based on an evaluation of the historical behavior of the broad financial markets and the Company's investment portfolio, taking into consideration input from the plans' investment consultant and actuary regarding expected long-term market conditions and investment management performance.

*Case 17-7 (concluded)*

The weighted-average asset allocations for our pension plans at December 31, 2003 and 2002, by asset category are as follows:

|  | **Plan Assets at December 31** | |
|---|---|---|
| **Asset Category** | **2003** | **2002** |
| Equity securities | 60% | 58% |
| Fixed income | 35 | 37 |
| Other | 5 | 5 |
| Total | 100% | 100% |

Our targeted allocation of assets to the following fund types: 60% equities, 35% fixed income and 5% other, with expected long-term rates of return of 10%, 7.5% and 15%, respectively.

We believe that the long-term asset allocation on average will approximate the targeted allocation and regularly review the actual asset allocation to periodically rebalance the investments to the targeted allocation when appropriate. Pension expense is reduced by the expected return on plan assets, which is measured by assuming the market-related value of plan assets increases at the expected rate of return. The market-related value is a calculated value that phases in differences between the expected rate of return and the actual return over a period of five years.

We expect to contribute approximately $1.1 billion to our defined benefit pension plan trusts and approximately $200 million to our other benefit plans in 2004. In addition, the following benefit payments, which reflect expected future service, as appropriate, are expected to be paid from the trusts:

|  | **Pension Benefits** | **Other Benefits** |
|---|---|---|
| 2004 | $ 795 | $ 225 |
| 2005 | 809 | 235 |
| 2006 | 826 | 230 |
| 2007 | 845 | 235 |
| 2008 | 854 | 235 |
| Years 2009 - 2013 | 4,446 | 1,152 |

# Real World Case 17-8

## Requirement 1

A pension plan is underfunded when the obligation (PBO) exceeds the resources available to satisfy that obligation (plan assets) and overfunded when the opposite is the case. FedEx's plans are underfunded. The PBO exceeds plan assets in both years reported. Note that when the obligation is measured as the Accumulated Benefit Obligation (ABO), plan assets exceed the obligation in 2004.

## Requirement 2

Neither the PBO nor the plan assets is reported in the balance sheets. The difference between the pension expense and the cash contribution each period is debited or credited, depending on the situation, to a single account: prepaid (accrued) pension cost. When the account has a *debit* balance it represents a cumulative overpayment and is reported as an asset – "prepaid pension cost." When it has a *credit* balance it represents a cumulative underpayment and is reported as a liability – "accrued pension cost." As indicated in Note 12, FedEx reports an asset (apparently among "other assets") of $907,000,000 in 2004 and $1,071,000,000 in 2003, both amounts far less than either the PBO or plan assets.

## Requirement 3

FedEx reports three actuarial assumptions used in its pension calculations:

| Pension Plans | 2004 | 2003 |
|---|---|---|
| Discount rate | 6.78% | 6.99% |
| Rate of increase in future compensation levels | 3.15% | 3.15% |
| Expected long-term rate of return on assets | 9.10% | 10.10% |

- The reported decrease in the discount rate from 2003 to 2004 increased FedEx's projected benefit obligation. The lower the discount rate in a present value calculation, the higher the present value.
- There was no change in FedEx's rate of increase in future compensation from 2003 to 2004. However, if FedEx had reported decrease in the rate of increase in future compensation levels it would have decreased FedEx's PBO. Lower compensation estimates in the pension formula result in lower estimates of retirement benefits and thus in the PV of those benefits.
- The expected long-term rate of return on assets will not directly affect FedEx's projected benefit obligation. It affects instead the plan assets and pension expense.

# Real World Case 17-9

## Requirement 1

The increase in a company's PBO attributable to making a plan amendment retroactive is referred to as the prior service cost. Prior service cost adds to the cost of having a pension plan. Amending a pension plan typically is done with the idea that future operations will benefit from having done so. Thus, the cost is not recognized as pension expense entirely in the year the plan is amended, but is recognized as pension expense over the time that the employees who benefited from the retroactive amendment will work for the company in the future. In GM's case, that may be a relatively short time. Apparently, a motive for GM's amendment was the expectation that employees would retire early and take advantage of the limited time offer.

## Requirement 2

The amendment increased GM's pension obligation. GM's pension expense will be higher each year for as long as the prior service cost is amortized. Presumably, in this instance, GM expects the bulk, if not all, of the cost to be expensed in the first year.

# Research Case 17-10

## Requirement 1

Normally, a company's net periodic pension cost represents an expense and therefore decreases earnings. Often, though, circumstances cause this element of the income statement to actually *increase* reported earnings. This occurs when the "expected return on assets," a negative component of pension expense, is higher than the combined total of the other components.

## Requirement 2

Qwest's 2003 income statement does not specifically report the effect of the pension plan. Any effect apparently is included in another item.

## Requirement 3

The note on employee benefits indicates that the pension plan contributed $158 million to reported earnings in 2003.

| | |
|---|---:|
| Service cost | $ 170 |
| Interest cost | 601 |
| Expected return on plan assets. | (858) |
| Amortization of transition asset* | (71) |
| Net (credit) cost | $(158) |

The major contributor to this effect is the Expected return on plan assets of over a billion dollars.

* A transition amount created when companies initially adopted SFAS 87 was amortized to earnings. For most companies, this effect will end in 2007.

## Case 17-10 (concluded)

## Requirement 4

Companies must report the actuarial assumptions used to make estimates concerning pension plans. Qwest reported these assumptions at the beginning of years:

|  | **2003** | **2002** |
|---|---|---|
| Discount rate | 6.75% | 7.25% |
| Average rate of compensation increase | 4.65% | 4.65% |
| Expected long-term rate of return on plan assets | 9.00% | 9.40% |

The two changes reported by Quest do impact the effect of the pension plan on reported earnings.

- The reported decrease in the discount rate from 2002 to 2003 increased the projected benefit obligation. The lower the discount rate in a present value calculation, the higher the present value. This will increase the service cost and interest cost components of the net pension cost (credit).

- The rate of increase in future compensation levels did not change.

- The reported decrease in the expected long-term rate of return on assets directly affects the net pension cost (credit). The lower the rate, the lower the "expected return on assets," a negative component of the net pension cost (credit).

# Integrating Case 17-11

## Requirement 1

| | ($ in millions) |
|---|---|
| Service cost | $43 |
| Interest cost | 32 |
| Actual return on the plan assets | (none) |
| *Adjusted for: gain or loss on the plan assets* | none |
| Amortization of prior service cost | none |
| Amortization of net loss or net gain | none |
| Amortization of transition liability ($275 ÷ 25 yrs) | 11 |
| **Postretirement benefit expense** | **$86** |

## Requirement 2

| | ($ in millions) |
|---|---|
| Postretirement benefit expense (determined above)................ | 86 |
| Accrued postretirement benefit cost (difference) .............. | 76 |
| Cash (retiree benefits paid)..................................... | 10 |

## Requirement 3

| | | |
|---|---|---|
| Income tax expense (to balance)............................................ | 129.6 | |
| Deferred tax asset ([$86 – 10] x 40%).................................... | 30.4 | |
| Income tax payable ($400 x 40%)........................................ | | 160 |

## Requirement 4

| | ($ in millions) | |
|---|---|---|
| **Postretirement benefit expense:** | | |
| Postretirement benefit expense ($43 + 32 + 275) ................... | 350 | |
| Accrued postretirement benefit cost (difference) .............. | | 340 |
| Cash (retiree benefits paid)...................................... | | 10 |
| **Tax expense:** | | |
| Income tax expense (to balance)............................................ | 24 | |
| Deferred tax asset ([$350 – 10] x 40%).................................... | 136 | |
| Income tax payable ($400 x 40%)........................................ | | 160 |

# International Case 17-12

The report should indicate similarities and differences between the United States and the chosen country focusing on the following issues:

a.  Depending on the country chosen, the financial statement effect may be minimal. In many countries, postretirement benefits other than pensions are uncommon. For example, in Japan the profusion of government-sponsored plans means most Japanese companies choose not to provide separate benefits.

b.  In the United States, accrual of these benefits in a manner similar to pensions is required. Benefits are commonly provided in Canada, but three accounting treatments are permitted: (1) accrual, (2) pay-as-you-go, and (3) accrual only when employees retire. The method used must be disclosed. Accounting for these benefits in the United Kingdom is similar to the United States. Little official guidance is offered in most other countries.

The report might also comment whether cultural differences are likely contributors to the differences observed.

# Research Case 17-13

The specification of postretirement benefit coverage in the Content Specification Outline will depend on the date the website is accessed.

The examination structure comprises four separately scored sections:
- Auditing & Attestation
- Business Environment & Concepts
- Financial Accounting & Reporting (business enterprises, not-for-profit organizations, and governmental entities)
- Regulation (professional responsibilities, business law, and taxation)

Postretirement benefits are not specifically mentioned by name. However, the content specification outline indicates testing of standards for presentation and disclosure in the balance sheet and of comprehensive income and, more specifically, employee benefits are tested in the Financial Accounting & Reporting section.

The education requirements to sit for the CPA exam vary somewhat from state to state. In Tennessee, examination candidates must have a minimum of 150 semester (225 quarter) hours which includes;

- a baccalaureate or higher degree from a Board recognized academic institution,

- 24 semester hours in accounting, and

- 24 semester hours in general business subjects.

Educational requirements must be met within 120 days following the examination or grades will be voided.

# Analysis Case 17-14

> **Note 12: Employee Benefit Plans (in part)**
> Certain of our subsidiaries offer medical, dental and vision coverage to eligible U.S. retirees and their eligible dependents. U.S. employees covered by the principal plan become eligible for these benefits at age 55 and older, if they have permanent, continuous service of at least 10 years after attainment of age 45 if hired prior to January 1, 1988, or at least 20 years after attainment of age 35 if hired on or after January 1, 1988.

1. Note 12 above tells us that FedEx provides its retirees medical and dental coverage to eligible U.S. domestic retirees and their eligible dependents. Employees become eligible for these benefits at age 55 and older, if they have permanent, continuous service with the Company of at least 10 years after attainment of age 45 if hired prior to January 1, 1988, or at least 20 years after attainment of age 35, if hired on or after January 1, 1988.

2. When Federal Express adopted SFAS 106, it chose to expense the transition cost immediately. We know that because there is no unrecognized transition cost reported and no amortization of this amount in the calculation of postretirement benefit cost and because there is zero unrecognized transition amount indicated for postretirement benefits.

3. The postretirement benefit plan is not funded. No plan assets are reported and no return on plan assets is included in the calculation of postretirement benefit cost.

# Chapter 18  Shareholders' Equity

## QUESTIONS FOR REVIEW OF KEY TOPICS

### Question 18-1
The two primary sources of shareholders' equity are amounts *invested* by shareholders in the corporation and amounts *earned* by the corporation on behalf of its shareholders. Invested capital is reported as **paid-in capital** and earned capital is reported as **retained earnings**.

### Question 18-2
The statement of shareholders' equity reports the transactions that cause *changes* in its shareholders' equity account balances. It shows the beginning and ending balances in primary shareholders' equity accounts and any changes that occur during the years reported. Typical reasons for changes are the sale of additional shares of stock, the acquisition of treasury stock, net income, and the declaration of dividends.

### Question 18-3
Comprehensive income is a broader view of the change in shareholders' equity than traditional net income. It is the total *nonowner* change in equity for a reporting period. It encompasses all changes in equity except those caused by transactions with owners. Transactions between the corporation and its owners (shareholders) primarily include dividends and the sale or purchase of shares of the company's stock. Most nonowner changes (e. g., revenues and expenses) are reported in the income statement. So, the changes other than the ones that are part of traditional net income are those reported as "other comprehensive income."

Two attributes of other comprehensive income are reported: (1) components of comprehensive income *created during the reporting period* and (2) the comprehensive income *accumulated* over the current and prior periods. The components of comprehensive income *created during the reporting period* - can be reported either (a) as an additional section of the income statement, (b) as part of the statement of shareholders' equity, or (c) in a disclosure note. Regardless of the choice a company makes, the presentation will report net income, other components of comprehensive income, and total comprehensive income. The second attribute - the comprehensive income *accumulated* over the current and prior periods – is reported as a separate component of shareholders' equity. This amount represents the *cumulative* sum of the changes in each component created during each reporting period throughout all prior years.

## Answers to Questions (continued)

### Question 18-4
The three primary ways a company can be organized are (1) a *single proprietorship*, (2) a *partnership*, or (3) a *corporation*. Transactions are accounted for the same regardless of the form of business organization with the exception of the method of accounting for capital – the ownership interest in the company. Several capital accounts (as discussed in this chapter) are used to record changes in ownership interests for a corporation, rather than recording all changes in ownership interests in a single capital account for each owner, as we do for single proprietorships and partnerships.

### Question 18-5
In the eyes of the law, a corporation is a separate legal entity – separate and distinct from its owners. The owners are not personally liable for debts of the corporation. So, shareholders generally may not lose more than the amounts they invest when they purchase shares. This is perhaps the single most important advantage of corporate organization over a proprietorship or a partnership.

### Question 18-6
"Not-for-profit" corporations, such as churches, hospitals, universities, and charities, are not organized for profit and do not sell stock. Some *not-for-profit* corporations, such as the Federal Deposit Insurance Corporation (FDIC), are government owned.

### Question 18-7
Corporations that are organized for profit may be publicly held or privately (or closely) held. The stock of *publicly held* corporations is available for purchase by the general public. Shares might be traded on organized national stock exchanges available "over-the-counter" from securities dealers. *Privately held* companies' shares are held by only a few individuals and are not available to the general public.

### Question 18-8
Corporations are formed in accordance with the corporation laws of *individual states*. The Model Business Corporation Act serves as the guide to states in the development of their corporation statutes, presently as the model for the majority of states.

### Question 18-9
The ownership rights held by common shareholders, unless specifically withheld by agreement with the shareholders, are:
a. The right to vote on policy issues.
b. The right to share in profits when dividends are declared (in proportion to the percentage of shares owned by the shareholder).
c. The right to share in the distribution of any assets remaining at liquidation after other claims are satisfied.

## Question 18-10

The "preemptive right" is the right to maintain one's percentage share of ownership when new shares are issued. When granted, each shareholder is offered the opportunity to buy the same percentage of any new shares issued as the percentage of shares he/she owns at the time. For reasons of practicality, the preemptive right usually is excluded.

## Question 18-11

The typical rights of preferred shares usually include one or both of the following:
a. A *preference* to a predesignated amount of dividends, i.e., a stated dollar amount per share or % of par value per share. This means that when the board of directors of a corporation declares dividends, preferred shareholders will receive the specified dividend prior to any dividends being paid to common shareholders.
b. A *preference* over common shareholders in the distribution of assets in the event the corporation is dissolved.

## Question 18-12

If preferred shares are noncumulative, dividends not declared in any given year need never be paid. However, if cumulative, when the specified dividend is *not* paid in a given year, the unpaid dividends *accumulate* and must be made up in a *later dividend year* before any dividends are paid on common shares. These unpaid dividends are called "dividends in arrears."

## Question 18-13

Par value was defined by early corporation laws as the amount of net assets not available for distribution to shareholders (as dividends or otherwise). However, now the concepts of "par value" and "legal capital" have been eliminated entirely from the Model Business Corporation Act. Most shares continue to bear arbitrarily designated par values, typically nominal amounts. Although many states already have adopted these provisions, most established corporations issued shares prior to changes in the state statutes. So, most companies still have par value shares outstanding and continue to issue previously authorized par value shares.

## Question 18-14

An argument can be made that, when shares are issued without restriction at the time of sale, this account is an *asset*, similar to accounts receivable. However, when shares are withheld or restricted until the selling price is received, the receivable should be reported as a contra equity account – a *reduction in paid-in capital*. This is the prevailing practice. This means reporting total paid-in capital only to the extent that unrestricted shares are outstanding. This is the preferred practice.

## Question 18-15

The measurement objective is that the transaction should be recorded at fair market value. This might be the fair value of the shares or of the noncash assets or services received, whichever evidence of fair market value seems more clearly evident. This is consistent with the general practice of recording any noncash transaction at market value.

## Answers to Questions (continued)

### Question 18-16

The cash received usually is the sum of the separate market values of the separate securities. However, when the total selling price is not equal to the sum of the separate market prices, the total selling price is allocated in proportion to their relative market values.

### Question 18-17

Share issue costs reduce the net cash proceeds from selling the shares and thus paid-in capital – excess of par. On the other hand, debt issue costs are recorded in a separate "debt issue costs" account and amortized to expense over the life of the debt. The difference often is justified by the presumption that share issue costs and debt issue costs are fundamentally different because a debt issue has a fixed maturity, but that selling shares represents a *perpetual* equity interest. Concept Statement 6 disagrees, stating that debt issue costs should be treated the same way as *share* issue costs. But, Concept Statements do not constitute GAAP, and the currently prescribed practice is to record debt issue costs as assets and expense the asset over the maturity of the debt.

### Question 18-18

The same accounts that previously were increased when the shares were sold are decreased when the shares are retired. Specifically, common (or preferred) stock and paid-in capital – excess of par are reduced by the same amounts they were increased by when the shares were originally sold.

If the cash paid to repurchase the shares differs from the amount originally paid in, accounting for the difference depends on whether the cash paid to repurchase the shares is less than or more than the price previously received when the shares were sold. When less cash is distributed to shareholders to retire shares than originally paid in, some of the original investment remains and is labeled paid-in capital – share repurchase. When more cash is distributed to shareholders to retire shares than originally was paid in for those shares, the additional amount is viewed as a dividend on the original investment, and thus a reduction of retained earnings (unless previous share repurchases have created a balance in paid-in capital – share repurchase which would be reduced first).

### Question 18-19

The purchase of treasury stock and its subsequent resale are considered to be a "single transaction." The purchase of treasury stock is perceived as a temporary reduction of shareholders' equity, to be reversed later when the treasury stock is resold, so the cost of acquiring the shares is "temporarily" debited to the treasury stock account. Allocating the effects to specific shareholders' equity accounts is deferred until the shares are subsequently reissued.

# Answers to Questions (concluded)

## Question 18-20
For a stock dividend of less than 25%, a "small" stock dividend, the fair market value of the additional shares distributed is transferred from retained earnings to paid-in capital  The reduction in retained earnings is the same amount as if *cash* dividends were paid equal to the market value of the shares issued. The treatment is consistent with the belief that per share prices remain unchanged by stock dividends.

This is not logical.  If the value of each share were to remain the same when additional shares are distributed without compensation, the *total value* of the company would grow simply because additional stock certificates are distributed.   Instead, the market price per share will decline in proportion to the increase in the number of shares distributed in a stock dividend.

## Question 18-21
The effect and maybe the motivation for the stock split is to reduce the per share market price (by half).  This will likely increase the stock's *marketability* by making it attractive to a larger number of potential investors.  The appropriate accounting treatment of a stock split is to make no journal entry, which avoids the reclassification of "earned" capital as "invested" capital.  However, if the stock distribution is referred to as a "stock split effected in the form of a stock dividend," and the *per share* par value of the shares is *not* changed, a journal entry is recorded that increases the common stock account by the par value of the additional shares.  To avoid reducing retained earnings Brandon can reduce (debit) paid-in capital – excess of par to offset the credit to common stock, although it's permissible to debit retained earnings.

## Question 18-22
When a company *decreases*, rather than increases, its outstanding shares a **reverse stock split** occurs.  A 1 for 2 reverse stock split would cause one million $1 par shares to become one-half million $2 par shares.  No journal entry would be recorded, so no account balances will change.  But the market price per share would double, and the par amount per share would double.

## Question 18-23
You would be entitled to 3.2 shares (4% x 80 shares).  Since cash payments usually are made when shareholders are entitled to fractions of whole shares, you probably would receive 3 shares and cash equal to the market value of $1/5$ of one share.  Sometimes fractional share rights are issued for the partial shares, which would entitle you to a fractional share right for $1/5$ of a share.

## Question 18-24
A quasi reorganization allows a company to (1) write down inflated asset values and (2) eliminate an accumulated deficit in retained earnings.  The following steps are taken:
1. Assets and liabilities are *revalued* to reflect their fair *market values*, with corresponding credits or debits to *retained earnings*.  This may temporarily *increase the deficit*.
2. The debit balance in retained earnings is eliminated against additional paid-in capital.  When *additional paid-in capital* is not sufficient to absorb the entire deficit, capital stock is debited.
3. Disclosure is provided to indicate the date the deficit was eliminated and when the new accumulation of earnings began.

# BRIEF EXERCISES

## Brief Exercise 18-1

Two attributes of other comprehensive income are reported: (1) components of comprehensive income *created during the reporting period* ($15 million in this instance) and (2) the comprehensive income *accumulated* over the current and prior periods ($50 million at the end of this year).

The $50 million represents the *cumulative* sum of the changes in each component created during each reporting period (the disclosure note) throughout all prior years. Since this amount increased by $15 million, the balance must have been $35 million last year.

## Brief Exercise 18-2

|  | ($ in millions) |  |
| --- | --- | --- |
| Cash (8 million shares x $12 per share) ................................. | 96 | |
| Common stock (8 million shares x $1 par per share)............... | | 8 |
| Paid-in capital – excess of par (remainder) ................... | | 88 |

# Brief Exercise 18-3

Lewelling's paid-in capital – excess of par will increase by $860,000: 4,000 hours x $240 less $100,000 par.

*Journal entry (not required):*

| | | |
|---|---|---|
| Legal expense (4,000 hours x $240)..................................... | 960,000 | |
|    Common stock (100,000 shares x $1 par per share) ............... | | 100,000 |
|    Paid-in capital – excess of par (remainder).................... | | 860,000 |

# Brief Exercise 18-4

Horton's total paid-in capital will decline by $17 million, the price paid to buy back the shares.

*Journal entry (not required):*

| | ($ in millions) | |
|---|---|---|
| Common stock (2 million shares x $1 par)................................. | 2 | |
| Paid-in capital – excess of par (2 million shares x $9*) ................ | 18 | |
|    Paid-in capital – share repurchase (difference).................... | | 3 |
|    Cash (2 million shares x $8.50 per share)................................. | | 17 |

* Paid-in capital – excess of par: $900 ÷ 100 million shares

# Brief Exercise 18-5

Agee's total paid-in capital will decline by $18 million because recording the transaction involves a $1 million reduction of retained earnings and an $18 million reduction in paid-in capital accounts.

## *Journal entries (not required):*

**First buyback**                                                      ($ in millions)
Common stock (1 million shares x $1 par) .................................. 1
Paid-in capital – excess of par (1 million shares x $15*)............ 15
    Paid-in capital – share repurchase (difference) ...................     2
    Cash (1 million shares x $14) .................................................     14
  * $16 - $1 par

**Second buyback**
Common stock (1 million shares x $1 par) .................................. 1
Paid-in capital – excess of par (1 million shares x $15*)............ 15
Paid-in capital – share repurchase (balance from first buyback) . 2
Retained earnings (difference) ................................................. 1
    Cash (1 million shares x $19) .................................................     19
  * $16 - $1 par

# Brief Exercise 18-6

Jennings' retained earnings will decline by $2 million because the $67 million sale price is less than the sum of the cost of the treasury stock ($70 million) and paid-in capital from the previous treasury stock sale ($1 million).

*Journal entries (not required):*

| **Purchase of treasury stock** | ($ in millions) | |
|---|---|---|
| Treasury stock (2 million shares x $70)..................................... | 140 | |
|   Cash........................................................................ | | 140 |

| **First sale of treasury stock** | | |
|---|---|---|
| Cash (1 million shares x $71)..................................... | 71 | |
|   Treasury stock (1 million shares x $70)............................... | | 70 |
|   Paid-in capital – share repurchase (remainder)..................... | | 1 |

| **Second sale of treasury stock** | | |
|---|---|---|
| Cash (1 million shares x $67)..................................... | 67 | |
| Paid-in capital – share repurchase (balance from first sale) ....... | 1 | |
| Retained earnings (remainder) ..................................... | 2 | |
|   Treasury stock (1 million shares x $70)................................ | | 70 |

# Brief Exercise 18-7

Cox' paid-in capital – share repurchase will increase by $7 million as determined in the following journal entry:

|  | ($ in millions) | |
|---|---|---|
| Cash (1 million shares x $29) ....................................................... | 29 | |
|   Paid-in capital – share repurchase (difference) .................... | | 7 |
|   Treasury stock (1 million shares x $22*) ............................... | | 22 |

   * 2 million shares x $20 =  $40 million
    <u>1</u> million shares x $26 =   <u>26</u> million
    3 million shares        $66 million

   $66 million ÷ 3 million shares = $22 average cost per share


# Brief Exercise 18-8

Cox' paid-in capital – share repurchase will increase by $9 million as determined in the following journal entry:

|  | ($ in millions) | |
|---|---|---|
| Cash (1 million shares x $29) ....................................................... | 29 | |
|   Paid-in capital – share repurchase (difference) .................... | | 9 |
|   Treasury stock (1 million shares x $20*) ............................... | | 20 |

   * 2 million shares x $20 =  $40 million (first million at $20)
    1 million shares x $26 =   <u>26</u> million
                       $66 million

# Brief Exercise 18-9

| | ($ in millions) | |
|---|---|---|
| **Declaration date** | | |
| Retained earnings............................................................. | 868.96 | |
| Cash dividends payable (10,862 million shares x $.08) ..... | | 868.96 |
| **Date of record** | | |
| no entry | | |
| **Payment date** | | |
| Cash dividends payable ................................................... | 868.96 | |
| Cash ............................................................................. | | 868.96 |

# Brief Exercise 18-10

| | | |
|---|---|---|
| **Declaration date** | | |
| Loss on investment ($37,000 - 35,000) ............................. | 2,000 | |
| Investment in GE stock .................................................. | | 2,000 |
| Retained earnings (1,000 shares at $35 per share)...................... | 35,000 | |
| Property dividends payable ........................................... | | 35,000 |
| **Payment date** | | |
| Property dividends payable ............................................. | 35,000 | |
| Investment in GE stock ................................................. | | 35,000 |

# Brief Exercise 18-11

| | ($ in millions) | |
|---|---|---|
| Retained earnings (3 million* shares at $25 per share) .............. | 75 | |
| Common stock (3 million* shares at $1 par per share) ........ | | 3 |
| Paid-in capital – excess of par (remainder)..................... | | 72 |

* 5% x 60 million shares = 3 million shares

# Brief Exercise 18-12

If a stock split is not to be effected in the form of a stock dividend, no entry is recorded. Since the shares double, but the balance in the common stock account is not changed, the par per share is reduced, to **$.50** in this instance.


# Brief Exercise 18-13

| | | |
|---|---|---|
| Paid-in capital – excess of par | 60 | |
| Common stock (60 million shares* x $1 par per share) | | 60 |

\* 100% x 60 million shares = 60 million shares

If the *per share* par value of the shares is *not* to be changed, the stock distribution is referred to as a "stock split effected in the form of a stock dividend." In that case, the journal entry increases the common stock account by the par value of the additional shares. This prevents the increase in shares from reducing (by half in this case) the par per share. The par is $1 before and after the split.

# EXERCISES

## Exercise 18-1

### Requirement 1

Comprehensive income is a more expansive view of the change in shareholders' equity than traditional net income. It is the total *nonowner* change in equity for a reporting period. In fact, it encompasses all changes in equity other than from transactions with owners. Transactions between the corporation and its shareholders primarily include dividends and the sale or purchase of shares of the company's stock. Most nonowner changes are reported in the income statement. So, the changes other than those that are part of traditional net income are the ones reported as "other comprehensive income."

### Requirement 2

Two attributes of other comprehensive income are reported: (1) components of comprehensive income *created during the reporting period* and (2) the comprehensive income *accumulated* over the current and prior periods.

The second measure - the comprehensive income *accumulated* over the current and prior periods – is reported in the balance sheet as a separate component of shareholders' equity. This is what Kaufman reported in its balance sheet ($107 million in 2006). Be sure to realize this amount represents the *cumulative* sum of the changes in each component created during each reporting period (the disclosure note) throughout all prior years.

## Exercise 18-1 (continued)

### Requirement 3

Kaufman's 2006 balance sheet amount ($107 million) differs from the 2006 amount reported in the disclosure note. On the other hand, the comprehensive income *created during the reporting period* can be reported either (a) as an additional section of the income statement, (b) as part of the statement of shareholders' equity, or (c) in a disclosure note. This is the measure of comprehensive income Kaufman reported in the disclosure note. Regardless of the placement a company chooses, the presentation is similar. It will report net income, other components of comprehensive income, and total comprehensive income, similar to the following:

|  | ($ in millions) |  |
|---|---|---|
| Net income |  | $xxx |
| Other comprehensive income: |  |  |
| Net unrealized holding gains (losses) on investments (net of tax)† | $ x |  |
| Net unrecognized loss on pensions (net of tax)‡ | (x) |  |
| Deferred gains (losses) from derivatives (net of tax)§ | x |  |
| Gains (losses) from foreign currency translation (net of tax)* | x | xx |
| Comprehensive income |  | $xxx |

†   Changes in the market value of securities available-for-sale.

‡   Reporting a pension liability sometimes requires recording this (described in Chapter 17). It often is called pension liability adjustment.

§   When a derivative designated as a cash flow hedge is adjusted to fair value, the gain or loss is deferred as a component of comprehensive income and included in earnings later, at the same time as earnings are affected by the hedged transaction (described in the Derivatives Appendix to the text).

*   Gains or losses from changes in foreign currency exchange rates. The amount could be an addition to or reduction in shareholders' equity. (This item is discussed elsewhere in your accounting curriculum.)

Notice that each component is reported net of its related income tax expense or income tax benefit.

## Exercise 18-1 (concluded)

### Requirement 4

From the information Kaufman's financial statements provide, we can determine how the company calculated the $107 million accumulated other comprehensive income in 2006:

|  | ($ in millions) |
|---|---|
| Accumulated other comprehensive income, 2005 | $75 |
| Change in net unrealized gains on investments | 34 |
| Change in "other" | (2) |
| Accumulated other comprehensive income, 2006 | $ 107 |

# Exercise 18-2

| | | |
|---|---|---|
| Cash (3 million shares x $17.15 per share) ............................. | 51,450,000 | |
| Common stock (3 million shares x $.01 par per share)........ | | 30,000 |
| Paid-in capital – excess of par (remainder)................... | | 51,420,000 |

# Exercise 18-3

## Requirement 1

|  | ($ in millions) |
|---|---|
| Cash (28 million shares x $20 per share) .................................................. | 560 |
|    Common stock (28 million shares x $1 par per share) ......................... | 28 |
|    Paid-in capital – excess of par (remainder) ..................................... | 532 |

## Requirement 2

|  | ($ in millions) |
|---|---|
| Cash (50% x $560 million) ..................................................................... | 280 |
| Receivable from share purchase contract (50% x $560 million).......... | 280 |
|    Common stock (28 million shares x $1 par per share) ......................... | 28 |
|    Paid-in capital – excess of par (remainder) ..................................... | 532 |

## Requirement 3

| **Shareholders' equity:** | ($ in millions) | |
|---|---|---|
| Common stock, 28 million shares at $1 par ................................... | $ 28 | |
| Paid-in capital – excess of par........................................................ | 532 | |
|    Less:  Receivable from share purchase contract.......................... | (280) | $280 |
| Retained earnings ....................................................................... | | 50 |
| *Total shareholders' equity* ......................................................... | | $330 |

## Requirement 4

|  | ($ in millions) |
|---|---|
| Cash (50% x $560 million) ..................................................................... | 280 |
|    Receivable from share purchase contract (50% x $560 million) ....... | 280 |

## Requirement 5

| **Shareholders' equity:** | ($ in millions) |
|---|---|
| Common stock, 28 million shares at $1 par ................................... | $ 28 |
| Paid-in capital – excess of par........................................................ | 532 |
| Retained earnings ....................................................................... | 115 |
| *Total shareholders' equity* ......................................................... | $675 |

# Exercise 18-4

**February 12**

| | | |
|---|---|---|
| Cash (2 million shares x $9 per share) ............................ | 18,000,000 | |
| Common stock (2 million shares x $1 par)................... | | 2,000,000 |
| Paid-in capital – excess of par (difference)................... | | 16,000,000 |

**February 13**

| | | |
|---|---|---|
| Legal expenses (40,000 shares x $9 per share) ................. | 360,000 | |
| Common stock (40,000 shares x $1 par)...................... | | 40,000 |
| Paid-in capital – excess of par (difference)................... | | 320,000 |

Note: Because 2 million shares sold the previous day for $9 per share, it's reasonable to assume a $9 per share fair value.

**February 13**

| | | |
|---|---|---|
| Cash....................................................................... | 945,000 | |
| Common stock (80,000 shares x $1 par) ..................... | | 80,000 |
| Paid-in capital – excess of par, common*.............. | | 640,000 |
| Preferred stock (4,000 shares x $50 par)...................... | | 200,000 |
| Paid-in capital – excess of par, preferred**............ | | 25,000 |

\*   80,000 shares x [$9 market value - $1 par]

\*\*  Since the value of the common shares is known ($720,000), the market value of the preferred ($225,000) is assumed from the total selling price ($945,000).

**November 15**

| | | |
|---|---|---|
| Property, plant, and equipment (cash value) ................. | 3,688,000 | |
| Common stock (380,000 shares at $1 par per share) ...... | | 380,000 |
| Paid-in capital – excess of par (difference)................ | | 3,308,000 |

# Exercise 18-5

Williams Industries must report the 20 million Class B shares among its long-term liabilities in its balance sheet, not as part of shareholders' equity. The "triggering event," the death of J.P Williams, is certain to occur even though its timing may not be. A share or other financial instrument is considered to be mandatorily redeemable if it embodies an unconditional obligation that requires the issuer to redeem the instrument with cash or other assets at a specified or determinable date or upon an *event certain to occur*. Events certain to occur include the death or termination of employment of an individual, since both events, like taxes, are inevitable.

Because Williams has the right *but not the obligation* to repurchase the Class A shares if a change in ownership of the voting common shares changes, there is no unconditional obligation to repurchase the Class B shares. They are classified as equity.

# Exercise 18-6

## Requirement 1

|  | ($ in millions) |
| --- | --- |
| Cash ($424 million – $2 million) ................................................. | 422 |
|     Common stock (15 million shares at $1 par per share) .............. | 15 |
|     Paid-in capital – excess of par (difference) ......................... | 407 |

## Requirement 2

In recording the sale of shares above, the cost of services related to the sale reduced the net proceeds from selling the shares. Since paid-in capital – excess of par is credited for the excess of the proceeds over the par amount of the shares sold, the effect of share issue costs is to reduce the amount credited to that account. On the other hand, the costs associated with a debt issue are recorded in a separate "debt issue costs" account and amortized to expense over the life of the debt (Chapter 14).

Some argue that share issue costs and debt issue costs are fundamentally different. This view is that a debt issue has a fixed maturity so, like interest expense, debt issue costs are part of the expense of borrowing funds for that period of time (recorded in a separate expense account – "debt issue expense".) On the other hand, selling shares represents a perpetual equity interest. Just as dividends paid on that capital investment are not an expense, neither are the share issue costs of obtaining that capital investment.

Expensing debt issue costs presently is required by GAAP. However, the FASB has suggested in Concept Statement 6 that those costs should be treated the same way as share issue costs, meaning that the debt issue costs would reduce the recorded amount of the debt instead of being recorded separately as an asset. Since Concept Statements do not constitute GAAP, until a new FASB Standard is issued to supersede APB Opinion 21, the accepted practice is to record debt issue costs as assets and expense the asset over the maturity of the debt.

# Exercise 18-7

### 1.  January 7, 2006

|  | ($ in millions) | |
|---|---|---|
| Common stock (2 million shares x $1 par) ................................. | 2 | |
| Paid-in capital – excess of par (2 million shares x $3*) ................ | 6 | |
| Retained earnings (difference) .................................................. | 2 | |
|    Cash (2 million shares x $5 per share)..................................... | | 10 |

  * Paid-in capital – excess of par: $300 ÷ 100 million shares

### 2.  August 23, 2006

| | | |
|---|---|---|
| Common stock (4 million shares x $1 par) ................................. | 4 | |
| Paid-in capital – excess of par (4 million shares x $3) ................ | 12 | |
|    Paid-in capital – share repurchase (difference) .................... | | 2 |
|    Cash (4 million shares x $3.50 per share) ............................... | | 14 |

### 3.  July 25, 2007

| | | |
|---|---|---|
| Cash (3 million shares x $6 per share)..................................... | 18 | |
|    Common stock (3 million shares x $1 par) ............................. | | 3 |
|    Paid-in capital – excess of par (difference)............................ | | 15 |

# Exercise 18-8

**1. January 2, 2006**            ($ in millions)

| | | |
|---|---:|---:|
| Common stock (10 million shares x $1 par) ............................... | 10 | |
| Paid-in capital – excess of par (10 million shares x $33*).......... | 330 | |
|    Paid-in capital – share repurchase (difference)..................... | | 15 |
|    Cash (10 million shares x $32.50)............................................ | | 325 |

  * $34 - $1 par

**2. March 3, 2006**

| | | |
|---|---:|---:|
| Common stock (10 million shares x $1) ..................................... | 10 | |
| Paid-in capital – excess of par (10 million shares x $33*) ............ | 330 | |
| Paid-in capital – share repurchase (available balance) .............. | 15 | |
| Retained earnings (remainder) ................................................. | 5 | |
|    Cash  (10 million shares x $36) ............................................... | | 360 |

  * $34 - $1 par

**3. August 13, 2006**

| | | |
|---|---:|---:|
| Cash (1 million shares x $42)...................................................... | 42 | |
|    Common stock (1 million shares x $1) ..................................... | | 1 |
|    Paid-in capital – excess of par (remainder)........................... | | 41 |

**4. December 15, 2006**

| | | |
|---|---:|---:|
| Cash (2 million shares x $36)...................................................... | 72 | |
|    Common stock (2 million shares x $1) ..................................... | | 2 |
|    Paid-in capital – excess of par (remainder)........................... | | 70 |

# Exercise 18-9

### 1. January 23, 2006

|  |  | ($ in millions) |
|---|---|---|
| Treasury stock (10 million shares x $20)............................................ | 200 |  |
|    Cash ..................................................................................................... |  | 200 |

### 2. September 3, 2006

| | | |
|---|---|---|
| Cash (1 million shares x $21) ................................................................ | 21 | |
|    Treasury stock (1 million shares x $20) ................................................ | | 20 |
|    Paid-in capital – share repurchase (remainder) ..................... | | 1 |

### 3. November 4, 2006

| | | |
|---|---|---|
| Cash (1 million shares x $18) ................................................................ | 18 | |
| Paid-in capital – share repurchase (from 2.) ............................ | 1 | |
| Retained earnings (remainder) ....................................................... | 1 | |
|    Treasury stock (1 million shares x $20) ................................................ | | 20 |

# Exercise 18-10

### 1. February 12, 2006

|  | ($ in millions) | |
|---|---|---|
| Treasury stock (1 million shares x $13)................................. | 13 | |
| Cash..................................................................... | | 13 |

### 2. June 9, 2007

| | | |
|---|---|---|
| Treasury stock (2 million shares x $10).................................. | 20 | |
| Cash..................................................................... | | 20 |

### 3. May 25, 2008

| | | |
|---|---|---|
| Cash (2 million shares x $15)........................................... | 30 | |
| Paid-in capital – share repurchase (difference).................... | | 8 |
| Treasury stock (2 million shares x $11*)............................... | | 22 |

```
* 1 million shares x $13 =  $13 million
  2 million shares x $10 =   20 million
  3 million shares          $33 million
```

$33 million ÷ 3 million shares = $11 average cost per share

### 4. May 25, 2008

| | | |
|---|---|---|
| Cash (2 million shares x $15)........................................... | 30 | |
| Paid-in capital – share repurchase (difference).................... | | 7 |
| Treasury stock (FIFO cost*)............................................. | | 23 |

```
* 1 million shares x $13 =  $13 million
  1 million shares x $10 =   10 million
                             $23 million
```

# Exercise 18-11

## Requirement 1

Method A – Reacquired shares are treated as treasury stock.

Method B – Reacquired shares are retired with their status restored to that of authorized but unissued shares.

## Requirement 2

Reacquired shares that are retired have their status restored to that of authorized but *unissued* shares. Although theoretically identical to retired shares, treasury shares are treated as *issued*, but *not outstanding* shares – at the same time both (a) issued and (b) not outstanding. This artificial status has provided companies an effective device to evade the superficial constraints imposed on par value shares.

Treasury stock is reported as a reduction in *total* shareholders' equity, not associated with any specific shareholders' equity account. By either method *total* shareholders' equity is the same. Retiring shares clearly is conceptually superior because it effectively restores the shares to the status of being authorized, but unissued, shares.

Treated as treasury stock, the *cost* of acquiring the shares is "temporarily" debited to the treasury stock account. Recording the effects on specific shareholders' equity accounts is delayed until later when the shares are reissued. In the meantime, the shares assume the artificial status of being neither unissued nor outstanding.

# Exercise 18-12

This is a change in accounting principle.

|  | ($ in millions) |
|---|---|
| Common stock ($1 par x 4 million shares retired) .......................... | 4 |
| Paid-in capital – excess of par (average amount above par at which the retired shares originally sold: $800 million................... | |
| ÷ 200 million shares = $4; $4 x 4 million shares retired).............. | 16 |
| Retained earnings (difference) ..................................................... | 5 |
| Treasury stock (cost of the shares retired) ................................. | 25 |

UMC applies the new way of reporting reacquired shares retrospectively; that is, to all prior periods as if it always had used that method. In other words, all financial statement amounts for individual periods affected by the change and that are included for comparison with the current financial statements are revised.

In each prior period reported, then, UMC would reduce Common stock by $4 million, Paid-in capital – excess of par by $16 million, Retained earnings by $5 million, and Treasury stock by $25 million.

The effect of the change on each line item affected should be disclosed for each period reported as well as any adjustment for periods prior to those reported. Also, the nature of and justification for the change should be described in the disclosure notes.

# Exercise 18-13

1. a
2. c

# Exercise 18-14
## Requirement 1.

### Retirement of common shares                                      ($ in millions)

| | | |
|---|---|---|
| Common stock (5 million shares x $1 par per share).................... | 5 | |
| Paid-in capital – excess of par ($22 – 5 – 2)........................... | 15 | |
| Retained earnings (given) ..................................,...................... | 2 | |
| Cash (given) ................................................................ | | 22 |

### Net income closed to retained earnings

| | | |
|---|---|---|
| Income summary ......................................................... | 88 | |
| Retained earnings (given) ......................................... | | 88 |

### Declaration of a cash dividend

| | | |
|---|---|---|
| Retained earnings (given) .......................................... | 33 | |
| Cash ............................................................................. | | 33 |

### Declaration of a stock dividend

| | | |
|---|---|---|
| Retained earnings (given) .......................................... | 20 | |
| Common stock ([105-5] x 4%) million shares at $1 par per share) | | 4 |
| Paid-in capital – excess of par (difference) ........................ | | 16 |

## Requirement 2.

Brenner-Jude Corporation
Statement of Retained Earnings
FOR THE YEAR ENDED DECEMBER 31, 2006

($ in millions)

| | |
|---|---|
| **Balance at January 1** | $ 90 |
| Net income for the year | 88 |
| *Deductions*: | |
| Retirement of common stock | (2) |
| Cash dividends of $.33 per share | (33) |
| 4% stock dividend | (20) |
| **Balance at December 31** | $123 |

# Exercise 18-15

|      | Preferred      | Common                    |
|------|----------------|---------------------------|
| 2006 | $ 8 million    | $ 0                       |
| 2007 | 20 million*    | 0                         |
| 2008 | 20 million**   | 130 million (remainder)   |

*   $8 million dividends in arrears plus $12 million of the $16 million current preference.

**  $4 million dividends in arrears plus the $16 million current preference.


# Exercise 18-16

**April 1, 2006**

| Retained earnings (300,000* shares at $30 per share)............... | 9,000,000 |           |
|-------------------------------------------------------------------|-----------|-----------|
| Common stock (300,000* shares at $1 par per share) ......... |           | 300,000   |
| Paid-in capital – excess of par (remainder).................... |           | 8,700,000 |

* 10% x 3 million shares issued and outstanding

or, alternatively:

**April 1, 2006**

| Retained earnings .................................................................... | 9,000,000 |           |
|---------------------------------------------------------------------------------------|-----------|-----------|
| Common stock dividends distributable........................ |           | 300,000   |
| Paid-in capital – excess of par ..................................... |           | 8,700,000 |

**June 1, 2006**

| Common stock dividends distributable ............................... | 300,000 |         |
|--------------------------------------------------------------------|---------|---------|
| Common stock ................................................................ |         | 300,000 |

# Exercise 18-17

## Requirement 1.

| | | |
|---|---|---|
| Paid-in capital – excess of par | 24,500 | |
|   Common stock (24.5 million shares* x $.001 par per share) | | 24,500 |

\* 100% x 24.5 million shares = 24.5 million shares

## Requirement 2.

If the *per share* par value of the shares is *not* to be changed, the stock distribution is referred to as a "stock split effected in the form of a stock dividend." In that case, the journal entry in requirement 1 increases the common stock account by the par value of the additional shares. This prevents the increase in shares from reducing (by half in this case) the par per share.

## Requirement 3.

If Hanmi's stock price had been $36 at the time of the split, its approximate value after the split (other things equal) would be $18. The same pie is sliced into twice as many pieces, so each piece is worth half as much.

# Exercise 18-18

## Requirement 1

A stock dividend or stock split usually results in some shareholders being entitled to fractions of whole shares. For instance, if a company declares a 25% stock dividend, or equivalently a 5 for 4 stock split, a shareholder owning 10 shares would be entitled to 2 $^1/_2$ shares. Another shareholder with 15 shares would be entitled to 3 $^3/_4$ shares. Paying shareholders the cash equivalent of the fractional shares simplifies matters for both the corporation and shareholders.

## Requirement 2

|  | ($ in millions) |
|---|---|
| Retained earnings (36 million* x $21 per share)............................. | 756 |
|     Common stock ([36 million* – 2 million] x $1 par) ................ | 34 |
|     Paid-in capital – excess of par | |
|         ([36 million* – 2 million] x [$21 - 1 = $20 per share]).............. | 680 |
|     Cash (2 million shares at $21 market price per share) ................. | 42 |

* 4% x 900 million shares = 36 million additional shares

# Exercise 18-19

## Requirement 1

### a. March 3 – declaration date

Investment in Leasco International stock .......................  20,000
    Gain on appreciation of investment ($720,000 - $700,000)      20,000

Retained earnings (240,000 shares at $3 per share) ...................  720,000
    Property dividends payable ...........................................      720,000

### March 15 – date of record
        no entry

### March 31 – payment date
Property dividends payable ..............................................  720,000
    Investment in Leasco International stock ...................      720,000

### b. May 3
Paid-in capital – excess of par, common*.........................  90,000
    Common stock (25% x [364,000 - 4,000] shares at $1 par) ..      90,000

    *alternatively, retained earnings may be debited.

### c. July 5
Retained earnings (9,000* x $11 per share)..............................  99,000
    Common stock (9,000* x $1 par) .......................................      9,000
    Paid-in capital – excess of par, common (difference) .....      90,000

    * 2% x [360,000 + 90,000 shares] = 9,000 additional shares

*Exercise 18-19 (concluded)*

**d. December 1 – declaration date**
| | | |
|---|---:|---:|
| Retained earnings.......................................................... | 7,920 | |
|   Cash dividends payable ($90,000 par x 8.8%) ................ | | 7,920 |

**December 20 – date of record**
      no entry

**December 28 – payment date**
| | | |
|---|---:|---:|
| Cash dividends payable ...................................................... | 7,920 | |
|   Cash ......................................................................... | | 7,920 |

**e. December 1 – declaration date**
| | | |
|---|---:|---:|
| Retained earnings.......................................................... | 229,500 | |
|   Cash dividends payable (459,000* x $.50) ..................... | | 229,500 |

\* 360,000 + 90,000 + 9,000 = 459,000 shares

**December 20 – date of record**
      no entry

**December 28 – payment date**
| | | |
|---|---:|---:|
| Cash dividends payable ...................................................... | 229,500 | |
|   Cash ......................................................................... | | 229,500 |

**Requirement 2**
  **Paid-in capital:**

| | | |
|---|---:|---|
| Preferred stock, 8.8%, 90,000 shares at $1 par ............ | $   90,000 | |
| Common stock, 463,000[1] shares at $1 par ................. | 463,000 | |
| Paid-in capital – excess of par, preferred ..................... | 1,437,000 | |
| Paid-in capital – excess of par, common....................... | 2,574,000 | [2] |
| **Retained earnings...........................................** | 9,488,580 | [3] |
| Treasury stock, at cost; 4,000 common shares ............ | (44,000) | |
| *Total shareholders' equity*........................................ | $14,008,580 | |

[1] 364,000 + 90,000 + 9,000 = 463,000 shares
[2] $2,574,000 - 90,000 + 90,000 = $2,574,000
[3] $9,735,000 - 720,000 - 99,000 - 7,920 - 229,500 + 810,000 = $9,488,580

# Exercise 18-20

1.  d
2.  b
3.  a

# Exercise 18-21

The return on shareholders' equity is computed by dividing net income by average shareholders' equity.

$$[\$200 - 120]^* \div ([\$600 + 520] / 2) = \underline{14.29\%}$$

> \* increase in retained earnings, which equals net income since no dividends were paid

The ratio is a summary measure of profitability often used by investors and potential investors, particularly common shareholders. It measures the ability of company management to generate net income from the resources that owners provide.

However, because shareholders' equity is a measure of the *book value* of equity, investors often relate earnings to the market value of equity, calculating the earnings-price ratio. Information available in the exercise is insufficient to do so.

# Exercise 18-22

**AMTC**

| | | |
|---|---|---|
| Cash (7.5 million shares x $13.546).................... | 101,595,000 | |
| Common stock (7.5 million sh. x $.001 par) .. | | 7,500 |
| Paid-in capital – excess of par (difference)..... | | 101,587,500 |

**PSI**

| | | |
|---|---|---|
| Cash (9 million shares x $15.20)........................ | 136,800,000 | |
| Common stock (9 million shares x $.01 par) . | | 90,000 |
| Paid-in capital – excess of par (difference)..... | | 136,710,000 |

# Exercise 18-23

## Requirement 1

|  | ($ in millions) | |
|---|---|---|
| Common stock (10.5 million shares x $.01) ........... | .105 | |
| Paid-in capital – excess of par (10.5 million shares x $36.12) | 379.260 | |
| Retained earnings (difference) | 618.135 | |
| Cash ($1 billion / $95 = 10.5 million shares) | | 997.500 |

Note: This assumes ConocoPhillips retires the shares it buys back rather than accounting for them as treasury stock. If it treated the shares as treasury stock the entry would be:

| | | |
|---|---|---|
| Treasury stock | 997.5 | |
| Cash | | 997.5 |

## Requirement 2

ConocoPhillips is referring to the fact that stock options and stock awards increase the number of shares and thus decrease earnings per share, other things being equal. This effect would partially be offset by decreasing the number of shares through share repurchase.

# Exercise 18-24

1. **b.** Par value represents a stock's legal capital. It is an arbitrary value assigned to stock before it is issued. Par value represents a shareholder's liability ceiling because, as long as the par value has been paid in to the corporation, the shareholders obtain the benefits of limited liability.

2. **c.** Common shareholders usually have preemptive rights, which means they have the right to purchase any new issues of stock in proportion to their current ownership percentages. The purpose of a preemptive right is to allow shareholders to maintain their current percentages of ownership. Given that Smith had 2,000,000 shares outstanding ($10,000,000 / $5), an investor with 20,000 shares has a 1% ownership. Hence, this investor must be allowed to purchase 4,000 (1% x 400,000 shares) of the additional shares.

3. **b.** A stock dividend is a transfer of equity from retained earnings to paid-in capital. The debit is to retained earnings, and the credits are to common stock and additional paid-in capital. More shares are outstanding following the stock dividend, but every shareholder maintains the same percentage of ownership. In effect, a stock dividend divides the pie (the corporation) into more pieces, but the pie is still the same size. Hence, a corporation will have a lower EPS and a lower carrying amount per share following a stock dividend, but every shareholder will be just as well off as previously.

# PROBLEMS

## Problem 18-1

### PART A
**Jan. 9**

|  | ($ in millions) | |
|---|---|---|
| Cash (40 million shares x $20 per share)............................................. | 800 | |
| Common stock (40 million shares x $1 par) ............................ | | 40 |
| Paid-in capital – excess of par (difference) ............................. | | 760 |

**Mar. 11**

| Equipment (5,000 shares x $20 per share)......................... | 100,000 | |
|---|---|---|
| Common stock (5,000 shares x $1 par)......................... | | 5,000 |
| Paid-in capital – excess of par (difference)................... | | 95,000 |

### PART B
**Jan. 12**

|  | ($ in millions) | |
|---|---|---|
| Land ....................................................................................... | 2 | |
| Revenue – donation of land ................................................. | | 2 |

Note: Donated assets are recorded as revenue at the fair value of the assets received, not paid-in capital (SFAS 116). This is discussed in Chapter 10.

**Sept. 1**

|  | ($ in millions) | |
|---|---|---|
| Common stock (2 million shares x $1 par)................................. | 2 | |
| Paid-in capital – excess of par | | |
| (2 million shares x $19) ....................................................... | 38 | |
| Retained earnings (difference) ................................................ | 10 | |
| Cash......................................................................................... | | 50 |

**Dec. 1**

|  | ($ in millions) | |
|---|---|---|
| Cash........................................................................................ | 26 | |
| Common stock ....................................................................... | | 1 |
| Paid-in capital – excess of par ............................................. | | 25 |

# Problem 18-2

## Requirement 1

### a. February 5, 2006

($ in millions)

| Retirement | | Treasury Stock | |
|---|---|---|---|

| Retirement | | | | Treasury Stock | | |
|---|---|---|---|---|---|---|
| Common stock (6 million sh. x $1) | 6 | | | Treasury stock (6 million sh. x $10) | 60 | |
| Paid-in capital – excess of par | | | | Cash | | 60 |
| (6 million shares x $7*) | 42 | | | | | |
| Paid-in capital – share repurchase | 1 | | | | | |
| Retained earnings (plug) | 11 | | | | | |
| Cash | | 60 | | | | |

*Paid-in capital – excess of par:  $1,680 ÷ 240

### b. July 9, 2006

| | | | | | |
|---|---|---|---|---|---|
| Cash (2 million sh. x $12) | 24 | | Cash (2 million sh. x $12) | 24 | |
| Common stock (2 million sh. x $1) | | 2 | Treasury stock (2 million sh. x $10) | | 20 |
| Paid-in capital – excess of par | | 22 | Paid-in capital–sh. repurchase | | 4 |

### c. November 14, 2008

| | | | | | |
|---|---|---|---|---|---|
| Cash (2 million sh. x $7) | 14 | | Cash (2 million sh. x $7) | 14 | |
| Common stock (2 million sh. x $1) | | 2 | Paid-in cap.- sh. repurchase ($1 + 4 ) | 5 | |
| Paid-in capital – excess of par | | 12 | Retained earnings (plug) | 1 | |
| | | | Treasury stock (2 million sh. x $10) | | 20 |

*Problem 18-2 (concluded)*

**Requirement 2**

| Shareholders' Equity | | $ in millions |
|---|---|---|
| | **Retirement** | **Treasury Stock** |
| **Paid-in capital:** | | |
| Common stock, 240 million shares at $1 par, .............. | $ 238 | $ 240 |
| Paid-in capital – excess of par ...................................... | 1,672 * | 1,680 |
| Paid-in capital – share repurchase ................................ | 0 | 0 |
| **Retained earnings**............................................................ | 1,089 ** | 1,099 *** |
| Less:  treasury stock, 2 million shares (at cost).......... | | (20) |
| *Total shareholders' equity* .............................................. | $2,999 | $2,999 |

\*   1,680 - 42 + 22 + 12
\*\*   1,100 - 11
\*\*\* 1,100 - 1

or, alternatively:

| | **Retirement** | **Treasury Stock** |
|---|---|---|
| **Paid-in capital:** | | |
| Common stock, 240 million shares at $1 par, .............. | $ 238 | $ 240 |
| Additional paid-in capital ............................................. | 1,672 * | 1,680 |
| **Retained earnings**........................................................... | 1,089 ** | 1,099 *** |
| Less:  treasury stock, 2 million shares (at cost).......... | | (20) |
| *Total shareholders' equity* .............................................. | $2,999 | $2,999 |

\*   1,680 - 42 + 22 + 12
\*\*   1,100 - 11
\*\*\* 1,100 - 1

# Problem 18-3

**Requirement 1**

### February 15, 2006
**(a) Retired**

| | | |
|---|---:|---:|
| Common stock (300,000 shares x $1 par)........................ | 300,000 | |
| Paid-in capital – excess of par | | |
| (300,000 shares x $5) ................................... | 1,500,000 | |
| Retained earnings (difference)........................................ | 600,000 | |
| Cash (300,000 shares x $8) ........................................ | | 2,400,000 |

**(b) Accounted for as treasury stock**

| | | |
|---|---:|---:|
| Treasury stock (300,000 shares x $8).............................. | 2,400,000 | |
| Cash (300,000 shares x $8) ........................................ | | 2,400,000 |

### February 17, 2007
**(a) Retired**

| | | |
|---|---:|---:|
| Common stock (300,000 shares x $1 par)........................ | 300,000 | |
| Paid-in capital – excess of par | | |
| (300,000 shares x $5) ..................................... | 1,500,000 | |
| Paid-in capital – share repurchase (difference) .......... | | 150,000 |
| Cash (300,000 shares x $5.50)...................................... | | 1,650,000 |

**(b) Accounted for as treasury stock**

| | | |
|---|---:|---:|
| Treasury stock (300,000 shares x $5.50) .......................... | 1,650,000 | |
| Cash (300,000 shares x $5.50)....................................... | | 1,650,000 |

*Problem 18-3 (concluded)*

**November 9, 2008**

**(a) Retired**

| | | |
|---|---:|---:|
| Cash (200,000 shares x $7)............................................ | 1,400,000 | |
| Common stock (200,000 shares x $1 par) ..................... | | 200,000 |
| Paid-in capital – excess of par (difference)................ | | 1,200,000 |

**(b) Accounted for as treasury stock**

| | | |
|---|---:|---:|
| Cash (200,000 shares x $7)............................................. | 1,400,000 | |
| Retained earnings........................................................... | 200,000 | |
| Treasury stock (200,000 shares x $8 FIFO cost) ............ | | 1,600,000 |

## Requirement 2
### Shareholders' Equity

| | SHARES RETIRED | TREASURY STOCK |
|---|---:|---:|
| **Paid-in capital:** | | |
| Common stock, $1 par, ......................................... | $ 5,600,000 | $ 6,000,000 |
| Paid-in capital – excess of par .............................. | 28,200,000 | 30,000,000 |
| Paid-in capital – share repurchase......................... | 150,000 | 0 |
| **Retained earnings**............................................. | 130,900,000* | 131,300,000** |
| Less: treasury stock, 400,000 shares (at cost) ... | | (2,450,000) |
| *Total shareholders' equity* ................................... | $164,850,000 | $164,850,000 |

\* $86,500,000 - 600,000 + 14,000,000 + 15,000,000 + 16,000,000
\*\*$86,500,000 + 14,000,000 + 15,000,000 + 16,000,000 - 200,000

  or, alternatively:

| | SHARES RETIRED | TREASURY STOCK |
|---|---:|---:|
| **Paid-in capital:** | | |
| Common stock, $1 par, ......................................... | $ 5,600,000 | $ 6,000,000 |
| Additional paid-in capital ...................................... | 28,350,000 | 30,000,000 |
| **Retained earnings**............................................. | 130,900,000* | 131,300,000** |
| Less: treasury stock, 400,000 shares (at cost) ... | | (2,450,000) |
| *Total shareholders' equity* ................................... | $164,850,000 | $164,850,000 |

# Problem 18-4

**2004**

| | | |
|---|---:|---:|
| Retained earnings .................................................... | 160,500 | |
|    Income summary .................................................... | | 160,500 |

**2005**

| | | |
|---|---:|---:|
| Income summary .......................................................... | 2,240,900 | |
|    Retained earnings .................................................. | | 2,240,900 |

| | | |
|---|---:|---:|
| Common stock (110,000 shares at $1 par per share)............. | 110,000 | |
| Paid-in capital – excess of par (110,000 shares x $4)........ | 440,000 | |
| Retained earnings (given) .............................................. | 212,660 | |
|    Cash (total)................................................................ | | 762,660 |

       \* Paid-in capital – excess of par: $7,420 ÷ 1,855 = $4

| | | |
|---|---:|---:|
| Retained earnings (given) .............................................. | 698,000 | |
|    Cash dividends payable ............................................. | | 698,000 |

| | | |
|---|---:|---:|
| Cash dividends payable ................................................ | 698,000 | |
|    Cash .......................................................................... | | 698,000 |

**2006**

| | | |
|---|---:|---:|
| Income summary .......................................................... | 3,308,700 | |
|    Retained earnings .................................................. | | 3,308,700 |

| | | |
|---|---:|---:|
| Retained earnings (given) .............................................. | 242,000 | |
|    Common stock (34,900 shares at $1 par per share) ........ | | 34,900 |
|    Paid-in capital – excess of par (difference) ................ | | 207,100 |

| | | |
|---|---:|---:|
| Retained earnings ........................................................ | 889,950 | |
|    Cash dividends payable ............................................. | | 889,950 |

| | | |
|---|---:|---:|
| Cash dividends payable ................................................ | 889,950 | |
|    Cash .......................................................................... | | 889,950 |

# Problem 18-5

**Requirement 1**

**2006**

**a. November 1 – declaration date**

| | | |
|---|---|---|
| Retained earnings....................................................... | 84,000,000 | |
| Cash dividends payable (105 million shares at $.80/share) | | 84,000,000 |

**November 15 – date of record**

no entry

**December 1 – payment date**

| | | |
|---|---|---|
| Cash dividends payable ............................................... | 84,000,000 | |
| Cash ......................................................................... | | 84,000,000 |

**2007**

**b. March 1 – declaration date**

| | | |
|---|---|---|
| Investment in Warner bonds......................................... | 300,000 | |
| Gain on appreciation of investment | | |
| ($1.6 million - 1.3 million)......................................... | | 300,000 |

| | | |
|---|---|---|
| Retained earnings ....................................................... | 1,600,000 | |
| Property dividends payable ...................................... | | 1,600,000 |

**March 13– date of record**

no entry

**April 5– payment date**

| | | |
|---|---|---|
| Property dividends payable ......................................... | 1,600,000 | |
| Investment in Warner bonds ...................................... | | 1,600,000 |

**c. July 12**

| | | |
|---|---|---|
| Retained earnings (5,250,000* x $21 per share).............. | 110,250,000 | |
| Common stock ([5,250,000* – 250,000] x $1 par) .... | | 5,000,000 |
| Paid-in capital – excess of par | | |
| ([5,250,000* – 250,000] x $20 per share).................. | | 100,000,000 |
| Cash (250,000 shares at $21 market price per share)..... | | 5,250,000 |

\* 5% x 105,000,000 shares = 5,250,000 additional shares

# Problem 18-5 (continued)

**d. November 1 – declaration date**

| | | |
|---|---|---|
| Retained earnings .......................................................... | 88,000,000 | |
|     Cash dividends payable (110,000,000* x $.80).............. | | 88,000,000 |

    * 105,000,000 + 5,000,000 = 110,000,000 shares

**November 15 – date of record**
         no entry

**December 1 – payment date**

| | | |
|---|---|---|
| Cash dividends payable ............................................... | 88,000,000 | |
|     Cash ...................................................................... | | 88,000,000 |

## 2008

**e. January 15**

| | | |
|---|---|---|
| Paid-in capital – excess of par..................................... | 55,000,000 | |
|     Common stock (55,000,000* shares at $1 par) .............. | | 55,000,000 |

       * 110,000,000 shares x 50% = 55,000,000 shares

**f. November 1 – declaration date**

| | | |
|---|---|---|
| Retained earnings ......................................................... | 107,250,000 | |
|     Cash dividends payable (165,000,000 * x $.65)............. | | 107,250,000 |

    * 105,000,000 + 5,000,000 + 55,000,000 = 165,000,000 shares

**November 15 – date of record**
         no entry

**December 1 – payment date**

| | | |
|---|---|---|
| Cash dividends payable ............................................... | 107,250,000 | |
|     Cash ...................................................................... | | 107,250,000 |

# Problem 18-5 (concluded)

## Requirement 2

### Branch-Rickie Corporation
### Statement of Shareholders' Equity
For the Years Ended Dec. 31, 2006, 2007, and 2008 ($ in 000s)

| | Common Stock | Additional Paid-in Capital | Retained Earnings | Total Shareholders' Equity |
|---|---|---|---|---|
| **Jan. 1, 2006** | **105,000** | **630,000** | **970,000** | **1,705,000** |
| Net income | | | 330,000 | 330,000 |
| Cash dividends | | | (84,000) | (84,000) |
| **Dec. 31, 2006** | **105,000** | **630,000** | **1,216,000** | **1,951,000** |
| Property dividends | | | (1,600) | (1,600) |
| Common stock dividend | 5,000 | 100,000 | (110,250) | (5,250) |
| Net income | | | 395,000 | 395,000 |
| Cash dividends | | | (88,000) | (88,000) |
| **Dec. 31, 2007** | **110,000** | **730,000** | **1,411,150** | **2,251,150** |
| 3 for 2 split effected in the form of a stock dividend | 55,000 | (55,000) | | |
| Net income | | | 455,000 | 455,000 |
| Cash dividends | | | (107,250) | (107,250) |
| **Dec. 31, 2008** | **165,000** | **675,000** | **1,758,900** | **2,598,900** |

# Problem 18-6

| **2006** | | ($ in millions) |
|---|---|---|
| Cash ......................................................................... | 120 | |
| Receivable from share purchase contract ........................... | 360 | |
|    Preferred stock (1 million shares x $10 par per share) .............. | | 10 |
|    Paid-in capital – excess of par, preferred .......................... | | 470 |
| | | |
| Cash ......................................................................... | 70 | |
|    Common stock (7 million shares x $1 par per share) ................ | | 7 |
|    Paid-in capital – excess of par, common .......................... | | 63 |
| | | |
| Retained earnings ......................................................... | 1 | |
|    Cash dividends payable, preferred .................................. | | 1 |
| | | |
| Cash dividends payable, preferred ..................................... | 1 | |
|    Cash ................................................................ | | 1 |
| | | |
| Retained earnings ......................................................... | 16 | |
|    Cash dividends payable, common .................................... | | 16 |
| | | |
| Cash dividends payable, common ....................................... | 16 | |
|    Cash ................................................................ | | 16 |
| | | |
| Income summary ........................................................... | 290 | |
|    Retained earnings ................................................. | | 290 |

| **2007** | | ($ in millions) |
|---|---|---|
| Cash ......................................................................... | 360 | |
|    Receivable from share purchase contract .......................... | | 360 |
| | | |
| Common stock (3 million shares x $1 par) ............................. | 3 | |
| Paid-in capital – excess of par (3 million shares x $9*) ............. | 27 | |
| Retained earnings (given) ............................................... | 20 | |
|    Cash (total) ....................................................... | | 50 |

   * [$495 million + $63 million] ÷ [55 million + 7 million shares]
     = $9 weighted average amount per share in excess of par

# Problem 18-6 (concluded)

|  | ($ in millions) | |
|---|---|---|
| Retained earnings................................................................ | 1 | |
|    Cash dividends payable, preferred .................................. | | 1 |
| | | |
| Cash dividends payable, preferred .................................... | 1 | |
|    Cash ............................................................................... | | 1 |
| | | |
| Retained earnings................................................................ | 20 | |
|    Cash dividends payable, common .................................... | | 20 |
| | | |
| Cash dividends payable, common ...................................... | 20 | |
|    Cash .............................................................................. | | 20 |
| | | |
| Paid-in capital – excess of par, preferred ........................... | 5 | |
|    Preferred stock ............................................................. | | 5 |
| | | |
| Income summary............................................................... | 380 | |
|    Retained earnings ......................................................... | | 380 |

| **2008** | ($ in millions) | |
|---|---|---|
| Retained earnings ............................................................... | 65 | |
|    Common stock ............................................................... | | 6 |
|    Paid-in capital – excess of par, common......................... | | 59 |
| | | |
| Retained earnings................................................................ | 1 | |
|    Cash dividends payable, preferred .................................. | | 1 |
| | | |
| Cash dividends payable, preferred .................................... | 1 | |
|    Cash ............................................................................... | | 1 |
| | | |
| Retained earnings................................................................ | 22 | |
|    Cash dividends payable, common .................................... | | 22 |
| | | |
| Cash dividends payable, common ...................................... | 22 | |
|    Cash .............................................................................. | | 22 |
| | | |
| Income summary............................................................... | 412 | |
|    Retained earnings ......................................................... | | 412 |

# Problem 18-7

### Requirement 1

The statement of shareholders' equity explains why and how the various shareholders' equity items on the balance sheet change from year to year. The statement shows the beginning and ending balances in primary shareholders' equity accounts and any changes that occur during the years reported (usually three years). Typical reasons for changes are the sale of additional shares of stock, the acquisition of treasury stock, net income, and the declaration of dividends.

### Requirement 2

HP accounts for its share repurchases by formally retiring them. The Statement of Shareholders' Equity reports the repurchase of common stock and yet has no column in the Statement of Shareholders' Equity for treasury stock. If the buybacks were viewed as the purchase of treasury shares, a Treasury Stock account would have been employed.

### Requirement 3

The price HP paid for the shares repurchased in 2004 was *more* than the average price at which HP had sold the shares previously. We know this because the Statement of Shareholders' Equity reports a reduction in retained earnings resulting from that transaction. This occurs only when the cash paid exceeds the reduction in Common stock and Paid-in capital – excess of par:

|  | ($ in millions) |
|---|---|
| Common stock (172,468,000 shares x $.01 par per share).... | 1 |
| Additional paid-in capital*(given)................................. | 3,100 |
| Retained earnings (given) ............................................... | 208 |
| Cash (given: change in total shareholders' equity) ............ | 3,309 |

*consisting of Paid-in capital – excess of par (shares x paid-in per share in excess of par when sold), and possibly Paid-in capital – share repurchase (if any balance remained from previous buybacks when the cash paid was *less* than the selling price.)

## Requirement 4

Comprehensive income is the total *nonowner* change in equity for a reporting period. It encompasses all changes in equity other than from transactions with owners. Transactions between the corporation and its owners primarily include dividends and the sale or purchase of shares of the company's stock. Most nonowner changes are reported in the income statement ($3,497 million for HP). The changes other than those that are part of traditional net income are reported as "Other comprehensive income."

## Requirement 5

The change in Comprehensive income in 2004 was due to (1) net income ($3,497 million), (2) a net unrealized loss on investment securities classified as available for sale ($20 million), (3) a deferred gain from derivatives ($28 million), (4) an adjustment of the minimum pension liability ($13 million), and (5) foreign currency translation gain ($21 million). Each of the last four items is considered *other comprehensive income* and not discussed in detail in this chapter. Here's a summary:

> For reporting purposes, investments in marketable equity securities are categorized as either (a) held-to-maturity, (b) trading securities, or (c) available for sale. Trading securities and securities available for sale are reported at their fair values. The holding gains and losses from writing these securities available for sale up or down to fair value are not reported in the income statement, but instead are reported as a component of Other comprehensive income in the balance sheet. (described in Chapter 12).
>
> When a derivative designated as a cash flow hedge is adjusted to fair value, the gain or loss is deferred as a component of comprehensive income and included in earnings later, at the same time as earnings are affected by the hedged transaction (described in the Derivatives Appendix to the text).

## Problem 18-7 *(concluded)*

Reporting an additional minimum pension liability sometimes requires a reduction in shareholders' equity (see Chapter 17). The intangible pension asset debited when an additional minimum pension liability is increased represents future economic benefits as would arise from employee goodwill associated with incurring a prior service cost by, say, amending the pension formula to be more generous. However, the minimum liability adjustment is to cover an underfunded pension plan (ABO exceeds plan assets). The portion of the underfunding due to the obligation including prior service cost is appropriately represented by an intangible asset, but any portion of the underfunding due to the obligation including unrecognized net losses is not. If not reported as an intangible asset, then, where should it be reported? As we noted in Chapter 17, pension gains and losses are not recognized currently in earnings. Neither are gains and losses from adjusting securities available-for-sale recognized currently in earnings, as noted above. Consistent with reporting unrealized gains and losses from adjusting investment securities to fair value as part of *other comprehensive income*, we also report unrealized losses from adjusting the pension liability as part of *other comprehensive income.*

Gains and losses from changes in foreign currency exchange rates are discussed elsewhere in your accounting curriculum, but also are included in *other comprehensive income* but not net income.

The components of comprehensive income *created during the reporting period* can be reported either (a) as an additional section of the income statement, (b) as part of the statement of shareholders' equity (as HP does), or (c) in a disclosure note. Regardless of the placement a company chooses, the presentation is similar. It will report net income, other components of comprehensive income, and total comprehensive income. This is the measure of comprehensive income HP reported in the Statement of Shareholders' Equity.

The comprehensive income *accumulated* over the current and prior periods is reported as a separate component of shareholders' equity. In HP's case, this amount is a net loss of **$243 million**. This amount represents the *cumulative* sum of the changes in each component created during each reporting period throughout all prior years.

# Problem 18-8

## Requirement 1

| | | |
|---|---|---|
| Cash ($385,000 – 1,500) .................................................... | 383,500 | |
|     Common stock (30,000 shares at $1 par per share)................. | | 30,000 |
|     Paid-in capital – excess of par (remainder)........................ | | 353,500 |

## Requirement 2

| | | |
|---|---|---|
| Retained earnings............................................................ | 60,000 | |
|     Cash dividends payable (30,000 shares x $2) ..................... | | 60,000 |

## Requirement 3

| | | |
|---|---|---|
| Cash dividends payable ..................................................... | 60,000 | |
|     Cash ........................................................................ | | 60,000 |

## Requirement 4

| | | |
|---|---|---|
| Common stock (10% x $30,000) ............................................ | 3,000 | |
| Paid-in capital – excess of par (10% x $353,500)...................... | 35,350 | |
| Retained earnings (difference) ............................................. | 1,150 | |
|     Cash (given)............................................................... | | 39,500 |

# Problem 18-9

**Assumption A – noncumulative**

|  | **Preferred** | **Common** |  |  |
|---|---|---|---|---|
|  |  |  | *Total* | $150 |
| *Current preference* | $10 (10% x $100) |  |  | (10) |
|  |  |  |  | $140 |
| *Remainder to common* |  | $140 |  | (140) |
|  |  |  |  | 0 |
| *Allocation* | $10 | $140 |  |  |

**Assumption B – cumulative**

|  | **Preferred** | **Common** |  |  |
|---|---|---|---|---|
|  |  |  | *Total* | $150 |
| *Dividends in arrears:* |  |  |  |  |
| -2004 | $10 (10% x $100) |  |  | (10) |
| -2005 | 10 (10% x $100) |  |  | (10) |
| *Current preference* | 10 (10% x $100) |  |  | (10) |
|  |  |  |  | $120 |
| *Remainder to common* |  | $120 |  | (120) |
|  |  |  |  | 0 |
| *Allocation* | $30 | $120 |  |  |

# Problem 18-10

### Transactions

| | | |
|---|---|---|
| N | 1. | Sale of common stock |
| N | 2. | Purchase of treasury stock at a cost *less* than the original issue price |
| N | 3. | Purchase of treasury stock at a cost *greater* than the original issue price |
| D | 4. | Declaration of a property dividend |
| N | 5. | Sale of treasury stock for *more* than cost |
| D | 6. | Sale of treasury stock for *less* than cost |
| I | 7. | Net income for the year |
| D | 8. | Declaration of a cash dividend |
| N | 9. | Payment of a previously declared cash dividend |
| N | 10. | Issuance of convertible bonds for cash |
| D | 11. | Declaration and distribution of a 5% stock dividend |
| N | 12. | Retirement of common stock at a cost *less* than the original issue price |
| D | 13. | Retirement of common stock at a cost *greater* than the original issue price |
| N(orD) | 14. | A stock split effected in the form of a stock dividend |
| N | 15. | A stock split in which the par value per share is reduced (not effected in the form of a stock dividend) |
| D | 16. | A net loss for the year |

# Problem 18-11

A stock dividend is the distribution of *additional shares of stock* to *current* shareholders of the corporation. The investor receives no assets, only additional shares. Because each shareholder receives the same *percentage* increase in shares, an investor's proportional interest in (percentage ownership of) the investee corporation remains unchanged. So, when additional shares are received from a stock dividend, no journal entry is needed. The same investment is simply represented by a larger number of shares. Of course, the investment *per share* is now less, an effect that must be considered if a portion of the investment is sold.

| | ($ in millions) |
|---|---|
| **To record the investment** | |
| Investment in L&K Corporation shares ............................... | 52.8 |
|    Cash (1.2 million shares x $44)................................................. | 52.8 |

| | |
|---|---|
| **To record the sale of shares**.......................... | |
| Cash (200,000 shares x $46)........................................................ | 9.2 |
|    Investment in L&K shares (200,000 shares x $44).................. | 8.8 |
|    Gain on sale of investments (difference) ............................. | .4 |

**10% stock dividend**

There is no entry for the stock dividend, but a new investment *per share* must be calculated for use later when the shares are sold:

$$\frac{\$44 \text{ million}^*}{1,000,000 \text{ shares} \times 1.10} = \$40 \text{ per share}$$

\* $52.8 - 8.8 = $44

| | |
|---|---|
| **To record the sale of shares** | |
| Cash (100,000 shares x $43)......................................................... | 4.3 |
|    Investment in L&K shares (100,000 shares x **$40**).................. | 4.0 |
|    Gain on sale of investments (difference) ............................. | .3 |

Note: If a financial reporting date falls between the acquisition and sale of shares, and the investment is adjusted to fair value on that date, the treatment of the stock dividend would be the same. That is, the new investment *per share* still would be the investment balance divided by the number of shares after the stock dividend. But the investment balance now would be its *fair value* on the last reporting date rather than its *cost*.

# Problem 18-12

## Part A

### Requirement 1

**January 2**

| | | |
|---|---|---|
| Cash (amount received)..................................................... | 30,000,000 | |
|     Common stock ($1 par x 3,000,000 shares)...................... | | 3,000,000 |
|     Paid-in capital – excess of par, common (difference)... | | 27,000,000 |

**January 2**

| | | |
|---|---|---|
| Cash (amount received)..................................................... | 20,000,000 | |
|     Preferred stock ($5 par x 1,000,000 shares)......................... | | 5,000,000 |
|     Paid-in capital – excess of par, preferred (difference).. | | 15,000,000 |

### Requirement 2

**Nicklaus Corporation**
**Balance Sheet-Shareholders' Equity Section**
**March 31, 2006**

**Shareholders' equity**

| | |
|---|---|
| Preferred stock, $5 par, authorized 1,000,000 shares, issued and outstanding 1,000,000 shares | $ 5,000,000 |
| Common stock, $1 par, authorized 5,000,000 shares, issued and outstanding 3,000,000 shares | 3,000,000 |
| Paid-in capital – excess of par | 42,000,000 |
| Retained earnings | 1,000,000 |
| | |
| Total shareholders' equity | $51,000,000 |

***Problem 18-12 (continued)***
**Part B**

**Requirement 1**

**June 30**

| | | |
|---|---|---|
| Treasury stock ($12 x 200,000 shares)............................... | 2,400,000 | |
|     Cash ......................................................................... | | 2,400,000 |

**July 31**

| | | |
|---|---|---|
| Cash ($15 x 50,000 shares) ...................................... | 750,000 | |
|     Treasury stock ($12 x 50,000 shares)............................ | | 600,000 |
|     Paid-in capital – share repurchase | | |
|       [($15-$12) x 50,000 shares]............................................ | | 150,000 |

**September 30**

| | | |
|---|---|---|
| Cash ($10 x 50,000 shares) ...................................... | 500,000 | |
| Paid-in capital – share repurchase | | |
|     [($12-$10) x 50,000 shares]............................................ | 100,000 | |
|     Treasury stock ($12 x 50,000 shares)............................ | | 600,000 |

**Requirement 2**

**Nicklaus Corporation**
**Balance Sheet - Shareholders' Equity Section**
**September 30, 2006**

**Shareholders' equity**

| | |
|---|---|
| Preferred stock, $5 par, authorized 1,000,000 shares, issued and outstanding 1,000,000 shares | $ 5,000,000 |
| Common stock, $1 par, authorized 5,000,000 shares issued 3,000,000 shares, 2,900,000[1] shares outstanding | 3,000,000 |
| Paid-in capital – excess of par | 42,000,000 |
| Paid-in capital – share repurchase[2] | 50,000 |
| Retained earnings[3] | 4,000,000 |
| | $54,050,000 |
| Less: Treasury stock (200,000 shares at cost) | (1,200,000) |
|     Total shareholders' equity | $52,850,000 |

[1] 3,000,000 - 200,000 + 50,000 + 50,000

[2] $150,000 - 100,000

[3] $1,000,000 + 3,000,000

# Problem 18-12 (continued)

## Part C

### Requirement 1

**October 1**
NO ENTRY

**November 1**

| | | |
|---|---|---|
| Retained earnings............................................................ | 540,000 | |
|    Dividends payable – common ($.05 x 5,800,000[1]) ........ | | 290,000 |
|    Dividends payable – preferred ($.25 x 1,000,000) ......... | | 250,000 |

**November 15**
NO ENTRY

**December 1**

| | | |
|---|---|---|
| Dividends payable – common ........................................ | 290,000 | |
| Dividends payable – preferred ...................................... | 250,000 | |
|    Cash...................................................................... | | 540,000 |

**Note:** Dividends are not paid on shares held in the treasury. Cash dividends are paid only on the 5,800,000 common shares outstanding.

**December 2**

| | | |
|---|---|---|
| Retained earnings ($10 fair value x 58,000 shares[2]) | 580,000 | |
|    Common stock dividends | | |
|      distributable ($.50 par x 58,000 shares) ...................... | | 29,000 |
|    Paid-in capital – excess of par, common (difference)... | | 551,000 |

**December 28**

| | | |
|---|---|---|
| Common stock dividends distributable ........................ | 29,000 | |
|    Common stock ....................................................... | | 29,000 |

[1] (3,000,000 - 200,000 + 50,000 + 50,000) x 2 = 5,800,000 shares

[2] 1% x 5,800,000 shares

*Problem 18-12 (continued)*

**Requirement 2**

**Nicklaus Corporation**
**Balance Sheet-Shareholders' Equity Section**
**December 31, 2006**

**Shareholders' equity**

| | |
|---|---:|
| Preferred stock, $5 par, authorized 1,000,000 shares, issued and outstanding 1,000,000 shares | $ 5,000,000 |
| Common stock, $.50 par, authorized 10,000,000 shares, issued 6,058,000 shares and 5,858,000[1] shares outstanding | 3,029,000 |
| Paid-in capital – excess of par[2] | 42,551,000 |
| Paid-in capital – share repurchase | 50,000 |
| Retained earnings[3] | 5,380,000 |
| | $56,010,000 |
| Less: Treasury stock (100,000 shares at cost) | (1,200,000) |
| Total shareholders' equity | $54,810,000 |

[1] 5,800,000 + 58,000

[2] $27,000,000 + 15,000,000 + 551,000

[3] $4,000,000 - 540,000 - 580,000 + 2,500,000

**Problem 18-12 (concluded)**

**Requirement 3**

Nicklaus Corporation
**Statement of Shareholders' Equity**
For the Year Ended Dec. 31, 2006
($ in 000s)

|  | Preferred Stock | Common Stock | Additional Paid-in Capital | Retained Earnings | Treasury Stock (at cost) | Total Share-holders' Equity |
|---|---|---|---|---|---|---|
| **Jan. 2, 2006** | — | — | — | — | — | — |
| Issuance of preferred stock | 5,000 | | 15,000 | | | 20,000 |
| Issuance of common stock | | 3,000 | 27,000 | | | 30,000 |
| Purchase of treasury stock | | | | | (2,400) | (2,400) |
| Sale of treasury stock | | | 50 | | 1,200 | 1,250 |
| Net income | | | | 6,500 | | 6,500 |
| Common cash dividends | | | | (290) | | (290) |
| Preferred cash dividends | | | | (250) | | (250) |
| Stock dividend | | 29 | 551 | (580) | | 0 |
| **Dec. 31, 2006** | 5,000 | 3,029 | 42,601 | 5,380 | (1,200) | 54,810 |

# Problem 18-13

## Requirement 1

**To revalue assets:**

| | | |
|---|---|---|
| Retained earnings ................................................................. | 105 | |
|    Inventory ........................................................................ | | 105 |

| | | |
|---|---|---|
| Land............................................................................................ | 5 | |
|    Retained earnings ................................................................. | | 5 |

**To eliminate a portion of the deficit against available additional paid-in capital:**

| | | |
|---|---|---|
| Additional paid-in capital...................................................... | 60 | |
|    Retained earnings ................................................................. | | 60 |

**To eliminate the remainder of the deficit against common stock:**

| | | |
|---|---|---|
| Common stock.......................................................................... | 240 | |
|    Retained earnings ................................................................. | | 240 |

## Requirement 2

Champion Chemical Corporation
BALANCE SHEET
At January 1, 2006 ($ in millions)

| | |
|---|---|
| Cash | $ 20 |
| Receivables | 40 |
| Inventory | 125 |
| Land | 45 |
| Buildings and equipment (net) | 90 |
| | $320 |
| | |
| Liabilities | $240 |
| Common stock (320 million shares at $.25 par ) | 80 |
| Additional paid-in capital | 0 |
| Retained earnings (deficit) | (0) |
| | $320 |

# CASES

## Real World Case 18-1

### Requirement 1.

Assuming the shares are issued at the midpoint of the price range indicated, $14.50 per share, Dolby Laboratories would raise $14.50 x 27.5 million shares = $398.75 million before any underwriting discount and offering expenses

### Requirement 2.

|  | $ in millions |
| --- | --- |
| Cash (determined above)........................................................... | 398.750 |
|     Common stock (27.5 million shares x $.01 par)...................... | .275 |
|     Paid-in capital – excess of par (difference)......................... | 398.475 |

# Analysis Case 18-2

Sessel's Department Stores, Inc.
**Statement of Shareholders' Equity**
For the Years Ended December 31, 2006, 2005, and 2004
($ in 000s)

| | Preferred Stock | | Common Stock | Additional Paid-in Capital | Retained Earnings | Total Share-holders' Equity |
|---|---|---|---|---|---|---|
| | Series A | Series B | | | | |
| **Dec. 31, 2003** | $ – | $ – | **$1,288** | **$ 88,468** | **$19,178** | **$108,934** |
| Net income | | | | | 13,494 | 13,494 |
| Issuance of common stock | | | 12 | 814 | | 826 |
| **Dec. 31, 2004** | | | **1,300** | **89,282** | **32,672** | **123,254** |
| Net income | | | | | 12,126 | 12,126 |
| Issuance of common stock | | | 558 | 112,148 | | 112,706 |
| **Dec. 31, 2005** | | | **1,858** | **201,430** | **44,798** | **248,086** |
| Net income | | | | | 32,256[1] | 32,256 |
| Issuance of shares | 57,700 | 6,592 | 104[4] | 20,002[5] | | 84,398 |
| Conversion of Series B preferred stock | | (6,592) | 32[2] | 6,560[3] | | |
| Preferred dividends | | | | | (3,388) | (3,388) |
| **Dec. 31, 2006** | **$57,700** | **$ –** | **$1,994** | **$227,992** | **$73,666** | **$361,352** |

[1] [$73,666,000 – 44,798,000] + 3,388,000 = $32,256,000
[2] 320,000 shares x $.10 par = $32,000
[3] $6,592,000 - 32,000 = $6,560,000
[4] [$1,994,000 – 1,858,000] - 32,000 = $104,000
[5] [$227,992,000 – 201,430,000] – 6,560,000 = $20,002,000

# Communication Case 18-3

This case encourages students to consider the larger question of the factors that differentiate whether financial instruments qualify for recognition as assets or part of equity. It also requires them to carefully consider the profession's definitions of those elements. You may wish to suggest to your students that they consult the FASB 1990 Discussion Memorandum, "Distinguishing between Liability and Equity Instruments and Accounting for Instruments with Characteristics of Both," which sets forth the most common arguments on the issues in this case. Or, you may prefer that they think for themselves and approach the issue from scratch.

There is no right or wrong answer. Both views can and often are convincingly defended. The process of developing and synthesizing the arguments will likely be more beneficial than any single solution. Each student should benefit from participating in the process, interacting first with his or her partner, then with the class as a whole. It is important that each student actively participate in the process. Domination by one or two individuals should be discouraged.

**Arguments brought out in the FASB DM include the following:**

Some argue that receivables held for stock issued or to be issued are assets that should be recognized and reported as such. Others contend that, unless payment has been received before the financial statements are issued or unless there is strong evidence of intent and ability to pay, the receivables should be reported as a reduction of stockholders' equity (par. 174).

At least for public companies, present practice follows the second view, except in very limited circumstances when there is substantial evidence of ability and intent to pay within a reasonably short period of time. (par. 175).

An enterprise that offers a stock subscription puts aside stock to be issued in exchange for the subscriber's promise to pay for the shares. When all the consideration is received, the stock is issued. The Revised Model Business Corporation Act provides that the purchaser of shares is liable to the corporation for the consideration for which shares were authorized to be issued. The Act also provides that post-incorporation stock subscriptions are simple contracts and are therefore subject to contract law. Under contract law, "a corporation may compel a stock subscriber to make payment to the corporation, on call, in accordance with the terms of the subscription agreement." In other words, a corporation has a legally enforceable claim against one who subscribes to an issue of its stock (par. 176).

## Case 18-3 (concluded)

The Act specifically validates "any tangible or intangible property or benefit to the corporation" as consideration for the issue of shares. As discussed above, it also provides that a stockholder is obligated to pay the consideration established in the agreement. While notes receivable are valid consideration for the issuance of shares, the Act adds that the company may restrict transfer of those shares until the note is paid. If payment is not made, the restricted shares can be canceled. However, if shares are issued without restriction, "they are validly issued insofar as the adequacy of consideration is concerned." Although the stockholder's obligation to pay for the stock was satisfied with the note and the shares issued therefore cannot be canceled, the stockholder has a continuing obligation under the note (par. 178).

### Arguments Supporting View 1:

Proponents of the view that receivables for stock should be deducted from equity note that the enterprise's ultimate recourse if the receivable is not collected may be to not issue the stock subscribed or to cancel restricted stock issued for a note. In addition, some argue that the enterprise may not intend to pursue collection from an owner. They contend that collection of the receivable therefore is sufficiently uncertain that the receivable does not qualify as a recognizable asset. Further, receivables for stock differ from other receivables because receivables for stock are not obtained in exchange for transferring assets or providing services, which some consider to be significant (par. 179).

### Arguments Supporting View 2:

Proponents of the view that receivables for stock are recognizable assets argue that the receivables fit the definition of assets in Concepts Statement 6 because they embody probable future economic benefits. Receivables for stock issued or to be issued are legally binding, giving the enterprise a legally enforceable claim against the purchaser of the shares. Concepts Statement 6 says that although assets usually are obtained at a cost, that feature is not an essential characteristic of assets. Therefore, a receivable is not disqualified from being an asset merely because it was obtained in exchange for stock rather than in exchange for an asset (par. 180).

Proponents also argue that the question of collectibility does not require equity treatment. Collectibility of all receivables needs to be assessed regularly and provision made for uncollectible amounts. Assessment of the collectibility of a receivable from an owner should consider all pertinent factors, including the enterprise's intent to pursue collection. Moreover, receivables for stock issued or to be issued might be displayed separately from other receivables to inform investors and creditors of the nature of the receivables (par. 181).

# Research Case 18-4

## Requirement 1.
Cisco reports Accumulated other comprehensive income (loss) in its balance sheet as a component of shareholders' equity as follows:

| | ($ in millions) | |
| Shareholders' equity: | **2004** | **2003** |
|---|---|---|
| Preferred stock | | |
| Common stock and additional paid-in capital | 22,450 | 21,116 |
| Retained earnings | 3,164 | 6,559 |
| Accumulated other comprehensive income (loss) | 212 | 354 |
| *Total shareholders' equity* | $25,826 | $28,029 |

## Requirement 2.
Cisco relies on SFAS Number 130, *"Reporting Comprehensive Income"* when reporting comprehensive income. The requirement became effective for fiscal years beginning after December 15, 1997.

## Requirement 3.
    **Comprehensive income** is a more expansive view of the change in shareholders' equity than traditional net income. It is the total *nonowner* change in equity for a reporting period. In fact, it encompasses all changes in equity other than from transactions with owners. Transactions between the corporation and its shareholders primarily include dividends and the sale or purchase of shares of the company's stock. Most nonowner changes are reported in the income statement. So, the changes other than those that are part of traditional net income are the ones reported as "other comprehensive income." Two attributes of other comprehensive income are reported: (1) components of comprehensive income *created during the reporting period* and (2) the comprehensive income *accumulated* over the current and prior periods.

    The first of these - components of comprehensive income *created during the reporting period* - can be reported either (a) as an additional section of the income statement, (b) as part of the statement of shareholders' equity, or (c) in a disclosure note. Regardless of the placement a company chooses, the presentation is similar. It will report net income, other components of comprehensive income, and total comprehensive income, similar to the following:

## Case 18-4 (continued)

|  | ($ in millions) |
|---|---|
| Net income | $xxx |
| Other comprehensive income: | |
|   Net unrealized holding gains (losses) on investments (net of tax)† | $ x |
|   Net unrecognized loss on pensions (net of tax)‡ | (x) |
|   Deferred gains (losses) from derivatives (net of tax)§ | x |
|   Gains (losses) from foreign currency translation (net of tax)* | x    xx |
| Comprehensive income | $xxx |

†   Changes in the market value of securities available-for-sale.

‡   Reporting a pension liability sometimes requires recording this (described in Chapter 17). It often is called pension liability adjustment.

§   When a derivative designated as a cash flow hedge is adjusted to fair value, the gain or loss is deferred as a component of comprehensive income and included in earnings later, at the same time as earnings are affected by the hedged transaction (described in the Derivatives Appendix to the text).

*   Gains or losses from changes in foreign currency exchange rates. The amount could be an addition to or reduction in shareholders' equity. (This item is discussed elsewhere in your accounting curriculum.)

This is the measure of comprehensive income Cisco reported in the disclosure note. Notice that each component is reported net of its related income tax expense or income tax benefit.

The second measure - the comprehensive income *accumulated* over the current and prior periods – is reported as a separate component of shareholders' equity. This is what Cisco reported in its balance sheet as indicated in Requirement 1 ($212 million in 2004). Be sure to realize this amount represents the *cumulative* sum of the changes in each component created during each reporting period (the disclosure note) throughout all prior years.

## Case 18-4 (concluded)

### Requirement 4.
The primary component of Other comprehensive Income for Cisco Is "Change in net unrealized gains on investments." For reporting purposes, investments in marketable equity securities are categorized as either (a) held-to-maturity, (b) trading securities, or (c) available for sale. Trading securities and securities available for sale are reported at their fair values. The holding gains and losses from writing these securities available for sale up or down to fair value are not reported in the income statement, but instead are reported as a component of Other comprehensive income in the balance sheet. This makes up the greatest part of Cisco's Other comprehensive income. From the information Cisco's financial statements provide, we can determine how the company calculated the $212 million accumulated other comprehensive income in fiscal 2004:

|  | ($ in millions) |
|---|---|
| Accumulated other comprehensive income (loss), 2003 | $354 |
| Change in net unrealized gains on investments | (77) |
| Change in "other" | 19 |
| Minority interest | (84) |
| Accumulated other comprehensive income (loss), 2004 | $ 212 |

### Requirement 5.
Nonowner changes other than those that are part of traditional net income are the ones reported as "other comprehensive income." As described in Requirement 3, besides changes in the market value of securities available for sale, these changes might include Net unrecognized loss on pensions, Deferred gain (loss) from derivatives, and Gains (losses) from foreign currency translation.

# Judgment Case 18-5

## Requirement 1

Alcoa has two choices of how to account for the buyback:
1. The shares can be formally retired.
2. The shares can be called "treasury stock"

Regardless of the choice, total shareholders' equity will be the same. Cash is paid to repurchase stock so the effect is to *decrease* both cash and shareholders' equity. However, the choice does affect how individual shareholders' accounts are reported in the balance sheet.

Formally retiring shares restores the balances in both the Common stock account and Paid-in capital – excess of par to what those balances would have been if the shares never had been issued at all. Any net increase in assets resulting from the sale and subsequent repurchase is reflected as Paid-in capital – share repurchase. On the other hand, any net decrease in assets resulting from the sale and subsequent repurchase is reflected as a reduction in retained earnings.

In contrast, when a share repurchase is viewed as treasury stock, the cost of the treasury stock is simply reported as a reduction in total shareholders' equity. Alcoa would account for the purchase of the treasury stock by debiting treasury stock and crediting cash for the cost of the purchase. The treasury stock should be presented separately in the shareholders' equity section of Alcoa's balance sheet as an unallocated reduction of shareholders' equity. These shares are considered issued but not part of common stock outstanding.

If later resold for an amount greater than cost, Alcoa should account for the sale of the treasury stock by debiting cash for the selling price, crediting treasury stock for cost, and crediting additional paid-in capital from reacquired stock for the excess of the selling price over the cost. On the other hand, if the shares were retired, Alcoa would simply record any subsequent sale as it would the sale of any new shares.

## Requirement 2

Alcoa can choose not to make any journal entry for the stock split. Alternatively, Alcoa can choose to effect the split "in the form of a stock dividend." In that case, Alcoa would account for the stock split by debiting paid-in capital for the par per share multiplied by the shares distributed. Total shareholders' equity does not change. This prevents the par per share from changing. Alcoa should then credit common stock for the same amount.

## Case 18-5 (concluded)

### Requirement 3

Alcoa should account for the cash dividend on the declaration date by debiting retained earnings and crediting cash dividends payable for $.25 per share multiplied by the number of shares outstanding. A cash dividend is a distribution to the corporation's shareholders. The liability for this distribution is incurred on the declaration date, and it is a current liability because it is payable within one year. The effect of the cash dividend on Alcoa's balance sheet is an increase in current liabilities and a decrease in retained earnings.

# Communication Case 18-6

*sample memo:*

## Memorandum

**To:**   Les Kramer
         Supervisor
**From:** {your name}
**Re:**   Share issue costs
**Date:** {current date}

This memo is in response to your request for information about how IBR accounted for share issue costs in its recent equity offering. When a company sells shares, it obtains the legal, promotional, and accounting services necessary to effect the sale. The cost of these services reduces the net proceeds from selling the shares. Paid-in capital – excess of par is credited for the excess of the proceeds over the par value of the shares sold. Thus, the effect of share issue costs is to reduce the amount credited to that account.

This treatment differs from how *debt issue costs* are recorded. The costs associated with a debt issue are recorded in a separate "debt issue costs" account and amortized to expense over the life of the debt.

In IBR's case, the shares sold for a total of $53.289 million (2,395,000 shares times $22.25 per share). Since paid-in capital – excess of par is credited for the excess of the $50.2 million net proceeds over the par amount of the shares sold, the effect of share issue costs (underwriting discount and offering expenses) is to reduce the amount credited to that account. In particular, IBR would have recorded the following journal entry upon the issue of the shares.

|  |  |  |
|---|---|---|
|  |  | ($ in 000s) |
| Cash (given) .................................................................... | 50,200.0 |  |
| Common stock ($.10 par x 2,395 shares) ................... |  | 239.5 |
| Paid-in capital – excess of par  (difference) ............ |  | 49,960.5* |

*   This amount reflects the reduction for share issue costs (underwriting
    discount and offering expenses).

Please let me know if I can provide you additional information.

## Suggested Grading Concepts And Grading Scheme:

**Content** (80% )

_____  30  Accounting for share issue costs.

  ____ Nature of costs.

  ____ Reduces the net proceeds from selling the shares.

  ____ Effect of share issue costs is to reduce the amount credited to paid-in capital.

_____  10  "Debt issue costs" recorded in a separate account and amortized to expense over the life of the debt.

_____  10  IBR's accounting.

  ____ Paid-in capital – excess of par is credited for the excess of the $50.2 million net proceeds over the par amount of the shares sold.

_____  30  Journal entry.

  ____ Cash $50,200,000.

  ____ Common stock $239,500.

  ____ Paid-in capital – excess of par $49,960,500.

_____  **Bonus (5)** The FASB has suggested in Concept Statement 6 that debt issue costs should be treated the same way as *share* issue costs. But Concept Statements do not constitute GAAP, so until a new FASB Standard is issued to supersede APB Opinion 21, the prescribed practice is to record debt issue costs as assets and expense the asset over the maturity of the debt.

_____  80-85 points

**Writing** (20%)

_____  5  Terminology and tone appropriate to the audience of supervisor.

_____  6  Organization permits ease of understanding.

  ____ Introduction that states purpose.

  ____ Paragraphs separate main points.

_____  9  English.

  ____ Word selection.

  ____ Spelling.

  ____ Grammar.

_____  20 points

# Analysis Case 18-7

### Requirement 1

The ratio is computed by dividing net income by average shareholders' equity.

$$
\begin{aligned}
\textbf{Rate of return on} \quad &= \quad \frac{\text{Net income}}{\text{Average shareholders' equity}} \\[2mm]
\textbf{shareholders' equity} & \\[4mm]
&= \quad \frac{\$487}{[\$2,931 + 2,671]\,/\,2} \\[4mm]
&= \quad \underline{17.4\%}
\end{aligned}
$$

*NYSE average* $= 18.8\%$

The return on shareholders' equity is an important ratio for the owners of a company. It measures the ability of company management to generate net income from the resources that owners provide. IGF's return is comparable to other firms, although slightly less. Like most ratios, though, it should not be viewed in isolation. For example, when the return on shareholders' equity is greater than the return on assets, management is using debt funds to enhance the earnings for stockholders. The return on assets is a measure of a company's ability to use assets profitably, *regardless of how the assets were financed*. It is computed by dividing net income by average total assets.

$$
\begin{aligned}
\textbf{Rate of return on} \quad &= \quad \frac{\text{Net income}}{\text{Average total assets}} \\[2mm]
\textbf{assets} & \\[4mm]
&= \quad \frac{\$487}{[\$5,345 + 4,684]\,/\,2} \\[4mm]
&= \quad \underline{9.7\%}
\end{aligned}
$$

IGF is in this enviable position and therefore has *favorable* financial leverage. We discussed financial leverage in Chapter 14.

# Case 18-7 (concluded)

## Requirement 2

Earnings per share, in its simplest form, is simply a firm's net income divided by the number of shares outstanding throughout the year. It expresses a firm's profitability on a per share basis.

$$\text{Earnings per share} = \frac{\text{Income available to common shareholders}}{\text{Average shares outstanding}}$$

$$= \frac{\$487}{181}$$

$$= \underline{\$2.69}$$

To complement the return on shareholders' equity ratio, analysts sometimes calculate the earnings-price ratio in order to relate earnings to the market value of equity. This ratio is the earnings per share divided by the market price per share:

$$\text{Earnings-price ratio} = \frac{\text{Earnings per share}}{\text{Market price per share}}$$

$$= \frac{\$2.69}{\$47}$$

$$= \underline{5.7\%}$$

The earnings-price ratio measures the return on the market value of common stock. Remember, shareholders' equity is a measure of the *book value* of equity. The market value of a share of stock (or of total shareholders' equity) usually is different from its book value. IGF's return on market value is somewhat higher than the average return for the stocks listed on the New York Stock Exchange in a comparable time period (5.4%). So, even though the return on book value is a little lower than average, a closer look at the return to market value shows IGF to be at least in line with its industry.

# International Case 18-8

The report should indicate similarities and differences between the United States and the chosen country focusing on the following issues:

a. How shareholders' equity is defined.
b. The categories by which it is reported in the financial statements.
c. What if any requirements exist to separately maintain "legal capital."
d. Restrictions on dividend payments and how dividends are reported.
e. Whether a Statement of Shareholders' Equity, or equivalent, is reported.

# Ethics Case 18-9

Discussion should include these elements.

**Return on assets:**
Rate of return on assets is net income divided by assets. The lower the asset base, the higher the percentage return.

A noncash transaction should be recorded at fair value. This should be the fair value of the consideration given or the asset (in this case) received. The asset has no readily available fair value because it is custom-made. The value of debt the Swiss firm is asking for probably provides a good indication of the fair value of the asset.

**Ethical Dilemma:**
Is the desire to boost return justification for questionable accounting treatment of the transaction?

**Who is affected?**
Benson
Sharp
Other managers?
The company's auditor, if any. This is a private company.
Shareholders (probably few)
The employees
The creditors

# Research Case 18-10

The results students report will vary depending on the companies chosen. It can be interesting to have students compare in class their findings with those of their classmates.

Typical items that affect retained earnings are dividends (cash, property, or stock) and net income or loss. Treasury stock or retired stock transactions also affect retained earnings.

Typical transactions that affect common stock are new stock issues, treasury stock or retired stock transactions, and conversions of other securities into common stock. Were any of these transactions identified in requirement 3 also?

The statement of shareholders' equity explains why and how the various shareholders' equity items on the balance sheet change from year to year.

# Real World Case 18-11

## Requirement 1

Since the base amount of the preferred shares is $25 and the dividend preference is 6.785%, the dividends paid annually to a preferred shareholder owning 100 shares are: $25 x 100 shares x 6.785% = $169.63.

## Requirement 2

If dividends are not paid in 2005 and 2006, but are paid in 2007, the shareholder will receive $169.63 x 3 = $508.89. The prior years' unpaid dividends are paid because the shares are *cumulative*. Otherwise, only the $169.63 current year dividend would be paid. When preferred shares are cumulative, this means that if the specified dividend is *not* paid in a given year, the unpaid dividends (called "dividends in arrears") *accumulate* and must be made up in a *later dividend year* before any dividends are paid on common shares.

## Requirement 3

If the investor chooses to convert the shares in 2005, the investor will receive $25/$30.31 x 100 shares = 82.48 shares of common stock for his/her 100 shares. The .48 fractional share likely would be paid in cash equal to the current market price per share times .48.

## Requirement 4

If AMCON chooses to redeem the shares in 2006, the investor will be paid $2,800 for his/her 100 shares: 100 shares at the redemption price of $28 ($25 x 112%).

# Communication Case 18-12

You may wish to suggest to your students that they consult the FASB 1990 Discussion Memorandum, "Distinguishing between Liability and Equity Instruments and Accounting for Instruments with Characteristics of Both," which sets forth the most common arguments on the issues in this case. Or, you may prefer that they think for themselves and approach the issue from scratch.

There is no right or wrong answer. Both views can and often are convincingly defended. The process of developing and synthesizing the arguments will likely be more beneficial than any single solution. Each student should benefit from participating in the process, interacting first with his or her partner, then with the class as a whole. It is important that each student actively participate in the process. Domination by one or two individuals should be discouraged.

A significant benefit of this case is its forcing students' consideration and acceptance of the fact that both liabilities and equities are claims to an enterprise's assets. It also requires them to carefully consider the profession's definitions of those elements. Arguments brought out in the FASB DM include the following:

## Arguments Supporting View 1:

Some students likely will argue that convertible bonds and other similar instruments can be appropriately classified in the two existing categories on the basis of existing distinctions and definitions. For instance, they might focus on the characteristic of a liability that requires that the enterprise issuing it have little or no discretion to avoid the future sacrifice of economic benefits.

Concepts Statement 6 defines liabilities as:

. . . probable future sacrifices of economic benefits arising from present obligations of a particular entity to transfer assets or provide services to other entities in the future as a result of past transactions or events. [paragraph 35]

Three essential characteristics of a liability are:

a. It embodies a present duty or responsibility to one or more other entities for settlement by probable future transfer or use of assets at a specified or determinable date, on occurrence of a specified event, or on demand.

b. The duty or responsibility obligates a particular entity, leaving it little or no discretion to avoid the future sacrifice.

c. The transaction or other event obligating the entity has already happened.

## Case 18-12 (continued)

Equity of a business enterprise is defined simply as the residual interest: the difference between an enterprise's assets and its liabilities. The essential characteristics of equity focus on the conditions for transferring assets to the holders of equity interests. Usually, a company is not obligated to transfer assets to owners except in the event of liquidation unless it voluntarily acts to do so, such as by declaring a dividend. A company's liabilities and equity are mutually exclusive claims to or interests in its assets by others, and liabilities take precedence over ownership interests.

A company may have two or more classes of equity, such as preferred stock and common stock; no class has an unconditional right to receive distributions of assets other than in liquidation and then only after all liabilities have been settled. That is the essential distinction between liabilities and equity. A liability entails an obligation to transfer assets or provide services in the future, while an equity instrument does not.

The distinction between liabilities and equity is important to reported financial position. So, whether an issue of convertible bonds is classified as a liability or as equity affects both reported amounts of total liabilities and equity and summary amounts based on those amounts, such as ratios. The distinction also is critical in measuring income. *Comprehensive income* is defined in Concepts Statement 6 to include all changes in equity during a period other than those resulting from transactions with owners. Income includes only inflows in excess of the amount needed to maintain capital. Without a distinction between the claims of creditors and those of owners, measurement of income is not possible.

Reported income also is affected. Convertible bonds have features of both debt (fixed interest and principal payments) and equity (ability to participate in the benefits of stock ownership). If convertible bonds are treated as an equity instrument, the interest payments are not deducted in determining the issuer's net income. However, if they are deemed to be liability, the interest would be reported as an expense and deducted in determining net income.

### Arguments Supporting View 2:

Arguments here center on the "entity theory" of accounting first proposed by W. A. Paton in 1922 which views the accounting equation as:

$$\text{Assets} = \text{Equities}$$

with equities including both what are termed liabilities and equity in the current conceptual framework. A central feature of this theory is that profits are determined with reference to all capital suppliers. That is, profits are determined before deducting either interest or dividends. Both interest and dividends, and income taxes as well, are treated as distributions of profits.

Examples of possible formats of a balance sheet and an income statement under this alternative suggested by the DM follow.

### Balance Sheet

| | | | | |
|---|---|---|---|---|
| Cash | $ 2,050 | | Accounts payable | $1,200 |
| Investments | 5,000 | | Mortgage | 4,000 |
| Inventory | 7,000 | | Bonds | 5,000 |
| Plant and | | | Preferred stock | 5,000 |
| equipment | 15,000 | | Common stock | 4,800 |
| | | | Retained earnings | 9,050 |
| | | | Total equities | 18,850 |
| | | | Total liabilities | |
| Total assets | $29,050 | | and equities | $29,050 |

### Income Statement

| | |
|---|---|
| Sales | $30,000 |
| Cost of goods sold | 10,000 |
| Selling and other expenses | 4,000 |
| Excess of revenues over expenses | $16,000 |
| | |
| Interest on mortgage | 300 |
| Interest on bonds | 400 |
| Income taxes | 5,000 |
| Preferred dividends | 450 |
| Earnings attributable to common stock | $9,850 |
| Common dividends | 800 |
| Earnings retained | $9,050 |

**Case 18-12 (concluded)**

*or, alternatively:*

| | |
|---|---:|
| Sales | $30,000 |
| Cost of goods sold | 10,000 |
| Selling and other expenses | 4,000 |
| Enterprise net income | $16,000 |
| | |
| Interest on mortgage | 300 |
| Interest on bonds | 400 |
| Income taxes | 5,000 |
| Preferred dividends | 450 |
| Common dividends | 800 |
| Earnings retained | $9,050 |

Many issues would have to be resolved if this approach were to be seriously pursued. For instance, would all present liabilities be treated as "equities"; if not, which would be treated differently? Today the distinction between short-term and long-term is not considered to be particularly relevant for at least some companies, so it might be questionable to distinguish on that basis. Another possibility would be to treat only liabilities incurred in exchange for cash proceeds as "equities." However, labor, inventory, and the like also are "capital" in a broad sense, so it may be hard to justify treating obligations incurred to acquire them differently from obligations to pay cash.

The concept of income under this approach is another question. Would an attempt to eliminate the line between liabilities and equity make it inappropriate to attempt to measure income, or would it merely change the underlying concept and measure of net income? These are only two possible questions, but students favoring Alternative 2 should discuss its overall effect on the financial statements, including the concept and measurement of income.

# Chapter 19    Share-Based Compensation and Earnings per Share

## QUESTIONS FOR REVIEW OF KEY TOPICS

### Question 19-1

Restricted stock refers to shares actually awarded in the name of an employee, although the employer might retain physical possession of the shares. Typically, the employee has all rights of a shareholder, but the shares are subject to certain restrictions or forfeiture. Usually the employee is not free to sell the shares during the restriction period. Restricted shares usually are subject to forfeiture by the employee if employment is terminated between the date of grant and a specified vesting date. Restrictions provide the employee incentive to remain with the company.

Compensation cost is the fair value of the restricted stock at the grant date and is equal to the market price of unrestricted shares of the same stock. The fair value of shares awarded under a restricted stock award plan is accrued to compensation expense over the service period for which participants receive the shares. This usually is the period from the date of grant to when restrictions are lifted (the vesting date).

### Question 19-2

The fair value of a stock option is determined by employing a recognized option pricing model. The option pricing model should take into account the (1) exercise price of the option, (2) expected term of the option, (3) current market price of the stock, (4) expected dividends, (5) expected risk-free rate of return during the term of the option, and (6) expected volatility of the stock.

### Question 19-3

The recipient pays no tax at the time of the grant or the exercise of the options under an incentive plan. Instead, the tax on the difference between the option price and the market price at the exercise date is paid on the date any shares acquired are subsequently sold. The employer gets no tax deduction at all.

The employee cannot delay paying tax under a nonqualified plan. The tax that could be deferred until the shares are sold under an incentive plan must be paid at the exercise date under a nonqualified plan. On the other hand, the employer is allowed to deduct the difference between the option price and the market price on the exercise date. Thus, a nonqualified plan offers favorable tax treatment to the employer, while an incentive plan offers favorable tax treatment to the employee.

# Answers to Questions *(continued)*

## Question 19-4

The fair value of stock options has two essential components: (1) intrinsic value and (2) time value. "Intrinsic value" is the benefit the holder of an option would realize by exercising the option rather than buying the underlying stock directly. For example, an option that allows an employee to buy $13 stock for $8 has an intrinsic value of $5. "Time value" exists so long as time remains before expiration because the market price of the underlying stock may yet rise and create additional intrinsic value.

## Question 19-5

For performance-based options initial estimates of compensation cost as well as subsequent revisions of that estimate take into account the likelihood of both forfeitures and achieving performance targets. If it is probable that the performance target will be met, we recognize compensation over the vesting period at fair value. If achieving the target is not probable, no compensation is recorded. Probability is reassessed each period.

If the award contains a market condition (e.g., a share option with an exercisability requirement based on the stock price reaching a specified level), then no special accounting is required. The fair value estimate of the share option already implicitly reflects market conditions due to the nature of share option pricing models. Thus, we recognize compensation expense regardless of when, if ever, the market condition is met.

## Question 19-6

The accounting treatment of SARs depends on whether the award is considered an equity instrument or a liability. If the employer can choose to settle in shares rather than cash, the award is considered to be equity. If the employee will receive cash or can choose to receive cash, the award is considered to be a liability. This is the case with the LTV plan. As a result, the amount of compensation and related liability is continually adjusted to reflect changes in the fair value of the SARs until the liability is finally settled. The expense each period is the percentage of the total liability earned to date by recipients of the SARs (based on the elapsed percentage of the service period), minus any amounts expensed in prior periods. Both compensation expense and the liability are adjusted each period until the SARs ultimately either are exercised or lapse.

## Question 19-7

A firm has a simple capital structure if it has no potential common shares outstanding. These are securities that are not yet common stock, but might become common stock if exercised or converted. Thus, they could potentially dilute (meaning reduce) earnings per share.

For a firm with a simple capital structure, EPS is simply *earnings available to common shareholders* divided by the *weighted-average number of common shares outstanding*.

*Answers to Questions (continued)*

## Question 19-8

There is a fundamental difference between the increase in shares caused by stock dividends and stock splits and an increase from selling new shares. When additional shares are *sold*, both the assets of the firm and shareholders' equity are increased by an additional investment by owners. On the other hand, stock dividends or stock splits merely increase the number of shares without affecting the firm's assets. As a consequence, the same "pie" is divided into more pieces resulting in a larger number of less valuable shares. Shares outstanding prior to a stock dividend or stock split are *retroactively restated* to reflect the increase in shares, as if the distribution occurred at the beginning of the period. On the other hand, any new shares issued are "time-weighted' by the fraction of the period they were outstanding and then added to the number of shares outstanding for the entire period.

## Question 19-9

The weighted-average number of shares for calculating EPS would be 104,500 determined as follows:

$$100{,}000 \quad (1.05) \quad - \quad 1{,}200\,(^5/_{12}) \quad = \quad 104{,}500 \text{ shares}$$

| 100,000 | (1.05) | 1,200 (⁵/₁₂) |
|---|---|---|
| shares | stock | treasury |
| at Jan. 1 | dividend | shares |
|  | adjustment |  |

The 1,200 shares retired are weighted by $(^5/_{12})$ to reflect the fact they were not outstanding the last five months of the year. Purchases of shares that occur after a stock dividend or split are not affected by the distribution.

## Question 19-10

Preferred dividends are deducted from the numerator in the EPS fraction so that "earnings available to *common* shareholders" will be divided by the weighted-average number of *common* shares. An exception would be when the preferred stock is *noncumulative* and no dividends were declared in the reporting period. Another time the deduction is not made is when the preferred stock is convertible and the calculation of EPS assumes the preferred stock has been converted and therefore no dividends are paid.

## Question 19-11

Basic EPS does not reflect the dilutive effect of potential common shares. On the other hand, diluted EPS incorporates the dilutive effect of *all* potential common shares, if the effect is not antidilutive.

## Question 19-12

When calculating diluted EPS, we assume that the shares specified by stock options, warrants, and rights are issued at the exercise price and that the proceeds are used to buy back as treasury stock as many of those shares as could be acquired at the average market price during the reporting period.

## Answers to Questions (continued)

### Question 19-13
The potentially dilutive effect of convertible bonds is reflected in diluted EPS calculations by assuming the bonds were converted into common stock. The conversion is assumed to have occurred at the beginning of the period, or at the time the convertible bonds were issued, if later. When conversion is assumed, the additional common shares that would have been issued upon conversion are added to the denominator of the EPS fraction. The *numerator* is increased by the after-tax interest that would have been avoided if the bonds really had not been outstanding. This effect is reflected in diluted EPS calculations only if the effect is dilutive.

### Question 19-14
The potentially dilutive effect of convertible preferred stock is reflected in diluted EPS calculations by assuming the preferred stock was converted into common stock, just as is done with convertible bonds. The conversion is assumed to have occurred at the beginning of the period, or at the time the convertible preferred stock was issued, if later.

When conversion is assumed, the additional common shares that would have been issued upon conversion are added to the denominator of the EPS fraction. Since EPS are calculated as if the preferred shares had been converted into common shares, there would be no dividends on the preferred stock; so, earnings available to common shareholders are increased in the calculation by the dividends that otherwise would have been distributed to preferred shareholders. This is similar to the way after-tax interest would be added back to net income if the securities were convertible bonds. The difference is that dividends have no tax effect to consider. This effect is reflected in diluted EPS calculations only if the effect is dilutive.

### Question 19-15
The order in which convertible securities are included in the dilutive EPS calculation is determined by comparing the incremental effect of their conversion. They should be included in numerical order, beginning with the *lowest* incremental effect (that is, the most dilutive).

# Answers to Questions (concluded)

## Question 19-16

Contingently issuable shares are considered outstanding in the computation of *diluted* EPS when they will later be issued upon the mere passage of time or because of conditions that currently are met. If this year's operating income were $2.2 million, the additional shares would be considered outstanding in the computation of *diluted* EPS by simply adding 50,000 additional shares to the denominator of the EPS fraction:

### Contingently issuable shares:

$$\frac{\text{no numerator adjustment}}{+\,50,000 \text{ additional shares}}$$

If conditions specified for issuance are *not yet met*, the additional shares are ignored in the calculation. This would be the case if this year's operating income had been $2 million.

## Question 19-17

The calculation of diluted EPS assumes convertible bonds had been converted at the beginning of the year (unless they actually were issued later). If they actually had been converted, the *actual* conversion would cause an actual increase in shares at the conversion date. These additional shares would be time-weighted for the remainder of the year. The numerator would be higher because net income actually would be increased by the after-tax interest saved on the bonds for that period. But the calculation also would *assume* conversion for the period before the actual conversion date because they were potentially dilutive during that period. The shares *assumed* outstanding would be time-weighted for the fraction of the year before the conversion, and the numerator would be increased by the after-tax interest *assumed* saved on the bonds for the same period.

## Question 19-18

EPS data (both basic and diluted for a complex capital structure) must be reported on the face of the income statement for income from continuing operations and net income. Per share numbers for discontinued operations and extraordinary items also should be reported either on the face of the income statement or in related disclosure notes when these components of net income are present.

## Question 19-19

Disclosure notes should include (a) a summary description of the rights and privileges of the company's various securities and (b) supplemental EPS data for transactions that occur after the balance sheet date that result in a material change to the number of shares outstanding at the balance sheet date, and (c) a reconciliation of the numerator and denominator used in the basic EPS computations to the numerator and the denominator used in the diluted EPS computations.

# BRIEF EXERCISES

## Brief Exercise 19-1

$6     fair value per share

x   8 million   shares granted

= **$48 million**   fair value of award

The $48 million total compensation is expensed equally over the three-year vesting period, reducing earnings by **$16 million** each year.

## Brief Exercise 19-2

$5     fair value per option

x   12 million   options granted

= **$60 million**   fair value of award

The $60 million total compensation is expensed equally over the three-year vesting period, reducing earnings by **$20 million** each year.

## Brief Exercise 19-3

The company should adjust the cumulative amount of compensation expense recorded to date in the year the estimate changes.

**2007**

Compensation expense ([$60 x 95% x 2/3] – $20)...................   18

  Paid-in capital –stock options .............................................     18

**2008**

Compensation expense ([$60 x 95% x 3/3] – $20 – $18) .......   19

  Paid-in capital –stock options .............................................     19

Note that this approach is contrary to the usual way companies account for changes in estimates. For instance, assume a company acquires a 3-year depreciable asset having no estimated residual value. The $60 million depreciable cost would be depreciated straight-line at $20 million over the three-year useful life. If the estimated residual value changes after one year to 5% of cost, the new estimated depreciable cost of $57 would be reduced by the $20 million depreciation recorded the first year, and the remaining $37 million would be depreciated equally, $18.5 million per year, over the remaining two years.

# Brief Exercise 19-4

|  | ($ in millions) |  |
|---|---|---|
| Cash ($17 exercise price x 12 million shares) ...................... | 204 |  |
| Paid-in capital - stock options (account balance) ............ | 60 |  |
| Common stock (12 million shares at $1 par per share) .... |  | 12 |
| Paid-in capital – excess of par (remainder) ................... |  | 252 |

Note: The market price at exercise is irrelevant.

# Brief Exercise 19-5

| Paid-in capital - stock options (account balance) ............ | 60 |  |
|---|---|---|
| Paid-in capital – expiration of stock options .......... |  | 60 |

# Brief Exercise 19-6

The estimate of the total compensation would be:

| 100,000 | x | $6 | = | $600,000 |
|---|---|---|---|---|
| options |  | fair |  | estimated |
| expected |  | value |  | total |
| to vest |  |  |  | compensation |

One-third of that amount, or $200,000, will be recorded in each of the three years.

# Brief Exercise 19-7

The new estimate of the total compensation would change to:

| 0 | x | $6 | = | $0 |
|---|---|---|---|---|
| options |  | fair |  | estimated |
| expected |  | value |  | total |
| to vest |  |  |  | compensation |

In that case, Farmer would reverse the $200,000 expensed in 2006 because no compensation can be recognized for options that don't vest due to performance targets not being met, and that's the new expectation.

# Brief Exercise 19-8

In that case, in 2007, the revised estimate of the total compensation would change to $600,000:

| 100,000 | x | $6 | = | $600,000 |
|---|---|---|---|---|
| options | | fair | | estimated |
| expected | | value | | total |
| to vest | | | | compensation |

Farmer would reflect the cumulative effect on compensation in 2007 earnings and record compensation thereafter:

**2007**

| | | |
|---|---|---|
| Compensation expense ([$600,000 x 2/3] - $0) | 400,000 | |
| Paid-in capital –stock options ................. | | 400,000 |

**2008**

| | | |
|---|---|---|
| Compensation expense ([$600,000 x 3/3] - $400,000) | 200,000 | |
| Paid-in capital –stock options ................. | | 200,000 |

# Brief Exercise 19-9

If an award contains a market condition such as the stock price reaching a specified level, then no special accounting is required. The fair value estimate of the share option ($6) already implicitly reflects market conditions due to the nature of share option pricing models. So, Farmer recognizes compensation expense regardless of when, if ever, the market condition is met. The estimate of the total compensation would be:

| 100,000 | x | $6 | = | $600,000 |
|---|---|---|---|---|
| options | | fair | | estimated |
| expected | | value | | total |
| to vest | | | | compensation |

One-third of that amount, or $200,000, will be recorded in each of the three years.

# Brief Exercise 19-10

(amounts in millions, except per share amount)

$$\frac{\underset{\substack{\text{net} \\ \text{income}}}{\$741}}{\underset{\substack{\text{shares} \\ \text{at Jan. 1}}}{544} \quad \underset{\substack{\text{new} \\ \text{shares}}}{+ 36\,(^{10}/_{12})} \quad \underset{\substack{\text{shares} \\ \text{retired}}}{- 6\,(^{8}/_{12})}} = \underset{\substack{\text{Earnings} \\ \text{Per Share}}}{\frac{\$741}{570} = \$1.30}$$

# Brief Exercise 19-11

(amounts in millions, except per share amount)

$$\frac{\underset{\substack{\text{net} \\ \text{income}}}{\$426} \quad \underset{\substack{\text{preferred} \\ \text{dividends}}}{- \$16}}{\underset{\substack{\text{common} \\ \text{shares}}}{820}} = \underset{\substack{\text{Earnings} \\ \text{Per Share}}}{\frac{\$410}{820} = \$.50}$$

Since the preferred stock is cumulative, the dividends (8% x $200 million = $16 million) are deducted even though no dividends were declared. There are no potential common shares, so a single calculation of EPS is appropriate.

# Brief Exercise 19-12

$$24,000 \text{ shares} - 20,000 \text{ shares}^* = 4,000 \text{ shares}$$

**\*Purchase of treasury shares**

$$
\begin{array}{rl}
 & 24,000 \text{ shares} \\
\times & \underline{\quad\$50\ \text{(exercise price)}} \\
 & \$1,200,000 \\
\div & \underline{\quad\$60\ \text{(average market price)}} \\
 & 20,000 \text{ shares}
\end{array}
$$

# Brief Exercise 19-13

(amounts in thousands, except per share amounts)

## Basic EPS

$$
\frac{\overset{\substack{\text{net} \\ \text{income}}}{\$1,500} \ \overset{\substack{\text{preferred} \\ \text{dividends}}}{-\ \$60}}{\underset{\substack{\text{shares} \\ \text{at Jan. 1}}}{800}} = \frac{\$1,440}{800} = \$1.80
$$

## Diluted EPS

$$
\frac{\overset{\substack{\text{net} \\ \text{income}}}{\$1,500}}{\underset{\substack{\text{shares} \\ \text{at Jan. 1}}}{800} \ \underset{\substack{\text{conversion}^* \\ \text{of preferred} \\ \text{shares}}}{+\ 200}} = \frac{\$1,500}{1,000} = \$1.50
$$

- The preferred shares are considered converted when calculating diluted EPS. If converted, there would be no preferred dividends.

# EXERCISES

## Exercise 19-1

**Requirement 1**

| | |
|---|---|
| $5 | fair value per share |
| x   16 million | shares granted |
| = $80 million | fair value of award |

**Requirement 2**

**December 31, 2006**  ($ in millions)

| | | |
|---|---|---|
| Compensation expense ($80 million ÷ 2 years)... | 40 | |
| Paid-in capital – restricted stock ............... | | 40 |

**December 31, 2007**

| | | |
|---|---|---|
| Compensation expense ($80 million ÷ 2 years)... | 40 | |
| Paid-in capital – restricted stock ............... | | 40 |
| | | |
| Paid-in capital – restricted stock.................... | 80 | |
| Common stock (16 million shares x $1 par) ..... | | 16 |
| Paid-in capital – excess of par (remainder)... | | 64 |

# Exercise 19-2

## Requirement 1

$2.50     fair value per share
x   12 million     shares granted
= $30 million     fair value of award

## Requirement 2

no entry

## Requirement 3

|  | ($ in millions) |  |
|---|---|---|
| Compensation expense ($30 million ÷ 3 years) ... | 10 |  |
| Paid-in capital – restricted stock ................. |  | 10 |

## Requirement 4

|  |  |  |
|---|---|---|
| Compensation expense ($30 million ÷ 3 years) ... | 10 |  |
| Paid-in capital – restricted stock ................. |  | 10 |

## Requirement 5

|  |  |  |
|---|---|---|
| Compensation expense ($30 million ÷ 3 years) ... | 10 |  |
| Paid-in capital – restricted stock ................. |  | 10 |

## Requirement 6

|  |  |  |
|---|---|---|
| Paid-in capital – restricted stock ..................... | 30 |  |
| Common stock (12 million shares x $1 par)...... |  | 12 |
| Paid-in capital – excess of par (remainder) ... |  | 18 |

# Exercise 19-3

## Requirement 1

$22.50       fair value per share
x    4 million    shares granted
= $90 million    fair value of award

## Requirement 2

no entry

## Requirement 3

| | ($ in millions) |
|---|---|
| Compensation expense ($90 million ÷ 3 years)... | 30 |
| Paid-in capital – restricted stock ................ | 30 |

## Requirement 4

$22.50       fair value per share
x    4 million    shares granted
x    90%      100% – 10% forfeiture rate
=   $81 million    fair value of award

# Exercise 19-4

**Requirement 1**

| | |
|---|---|
| $3 | fair value per option |
| x    4 million | options granted |
| = $12 million | total compensation |

**Requirement 2**

no entry

**Requirement 3**

|  | ($ in millions) | |
|---|---|---|
| Compensation expense ($12 million ÷ 2 years) ... | 6 | |
| Paid-in capital – stock options .................... | | 6 |

**Requirement 4**

|  |  | |
|---|---|---|
| Compensation expense ($12 million ÷ 2 years) ... | 6 | |
| Paid-in capital – stock options .................... | | 6 |

# Exercise 19-5

## Requirement 1

At January 1, 2006, the estimated value of the award is:

| | |
|---|---|
| $3 | estimated fair value per option |
| x  25 million | options granted |
| = $75 million | total compensation |

## Requirement 2

| | ($ in millions) |
|---|---|
| Compensation expense ($75 million ÷ 3 years)............................ | 25.0 |
|    Paid-in capital – stock options ............................................. | 25.0 |

## Requirement 3

Adams-Menke should adjust the cumulative amount of compensation expense recorded to date in the year the estimate changes.

**2007**

| | |
|---|---|
| Compensation expense ([$75 x 94% x 2/3] – $25)................... | 22 |
|    Paid-in capital –stock options ............................................. | 22 |

**2008**

| | |
|---|---|
| Compensation expense ([$75 x 94% x 3/3] – $25 – $22)........ | 23.5 |
|    Paid-in capital –stock options ............................................. | 23.5 |

Note that this approach is contrary to the usual way companies account for changes in estimates. For instance, assume a company acquires a 3-year depreciable asset having no estimated residual value. The $75 million depreciable cost would be depreciated straight-line at $25 million over the three-year useful life. If the estimated residual value changes after one year to 6% of cost, the new estimated depreciable cost of $70.5 would be reduced by the $25 million depreciation recorded the first year, and the remaining $45.5 million would be depreciated equally, $22.75 million per year, over the remaining two years.

# Exercise 19-6

## Requirement 1

At January 1, 2006, the estimated value of the award is:

| | |
|---|---|
| $1 | estimated fair value per option |
| x 40 million | options granted |
| = $40 million | fair value of award |

## Requirement 2

|  | ($ in millions) |  |
|---|---|---|
| Compensation expense ($40 million ÷ 2 years) ... | 20 | |
|    Paid-in capital – stock options ................... | | 20 |

## Requirement 3

|  |  |  |
|---|---|---|
| Compensation expense ($40 million ÷ 2 years) ... | 20 | |
|    Paid-in capital – stock options ................... | | 20 |

## Requirement 4

|  |  |  |
|---|---|---|
| Cash ($8 exercise price x 30 million shares) ........................ | 240 | |
| Paid-in capital - stock options | | |
|    ($3/4$ account balance of $40 million) ................................ | 30 | |
|      Common stock (30 million shares at $1 par per share) .... | | 30 |
|      Paid-in capital – excess of par (remainder)................... | | 240 |

Note: The market price at exercise is irrelevant.

## Requirement 5

|  |  |  |
|---|---|---|
| Paid-in capital – stock options ($40 -30 million) ............ | 10 | |
|    Paid-in capital – expiration of stock options .......... | | 10 |

# Exercise 19-7

## Requirement 1

At January 1, 2006, the total compensation is measured as:

| | | |
|---|---|---|
| | $ 3 | fair value per option |
| x | 12 million | options granted |
| = | $36 million | intrinsic value of award |

## Requirement 2

**December 31, 2006, 2007, 2008**

|  | ($ in millions) |  |
|---|---|---|
| Compensation expense ($36 million ÷ 3 years)................ | 12 | |
| Paid-in capital – stock options.................................. | | 12 |

## Requirement 3

|  |  |  |
|---|---|---|
| Cash ($11 exercise price x 12 million shares) ...................... | 132 | |
| Paid-in capital - stock options ($12 million x 3 years)..... | 36 | |
| Common stock (12 million shares at $1 par per share).... | | 12 |
| Paid-in capital – excess of par (to balance)................... | | 156 |

Note: The market price at exercise is irrelevant.

# Exercise 19-8

## Requirement 1
The SARs are considered to be equity because IE will settle in shares of IE stock at exercise

**January 1, 2006**
No entry
*Calculate total compensation expense:*

$$
\begin{array}{ll}
\$\ 3 & \text{estimated fair value per SAR} \\
\underline{\text{x}\ \ 24\ \text{million}} & \text{SARs granted} \\
= \$72\ \text{million} & \text{total compensation}
\end{array}
$$

The total compensation is allocated to expense over the 4-year service (vesting) period: 2006 – 2009
$72 million ÷ 4 years = $18 million per year

## Requirement 2

| **December 31, 2006, 2007, 2008, 2009** | ($ in millions) | |
|---|---|---|
| Compensation expense ($72 million ÷ 4 years) | 18 | |
|    Paid-in capital – SAR plan | | 18 |

## Requirement 3
The total compensation is measured once – at the grant date – and is not re-measured subsequently.

## Requirement 4

| **June 6, 2011** | | |
|---|---|---|
| Paid-in capital – SAR plan (account balance) | 72 | |
|    Common stock ($1 par x 24 million shares) | | 24 |
|    Paid-in capital – in excess of par (to balance) | | 48 |

# Exercise 19-9

## Requirement 1

The SARs are considered to be a liability because employees can elect to receive cash at exercise.

**January 1, 2006**
No entry

## Requirement 2

| | ($ in millions) | |
|---|---|---|
| **December 31, 2006** | | |
| Compensation expense ($4 x 24 million x 1/4) | 24 | |
|     Liability – SAR plan | | 24 |
| | | |
| **December 31, 2007** | | |
| Compensation expense ([$3 x 24 million x 2/4] - 24) | 12 | |
|     Liability – SAR plan | | 12 |
| | | |
| **December 31, 2008** | | |
| Compensation expense ([$4 x 24 million x 3/4] – 24 – 12) | 36 | |
|     Liability – SAR plan | | 36 |
| | | |
| **December 31, 2009** | | |
| Liability – SAR plan | 12 | |
|     Compensation expense ([$2.50 x 24 million x 4/4] –24 –12 –36) | | 12 |

## Requirement 3

| | | |
|---|---|---|
| **December 31, 2010** | | |
| Compensation expense ([$3 x 24 million x all] –24 –12 –36 +12) | 12 | |
|     Liability – SAR plan | | 12 |

## Requirement 4

| | | |
|---|---|---|
| **June 6, 2011** | | |
| Compensation expense ([($50-46) x 24 million x all] –24–12–36+12–12) | 24 | |
|     Liability – SAR plan | | 24 |
| | | |
| Liability – SAR plan (account balance) | 96 | |
|     Cash | | 96 |

# Exercise 19-10

| | | |
|---|---|---|
| Cash ($12 x 50,000 x 85%) | 510,000 | |
| Compensation expense ($12 x 50,000 x 15%) | 90,000 | |
| Common stock ($1 x 50,000) | | 50,000 |
| Paid-in capital - in excess of par ($11 x 50,000) | | 550,000 |

# Exercise 19-11

(amounts in thousands, except per share amount)

$$\frac{\substack{\text{net} \\ \text{income} \\ \$655}}{\underset{\substack{\text{shares} \\ \text{at Jan. 1}}}{900(1.05)} + \underset{\substack{\text{new} \\ \text{shares}}}{60\,(^8/_{12})}\,(1.05) + \underset{\substack{\text{new} \\ \text{shares}}}{72\,(^7/_{12})}} = \frac{\$655}{1,029} = \$.64$$

↑___ stock dividend ___↑
adjustment

**Earnings Per Share**

# Exercise 19-12

(amounts in thousands, except per share amount)

$$\frac{\underset{\text{income}}{\text{net}}\quad \underset{\text{dividends}}{\text{preferred}}}{\underset{\substack{\text{shares}\\\text{at Jan. 1}}}{800}\quad\underset{\substack{\text{stock dividend}\\\text{adjustment}}}{(1.25)}} = \frac{\$1,950}{1,000} = \underset{\substack{\textbf{Earnings}\\\textbf{Per Share}}}{\$1.95}$$

$$\$2,000 \quad -\$50$$

# Exercise 19-13

(amounts in thousands, except per share amount)

$$\frac{\underset{\text{loss}}{\text{net}}\quad \underset{\text{dividends}}{\text{preferred}}}{\underset{\substack{\text{shares}\\\text{at Jan. 1}}}{373}\quad\underset{\substack{\text{new}\\\text{shares}}}{+\,12\,(^7/_{12})}} = \frac{-\$190}{380} = \underset{\substack{\textbf{Net Loss}\\\textbf{Per Share}}}{(\$.50)}$$

$$-\$114 \quad -\$76^1$$

[1] 9.5% x $800* = $76

*8,000 shares x $100 par = $800,000

# Exercise 19-14

## 1. EPS in 2006

(amounts in thousands, except per share amount)

$$\frac{\underset{\substack{\text{net} \\ \text{income}}}{\$400}}{\underset{\substack{\text{shares} \\ \text{at Jan. 1}}}{202} \quad \underset{\substack{\text{treasury} \\ \text{shares}}}{-6\,(^{10}/_{12})} \quad \underset{\substack{\text{treasury shares} \\ \text{sold}}}{+6\,(^{2}/_{12})} \quad \underset{\substack{\text{new} \\ \text{shares}}}{+24\,(^{1}/_{12})}} \qquad \frac{\$400}{200} = \underset{\substack{\text{Earnings} \\ \text{Per Share}}}{\$2.00}$$

## 2. EPS in 2007

(amounts in thousands, except per share amount)

$$\frac{\underset{\substack{\text{net} \\ \text{income}}}{\$400}}{\underset{\substack{\text{shares} \\ \text{at Jan. 1}}}{(202 \quad -6 \quad +6 \quad +24)} \quad \underset{\substack{\text{stock dividend} \\ \text{adjustment}}}{\text{x} \;\; (2.00)}} \qquad \frac{\$400}{452} = \underset{\substack{\text{Earnings} \\ \text{Per Share}}}{\$.88}$$

## 3. 2006 EPS in the 2007 comparative financial statements

(amounts in thousands, except per share amount)

$$\frac{\underset{\substack{\text{net} \\ \text{income}}}{\$400}}{\underset{\substack{\text{weighted-average shares} \\ \text{as previously calculated}}}{200} \quad \underset{\substack{\text{stock dividend} \\ \text{adjustment}}}{\text{x} \;\; (2.00)}} \qquad \frac{\$400}{400} = \underset{\substack{\text{Earnings} \\ \text{Per Share}}}{\$1.00}$$

# Exercise 19-15

(amounts in millions, except per share amount)

$$\frac{\overset{\substack{\text{net} \\ \text{income}}}{\$150} \quad \overset{\substack{\text{preferred} \\ \text{dividends}}}{- \$27^1}}{\underset{\substack{\text{shares} \\ \text{at Jan. 1}}}{200\,(1.05)} \quad \underset{\substack{\text{treasury} \\ \text{shares}}}{- 24\,(^{10}/_{12})\,(1.05)} \quad \underset{\substack{\text{new} \\ \text{shares}}}{+ 4\,(^{3}/_{12})}} = \frac{\$123}{190} = \overset{\substack{\textbf{Earnings} \\ \textbf{Per Share}}}{\$.65}$$

$\uparrow$ ___ stock dividend ___ $\uparrow$
adjustment

[1] 9% x $300 = $27

# Exercise 19-16

(amounts in millions, except per share amount)

**Basic EPS**

$$\frac{\overset{\substack{\text{net}\\\text{income}}}{\$150} \quad \overset{\substack{\text{preferred}\\\text{dividends}}}{-\ \$27}}{\underset{\substack{\text{shares}\\\text{at Jan. 1}}}{200}\ (1.05)\ \underset{\substack{\text{treasury}\\\text{shares}}}{-\ 24\ (^{10}/_{12})\ (1.05)}\ \underset{\substack{\text{new}\\\text{shares}}}{+\ 4\ (^{3}/_{12})}} = \frac{\$123}{190} = \$.65$$

↑___ stock dividend ___↑
adjustment

**Diluted EPS**

$$\frac{\overset{\substack{\text{net}\\\text{income}}}{\$150} \quad \overset{\substack{\text{preferred}\\\text{dividends}}}{-\ \$27}}{\underset{\substack{\text{shares}\\\text{at Jan. 1}}}{200}\ (1.05)\ \underset{\substack{\text{treasury}\\\text{shares}}}{-\ 24\ (^{10}/_{12})\ (1.05)}\ \underset{\substack{\text{new}\\\text{shares}}}{+\ 4\ (^{3}/_{12})}\ \underset{\substack{\text{assumed exercise}\\\text{of options}}}{+\ (30 - 24^{*})}} = \frac{\$123}{196} = \$.63$$

↑___ stock dividend ___↑
adjustment

**\*Purchase of treasury stock**

$$
\begin{array}{ll}
 & \text{30 million shares} \\
\text{x} & \underline{\ \$56\ }\text{(exercise price)} \\
 & \$1,680\text{ million} \\
\div & \underline{\ \$70\ }\text{(average market price)} \\
 & \text{24 million shares}
\end{array}
$$

# Exercise 19-17

(amounts in millions, except per share amount)

**Basic EPS**

$$\frac{\overset{\substack{\text{net} \\ \text{income}}}{\$150} \quad \overset{\substack{\text{preferred} \\ \text{dividends}}}{- \$27}}{\underset{\substack{\text{shares} \\ \text{at Jan. 1}}}{200} \ (1.05) \ \underset{\substack{\text{treasury} \\ \text{shares}}}{- \ 24 \ (^{10}/_{12}) \ (1.05)} \ \underset{\substack{\text{new} \\ \text{shares}}}{+ 4 \ (^{3}/_{12})} \ \underset{\substack{\text{actual exercise} \\ \text{of options}}}{+ 30(^{4}/_{12})}} = \frac{\$123}{200} = \$.62$$

↑___ stock dividend ___↑
adjustment

**Diluted EPS**

$$\frac{\overset{\substack{\text{net} \\ \text{income}}}{\$150} \quad \overset{\substack{\text{preferred} \\ \text{dividends}}}{- \$27}}{\underset{\substack{\text{shares} \\ \text{at Jan. 1}}}{200 \ (1.05)} \ \underset{\substack{\text{treasury} \\ \text{shares}}}{- 24(^{10}/_{12}) \ (1.05)} \ \underset{\substack{\text{new} \\ \text{shares}}}{+ 4(^{3}/_{12})} \ \underset{\substack{\text{assumed exercise} \\ \text{of options}}}{+ (30 - 24^{*})(^{8}/_{12})} \ \underset{\substack{\text{actual exercise} \\ \text{of options}}}{+ 30(^{4}/_{12})}} = \frac{\$123}{204} = \$.60$$

↑___ stock dividend ___↑
adjustment

**\*Purchase of treasury stock**

      30 million shares

x    <u>$56</u> (exercise price)

    $1,680 million

÷    <u>$70</u> (average market price)

    24 million shares

# Exercise 19-18

(amounts in millions, except per share amount)

**Basic EPS**

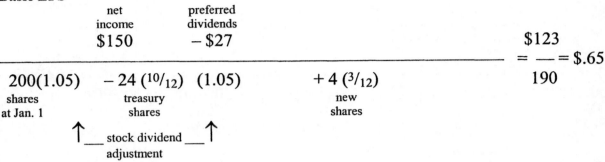

$$\frac{\underset{\substack{\text{net} \\ \text{income}}}{\$150} \quad \underset{\substack{\text{preferred} \\ \text{dividends}}}{-\,\$27}}{\underset{\substack{\text{shares} \\ \text{at Jan. 1}}}{200(1.05)} \quad \underset{\substack{\text{treasury} \\ \text{shares}}}{-\,24\,(^{10}/_{12})} \quad (1.05) \quad \underset{\substack{\text{new} \\ \text{shares}}}{+\,4\,(^{3}/_{12})}} = \frac{\$123}{190} = \$.65$$

stock dividend adjustment

**Diluted EPS**

$$\frac{\underset{\substack{\text{net} \\ \text{income}}}{\$150} \; \underset{\substack{\text{preferred} \\ \text{dividends}}}{-\,\$27} \; + \; \underset{\substack{\text{after-tax} \\ \text{interest savings}}}{\$5^* - 40\%\,(\$5^*)}}{\underset{\substack{\text{shares} \\ \text{at Jan. 1}}}{200\,(1.05)} \underset{\substack{\text{treasury} \\ \text{shares}}}{-\,24\,(^{10}/_{12})} (1.05) \underset{\substack{\text{new} \\ \text{shares}}}{+\,4\,(^{3}/_{12})} \underset{\substack{\text{exercise} \\ \text{of options}}}{+\,(30 - 24^{**})} \underset{\substack{\text{conversion} \\ \text{of bonds}}}{+\,6}} = \frac{\$126}{202} = \$.62$$

stock dividend adjustment

$^*8\% \times \$62.5$ million $= \$5$ million interest

**\*\*Purchase of treasury stock**

$$
\begin{array}{rl}
& 30 \text{ million shares} \\
\times & \underline{\$56}\text{ (exercise price)} \\
& \$1{,}680 \text{ million} \\
\div & \underline{\$70}\text{ (average market price)} \\
& 24 \text{ million shares}
\end{array}
$$

# Exercise 19-19

(amounts in thousands, except per share amounts)

## Basic EPS

$$\frac{\underset{\substack{\text{net} \\ \text{income}}}{\$500} \quad \underset{\substack{\text{preferred} \\ \text{dividends}}}{-60^*}}{\underset{\substack{100 \\ \text{shares} \\ \text{at Jan. 1}}}{}} = \frac{\$440}{100} = \$4.40$$

## Diluted EPS

$$\frac{\underset{\substack{\text{net} \\ \text{income}}}{\$500} \quad \underset{\substack{\text{preferred} \\ \text{dividends}}}{-60^*} \quad \underset{\substack{\text{preferred} \\ \text{dividends}}}{+60^*} \quad \underset{\substack{\text{after-tax} \\ \text{interest savings}}}{+\$100^{**} - 40\%\,(\$100)}}{\underset{\substack{100 \\ \text{shares} \\ \text{at Jan. 1}}}{} \quad \underset{\substack{+32 \\ \text{conversion} \\ \text{of preferred} \\ \text{stock}}}{} \quad \underset{\substack{+30 \\ \text{conversion} \\ \text{of bonds}}}{}} = \frac{\$560}{162} = \$3.46$$

\* 12,000 shares x $5
\*\* $1,000,000 x 10%

# Exercise 19-20

(amounts in thousands, except per share amount)

## Basic EPS

$$\frac{\underset{\substack{\text{net} \\ \text{income}}}{\$720}}{\underset{\substack{\text{shares} \\ \text{at Jan. 1}}}{80} + \underset{\substack{\text{new} \\ \text{shares}}}{15\,(^4/_{12})}} = \frac{\$720}{85} = \$8.47$$

## Diluted EPS

$$\frac{\underset{\substack{\text{net} \\ \text{income}}}{\$720}}{\underset{\substack{\text{shares} \\ \text{at Jan. 1}}}{80} + \underset{\substack{\text{new} \\ \text{shares}}}{15\,(^4/_{12})} + \underset{\substack{\text{exercise} \\ \text{of warrants}}}{(24 - 20)^*}} = \frac{\$720}{89} = \$8.09$$

### *Purchase of treasury shares

|     |           |                        |
|-----|-----------|------------------------|
|     | 24,000    | shares                 |
| x   | $37.50    | (exercise price)       |
|     | $900,000  |                        |
| ÷   | $45       | (average market price) |
|     | 20,000    | shares                 |

# Exercise 19-21

(amounts in millions, except per share amounts)

## Basic EPS

$$\frac{\overset{\text{net income}}{\$148}}{\underset{\substack{\text{shares} \\ \text{at Jan. 1}}}{35} + \underset{\substack{\text{new} \\ \text{shares}}}{4\,(^9/_{12})}} = \frac{\$148}{38} = \$3.89$$

## Diluted EPS

$$\frac{\overset{\text{net income}}{\$148}}{\underset{\substack{\text{shares} \\ \text{at Jan. 1}}}{35} + \underset{\substack{\text{new} \\ \text{shares}}}{4\,(^9/_{12})} + \underset{\substack{\text{additional} \\ \text{shares}}}{1}} = \frac{\$148}{39} = \$3.79$$

Because the conditions are met for issuing 1 million shares, those shares are assumed issued for diluted EPS. Conditions for the other 1 million shares are not yet met, so as they are ignored.

# Exercise 19-22

(amounts in thousands, except per share amounts)

## Basic EPS

$$\frac{\substack{\text{net} \\ \text{income} \\ \$2,000}}{\underset{\substack{\text{shares} \\ \text{at Jan. 1}}}{600} + \underset{\substack{\text{new} \\ \text{shares}}}{100\,(^9/_{12})}} = \frac{\$2,000}{675} = \$2.96$$

## Diluted EPS

$$\frac{\substack{\text{net} \\ \text{income} \\ \$2,000}}{\underset{\substack{\text{shares} \\ \text{at Jan. 1}}}{600} + \underset{\substack{\text{new} \\ \text{shares}}}{100\,(^9/_{12})} + \underset{\substack{\text{contingent} \\ \text{shares}^*}}{4 \times 10} + \underset{\substack{\text{contingent} \\ \text{shares}^{**}}}{15}} = \frac{\$2,000}{730} = \$2.74$$

\* Because the conditions currently are met (i.e., market price exceeds $48) for issuing 10,000 shares in each of the next 4 years, those shares are assumed issued for diluted EPS.

\*\* The condition for the other 15,000 shares also is met (the controller is employed), so those shares are assumed issued for diluted EPS.

# Exercise 19-23

| List A | List B |
|---|---|
| __e__ 1. Subtract preferred dividends. | a. Options exercised. |
| __m__ 2. Time-weighted by $^5/_{12}$. | b. Simple capital structure. |
| __a__ 3. Time-weighted shares assumed issued plus time-weighted-actual shares. | c. Basic EPS. |
| | d. Convertible preferred stock. |
| __i__ 4. Midyear event treated as if it occurred at the beginning of the reporting period. | e. Earnings available to common shareholders. |
| | f. Antidilutive. |
| __l__ 5. Preferred dividends do not reduce earnings. | g. Increased marketability. |
| | h. Extraordinary items. |
| __b__ 6. Single EPS presentation. | i. Stock dividend. |
| __g__ 7. Stock split. | j. Add after-tax interest to numerator. |
| __d__ 8. Potentially dilutive security. | k. Diluted EPS. |
| __f__ 9. Exercise price exceeds market price. | l. Noncumulative, undeclared preferred dividends. |
| __c__ 10. No dilution assumed. | |
| __j__ 11. Convertible bonds. | m. Common shares retired in August. |
| __n__ 12. Contingently issuable shares. | n. Include in diluted EPS when conditions for issuance are met. |
| __k__ 13. Maximum potential dilution. | |
| __h__ 14. Shown between per share amounts for net income and for income from continuing operations. | |

# Exercise 19-24

1. **d.** A noncompensatory plan is defined as one in which substantially all full-time employees participate, the stock available to each employee is equal or is based on salary, the option exercise period is reasonable, and the discount from market is not greater than reasonable in an offer to shareholders or others. Noncompensatory plans do not provide for the achievement of certain performance criteria.

2. **b.** A compensatory stock option plan involves the issuance of stock in whole or in part for employee services. The compensation cost should be recognized as an expense of one or more periods in which the employee performed services.

# PROBLEMS

## Problem 19-1

### Requirement 1

The measurement date is always is the date of grant.

### Requirement 2

| | |
|---|---|
| $ 6 | estimated fair value per option |
| x    20 million | options granted |
| = $120 million | fair value of award |

The total compensation is to be allocated to expense over the 3-year service (vesting) period: 2006 - 2008

$120 million ÷ 3 years = $40 million per year

### Requirement 3

Ensor should adjust the cumulative amount of compensation expense recorded to date in the year the estimate changes.

**2007**

| | | |
|---|---|---|
| Compensation expense ([$120 x 90% x 2/3] – $40)................ | 32 | |
| Paid-in capital –stock options ............................................... | | 32 |

**2008**

| | | |
|---|---|---|
| Compensation expense ([$120 x 90% x 3/3] – $40 – $32) ..... | 36 | |
| Paid-in capital –stock options ............................................... | | 36 |

# Problem 19-1 (concluded)

## Requirement 4

This approach is contrary to the usual way companies account for changes in estimates. For instance, assume a company acquires a 3-year depreciable asset having no estimated residual value for $120 million. The $120 million depreciable cost would be depreciated straight-line at $40 million over the three-year useful life. If the estimated residual value changes after one year to 10% of cost, the new estimated depreciable cost of $108 would be reduced by the $40 million depreciation recorded the first year, and the remaining $68 million would be depreciated equally, $34 million per year, over the remaining two years.

## Requirement 5

| | | |
|---|---|---|
| Cash ($15 x 80% = $12 exercise price x 18 million shares).... | 216 | |
| Paid-in capital - stock options (account balance of $108 million) | 108 | |
|    Common stock (2 million shares at $1 par per share)...... | | 18 |
|    Paid-in capital – excess of par (remainder)................... | | 306 |

Note: The market price at exercise is irrelevant.

# Problem 19-2

## Requirement 1

At January 1, 2006, the estimated value of the award is:

| | |
|---|---|
| $2 | estimated fair value per option |
| x   40 million | options granted |
| = $80 million | total compensation |

## Requirement 2

| | ($ in millions) |
|---|---|
| Compensation expense ($80 million ÷ 2 years) ... | 40 |
| Paid-in capital – stock options .................... | 40 |
| | |
| Deferred tax asset ($40 million x 40%) ............... | 16 |
| Tax expense ................................. | 16 |

**Note:** Since the plan does *not* qualify as an incentive plan, Walters will deduct the difference between the exercise price and the market price at the exercise date. Recall from Chapter 16 that this creates a temporary difference between accounting income (for which compensation expense is recorded currently) and taxable income (for which the tax deduction is taken later upon the exercise of the options). Under FASB 123(r), we assume the temporary difference is the cumulative amount expensed for the options, $40 million at this point. So, the deferred tax benefit is 40% x $40 million.

## Requirement 3

| | |
|---|---|
| Compensation expense ($80 million ÷ 2 years) ... | 40 |
| Paid-in capital – stock options .................... | 40 |
| | |
| Deferred tax asset ($40 million x 40%) ............... | 16 |
| Tax expense ................................. | 16 |

## Problem 19-2 (concluded)

### Requirement 4

|  | ($ in millions) | |
|---|---|---|
| Cash ($8 exercise price x 40 million shares)......................... | 320 | |
| Paid-in capital - stock options (account balance)............. | 80 | |
|    Common stock (40 million shares at $1 par per share)..... | | 40 |
|    Paid-in capital – excess of par (to balance).................... | | 360 |
|  | | |
| Income taxes payable ([$12 - 8] x 40 million shares x 40%) | 64 | |
|    Deferred tax asset (2 years x $16 million) ...................... | | 32 |
|    Paid-in capital - tax effect of stock options (remainder) | | 32 |

### Requirement 5

| | | |
|---|---|---|
| Compensation expense ($80 million ÷ 2 years)................ | 40 | |
|    Paid-in capital – stock options................................ | | 40 |

No deferred tax asset is recorded because an incentive plan does not provide the employer a tax deduction.

### Requirement 6

| | | |
|---|---|---|
| Cash ($8 exercise price x 40 million shares)....................... | 320 | |
| Paid-in capital - stock options (account balance)............ | 80 | |
|    Common stock (40 million shares at $1 par per share).... | | 40 |
|    Paid-in capital – excess of par (to balance).................. | | 360 |

No tax effect because an incentive plan does not provide the employer a tax deduction.

# Problem 19-3

## Requirement 1

At January 1, 2006, the total compensation is measured as:

|   | | |
|---|---|---|
| | $ 6 | fair value per option |
| x | 6 million | options granted |
| = | $36 million | fair value of award |

## Requirement 2

### Dec. 31, 2006, 2007, 2008

| | ($ in millions) | |
|---|---|---|
| Compensation expense ($36 million ÷ 3 years) ... | 12.0 | |
| Paid-in capital – stock options ..................... | | 12.0 |
| | | |
| Deferred tax asset ($12 million x 40%) .............. | 4.8 | |
| Tax expense ................................................. | | 4.8 |

> **Note:** Since the plan does *not* qualify as an incentive plan, JBL will deduct the difference between the exercise price and the market price at the exercise date. Recall from Chapter 16 that this creates a temporary difference between accounting income (for which compensation expense is recorded currently) and taxable income (for which the tax deduction is taken later upon the exercise of the options). Under FASB 123, we assume the temporary difference is the cumulative amount expensed for the options, $12 million, $24 million, and $36 million at Dec. 31, 2006, 2007, and 2008, respectively. So, the deferred tax benefit is 40% of that amount each year.

## Requirement 3

### August 21, 2010

| | ($ in millions) | |
|---|---|---|
| Cash ($22 exercise price x 6 million shares) ................................. | 132.0 | |
| Paid-in capital - stock options (account balance)....................... | 36.0 | |
| Common stock (6 million shares at $1 par per share) ................ | | 6.0 |
| Paid-in capital – excess of par (to balance)............................ | | 162.0 |
| | | |
| Income taxes payable ([$27 - 22] x 6 million shares x 40%)......... | 12.0 | |
| Paid-in capital - tax effect of stock options (remainder).......... | 2.4 | |
| Deferred tax asset (3 years x $4.8 million)......... .................... | | 14.4 |

# Problem 19-4

## Requirement 1

No entry until the end of the reporting period, but compensation must be estimated at the grant date:

| 1 million | x | $12 | = | $12 million |
|-----------|---|-----|---|-------------|
| options expected to vest | | fair value | | estimated total compensation |

## Requirement 2

**December 31, 2006, 2007, 2008, 2009**          ($ in millions)
Compensation expense ($12 million x ¼)......   3
      Paid-in capital – stock options....................          3

## Requirement 3

If, after two years, LCI estimates that it is *not* probable that the performance goals will be met, then the new estimate of the total compensation would change to:

| 0 | x | $12 | = | $0 |
|---|---|-----|---|-----|
| options expected to vest | | fair value | | estimated total compensation |

In that case, LCI would reverse the $6 million expensed in 2006-2007 because no compensation can be recognized for options that don't vest due to performance targets not being met, and that's the new expectation.

**December 31, 2008**                     ($ in millions)
Paid-in capital – stock options........................   6
      Compensation expense .............................          6

**December 31, 2009**
No entry

# Problem 19-5

## 1. Net loss per share for the year ended December 31, 2006:

(amounts in millions, except per share amount)

$$\frac{\underset{\substack{\text{net} \\ \text{loss}}}{-\$140} \quad \underset{\substack{\text{preferred} \\ \text{dividends}}}{-\$160^1}}{\underset{\substack{\text{shares} \\ \text{at Jan. 1}}}{600\,(1.05)} \quad \underset{\substack{\text{treasury} \\ \text{shares}}}{-30\,(^8/_{12})\,(1.05)} \quad \underset{\substack{\text{new} \\ \text{shares}}}{+12\,(^4/_{12})}} = \frac{-\$300}{613} = (\$.49) \quad \text{Net Loss Per Share}$$

↑___ stock dividend ___↑
adjustment

## 2. Per share amount of income or loss from continuing operations for the year ended December 31, 2006:

(amounts in millions, except per share amount)

$$\frac{\underset{\substack{\text{operating} \\ \text{income}}}{\$260^2} \quad \underset{\substack{\text{preferred} \\ \text{dividends}}}{-\$160^1}}{\underset{\substack{\text{shares} \\ \text{at Jan. 1}}}{600(1.05)} \quad \underset{\substack{\text{treasury} \\ \text{shares}}}{-30\,(^8/_{12})\,(1.05)} \quad \underset{\substack{\text{new} \\ \text{shares}}}{+12\,(^4/_{12})}} = \frac{\$100}{613} = \$.16 \quad \text{Income from Continuing Operations Per Share}$$

↑___ stock dividend ___↑
adjustment

[1] 20 million shares x $100 x 8% = $160 million
[2] $400 – $140 = $260 million

# Problem 19-5 (concluded)

## 3. 2006 and 2005 comparative income statements:

(amounts in millions, except per share amount)

|  | 2006 | 2005 |
|---|---|---|
| **Earnings (Loss) Per Common Share:** | | |
| Income (loss) from operations before extraordinary items | $ .16 | $.71 |
| Extraordinary loss from litigation settlement | (.65) | — |
| Net income (loss) | ($ .49) | $.71 |

Note: The weighted-average number of common shares in 2005 should be adjusted for the stock dividend in 2006 for the purpose of reporting 2005 EPS in subsequent years for comparative purposes:

$$\frac{\text{net income} \quad \$450}{\underset{\substack{\text{shares} \\ \text{at Jan. 1}}}{600} \quad \underset{\substack{\text{stock dividend} \\ \text{adjustment}}}{(1.05)}} = \frac{\$450}{630} = \$.71 \quad \text{Earnings Per Share}$$

# Problem 19-6

## 2004

$$\frac{\overset{\text{net}}{\underset{\text{loss}}{-\$160,500}}}{\underset{\text{shares}}{1,855,000}} \quad \overset{\text{Net Loss}}{\underset{\text{Per Share}}{}} = (\$.09)$$

## 2005

$$\frac{\overset{\text{net}}{\underset{\text{income}}{\$2,240,900}}}{\underset{\underset{\text{at Jan. 1}}{\text{shares}}}{1,855,000} \;\; \underset{\underset{\text{shares}}{\text{retired}}}{- \, 110,000 \, (^3/_{12})}} = \frac{\$2,240,900}{1,827,500} = \$1.23 \quad \overset{\text{Earnings}}{\underset{\text{Per Share}}{}}$$

## 2006

$$\frac{\overset{\text{net}}{\underset{\text{income}}{\$3,308,700}}}{\underset{\underset{\text{at Jan. 1}}{\text{shares}}}{1,745,000^*} \;\; \underset{\underset{\text{adjustment}}{\text{stock dividend}}}{\text{x } (1.02)^{**}}} = \frac{\$3,308,700}{1,779,900} = \$1.86 \quad \overset{\text{Earnings}}{\underset{\text{Per Share}}{}}$$

\*    1,855,000 − 110,000 = 1,745,000 shares

\*\*   This is a 2% stock dividend: 34,900 ÷ 1,745,000 = 2%. Alternatively, the additional 34,900 shares could be simply added to the 1,745,000 initial shares outstanding.

# Problem 19-7

(amounts in millions, except per share amount)

## 2004

$$\frac{\underset{\substack{\text{net} \\ \text{income}}}{\$290} \quad \underset{\substack{\text{preferred} \\ \text{dividends}}}{-\$1}}{\underset{\substack{\text{shares} \\ \text{at Jan. 1}}}{55} \quad \underset{\substack{\text{new} \\ \text{shares}}}{+9\,(^6/_{12})}} = \frac{\$289}{59.5} = \underset{\substack{\text{Earnings} \\ \text{Per Share}}}{\$4.86}$$

## 2005

$$\frac{\underset{\substack{\text{net} \\ \text{income}}}{\$380} \quad \underset{\substack{\text{preferred} \\ \text{dividends}}}{-\$1}}{\underset{\substack{\text{shares} \\ \text{at Jan. 1}}}{64\,(1.50)} \quad \underset{\substack{\text{retired} \\ \text{shares}}}{-4\,(^9/_{12})\,(1.50)}} = \frac{\$379}{91.5} = \underset{\substack{\text{Earnings} \\ \text{Per Share}}}{\$4.14}$$

↑___ stock split ___↑
adjustment

## 2006

$$\frac{\underset{\substack{\text{net} \\ \text{income}}}{\$412} \quad \underset{\substack{\text{preferred} \\ \text{dividends}}}{-\$2}}{\underset{\substack{\text{shares} \\ \text{at Jan. 1}}}{90} \quad \underset{\substack{\text{stock dividend} \\ \text{adjustment}}}{(1.10)} \quad \underset{\substack{\text{new} \\ \text{shares}}}{+3\,(^4/_{12})}} = \frac{\$410}{100} = \underset{\substack{\text{Earnings} \\ \text{Per Share}}}{\$4.10}$$

# Problem 19-8

(amounts in thousands, except per share amount)

$$\frac{\overset{\substack{\text{net}\\ \text{income}}}{\$2,100} \quad \overset{\substack{\text{preferred}\\ \text{dividends}}}{- \$75}}{\underset{\substack{\text{shares}\\ \text{at Jan. 1}}}{600 \;\; (1.04)} \quad + \underset{\substack{\text{new}\\ \text{shares}}}{60 \; (^{10}/_{12}) \; (1.04)} \quad - \underset{\substack{\text{shares}\\ \text{retired}}}{2 \; (^{6}/_{12})}} = \frac{\overset{\substack{\textbf{Earnings}\\ \textbf{Per Share}}}{\$2,025}}{675} = \$3.00$$

↑___ stock dividend ___↑
adjustment

# Problem 19-9

The options issued in 2004 are not considered when calculating 2006 EPS because the exercise price ($33) is not less than the 2006 average market price of $32 (although they would have been considered when calculating 2004 or 2005 EPS if the average price those years had been more than $33).

The options issued in 2006 do not affect the calculation of 2006 EPS because they were issued at December 31. Options are assumed exercised at the beginning of the year or when granted, whichever is later — when granted, in this case. So, the fraction of the year the shares are assumed outstanding is $0/12$, meaning no increase in the weighted-average shares.

The options issued in 2005 are considered exercised for 8,000 shares when calculating 2006 EPS because the exercise price ($24) is less than the 2006 average market price of $32. Treasury shares are assumed repurchased at the average price for diluted EPS:

$$
\begin{array}{rll}
& 8,000 & \text{shares} \\
\times & \underline{\$24} & \text{(exercise price)} \\
& \$192,000 & \\
\div & \underline{\$32} & \text{(average market price)} \\
& 6,000 & \text{shares}
\end{array}
$$

## Problem 19-9 (concluded)

(amounts in thousands, except per share amount)

### Basic EPS

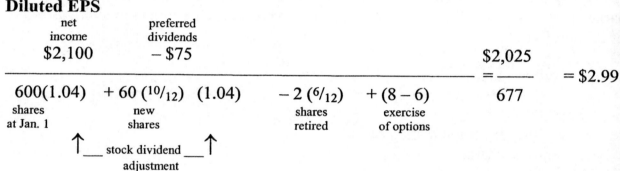

$$\frac{\underset{\$2,100}{\overset{\text{net}}{\underset{\text{income}}{}}} - \underset{\$75}{\overset{\text{preferred}}{\underset{\text{dividends}}{}}}}{\underset{\substack{\text{shares}\\\text{at Jan. 1}}}{600(1.04)} + \underset{\substack{\text{new}\\\text{shares}}}{60\,(^{10}/_{12})}\,(1.04) \;\underset{\substack{\text{shares}\\\text{retired}}}{-\,2\,(^6/_{12})}} = \frac{\$2,025}{675} = \$3.00$$

↑___ stock dividend ___↑
adjustment

### Diluted EPS

$$\frac{\underset{\$2,100}{\overset{\text{net}}{\underset{\text{income}}{}}} - \underset{\$75}{\overset{\text{preferred}}{\underset{\text{dividends}}{}}}}{\underset{\substack{\text{shares}\\\text{at Jan. 1}}}{600(1.04)} + \underset{\substack{\text{new}\\\text{shares}}}{60\,(^{10}/_{12})}\,(1.04) \;\underset{\substack{\text{shares}\\\text{retired}}}{-\,2\,(^6/_{12})} \;\underset{\substack{\text{exercise}\\\text{of options}}}{+\,(8-6)}} = \frac{\$2,025}{677} = \$2.99$$

↑___ stock dividend ___↑
adjustment

# Problem 19-10

The options issued in 2004 are not considered when calculating 2006 EPS because the exercise price ($33) is not less than the 2006 average market price of $32 (although they would have been considered when calculating 2004 or 2005 EPS if the average price those years had been more than $33).

The options issued in 2006 do not affect the calculation of 2006 EPS because they were issued at December 31. Options are assumed exercised at the beginning of the year or when granted, whichever is later — when granted, in this case. So, the fraction of the year the shares are assumed outstanding is $0/12$, meaning no increase in the weighted-average shares.

The options issued in 2005 are considered exercised for 8,000 shares when calculating 2006 EPS because the exercise price ($24) is less than the 2006 average market price of $32. Treasury shares are assumed repurchased at the average price for diluted EPS:

|   | 8,000 | shares |
|---|---|---|
| x | $24 | (exercise price) |
|   | $192,000 | |
| ÷ | $32 | (average market price) |
|   | 6,000 | shares |

# Problem 19-10 (concluded)

(amounts in thousands, except per share amounts)

## Basic EPS

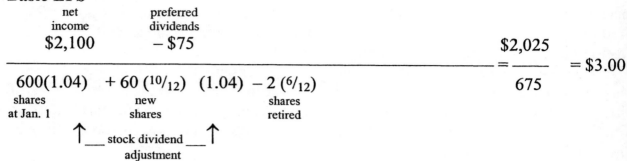

$$\frac{\underset{\substack{\text{net} \\ \text{income}}}{\$2,100} \quad \underset{\substack{\text{preferred} \\ \text{dividends}}}{-\$75}}{\underset{\substack{\text{shares} \\ \text{at Jan. 1}}}{600(1.04)} \quad \underset{\substack{\text{new} \\ \text{shares}}}{+60\,(^{10}/_{12})} \quad (1.04) \quad \underset{\substack{\text{shares} \\ \text{retired}}}{-2\,(^{6}/_{12})}} = \frac{\$2,025}{675} = \$3.00$$

↑___ stock dividend ___↑
adjustment

## Diluted EPS

$$\frac{\underset{\substack{\text{net} \\ \text{income}}}{\$2,100} \quad \underset{\substack{\text{preferred} \\ \text{dividends}}}{-\$75} \qquad \underset{\substack{\text{after-tax} \\ \text{interest savings}}}{+\$80-40\%(\$80)}}{\underset{\substack{\text{shares} \\ \text{at Jan. 1}}}{600(1.04)} \; \underset{\substack{\text{new} \\ \text{shares}}}{+60(^{10}/_{12})} \, (1.04) \, \underset{\substack{\text{shares} \\ \text{retired}}}{-2\,(^{6}/_{12})} \, \underset{\substack{\text{exercise} \\ \text{of options}}}{+(8-6)} \, \underset{\substack{\text{contingent} \\ \text{shares}}}{+23^*} \, \underset{\substack{\text{conversion} \\ \text{of bonds}}}{+24^{**}}} = \frac{\$2,073}{724} = \$2.86$$

↑___ stock dividend ___↑
adjustment

\* The contingently issuable shares are considered issued when calculating diluted EPS because the condition for issuance (Merrill net income > $500,000) currently is being met.

\*\* The bonds are considered converted when calculating diluted EPS: 800 bonds x 30 shares = 24,000 shares upon conversion. Interest = $800,000 x 10% = $80,000.

# Problem 19-11

## Requirement 1

(amounts in thousands, except per share amount)

### Basic EPS:

$$\frac{\overset{\text{net income}}{\$150} \quad \overset{\substack{\text{preferred}\\\text{dividends}}}{-\,\$77}}{\underset{\substack{\text{weighted-average}\\\text{shares}}}{40}} = \frac{\$73}{40} = \$1.83$$

### With conversion of preferred stock (Diluted EPS):

$$\frac{\overset{\text{net income}}{\$150}}{\underset{\substack{\text{weighted-average}\\\text{shares}}}{40} \quad \underset{\substack{\text{conversion}\\\text{of preferred}\\\text{shares}}}{+\,20}} = \frac{\$150}{60} = \$2.50$$

Since the assumed conversion of the convertible preferred stock causes EPS to increase, it is **antidilutive** and therefore ignored when calculating EPS.

*Problem 19-11 (concluded)*

## Requirement 2

**Basic EPS:**

$$\frac{\overset{\text{net income}}{\$150}}{\underset{\substack{\text{weighted-average} \\ \text{shares}}}{40}} = \$3.75$$

**With conversion of bonds:**

$$\frac{\overset{\text{net income}}{\$150} + \overset{\substack{\text{after-tax} \\ \text{interest savings}}}{\$40 - 40\% \, (\$40)}}{\underset{\substack{\text{weighted-average} \\ \text{shares}}}{40} + \underset{\substack{\text{conversion} \\ \text{of bonds}}}{5}} = \frac{\$174}{45} = \$3.87$$

Since the assumed conversion of the convertible bonds causes EPS to increase, it is **antidilutive** and therefore ignored when calculating EPS.

## Requirement 3

Since the exercise price is less than average market price, the options are **not** antidilutive and therefore assumed exercised when calculating diluted EPS.

## Requirement 4

Since the exercise price is higher than the average market price, the warrants are **antidilutive** and therefore ignored when calculating diluted EPS.

## Requirement 5

The 5,000 shares are added to the denominator when calculating diluted EPS since 2006 net income is higher than the conditional amount. Since only the denominator is increased, the effect is **not** antidilutive.

# Problem 19-12

(amounts in millions, except per share amounts)

## Basic EPS

$$\frac{\substack{\text{net} \\ \text{income} \\ \$560}}{\underset{\substack{\text{shares} \\ \text{at Jan. 1}}}{400} \quad \underset{\substack{\text{new} \\ \text{shares}}}{-30\,(^4/_{12})}} = \frac{\$560}{390} = \$1.44$$

## Diluted EPS

$$\frac{\substack{\text{net} \\ \text{income} \\ \$560} \qquad \overset{\substack{\text{after-tax}^* \\ \text{interest savings}}}{+\$30 - 40\%\,(\$30)}}{\underset{\substack{\text{shares} \\ \text{at Jan. 1}}}{400} \quad \underset{\substack{\text{new} \\ \text{shares}}}{-30\,(^4/_{12})} \quad \underset{\substack{\text{conversion} \\ \text{of bonds}}}{+36}} = \frac{\$578}{426} = \$1.36$$

*Interest on the bonds = $300 million x 10% = $30 million. If the bonds were not outstanding, interest expense would have been $30 million lower, and tax expense would have been 40% x $30 million, or $12 million higher, a net after-tax savings of $18 million.

# Problem 19-13

(amounts in thousands, except per share amounts)

## Basic EPS

$$\frac{\overset{\substack{\text{net} \\ \text{income}}}{\$650} \quad \overset{\substack{\text{preferred} \\ \text{dividends}}}{-\$40^*}}{\underset{\substack{\text{shares} \\ \text{at Jan. 1}}}{440} \quad \underset{\substack{\text{new} \\ \text{shares}}}{+16\,(^3/_{12})}} = \frac{\$610}{444} = \$1.37$$

## Diluted EPS

$$\frac{\overset{\substack{\text{net} \\ \text{income}}}{\$650} \quad \overset{\substack{\text{preferred} \\ \text{dividends}}}{-\$40^*} \qquad \overset{\substack{\text{preferred} \\ \text{dividends}}}{+40^*}}{\underset{\substack{\text{shares} \\ \text{at Jan. 1}}}{440} \quad \underset{\substack{\text{new} \\ \text{shares}}}{+16\,(^3/_{12})} \quad \underset{\substack{\text{exercise} \\ \text{of options}}}{+(20-15^{**})} \quad \underset{\substack{\text{conversion} \\ \text{of preferred} \\ \text{shares}}}{+40}} = \frac{\$650}{489} = \$1.33$$

\* 4,000 shares x $100 par x 10% = $40,000

**\*\*Assumed purchase of treasury shares**

$$
\begin{array}{rll}
 & 20{,}000 & \text{shares} \\
\text{x} & \underline{\quad\$30\quad} & \text{(exercise price)} \\
 & \$600{,}000 & \\
\div & \underline{\quad\$40\quad} & \text{(average market price)} \\
 & 15{,}000 & \text{shares}
\end{array}
$$

# Problem 19-14

(amounts in millions, except per share amounts)

## Basic EPS

$$\frac{\overset{\text{net income}}{\$1,476} \quad \overset{\text{preferred dividends}}{- \$60^*}}{\underset{\substack{\text{shares} \\ \text{at Jan. 1}}}{600} \quad \underset{\substack{\text{new} \\ \text{shares}}}{+ 72 \, (^4/_{12})}} = \frac{\$1,416}{624} = \$2.27$$

## Diluted EPS

$$\frac{\overset{\text{net income}}{\$1,476} \quad \overset{\text{preferred dividends}}{- \$60^*} \quad \quad \quad \overset{\substack{\text{after-tax} \\ \text{Interest savings}}}{+ \$160 - 40\% \, (\$160)}}{\underset{\substack{\text{shares} \\ \text{at Jan. 1}}}{600} \quad \underset{\substack{\text{new} \\ \text{shares}}}{+ 72 \, (^4/_{12})} \quad \underset{\substack{\text{exercise} \\ \text{of options}}}{+ (60 - 40)^{**}} \quad \underset{\substack{\text{conversion} \\ \text{of bonds}}}{+ 80}} = \frac{\$1,512}{724} = \$2.09$$

*Preferred dividends: 6% x $50 x 20 million shares = $60 million

**Computation of Treasury Shares:

| | |
|---|---|
| 60 million | shares |
| x  $12 | exercise price |
| $720 million | proceeds |
| ÷    $18 | average share price |
| 40 million | treasury shares |

# CASES

## Real World Case 19-1

### Requirement 1

The shares are restricted in such a way as to provide some incentive to the recipient. Dell's restricted stock award plans are *tied to continued employment*. The shares are subject to forfeiture by the employee if employment is terminated within seven years from the date of grant. These restrictions give the employee incentive to remain with the company until rights to the shares vest.

### Requirement 2

**2002 grant**

| | |
|---|---|
| $24 | fair value per share |
| x    2.1 million | shares granted |
| = $50.4 million | fair value of award |
| /    7 years | service period |
| $ 7.2 million | annual compensation expense |

**2003 grant**

| | |
|---|---|
| $25 | fair value per share |
| x    0.3 million | shares granted |
| = $7.5 million | fair value of award |
| /    7 years | service period |
| $ 1.1 million | annual compensation expense |

**2004 grant**

| | |
|---|---|
| $28 | fair value per share |
| x    0.6 million | shares granted |
| = $16.8 million | fair value of award |
| /    7 years | service period |
| $ 2.4 million | annual compensation expense |

**2004 expense**

| | |
|---|---|
| $ 7.2 million | 2002 grant |
| 1.1 million | 2003 grant |
| 2.4 million | 2004 grant |
| **$10.7 million** | 2004 compensation expense |

# Communication Case 19-2

## Suggested Grading Concepts and Grading Scheme:

**Content** (80% )

_____  30  Measurement of compensation.

    _____ Compensation cost should be measured at the date of grant.

    _____ Fair value of the stock options.

    _____ Estimated by employing a recognized option pricing model.

    _____ Value per option times number of options.

    _____ Can be adjusted for estimated forfeiture rate.

    _____ No entry on grant date.

_____  25  Determination of compensation expense.

    _____ Expensed over the period of service for which the
options are given, 2006 - 2008.

    _____ Debit compensation expense.

    _____ Credit paid-in capital – stock options.

    _____ Not adjusted when the price of the underlying stock changes.

_____  15  Effect of forfeiture before vesting.

    _____ Reduce compensation expense in forfeiture period
for the cumulative effect of the revised estimate.

    _____ Revise compensation expense for remaining service period.

_____  10  Effect of forfeiture after vesting.

    _____ Paid-in capital - stock options becomes Paid-in
capital - expiration of stock options.

    _____ Compensation expense of previous periods cannot be reversed
for vested options.

**Bonus (5)** Option pricing model considers:

    Exercise price of the option.

    Expected term of the option.

    Current market price of the stock.

    Expected dividends.

    Expected risk-free rate of return.

    Expected volatility of the stock.

_____  80-85 points

## Case 19-2 (concluded)

**Writing** (20%)

| | | |
|---|---|---|
| _____ | 5 | Terminology and tone appropriate to the audience of controller. |
| _____ | 6 | Organization permits ease of understanding. |

          _____ introduction that states purpose.

          _____ paragraphs separate main points.

| | | |
|---|---|---|
| _____ | 9 | English. |

          _____ word selection.

          _____ spelling.

          _____ grammar.

_____      20 points

# Ethics Case 19-3

Discussion should include these elements:

**Facts:**

The choice of method will affect earnings. FIFO will increase reported net income.

FIFO will cause an increase in taxes paid.

Company managers stand to benefit from the change.

The auditor risks negative consequences if the change is challenged.

**Ethical Dilemma:**

Is the auditor's obligation to challenge the questionable change in methods greater than the obligation to the financial interests of the CPA firm and its client?

**Who is affected?**

You, the auditor

Managers

CPA firm (lost fees? reputation? legal action?)

Shareholders

Potential shareholders

[From research performed in this area, it is not clear that accounting changes that increase earnings without any real economic (cash flow) effect will have the desired effect of increasing share price. In fact, the preponderance of such research indicates that the market "sees through" cosmetic accounting changes. Nevertheless, there is plenty of evidence, at least anecdotal, that managers attempt to fool the market. Some efforts to manage earnings may not be an attempt to affect share prices, but to avoid violating terms of contracts based on earnings or related balance sheet items. Some may be to favorably affect terms of compensation agreements.]

The employees

The creditors

# Real World Case 19-4

### Requirement 1

Whether an incentive plan is a stock option plan, a stock award plan, a stock appreciation rights (SARs) plan, or one of the various similar plans, the intention is to provide compensation to designated employees, while at the same time providing those employees with some sort of performance incentive. Likewise, our reporting objectives in accounting for these plans are the same for each: (1) to determine the fair value of the compensation and (2) to expense that compensation over the periods in which participants perform services.

### Requirement 2

The $29 million GE reported as share-based expense in the third quarter of 2004 is that period's portion of the value of options granted in 2004 and prior years. Each reporting period, GE determines the value of the options granted that period and expenses that compensation over the periods in which participants perform services, usually the vesting period for the options. So, for instance, if options granted in 2002 had a value of $40 million and a 4-year vesting period, $10 million / 4 quarters = $2.5 million of that amount would be part of the $29 million expensed in the third quarter of 2004.

# Judgment Case 19-5

Although net income declined during the period, a combination of events caused EPS to increase in spite of declining profits. Specifically, retiring the preferred shares increased earnings available to common shareholders; retiring common shares and retiring convertible debt each decreased the weighted-average number of common shares. The following calculations show the effect of these events:

(amounts in millions, except per share amount)

**2004**

$$\frac{\underset{\substack{\text{net} \\ \text{income}}}{\$145} - \underset{\substack{\text{preferred} \\ \text{dividends}}}{\$16^*}}{\underset{\substack{\text{shares} \\ \text{at Jan. 1}}}{60}} = \frac{\$129}{60} = \$2.15 \quad \begin{array}{c} \textbf{Basic} \\ \textbf{EPS} \end{array}$$

$$\frac{\underset{\substack{\text{net} \\ \text{income}}}{\$145} - \underset{\substack{\text{preferred} \\ \text{dividends}}}{\$16^*} + \underset{\substack{\text{after-tax} \\ \text{interest savings}}}{\$5 - 40\%\,(\$5)}}{\underset{\substack{\text{shares} \\ \text{at Jan. 1}}}{60} + \underset{\substack{\text{conversion} \\ \text{of bonds}}}{9}} = \frac{\$132}{69} = \$1.91 \quad \begin{array}{c} \textbf{Diluted} \\ \textbf{EPS} \end{array}$$

\* 8% x [$10 x 20 million] = $16

## Case 19-5 *(concluded)*

**2005**

$$\frac{\underset{\substack{\text{net}\\\text{income}}}{\$134} - \underset{\substack{\text{preferred}\\\text{dividends}}}{\$12\ddagger}}{\underset{\substack{\text{shares}\\\text{at Jan. 1}}}{60} - \underset{\substack{\text{retired}\\\text{shares}}}{12\,(^{10}/_{12})}} = \frac{\$122}{50} = \$2.44 \quad \substack{\textbf{Basic}\\\textbf{EPS}}$$

$$\frac{\underset{\substack{\text{net}\\\text{income}}}{\$134} - \underset{\substack{\text{preferred}\\\text{dividends}}}{\$12\ddagger} + \underset{\substack{\text{after-tax}\\\text{interest savings}}}{\$5 - 40\%\,(\$5)}}{\underset{\substack{\text{shares}\\\text{at Jan. 1}}}{60} - \underset{\substack{\text{retired}\\\text{shares}}}{12\,(^{10}/_{12})} + \underset{\substack{\text{conversion}\\\text{of bonds}}}{9}} = \frac{\$125}{59} = \$2.12 \quad \substack{\textbf{Diluted}\\\textbf{EPS}}$$

**2006**

$$\frac{\underset{\substack{\text{net}\\\text{income}}}{\$95}}{\underset{\substack{\text{shares}\\\text{at Jan. 1}}}{48\pm} - \underset{\substack{\text{retired}\\\text{shares}}}{12\,(^{10}/_{12})}} = \frac{\$95}{38} = \$2.50 \quad \substack{\textbf{Basic}\\\textbf{EPS}}$$

$$\frac{\underset{\substack{\text{net}\\\text{income}}}{\$95}}{\underset{\substack{\text{shares}\\\text{at Jan. 1}}}{48} - \underset{\substack{\text{retired}\\\text{shares}}}{12\,(^{10}/_{12})}} = \frac{\$95}{38} = \$2.50 \quad \substack{\textbf{Diluted}\\\textbf{EPS}}$$

$\ddagger$ $16 - (^{6}/_{12} \times 8\% \times [\$10 \times 20 \text{ million} \times {}^{1}/_{2}])$: calculation reflects the retirement of half the shares on July 1

$\pm$ 60 - 12

# Communication Case 19-6

## Suggested Grading Concepts and Grading Scheme:

**Content** (80% )

_____    60    Convertible securities are included in the computation.

         _____ Of *diluted* earnings per share.

         _____ By assuming they were converted, the "if-converted" method, as it's called.

         _____ The *denominator* of the EPS fraction is increased by the additional common shares that would have been issued upon conversion.

         _____ The *numerator* is increased by the *interest* (after-tax) or *preferred dividends* that would have been avoided.

_____    20    Antidilutive securities.

         _____ Antidilutive means EPS increases rather than decreases.

         _____ Ignored when calculating earnings per share.

_____    **Bonus (4)** Provides detail regarding the tax effect calculation for convertible bonds.

         _____ Interest on bonds is tax deductible.

         _____ Tax expense will increase by the tax rate times interest.

_____    80-84 points


**Writing** (20%)

_____    5    Terminology and tone appropriate to the audience of division managers.

_____    6    Organization permits ease of understanding.

         _____ Introduction that states purpose.

         _____ Paragraphs separate main points.

_____    9    English

         _____ Word selection.

         _____ Spelling.

         _____ Grammar.

_____    20 points

# Real World Case 19-7

## Requirement 1

The disclosure note refers to adjustments for "stock options and other." Other potential common shares might include convertible securities and contingently issuable shares.

Stock options give their holders the right to to purchase common stock at a specified *exercise price*. The dilution that would result from their exercise should be reflected in the calculation of *diluted* EPS, but not *basic* EPS. To include the dilutive effect of a security means to calculate EPS *as if* the potential increase in shares already has occurred (even though it hasn't yet). So, for stock options, we "pretend" the options have been exercised. In fact, we assume the options were exercised at the beginning of the reporting period, or when the options were issued if that's later. We then assume the cash proceeds from selling the new shares at the exercise price are used to buy back as many shares as possible at the shares' average market price during the year.

Similarly, we would assume convertible securities had been converted into shares. This means adding the new shares to the denominator and increasing the numerator by the after-tax effect of the convertible security not being outstanding.

When an agreement specifies that additional shares of common stock will be issued contingent upon the occurrence of some future circumstance, perhaps issuable to shareholders of an acquired company, certain key executives, or others in the event a certain level of performance is achieved. Contingent performance may be a desired level of income, a target stock price, or some other measurable activity level. When calculating EPS, contingently issuable shares are considered to be outstanding in the computation of *diluted* EPS if shares are to be issued merely as a result of time passing, or if some target performance level already is being met (assumed to remain at existing levels until the end of the contingency period). For example, if shares will be issued at a future date if a certain level of income is achieved and that level of income or more was already earned this year, those additional shares are simply added to the denominator of the diluted EPS fraction. The shares should be included in both basic and diluted EPS if *all* conditions have actually been met so that there is *no* circumstance under which those shares would not be issued. In essence, these are *no longer contingent shares*.

# Case 19-7 (concluded)

## Requirement 2

Sometimes, the effect of the exercise of options would be to *increase*, rather than decrease, EPS. These we refer to as "antidilutive" securities. Such options are ignored when calculating both basic and diluted EPS. For example, when we adjust shares for the effect of the options being exercised, we apply what's called the "treasury stock" method. The number of shares assumed repurchased is fewer than the number of shares assumed sold any time the buy-back (average market) price is higher than the exercise price. In those cases, there will be a net increase in the number of shares so earnings per share will decline. This was the case for Clorox's options referred to in the note. On the other hand, if the exercise price is *higher* than the market price, to assume shares are sold at the exercise price and repurchased at the market price would mean buying back more shares than were sold. This would produce a net *decrease* in the number of shares. EPS would increase, not decrease, if we were to assume the exercise of stock options. These would have an antidilutive effect and would not be considered exercised. For that matter, a rational investor would not exercise options at an exercise price higher than the current market price anyway. We don't include them because the intent of reporting diluted EPS is to report the extent to which EPS would be diluted, or reduced, if the potential common shares actually had become shares.

## Requirement 3

Here is the presentation of basic and diluted earnings per share for 2004, 2003, and 2002 that Clorox reports in its 2004 annual report.

| Net Income Per Common Share | 2004 | 2003 | 2002 |
|---|---|---|---|
| **Basic:** | | | |
| Continuing operations | $2.58* | $2.36 | $1.54 |
| Discontinued operations | 0.01** | (0.10) | (0.15) |
| | $2.59 | $2.26 | $1.39 |
| **Diluted:** | | | |
| Continuing operations | $2.55‡ | $2.33 | $1.52 |
| Discontinued operations | 0.01± | (0.10) | (0.15) |
| | $2.56 | $2.23 | $1.37 |

  *  $546,000/211,683 = $2.58
 ** $3,000/211,683 = $0.01
 ‡  $546,000/214,371= $2.55
 ±  $3,000/214,371= $0.01

# Analysis Case 19-8

## Requirement 1

In its simplest form, earnings per share is merely a firm's net income divided by the number of shares outstanding throughout the year.

$$\text{Earnings per share} = \frac{\text{Income available to common shareholders}}{\text{Weighted-average shares outstanding}}$$

$$= \frac{\$487}{181}$$

$$= \underline{\$2.69}$$

## Requirement 2

$$\text{Price-earnings ratio} = \frac{\text{Market price per share}}{\text{Earnings per share}}$$

$$= \frac{\$47.00}{\$2.69}$$

$$= \underline{17.5}$$

The ratio is a measure of the market's perception of the "quality" of a company's earnings. It indicates the price multiple the capital market is willing to pay for the company's earnings. In a way, this ratio reflects the market's perceptions of the company's growth potential, stability, and relative risk in that the ratio relates these performance measures with the external judgment of the marketplace concerning the value of the firm.

The calculation indicates that IGF's share price represents $17.50 for every dollar of earnings. In that regard, it measures the "quality" of earnings in the sense that it represents the market's expectation of *future* earnings as indicated by current earnings. We should be aware, though, that a ratio might be low, not because earnings expectations are low, but because of abnormally elevated current earnings, or, the ratio might be high, not because earnings expectations are high, but because the company's current earnings are temporarily depressed.

## Case 19-8 (concluded)

### Requirement 3

The dividend payout ratio expresses the percentage of earnings that is distributed to shareholders as dividends. To calculate the ratio for IGF with the information provided, we must estimate dividends from analysis of the retained earnings account:

|  | Retained Earnings | |
|---|---|---|
|  | 2,428 | |
|  | 487 | Net income |
| Dividends ? | | |
|  | 2,730 | |

Dividends apparently were $185,000,000. Dividends per share, then, would be $185 / 181 = $1.02

$$\textbf{Dividend payout ratio} \quad = \quad \frac{\text{Cash dividends per share}}{\text{Earnings per share}}$$

$$= \quad \frac{\$1.02}{\$2.69}$$

$$= \quad \underline{37.9\%}$$

IGF paid cash dividends of $1.02 cents per share during the most recent year, almost 38% of earnings. The ratio provides an indication of the firm's reinvestment strategy. If the payout ratio is low, it suggests that the company retains a large portion of earnings for reinvestment for purposes such as new facilities and current operations. Sometimes, though, the ratio just reflects managerial strategy regarding the mix of internal versus external financing. Investors who, for tax or other reasons, prefer current income over market price appreciation, or vice versa, are particularly interested in this ratio.

# Ethics Case 19-9

Discussion should include these elements.

## Effect of share repurchase on EPS.

Reducing the number of shares will increase earnings *per share*. That impact will be lessened, though, the closer to the end of the year the shares are bought due to the way the share reduction is "time-weighted" for the fraction of the year they are not outstanding.

## Ethical Dilemma:

Apparently, a more productive use for available funds will be offered by Barber. How does a less-than-optimal use of company funds compare with the perceived need to maintain a record of increasing reported EPS?

## Who is affected?

Mashburn

Lane

Managers under the bonus plan

Shareholders

Potential shareholders

Employees

Creditors

# Integrating Case 19-10

## Requirement 1

The 949 million options outstanding will not affect basic EPS. Only shares actually issued upon the exercise of options affect that calculation. However, *diluted* EPS will reflect the potential dilution from the assumed exercise of those options. Specifically, that calculation assumes the outstanding options had been exercised at the beginning of the year, or when the options were issued for those granted during the current period. The assumed proceeds from the exercise would be assumed to be used to buy back as many of the 949 million shares as could be purchased at the average market price of the shares.

## Requirement 2

If there were no actual changes in shares, and no potential common shares other than options, we could explain the difference as follows:

| | |
|---|---|
| 949 million | shares assumed issued upon the exercise of the options at the beginning of the period |
| (91 million) | difference in shares used in diluted and basic EPS calculations (10,894 million – 10,803 million) |
| 858 million | shares assumed repurchased at the average market price per share |

Note: The restrictive assumptions were made for convenience. Microsoft's dilutive potential common shares were due primarily to stock options, but partly also to other potential common shares. Also, Microsoft's shares actually did change in fiscal 2004 as a result of common stock repurchases and the actual exercise of options. Also, the options outstanding changed during the year as follows:

| | |
|---|---|
| Balance, June 30, 2003 | 1,549 |
| Granted | 2 |
| Exercised | (198) |
| Transferred under transfer program | (345) |
| Canceled | (59) |
| Balance, June 30, 2004 | 949 |

# Research Case 19-11

The results students report will vary somewhat depending on the dates and times quotes were accessed. It is unlikely, though, that their relative comparisons or conclusions will differ.

The PE ratio is the market price per share divided by the earning per share. It measures the market's perception of the "quality" of a company's earnings by indicating the price multiple the capital market is willing to pay for the company's earnings. The ratio reflects the information provided by all financial information in that the market price reflects analysts' perceptions of the company's growth potential, stability, and relative risk. The price-earnings ratio relates these performance measures with the external judgment of the marketplace concerning the value of the firm. The ratio measures the "quality" of earnings in the sense that it represents the market's expectation of *future* earnings as indicated by current earnings. Caution is called for in comparing price-earnings ratios. Historically, the ratio for both companies has been relatively high, reflecting growth expectations.

# Analysis Case 19-12

## Requirement 1

The price-earnings ratio is simply the market price per share divided by the earnings per share. For Kellogg, the ratio is:

$$\$44.66 \div \$2.14 = 20.9$$

It purports to measure the market's perception of the "quality" of a company's earnings by indicating the price multiple the securities market is willing to pay for the company's earnings. The P/E ratio reflects analysts' perceptions of the company's growth potential, stability, and relative risk by relating these performance measures with the external judgment of the marketplace in regard to the value of the company.

Care is needed when evaluating price-earnings ratios. Like other ratios, it is best evaluated in context of P/E ratios of earlier periods and other, similar companies. For example, the P/E ratio of General Mills, Kellogg's prime competitor was 18.9 at the same time. Neither is high relative to the average P/E ratio for all companies at the time, which was 20.2.

## Requirement 2

The dividend payout ratio expresses the percentage of earnings that is distributed to shareholders as dividends. The ratio is calculated by dividing dividends per common share by the earnings per share. For Kellogg's most recent 12 months, the ratio is:

$$(\$.2525 \times 4) \div (\$2.14) = 47\%$$

Relative to the average company, this payout percentage is quite high. It slightly higher than General Mills, Kellogg's prime competitor. General Mills' payout ratio was 44% at the same time. Historically, both companies and the industry in general have relatively high dividend payouts. This ratio provides an indication of a firm's reinvestment strategy. A low payout percentage suggests that a company is retaining a large portion of earnings for reinvestment in new projects. Low ratios often are found in growth industries. High payouts, like those of General Mills and Kellogg, often are found in mature industries. Sometimes, the ratio is just an indication of management strategy related to the mix of internal versus external financing. A high ratio is preferred by investors who, for tax or other reasons, prefer current income to market price appreciation.

# Analysis Case 19-13

### Requirement 1
When calculating basic earnings per share, the numerator in the computation is the earnings available to common shareholders. This will be net income reduced by dividends payable to preferred shareholders. Since the preferred stock is *cumulative* we subtract preferred dividends even if not declared. Because unpaid dividends accumulate to be paid in a future year when (if) dividends are subsequently declared, the presumption is that, although the year's dividend preference isn't distributed this year, it eventually will be paid.

### Requirement 2
When calculating basic earnings per share, the denominator in the computation is the weighted-average number of common shares outstanding during 2006. Thus, the 8 million shares outstanding at January 1, 2006, plus a portion of the shares sold will result in the weighted-average number of shares outstanding for calculating basic EPS. The 3 million common shares issued during 2006 must be included in computing the weighted-average number of shares outstanding. The 3 million shares will be weighted one-third because they were outstanding only for the four months of 2006. The 1 million common shares issued upon the exercise of stock options must be included in computing the weighted-average number of shares outstanding. The 1 million shares will be weighted one-half because they were outstanding only for the six months of 2006.

### Requirement 3
When calculating diluted earnings per share, the numerator in the computation is the earnings available to common shareholders. Proactive will not reduce net income by dividends payable to preferred shareholders because it will treat the convertible preferred stock as if the preferred shares were converted and 4 million common shares were outstanding, unless including these shares in the denominator would increase earnings per share (be antidilutive). This means that it would not reduce the numerator for the preferred dividends as it would do if the preferred shares were assumed outstanding, as in calculating basic EPS.

## Case 19-13 (continued)

### Requirement 4

When calculating diluted earnings per share, the denominator in the computation is the weighted-average number of common shares outstanding during the reporting period. But since potential common shares exist in a complex capital structure, as in this situation, the calculation of the denominator becomes more involved.

We begin by determining the weighted-average of the number of common shares outstanding during 2006, the 8 million shares outstanding at January 1, 2006, plus a portion of the shares sold. The 3 million common shares issued during 2006 must be included in computing the weighted-average number of shares outstanding. The 3 million shares will be weighted one-third because they were outstanding only for the four months of 2006. The 1 million common shares issued upon the exercise of stock options must be included in computing the weighted-average number of shares outstanding. The 1 million shares will be weighted one-half because they were outstanding only for the six months of 2006.

For diluted EPS, two adjustments are needed to the denominator. First, we treat the convertible preferred stock as if the preferred shares were converted and 4 million additional common shares were outstanding, unless including these shares in the denominator would increase earnings per share (be antidilutive). As noted in requirement 2, this means also that we would not reduce the numerator for the preferred dividends as we would do if the preferred shares were assumed still outstanding.

Second, we treat the stock options outstanding under the employee stock option plan as having been exercised. The number of common shares represented by the options outstanding should be computed by application of the treasury stock method. By this method, earnings per share is computed as if the options were exercised at the beginning of the period (or at time of issue, if later) and as if the cash received were used to purchase common stock at the average market price during the period. The weighted-average number of shares outstanding for 2006 includes (a) the 1 million shares represented by the 1 million options outstanding for the full year, plus (b) a time-weighted proportion of the 1 million exercised in 2006, and (c) a time-weighted proportion of the 1.5 million granted during 2006. We cannot determine the weighted-average number of options outstanding from the data provided because no exercise or grant dates were given.

The 1 million shares issued when the options were exercised during 2006 must be included in the computation of the weighted-average number of shares outstanding from the date exercised to the year-end. Again, we cannot determine this number because the exercise dates were not given.

## Case 19-13 (concluded)

Note that the options outstanding for only part of the reporting period are included in the denominator on a time-weighted basis. For the 1.5 million options *granted* during the year, the denominator would include the appropriate *incremental* shares x the appropriate time-weighting fraction. Likewise, for the options *exercised* during the year, the weighted average shares should include (a) the appropriate *incremental* shares x the appropriate time-weighting fraction for the period prior to actual exercise and (b) the appropriate *actual* shares issued x the appropriate time-weighting fraction for the period after the exercise.

# Real World Case 19-14

## Requirement 1

The note indicates that "diluted net loss per common share is computed using the weighted average number of common and dilutive common equivalent shares outstanding during the period." Securities like stock options or convertible bonds, while not being common stock, may become common stock through their exercise or conversion. As a result, they may dilute (reduce) earnings per share and therefore are called "potential common shares." Diluted EPS incorporates the dilutive effect of all potential common shares.

## Requirement 2

In fiscal 2004, Sun would have added 30 million potential common shares to the "basic weighted average shares outstanding to compute the diluted weighted average shares outstanding" for its 603 million stock options. To include the dilutive effect of a security means to calculate EPS *as if* the potential increase in shares already has occurred, even though it hasn't yet. Therefore, for its stock options Sun "pretends" the options have been exercised. Specifically, it assumed the options were exercised at the beginning of the reporting period, or when the options were issued if that's later. Sun assumed the cash proceeds from selling the new shares at the exercise price were used to buy back as many shares as possible at the shares' average market price during the year. The net difference, shares issued (603 million) minus shares repurchased, was 30 million shares, so the shares assumed repurchased must have been 573 million.

## Requirement 3

In fiscal 2004, Sun does not include dilutive potential common shares from employee stock options. The reason is stated in the disclosure note: "due to our net loss, .... their inclusion would have been anti-dilutive. If Sun had included the 30 million dilutive potential common shares from employee stock options, the loss per share would have declined from ($.118) to ($.117), ($388) / [3,277 + 30]. Whenever a company reports a net loss, as Sun did, it reports a loss per share. In that situation, stock options that otherwise are dilutive will be antidilutive. The *loss* per share *declines*. This represents an *increase* in performance – not a dilution of performance. The options would be considered antidilutive, then, and not included in the calculation of the net loss per share.

# Real World Case 19-15

## Requirement 1

Meg's questions imply that she thinks you will get cash dividends of 26 cents share. Earnings per share, though, is a way to summarize the performance o business enterprises into a single number. It is simply earnings expressed on a pe share basis. It does not imply anything about cash dividends. Whether some, all, o none of the earnings are distributed depends on the company's reinvestmen strategy. A dividend payout ratio expresses the percentage of earnings that i distributed to shareholders as dividends.

## Requirement 2

The press release says, "Earnings per share for the prior-year period have beer adjusted to reflect the company's three-for-two stock split distributed in Ma 2004." When calculating earnings per share, shares outstanding prior to a stocl split (or stock dividend) are retroactively restated to reflect the increase in share (50% in this instance). That is, it is treated as if the May split occurred at the beginning of the year. When reported again for comparison purposes in the comparative income statements, the year earlier figure also would be restated to reflect the 3-for-2 stock split. Otherwise we would be comparing apples and oranges.

## Requirement 3

The press release indicates that Sonic may repurchase up to $60 million of its stock. If the number of shares changes, it's necessary to find the weighted average of the shares outstanding during the period the earnings were generated. If shares are reacquired during a period (either retired or as treasury stock), Sonic wil reduce the weighted-average number of shares. The company time-weights the number of reacquired shares for the fraction of the year they were not outstanding prior to subtracting from the number of shares outstanding during the period.

## Requirement 4

Yes, it is. If we don't take into account the dilutive effect of the share increase we might mislead investors and creditors. So, in addition to basic EPS, we also calculate diluted EPS to include the dilutive effect of options and other potential common shares. This means to calculate EPS as if the potential increase in shares already has occurred (even though it hasn't yet). For Sonic's stock options, the calculation assumes the options were exercised at the beginning of the reporting period. Then the cash proceeds from selling the new shares are used to buy back as many shares as possible at the shares' average market price during the year.

# Chapter 20 — Accounting Changes and Error Corrections

## QUESTIONS FOR REVIEW OF KEY TOPICS

### Question 20-1
Accounting changes are categorized as:
1. Changes in **principle** (when companies switch from one acceptable accounting method to another)
2. Changes in **estimate** (when new information causes companies to revise estimates made previously)
3. Changes in **reporting entity** (the group of companies comprising the reporting entity changes)

### Question 20-2
Accounting changes can be accounted for:
1. Retrospectively (prior years revised),

or 2. Prospectively (only current and future years affected).

### Question 20-3
In general, we report voluntary changes in accounting principles retrospectively. This means revising all previous period's financial statements as if the new method were used in those periods. In other words, for each year in the comparative statements reported, we revise the balance of each account affected. Specifically, we make those statements appear as if the newly adopted accounting method had been applied all along. Also, if retained earnings is one of the accounts whose balance requires adjustment (and it usually is), we revise the beginning balance of retained earnings for the earliest period reported in the comparative statements of shareholders' equity (or statements of retained earnings if they're presented instead). Then we create a journal entry to adjust all account balances affected as of the date of the change. In the first set of financial statements after the change, a disclosure note would describe the change and justify the new method as preferable. It also would describe the effects of the change on all items affected, including the fact that the retained earnings balance was revised in the statement of shareholders' equity.

# Question 20-4

Lynch should report its change in depreciation method as a change in estimate, rather than as a change in accounting principle. This is because a change in depreciation method is considered a change in accounting estimate reflected by a change in accounting principle. In other words, a change in the depreciation method is adopted to reflect a change in (a) estimated future benefits from the asset, (b) the pattern of receiving those benefits, or (c) the company's knowledge about those benefits. The effect of the change in depreciation method is inseparable from the effect of the change in accounting estimate. Such changes frequently are related to the ongoing process of obtaining new information and revising estimates and, accordingly, are actually changes in estimates not unlike changing the estimated useful life of a depreciable asset. Logically, the two events should be reported the same way.

Accordingly, Lynch reports the change prospectively; previous financial statements are not revised. Instead, the company simply employs the straight-line method from then on. The undepreciated cost remaining at the time of the change would be depreciated straight-line over the remaining useful life. A disclosure note should justify that the change is preferable and describe the effect of a change on any financial statement line items and per share amounts affected for all periods reported.

# Question 20-5

In general, we report voluntary changes in accounting principles retrospectively. This means Sugarbaker will revise all previous period's financial statements, including 2005, as if the average cost method always had been used. Sugarbaker will revise cost of goods sold for 2005 as well as any other income statement amounts affected by that revision, including income taxes and net income.

Since the change affects income, retained earnings also changes. Sugarbaker reflects the cumulative prior year difference in cost of goods sold (after tax) as a difference in prior years' income and therefore in the balance in retained earnings. It also revises inventory in the balance sheet.

The company also will revise deferred taxes. Income tax effect is reflected in the deferred income tax asset because retrospectively decreasing accounting income, but not taxable income, creates a temporary difference between the two that will reverse over time as the unsold inventory becomes cost of goods sold. When that happens, taxable income will become lower than accounting income – a future deductible amount, creating a deferred tax asset. Recall from Chapter 16 that in the meantime, the temporary difference is reflected in the deferred tax asset.

*Answers to Questions (continued)*

## Question 20-6

Voluntary changes in accounting principles usually are reported retrospectively. We don't report changes in depreciation method that way, though, because such changes are considered to be *changes in estimate* and thus reported prospectively.

Also, it's not practicable to report some changes in principle retrospectively because insufficient information is available. Revising balances in prior years means knowing what those balances should be. For instance, suppose we're switching from the FIFO method of inventory costing to the LIFO method. Recall that LIFO inventory consists of "layers" added in prior years at costs existing in those years. So, if FIFO has been used, the company probably hasn't kept track of those costs. Accounting records of prior years typically are inadequate to report the change retrospectively, so a company changing to LIFO usually reports the change prospectively. The beginning inventory in the year the LIFO method is adopted becomes the base year inventory for all future LIFO calculations.

Another exception is when an FASB Statement or other authoritative pronouncement requires prospective application for specific changes in accounting methods. For example, when there's a change from the equity method to another method of accounting for long-term investments, APBO No. 18 requires the prospective application of the new method. From Chapter 12, recall that if an investor's level of influence over an investee changes, it may be necessary to change from the equity method to another method. This might happen if a sale of shares causes the investor's ownership interest to fall from, say, 20% to 10%, resulting in the equity method no longer being appropriate. In such a case, we make no adjustment to the carrying amount of the investment, but instead, simply discontinue the equity method and apply the new method applied from then on. The existing balance in the investment account when the equity method is discontinued serves as the new "cost" basis from then on.

## Question 20-7

Accounting records of prior years usually are inadequate to determine the cumulative income effect of the change for prior years when a company changes *to the LIFO inventory* method from another inventory method. For example, it would be necessary to make assumptions as to when specific LIFO inventory layers were created in years prior to the change. Accordingly, a company changing to LIFO generally does not revise the balance in retained earnings. Rather, the beginning inventory in the year the LIFO method is adopted becomes the base year inventory for all future LIFO calculations. A disclosure note would be included in the financial statements describing the nature of and justification for the change as well as an explanation as to why retrospective application was impracticable.

## Question 20-8

A change in estimate is accounted for prospectively. When a company revises an estimate previous financial statements are *not* revised. Rather, the company simply incorporates the new estimate in any related accounting determinations from then on. The unamortized cost remaining after three years would be amortized over the new estimate of the useful life. A disclosure note should describe the effect of a change in estimate on income before extraordinary items, net income and related per share amounts for the current period.

## Question 20-9

When it's not possible to distinguish between a change in principle and a change in estimate, the change should be treated as a change in estimate.

## Question 20-10

The situations deemed to constitute a change in reporting entity are (1) presenting consolidated financial statements in place of statements of individual companies and (2) changing the specific companies that comprise the group for which consolidated or combined statements are prepared.

## Question 20-11

Ford reported the situation as a change in reporting entity. This means recasting all previous period's financial statements as if the new reporting entity existed in those periods. In the first set of financial statements after the change, a disclosure note describes the nature of the change and the reason it occurred. Also, the effect of the change on net income, income before extraordinary items and related per share amounts is indicated for all periods presented.

## Question 20-12

When an error is discovered, previous years' financial statements that were incorrect as a result of the error are *retrospectively restated* to reflect the correction. Any account balances that currently are incorrect as a result of the error should be corrected by a journal entry. Also, if retained earnings is one of the accounts whose balance is incorrect, the correction is reported as a "*prior period adjustment*" to the beginning balance in a Statement of Shareholders' Equity (or Statement of Retained Earnings if that's presented instead). A *disclosure note* is needed also to describe the nature of the error and the impact of its correction on operations.

## Question 20-13

If merchandise inventory is understated at the end of 2005, that year's cost of goods sold would be overstated, causing 2005 net income to be understated. Because 2005 ending inventory is 2006 beginning inventory, the opposite effect on net income would occur in 2006. 2006 cost of goods sold would be understated, causing 2006 net income to be overstated by the same amount it was understated the year before.

# Answers to Questions (concluded)

## Question 20-14

The error would have caused the previous year's expenses to be *overstated*, and therefore its net income to be *understated*. Therefore, retained earnings would be *understated* as a result of the error. So, the correction to that account would be reported as a *"prior period adjustment"* (increase in this case) to the beginning retained earnings balance in the retained earnings column of the Statement of Shareholders' Equity.

## Question 20-15

During the two-year period, insurance expense would have been *overstated* by $30,000, so net income during the period was *understated* by $30,000. This means retained earnings is currently *understated* by that amount. During the two-year period, prepaid insurance would have been understated, and continues to be understated by $30,000. So, a correcting entry would debit prepaid insurance and credit retained earnings. Also, the financial statements that were incorrect as a result of the error would be *retrospectively restated* to report the prepaid insurance acquired and reflect the correct amount of insurance expense when those statements are reported again for comparative purposes in the current annual report. A *"prior period adjustment"* to retained earnings would be reported since retained earnings is one of the accounts incorrect as a result of the error. And, a *disclosure note* should describe the nature of the error and the impact of its correction on each year's net income, income before extraordinary items, and earnings per share.

## Question 20-16

If the error in the previous question is not discovered until the insurance coverage has expired, *no correcting entry at all would be needed*. By then, the sum of the omitted insurance expense amounts ($10,000 x 5 years) would equal the expense incorrectly recorded when the error occurred, so the retained earnings balance would be the same as if the error never had occurred. Also, the asset – prepaid insurance – would have expired so it also would not need to be recorded. Of course, any statements of prior years that were affected and are reported again in comparative statements still would be restated, and a footnote would describe the error.

# BRIEF EXERCISES

## Brief Exercise 20-1

**Requirement 1**

| To record the change: | ($ in millions) | |
|---|---|---|
| Retained earnings ............................................................................. | 8.2 | |
| Inventory ($32 million – 23.8 million)...................................... | | 8.2 |

**Requirement 2**

Carney applies the average cost method retrospectively; that is, to all prior periods as if it always had used that method. In other words, all financial statement amounts for individual periods that are included for comparison with the current financial statements are revised for period-specific effects of the change.

Then, the cumulative effects of the new method on periods prior to those presented are reflected in the reported balances of the assets and liabilities affected as of the beginning of the first period reported and a corresponding adjustment is made to the opening balance of retained earnings for that period. Let's say Carney reports 2006-2004 comparative statements of shareholders' equity. The $8.2 million adjustment above is due to differences prior to the 2006 change. The portion of that amount due to differences prior to 2004 is subtracted from the opening balance of retained earnings for 2004.

The effect of the change on each line item affected should be disclosed for each period reported as well as any adjustment for periods prior to those reported. Also, the nature of and justification for the change should be described in the disclosure notes.

## Brief Exercise 20-2

| To record the change: | ($ in millions) | |
|---|---|---|
| Inventory ($47.6 million – 64 million)........................................... | 16.4 | |
| Retained earnings ...................................................................... | | 16.4 |

# Brief Exercise 20-3

When a company changes *to the LIFO inventory* method from another inventory method, accounting records of prior years often are inadequate to determine the cumulative income effect of the change for prior years. For instance, it would be necessary to make assumptions as to when specific LIFO inventory layers were created in years prior to the change. So, a company changing *to* LIFO generally does not revise the balance in retained earnings. This is the case for Dorsey Markets. No entry is made. Instead, the beginning inventory in the year the LIFO method is adopted ($96 million for Dorsey) becomes the base year inventory for all future LIFO calculations. A disclosure note would be included in the financial statements describing the nature of and justification for the change as well as an explanation as to why retrospective application was impracticable.

# Brief Exercise 20-4

A change in depreciation method is considered a change in accounting estimate resulting from a change in accounting principle. In other words, a change in the depreciation method is similar to changing the economic useful life of a depreciable asset, and therefore the two events should be reported the same way. Accordingly, Irwin reports the change prospectively; previous financial statements are not revised. Instead, the company simply employs the straight-line method from then on. The undepreciated cost remaining at the time of the change would be depreciated straight-line over the remaining useful life.

|  | ($ in millions) |
|---|---|
| Asset's cost | $35.0 |
| Accumulated depreciation to date (calculated below) | (16.2) |
| Undepreciated cost, Jan. 1, 2006 | $18.8 |
| Estimated residual value | (2.0) |
| To be depreciated over remaining 7 years | $16.8 |
|  | 7   years |
| Annual straight-line depreciation 2006-12 | $ 2.4 |

## Calculation of SYD depreciation

$\dfrac{(10+9+8)}{55*}$ x [$35 -2] million) = $16.2 million

* $n (n = 1) \div 2 = 10 (11) \div 2 = 55$

## Adjusting entry (2006 depreciation):

|  | ($ in millions) |
|---|---|
| Depreciation expense (calculated above) ............................................. | 2.4 |
| Accumulated depreciation............................................................. | 2.4 |

# Brief Exercise 20-5

A change in depreciation method is considered a change in accounting estimate resulting from a change in accounting principle. In other words, a change in the depreciation method is similar to changing the economic useful life of a depreciable asset, and therefore the two events should be reported the same way. Accordingly, Irwin reports the change prospectively; previous financial statements are not revised. Instead, the undepreciated cost remaining at the time of the change would be depreciated by the sum-of-the-years'-digits method over the remaining useful life.

|  | ($ in millions) |
|---|---|
| Asset's cost | $35.0 |
| Accumulated depreciation to date (calculated below) | (9.9) |
| Undepreciated cost, Jan. 1, 2006 | $25.1 |
| Estimated residual value | (2.0) |
| To be depreciated over remaining 7 years | $23.1 |

## Calculation of straight-line depreciation to date

($35 -2) ÷ 10 years = $3.3 x 3 years = $9.9

## Adjusting entry (2006 depreciation):

|  | ($ in millions) |
|---|---|
| Depreciation expense (calculated below) ............................................... | 5.78 |
| Accumulated depreciation .............................................................. | 5.78 |

## Calculation of SYD depreciation

$\frac{7}{28*}$ x 23.1 million = $5.775 million

* n (n + 1) ÷ 2 = 7 (8) ÷ 2 = 28

# Brief Exercise 20-6

When an estimate is revised as new information comes to light, accounting for the change in estimate is quite straightforward. We do not recast prior years' financial statements to reflect the new estimate. Instead, we merely incorporate the new estimate in any related accounting determinations from there on. If the effect of the change in estimate is material, the effect on net income and earnings per share must be disclosed in a note, along with the justification for the change.

|  | ($ in millions) |
|---|---|
| Amortization expense (determined below).. | 5 |
| Patent ..................................................... | 5 |

## Calculation of annual amortization after the estimate change:

|  | ($ in millions) |  |
|---|---|---|
|  | $18 | Cost |
| $2 |  | Previous annual amortization ($18 ÷ 9 years) |
| x 4 years | 8 | Amortization to date (2002-2005) |
|  | $10 | Unamortized cost (balance in the patent account) |
|  | ÷ 2 | Estimated remaining life (6 years – 4 years) |
|  | $ 5 | New annual amortization |

# Brief Exercise 20-7

**To correct the error:**

| | | |
|---|---|---|
| Machinery ................................................................. | 65,000 | |
| Buildings ................................................................. | | 65,000 |

**Other step(s) that would be taken in connection with the error:**

When comparative balance sheets are reported that include 2005, the 2005 balance sheet would be restated to reflect the correction. A disclosure note should describe the error and the impact of its correction on each year's net income, income before extraordinary items, and earnings per share. In this case, because the machine was purchased at the end of 2005, depreciation in 2005 is correct and net income for 2005 is not impacted by the error.

# Brief Exercise 20-8

**Requirement 1**
    **Analysis:**

| | Correct<br>(Should Have Been Recorded) | | Incorrect<br>(As Recorded) |
|---|---|---|---|

| | | | | |
|---|---|---|---|---|
| 2003 | Equipment | 350,000 | | Expense | 350,000 |
| | Cash | | 350,000 | Cash | 350,000 |

2003   Expense     70,000         depreciation entry omitted
       Accum. deprec.     70,000

2004   Expense     70,000         depreciation entry omitted
       Accum. deprec.     70,000

2005   Expense     70,000         depreciation entry omitted
       Accum. deprec.     70,000

During the three year period, depreciation expense was *understated* by $210,000, but other expenses were *overstated* by $350,000, so net income during the period was *understated* by $140,000, which means retained earnings is currently *understated* by that amount.

During the three year period, accumulated depreciation was understated, and continues to be understated by $210,000.

**To correct incorrect accounts**
Equipment ......................................................... 350,000
    Accumulated depreciation ($70,000 x 3 years)        210,000
    Retained earnings ($350,000 – 140,000).......        140,000

# Brief Exercise 20-9

No correcting entry would be required because, after five years, the accounts would show appropriate balances.

# Brief Exercise 20-10

**Error a**

**1.**

**2005 Income Statement:** Expenses understated, net income overstated.
**2005 Balance Sheet:** Liabilities understated, retained earnings overstated.

| | ($ in millions) |
|---|---|
| Retained earnings................................................................. | 2 |
|     Wages expense ................................................................. | 2 |

**2.** The 2005 financial statements that were incorrect as a result of the error would be *retrospectively restated* to reflect the correct wages expense, (income tax expense if taxes are considered), net income, and retained earnings when those statements are reported again for comparative purposes in the 2006 annual report.

**3.** Because retained earnings is one of the accounts incorrectly stated accounts, the correction to that account is reported as a *prior period adjustment* to the 2006 beginning retained earnings balance in the comparative statements of shareholders' equity.

**4.** Also, a *disclosure note* should describe the nature of the error and the impact of its correction on each year's net income, income before extraordinary items, and earnings per share.

## Brief Exercise 20-10 (concluded)

## Error b

1. To include the $3 million in year 2006 purchases and increase retained earnings to what it would have been if 2005 cost of goods sold had not included the $3 million purchases.

```
Analysis:
            2005                              2006
     Beginning inventory             Beginning inventory
     Purchases            O          Purchases            U
     Less: Ending inventory
     Cost of goods sold   O

     Revenues
     Less: Cost of goods sold O               U = Understated
     Less: Other expenses                     O = Overstated
     Net income           U
       ↓
     Retained earnings    U
                                          ($ in millions)
Purchases ....................................     3
     Retained earnings .......................        3
```

2. The 2005 financial statements that were incorrect as a result of the error would be *retrospectively restated* to reflect the correct cost of goods sold, (income tax expense if taxes are considered), net income, and retained earnings when those statements are reported again for comparative purposes in the 2006 annual report.

3. Because retained earnings is one of the accounts incorrectly stated accounts, the correction to that account is reported as a *prior period adjustment* to the 2005 retained earnings balance in the comparative statements of shareholders' equity.

4. Also, a *disclosure note* should describe the nature of the error and the impact of its correction on each year's net income, income before extraordinary items, and earnings per share.

# EXERCISES

## Exercise 20-1
### Requirement 1

| January 1, 2006 | | ($ in millions) |
|---|---|---|
| Retained earnings............................................................... | | 30 |
| Inventory (cumulative effect) * ................................................ | | 30 |

| | **2005** | **2004** | **Total** |
|---|---|---|---|
| * Cost of goods sold (FIFO)......................................... | 40 | 38 | |
| Cost of goods sold (average) ...................................... | 56 | 52 | |
| Difference ................................................................. | 16 | 14 | **30** |

Since the cost of goods available for sale each period is the sum of the cost of goods *sold* and the cost of goods *unsold* (inventory), a $30 million difference ($16 + 14) in cost of goods sold due to using FIFO rather than Average means there also is a $30 million difference in inventory. The cumulative prior year difference in cost of goods sold is reflected as a difference in prior years' income and therefore the balance in retained earnings.

### Requirement 2

| COMPARATIVE INCOME STATEMENTS | | |
|---|---|---|
| ($ in millions) | **2006** | **2005** |
| Revenues | $420 | $390 |
| Cost of goods sold (average) | (62) | (56) |
| Operating expenses | (254) | (250) |
| Net income | $104 | $ 84 |

### Requirement 3

**Calculations** ($ in millions):

| | 2004 |
|---|---|
| Revenues | $380 |
| Cost of goods sold (FIFO) | (38) |
| Operating expenses | (242) |
| Net income | $100 |
| Dividends | (20) |
| Retained earnings, Jan. 1, 2004 | 0 |
| Retained earnings, Jan. 1, 2005 | $ 80 |

## Exercise 20-1 (concluded)

### Requirement 4

**Calculations** ($ in millions):

|  | 2004 | | |
|---|---|---|---|
|  | **FIFO** | **Average** | **Difference** |
| Revenues | $380 | $380 | |
| Cost of goods sold | (38) | (52) | |
| Operating expenses | (242) | (242) | |
| Net income | $100 | $ 86 | $14 |

### Comparative Statements of Shareholders' Equity (not required)

| ($ in millions) | Common Stock | Additional Paid-in Capital | Retained Earnings | Total Shareholders' Equity |
|---|---|---|---|---|
| **Jan. 1, 2005*** | | | 66 | |
| Net income | | | 84** | |
| Dividends | | | (20) | |
| **Jan. 1, 2006** | | | 130 | |
| Net income | | | 104** | |
| Dividends | | | (20) | |
| **Jan. 1, 2007** | | | 214 | |

\* Decreased from $80 million to $66 million to reflect the effect of the change in inventory methods.

**\*\*Calculations** ($ in millions):

|  | 2006 | 2005 |
|---|---|---|
| Revenues | $420 | $390 |
| Cost of goods sold (average) | (62) | (56) |
| Operating expenses | (254) | (250) |
| Net income | $104 | $ 84 |

# Exercise 20-2

## Requirement 1

| | |
|---|---:|
| Balance at January 1, 2006, using LIFO | $780,000 |

*Prior to 2006, using FIFO:*
Inventory would have been *higher* by $60,000, so
Cost of goods sold would have been *lower* by $60,000, so

| | | |
|---|---:|---:|
| Pretax income would have been *higher* by: | $60,000 | |
| Less: income tax at 40% | (24,000) | |
| Cumulative net income and thus retained earnings would have been *higher* by: | | 36,000 |
| Balance at January 1, 2006, using FIFO | | $816,000 |

## Requirement 2

### January 1, 2006

| | | |
|---|---:|---:|
| Inventory (additional inventory if FIFO had been used) ...................... | 60,000 | |
| Retained earnings (additional net income if FIFO had been used).. | | 36,000 |
| Deferred tax liability (40% x $60,000)....................................... | | 24,000 |

# Exercise 20-3

## Requirement 1

($ in millions)

| | | |
|---|---:|---:|
| Construction in process (additional amount due to the new method: $7 million + 3 million) ............................................. | 10 | |
| Deferred tax liability ($10 million x 40%)......................................... | | 4 |
| Retained earnings (difference) ....................................................... | | 6 |

Retained earnings is increased by $6 million because the net income in years prior to 2006 would have been higher by that amount.

## Requirement 2

| | 2006 | 2005 |
|---|---:|---:|
| Income before income taxes | $10.0 | $8.0 |
| Income tax expense (40%) | (4.0) | (3.2) |
| Net Income | $ 6.0 | $4.8 |

## Exercise 20-3 (continued)

### Requirement 3

Besides net income, which was reported in 2005 as $3 million ($5 million less tax) and now revised to $4.8 million, other amounts that would be revised to reflect accounting by the percentage - of - completion method are:

Earnings per share
Income tax expense (and income before income taxes)
Construction in process (and total assets)
Deferred tax liability (and total liabilities)
Retained earnings (and total shareholders' equity)

The reason for the adjustment to deferred tax liability requires some explanation. Remember from Chapter 16 that when taxable income is less than pretax accounting income because of a "temporary difference," a deferred tax liability is recorded. This liability reflects the tax that eventually will be paid when the difference later reverses and taxable income is higher than pretax accounting income. Here, construction income would have been higher during years prior to 2006 if accounting income had been based on the percentage-of-completion method. So, we need to increase the deferred tax liability from what it is now to what it would have been if percentage-of-completion had been used previously. Here's another way to view it. For financial reporting purposes, but not for tax, we are now retrospectively recognizing income not previously recorded under the earlier completed contract method. In a future year, when the contract is completed and that income is recognized for tax purposes, taxable income will be higher than accounting income. When taxable income will be higher than accounting income as a temporary difference reverses, we a have "future taxable amount," and record a deferred tax liability.

If we were switching the other way, from percentage-of-completion to the completed contract method, we would record a deferred tax asset instead. For financial reporting purposes, but not for tax, we would be retrospectively eliminating income previously recorded under the percentage-of-completion method. In a future year, when the contract is completed and that income is recognized for financial reporting purposes, accounting income will be higher than taxable income. When taxable income will be less than accounting income as a temporary difference reverses, we have a "future deductible amount" and record a deferred tax asset.

*Exercise 20-3 (concluded)*
**Requirement 4**

In the retained earnings column of the comparative statements of shareholders' equity, the beginning balance of 2005 retained earnings is revised to include any portion of the cumulative income effect attributable to years prior to 2005. The adjusted balance is then followed by any increases or decreases to retained earnings during the year (net income, dividends, etc.).

For example, if retained earnings had been reported at the end of 2004 as $9 million (reflecting the completed contract method) and dividends of $1 million were paid each year, retained earnings would be adjusted as follows (not required):

Long Island Construction Company
**Statement of Shareholders' Equity**
For the Years Ended Dec. 31, 2006 and 2005

($ in millions)

|  | Common Stock | Additional Paid-in Capital | Retained Earnings | Total Shareholders' Equity |
|---|---|---|---|---|
| **Balance at Jan. 1** |  |  | **13.2*** |  |
| Net income |  |  | 4.8 |  |
| Cash dividends |  |  | (1.0) |  |
| **Balance at Dec. 31, 2005** |  |  | **17.0** |  |
| Net income |  |  | 6.0 |  |
| Cash dividends |  |  | (1.0) |  |
| **Balance at Dec. 31, 2006** |  |  | **22.0** |  |

* $9 million increased by $4.2 million, the $7 million difference in income before 2005, less 40% income tax.

# Exercise 20-4

  EP         1. Change from declining balance depreciation to straight-line.

  E         2. Change in the estimated useful life of office equipment.

  E         3. Technological advance that renders worthless a patent with an unamortized cost of $45,000.

  PR        4. Change from determining lower of cost or market for inventories by the individual item approach to the aggregate approach.

  PR        5. Change from LIFO inventory costing to weighted-average inventory costing.

  E         6. Settling a lawsuit for less than the amount accrued previously as a loss contingency.

  R         7. Including in the consolidated financial statements a subsidiary acquired several years earlier that was appropriately not included in previous years.

  N *      8. Change by a retail store from reporting bad debt expense on a pay-as-you-go basis to the allowance method.

  PR        9. A shift of certain manufacturing overhead costs to inventory that previously were expensed as incurred to more accurately measure cost of goods sold. (Either method is generally acceptable.)

  E       10. Pension plan assets for a defined benefit pension plan achieving a rate of return in excess of the amount anticipated.

*Error correction: change from an unacceptable method to GAAP.

# Exercise 20-5

This is a change in accounting principle.

|  | ($ in millions) |
|---|---|
| Common stock ($1 par x 4 million shares retired) ........................ | 4 |
| Paid-in capital – excess of par (average amount above par at which the retired shares originally sold: $800 million.................. ÷ 200 million shares = $4; $4 x 4 million shares retired).............. | 16 |
| Retained earnings (difference) ..................................................... | 5 |
|     Treasury stock (cost of the shares retired) .............................. | 25 |

UMC applies the new way of reporting reacquired shares retrospectively; that is, to all prior periods as if it always had used that method. In other words, all financial statement amounts for individual periods affected by the change and that are included for comparison with the current financial statements are revised.

In each prior period reported, then, UMC would reduce Common stock by $4 million, Paid-in capital – excess of par by $16 million, Retained earnings by $5 million, and Treasury stock by $25 million.

The effect of the change on each line item affected should be disclosed for each period reported as well as any adjustment for periods prior to those reported. Also, the nature of and justification for the change should be described in the disclosure notes.

# Exercise 20-6

**Requirement 1**

|  | ($ in millions) |
|---|---|
| Investment in equity securities ($48 million – 31 million)........... | 17 |
|     Retained earnings (investment revenue from the equity method). | 17 |

**Requirement 2**

    Financial statements would be recast to reflect the equity method for each year reported for comparative purposes. A disclosure note also should describe the change, justify the switch, and indicate its effects on all financial statement items.

**Requirement 3**

    When a company changes *from* the equity method, *no adjustment* is made to the carrying amount of the investment. Instead, the equity method is simply discontinued, and the new method is applied from then on. The balance in the investment account when the equity method is discontinued would serve as the new "cost" basis for writing the investment up or down to market value in the next set of financial statements. There also would be no revision of prior years, but the change should be described in a disclosure note.

# Exercise 20-7

## Requirement 1

**To record the change:** ($ in millions)

Retained earnings (cost of goods sold higher; 2005 net income lower)    6

     Inventory (cost of goods sold higher; inventory lower)...............    6

## Requirement 2

Moulton is unable to apply the LIFO cost method retrospectively. It does, however, have sufficient information to apply the new method prospectively *beginning in 2005*. So, the company reports numbers for years beginning in 2005 as if it had carried forward the 2004 ending balance in inventory (measured on the FIFO inventory costing basis) and then had begun applying LIFO as of January 1, 2005.

A journal entry is needed to revise retained earnings and inventory to balances that would have resulted from using LIFO beginning in 2005 (requirement 1). Information available doesn't allow recording and reporting the cumulative effects of the new method on periods prior to 2005.

The effect of the change on each line item affected should be disclosed for each period reported. Also, the nature of and justification for the change should be described, as well as the reasons full retrospective application was impracticable.

## Requirement 3

| ($ in millions) | **2006** | **2005** | **2004** |
|---|---|---|---|
| Net income | $80 | $78 | $82 |
| | LIFO | LIFO (revised) | FIFO |

# Exercise 20-8

## Requirement 1

**To record the change:** ($ in millions)

Retained earnings ($23 million plus $7 million) .......................... 30

    Inventory (cost of goods sold higher; inventory lower) ............... 30

## Requirement 2

If it is impracticable to revise all specific years reported, a change is applied retrospectively as of the earliest year practicable. Wolfgang has information that would allow it to revise all assets and liabilities on the basis of LIFO for 2005 in its comparative statements, but not for 2004. So, the company should report 2005 statement amounts (revised) and 2006 statement amounts (reported for the first time) based on LIFO, but not revise 2004 numbers. Then, it should revise reported account balances retrospectively as of the beginning of 2005 since that's the earliest date it's practicable to do so.

A journal entry is needed at the beginning of 2006 to adjust retained earnings and inventory to balances that would have resulted from using LIFO all along. This is the cumulative income effects prior to 2005 ($23 million), plus the income effects of 2005 ($7 million).

The effect of the change on each line item affected should be disclosed for each period reported. Also, the nature of and justification for the change should be described, as well as the reasons full retrospective application was impracticable.

## Requirement 3

| ($ in millions) | 2006 | 2005 | 2004 |
|---|---|---|---|
| Net income | $90 | $87 | $92 |
| | LIFO | LIFO (revised) | FIFO |

# Exercise 20-9

## Requirement 1

In general, we report voluntary changes in accounting principles retrospectively. However, a change in depreciation method is considered a change in accounting estimate resulting from a change in accounting principle. In other words, a change in the depreciation method reflects a change in the (a) estimated future benefits from the asset, (b) the pattern of receiving those benefits, or (c) the company's knowledge about those benefits, and therefore the two events should be reported the same way. Accordingly, Clinton reports the change prospectively; previous financial statements are not revised. Instead, the company simply employs the straight-line method from now on. The undepreciated cost remaining at the time of the change would be depreciated straight-line over the remaining useful life. A disclosure note should justify that the change is preferable and describe the effect of the change on any financial statement line items and per share amounts affected for all periods reported.

## Requirement 2

| | |
|---|---|
| Asset's cost | $2,560,000 |
| Accumulated depreciation to date (given) | (1,650,000) |
| Undepreciated cost, Jan. 1, 2006 | $ 910,000 |
| Estimated residual value | (160,000) |
| To be depreciated over remaining 3 years | $ 750,000 |
| | 3 years |
| Annual straight-line depreciation 2006-5 | $ 250,000 |

## Adjusting entry:

| | | |
|---|---|---|
| Depreciation expense (calculated above)............................ | 250,000 | |
| Accumulated depreciation ...................................... | | 250,000 |

# Exercise 20-10

## Requirement 1

In general, we report voluntary changes in accounting principles retrospectively. However, a change in depreciation method is considered a change in accounting estimate resulting from a change in accounting principle. In other words, a change in the depreciation method reflects a change in the (a) estimated future benefits from the asset, (b) the pattern of receiving those benefits, or (c) the company's knowledge about those benefits, and therefore the two events should be reported the same way. Accordingly, Canliss reports the change prospectively; previous financial statements are not revised. Instead, the company simply employs the SYD method from now on. The undepreciated cost remaining at the time of the change would be depreciated by the SYD method over the remaining useful life (3 years). A disclosure note should justify that the change is preferable and describe the effect of the change on any financial statement line items and per share amounts affected for all periods reported.

## Requirement 2

| | |
|---|---|
| Asset's cost | $800,000 |
| Accumulated depreciation to date ($160,000 x 2) | (320,000) |
| To be depreciated over remaining 3 years | $ 480,000 |

2006 SYD depreciation: $\dfrac{3}{(3+2+1)}$ x $480,000 = $240,000

## Adjusting entry:

| | | |
|---|---|---|
| Depreciation expense (calculated above) .......................... | 240,000 | |
|     Accumulated depreciation ........................................ | | 240,000 |

## Not required:

2007 SYD depreciation: $\dfrac{2}{(3+2+1)}$ x $480,000 = $160,000

2008 SYD depreciation: $\dfrac{1}{(3+2+1)}$ x $480,000 = $80,000

# Exercise 20-11

1. d
2. b

# Exercise 20-12

## Requirement 1

### April 1, 2006

| | | |
|---|---|---|
| Cash........................................................................... | 36,000 | |
|    Receivable - royalty revenue ............................................ | | 31,000 |
|    Royalty revenue ................................................................... | | 5,000 |

### October 1, 2006

| | | |
|---|---|---|
| Cash........................................................................... | 40,000 | |
|    Royalty revenue ................................................................... | | 40,000 |

### December 31, 2006

| | | |
|---|---|---|
| Receivable - royalty revenue ............................................ | 50,000 | |
|    Royalty revenue ($500,000 x 10%) ........................................ | | 50,000 |

## Requirement 2

The fact that more royalty revenue was received in April than anticipated in December represents a change in estimate. No adjustments are made to any 2005 financial statements.

# Exercise 20-13

1. This is a change in estimate.

**To revise the liability on the basis of the new estimate:**
Liability - litigation ($1,000,000 – 600,000)................... 400,000
    Gain – litigation.......................................................             400,000

2. A disclosure note should describe the effect of a change in estimate on income before extraordinary items, net income, and related per-share amounts for the current period.

# Exercise 20-14

## Requirement 1

**Accrued liability and expense**
Warranty expense (3% x $3,600,000)............................................... 108,000
    Estimated warranty liability ...............................................         108,000

**Actual expenditures (summary entry)**
Estimated warranty liability ................................................. 88,000
    Cash, wages payable, parts and supplies, etc. ...................         88,000

## Requirement 2

**Actual expenditures (summary entry)**
Estimated warranty liability ($50,000 – $23,000) ..................... 27,000
Loss on product warranty (3% – 2%] x $2,500,000)................... 25,000
    Cash, wages payable, parts and supplies, etc. ...................         52,000*
        *(3% x $2,500,000) – $23,000 = $52,000

# Exercise 20-15

A deferred tax liability is established using the currently enacted tax rate for the year(s) a temporary difference is expected to reverse. In this case that rate was 40%. The change in the tax law in 2007 constitutes a change in estimate. The deferred tax liability is simply revised to reflect the new rate.

|  | ($ in millions) |
| --- | --- |
| Income tax expense (to balance) .............................................. | 10 |
| Deferred tax liability ($20 million x [40% – 30%])....................... | 2 |
| Income tax payable ($30 million x 40%)................................. | 12 |

When a company revises a previous estimate, prior financial statements are *not* revised. No adjustment is made to existing accounts. A disclosure note should describe the effect of a change in estimate on income before extraordinary items, net income, and related per-share amounts for the current period.

# Exercise 20-16

## Requirement 1

This is a change in accounting estimate.

## Requirement 2
When an estimate is revised as new information comes to light, accounting for the change in estimate is quite straightforward. We do not recast prior years' financial statements to reflect the new estimate. Instead, we merely incorporate the new estimate in any related accounting determinations from there on. If the after-tax income effect of the change in estimate is material, the effect on net income and earnings per share must be disclosed in a note, along with the justification for the change.

## Requirement 3

|  |  |  |
| --- | --- | --- |
|  | $800,000 | Cost |
| $160,000 |  | Old annual depreciation ($800,000 ÷ 5 years) |
| x 2 years | 320,000 | Depreciation to date (2004-2005) |
|  | 480,000 | Book value |
|  | ÷ 6 | New estimated remaining life (8 years - 2 years) |
|  | $ 80,000 | New annual depreciation |

# Exercise 20-17

## Requirement 1

Depreciation expense (determined below) .. 3,088
    Accumulated depreciation ................... 3,088

### Calculation of annual depreciation after the estimate change:

|  | $40,000 | Cost |
| $7,200 | | Old annual depreciation ($36,000 ÷ 5 years) |
| x 2 years | 14,400 | Depreciation to date (2004-2005) |
| | $25,600 | Book value |
| | 900 | Revised residual value |
| | $24,700 | Revised depreciable base |
| | ÷ 8 | Estimated remaining life (10 years - 2 years) |
| | $ 3,088 | New annual depreciation |

## Requirement 2

Depreciation expense (determined below) .. 3,889
    Accumulated depreciation................... 3,889

### Calculation of annual depreciation after the estimate change:

|  | $40,000 | Cost |
| | | Previous depreciation: |
| $12,000 | | 2004: ($36,000 x 5/15) |
| 9,600 | | 2005: ($36,000 x 4/15) |
| | 21,600 | Depreciation to date (2004-2005) |
| | $18,400 | Book value |
| | 900 | Revised residual value |
| | $17,500 | Revised depreciable base |
| | x 8/36* | Estimated remaining life - 8 years |
| | $ 3,889 | 2006 depreciation |

$$* n (n + 1) / 2 = 8 (9) / 2 = 36$$

# Exercise 20-18

## Requirement 1

The 2004 error caused 2004 net income to be *understated*, but since 2004 ending inventory is 2005 beginning inventory, 2005 net income was *overstated* the same amount. So, the income statement was misstated for 2004 and 2005, but the balance sheet (retained earnings) was incorrect only for 2004. After that, no account balances are incorrect due to the 2004 error.

**Analysis:**                                                U = Understated
                                                             O = Overstated

| **2004** | | | **2005** | |
|---|---|---|---|---|
| Beginning inventory | | → | Beginning inventory | U |
| Plus: net purchases | | ↑ | Plus: net purchases | |
| Less: ending inventory | U | → | Less: ending inventory | |
| Cost of goods sold | O | | Cost of goods sold | U |
| | | | | |
| Revenues | | | Revenues | |
| Less: cost of goods sold | O | | Less: cost of goods sold | U |
| Less: other expenses | | | Less: other expenses | |
| Net income | U | | Net income | O |
| ↓ | | | ↓ | |
| Retained earnings | U | | Retained earnings | ***corrected*** |

# Exercise 20-18 (concluded)

However, the 2005 error has not yet self-corrected. Both retained earnings and inventory still are overstated as a result of the second error.

<table>
<tr><td>**Analysis:**</td><td></td><td>U = Understated</td></tr>
<tr><td></td><td></td><td>O = Overstated</td></tr>
</table>

**2005**

| | |
|---|---|
| Beginning inventory | |
| Plus: net purchases | |
| Less: ending inventory | O |
| Cost of goods sold | U |
| | |
| Revenues | |
| Less: cost of goods sold | U |
| Less: other expenses | |
| Net income | O |
| ↓ | |
| Retained earnings | O |

## Requirement 2

| | | |
|---|---|---|
| Retained earnings (overstatement of 2005 income) ........................ | 150,000 | |
|     Inventory (overstatement of 2006 beginning inventory) .............. | | 150,000 |

## Requirement 3

The financial statements that were incorrect as a result of both errors (effect of one error in 2004 and effect of two errors in 2005) would be *retrospectively restated* to report the correct inventory amounts, cost of goods sold, income, and retained earnings when those statements are reported again for comparative purposes in the current annual report. A *"prior period adjustment"* to retained earnings would be reported, and a *disclosure note* should describe the nature of the error and the impact of its correction on each year's net income, income before extraordinary items, and earnings per share.

# Exercise 20-19

**1. Error discovered before the books are adjusted or closed in 2006.**

| | | |
|---|---|---|
| Investments ($100,000 – 80,000)............................................................ | 20,000 | |
|    Gain on sale of investments................................................. | | 20,000 |

**2. Error not discovered until early 2007.**

| | | |
|---|---|---|
| Investments ($100,000 – 80,000)............................................................ | 20,000 | |
|    Retained earnings............................................................... | | 20,000 |

# Exercise 20-20

## Requirement 1

The error caused both 2004 net income and 2005 net income to be *overstated*, s[ ]
retained earnings is overstated by a total of $85,000. Also, the note payable would b[ ]
*understated* by the same amount. Remember, the entry to record interest is:

| | | |
|---|---|---|
| Interest expense ............................................................................. | xxx | |
| Note payable (difference)........................................................... | xxx | |
|    Cash ................................................................................... | | xxx |

So, if interest expense is understated, the reduction in the note will be too much
causing the balance in that account to be understated.

## Requirement 2

| | | |
|---|---|---|
| Retained earnings (overstatement of 2004-05 income) ................. | 85,000 | |
|    Note payable (understatement determined above) ..................... | | 85,000 |

## Requirement 3

The financial statements that were incorrect as a result of the error would b[ ]
*retrospectively restated* to report the correct interest amounts, income, and retaine[ ]
earnings when those statements are reported again for comparative purposes in th[ ]
current annual report. A *"prior period adjustment"* to retained earnings would b[ ]
reported, and a *disclosure note* should describe the nature of the error and the impac[ ]
of its correction on each year's net income, income before extraordinary items, an[ ]
earnings per share.

# Exercise 20-21

1.  c
2.  a
3.  a

# Exercise 20-22

The 2006 interest expense is overstated by the extra interest recorded in February. Similarly, retained earnings is overstated the same amount because 2005 interest expense was understated when the accrued interest was not recorded.

**To correct the error:**

| | | |
|---|---:|---:|
| Retained earnings | 61,000 | |
|     Interest expense ($73,200 – $12,200*) | | 61,000 |

**2006 adjusting entry:**

| | | |
|---|---:|---:|
| Interest expense ($5/6$ x $73,200) | 61,000 | |
|     Discount on bonds payable ($5/6$ x $1,200) | | 1,000 |
|     Interest payable ($5/6$ x $72,000) | | 60,000 |

***ENTRIES THAT SHOULD HAVE BEEN RECORDED:***

**2005 adjusting entry:**

| | | |
|---|---:|---:|
| Interest expense ($5/6$ x $73,200) | 61,000 | |
|     Discount on bonds payable ($5/6$ x $1,200) | | 1,000 |
|     Interest payable ($5/6$ x $72,000) | | 60,000 |

**February 1, 2006:**

| | | |
|---|---:|---:|
| Interest expense ($1/6$ x $73,200) | 12,200 | |
| Interest payable ($5/6$ x $72,000) | 60,000 | |
|     Discount on bonds payable ($1/6$ x $1,200) | | 200 |
|     Cash ( given) | | 72,000 |

# Exercise 20-23

## Error a

**Income Statement:**  Expenses understated, net income overstated.
**Balance Sheet:**  Liabilities understated, retained earnings overstated.

| | | |
|---|---|---|
| Retained earnings ................................................................. | 1,800 | |
|    Office supplies expense ................................................... | | 1,800 |

## Error b

**Income Statement:**  Revenue overstated, net income overstated.
**Balance Sheet:**  Liabilities understated, retained earnings overstated.

| | | |
|---|---|---|
| Retained earnings ................................................................. | 90,000 | |
|    Rent revenue.................................................................... | | 90,000 |

## Error c

**Income Statement:**  Revenue understated, net income understated.
**Balance Sheet:**  Assets understated, retained earnings understated.

| | | |
|---|---|---|
| Interest revenue .................................................................. | 8,000 | |
|    Retained earnings ............................................................. | | 8,000 |

# Exercise 20-24

U = understated
O = overstated
NE = no effect

| | Cost of Goods Sold | Net Income | Retained Earnings |
|---|---|---|---|
| 1. Overstatement of ending inventory | U | O | O |
| 2. Overstatement of purchases | O | U | U |
| 3. Understatement of beginning inventory | U | O | O |
| 4. Freight-in charges are understated | U | O | O |
| 5. Understatement of ending inventory | O | U | U |
| 6. Understatement of purchases | U | O | O |
| 7. Overstatement of beginning inventory | O | U | U |
| 8. Understatement of purchases + understatement of ending inventory by the same amount | NE | NE | NE |

# Exercise 20-25

_F_       1. Change from expensing extraordinary repairs to capitalizing the expenditures.

_C_       2. Change in the residual value of machinery.

_B_       3. Change from FIFO inventory costing to LIFO inventory costing.

_C_       4. Change in the percentage used to determine bad debts.

_A_       5. Change from LIFO inventory costing to FIFO inventory costing.

_B_       6. Change from reporting an investment by the equity method to another method due to a reduction in the percentage of shares owned.

_E_       7. Change in the composition of a group of firms reporting on a consolidated basis.

_D_       8. Change from sum-of-the-years'-digits depreciation to straight-line.

_A_       9. Change from the percentage-of-completion method by a company in the long-term construction industry.

_C_       10. Change in actuarial assumptions for a defined benefit pension plan.

# Exercise 20-26

1. **a.** Prior-period adjustments (error corrections) are to be accounted for through retained earnings, not the income statement. Thus, the beginning balance of retained earnings should be credited for revenue that was erroneously not accrued in a prior period. The amount of the credit at May 31, 2007 is $91,800 (2006 accrued interest revenue)..

2. **d.** A change in the liability is merely a change in an estimate; it is not a change in principle. A change in estimate should be accounted for prospectively, that is, in the current and future periods.

3. **c.** The correction of an error in the financial statements of a prior period is accounted for and reported as a prior-period adjustment and excluded from the determination of net income for the current period (SFAS 16, *Prior Period Adjustment*).

# PROBLEMS

## Problem 20-1
### Requirement 1

**To record the change:**

| | | |
|---|---|---|
| Inventory ($155,000 – $120,000) ................................................. | 35,000 | |
| Deferred tax liability ($35,000 x 40%) ................................ | | 14,000 |
| Retained earnings (net effect) ............................................. | | 21,000 |

Note: For financial reporting purposes, but not for tax, the company is retrospectivel _increasing_ accounting income, but not taxable income. This creates a temporar difference between the two that will reverse over time as the unsold inventory become cost of goods sold. When that happens, taxable income will be higher than accountin income. When taxable income will be higher than accounting income as a temporar difference reverses, we have a "future taxable amount" and record a deferred tax liability.

### Requirement 2

| COMPARATIVE INCOME STATEMENTS | | |
|---|---|---|
| | **2006** | **2005** |
| Income before taxes | $525,000 | $399,000* |
| Income tax expense (40%) | (210,000) | (159,600) |
| Net income | $315,000 | $239,400 |
| **Earnings per share:** | | |
| Earnings per common share | $3.15 | $2.39 |

*$400,000   less   1,000‡   =   $399,000   if FIFO had been used

‡ **Calculation of decrease in 2005 pretax income:**

| | | | |
|---|---|---|---|
| $160,000 – $124,000 = | $36,000 | increase in 2005 beginning inventory |
| $155,000 – $120,000 = | (35,000) | increase in 2005 ending inventory |
| ↑          ↑ | $ 1,000 | increase in cost of goods sold/ |
| FIFO      average | | decrease in income |

# Problem 20-2

**Requirement 1**

| | | |
|---|---|---|
| Construction in process (additional amount due to the new method) | 39,000 | |
|    Deferred tax liability ($39,000* x 40%)................................ | | 15,600 |
|    Retained earnings (difference) ............................................. | | 23,400 |

\* Since the method used for tax purposes cannot be changed retrospectively for *prior* years, the switch for financial reporting purposes will cause a temporary difference between taxable income and pretax financial income in prior years when the method of determining pretax financial income in those years is changed – regardless of whether the tax method is changed for *future* years or not. When the temporary difference reverses, taxable income will be higher than accounting income. When taxable income will be higher than accounting income as a temporary difference reverses, we have a "future taxable amount" and record a deferred tax liability.

Retained earnings is increased by $23,400 because the net income for 2004 and 2005 would have been higher by that amount, and net income increases retained earnings.

**Requirement 2**

| | 2006 | 2005 |
|---|---|---|
| Income before income taxes | $51,000 | $45,000 |
|    Income tax expense (40%) | (20,400) | (18,000) |
| Net Income | $30,600 | $27,000 |
| | | |
| *Earnings per share*: | | |
|    (50,000 shares) | $.61 | $.54 |

**Problem 20-2 (concluded)**

**Requirement 3**

Pyramid Construction Company
**Statement of Shareholders' Equity**
For the Years Ended Dec. 31, 2006 and 2005

| | Common Stock | Additional Paid-in Capital | Retained Earnings | Total Shareholders' Equity |
|---|---|---|---|---|
| **Balance at Jan. 1 *** | **50,000** | **180,000** | **54,000** | **284,000** |
| Net income | | | 27,000 | 27,000 |
| Cash dividends | | | (10,000) | (10,000) |
| **Balance at Dec. 31, 2005** | **50,000** | **180,000** | **71,000** | **301,000** |
| Net income | | | 30,600 | 30,600 |
| Cash dividends | | | (10,000) | (10,000) |
| **Balance at Dec. 31, 2006** | **50,000** | **180,000** | **91,600** | **321,600** |

* Retained earnings at the beginning of 2005 (end of 2004) is increased by $18,000 because the net income for 2004 would have been higher by that amount, and net income increases retained earnings.

# Problem 20-3

1. This is a change in accounting principle to be recorded ***retrospectively***.

|  | ($ in 000s) |
|---|---|
| Retained earnings ($3,550 – 3,140) ........................................... | 410 |
| Inventory (reduction to Average)............................................. | 410 |

Weihrich will recast its financial statements to appear as if the average method always had been used. It also will reduce retained earnings to the balance it would have had if the average method had been used previously; that is, by the cumulative income difference between the average and FIFO methods. Simultaneously, inventory is reduced to the balance it would have had if the average method had always been used. A disclosure note should justify that the change is preferable and describe the effect of the change on any financial statement line items and per share amounts affected for all periods reported.

2. This is a change in accounting principle to be recorded ***retrospectively***.

|  | ($ in 000s) |
|---|---|
| Inventory (increase to average cost)................................................. | 730 |
| Retained earnings ($3,550 – 2,820) ....................................... | 730 |

In its comparative 2006-2005 financial statements, Weihrich should report numbers for 2005 as if it had carried forward the 2004 ending balance in inventory (measured on the previous FIFO inventory costing basis) and then had begun applying LIFO as of January 1, 2005. There would be no adjustment to accounts for the cumulative income effect of not using LIFO prior to that.

3. This is a change in accounting principle that usually is reported ***prospectively***.

No entry is needed to record the change.

When a company changes *to the LIFO inventory method* from another inventory method, it usually does not report the change retrospectively. Instead, the base year inventory for all future LIFO calculations is the beginning inventory in the year the LIFO method is adopted. A footnote should describe the nature of and justification for the change as well as an explanation as to why retrospective application was impracticable.

# Problem 20-4

## Requirement 1

**To record the change:**

| | | |
|---|---|---|
| Retained earnings (net effect) ................................................. | 12,000 | |
| Deferred tax asset ($20,000 x 40%) .......................................... | 8,000 | |
| Inventory ($150,000 – $130,000) .............................................. | | 20,000 |

Note: For financial reporting purposes, but not for tax, the company is retrospectively *decreasing* accounting income, but not taxable income. This creates a temporary difference between the two that will reverse over time as the unsold inventory becomes cost of goods sold. When that happens, taxable income will be lower than accounting income. When taxable income will be lower than accounting income as a temporary difference reverses, we have a "future deductible amount" and record a deferred tax asset.

## Requirement 2

Rockwell will recast its financial statements to appear as if the average method always had been used. This will include reporting cost of goods sold in the income statement and inventory in the balance sheet for 2006 using the newly adopted average method.

*Average cost method cost of goods sold:*

| | | |
|---|---|---|
| Beginning inventory (5,000 units) | | $130,000 |
| Purchases: | | |
| 5,000 units @ $36 | $180,000 | |
| 5,000 units @ $40 | 200,000 | 380,000 |
| Cost of goods available for sale (15,000 units) | | 510,000 |
| Less ending inventory (below) | | (238,000) |
| Cost of goods sold | | **$272,000** |

*Cost of ending inventory:*

$$\text{Weighted average unit cost} = \frac{\$510,000}{15,000 \text{ units}} = \$34$$

Inventory: 7,000 units x $34 = **$238,000**

# Problem 20-5

## Requirement 1

### January 1, 2006

|  |  | ($ in millions) |
|---|---|---|
| Inventory (additional inventory if FIFO had been used) ...................... | | 20 |
| Retained earnings (additional net income if FIFO had been used).. | | 12* |
| Deferred tax payable (40% x $20 million)................................. | | 8 |

**\* Prior to 2006, using FIFO:**

Inventory would have been *higher* by $20, so
Cost of goods sold would have been *lower* by $20, so

| | |
|---|---|
| Pretax income would have been *higher* by: | $20 |
| Less: income tax at 40% | (8) |
| Cumulative net income and thus retained earnings would have been *higher* by: | $12 |

For financial reporting purposes, but not for tax, the company is retrospectively increasing accounting income, but not taxable income. This creates a temporary difference between the two that will reverse over time as the unsold inventory becomes cost of goods sold. When that happens, taxable income will be higher than accounting income. When taxable income will be higher than accounting income as a temporary difference reverses, we have a "future taxable amount" and record a deferred tax liability.

## Requirement 2

Net income, which was reported in 2005 as $28 million would be revised to $30 million in the 2006-2005 comparative income statements. Net income in 2006 would simply be reported at $36 million, the amount resulting from using the new method (FIFO). The comparative income statements and balance sheets also would be recast to reflect the balances as if the FIFO method had been used in prior years.

## Problem 20-5 (concluded)

**Requirement 3**

### Fantasy Fashions
### Statement of Shareholders' Equity
### For the Years Ended Dec. 31, 2006 and 2005

($ in millions)

| | Common Stock | Additional Paid-in Capital | Retained Earnings | Total Shareholders' Equity |
|---|---|---|---|---|
| **Balance at Jan. 1, 2005** | | | 250[1] | |
| Net income (revised to FIFO) | | | 30 [2] | |
| Cash dividends | | | (8) | |
| **Balance at Dec. 31, 2005** | | | 272 | |
| Net income (using FIFO) | | | 36 [2] | |
| Cash dividends | | | (8) | |
| **Balance at Dec. 31, 2006** | | | 300 | |

[1] $240 million plus the difference in net income before 2005: $250 - 240

[2] given

A disclosure note would describe the change and justify the new method as preferable. It also would describe the effects of the change on all items affected, including the fact that the January 1, 2005, balance in the statement of shareholders' equity was revised by $10 million due to the change from the LIFO to the FIFO method of accounting for inventories.

If three-year comparative statements were provided, it would be the balance in retained earnings at the beginning of *2004* that would be revised for any portion of the cumulative income effect attributable to years *prior to 2004*. Retained earnings is revised for the earliest year reported in the comparative statements.

# Problem 20-6

## Requirement 1

A change in depreciation method is considered a change in accounting estimate resulting from a change in accounting principle. In other words, a change in the depreciation method is similar to changing the economic useful life of a depreciable asset, and therefore the two events should be reported the same way. Accordingly, Faulkner reports the change prospectively; previous financial statements are not revised. Instead, the company simply employs the straight-line method from then on. The undepreciated cost remaining at the time of the change would be depreciated straight-line over the remaining useful life.

| | |
|---|---|
| Asset's cost | $21,000 |
| Accumulated depreciation (SYD) to date (given) | (6,000) |
| Undepreciated cost, Jan. 1, 2006 | $15,000 |
| Estimated residual value | (1,000) |
| To be depreciated over remaining 8 years | $14,000 |
| | 8    years |
| Annual straight-line depreciation 2006-13 | $ 1,750 |

**Adjusting entry (2006 depreciation):**

Depreciation expense (calculated above)................................................. 1,750

     Accumulated depreciation .......................................................... 1,750

A disclosure note should justify that the change is preferable and describe the effect of a change on any financial statement line items and per share amounts affected for all periods reported.

## Problem 20-6 (concluded)

### Requirement 2

If Faulkner switched to sum-of-the-years'-digits with 8 years remaining, i reports the change prospectively; previous financial statements are not revised Instead, the company employs the SYD method from then on. The undepreciated cos remaining at the time of the change would be depreciated by the SYD method ove the remaining useful life.

| | |
|---|---:|
| Asset's cost | $21,000 |
| Accumulated depreciation (S-L) to date (given) | (4,000) |
| Undepreciated cost, Jan. 1, 2006 | $17,000 |
| Estimated residual value | (1,000) |
| To be depreciated over remaining 8 years | $16,000 |
| x | 8 / 36* |
| SYD depreciation 2006 | $ 3,556 |

$$* \, n\,(n+1)\,/\,2 = 8\,(9)\,/\,2 = 36$$

### Adjusting entry (2006 depreciation):

| | | |
|---|---:|---:|
| Depreciation expense (calculated above) ............................................. | 3,556 | |
| Accumulated depreciation ......................................................... | | 3,556 |

A disclosure note should justify that the change is preferable and describe the effect of the change on any financial statement line items and per share amounts affected for all periods reported.

# Problem 20-7

**Requirement 1**

**Cost of mineral mine**:

| | |
|---|---|
| Purchase price | $1,600,000 |
| Development costs | 600,000 |
| | $2,200,000 |

**Depletion**:

$$\text{Depletion per ton} = \frac{\$2,200,000 - 100,000}{400,000 \text{ tons}} = \$5.25 \text{ per ton}$$

2006 depletion = $5.25 x 50,000 tons = **$262,500**

*2007 depletion:*

$$\text{Revised depletion rate} = \frac{(\$2,200,000 - 262,500) - 100,000}{487,500 - 50,000 \text{ tons}} = \$4.20$$

2007 depletion = $4.20 x 80,000 tons = **$336,000**

**Depreciation:**

*Structures:*

$$\text{Depreciation per ton} = \frac{\$150,000}{400,000 \text{ tons}} = \$.375 \text{ per ton}$$

2006 depreciation = $.375 x 50,000 tons = **$18,750**

2007 depreciation:

$$\text{Revised depreciation rate} = \frac{\$150,000 - 18,750}{487,500 - 50,000 \text{ tons}} = \$.30$$

2007 depreciation = $.30 x 80,000 tons = **$24,000**

© The McGraw-Hill Companies, Inc., 2007
20-49
*Solutions Manual, Vol.2, Chapter 20*

## Problem 20-7 (concluded)

*Equipment:*

Depreciation per ton $= \dfrac{\$80{,}000 - 4{,}000}{400{,}000 \text{ tons}} = \$.19$ per ton

2006 depreciation $= \$.19 \times 50{,}000$ tons $= \mathbf{\$9{,}500}$

2007 depreciation:

Revised depreciation rate $= \dfrac{(\$80{,}000 - 9{,}500) - 4{,}000}{487{,}500 - 50{,}000 \text{ tons}} = \$.152$

2007 depreciation $= \$.152 \times 80{,}000$ tons $= \mathbf{\$12{,}160}$

## Requirement 2

### Mineral mine:

| | | |
|---|---|---|
| Cost | | $ 2,200,000 |
| Less accumulated depletion: | | |
| 2006 depletion | $262,500 | |
| 2007 depletion | 336,000 | 598,500 |
| Book value, 12/31/07 | | **$1,601,500** |

### Structures:

| | | |
|---|---|---|
| Cost | | $ 150,000 |
| Less accumulated depreciation: | | |
| 2006 depreciation | $18,750 | |
| 2007 depreciation | 24,000 | 42,750 |
| Book value, 12/31/07 | | **$107,250** |

### Equipment:

| | | |
|---|---|---|
| Cost | | $ 80,000 |
| Less accumulated depreciation: | | |
| 2006 depreciation | $ 9,500 | |
| 2007 depreciation | 12,160 | 21,660 |
| Book value, 12/31/07 | | **$58,340** |

# Problem 20-8

a. This is a change in estimate.

---

No entry is needed to record the change

**2006 adjusting entry:**

| | | |
|---|---|---|
| Warranty expense (2% x $4,000,000) .................................... | 80,000 | |
| Estimated warranty liability ..................................... | | 80,000 |

---

If the effect is material, a disclosure note should describe the effect of a change in estimate on income before extraordinary items, net income, and related per share amounts for the current period.

b. This is a change in estimate.

---

No entry is needed to record the change

**2006 adjusting entry:**

| | | |
|---|---|---|
| Depreciation expense (determined below) ..................... | 45,000 | |
| Accumulated depreciation ...................................... | | 45,000 |

---

**Calculation of annual depreciation after the estimate change:**

| | | |
|---|---|---|
| | $1,000,000 | Cost |
| $25,000 | | Old depreciation ($1,000,000 ÷ 40 years) |
| x 3 yrs | (75,000) | Depreciation to date (2003-2005) |
| | $ 925,000 | Undepreciated cost |
| | (700,000) | New estimated salvage value |
| | $ 225,000 | To be depreciated |
| | ÷ 5 | Estimated remaining life (5 years: 2006-2010) |
| | $ 45,000 | New annual depreciation |

A disclosure note should describe the effect of a change in estimate on income before extraordinary items, net income, and related per share amounts for the current period.

## Problem 20-8 (continued)

c. This is a change in accounting principle that usually is reported prospectively.

> No entry is needed to record the change.

When a company changes **to the LIFO inventory method** from another inventory method, accounting records usually are insufficient to determine the cumulative income effect of the change necessary to retrospectively revise accounts. So, a company changing to LIFO usually reports the beginning inventory in the year the LIFO method is adopted ($690,000 in this case) as the base year inventory for all future LIFO calculations. The disclosure required is a footnote to the financial statements describing the nature of and justification for the change as well as an explanation as to why the retrospective application was impracticable.

d. This is a change in accounting estimate resulting from a change in accounting principle.

> No entry is needed to record the change
>
> **2006 adjusting entry:**
> Depreciation expense (determined below) ..................... 24,000
>     Accumulated depreciation .......................................     24,000

# Problem 20-8 (concluded)

A change in depreciation method is considered a change in accounting estimate resulting from a change in accounting principle. Accordingly, the Hoffman Group reports the change prospectively; previous financial statements are not revised. Instead, the company simply employs the straight-line method from now on. The undepreciated cost remaining at the time of the change is depreciated straight-line over the remaining useful life.

| | ($ in 000s) |
|---|---|
| Asset's cost | $330 |
| Accumulated depreciation to date (calculated below) | (162) |
| Undepreciated cost, Jan. 1, 2006 | $168 |
| Estimated residual value | (0) |
| To be depreciated over remaining 7 years | $168 |
| | 7 years |
| Annual straight-line depreciation 2006-12 | $ 24 |

**Calculation of SYD depreciation:**

$$\frac{(10+9+8)}{55} \times \$330,000) = \$162,000$$

e. This is a change in estimate.

---

**To revise the liability on the basis of the new estimate:**

| | | |
|---|---|---|
| Loss – litigation .................................................... | 150,000 | |
| Liability - litigation ($350,000 – 200,000)......................... | | 150,000 |

---

A disclosure note should describe the effect of a change in estimate on income before extraordinary items, net income, and related per share amounts for the current period.

f. This is a change in accounting principle accounted for prospectively.

Because the change will be effective only for assets placed in service after the date of change, the change doesn't affect assets depreciated in prior periods. The nature of and justification for the change should be described in the disclosure notes. Also, the effect of the change on the current period's financial statements should be disclosed.

# Problem 20-9

_P_ _R_ 1. By acquiring additional stock, Wagner increased its investment in Wise, Inc. from a 12% interest to 25% and changed its method of accounting for the investment from an available-for-sale investment to the equity method.

_N_ _P_ 2. Wagner instituted a postretirement benefit plan for its employees in 2006 and adopted SFAS No. 106, "Accounting for Postretirement Benefit Plans Other than Pensions." Wagner had not previously had such a plan.

_EP_ _P_ 3. Wagner changed its method of depreciating computer equipment from the SYD method to the straight-line method.

_X_ _R_ 4. Wagner determined that a liability insurance premium it both paid and expensed in 2005 covered the 2005-2007 period.

_P_ _R_ 5. Wagner custom-manufactures farming equipment on a contract basis. Wagner switched its accounting for these long-term contracts from the completed-contract method to the percentage-of-completion method.

_E_ _P_ 6. Due to an unexpected relocation, Wagner determined that its office building previously to be depreciated over 45 years should be depreciated over 18 years.

_E_ _P_ 7. Wagner offers a three-year warranty on the farming equipment it sells. Manufacturing efficiencies caused Wagner to reduce its expectation of warranty costs from 2% of sales to 1% of sales.

_P_ _R_ 8. Wagner changed from LIFO to FIFO to account for its materials and work in process inventories.

_P_ _R_ 9. Wagner changed from FIFO to average cost to account for its equipment inventory.

_X_ _R_ 10. Wagner sells extended service contracts on some of its equipment sold. Wagner performs services related to these contracts over several years, so in 2006 Wagner changed from recognizing revenue from these service contracts on a cash basis to the accrual basis.

# Problem 20-10

## Requirement 1

**Analysis:**                                   U = Understated
                                                O = Overstated

|  | **2004** |  | **2005** |  |
|---|---|---|---|---|
| Beginning inventory | | → | Beginning inventory | U-6,000 |
| Plus: Net purchases | | ↑ | Plus: Net purchases | U-3,000 |
| Less: Ending inventory | U-6,000 | | Less: Ending inventory | O-9,000 |
| Cost of goods sold | O-6,000 | | Cost of goods sold | U-18,000 |
| | | | | |
| Revenues | | | Revenues | |
| Less: Cost of goods sold | O-6,000 | | Less: Cost of goods sold | U-18,000 |
| Less: Other expenses | | | Less: Other expenses | |
| Net income | U-6,000 | | Net income | O-18,000 |
| ↓ | | | ↓ | |
| Retained earnings | U-6,000 | | Retained earnings | O-12,000 |

## Requirement 2

| | | |
|---|---|---|
| Retained earnings.................................... | 12,000 | |
| Inventory.............................................. | | 9,000 |
| Purchases.............................................. | | 3,000 |

## Requirement 3

The financial statements that were incorrect as a result of both errors (effect of one error in 2004 and effect of three errors in 2005) would be *retrospectively restated* to report the correct inventory amounts, cost of goods sold, income, and retained earnings when those statements are reported again for comparative purposes in the 2006 annual report. A prior period adjustment to retained earnings would be reported, and a *disclosure note* should describe the nature of the error and the impact of its correction on each year's net income, income before extraordinary items, and earnings per share.

# Problem 20-11

**Requirement 1**

>    **Analysis:**

| | **Correct**<br>(Should Have Been Recorded) | | **Incorrect**<br>(As Recorded) | |
|---|---|---|---|---|
| 2004 Equipment | 1,900,000 | | Equipment 2,000,000 | |
| Expense | 100,000 | | Cash | 2,000,000 |
| Cash | | 2,000,000 | | |
| | | | | |
| 2004 Expense | 475,000 [1] | | Expense | 500,000 [2] |
| Accum. deprec. | | 475,000 | Accum. deprec. | 500,000 |
| | | | | |
| 2005 Expense | 356,250 [3] | | Expense | 375,000 [4] |
| Accum. deprec. | | 356,250 | Accum. deprec. | 375,000 |

>    [1] $1,900,000 x 25% (2 times the straight-line rate of 12.5%)
>    [2] $2,000,000 x 25%
>    [3] ($1,900,000 - 475,000) x 25%
>    [4] ($2,000,000 - 500,000 ) x 25%

During the two-year period, depreciation expense was *overstated* by $43,750, but other expenses were *understated* by $100,000, so net income during the period was *overstated* by $56,250, which means retained earnings is currently *overstated* by that amount.

During the two-year period, accumulated depreciation was overstated, and continues to be overstated by $43,750.

**To correct incorrect accounts**

| | | |
|---|---|---|
| Retained earnings ................................................ | 56,250 | |
| Accumulated depreciation ................................. | 43,750 | |
| Equipment........................................................ | | 100,000 |

## Problem 20-11 (concluded)

### Requirement 2

This is a change in accounting estimate resulting from a change in accounting principle.

No entry is needed to record the change

**2006 adjusting entry:**
Depreciation expense (determined below) ...................... 178,125
    Accumulated depreciation ....................................... 178,125

A change in depreciation method is considered a change in accounting estimate resulting from a change in accounting principle. Accordingly, the Collins Corporation reports the change prospectively; previous financial statements are not revised. Instead, the company simply employs the straight-line method from now on. The undepreciated cost remaining at the time of the change is depreciated straight-line over the remaining useful life.

| | |
|---|---:|
| Asset's cost (after correction) | $1,900,000 |
| Accumulated depreciation to date ($475,000 + 356,250) | (831,250) |
| Undepreciated cost, Jan. 1, 2006 | $1,068,750 |
| Estimated residual value | (0) |
| To be depreciated over remaining 6 years | $1,068,750 |
| | 6   years |
| Annual straight-line depreciation 2006-11 | $ 178,125 |

# Problem 20-12

a. This is a correction of an error.

> **To correct the error:**
> Prepaid insurance ($35,000 ÷ 5 yrs x 3 yrs: 2006-2008) ............ 21,000
>     Retained earnings* .................................................................... 21,000
>        *$35,000 – [$35,000 ÷ 5 years x 2 years: 2004-05]
>
> **2006 adjusting entry:**
> Insurance expense ($35,000 ÷ 5 years) ..................................... 7,000
>     Prepaid insurance ....................................................... 7,000

    The financial statements that were incorrect as a result of the error would be *retrospectively restated* to report the prepaid insurance acquired and reflect the correct amount of insurance expense when those statements are reported again for comparative purposes in the current annual report. A *"prior period adjustment"* to retained earnings would be reported, and a *disclosure note* should describe the nature of the error and the impact of its correction on each year's net income, income before extraordinary items, and earnings per share.

b. This is a change in estimate.

> No entry is needed to record the change
>
> **2006 adjusting entry:**
> Depreciation expense (determined below) .......................... 15,000
>     Accumulated depreciation ............................................. 15,000

## Calculation of annual depreciation after the estimate change:

|  | $600,000 | Cost |
|---|---|---|
| $12,500 |  | Old depreciation ([$600,000 – $100,000] ÷ 40 years) |
| x 10 yrs | (125,000) | Depreciation to date (1996-2005) |
|  | $475,000 | Undepreciated cost |
|  | (25,000) | New estimated salvage value |
|  | $450,000 | To be depreciated |
|  | ÷ 30 | Estimated remaining life (40 years – 10 years) |
|  | $ 15,000 | New annual depreciation |

*Problem 20-12 (continued)*

A disclosure note should describe the effect of a change in estimate on income before extraordinary items, net income, and related per share amounts for the current period.

c. This is a correction of an error.

| | | |
|---|---|---|
| **To correct the error:** | | |
| Retained earnings ................................................................ | 25,000 | |
| Inventory .............................................................................. | | 25,000 |

The financial statements that were incorrect as a result of the error would be *retrospectively restated* to report the correct inventory amounts, cost of goods sold, and retained earnings when those statements are reported again for comparative purposes in the current annual report. A *"prior period adjustment"* to retained earnings would be reported, and a *disclosure note* should describe the nature of the error and the impact of its correction on each year's net income, income before extraordinary items, and earnings per share.

d. This is a change in accounting principle and is reported retrospectively.

| | | |
|---|---|---|
| **To record the change:** | | |
| Inventory (given) ................................................................. | 960,000 | |
| Retained earnings ............................................................... | | 960,000 |

Most changes in accounting principle are accounted for retrospectively. Prior years' financial statements are recast to reflect the use of the new accounting method. The company should increase retained earnings to the balance it would have been if the FIFO method had been used previously; that is, by the cumulative income difference between the LIFO and FIFO methods. Simultaneously, inventory is increased to the balance it would have been if the FIFO method had always been used. A disclosure note should justify that the change is preferable and describe the effect of the change on any financial statement line items and per share amounts affected for all periods reported.

## Problem 20-12 (continued)

e. This is a correction of an error.

> **To correct the error:**
> Retained earnings ........................................................... 15,500
>     Compensation expense ...........................................           15,500

The 2005 financial statements that were incorrect as a result of the error would be *retrospectively restated* to report the correct compensation expense, net income and retained earnings when those statements are reported again for comparative purposes in the current annual report. A *"prior period adjustment"* to retained earnings would be reported, and a *disclosure note* should describe the nature of the error and the impact of its correction on each year's net income, income before extraordinary items, and earnings per share.

f. This is a change in estimate resulting from a change in accounting principle and is accounted for prospectively.

> No entry is needed to record the change
>
> **2006 adjusting entry:**
> Depreciation expense (calculated below) ............................... 57,600
>     Accumulated depreciation .............................................           57,600

A change in depreciation method is considered a change in accounting estimate resulting from a change in accounting principle. Accordingly, the Williams-Santana reports the change prospectively; previous financial statements are not revised. Instead, the company simply employs the straight-line method from now on. The undepreciated cost remaining at the time of the change is depreciated straight-line over the remaining useful life.

| | |
|---|---:|
| Undepreciated cost, Jan. 1, 2006 (given) | $460,800 |
| Estimated residual value | (0) |
| To be depreciated over remaining 8 years | $460,800 |
| | 8   years |
| Annual straight-line depreciation 2006-13 | $ 57,600 |

*Problem 20-12 (concluded)*

g.  This is a change in estimate.

---

No entry is needed to record the change

**2006 adjusting entry:**
Bad debt expense (.75% x $4,000,000) .............................. 30,000
    Allowance for uncollectible accounts .........................           30,000

---

If the effect is material, a disclosure note should describe the effect of a change in estimate on income before extraordinary items, net income, and related per share amounts for the current period.

h.  This is a correction of an error.

---

**To correct the error:**
Equipment (cost) ................................................................. 1,000,000
    Accumulated depreciation ([$1,000,000 ÷ 10] x 3 years)....     300,000
    Retained earnings ($1,000,000 – [$100,000 x 3 years])..........     700,000

**2006 adjusting entry:**
Depreciation expense ($1,000,000 ÷ 10) ............................. 100,000
    Accumulated depreciation .............................................     100,000

---

The financial statements that were incorrect as a result of the error would be *retrospectively restated* to report the correct depreciation, assets, and retained earnings when those statements are reported again for comparative purposes in the current annual report.  A *"prior period adjustment"* to retained earnings would be reported, and a *disclosure note* should describe the nature of the error and the impact of its correction on each year's net income, income before extraordinary items, and earnings per share.

# Problem 20-13

a. This is a correction of an error.

> **To correct the error:**
> Prepaid insurance ($35,000 ÷ 5 yrs x 3 yrs: 2006-2008) ........... 21,000
>     Income tax payable ($21,000 x 40%) .............................          8,400
>     Retained earnings* ..........................................      12,600
>       *($35,000 – [$35,000 ÷ 5 years x 2 years: 2004-05]) less $8,400 tax
>
> **2006 adjusting entry:**
> Insurance expense ($35,000 ÷ 5 years) ..................................... 7,000
>     Prepaid insurance ........................................................      7,000

The financial statements that were incorrect as a result of the error would be *retrospectively restated* to report the prepaid insurance acquired and reflect the correct amount of insurance expense when those statements are reported again for comparative purposes in the current annual report. A *"prior period adjustment"* to retained earnings would be reported, and a *disclosure note* should describe the nature of the error and the impact of its correction on each year's net income, income before extraordinary items, and earnings per share.

b. This is a change in estimate.

> No entry is needed to record the change
>
> **2006 adjusting entry:**
> Depreciation expense (determined below) ......................... 15,000
>     Accumulated depreciation ..............................................    15,000

**Calculation of annual depreciation after the change:**

|  | $600,000 | Cost |
|---|---|---|
| $12,500 |  | Old depreciation ([$600,000 – $100,000] ÷ 40 years) |
| x 10 yrs | (125,000) | Depreciation to date (1996-2005) |
|  | $475,000 | Undepreciated cost |
|  | (25,000) | New estimated salvage value |
|  | $450,000 | To be depreciated |
|  | ÷ 30 | Estimated remaining life (40 years – 10 years) |
|  | $ 15,000 | New annual depreciation |

*Problem 20-13 (continued)*

A disclosure note should describe the effect of a change in estimate on income before extraordinary items, net income, and related per share amounts for the current period.

c. This is a correction of an error.

| | | |
|---|---|---|
| **To correct the error:** | | |
| Retained earnings (net effect) ........................................ | 15,000 | |
| Refund - income tax ($25,000 x 40%) ............................ | 10,000 | |
| Inventory ....................................................................... | | 25,000 |

The financial statements that were incorrect as a result of the error would be *retrospectively restated* to report the correct inventory amounts, cost of goods sold, and retained earnings when those statements are reported again for comparative purposes in the current annual report. A *"prior period adjustment"* to retained earnings would be reported, and a *disclosure note* should describe the nature of the error and the impact of its correction on each year's net income, income before extraordinary items, and earnings per share.

d. This is a change in accounting principle and is reported retrospectively.

| | | |
|---|---|---|
| **To record the change:** | | |
| Inventory (given) ............................................................. | 960,000 | |
| Deferred tax liability ($960,000 x 40%) ............................ | | 384,000 |
| Retained earnings (net effect) ......................................... | | 576,000 |

Most changes in accounting principle are accounted for retrospectively. Prior years' financial statements are recast to reflect the use of the new accounting method. The company should increase retained earnings to the balance it would have been if the FIFO method had been used previously; that is, by the cumulative net income difference between the LIFO and FIFO methods. Simultaneously, inventory is increased to the balance it would have been if the FIFO method had always been used. A disclosure note should justify that the change is preferable and describe the effect of the change on any financial statement line items and per share amounts affected for all periods reported.

## Problem 20-13 (continued)

For financial reporting purposes, but not for tax, the company is retrospectively *increasing* accounting income, but not taxable income. This creates a temporary difference between the two that will reverse over time as the unsold inventory becomes cost of goods sold. When that happens, taxable income will be higher than accounting income. When taxable income will be higher than accounting income as a temporary difference reverses, we have a "future taxable amount" and record a deferred tax liability.

e. This is a correction of an error.

| | | |
|---|---|---|
| **To correct the error:** | | |
| Retained earnings (net effect) ........................................................ | 9,300 | |
| Refund - income tax ($15,500 x 40%) ..................................... | 6,200 | |
|     Compensation expense ........................................................... | | 15,500 |

The 2005 financial statements that were incorrect as a result of the error would be *retrospectively restated* to report the correct compensation expense, net income, and retained earnings when those statements are reported again for comparative purposes in the current annual report. A *"prior period adjustment"* to retained earnings would be reported, and a *disclosure note* should describe the nature of the error and the impact of its correction on each year's net income, income before extraordinary items, and earnings per share.

## Problem 20-13 (continued)

f. This is a change in estimate resulting from a change in accounting principle and is accounted for prospectively.

---

No entry is needed to record the change

**2006 adjusting entry:**
Depreciation expense (calculated below) ................................. 57,600
    Accumulated depreciation ...........................................     57,600

---

    A change in depreciation method is considered a change in accounting estimate resulting from a change in accounting principle. Accordingly, the Williams-Santana reports the change prospectively; previous financial statements are not revised. Instead, the company simply employs the straight-line method from now on. The undepreciated cost remaining at the time of the change is depreciated straight-line over the remaining useful life.

| | |
|---|---:|
| Undepreciated cost, Jan. 1, 2006 (given) | $460,800 |
| Estimated residual value | (0) |
| To be depreciated over remaining 8 years | $460,800 |
| | 8 years |
| Annual straight-line depreciation 2006-13 | $ 57,600 |

g. This is a change in estimate.

---

No entry is needed to record the change.

**2006 adjusting entry:**
Bad debt expense (.75% x $4,000,000) ................................. 30,000
    Allowance for uncollectible accounts .........................     30,000

---

    If the effect is material, a disclosure note should describe the effect of a change in estimate on income before extraordinary items, net income, and related per share amounts for the current period.

## Problem 20-13 (concluded)

h. This is a correction of an error.

---

**To correct the error:**

| | | |
|---|---:|---:|
| Equipment (cost) ............................................................. | 1,000,000 | |
|     Accumulated depreciation ([$1,000,000 ÷ 10] x 3 years) .... | | 300,000 |
|     Deferred tax liability ([$1,000,000 - $300,000] x 40%) ....... | | 280,000 |
|     Retained earnings | | |
|       ($1,000,000 – [$100,000 x 3 years]) less $280,000 tax ........... | | 420,000 |

**2006 adjusting entry:**

| | | |
|---|---:|---:|
| Depreciation expense ($1,000,000 ÷ 10) ............................. | 100,000 | |
|     Accumulated depreciation............................................. | | 100,000 |

---

The financial statements that were incorrect as a result of the error would be *retrospectively restated* to report the correct depreciation, assets, and retained earnings when those statements are reported again for comparative purposes in the current annual report. A *"prior period adjustment"* to retained earnings would be reported, and a *disclosure note* should describe the nature of the error and the impact of its correction on each year's net income, income before extraordinary items, and earnings per share.

# Problem 20-14
## Requirement 1
**a.**
|  |  | ($ in millions) |
|---|---|---|
| Inventory (understatement of 2006 beginning inventory)............... | 10 | |
|    Retained earnings (understatement of 2005 income) ................ | | 10 |

Note: The 2004 error requires no adjustment because it has self-corrected by 2006.

**b.**
|  |  |  |
|---|---|---|
| Liability – litigation (original estimate)........................................ | 7 | |
|    Gain – litigation ($7 million – 4 million)..................................... | | 3 |
|    Cash (actual settlement) ................................................................. | | 4 |

**c.**
|  |  |  |
|---|---|---|
| Retained earnings (2004-05 patent amortization) ........................... | 6 | |
|    Patent ([$18 million ÷ 6 yrs.] x 2)............................................... | | 6 |

**2006 adjusting entry:**
|  |  |  |
|---|---|---|
| Patent amortization expense ($18 million ÷ 6 years)  ............... | 3 | |
|    Patent ........................................................................................... | | 3 |

**d.**
No entry to record the change

**2006 adjusting entry:**
|  |  |  |
|---|---|---|
| Depreciation expense (determined below) ............................... | 4 | |
|    Accumulated depreciation ................................................. | | 4 |

### Calculation of annual depreciation after the change:

| | |
|---|---|
| $30 | Cost |
| (18) | Previous depreciation (calculated below*) |
| $12 | Undepreciated cost |
| (0) | Estimated residual value |
| $12 | To be depreciated |
| ÷ 3 yrs | Estimated remaining life |
| $ 4 | New annual depreciation |

**\*SYD:**
| | | |
|---|---|---|
| 2004 depreciation | $10 | ($30 x $5/15$) |
| 2005 depreciation | 8 | ($30 x $4/15$) |
| Accumulated depreciation | $18 | |

## Problem 20-14 (concluded)

### Requirement 2

|  | Assets | Liabilities | Shareholders' Equity | Net Income | Expenses |
|---|---|---|---|---|---|
| **2004** | $740 | $330 | $410 | $210 | $150 |
| 2004 inventory | (12) |  | (12) | (12) | 12 |
| Loss contingency |  | no adjustments to prior years |  |  |  |
| Patent amortization | (3) |  | (3) | (3) | 3 |
| Depreciation |  | no adjustments to prior years |  |  |  |
|  | $725 | $330 | $395 | $195 | $165 |
| **2005** | $820 | $400 | $420 | $230 | $175 |
| 2004 inventory |  |  |  | 12 | (12) |
| 2005 inventory | 10 |  | 10 | 10 | (10) |
| Loss contingency |  | no adjustments to prior years |  |  |  |
| Patent amortization | (6) |  | (6) | (3) | 3 |
| Depreciation |  | no adjustments to prior years |  |  |  |
|  | $824 | $400 | $424 | $249 | $156 |

# Problem 20-15

## 1a. To correct the error:

| | | |
|---|---:|---:|
| Equipment (cost) .................................................................... | 45,000 | |
|     Accumulated depreciation ([$45,000 ÷ 5] x 2 years)............. | | 18,000 |
|     Retained earnings ($45,000 – [$9,000 x 2 years])................... | | 27,000 |

**2006 adjusting entry:**

| | | |
|---|---:|---:|
| Depreciation expense ($45,000 ÷ 5) ........................................ | 9,000 | |
|     Accumulated depreciation .............................................. | | 9,000 |

## b. To reverse erroneous entry:

| | | |
|---|---:|---:|
| Cash .................................................................................. | 17,000 | |
|     Office supplies ............................................................. | | 17,000 |

**To record correct entry:**

| | | |
|---|---:|---:|
| Tools ................................................................................ | 17,000 | |
|     Cash .......................................................................... | | 17,000 |

Note: These entries can, of course, be combined.

## c. To correct the error:

| | | |
|---|---:|---:|
| Inventory .......................................................................... | 78,000 | |
|     Retained earnings ......................................................... | | 78,000 |

## d. To correct the error:

| | | |
|---|---:|---:|
| Retained earnings ([$12 x 2,000 shares] – $2,000) ..................... | 22,000 | |
|     Paid-in capital – excess of par........................................... | | 22,000 |

Note: A "small" stock dividend (<25%) requires that the market value of the additional shares be "capitalized.".

# Problem 20-15 (concluded)

## e. To correct the error:

| | | |
|---|---|---|
| Retained earnings (overstatement of 2005 income) .................. | 104,000 | |
|     Interest expense (overstatement of 2006 interest) ................. | | 104,000 |

**2006 adjusting entry:**

| | | |
|---|---|---|
| Interest expense ($4/6$ x $156,000) ........................................... | 104,000 | |
|     Interest payable ($4/6$ x $156,000)....................................... | | 104,000 |

## f. To correct the error:

| | | |
|---|---|---|
| Prepaid insurance ($72,000 ÷ 3 yrs x 2 years: 2006-2007) .......... | 48,000 | |
|     Retained earnings ($72,000 – [$72,000 ÷ 3 years]) .............. | | 48,000 |

**2006 adjusting entry:**

| | | |
|---|---|---|
| Insurance expense ($72,000 ÷ 3 years) ....................................... | 24,000 | |
|     Prepaid insurance ............................................................ | | 24,000 |

# CASES

## Judgment Case 20-1
### Situation I

1. A change in the depreciable lives of fixed assets is a change in accounting estimate.

2. The change in estimate should be reflected in the current period and in future periods. Unlike a change in accounting principle, the change in accounting estimate should not be applied retrospectively.

3. This change in accounting estimate will affect the balance sheet in that the accumulated depreciation in the current and future years will increase at a different rate than previously reported, and this will also be reflected in depreciation expense in the income statement in the current and future years.

4. A footnote should disclose the effect of the change in accounting estimate on income before extraordinary items, net income, and related per share amounts for the current period.

### Situation II

1. The change from reporting the investment in Allen to using a consolidated financial statement basis is a change in reporting entity.

2. A change in reporting entity is effected and disclosed by recasting all prior-period financial statements in accordance with the method of presenting the current financial statements of the new reporting entity. In the initial set of financial statements occurring after the change, the nature of and reason for the change must be disclosed by footnote, but subsequent financial statements need not repeat the disclosures.

3. The balance sheet will be affected by this change in that the investment account of the parent and the equity section of the subsidiary will be eliminated, intercompany accounts will be eliminated, and a goodwill account may arise. The income statement will be affected in that intercompany transactions will be eliminated.

## Case 20-1 (concluded)

4. The financial statements of the period of the change in the reporting entity should describe by footnote disclosure the nature of the change and the reason for it. In addition, the effect of the change in earnings before extraordinary items, net earnings, and related per share amounts should be disclosed for all periods presented. Financial statements of subsequent periods need not repeat the disclosures.

### Situation III

1. The change in the method of computing depreciation represents a change in estimate resulting from a change in accounting principle. This is because a change in the depreciation method is adopted to reflect a change in (a) estimated future benefits from the asset, (b) the pattern of receiving those benefits, or (c) the company's knowledge about those benefits. The effect of the change in depreciation method is inseparable from the effect of the change in accounting estimate. Such changes frequently are related to the ongoing process of obtaining new information and revising estimates and, accordingly, are actually changes in estimates not unlike changing the estimated useful life of a depreciable asset. Logically, the two events should be reported the same way. Accordingly, the company reports the change prospectively; previous financial statements are not recast. Instead, the company simply employs the straight-line method from then on. The undepreciated cost remaining at the time of the change would be depreciated straight-line over the remaining useful life.

2. The change should be reflected in the current period and in future periods. Unlike most changes in accounting principle, the change in accounting estimate should not be applied retrospectively.

3. This change will affect the balance sheet in that the accumulated depreciation in the current and future years will increase at a different rate than previously reported, and this will also be reflected in depreciation expense in the income statement in the current and future years.

4. Additionally, a disclosure note should justify that the change is preferable and describe the effect of a change on any financial statement line items and per share amounts affected for all periods reported.

# Analysis Case 20-2

## Requirement 1

DRS's change in depreciation method for computers represents a change in estimate resulting from a change in accounting principle. This is because a change in the depreciation method is adopted to reflect a change in (a) estimated future benefits from the asset, (b) the pattern of receiving those benefits, or (c) the company's knowledge about those benefits. Accordingly, the company reports the change prospectively; previous financial statements are not recast. Instead, the company simply employs the straight-line method from then on. The undepreciated cost remaining at the time of the change would be depreciated using the straight-line method over the remaining useful life

The change in residual value for the office building is a change in accounting estimate. The company reports the change prospectively; previous financial statements are not recast. Instead, the company simply employs the new residual value estimate from then on. The undepreciated cost remaining at the time of the change would be reduced by the new estimate of residual value and the resulting amount would be depreciated over the remaining useful life of the building.

DRS's change in the specific subsidiaries constituting the group of companies for which consolidated financial statements are presented is a change in reporting entity. A change in reporting entity is effected and disclosed by recasting all prior-period financial statements in accordance with the method of presenting the current financial statements of the new reporting entity. In the initial set of financial statements occurring after the change, the nature of and reason for the change must be disclosed by footnote, but subsequent financial statements need not repeat the disclosures.

## Requirement 2
Applying the same accounting principles from one reporting period to another enhances the comparability of accounting information across accounting periods. The FASB's conceptual framework describes consistency as one of the important qualitative characteristics of accounting information. When accounting changes occur, the usefulness of the comparative financial statements is enhanced with retrospective application of those changes, especially when assessing trends.

If a change in accounting principle occurs, the nature and effect of a change should be disclosed. Disclosure is desirable because of the presumption that an accounting principle once adopted will not change.

# Analysis Case 20-3

The change from cash basis recognition for service contract revenue to the accrual basis is a change from an unacceptable accounting principle to one that is generally accepted. So the change is considered an error correction. Ray should restate prior periods' financial statements and adjust retained earnings for the effect on January 1, 2006. Ray also should disclose the nature and details of the corrections in disclosure notes.

The change from accelerated depreciation for all future acquisitions is a change in accounting principle. Ray should disclose the nature and justification for the change in depreciation methods in the disclosure notes to the 2006 financial statements, along with the effect of the change on current year's income. There is no retrospective application because the change was made only for equipment acquired after January 1, 2006.

Ray's change from LIFO to FIFO is a change in accounting principle for which Ray should recast prior periods' financial statements to appear as if FIFO had been used all along. It also should state the nature and justification for the change in inventory method along with the effects of the change on financial statement components for all periods presented.

# Integrating Case 20-4

1. Webster's dollar-value LIFO inventory at December 31, 2007 and 2008, is calculated as follows:

| Year | Inventory at FIFO | Divided by Index | Inventory At Base Year Cost | Layers At Base Year Cost | Times Index | Inventory at DVL |
|------|------|------|------|------|------|------|
| 2006 | $300,000 | 1.00 | $300,000 | $300,000 | 1.00 | $300,000 |
| 2007 | $412,500 | 1.25 | $330,000 | $300,000 | 1.00 | $300,000 |
|      |      |      |      | 30,000 | 1.25 | 37,500 |
|      |      |      |      |      |      | $337,500 |
| 2008 | $585,000 | 1.50 | $390,000 | $300,000 | 1.00 | $300,000 |
|      |      |      |      | 30,000 | 1.25 | 37,500 |
|      |      |      |      | 60,000 | 1.50 | 90,000 |
|      |      |      |      |      |      | $427,500 |

2. When a company changes *to the LIFO inventory method* from another inventory method, accounting records usually are insufficient to determine the cumulative income effect of the change required to apply the new method retrospectively. So, a company changing to LIFO usually applies the change prospectively. The base year inventory for all future LIFO calculations is the beginning inventory in the year the LIFO method is adopted ($300,000 in this case). Disclosure required includes a footnote to the financial statements describing the nature of and justification for the change as well as an explanation as to why retrospective application was impracticable.

# Communication Case 20-5
## Suggested Grading Concepts and Grading Scheme:

**Content** (80% )

_____    20    Identifies the situation as a change in estimate.

           ____ The liability was originally (appropriately) estimated as $750,000.

           ____ The final settlement indicates the estimate should be revised.

_____    40    Describes the journal entry related to the change in amounts.

           ____ The liability must be reduced (a debit).

           ____ A gain should be recorded (a credit).

           ____ The amount of the gain should be $275,000 ($750,000 – $475,000).

_____    20    Indicates that additional disclosure is necessary.

_____    **Bonus (4)** Provides detail regarding the disclosure note.

           ____ A disclosure note should describe the effect of a change in estimate on key items.

           ____ The effect on income before extraordinary items, net income, and related per share amounts for the current period should be indicated.

_____    80-84 points

**Writing** (20%)

_____    5    Terminology and tone appropriate to the audience of a Vice President.

_____    6    Organization permits ease of understanding.

           ____ Introduction that states purpose.

           ____ Paragraphs separate main points.

_____    9    English.

           ____ Word selection.

           ____ Spelling.

           ____ Grammar.

_____    20 points

# Analysis Case 20-6

Larry apparently is referring to the fact that because the company now believes the useful lives of the assets are longer than before that depreciation calculated assuming the shorter 16 year life was overstated. Now by not recalculating a lower depreciation for earlier years, the undepreciated cost to allocate to future years is less than it would have been had depreciation been based on 20 years all along. The result is that depreciation following the change in estimate is less than it would have been had depreciation been based on 20 years all along. In other words, depreciation was "too high" before the change and "too low" after the change.

Larry is right if we accept his premise that depreciation was, in fact, "too high" before the change. That perspective enjoys the benefit of hindsight. When the original estimate was made, 16 years was considered the appropriate useful life. The accounting profession argues that as conditions change, estimates change, and that resulting inconsistencies are unavoidable. Therefore, changes in estimates are accounted for prospectively. When a company revises a previous estimate, prior financial statements are *not* revised. Instead, the company merely incorporates the new estimate in any related accounting determinations from then on. The result, however, is as Larry describes: the depreciation before the change is higher and the depreciation after the change is lower than it would have been if the new estimate had been used throughout.

# Ethics Case 20-7

Discussion should include these elements.

## How would the actions suggested contribute toward "softening" the bad news?

The choice of inventory method will affect earnings. FIFO will increase reported net income in a period of rising prices. However, FIFO also will cause an increase in taxes paid.

Less obvious would be a change in LIFO pools. By drastically increasing the number of LIFO pools, the company may be able to cause some LIFO liquidations. If so, cost of goods sold would be forced to include much older, lower costs, thereby increasing net income.

Changing estimates on depreciable lives, salvage values, pension assumptions, and others also can influence reported profits.

Academic research performed in this area would indicate that accounting changes that merely increase reported earnings without any real economic (or cash flow) effect will not produce the desired effect of increasing share price. Most research suggests that the stock market "sees through" purely cosmetic accounting changes. Quite a bit of evidence, though, at least anecdotal evidence, indicates that managers attempt to fool the market. Some efforts to manage earnings may not be an attempt to affect share prices, but to avoid violating terms of contracts based on earnings or related balance sheet items. Some may be to favorably affect terms of compensation agreements.

## Case 20-7 (concluded)

### Ethical Dilemma:

Is the auditor's obligation to challenge the questionable change in methods greater than the obligation to the financial interests of the CPA firm and its client?

### Who is affected?:

You, the auditor

Managers

CPA firm (lost fees? reputation? legal action?)

Shareholders

Potential shareholders

The employees

The creditors

Company managers, particularly the president, stand to benefit from the suggested actions.

The auditor risks negative consequences if the changes occur and are challenged.

# Research Case 20-8

The results students report will vary somewhat depending on the firms chosen However, disclosures of changes in actuarial assumptions for benefit plans are quite similar, following SFAS No. 132, "Employers' Disclosures About Pensions and Other Postretirement Benefits."

A recent disclosure for Delta Airlines follows:

We used the following actuarial assumptions to determine the actuarial present value of our APBO:

|  | Sept. 30, 2001 | Sept. 30, 2000 | March 31, 2000 |
|---|---|---|---|
| Weighted average discount rate | 7.75% | 8.25% | 8.25% |
| Assumed health care cost trend rate(*) | 6.25% | 7.00% | 7.00% |

(*) The assumed healthcare cost trend rate is assumed to decline gradually to 5.50% in 2003 and remain level thereafter.

A 1% change in the health care cost rate used in measuring the APBO at September 30, 2001 would have the following effects:

| (In Millions) | 1% Increase | 1% Decrease |
|---|---|---|
| Increase (decrease) in the total service and interest cost | $ 17 | $ (15) |
| Increase (decrease) in the APBO | 112 | (111) |

Under SFAS 132, this is typical. Delta did not disclose the specific effect of changing from 8.25% to 7.75% in 2001. Instead, regardless of the actual change, the effect of a 1% change in either direction is reported.

# Analysis Case 20-9

For changes not involving LIFO or changes from the LIFO method to another, the event is accounted for as a normal change in accounting principle. In general, we report voluntary changes in accounting principles retrospectively. This means revising all previous period's financial statements as if the new method were used in those periods. In other words, for each year in the comparative statements reported, we revise the balance of each account affected. More specifically, we make those statements appear as if the newly adopted accounting method had been applied all along. Also, if retained earnings is one of the accounts whose balance requires adjustment (and it usually is), we make an adjustment to the beginning balance of retained earnings for the earliest period reported in the comparative statements of shareholders' equity (or statements of retained earnings if they're presented instead). Then we create a journal entry to adjust all account balances affected as of the date of the change.

The advantage of retrospective application is to enhance comparability of the statements from year to year. The recast statements appear as if the newly adopted accounting method had been applied in all previous years.

Consistency and comparability suggest that accounting choices once made should be consistently followed from year to year. So, any change requires that the new method be justified as clearly more appropriate. In the first set of financial statements after the change, a disclosure note is needed to provide that justification. The footnote also should point out that comparative information has been revised and report any per share amounts affected for the current period and all prior periods presented.

When a company changes to the LIFO inventory method from any other method, it usually is impracticable to calculate the cumulative effect of the change. Revising balances in prior years would require knowing what those balances should be. LIFO inventory, though, consists of "layers" added in prior years at costs existing in those years. If another method has been used, the company probably hasn't kept a record of those costs. Accordingly, accounting records of prior years usually are inadequate to report the change retrospectively. Because of this difficulty, a company changing to LIFO usually does not report the change retrospectively. Instead, the base year inventory for all future LIFO calculations is the beginning inventory in the year the LIFO method is adopted. Then, the LIFO method is applied prospectively from that point on. The disclosure note must include an explanation as to why retrospective application was impracticable.

# Real World Case 20-10

## Requirement 1

We report most voluntary changes in accounting principles retrospectively. This means recasting all previous period's financial statements as if the new method were used in those periods. For each year in the comparative statements reported, we revise the balance of each account affected so that those statements appear as if the newly adopted accounting method had been applied all along. Then we create a journal entry to adjust all account balances affected as of the date of the change.

GAAP requires retrospective application to enhance comparability of the statements from year to year. The revised statements are made to appear as if the newly adopted accounting method (FIFO inventory costing in this case) had been applied in all previous years.

## Requirement 2

The note reports that the switch to the FIFO cost method caused a decrease in earnings per share of 2 cents for the first nine months of 2003. In order for FIFO to result in lower earnings (higher cost of goods sold) than LIFO (assuming the quantity of inventory did not change), the cost of inventory must have *decreased* during the year.

# Communication Case 20-11

## Requirement 1

---

**Change in Inventory Method**

During 2006, the Company changed the method of valuing its inventories from the first-in, first-out (FIFO) method, to the last-in, first-out (LIFO) method, determined by the retail method. To estimate the effects of changing retail prices on inventories, the Company utilizes internally developed price indexes. The impact of the change was to decrease 2006 net income by $13.2 million and to decrease earnings per share by $0.13. Management has determined that retrospective application of the change is impracticable because the cumulative effect of the change on prior years was not determinable.

The Company believes that the change to the LIFO method provides a more consistent matching of merchandise costs with sales revenue and also provides a more comparable basis of accounting with competitors.

---

Note: Because cost of goods sold would have been $22 million lower if the change had not been made, income before tax would have been $22 million higher, and net income would have been $13.2 million higher ($22 million multiplied by 60% [1 - .40]).

## Requirement 2

It usually is impracticable to calculate the cumulative effect of a change to LIFO. To do so would require assumptions as to when specific LIFO inventory layers were created in years prior to the change. Accounting records usually are inadequate for a company to create the appropriate LIFO inventory layers. That's why a change to LIFO usually can't be applied retrospectively.

# Judgment Case 20-12

Despite the self-correcting feature of certain inventory errors, the errors caus the financial statements of the year of the error as well as the financial statements i the subsequent year to be incorrect. For example, an overstatement of endin inventory at the end of 2005 will correct itself in 2006 and retained earnings at th end of 2006 will be correct. However, cost of goods sold and net income will b incorrect in both years. In addition, inventory and retained earnings on the 200: balance sheet will be incorrect.

If a *material* inventory error is discovered in an accounting period subsequent t the period in which the error is made, previous years' financial statements that wer incorrect as a result of the error are *retrospectively restated* to reflect the correction And, of course, any account balances that are incorrect as a result of the error ar corrected by journal entry. If retained earnings is one of the incorrect accounts, th correction is reported as a prior period adjustment to the beginning balance o retained earnings in the statement of shareholders' equity. In addition, a disclosur note is needed to describe the nature of the error and the impact of its correction o net income, income before extraordinary item, and earnings per share.

# Ethics Case 20-13

### Requirement 1
Bonuses will be negatively affected because if the error is corrected, a lowe ending inventory results in higher cost of goods sold and lower pre-tax income. The effect of the error would be an *overstatement* of income by $665,000 ($3,265,000 2,600,000).

### Requirement 2
It will be reported as a prior period adjustment to the beginning retained earning: balance for the year beginning July 1, 2006. Financial statements for the year ending June 30, 2006, will be restated to reflect the correct inventory amount, cost of goods sold, net income, and retained earnings.

### Requirement 3

### Ethical Dilemma:
Should John recognize his obligation to disclose the inventory error to Danville shareholders, the local bank, auditors, and taxing authorities or remain quiet, enabling him and other company employees to receive originally computed year-end bonuses?

# Chapter 21     The Statement of Cash Flows Revisited

## QUESTIONS FOR REVIEW OF KEY TOPICS

### Question 21-1

Every cash flow eventually affects the balance of one or more accounts on the balance sheet, and the cash flows related to income-producing activities also are represented on the income statement. The cash flows, though, are not necessarily reported in the period the cash flows occur. This is because the income statement measures activities on an *accrual* basis rather than a cash basis. The Statement of Cash Flows fills the information gap by reporting the cash flows directly and in the period the cash flows occur.

### Question 21-2

No. Although the Statement of Cash Flows has been a required financial statement only since 1988, the relatively recent requirement completes a "full-cycle" movement of accounting thought back to cash flow reporting, which was common practice several decades ago. Prior to the mid-1930s, the preparation of financial statements on a cash basis was common although today's cash flow reporting requirements are quite different from the cash flow reporting practiced during that earlier period (when emphasis was placed on cash-based income determination). Later, in 1971, APB Opinion 19 required a Statement of Changes in Financial Position that reported "funds flows" that could be defined as either cash or working capital.

### Question 21-3

No, an investment in treasury bills need not always be classified as a cash equivalent. A guideline – not a rule – for cash equivalents is that these investments must have a maturity date not longer than three months from the date of purchase. However, flexibility is permitted and each company must establish a policy regarding which short-term, highly liquid investments it classifies as cash equivalents. The designation must be consistent with the company's customary motivation for acquiring various investments and the policy should be described in disclosure notes.

### Question 21-4

Transactions that involve merely transfers from cash to cash equivalents such as the purchase of a three-month treasury bill, or from cash equivalents to cash such as the sale of a treasury bill, should not be reported on the Statement of Cash Flows. A dollar amount is simply transferred from one "cash" account to another "cash" account so that the *total* of cash and cash equivalents is not altered by such transactions. An exception is the sale of a cash equivalent at a gain or loss. In this case, the *total* of cash and cash equivalents actually increases or decreases. The increase or decrease is reported as a cash flow from operating activities.

# Answers to Questions (continued)

## Question 21-5

"Cash flows from operating activities" are both inflows and outflows of cash that result from th same activities that are reported on the income statement. However, the income statement report the activities on an accrual basis (revenues earned during the reporting period, *regardless of whe cash is received*, and the expenses incurred in generating those revenues, *regardless of when cash i paid*). Cash flows from operating activities, on the other hand, report those activities when the cas is exchanged (on a cash basis).

## Question 21-6

The generalization that "cash flows from operating activities" report all the elements of th income statement on a cash basis is not strictly true for all elements of the income statement. N cash effects are reported for depreciation and amortization neither of operational assets, nor for gain and losses from the sale of those assets. Cash outflows occur when operational assets are acquired and cash inflows occur when the assets are sold. However, the acquisition and subsequent resale o operational assets are classified as investing activities, rather than as operating activities.

## Question 21-7

"Cash flows from investing activities" are both outflows and inflows of cash due to th acquisition and disposition of assets. This classification includes cash payments to acquire (1 property, plant and equipment and other productive assets (2) investments in securities, and (3 nontrade receivables. When these assets later are liquidated, any cash receipts from their dispositio also are classified as investing activities. The four specific examples can come from an combination of these categories.

Two exceptions are inventories and cash equivalents. The purchase and sale of inventories ar not considered investing activities because inventories are purchased for the purpose of being sold a part of the firm's primary operations and are classified as operating activities. The purchase and sal of assets classified as cash equivalents are not reported on the Statement of Cash Flows unless th total of cash and cash equivalents changes from the sale of a cash equivalent at a gain or loss.

## Question 21-8

The payment of cash dividends to shareholders is classified as a financing activity, but payin interest to creditors is classified as an operating activity. This is because "cash flows from operatin activities" should reflect the cash effects of items that enter into the determination of net income Interest expense is a determinant of net income. A dividend, on the other hand, is a distribution o net income and not an expense.

## Question 21-9

A Statement of Cash Flows reports transactions that cause an increase or a decrease in cash. However, some transactions that do not increase or decrease cash, but which result in significant investing and financing activities, must be reported in related disclosures. Entering a significant investing activity and a significant financing activity as two parts of a single transaction does not limit the value of reporting these activities. Examples of noncash transactions that would be reported:

1. Acquiring an asset by incurring a debt payable to the seller.
2. Acquiring an asset by entering into a capital lease.
3. Converting debt into common stock or other equity securities.
4. Exchanging noncash assets or liabilities for other noncash assets or liabilities.

## Question 21-10

The acquisition of a building purchased by issuing a mortgage note payable in addition to a significant cash down payment is an example of a transaction involving an investing and financing activity that is part cash and part noncash. The cash portion would be reported under the caption "Cash flows from investing activities," and the noncash portion of the transaction would be reported as a "noncash investing and financing activity."

## Question 21-11

Perhaps the most noteworthy item reported on an income statement is net income–the amount by which revenues exceed expenses. The most noteworthy item reported on a Statement of Cash Flows is not the amount of net cash flows. In fact, this may be the least important number on the statement. The increase or decrease in cash can be seen easily on comparative balance sheets. The purpose of the Statement of Cash Flows is not to report that cash increased or decreased by a certain amount, but why cash increased or decreased by that amount. The individual cash inflows and outflows provide that information.

## Question 21-12

The spreadsheet entries shown in the two "changes" columns, which separate the beginning and ending balances, explain the increase or decrease in each account balance. Spreadsheet entries duplicate the actual journal entries used to record the transactions as they occurred during the year Recording spreadsheet entries simultaneously identifies and classifies the activities to be reported on the Statement of Cash Flows because in order for cash to increase or decrease, there must be a corresponding change in a noncash account. Thus, if we can identify the events and transactions that caused the change in each noncash account during the period, we will have identified all the operating, investing, and financing activities .

*Answers to Questions (continued)*

## Question 21-13

If sales revenue is $200,000, this does not necessarily mean that $200,000 cash was received from customers. Amounts reported on the income statement usually do not represent the cash effects of the items reported. By referring to the beginning and ending balances in accounts receivable, we see whether cash received from customers was more or less than $200,000. If accounts receivable increased during the year, some of the sales revenue earned must not yet have been collected. On the other hand, if accounts receivable decreased during the year, more must have been collected than the sales revenue earned.

## Question 21-14

When an asset is sold at a gain, the gain is not reported as a cash inflow from operating activities. A gain (or loss) is simply the difference between cash received in the sale of an asset and the book value of the asset – not a cash flow. The cash effect of the sale is reported as an investing activity. To report the gain as a cash flow from operating activities, in addition to reporting the entire cash flow from investing activities, would be to report the gain twice.

## Question 21-15

Whether or not a loss is extraordinary, it is not reported on the statement of cash flows, but the cash inflow from the sale is reported as an investing activity. However, the spreadsheet entry would be affected if the loss is extraordinary. The income tax effect of an extraordinary item is not reflected in income tax expense, but instead is separately reported as a reduction in the extraordinary item. For example, if a loss on the sale of an asset was due to an extraordinary event, the tax savings from that loss would be reported as a reduction in the extraordinary loss rather than as a reduction in income tax expense. This must be considered when determining the cash paid for income taxes.

## Question 21-16

When determining the amount of cash paid for income taxes, an increase in the deferred income tax liability account would indicate that less cash had been paid than the income tax expense reported. The difference represents the portion of the income tax expense whose payment is deferred to a later year. Notice that precisely the same analysis would apply for an increase in current income tax payable.

## Question 21-17

When using the indirect method of determining net cash flows from operating activities, the net cash increase or decrease from operating activities is derived indirectly by starting with reported net income and "working backwards" to convert that amount to a cash basis. Amounts that were subtracted in determining net income, but which did not reduce cash, are added back to net income to reverse the effect of the amounts having been subtracted. Bad debt expense is one example. Other examples are depreciation expense, amortization of other intangibles, depletion, and a loss on the sale of assets.

## Answers to Questions *(concluded)*

### Question 21-18

When using the indirect method of determining net cash flows from operating activities, when components of net income increase or decrease cash, but by an amount different from that reported on the income statement, net income is adjusted for changes in the balances of related balance sheet accounts to convert the effects of those items to a cash basis. For components of net income that increase or decrease cash by an amount exactly the same as that reported on the income statement, no adjustment of net income is required.

### Question 21-19

Either the direct method or the indirect method is permitted, but the FASB strongly encourages companies to report "cash flows from operating activities" by the direct method. The direct method reports specific operating cash receipts and operating cash payments, consistent with the primary objective of the Statement of Cash Flows. This allows investors and creditors to gain additional insight into the specific sources of cash receipts and payments from operating activities. Users also can more easily interpret and understand the information presented because the direct method avoids the confusion caused by reporting noncash items and other reconciling adjustments under the caption "cash flows from operating activities."

### Question 21-20

The direct and indirect methods are alternative approaches to deriving net cash flows from operating activities only. Regardless of which method is used for that purpose, the way cash flows from investing and financing activities are presented is precisely the same.

# BRIEF EXERCISES

## Brief Exercise 21-1

**Summary Entry** ($ in millions)

| | | |
|---|---|---|
| Cash (received from customers) | **38** | |
| Accounts receivable | | 5 |
| Sales revenue | | 33 |

## Brief Exercise 21-2

**Summary Entry** ($ in millions)

| | | |
|---|---|---|
| Cash (received from customers) | **39** | |
| Accounts receivable | 4 | |
| Bad debt expense | 2 | |
| Allowance for uncollectible accounts | | 1 |
| Sales revenue | | 44 |

## Brief Exercise 21-3

**Summary Entry** ($ in millions)

| | | |
|---|---|---|
| Cost of goods sold | 25 | |
| Inventory | 6 | |
| Accounts payable | | 5 |
| Cash (paid to suppliers of goods) | | **26** |

## Brief Exercise 21-4

**Summary Entry** ($ in millions)

| | | |
|---|---|---|
| Salaries expense | 17 | |
| Salaries payable | | 3 |
| Cash (paid to employees) | | **14** |

# Brief Exercise 21-5

|  | ($ in millions) | |
|---|---|---|
| Interest expense (10% x $^1/_2$ x $380) | 19 | |
|     Discount on bonds payable | | 1 |
|     Cash (paid to bondholders) (9% x $^1/_2$ x $400) | | **18** |

Agee would report the cash inflow of $380 million from the sale of the bonds as a cash inflow from financing activities in its statement of cash flows.

The $18 million cash interest paid is cash outflow from operating activities because interest is an income statement (operating) item.

# Brief Exercise 21-6

|  | ($ in millions) | |
|---|---|---|
| Interest expense (10% x $^1/_2$ x $380) | 19 | |
|     Discount on bonds payable | | 1 |
|     Cash (paid to bondholders) (9% x $^1/_2$ x $400) | | **18** |

Agee would report the cash inflow of $380 million from the sale of the bonds as a cash inflow from financing activities in its statement of cash flows.

The $1 million discount would be added back to net income as a noncash adjustment because the interest expense ($19 million) was subtracted in calculating net income and yet the cash interest paid was only $18 million.

# Brief Exercise 21-7

Merit would report the cash inflow of $41 million from the borrowing as a cash inflow from financing activities in its statement of cash flows.

Each installment payment includes both an amount that represents interest and an amount that represents a reduction of principal. In its statement of cash flows, then, Merit reports the interest portion ($2,870,000*) as a cash outflow from operating activities and the principal portion ($7,130,000*) as a cash outflow from financing activities.

**\*December 31, 2006**

| | | |
|---|---|---|
| Interest expense (7% x outstanding balance).... | 2,870,000 | |
| Note payable (difference)............................ | 7,130,000 | |
| Cash (given)............................................. | | 10,000,000 |

# Brief Exercise 21-8

| | ($ in millions) |
|---|---|
| Cash........................................................ | 35 |
| Gain on sale of land (difference)............. | 13 |
| Land (cost)............................................. | 22 |

Morgan would report the cash inflow of $35 million from the sale as a cash inflow from investing activities in its statement of cash flows.

The $13 million gain is not a cash flow and would not be reported when using the direct method. For that reason, when using the indirect method, the gain would be subtracted from net income (which includes the gain) to avoid double-counting it.

# Brief Exercise 21-9

**Cash Flows From Investing Activities:**

| | |
|---|---:|
| Proceeds from sale of marketable securities | $30 |
| Proceeds from sale of land | 15 |
| Purchase of equipment for cash | (25) |
| Purchase of patent | (12) |
| Net cash inflows from investing activities | $ 8 |

# Brief Exercise 21-10

**Cash Flows From Financing Activities:**

| | |
|---|---:|
| Sale of common shares | $40 |
| Purchase of treasury stock | (21) |
| Net cash inflows from financing activities | $19 |

# Brief Exercise 21-11

| | |
|---|---|
| Net income | $90 |
| ***Adjustments for noncash effects*:** | |
| Depreciation expense | 3 |
| Loss on sale of equipment | 2 |
| Increase in accounts receivable | (1) |
| Increase in accounts payable | 4 |
| Increase in inventory | (3) |
| **Net cash flows from** | |
| **operating activities** | $95 |

# Brief Exercise 21-12

| | |
|---|---|
| Net income | $60 |
| ***Adjustments for noncash effects*:** | |
| Amortization expense | 2 |
| Gain on sale of equipment | (1) |
| Decrease in accounts receivable | 2 |
| Decrease in accounts payable | (5) |
| Decrease in inventory | 4 |
| **Net cash flows from** | |
| **operating activities** | $62 |

# EXERCISES

## Exercise 21-1

| Example | | | |
|---|---|---|---|
| | **F** | 1. | Sale of common stock |
| | **I** | 2. | Sale of land |
| | **F** | 3. | Purchase of treasury stock |
| | **O** | 4. | Merchandise sales |
| | **F** | 5. | Issuance of a long-term note payable |
| | **O** | 6. | Purchase of merchandise |
| | **F** | 7. | Repayment of note payable |
| | **O** | 8. | Employee salaries |
| | **I** | 9. | Sale of equipment at a gain |
| | **F** | 10. | Issuance of bonds |
| | **I** | 11. | Acquisition of bonds of another corporation |
| | **O** | 12. | Payment of semiannual interest on bonds payable |
| | **F** | 13. | Payment of a cash dividend |
| | **I** | 14. | Purchase of building |
| | **I** | 15. | Collection of nontrade note receivable (principal amount) |
| | **I** | 16. | Loan to another firm |
| | **F** | 17. | Retirement of common stock |
| | **O** | 18. | Income taxes |
| | **F** | 19. | Issuance of a short-term note payable |
| | **I** | 20. | Sale of a copyright |

# Exercise 21-2

## Requirement 1

($ in millions)

### Inventory

| | | | |
|---|---|---|---|
| Beginning balance | 90 | | |
| Goods purchased | 303 | 300 | Cost of goods sold |
| | | | |
| Ending balance | 93 | | |

### Accounts Payable

| | | | |
|---|---|---|---|
| | | 14 | Beginning balance |
| Cash paid | **301** | 303 | Goods purchased |
| | | | |
| | | 16 | Ending balance |

## Requirement 2

| Summary Entry | ($ in millions) | |
|---|---|---|
| Cost of goods sold | 300 | |
| Inventory | 3 | |
|    Accounts payable | | 2 |
|    Cash (paid to suppliers of goods) | | **301** |

# Exercise 21-3

($ in millions)

| Situation | Sales revenue | Accounts receivable increase (decrease) | Bad debt expense | Allowance for uncollectible accounts increase (decrease) | Cash received from customers |
|---|---|---|---|---|---|
| 1 | 100 | -0- | -0- | -0- | **100** |

| 1. Summary Entry | | | | |
|---|---|---|---|---|
| Cash (received from customers) | | | **100** | |
| Sales revenue | | | | 100 |

| Situation | Sales revenue | Accounts receivable | Bad debt expense | Allowance | Cash received from customers |
|---|---|---|---|---|---|
| 2 | 100 | 5 | -0- | -0- | **95** |

| 2. Summary Entry | | | |
|---|---|---|---|
| Cash (received from customers) | | **95** | |
| Accounts receivable | | 5 | |
| Sales revenue | | | 100 |

| Situation | Sales revenue | Accounts receivable | Bad debt expense | Allowance | Cash received from customers |
|---|---|---|---|---|---|
| 3 | 100 | (5) | -0- | -0- | **105** |

| 3. Summary Entry | | | |
|---|---|---|---|
| Cash (received from customers) | | **105** | |
| Accounts receivable | | | 5 |
| Sales revenue | | | 100 |

| Situation | Sales revenue | Accounts receivable | Bad debt expense | Allowance | Cash received from customers |
|---|---|---|---|---|---|
| 4 | 100 | 5 | 2 | 2 | **95** |

| 4. Summary Entry | | | |
|---|---|---|---|
| Cash (received from customers) | | **95** | |
| Accounts receivable | | 5 | |
| Bad debt expense | | 2 | |
| Allowance for uncollectible accounts | | | 2 |
| Sales revenue | | | 100 |

*Exercise 21-3 (concluded)*

| Situation | Sales revenue | Accounts receivable increase (decrease) | Bad debt expense | Allowance for uncollectible accounts increase (decrease) | Cash received from customers |
|-----------|---------------|------------------------------------------|------------------|-----------------------------------------------------------|------------------------------|
| 5 | 100 | (5) | 2 | 1 | **104** |

| | | |
|---|---|---|
| **5.** **Summary Entry** | Cash (received from customers) | **104** | |
| | Bad debt expense | 2 | |
| | Allowance for uncollectible accounts | | 1 |
| | Accounts receivable | | 5 |
| | Sales revenue | | 100 |

| Situation | Sales revenue | Accounts receivable | Bad debt expense | Allowance for uncollectible accounts | Cash received from customers |
|-----------|---------------|---------------------|------------------|--------------------------------------|------------------------------|
| 6 | 100 | 5 | 2 | (1) | **92** |

| | | |
|---|---|---|
| **6.** **Summary Entry** | Cash (received from customers) | **92** | |
| | Bad debt expense | 2 | |
| | Allowance for uncollectible accounts | 1 | |
| | Accounts receivable | 5 | |
| | Sales revenue | | 100 |

# Exercise 21-4

| Situation | Sales revenue | Accounts receivable increase (decrease) | Bad debt expense | Allowance for uncollectible accounts increase (decrease) | Cash received from customers |
|---|---|---|---|---|---|
| 1 | 200 | -0- | -0- | -0- | **200** |

| | | | |
|---|---|---|---|
| **1. Summary Entry** | Cash (received from customers) | **200** | |
| |     Sales revenue | | 200 |

| Situation | Sales revenue | Accounts receivable increase (decrease) | Bad debt expense | Allowance for uncollectible accounts increase (decrease) | Cash received from customers |
|---|---|---|---|---|---|
| 2 | 200 | 10 | -0- | -0- | **190** |

| | | | |
|---|---|---|---|
| **2. Summary Entry** | Cash (received from customers) | **190** | |
| | Accounts receivable | 10 | |
| |     Sales revenue | | 200 |

| Situation | Sales revenue | Accounts receivable increase (decrease) | Bad debt expense | Allowance for uncollectible accounts increase (decrease) | Cash received from customers |
|---|---|---|---|---|---|
| 3 | 200 | 10 | 4 | 4 | **190** |

| | | | |
|---|---|---|---|
| **3. Summary Entry** | Cash (received from customers) | **190** | |
| | Accounts receivable | 10 | |
| | Bad debt expense | 4 | |
| |     Allowance for uncollectible accounts | | 4 |
| |     Sales revenue | | 200 |

| Situation | Sales revenue | Accounts receivable increase (decrease) | Bad debt expense | Allowance for uncollectible accounts increase (decrease) | Cash received from customers |
|---|---|---|---|---|---|
| 4 | 200 | 10 | 4 | (2) | **184** |

| | | | |
|---|---|---|---|
| **4. Summary Entry** | Cash (received from customers) | **184** | |
| | Accounts receivable | 10 | |
| | Bad debt expense | 4 | |
| | Allowance for uncollectible accounts | 2 | |
| |     Sales revenue | | 200 |

# Exercise 21-5

| Situation | Cost of goods sold | Inventory increase (decrease) | Accounts payable increase (decrease) | Cash paid to suppliers |
|:---:|:---:|:---:|:---:|:---:|
| 1 | 100 | 0 | 0 | 100 |

| | | | |
|---|---|---|---|
| 1. **Summary Entry** | Cost of goods sold | 100 | |
| | Cash (paid to suppliers of goods) | | 100 |

| Situation | Cost of goods sold | Inventory increase (decrease) | Accounts payable increase (decrease) | Cash paid to suppliers |
|:---:|:---:|:---:|:---:|:---:|
| 2 | 100 | 3 | 0 | 103 |

| | | | |
|---|---|---|---|
| 2. **Summary Entry** | Cost of goods sold | 100 | |
| | Inventory | 3 | |
| | Cash (paid to suppliers of goods) | | 103 |

| Situation | Cost of goods sold | Inventory increase (decrease) | Accounts payable increase (decrease) | Cash paid to suppliers |
|:---:|:---:|:---:|:---:|:---:|
| 3 | 100 | (3) | 0 | 97 |

| | | | |
|---|---|---|---|
| 3. **Summary Entry** | Cost of goods sold | 100 | |
| | Inventory | | 3 |
| | Cash (paid to suppliers of goods) | | 97 |

| Situation | Cost of goods sold | Inventory increase (decrease) | Accounts payable increase (decrease) | Cash paid to suppliers |
|:---:|:---:|:---:|:---:|:---:|
| 4 | 100 | 0 | 7 | 93 |

| | | | |
|---|---|---|---|
| 4. **Summary Entry** | Cost of goods sold | 100 | |
| | Accounts payable | | 7 |
| | Cash (paid to suppliers of goods) | | 93 |

| Situation | Cost of goods sold | Inventory increase (decrease) | Accounts payable increase (decrease) | Cash paid to suppliers |
|:---:|:---:|:---:|:---:|:---:|
| 5 | 100 | 0 | (7) | 107 |

| | | | |
|---|---|---|---|
| 5. **Summary Entry** | Cost of goods sold | 100 | |
| | Accounts payable | 7 | |
| | Cash (paid to suppliers of goods) | | 107 |

# Exercise 21-5 (concluded)

| Situation | Cost of goods sold | Inventory increase (decrease) | Accounts payable increase (decrease) | Cash paid to suppliers |
|-----------|--------------------|-------------------------------|--------------------------------------|------------------------|
| 6 | 100 | 3 | 7 | 96 |

| | | |
|---|---|---|
| **6.** Summary Entry | Cost of goods sold | 100 |
| | Inventory | 3 |
| |    Accounts payable | 7 |
| |    Cash (paid to suppliers of goods) | **96** |

| Situation | Cost of goods sold | Inventory increase (decrease) | Accounts payable increase (decrease) | Cash paid to suppliers |
|-----------|--------------------|-------------------------------|--------------------------------------|------------------------|
| 7 | 100 | 3 | (7) | **110** |

| | | |
|---|---|---|
| **7.** Summary Entry | Cost of goods sold | 100 |
| | Inventory | 3 |
| | Accounts payable | 7 |
| |    Cash (paid to suppliers of goods) | **110** |

| Situation | Cost of goods sold | Inventory increase (decrease) | Accounts payable increase (decrease) | Cash paid to suppliers |
|-----------|--------------------|-------------------------------|--------------------------------------|------------------------|
| 8 | 100 | (3) | (7) | **104** |

| | | |
|---|---|---|
| **8.** Summary Entry | Cost of goods sold | 100 |
| | Accounts payable | 7 |
| |    Inventory | 3 |
| |    Cash (paid to suppliers of goods) | **104** |

| Situation | Cost of goods sold | Inventory increase (decrease) | Accounts payable increase (decrease) | Cash paid to suppliers |
|-----------|--------------------|-------------------------------|--------------------------------------|------------------------|
| 9 | 100 | (3) | 7 | **90** |

| | | |
|---|---|---|
| **9.** Summary Entry | Cost of goods sold | 100 |
| |    Inventory | 3 |
| |    Accounts payable | 7 |
| |    Cash (paid to suppliers of goods) | **90** |

# Exercise 21-6

| Situation | Cost of goods sold | Inventory increase (decrease) | Accounts payable increase (decrease) | Cash paid to suppliers |
|-----------|--------------------|-------------------------------|--------------------------------------|------------------------|
| 1 | 200 | 0 | 0 | **200** |

| | | | | |
|---|---|---|---|---|
| **1.** **Summary Entry** | Cost of goods sold | | 200 | |
| | Cash (paid to suppliers of goods) | | | **200** |

| Situation | Cost of goods sold | Inventory increase (decrease) | Accounts payable increase (decrease) | Cash paid to suppliers |
|-----------|--------------------|-------------------------------|--------------------------------------|------------------------|
| 2 | 200 | 6 | 0 | **206** |

| | | | | |
|---|---|---|---|---|
| **2.** **Summary Entry** | Cost of goods sold | | 200 | |
| | Inventory | | 6 | |
| | Cash (paid to suppliers of goods) | | | **206** |

| Situation | Cost of goods sold | Inventory increase (decrease) | Accounts payable increase (decrease) | Cash paid to suppliers |
|-----------|--------------------|-------------------------------|--------------------------------------|------------------------|
| 3 | 200 | 0 | 14 | **186** |

| | | | | |
|---|---|---|---|---|
| **3.** **Summary Entry** | Cost of goods sold | | 200 | |
| | Accounts payable | | | 14 |
| | Cash (paid to suppliers of goods) | | | **186** |

| Situation | Cost of goods sold | Inventory increase (decrease) | Accounts payable increase (decrease) | Cash paid to suppliers |
|-----------|--------------------|-------------------------------|--------------------------------------|------------------------|
| 4 | 200 | 6 | 14 | **192** |

| | | | | |
|---|---|---|---|---|
| **4.** **Summary Entry** | Cost of goods sold | | 200 | |
| | Inventory | | 6 | |
| | Accounts payable | | | 14 |
| | Cash (paid to suppliers of goods) | | | **192** |

| Situation | Cost of goods sold | Inventory increase (decrease) | Accounts payable increase (decrease) | Cash paid to suppliers |
|-----------|--------------------|-------------------------------|--------------------------------------|------------------------|
| 5 | 200 | (6) | (14) | **208** |

| | | | | |
|---|---|---|---|---|
| **5.** **Summary Entry** | Cost of goods sold | | 200 | |
| | Accounts payable | | 14 | |
| | Inventory | | | 6 |
| | Cash (paid to suppliers of goods) | | | **208** |

# Exercise 21-7

| Situation | Bond interest expense | Bond interest payable increase (decrease) | Unamortized discount increase (decrease) | Cash paid for interest |
|:---:|:---:|:---:|:---:|:---:|
| 1 | 10 | 0 | 0 | **10** |

| | | | | |
|:---|:---|---:|---:|
| **1.** Summary Entry | Bond interest expense | 10 | |
| | Cash (paid to bondholders) | | **10** |

| Situation | Bond interest expense | Bond interest payable increase (decrease) | Unamortized discount increase (decrease) | Cash paid for interest |
|:---:|:---:|:---:|:---:|:---:|
| 2 | 10 | 2 | 0 | **8** |

| | | | | |
|:---|:---|---:|---:|
| **2.** Summary Entry | Bond interest expense | 10 | |
| | Bond interest payable | | 2 |
| | Cash (paid to bondholders) | | **8** |

| Situation | Bond interest expense | Bond interest payable increase (decrease) | Unamortized discount increase (decrease) | Cash paid for interest |
|:---:|:---:|:---:|:---:|:---:|
| 3 | 10 | (2) | 0 | **12** |

| | | | | |
|:---|:---|---:|---:|
| **3.** Summary Entry | Bond interest expense | 10 | |
| | Bond interest payable | 2 | |
| | Cash (paid to bondholders) | | **12** |

| Situation | Bond interest expense | Bond interest payable increase (decrease) | Unamortized discount increase (decrease) | Cash paid for interest |
|:---:|:---:|:---:|:---:|:---:|
| 4 | 10 | 0 | (3) | **7** |

| | | | | |
|:---|:---|---:|---:|
| **4.** Summary Entry | Bond interest expense | 10 | |
| | Discount on bonds payable | | 3 |
| | Cash (paid to bondholders) | | **7** |

## Exercise 21-7 (concluded)

| Situation | Bond interest expense | Bond interest payable increase (decrease) | Unamortized discount increase (decrease) | Cash paid for interest |
|:---:|:---:|:---:|:---:|:---:|
| 5 | 10 | 2 | (3) | 5 |

| | | | | |
|:---|:---|---:|---:|---:|
| **5.** Summary Entry | Bond interest expense | 10 | | |
| | Bond interest payable | | 2 | |
| | Discount on bonds payable | | 3 | |
| | Cash (paid to bondholders) | | 5 | |

| Situation | Bond interest expense | Bond interest payable increase (decrease) | Unamortized discount increase (decrease) | Cash paid for interest |
|:---:|:---:|:---:|:---:|:---:|
| 6 | 10 | (2) | (3) | 9 |

| | | | | |
|:---|:---|---:|---:|---:|
| **6.** Summary Entry | Bond interest expense | 10 | | |
| | Bond interest payable | 2 | | |
| | Discount on bonds payable | | 3 | |
| | Cash (paid to bondholders) | | 9 | |

# Exercise 21-8

| Situation | Bond interest expense | Bond interest payable increase (decrease) | Unamortized discount increase (decrease) | Cash paid for interest |
|-----------|-----------------------|-------------------------------------------|------------------------------------------|------------------------|
| 1 | 20 | 0 | 0 | **20** |

| | | | |
|---|---|---|---|
| **1. Summary Entry** | Bond interest expense | 20 | |
| | Cash (paid to bondholders) | | 20 |

| Situation | Bond interest expense | Bond interest payable increase (decrease) | Unamortized discount increase (decrease) | Cash paid for interest |
|-----------|-----------------------|-------------------------------------------|------------------------------------------|------------------------|
| 2 | 20 | 4 | 0 | **16** |

| | | | |
|---|---|---|---|
| **2. Summary Entry** | Bond interest expense | 20 | |
| | Bond interest payable | | 4 |
| | Cash (paid to bondholders) | | 16 |

| Situation | Bond interest expense | Bond interest payable increase (decrease) | Unamortized discount increase (decrease) | Cash paid for interest |
|-----------|-----------------------|-------------------------------------------|------------------------------------------|------------------------|
| 3 | 20 | 0 | (6) | **14** |

| | | | |
|---|---|---|---|
| **3. Summary Entry** | Bond interest expense | 20 | |
| | Discount on bonds payable | | 6 |
| | Cash (paid to bondholders) | | 14 |

| Situation | Bond interest expense | Bond interest payable increase (decrease) | Unamortized discount increase (decrease) | Cash paid for interest |
|-----------|-----------------------|-------------------------------------------|------------------------------------------|------------------------|
| 4 | 20 | (4) | (6) | **18** |

| | | | |
|---|---|---|---|
| **4. Summary Entry** | Bond interest expense | 20 | |
| | Bond interest payable | 4 | |
| | Discount on bonds payable | | 6 |
| | Cash (paid to bondholders) | | 18 |

# Exercise 21-9

| Situation | Income tax expense | Income tax payable increase (decrease) | Deferred tax liability increase (decrease) | Cash paid for taxes |
|-----------|-------------------|----------------------------------------|--------------------------------------------|---------------------|
| 1 | 10 | 0 | 0 | 10 |

**1. Summary Entry**

| | | |
|---|---|---|
| Income tax expense | 10 | |
| Cash (paid for income taxes) | | 10 |

| Situation | Income tax expense | Income tax payable increase (decrease) | Deferred tax liability increase (decrease) | Cash paid for taxes |
|-----------|-------------------|----------------------------------------|--------------------------------------------|---------------------|
| 2 | 10 | 3 | 0 | 7 |

**2. Summary Entry**

| | | |
|---|---|---|
| Income tax expense | 10 | |
| Income tax payable | | 3 |
| Cash (paid for income taxes) | | 7 |

| Situation | Income tax expense | Income tax payable increase (decrease) | Deferred tax liability increase (decrease) | Cash paid for taxes |
|-----------|-------------------|----------------------------------------|--------------------------------------------|---------------------|
| 3 | 10 | (3) | 0 | 13 |

**3. Summary Entry**

| | | |
|---|---|---|
| Income tax expense | 10 | |
| Income tax payable | 3 | |
| Cash (paid for income taxes) | | 13 |

| Situation | Income tax expense | Income tax payable increase (decrease) | Deferred tax liability increase (decrease) | Cash paid for taxes |
|-----------|-------------------|----------------------------------------|--------------------------------------------|---------------------|
| 4 | 10 | 0 | 2 | 8 |

**4. Summary Entry**

| | | |
|---|---|---|
| Income tax expense | 10 | |
| Deferred income tax liability | | 2 |
| Cash (paid for income taxes) | | 8 |

| Situation | Income tax expense | Income tax payable increase (decrease) | Deferred tax liability increase (decrease) | Cash paid for taxes |
|-----------|-------------------|----------------------------------------|--------------------------------------------|---------------------|
| 5 | 10 | 0 | (2) | 12 |

**5. Summary Entry**

| | | |
|---|---|---|
| Income tax expense | 10 | |
| Deferred income tax liability | 2 | |
| Cash (paid for income taxes) | | 12 |

# Exercise 21-9 (concluded)

| Situation | Income tax expense | Income tax payable increase (decrease) | Deferred tax liability increase (decrease) | Cash paid for taxes |
|---|---|---|---|---|
| 6 | 10 | 3 | 2 | 5 |

**6. Summary Entry**

| | | |
|---|---|---|
| Income tax expense | 10 | |
| Income tax payable | | 3 |
| Deferred income tax liability | | 2 |
| Cash (paid for income taxes) | | 5 |

| Situation | Income tax expense | Income tax payable increase (decrease) | Deferred tax liability increase (decrease) | Cash paid for taxes |
|---|---|---|---|---|
| 7 | 10 | 3 | (2) | 9 |

**7. Summary Entry**

| | | |
|---|---|---|
| Income tax expense | 10 | |
| Deferred income tax liability | 2 | |
| Income tax payable | | 3 |
| Cash (paid for income taxes) | | 9 |

| Situation | Income tax expense | Income tax payable increase (decrease) | Deferred tax liability increase (decrease) | Cash paid for taxes |
|---|---|---|---|---|
| 8 | 10 | (3) | (2) | 15 |

**8. Summary Entry**

| | | |
|---|---|---|
| Income tax expense | 10 | |
| Income tax payable | 3 | |
| Deferred income tax liability | 2 | |
| Cash (paid for income taxes) | | 15 |

| Situation | Income tax expense | Income tax payable increase (decrease) | Deferred tax liability increase (decrease) | Cash paid for taxes |
|---|---|---|---|---|
| 9 | 10 | (3) | 2 | 11 |

**9. Summary Entry**

| | | |
|---|---|---|
| Income tax expense | 10 | |
| Income tax payable | 3 | |
| Deferred income tax liability | | 2 |
| Cash (paid for income taxes) | | 11 |

# Exercise 21-10

| Situation | Income tax expense | Income tax payable increase (decrease) | Deferred tax liability increase (decrease) | Cash paid for taxes |
|---|---|---|---|---|
| 1 | 10 | 0 | 0 | **10** |

| | | | |
|---|---|---|---|
| **1.** Summary Entry | Income tax expense | 10 | |
| |     Cash (paid for income taxes) | | **10** |

| Situation | Income tax expense | Income tax payable | Deferred tax liability | Cash paid for taxes |
|---|---|---|---|---|
| 2 | 10 | 3 | 0 | **7** |

| | | | |
|---|---|---|---|
| **2.** Summary Entry | Income tax expense | 10 | |
| |     Income tax payable | | 3 |
| |     Cash (paid for income taxes) | | 7 |

| Situation | Income tax expense | Income tax payable | Deferred tax liability | Cash paid for taxes |
|---|---|---|---|---|
| 3 | 10 | 0 | (2) | **12** |

| | | | |
|---|---|---|---|
| **3.** Summary Entry | Income tax expense | 10 | |
| | Deferred income tax liability | 2 | |
| |     Cash (paid for income taxes) | | 12 |

| Situation | Income tax expense | Income tax payable | Deferred tax liability | Cash paid for taxes |
|---|---|---|---|---|
| 4 | 10 | 3 | 2 | **5** |

| | | | |
|---|---|---|---|
| **4.** Summary Entry | Income tax expense | 10 | |
| |     Income tax payable | | 3 |
| |     Deferred income tax liability | | 2 |
| |     Cash (paid for income taxes) | | 5 |

| Situation | Income tax expense | Income tax payable | Deferred tax liability | Cash paid for taxes |
|---|---|---|---|---|
| 5 | 10 | (3) | (2) | **15** |

| | | | |
|---|---|---|---|
| **5.** Summary Entry | Income tax expense | 10 | |
| | Income tax payable | 3 | |
| | Deferred income tax liability | 2 | |
| |     Cash (paid for income taxes) | | 15 |

# Exercise 21-11

Most would report the cash inflow of $566,589,440 from the sale of the bonds as a cash inflow from financing activities in its statement of cash flows.

The $64,000,000 cash interest paid [*], [**] is a cash outflow from operating activities because interest is an income statement (operating) item.

**June 30, 2006***

| | | |
|---|---|---|
| Interest expense (6% x $566,589,440)................... | 33,995,366 | |
|     Discount on bonds payable (difference)......... | | 1,995,366 |
|     Cash (5% x $640,000,000)............................. | | 32,000,000 |

**December 31, 2006****

| | | |
|---|---|---|
| Interest expense (6% x [$566,589,440 + 1,995,366]) | 34,115,088 | |
|     Discount on bonds payable (difference)......... | | 2,115,088 |
|     Cash (5% x $640,000,000)............................. | | 32,000,000 |

# Exercise 21-12

National would report the cash inflow of $4 million from the borrowing as a cash inflow from financing activities in its statement of cash flows.

Each installment payment includes both an amount that represents interest and an amount that represents a reduction of principal. In its statement of cash flows, then National reports the interest portion ($400,000*) as a cash outflow from operating activities and the principal portion ($861,881*) as a cash outflow from financing activities.

**\*December 31, 2006**

| | | |
|---|---|---|
| Interest expense (10% x outstanding balance) | 400,000 | |
| Note payable (difference) ........................... | 861,881 | |
| Cash (given) ............................................. | | 1,261,881 |

# Exercise 21-13

## Requirement 1

### Cash Flows From Investing Activities:

| | |
|---|---:|
| Proceeds from sale of land | $ 12 |
| Purchase of Microsoft common stock | (160) |
| Net cash outflows from investing activities | $(148) |

## Requirement 2

### Cash Flows From Financing Activities:

| | |
|---|---:|
| Payment for the early extinguishment of long-term bonds (carrying amount: $97 million) | $(102) |
| Proceeds from the sale of treasury stock (cost: $17 million) | 22 |
| Distribution of cash dividends declared in 2005 | (40) |
| Net cash outflows from financing activities | $(120) |

# Exercise 21-14

## Requirement 1

### Cash Flows From Investing Activities:

| | |
|---|---:|
| Proceeds from sale of equipment | $ 8 |
| Acquisition of building for cash | (7) |
| Purchase of marketable securities (not a cash equivalent) | (5) |
| Collection of note receivable with interest (principal amount) | 11 |
| Net cash inflows from investing activities | $ 7 |

## Requirement 2

### Cash Flows From Financing Activities:

| | |
|---|---:|
| Payment for the early extinguishment of long-term notes (book value: $50 million) | $ (54) |
| Sale of common shares | 176 |
| Retirement of common shares | (122) |
| Issuance of short-term note payable for cash | 10 |
| Distribution of cash dividends declared in 2005 | (30) |
| Net cash outflows from financing activities | $ (20) |

# Exercise 21-15

Wilson would report the $3,000,000* investment in the commercial food processor and its financing with a capital lease as a significant noncash investing and financing activity in the disclosure notes to the financial statements.

The $391,548 ($195,774 x 2) cash lease payments[*],[**] are divided into the interest portion and the principal portion. The interest portion, $84,127, is reported as cash outflows from operating activities. The principal portion, $195,774 + 111,647, is reported as cash outflows from financing activities.

Note:  By the indirect method of reporting cash flows from operating activities, Wilson would add back to net income the $150,000 depreciation expense since it didn't actually reduce cash. The $84,127 interest expense that reduced net income actually did reduce cash [the interest portion of the $391,548 ($195,774 x 2) cash lease payments], so for it, no adjustment to net income is necessary.

## Calculations:
### September 30, 2006*

| | | |
|---|---|---|
| Leased equipment (calculated below)...................... | 3,000,000 | |
| Lease payable (calculated below) ....................... | | 3,000,000 |
| | | |
| Lease payable ...................................................... | 195,774 | |
| Cash (rental payment) ....................................... | | 195,774 |

**Note:**
$195,774 x 15.3238[t] = $3,000,000
[t] present value of an annuity due of $1: n=20, i=3%

### December 31, 2006**

| | | |
|---|---|---|
| Interest expense (3% x [$3 million − 195,774]) .......... | 84,127 | |
| Lease payable (difference)....................................... | 111,647 | |
| Cash (lease payment)......................................... | | 195,774 |
| | | |
| Depreciation expense ($3 million / 5 years x ¼ year) .. | 150,000 | |
| Accumulated depreciation .............................. | | 150,000 |

# Exercise 21-16

Investing Activities:
Beilich would report the $600 million investment as a cash outflow among investing activities in its statement of cash flows.

Operating Activities:
By the direct method of reporting cash flows from operating activities, Beilich would report the $12 million cash dividend as a cash inflow from operating activities.

By the indirect method of reporting cash flows from operating activities, Beilich would subtract from net income the $60 million investment revenue since it didn't actually provide cash but would add the $12 million cash dividend. Alternatively, the company might just subtract the $48 million difference.

# Exercise 21-17

## RECONCILIATION OF NET INCOME TO
## NET CASH FLOWS FROM OPERATING ACTIVITIES

| | |
|---|---:|
| Net income | $50,000 |
| | |
| ***Adjustments for noncash effects:*** | |
| Depreciation expense | 7,000 |
| Increase in inventory | (1,500) |
| Decrease in salaries payable | (800) |
| Decrease in accounts receivable | 2,000 |
| Amortization of patent | 500 |
| Decrease in bond premium | (1,000) |
| Increase in accounts payable | 4,000 |
| **Net cash flows from** | |
| **operating activities** | $60,200 |

# Exercise 21-18

($ in millions)

**Net income closed to retained earnings**

Income summary ................................................................ 75

    Retained earnings (given) .......................................... 75

The operating activities summarized by this transaction are identified individually when we explain the changes in the components of net income. But including the entry on the spreadsheet is helpful in partially explaining the change in retained earnings.

**Cash dividend**

Retained earnings (given) .................................................. 25

    Cash ............................................................................ 25

This transaction identifies a $25 million cash outflow from financing activities.

**Stock dividend**

Retained earnings (given) .................................................. 16

    Common stock (1 million shares at $1 par per share) ............... 1

    Paid-in capital – excess of par (remainder) ...................... 15

This transaction does not represent a significant investing or financing activity, but including the entry on the spreadsheet is helpful in partially explaining changes in the balances of the three accounts affected.

**Property dividend**

Retained earnings (given) .................................................. 12

    Short-term investments ................................................ 12

This noncash transaction identifies both a $12 million financing activity (distribution of a dividend to shareholders) and a $12 million investing activity (disposition of an investment). Both are reported on the Statement of Cash Flows.

## Sale of treasury shares

Cash (difference)* ............................................................... 43
Retained earnings (given) ....................................................... 10
    Treasury stock (at cost, given) .............................................. 53

*This transaction identifies a $43 million cash inflow from financing activities.

# Exercise 21-19

## Income Statement

| | | |
|---|---:|---:|
| Sales | | $600[a] |
| Cost of goods sold | 360[b] | |
| Salaries expense | 78[c] | |
| Depreciation expense | 18[f] | |
| Insurance expense | 42[d] | |
| Loss on sale of land | 12[f] | |
| Income tax expense | 54[e] | (564) |
| **Net Income** | | $ 36 |

| [a] Summary Entry | Cash (received from customers) | 612 | |
|---|---|---:|---:|
| | Accounts receivable | | 12 |
| | Sales revenue | | **600** |

| [b] Summary Entry | Cost of goods sold | **360** | |
|---|---|---:|---:|
| | Inventory | 24 | |
| | Accounts payable | 36 | |
| | Cash (paid to suppliers of goods) | | 420 |

| [c] Summary Entry | Salaries expense | **78** | |
|---|---|---:|---:|
| | Salaries payable | | 12 |
| | Cash (paid to employees) | | 66 |

| [d] Summary Entry | Insurance expense | **42** | |
|---|---|---:|---:|
| | Prepaid insurance | | 18 |
| | Cash (paid for insurance) | | 24 |

| [e] Summary Entry | Income tax expense | **54** | |
|---|---|---:|---:|
| | Income tax payable | | 12 |
| | Cash (paid for income taxes) | | 42 |

[f] Depreciation expense and the loss on sale of land are noncash reductions in income.

# Exercise 21-20

## RECONCILIATION OF NET INCOME TO
## NET CASH FLOWS FROM OPERATING ACTIVITIES

| | |
|---|---:|
| **Net income** | $ 26 |
| *Adjustments for noncash effects*: | |
| Increase in accounts receivable | (54) |
| Increase (decrease) in inventory | 0 |
| Increase in accounts payable | 13 |
| Increase in salaries payable | 4 |
| Decrease in prepaid insurance | 6 |
| Depreciation expense | 11 |
| Depletion expense | 5 |
| Decrease in bond discount | 1 |
| Gain on sale of equipment | (25) |
| Loss on sale of land | 8 |
| Increase in income tax payable | 12 |
| **Net cash flows from operating activities** | $ 7 |

# Exercise 21-21
**Requirement 1:**

| a. Summary Entry | Cash (received from customers) | 311 | |
|---|---|---|---|
| | Accounts receivable | | 6 |
| | Sales revenue | | 305 |

| b. Summary Entry | Cost of goods sold | 185 | |
|---|---|---|---|
| | Inventory | 13 | |
| | Accounts payable | 8 | |
| | Cash (paid to suppliers of goods) | | 206 |

| c. Summary Entry | Salaries expense | 41 | |
|---|---|---|---|
| | Salaries payable | | 5 |
| | Cash (paid to employees) | | 36 |

| d. Summary Entry | Insurance expense | 19 | |
|---|---|---|---|
| | Prepaid insurance | | 9 |
| | Cash (paid for insurance) | | 10 |

| e. Summary Entry | Income tax expense | 22 | |
|---|---|---|---|
| | Income tax payable | | 20 |
| | Cash (paid for income taxes) | | 2 |

Depreciation expense and the loss on sale of land are not cash outflows.

**Requirement 2:**

**Cash Flows from Operating Activities:**

| | |
|---|---|
| Cash received from customers | $311 |
| Cash paid to suppliers | (206) |
| Cash paid to employees | (36) |
| Cash paid for insurance | (10) |
| Cash paid for income taxes | (2) |
| **Net cash flows from operating activities** | $57 |

# Exercise 21-22

## RECONCILIATION OF NET INCOME TO
## NET CASH FLOWS FROM OPERATING ACTIVITIES

| | |
|---|---:|
| **Net loss** | $ (5,000) |
| *Adjustments for noncash effects:* | |
| Depreciation expense | 6,000 |
| Increase in salaries payable | 500 |
| Decrease in accounts receivable | 2,000 |
| Increase in inventory | (2,300) |
| Amortization of patent | 300 |
| Reduction in discount on bonds | 200 |
| **Net cash flows from operating activities** | $1,700 |

# Exercise 21-23

## Direct Method

**Cash Flows from Operating Activities:**

| | |
|---|---:|
| Cash received from customers | $672 |
| Cash paid to suppliers | (234) |
| Cash paid to employees | (116) |
| Cash paid for interest | (15) |
| Cash decrease from sale of cash equivalents | (3) |
| Cash paid for income taxes | (81) |
| **Net cash flows from operating activities** | $223 |

# Exercise 21-24

## Indirect Method

Cash Flows from Operating Activities:

| | |
|---|---:|
| **Net income** | $ 86 |
| *Adjustments for noncash effects:* | |
| Decrease in accounts receivable | 12 |
| Decrease in inventory | 10 |
| Increase in accounts payable | 6 |
| Decrease in salaries payable | (6) |
| Increase in interest payable | 5 |
| Depreciation expense | 90 |
| Patent amortization expense | 5 |
| Extraordinary loss (earthquake damage) | 10 |
| Increase in income tax payable | 5 |
| **Net cash flows from operating activities** | **$223** |

# Exercise 21-25

## Direct Method

**Cash Flows from Operating Activities:**

| | |
|---|---:|
| Cash received from customers | $1,332 [a] |
| Cash decrease from sale of cash equivalents | (6) |
| Cash paid to suppliers | (484)[b] |
| Cash paid to employees | (226)[c] |
| Cash paid for interest | (35)[d] |
| Cash paid for income taxes | (187)[e] |
| **Net cash flows from operating activities** | **$ 394** |

Calculations using spreadsheet entries:

| a. Summary Entry | Cash (received from customers) | 1,332 | |
|---|---|---:|---:|
| | Accounts receivable | | 12 |
| | Sales revenue | | 1,320 |

| b. Summary Entry | Cost of goods sold | 500 | |
|---|---|---:|---:|
| | Inventory | | 10 |
| | Accounts payable | | 6 |
| | Cash (paid to suppliers of goods) | | 484 |

| c. Summary Entry | Salaries expense | 220 | |
|---|---|---:|---:|
| | Salaries payable | 6 | |
| | Cash (paid to employees) | | 226 |

| d. Summary Entry | Interest expense | 40 | |
|---|---|---:|---:|
| | Interest payable | | 5 |
| | Cash (paid for interest) | | 35 |

| e. Summary Entry | Income tax expense | 182 | |
|---|---|---:|---:|
| | Tax on E.O. gain | 10 | |
| | Income tax payable | | 5 |
| | Cash (paid for income taxes) | | 187 |

Depreciation expense, patent amortization, and the gain on early extinguishment of debt are not cash flows.

# Exercise 21-26
## Indirect Method

**Cash Flows From Operating Activities:**

| | |
|---|---:|
| **Net income** | **$192** |
| *Adjustments for noncash effects*: | |
| Depreciation expense | 180 |
| Patent amortization expense | 10 |
| Extraordinary gain (sale of subsidiary) | (20) |
| Decrease in accounts receivable | 12 |
| Decrease in inventory | 10 |
| Increase in accounts payable | 6 |
| Decrease in salaries payable | (6) |
| Increase in interest payable | 5 |
| Increase in income tax payable | 5 |
| **Net cash flows from operating activities** | **$394** |

# Exercise 21-27

## Red, Inc.
## Spreadsheet for the Statement of Cash Flows

| | Dec.31 2005 | Changes Debits | | Changes Credits | | Dec. 31 2006 |
|---|---|---|---|---|---|---|
| **Balance Sheet** | | | | | | |
| *Assets:* | | | | | | |
| Cash | 110 | | | (11) | 86 | 24 |
| Accounts receivable | 132 | (1) | 46 | | | 178 |
| Prepaid insurance | 3 | (4) | 4 | | | 7 |
| Inventory | 175 | (2) | 110 | | | 285 |
| Buildings and equipment | 350 | (6) | 230 | (7) | 180 | 400 |
| Less: Acc. depreciation | (240) | (7) | 171 | (3) | 50 | (119) |
| | 530 | | | | | 775 |
| | | | | | | |
| *Liabilities:* | | | | | | |
| Accounts payable | 100 | (2) | 13 | | | 87 |
| Accrued expenses payable | 11 | (4) | 5 | | | 6 |
| Notes payable | 0 | | | (8) | 50 | 50 |
| Bonds payable | 0 | | | (10) | 160 | 160 |
| | | | | | | |
| *Shareholders' Equity:* | | | | | | |
| Common stock | 400 | | | | | 400 |
| Retained earnings | 19 | (9) | 50 | (5) | 103 | 72 |
| | 530 | | | | | 775 |
| | | | | | | |
| **Income Statement** | | | | | | |
| *Revenues:* | | | | | | |
| Sales revenue | | | | (1) | 2,000 | 2,000 |
| *Expenses:* | | | | | | |
| Cost of goods sold | | (2) | 1,400 | | | 1,400 |
| Depreciation expense | | (3) | 50 | | | 50 |
| Operating expenses | | (4) | 447 | | | 447 |
| Net income | | (5) | 103 | | | 103 |

*Exercise 21-27 (continued)*

| | Dec.31 2005 | Changes Debits | Changes Credits | Dec. 31 2006 |
|---|---|---|---|---|
| **Spreadsheet for the Statement of Cash Flows** (continued) | | | | |
| **Statement of Cash Flows** | | | | |
| ***Operating activities:*** | | | | |
| *Cash inflows:* | | | | |
| From customers | | (1) 1,954 | | |
| *Cash outflows:* | | | | |
| To suppliers of goods | | | (2) 1,523 | |
| For operating expenses | | | (4) 456 | |
| **Net cash flows** | | | | (25) |
| ***Investing activities:*** | | | | |
| Purchase of equipment | | | (6) 230 | |
| Sale of equipment | | (7) 9 | | |
| **Net cash flows** | | | | (221) |
| ***Financing activities:*** | | | | |
| Issuance of note payable | | (8) 50 | | |
| Payment of cash dividends | | | (9) 50 | |
| Issuance of bonds payable | | (10) 160 | | |
| **Net cash flows** | | | | 160 |
| ***Net decrease in cash*** | | (11) 86 | | (86) |
| Totals | | 4,888 | 4,888 | |

*Exercise 21-27 (concluded)*

---

**Red, Inc.**
**Statement of Cash Flows**
For year ended December 31, 2006 ($ in millions)

**Cash flows from operating activities:**
*Cash inflows:*
From customers                                  $1,954
*Cash outflows:*
To suppliers of goods                          (1,523)
For operating expenses                           (456)
*Net cash flows from operating activities*                    $(25)

**Cash flows from investing activities:**
Purchase of equipment                            (230)
Sale of equipment                                   9
*Net cash flows from investing activities*                    (221)

**Cash flows from financing activities:**
Issuance of note payable                           50
Issuance of bonds payable                         160
Payment of cash dividends                         (50)
*Net cash flows from financing activities*                     160
   **Net decrease in cash**                                   (86)
Cash balance, January 1                                       110
Cash balance, December 31                                    $ 24

---

# Exercise 21-28

| | | |
|---|---|---|
| Pension expense (given) | 82 | |
| Prepaid (accrued) pension cost (difference | | |
|     between beginning credit balance and ending debit balance) | 6 | |
|       Cash (paid to the pension trustee) | | 88 |

# Exercise 21-29

1.   c
2.   a
3.   d

# Exercise 21-30

## Red, Inc.
## Spreadsheet for the Statement of Cash Flows

| | Dec.31 2005 | Changes Debits | | Changes Credits | | Dec. 31 2006 |
|---|---|---|---|---|---|---|
| **Balance Sheet** | | | | | | |
| ***Assets:*** | | | | | | |
| Cash | 110 | | | (13) | 86 | 24 |
| Accounts receivable | 132 | (3) | 46 | | | 178 |
| Prepaid insurance | 3 | (4) | 4 | | | 7 |
| Inventory | 175 | (5) | 110 | | | 285 |
| Buildings and equipment | 350 | (8) | 230 | (9) | 180 | 400 |
| Less: Acc. depreciation | (240) | (9) | 171 | (2) | 50 | (119) |
| | 530 | | | | | 775 |
| ***Liabilities:*** | | | | | | |
| Accounts payable | 100 | (6) | 13 | | | 87 |
| Accrued expenses payable | 11 | (7) | 5 | | | 6 |
| Notes payable | 0 | | | (10) | 50 | 50 |
| Bonds payable | 0 | | | (11) | 160 | 160 |
| ***Shareholders' Equity:*** | | | | | | |
| Common stock | 400 | | | | | 400 |
| Retained earnings | 19 | (12) | 50 | (1) | 103 | 72 |
| | 530 | | | | | 775 |

# Exercise 21-30 (continued)

| | Dec.31 2005 | Changes | | | | Dec. 31 2006 |
|---|---|---|---|---|---|---|
| | | **Debits** | | **Credits** | | |
| **Statement of Cash Flows** | | | | | | |
| Net income | | (1) 103 | | | | |
| *Adjustments for noncash effects:* | | | | | | |
| Depreciation expense | | (2) 50 | | | | |
| Increase in accounts receivable | | | | (3) | 46 | |
| Increase in prepaid insurance | | | | (4) | 4 | |
| Increase in inventory | | | | (5) | 110 | |
| Decrease in accounts payable | | | | (6) | 13 | |
| Decrease in accrued expenses | | | | (7) | 5 | |
| **Net cash flows** | | | | | | (25) |
| | | | | | | |
| *Investing activities:* | | | | | | |
| Purchase of equipment | | | | (8) | 230 | |
| Sale of equipment | | (9) 9 | | | | |
| **Net cash flows** | | | | | | (221) |
| | | | | | | |
| *Financing activities:* | | | | | | |
| Issuance of note payable | | (10) 50 | | | | |
| Issuance of bonds payable | | (11) 160 | | | | |
| Payment of cash dividends | | | | (12) | 50 | |
| **Net cash flows** | | | | | | 160 |
| *Net decrease in cash* | | (13) 86 | | | | (86) |
| Totals | | **1,087** | | **1,087** | | |

*Exercise 21-30 (concluded)*

---

### Red, Inc.
### Statement of Cash Flows
For year ended December 31, 2006 ($ in millions)

**Cash flows from operating activities:**

| | | |
|---|---|---|
| Net income | $ 103 | |
| *Adjustments for noncash effects:* | | |
| Depreciation expense | 50 | |
| Increase in accounts receivable | (46) | |
| Increase in prepaid insurance | (4) | |
| Increase in inventory | (110) | |
| Decrease in accounts payable | (13) | |
| Decrease in accrued expenses payable | (5) | |
| *Net cash flows from operating activities* | | $ (25) |
| | | |
| **Cash flows from investing activities:** | | |
| Purchase of equipment | (230) | |
| Sale of equipment | 9 | |
| *Net cash flows from investing activities* | | (221) |
| | | |
| **Cash flows from financing activities:** | | |
| Issuance of note payable | 50 | |
| Issuance of bonds payable | 160 | |
| Payment of cash dividends | (50) | |
| *Net cash flows from financing activities* | | 160 |
| | | |
| **Net decrease in cash** | | (86) |
| | | |
| Cash balance, January 1 | | 110 |
| Cash balance, December 31 | | $ 24 |

# Exercise 21-31

1. **d.** Under SFAS 95, a statement of cash flows should report as operating activities all transactions and other events not classified as investing or financing activities. In general, the cash flows from transactions and other events that enter into the determination of income are to be classified as operating. Distributions to owners (cash dividends on a company's own stock) are cash flows from financing, not operating, activities.

2. **a.** Investing activities include the lending of money and the collecting of those loans, and the acquisition, sale, or other disposal of securities that are not cash equivalents and of productive assets that are expected to generate revenue over a long period of time. Investing activities include the purchase of machinery and the sale of a building. The net inflow from these activities is $700,000 ($1,200,000 - $500,000). Financing activities include the issuance of preferred stock and the payment of dividends. The net inflow is $3,600,000 ($4,000,000 - $400,000). The conversion of bonds into common stock and the stock dividend do not affect cash.

3. **c.** Net operating cash flow may be determined by adjusting net income. Depreciation is an expense not directly affecting cash flows that should be added back to net income. The increase in accounts payable is added to net income because it indicates that an expense has been recorded but not paid. The gain on the sale of land is an inflow from an investing, not an operating activity and should be subtracted from net income. The dividends paid on preferred stock are cash outflows from financing, not operating, activities and do not require an adjustment. Thus, net cash flow from operations is $4,600,000 ($3,000,000 + $1,500,000 - $200,000 + $300,000).

# Exercise 21-32

## BALANCE SHEET ACCOUNTS

### Cash (Statement of Cash Flows )

| | | | | | |
|---|---|---|---|---|---|
| | | | 86 | | |

**Operating Activities:**

| | | | | | |
|---|---|---|---|---|---|
| From customers | (1) | 1,954 | 1,523 | (2) | To suppliers |
| | | | 456 | (4) | For expenses |

**Investing Activities:**

| | | | | | |
|---|---|---|---|---|---|
| | | | 230 | (6) | Purchase of equipment |
| Sale of equipment | (7) | 9 | | | |

**Financing Activities:**

| | | | | | |
|---|---|---|---|---|---|
| Issuance of notes | (8) | 50 | 50 | (9) | Payment of dividends |
| Issuance of bonds | (10) | 160 | | | |

| Accounts Receivable | | Prepaid Insurance | |
|---|---|---|---|
| 46 | | 4 | |
| (1) 46 | | (4) 4 | |

| Inventory | | Buildings and Equipment | |
|---|---|---|---|
| 110 | | 50 | |
| (2) 110 | | (6) 230 | 180 (7) |

| Accumulated Depreciation | | Accounts Payable | |
|---|---|---|---|
| 121 | | 13 | |
| (7) 171 | 50 (3) | (2) 13 | |

*Exercise 21-32 (continued)*

### Accrued Expenses Payable

| | |
|---|---|
| 5 | |
| (4)  5 | |

### Notes Payable

| | |
|---|---|
| | 50 |
| | 50  (8) |

### Bonds Payable

| | |
|---|---|
| | 160 |
| | 160  (10) |

### Retained Earnings

| | |
|---|---|
| | 53 |
| (9)  50 | 103  (5) |

## INCOME STATEMENT ACCOUNTS

### Sales

| | |
|---|---|
| | 2,000 |
| | 2,000  (1) |

### Cost of Goods Sold

| | |
|---|---|
| 1,400 | |
| (2)  1,400 | |

### Depreciation Expense

| | |
|---|---|
| 50 | |
| (3)  50 | |

### Operating Expenses

| | |
|---|---|
| 447 | |
| (4)  447 | |

### Net Income (Income Summary)

| | |
|---|---|
| 103 | |
| (5)  103 | |

*Exercise 21-32 (concluded)*

---

Red, Inc.
**Statement of Cash Flows**
For year ended December 31, 2006 ($ in millions)

**Cash flows from operating activities:**
*Cash inflows:*
  From customers $1,954
*Cash outflows:*
  To suppliers of goods (1,523)
  For operating expenses (456)
*Net cash flows from operating activities* $(25)

**Cash flows from investing activities:**
  Purchase of equipment (230)
  Sale of equipment 9
*Net cash flows from investing activities* (221)

**Cash flows from financing activities:**
  Issuance of note payable 50
  Issuance of bonds payable 160
  Payment of cash dividends (50)
*Net cash flows from financing activities* 160

  **Net decrease in cash** (86)

Cash balance, January 1 110
Cash balance, December 31 $ 24

---

# PROBLEMS

## Problem 21-1

### Classifications

| | |
|---|---|
| **+ I** | Investing activity (cash inflow) |
| **– I** | Investing activity (cash outflow |
| **+ F** | Financing activity (cash inflow) |
| **– F** | Financing activity (cash outflow) |
| **N** | Noncash investing and financing activity |
| **X** | Not reported as an investing and/or a financing activity |

### Transactions

| | | |
|---|---|---|
| *Example* | + I | 1. Sale of land |
| | + F | 2. Issuance of common stock for cash |
| | - F | 3. Purchase of treasury stock |
| | N | 4. Conversion of bonds payable to common stock |
| | N | 5. Lease of equipment by capital lease |
| | + I | 6. Sale of patent |
| | - I | 7. Acquisition of building for cash |
| | N | 8. Issuance of common stock for land |
| | + I | 9. Collection of note receivable (principal amount) |
| | + F | 10. Issuance of bonds |
| | X | 11. Issuance of stock dividend |
| | N | 12. Payment of property dividend |
| | - F | 13. Payment of cash dividends |
| | + F | 14. Issuance of short-term note payable for cash |
| | + F | 15. Issuance of long-term note payable for cash |
| | - I | 16. Purchase of marketable securities (not cash equivalent) |
| | - F | 17. Payment of note payable |
| | X | 18. Cash payment for 5-year insurance policy |
| | + I | 19. Sale of equipment |
| | N | 20. Issuance of note payable for equipment |
| | - I | 21. Acquisition of common stock of another corporation |
| | N | 22. Repayment of long-term debt by issuing common stock |
| | X | 23. Appropriation of retained earnings for plant expansion |
| | X | 24. Payment of semiannual interest on bonds payable |
| | - F | 25. Retirement of preferred stock |
| | - I | 26. Loan to another firm |
| | X | 27. Sale of inventory to customers |
| | X | 28. Purchase of marketable securities (cash equivalents) |

# Problem 21-2

## Wright Company
### Spreadsheet for the Statement of Cash Flows

| | Dec.31 2005 | Changes | | | Dec. 31 2006 |
|---|---|---|---|---|---|
| | | Debits | | Credits | |
| **Balance Sheet** | | | | | |
| *Assets:* | | | | | |
| Cash | 30 | (15) | 12 | | 42 |
| Accounts receivable | 75 | | | (1) 2 | 73 |
| Short-term investment | 15 | (9) | 25 | | 40 |
| Inventory | 70 | (2) | 5 | | 75 |
| Land | 60 | | | (6) 10 | 50 |
| Buildings and equipment | 400 | (10) | 150 | | 550 |
| Less: Acc. depreciation | (75) | | | (4) 40 | (115) |
| | 575 | | | | 715 |
| | | | | | |
| *Liabilities:* | | | | | |
| Accounts payable | 35 | (2) | 7 | | 28 |
| Salaries payable | 5 | (3) | 3 | | 2 |
| Interest payable | 3 | | | (5) 2 | 5 |
| Income tax payable | 12 | (7) | 3 | | 9 |
| Notes payable | 30 | (11) | 30 | | 0 |
| Bonds payable | 100 | | | (12) 60 | 160 |
| | | | | | |
| *Shareholders' Equity:* | | | | | |
| Common stock | 200 | | | (13) 50 | 250 |
| Paid-in capital-ex. of par | 100 | | | (13) 26 | 126 |
| Retained earnings | 90 | (14) | 35 | (8) 80 | 135 |
| | 575 | | | | 715 |
| **Statement of Income** | | | | | |
| *Revenues:* | | | | | |
| Sales revenue | | | | (1) 380 | 380 |
| *Expenses:* | | | | | |
| Cost of goods sold | | (2) | 130 | | (130) |
| Salaries expense | | (3) | 45 | | (45) |
| Depreciation expense | | (4) | 40 | | (40) |
| Interest expense | | (5) | 12 | | (12) |
| Loss on sale of land | | (6) | 3 | | (3) |
| Income tax expense | | (7) | 70 | | (70) |
| **Net income** | | (8) | 80 | | 80 |

## Problem 21-2 (continued)

| | Dec.31 2005 | Changes | | Dec. 31 2006 |
|---|---|---|---|---|
| | | **Debits** | **Credits** | |
| **Statement of Cash Flows** | | | | |
| *Operating activities:* | | | | |
| *Cash inflows:* | | | | |
| From customers | | (1) 382 | | |
| *Cash outflows:* | | | | |
| To suppliers of goods | | | (2) 142 | |
| To employees | | | (3) 48 | |
| For interest expense | | | (5) 10 | |
| For income taxes | | | (7) 73 | |
| **Net cash flows** | | | | 109 |
| | | | | |
| *Investing activities:* | | | | |
| Sale of land | | (6) 7 | | |
| Purchase of ST investment | | | (9) 25 | |
| Purchase of equipment | | | (10) 150 | |
| **Net cash flows** | | | | (168) |
| | | | | |
| *Financing activities:* | | | | |
| Repayment of notes payable | | | (11) 30 | |
| Sale of bonds payable | | (12) 60 | | |
| Sale of common stock | | (13) 76 | | |
| Payment of cash dividends | | | (14) 35 | |
| **Net cash flows** | | | | 71 |
| | | | | |
| *Net increase in cash* | | | (15) 12 | 12 |
| | | | | |
| Totals | | 1,175 | 1,175 | |

**Spreadsheet for the Statement of Cash Flows**
(continued)

*Problem 21-2 (concluded)*

---

Wright Company
**Statement of Cash Flows**
For year ended December 31, 2006 (in $000)

**Cash flows from operating activities:**
*Cash inflows:*
| | | |
|---|---|---|
| From customers | $382 | |
| *Cash outflows:* | | |
| To suppliers of goods | (142) | |
| To employees | (48) | |
| For interest expense | (10) | |
| For income taxes | (73) | |
| Net cash flows from operating activities | | $109 |

**Cash flows from investing activities:**
| | | |
|---|---|---|
| Sale of land | 7 | |
| Purchase of short-term investment | (25) | |
| Purchase of equipment | (150) | |
| Net cash flows from investing activities | | (168) |

**Cash flows from financing activities:**
| | | |
|---|---|---|
| Repayment of notes payable | (30) | |
| Sale of bonds payable | 60 | |
| Sale of common stock | 76 | |
| Payment of cash dividends | (35) | |
| Net cash flows from financing activities | | 71 |

| | | |
|---|---|---|
| **Net increase in cash** | | 12 |
| | | |
| Cash balance, January 1 | | 30 |
| Cash balance, December 31 | | $ 42 |

# Problem 21-3

## National Intercable Company
## Spreadsheet for the Statement of Cash Flows

| | Dec.31 2005 | Changes Debits | | | Changes Credits | | Dec. 31 2006 |
|---|---|---|---|---|---|---|---|
| **Balance Sheet** | | | | | | | |
| *Assets:* | | | | | | | |
| Cash | 55 | (18) | 17 | | | | 72 |
| Accounts receivable | 170 | (1) | 11 | | | | 181 |
|   Less: Allowance | (6) | | | | (1) | 2 | (8) |
| Prepaid insurance | 12 | | | | (8) | 5 | 7 |
| Inventory | 165 | (4) | 5 | | | | 170 |
| Long-term investment | 90 | (2) | 6 | | (3) | 30 | 66 |
| Land | 150 | | | | | | 150 |
| Buildings and equipment | 270 | (13) | 80 | X | (11) | 60 | 290 |
|   Less: Acc. depreciation | (75) | (11) | 15 | | (6) | 25 | (85) |
| Trademark | 25 | | | | (7) | 1 | 24 |
| | 856 | | | | | | 867 |
| | | | | | | | |
| *Liabilities:* | | | | | | | |
| Accounts payable | 45 | (4) | 15 | | | | 30 |
| Salaries payable | 8 | (5) | 5 | | | | 3 |
| Deferred tax liability | 15 | | | | (10) | 3 | 18 |
| Lease liability | 0 | | | X | (13) | 80 | 80 |
| Bonds payable | 275 | (14) | 130 | | | | 145 |
|   Less: Discount | (25) | | | | (9) | 3 | (22) |
| | | | | | | | |
| *Shareholders' Equity:* | | | | | | | |
| Common stock | 290 | | | | (15) | 20 | 310 |
| Paid-in capital-ex of par | 85 | | | | (15) | 10 | 95 |
| Preferred stock | 0 | | | | (16) | 50 | 50 |
| Retained earnings | 163 | (17) | 30 | | (12) | 25 | 158 |
| | 856 | | | | | | 867 |

X Noncash investing and financing activity

## Problem 21-3 *(continued)*

### Spreadsheet for the Statement of Cash Flows
### (continued)

| | Dec.31 2005 | Changes Debits | | Credits | | Dec. 31 2006 |
|---|---|---|---|---|---|---|
| **Statement of Income** | | | | | | |
| *Revenues:* | | | | | | |
| Sales revenue | | | (1) | 320 | | 320 |
| Investment revenue | | | (2) | 15 | | 15 |
| Gain on sale of investments | | | (3) | 5 | | 5 |
| *Expenses:* | | | | | | |
| Cost of goods sold | | (4) | 125 | | | (125) |
| Salaries expense | | (5) | 55 | | | (55) |
| Depreciation expense | | (6) | 25 | | | (25) |
| Trademark amortization | | (7) | 1 | | | (1) |
| Bad debt expense | | (1) | 7 | | | (7) |
| Insurance expense | | (8) | 13 | | | (13) |
| Bond interest expense | | (9) | 30 | | | (30) |
| Income tax expense | | (10) | 38 | | | (38) |
| Extraordinary loss (tornado) | | (11) | 42 | | | (42) |
| Less: Tax savings | | | | (10) | 21 | 21 |
| **Net income** | | (12) | 25 | | | 25 |

# Problem 21-3 (continued)

| | Dec.31 2005 | Changes Debits | | Changes Credits | | Dec. 31 2006 |
|---|---|---|---|---|---|---|
| **Statement of Cash Flows** | | | | | | |
| ***Operating activities:*** | | | | | | |
| *Cash inflows:* | | | | | | |
| From customers | | (1) | 304 | | | |
| From investment revenue | | (2) | 9 | | | |
| *Cash outflows:* | | | | | | |
| To suppliers of goods | | | | (4) | 145 | |
| To employees | | | | (5) | 60 | |
| For insurance expense | | | | (8) | 8 | |
| For bond interest expense | | | | (9) | 27 | |
| For income taxes | | | | (10) | 14 | |
| **Net cash flows** | | | | | | 59 |
| | | | | | | |
| ***Investing activities:*** | | | | | | |
| Sale of long-term investment | | (3) | 35 | | | |
| Sale of building parts | | (11) | 3 | | | |
| **Net cash flows** | | | | | | 38 |
| | | | | | | |
| ***Financing activities:*** | | | | | | |
| Retirement of bonds payable | | | | (14) | 130 | |
| Sale of common stock | | (15) | 30 | | | |
| Sale of preferred stock | | (16) | 50 | | | |
| Payment of cash dividends | | | | (17) | 30 | |
| **Net cash flows** | | | | | | (80) |
| | | | | | | |
| ***Net increase in cash*** | | | | (18) | 17 | 17 |
| | | | | | | |
| Totals | | | 1,106 | | 1,106 | |

*Problem 21-3 (concluded)*

---

National Intercable Company
**Statement of Cash Flows**
For year ended December 31, 2006 ($ in millions)

**Cash flows from operating activities:**
*Cash inflows:*
From customers ................................................... $304
From investment revenue ....................................... 9
*Cash outflows:*
To suppliers of goods ........................................... (145)
To employees ..................................................... (60)
For insurance expense ........................................... (8)
For bond interest expense ....................................... (27)
For income taxes ................................................. (14)
*Net cash flows from operating activities* ............... $ 59

**Cash flows from investing activities:**
Sale of building parts ........................................... 3
Sale of long-term investment ................................... 35
*Net cash flows from investing activities* ............... 38

**Cash flows from financing activities:**
Retirement of bonds payable ................................... (130)
Sale of common stock ........................................... 30
Sale of preferred stock ......................................... 50
Payment of cash dividends ..................................... (30)
*Net cash flows from financing activities* ............... (80)

 Net increase in cash ......................................... 17

Cash balance, January 1 ........................................ 55
Cash balance, December 31 .................................... $ 72

**Noncash investing and financing activities:**

Acquired $80 million of equipment by 7-year capital lease.

---

# Problem 21-4

| | Dec.31 2005 | Changes Debits | | Changes Credits | | Dec. 31 2006 |
|---|---|---|---|---|---|---|
| **Dux Company** | | | | | | |
| **Spreadsheet for the Statement of Cash Flows** | | | | | | |
| **Balance Sheet** | | | | | | |
| *Assets:* | | | | | | |
| Cash | 20 | (17) | 13 | | | 33 |
| Accounts receivable | 50 | | | (1) | 2 | 48 |
| Less: Allowance | (3) | | | (1) | 1 | (4) |
| Dividends receivable | 2 | (2) | 1 | | | 3 |
| Inventory | 50 | (3) | 5 | | | 55 |
| Long-term investment | 10 | (10) | 5 | | | 15 |
| Land | 40 | (11) | 30 X | | | 70 |
| Buildings and equipment | 250 | (12) | 15 | (7) | 40 | 225 |
| Less: Acc. depreciation | (50) | (7) | 30 | (5) | 5 | (25) |
| | 369 | | | | | 420 |
| *Liabilities:* | | | | | | |
| Accounts payable | 20 | (3) | 7 | | | 13 |
| Salaries payable | 5 | (4) | 3 | | | 2 |
| Interest payable | 2 | | | (6) | 2 | 4 |
| Income tax payable | 8 | (8) | 1 | | | 7 |
| Notes payable | 0 | | | X (11) | 30 | 30 |
| Bonds payable | 70 | | | (13) | 25 | 95 |
| Less: Discount on bonds | (3) | | | (6) | 1 | (2) |
| *Shareholders' Equity:* | | | | | | |
| Common stock | 200 | | | (14) | 10 | 210 |
| Paid-in capital-ex. of par | 20 | | | (14) | 4 | 24 |
| Retained earnings | 47 | (14) | 14 | | | |
| | | (15) | 13 | (9) | 25 | 45 |
| Less: Treasury stock | 0 | (16) | 8 | | | (8) |
| | 369 | | | | | 420 |

X Noncash investing and financing activity

## Spreadsheet for the Statement of Cash Flows (continued)

| | Dec.31 2005 | Changes Debits | | Changes Credits | | Dec. 31 2006 |
|---|---|---|---|---|---|---|
| **Statement of Income** | | | | | | |
| *Revenues:* | | | | | | |
| Sales revenue | | | | (1) | 200 | 200 |
| Dividend revenue | | | | (2) | 3 | 3 |
| *Expenses:* | | | | | | |
| Cost of goods sold | | (3) | 120 | | | (120) |
| Salaries expense | | (4) | 25 | | | (25) |
| Depreciation expense | | (5) | 5 | | | (5) |
| Bad debt expense | | (1) | 1 | | | (1) |
| Interest expense | | (6) | 8 | | | (8) |
| Loss on sale of building | | (7) | 3 | | | (3) |
| Income tax expense | | (8) | 16 | | | (16) |
| **Net income** | | (9) | 25 | | | 25 |
| **Statement of Cash Flows** | | | | | | |
| *Operating activities:* | | | | | | |
| *Cash inflows:* | | | | | | |
| From customers | | (1) | 202 | | | |
| From dividends received | | (2) | 2 | | | |
| *Cash outflows:* | | | | | | |
| To suppliers of goods | | | | (3) | 132 | |
| To employees | | | | (4) | 28 | |
| For interest expense | | | | (6) | 5 | |
| For income taxes | | | | (8) | 17 | |
| **Net cash flows** | | | | | | 22 |
| *Investing activities:* | | | | | | |
| Sale of building | | (7) | 7 | | | |
| Purchase of LT investment | | | | (10) | 5 | |
| Purchase of equipment | | | | (12) | 15 | |
| **Net cash flows** | | | | | | (13) |
| *Financing activities:* | | | | | | |
| Sale of bonds payable | | (13) | 25 | | | |
| Payment of cash dividends | | | | (15) | 13 | |
| Purchase of treasury stock | | | | (16) | 8 | |
| **Net cash flows** | | | | | | 4 |
| *Net increase in cash* | | | | (17) | 13 | 13 |
| Totals | | | 584 | | 584 | |

*Problem 21-4 (concluded)*

---

Dux Company
**Statement of Cash Flows**
For year ended December 31, 2006 ($ in 000s)

**Cash flows from operating activities:**
*Cash inflows:*

| | | |
|---|---:|---:|
| From customers | $202 | |
| From dividends received | 2 | |
| *Cash outflows:* | | |
| To suppliers of goods | (132) | |
| To employees | (28) | |
| For interest expense | (5) | |
| For income taxes | (17) | |
| *Net cash flows from operating activities* | | $22 |
| | | |
| **Cash flows from investing activities:** | | |
| Sale of building | 7 | |
| Purchase of long-term investment | (5) | |
| Purchase of equipment | (15) | |
| *Net cash flows from investing activities* | | (13) |
| | | |
| **Cash flows from financing activities:** | | |
| Sale of bonds payable | 25 | |
| Payment of cash dividends | (13) | |
| Purchase of treasury stock | (8) | |
| *Net cash flows from financing activities* | | 4 |
| | | |
| **Net increase in cash** | | 13 |
| | | |
| Cash balance, January 1 | | 20 |
| Cash balance, December 31 | | $33 |

**Noncash investing and financing activities:**

Acquired $30,000 of land by issuing a 13%, 7-year note.   $30

---

# Problem 21-5

## Metagrobolize Industries
## Spreadsheet for the Statement of Cash Flows

| | Dec.31 2005 | Debits | | Credits | | Dec. 31 2006 |
|---|---|---|---|---|---|---|
| **Balance Sheet** | | | | | | |
| *Assets:* | | | | | | |
| Cash | 375 | (14) 225 | | | | 600 |
| Accounts receivable | 450 | (1) 150 | | | | 600 |
| Inventory | 525 | (4) 375 | | | | 900 |
| Land | 600 | (2) 150 | X | (3) | 75 | 675 |
| Building | 900 | | | | | 900 |
| Less: Acc. depreciation | (270) | | | (5) | 30 | (300) |
| Equipment | 2,250 | (11) 900 | | (7) | 300 | 2,850 |
| Less: Acc. depreciation | (480) | (7) 270 | | (6) | 315 | (525) |
| Patent | 1,500 | | | (8) | 300 | 1,200 |
| | 5,850 | | | | | 6,900 |
| *Liabilities:* | | | | | | |
| Accounts payable | 450 | | | (4) | 300 | 750 |
| Accrued expenses | 225 | | | (9) | 75 | 300 |
| Lease liability – land | 0 | | X (2) | 150 | | 150 |
| *Shareholders' Equity:* | | | | | | |
| Common stock | 3,000 | | | (12) | 150 | 3,150 |
| Paid-in capital-ex. of par | 675 | | | (12) | 75 | 750 |
| Retained earnings | 1,500 | (12) 225 | | (10) | 975 | |
| | | (13) 450 | | | | 1,800 |
| | 5,850 | | | | | 6,900 |
| **Income Statement** | | | | | | |
| *Revenues:* | | | | | | |
| Sales revenue | | | | (1) | 2,645 | 2,645 |
| Gain on sale of land | | | | (3) | 90 | 90 |
| *Expenses:* | | | | | | |
| Cost of goods sold | | (4) 600 | | | | (600) |
| Depreciation expense-build. | | (5) 30 | | | | (30) |
| Depreciation expense-equip. | | (6) 315 | | | | (315) |
| Loss on sale of equipment | | (7) 15 | | | | (15) |
| Amortization of patent | | (8) 300 | | | | (300) |
| Operating expenses | | (9) 500 | | | | (500) |
| Net income | | (10) 975 | | | | 975 |

**Problem 21-5 (continued)**

<table>
<tr><td colspan="6" align="center">**Spreadsheet for the Statement of Cash Flows**<br>(continued)</td></tr>
<tr><td></td><td>Dec.31<br>2005</td><td colspan="2" align="center">Changes</td><td></td><td>Dec. 31<br>2006</td></tr>
<tr><td></td><td></td><td>*Debits*</td><td></td><td>*Credits*</td><td></td></tr>
<tr><td>**Statement of Cash Flows**</td><td></td><td></td><td></td><td></td><td></td></tr>
<tr><td>*Operating activities:*</td><td></td><td></td><td></td><td></td><td></td></tr>
<tr><td>*Cash inflows:*</td><td></td><td></td><td></td><td></td><td></td></tr>
<tr><td>From customers</td><td></td><td>(1)2,495</td><td></td><td></td><td></td></tr>
<tr><td>*Cash outflows:*</td><td></td><td></td><td></td><td></td><td></td></tr>
<tr><td>To suppliers of goods</td><td></td><td></td><td>(4)</td><td>675</td><td></td></tr>
<tr><td>For operating expenses</td><td></td><td></td><td>(9)</td><td>425</td><td></td></tr>
<tr><td>**Net cash flows**</td><td></td><td></td><td></td><td></td><td>1,395</td></tr>
<tr><td></td><td></td><td></td><td></td><td></td><td></td></tr>
<tr><td>*Investing activities:*</td><td></td><td></td><td></td><td></td><td></td></tr>
<tr><td>Purchase of equipment</td><td></td><td></td><td>(11)</td><td>900</td><td></td></tr>
<tr><td>Sale of land</td><td></td><td>(3) 165</td><td></td><td></td><td></td></tr>
<tr><td>Sale of equipment</td><td></td><td>(7) 15</td><td></td><td></td><td></td></tr>
<tr><td>**Net cash flows**</td><td></td><td></td><td></td><td></td><td>(720)</td></tr>
<tr><td></td><td></td><td></td><td></td><td></td><td></td></tr>
<tr><td>*Financing activities:*</td><td></td><td></td><td></td><td></td><td></td></tr>
<tr><td>Payment of cash dividends</td><td></td><td></td><td>(13)</td><td>450</td><td></td></tr>
<tr><td>**Net cash flows**</td><td></td><td></td><td></td><td></td><td>(450)</td></tr>
<tr><td>*Net increase in cash*</td><td></td><td></td><td>(14)</td><td>225</td><td>225</td></tr>
<tr><td>Totals</td><td></td><td>8,155</td><td></td><td>8,155</td><td></td></tr>
</table>

X Noncash investing and financing activity

*Problem 21-5 (concluded)*

Metagrobolize Industries
**Statement of Cash Flows**
For year ended December 31, 2006 ($ in 000)

**Cash flows from operating activities:**
*Cash inflows:*
  From customers                                              $2,495
*Cash outflows:*
  To suppliers of goods                                        (675)
  For operating expenses                                      __(425)__
*Net cash flows from operating activities*                                    $1,395

**Cash flows from investing activities:**
  Purchase of equipment                                        (900)
  Sale of land                                                  165
  Sale of equipment                                           __15__
*Net cash flows from investing activities*                                     (720)

**Cash flows from financing activities:**
  Payment of cash dividends                                   __(450)__
*Net cash flows from financing activities*                                    __(450)__

  **Net increase in cash**                                                     225

Cash balance, January 1                                                       __375__
Cash balance, December 31                                                   $ __600__

**Noncash investing and financing activities:**

Land acquired by capital lease                                                $150

# Problem 21-6

## Requirement 1

| a. **Summary Entry** | Cash (received from customers) | 153 | |
|---|---|---|---|
| | Bad debt expense | 2 | |
| |     Accounts receivable | | 3 |
| |     Allowance for uncollectible accts. | | 2 |
| |     Sales revenue | | 150 |

| b. **Summary Entry** | Cost of goods sold | 90 | |
|---|---|---|---|
| | Inventory | 6 | |
| |     Accounts payable | | 9 |
| |     Cash (paid to suppliers of goods) | | 87 |

| c. **Summary Entry** | Salaries expense | 20 | |
|---|---|---|---|
| |     Salaries payable | | 3 |
| |     Cash (paid to employees) | | 17 |

| d. **Summary Entry** | Interest expense | 6 | |
|---|---|---|---|
| |     Discount on bonds payable | | 3 |
| |     Cash (paid for interest) | | 3 |

| e. **Summary Entry** | Insurance expense | 10 | |
|---|---|---|---|
| |     Prepaid insurance | | 2 |
| |     Cash (paid for insurance ) | | 8 |

| f. **Summary Entry** | Income tax expense | 13 | |
|---|---|---|---|
| |     Income tax payable | | 6 |
| |     Cash (paid for income taxes) | | 7 |

Depreciation expense, bad debt expense, the gain on sale of equipment, and the loss on sale of land are not cash outflows.

## Problem 21-6 (concluded)

## Requirement 2

**Cash Flows From Operating Activities:**

| | |
|---|---:|
| Cash received from customers | $153 |
| Cash paid to suppliers | (87) |
| Cash paid to employees | (17) |
| Cash paid for interest | (3) |
| Cash paid for insurance | (8) |
| Cash paid for income taxes | (7) |
| | |
| **Net cash flows from operating activities** | **$ 31** |

# Problem 21-7

**Cash Flows from Operating Activities:**

| | |
|---|---:|
| Cash received from customers | $316[a] |
| Cash increase from sale of cash equivalents | 2[b] |
| Cash paid to suppliers | (114)[c] |
| Cash paid to employees | (34)[d] |
| Cash paid for interest | (11)[e] |
| Cash paid for insurance | (16)[f] |
| Cash paid for income taxes | (52)[g] |
| **Net cash flows from operating activities** | **$ 91** |

| **a.** Summary Entry | Cash (received from customers) | 316 | |
|---|---|---:|---:|
| | Accounts receivable | | 6 |
| | Sales revenue | | 310 |

**b.**

The gain on sale of cash equivalents indicates that total cash increased as a result of converting cash in one form (say a $10 million treasury bill) to cash in another form (checking account)*:

| Summary Entry | Cash [checking account] | 12 | |
|---|---|---:|---:|
| | Gain on sale of cash equivalents | | 2 |
| | Cash [treasury bill] | | 10 |

[*Any other example you think of that involves a gain on sale of cash equivalents would work as well.]

| **c.** Summary Entry | Cost of goods sold | 120 | |
|---|---|---:|---:|
| | Inventory | 12 | |
| | Accounts payable | | 18 |
| | Cash (paid to suppliers of goods) | | 114 |

| **d.** Summary Entry | Salaries expense | 40 | |
|---|---|---:|---:|
| | Salaries payable | | 6 |
| | Cash (paid to employees) | | 34 |

| **e.** Summary Entry | Interest expense | 12 | |
|---|---|---:|---:|
| | Discount on bonds payable | | 1 |
| | Cash (paid for interest) | | 11 |

# Problem 21-7 (concluded)

| f. Summary Entry | Insurance expense | 20 | |
|---|---|---|---|
| | Prepaid insurance | | 4 |
| | Cash (paid for insurance ) | | **16** |

| g. Summary Entry | Income tax expense [on ordinary income] | 50 | |
|---|---|---|---|
| | Income tax expense - on extraordinary gain | 12 | |
| | Income tax payable | | 10 |
| | Cash (paid for income taxes) | | **52** |

Depreciation expense, patent amortization expense, the loss on sale of land, and the gain are neither cash inflows nor outflows.

# Problem 21-8

## Direct Method

**Cash Flows From Operating Activities:**

| | |
|---|---:|
| Cash received from customers | $692 |
| Cash paid to suppliers | (103) |
| Cash paid to employees | (111) |
| Cash paid for insurance | (18) |
| Cash paid for interest | (40) |
| Cash paid for income taxes | (70) |

**Net cash flows from
operating activities**            $350

## Indirect Method

**Cash Flows From Operating Activities:**

| | |
|---|---:|
| **Net income** | $ 88 |
| ***Adjustments for noncash effects:*** | |
| Increase in accounts receivable | (108) |
| Decrease in inventory | 104 |
| Increase in accounts payable | 93 |
| Increase in salaries payable | 9 |
| Decrease in prepaid insurance | 22 |
| Depreciation expense | 123 |
| Decrease in bond discount | 10 |
| Gain on sale of buildings | (11) |
| Loss on sale of machinery | 12 |
| Deferred income tax liability | 8 |
| **Net cash flows from operating activities** | $350 |

# Problem 21-9

## Direct Method

**Cash Flows From Operating Activities:**

| | |
|---|---:|
| Cash received from customers | $914 |
| Cash increase from sale of cash equivalents | 4 |
| Cash paid to suppliers | (384) |
| Cash paid to employees | (228) |
| Cash paid for interest | (35) |
| Cash paid for income taxes | (54) |
| **Net cash flows from operating activities** | **$217** |

## Indirect Method

**Cash Flows From Operating Activities:**

| | |
|---|---:|
| **Net income** | **$  40** |
| *Adjustments for noncash effects:* | |
| Decrease in accounts receivable | 14 |
| Increase in inventory | (10) |
| Decrease in accounts payable | (24) |
| Decrease in salaries payable | (8) |
| Increase in interest payable | 5 |
| Depreciation expense | 190 |
| Bad debt expense | 12 |
| Extraordinary loss (flood damage) | 12 |
| Decrease in income tax payable | (14) |
| **Net cash flows from operating activities** | **$217** |

# Problem 21-10

| | | |
|---|---|---:|
| 1. | Cash received from customers | $306 |
| 2. | Cost of goods sold | $180 |
| 3. | ?        in salaries payable | Increase |
| 4. | Cash paid for depreciation | 0 |
| | [Not reported – no cash effect] | |
| 5. | Interest expense | $12 |
| 6. | Cash paid for insurance | $12 |
| 7. | Increase in income tax payable | $6 |
| 8. | Net income | $27 |

# Problem 21-11

## Arduous Company
## Spreadsheet for the Statement of Cash Flows

| | Dec.31 2005 | | Changes Debits | | | Changes Credits | Dec. 31 2006 |
|---|---|---|---|---|---|---|---|
| **Balance Sheet** | | | | | | | |
| *Assets:* | | | | | | | |
| Cash | 81 | (21) | 35 | | | | 116 |
| Accounts receivable | 202 | | | | (1) | 2 | 200 |
| Less: Allowance | (8) | | | | (1) | 2 | (10) |
| Investment rev. receivable | 4 | (2) | 2 | | | | 6 |
| Inventory | 200 | (4) | 5 | | | | 205 |
| Prepaid insurance | 8 | | | | (8) | 4 | 4 |
| Long-term investment | 125 | (2) | 6 | | | | |
| | | (13) | 25 | | | | 156 |
| Land | 150 | (14) | 46 | X | | | 196 |
| Buildings and equipment | 400 | (15) | 82 | X | (11) | 70 | 412 |
| Less: Acc. depreciation | (120) | (11) | 35 | | (6) | 12 | (97) |
| Patent | 32 | | | | (7) | 2 | 30 |
| | 1,074 | | | | | | 1,218 |
| *Liabilities:* | | | | | | | |
| Accounts payable | 65 | (4) | 15 | | | | 50 |
| Salaries payable | 11 | (5) | 5 | | | | 6 |
| Bond interest payable | 4 | | | | (9) | 4 | 8 |
| Income tax payable | 14 | (10) | 2 | | | | 12 |
| Deferred tax liability | 8 | | | | (10) | 3 | 11 |
| Notes payable | 0 | | | | X (14) | 23 | 23 |
| Lease liability | 0 | | | | X (15) | 82 | 82 |
| Bonds payable | 275 | (16) | 60 | | | | 215 |
| Less: Discount | (25) | | | | (9) | 3 | (22) |
| *Shareholders' Equity:* | | | | | | | |
| Common stock | 410 | | | | (17) | 20 | 430 |
| Paid-in capital-ex. of par | 85 | | | | (17) | 10 | 95 |
| Preferred stock | 0 | | | | (18) | 75 | 75 |
| Retained earnings | 227 | (17) | 30 | | | | |
| | | (19) | 22 | | (12) | 67 | 242 |
| Less: Treasury stock | 0 | (20) | 9 | | | | (9) |
| | 1,074 | | | | | | 1,218 |

**Problem 21-11 (continued)**

## Spreadsheet for the Statement of Cash Flows
### (continued)

| | Dec.31 2005 | Changes Debits | | Changes Credits | | Dec. 31 2006 |
|---|---|---|---|---|---|---|
| **Statement of Income** | | | | | | |
| *Revenues:* | | | | | | |
| Sales revenue | | | | (1) | 410 | 410 |
| Investment revenue | | | | (2) | 11 | 11 |
| Gain on sale of treasury bills | | | | (3) | 2 | 2 |
| *Expenses:* | | | | | | |
| Cost of goods sold | | (4) | 180 | | | (180) |
| Salaries expense | | (5) | 65 | | | (65) |
| Depreciation expense | | (6) | 12 | | | (12) |
| Patent amortization expense | | (7) | 2 | | | (2) |
| Bad debt expense | | (1) | 8 | | | (8) |
| Insurance expense | | (8) | 7 | | | (7) |
| Bond interest expense | | (9) | 28 | | | (28) |
| Income tax expense | | (10) | 45 | | | (45) |
| Extraordinary loss (flood) | | (11) | 18 | | | (18) |
| Less: Tax savings | | | | (10) | 9 | 9 |
| **Net income** | | (12) | 67 | | | 67 |

X Noncash investing and financing activity

## Problem 21-11 (continued)

### Spreadsheet for the Statement of Cash Flows
#### (continued)

| | Dec.31 2005 | Changes Debits | Changes Credits | Dec. 31 2006 |
|---|---|---|---|---|
| **Statement of Cash Flows** | | | | |
| ***Operating activities:*** | | | | |
| *Cash inflows:* | | | | |
| From customers | | (1) 406 | | |
| From investment revenue | | (2) 3 | | |
| From sale of cash equivalents | | (3) 2 | | |
| *Cash outflows:* | | | | |
| To suppliers of goods | | | (4) 200 | |
| To employees | | | (5) 70 | |
| For insurance expense | | | (8) 3 | |
| For bond interest expense | | | (9) 21 | |
| For income taxes | | | (10) 35 | |
| **Net cash flows** | | | | 82 |
| | | | | |
| ***Investing activities:*** | | | | |
| Sale of machine components | | (11) 17 | | |
| Purchase of LT investment | | | (13) 25 | |
| Purchase of land | | | (14) 23 | |
| **Net cash flows** | | | | (31) |
| | | | | |
| ***Financing activities:*** | | | | |
| Retirement of bonds payable | | | (16) 60 | |
| Sale of preferred stock | | (18) 75 | | |
| Payment of cash dividends | | | (19) 22 | |
| Purchase of treasury stock | | | (20) 9 | |
| **Net cash flows** | | | | (16) |
| | | | | |
| ***Net increase in cash*** | | | (21) 35 | 35 |
| Totals | | 1,314 | 1,314 | |

## Problem 21-11 (concluded)

Arduous Company
**Statement of Cash Flows**
For year ended December 31, 2006 ($ in millions)

**Cash flows from operating activities:**
*Cash inflows:*

| | |
|---|---:|
| From customers | $406 |
| From investment revenue | 3 |
| From sale of cash equivalents | 2 |

*Cash outflows:*

| | |
|---|---:|
| To suppliers of goods | (200) |
| To employees | (70) |
| For insurance expense | (3) |
| For bond interest expense | (21) |
| For income taxes | (35) |
| Net cash flows from operating activities | $ 82 |

**Cash flows from investing activities:**

| | |
|---|---:|
| Sale of machine components | 17 |
| Purchase of long-term investment | (25) |
| Purchase of land | (23) |
| Net cash flows from investing activities | (31) |

**Cash flows from financing activities:**

| | |
|---|---:|
| Retirement of bonds payable | (60) |
| Sale of preferred stock | 75 |
| Payment of cash dividends | (22) |
| Purchase of treasury stock | (9) |
| Net cash flows from financing activities | (16) |
| Net increase in cash | 35 |
| Cash balance, January 1 | 81 |
| Cash balance, December 31 | $116 |

**Noncash investing and financing activities:**

Acquired $82 million building by 15-year capital lease.

Acquired $46 million of land by issuing cash and a 15%, 4-year note as follows:

| | |
|---|---:|
| Cost of land | $46 |
| Cash paid | 23 |
| Note issued | $23 |

# Problem 21-12

## Requirement 1

### Retirement of common shares

($ in millions)

| | |
|---|---|
| Common stock (5 million shares x $1 par per share) ............................. | 5 |
| Paid-in capital – excess of par ($22 – 5 – 2)................................... | 15 |
| Retained earnings (given)........................................................... | 2 |
|    Cash (given)* ...................................................................... | 22 |

*This transaction identifies a $22 million cash outflow from financing activities.

### Net income closed to retained earnings

| | |
|---|---|
| Income summary ........................................................................ | 88 |
|    Retained earnings (given) .......................................................... | 88 |

*The operating activities summarized by this transaction are identified individually when we explain the changes in the components of net income. But including the entry on the spreadsheet is helpful in partially explaining change in retained earnings.

### Declaration of a cash dividend

| | |
|---|---|
| Retained earnings (given)............................................................ | 33 |
|    Cash ..................................................................................... | 33 |

*This transaction identifies a $33 million cash outflow from financing activities.

### Declaration of a stock dividend

| | |
|---|---|
| Retained earnings (given)........................................................... | 20 |
|    Common stock ([105-5] x 4%) million shares at $1 par per share) .......... | 4 |
|    Paid-in capital – excess of par (difference) ............................... | 16 |

*This transaction does not represent a significant investing nor financing activity, but including the entry on the spreadsheet is helpful in partially explaining changes in the balances of the two accounts affected.

**Requirement 2**

## Brenner-Jude Corporation
## Statements of Retained Earnings
FOR THE YEAR ENDED DECEMBER 31, 2006

($ in millions)

| | |
|---|---|
| **Balance at January 1** | $ 90 |
| Net income for the year | 88 |
| *Deductions*: | |
| Retirement of common stock | (2) |
| Cash dividends of $.33 per share | (33) |
| 4% stock dividend | (20) |
| **Balance at December 31** | $123 |

# Problem 21-13

|  | Amount | Category |
|---|---|---|
| 1. Cash collections from customers (direct method). | $145,000[1] | O |
| 2. Payments for purchase of property, plant, and equipment. | $ 50,000[2] | I |
| 3. Proceeds from sale of equipment. | $ 31,000[3] | I |
| 4. Cash dividends paid. | $ 12,000[4] | F |
| 5. Redemption of bonds payable. | $ 17,000[5] | F |

[1] **Summary Entry**

| | | |
|---|---|---|
| Cash (received from customers) | **145,000** | |
| Accounts receivable ($34,000 - 24,000) | 10,000 | |
| Sales revenue (given) | | 155,000 |

### [2]P, P, & E

| | | | |
|---|---|---|---|
| Beginning balance | 247 | | |
| Acquired with B/P | 20 | | |
| | | 40 | Equipment sold |
| Purchased | **?** | | |
| Ending balance | 277 | | |

$277,000 + 40,000 - 247,000 - 20,000 = \textbf{\$50,000}$

[3] **Summary Entry**

| | | |
|---|---|---|
| Cash (sale of equipment) | **31,000** | |
| Accumulated depreciation (determined below) | 22,000 | |
| P, P, & E (given) | | 40,000 |
| Gain on sale of equipment (given) | | 13,000 |

### Accumulated Depreciation

| | | | |
|---|---|---|---|
| | | 167 | Beginning balance |
| | | 33 | Depreciation expense |
| Equipment sold | **?** | | |
| | | 178 | Ending balance |

$167,000 + 33,000 - 178,000 = \$22,000$

# Problem 21-13 (concluded)

[4] **Summary Entry**

| | | |
|---|---|---|
| Retained earnings (determined below) | 15,000 | |
|     Dividends payable ($8,000 - 5,000) | | 3,000 |
|     Cash (paid for dividends) | | **12,000** |

## Retained Earnings

| | | | |
|---|---|---|---|
| | | 91 | Beginning balance |
| | | 28 | Net income |
| Dividends declared | **?** | | |
| | | 104 | Ending balance |

$91,000 + 28,000 - 104,000 = $15,000

[5] **Summary Entry**

| | | |
|---|---|---|
| Bonds payable (determined below) | 17,000 | |
|     Cash | | **17,000** |

## Bonds payable

| | | | |
|---|---|---|---|
| | | 46 | Beginning balance |
| | | 20 | Issued for P, P, & E |
| Bonds redeemed | **?** | | |
| | | 49 | Ending balance |

$46,000 + 20,000 - 49,000 = $17,000

# Problem 21-14

## Surmise Company
## Spreadsheet for the Statement of Cash Flows

| | Dec.31 2005 | Debits | | | Credits | | Dec. 31 2006 |
|---|---|---|---|---|---|---|---|
| **Balance Sheet** | | | | | | | |
| *Assets:* | | | | | | | |
| Cash | 40 | (16) | 5 | | | | 45 |
| Accounts receivable | 96 | | | (5) | | 4 | 92 |
| Less: Allowance | (4) | | | (3) | | 8 | (12) |
| Prepaid expenses | 5 | (8) | 3 | | | | 8 |
| Inventory | 130 | (6) | 15 | | | | 145 |
| Long-term investment | 40 | (10) | 40 | | | | 80 |
| Land | 100 | | | | | | 100 |
| Buildings and equip. | 300 | (11) | 111 X | | | | 411 |
| Less: Acc. depreciation | (120) | | | (2) | | 22 | (142) |
| Patent | 17 | | | (4) | | 1 | 16 |
| | 604 | | | | | | 743 |
| *Liabilities:* | | | | | | | |
| Accounts payable | 32 | (7) | 15 | | | | 17 |
| Accrued liabilities | 10 | (9) | 12 | | | | (2) |
| Notes payable | 0 | | | (12) | | 35 | 35 |
| Lease liability | 0 | | | X (11) | | 111 | 111 |
| Bonds payable | 125 | (13) | 60 | | | | 65 |
| *Shareholders' Equity:* | | | | | | | |
| Common stock | 50 | | | (14) | | 10 | 60 |
| Paid-in capital-ex. of par | 205 | | | (14) | | 40 | 245 |
| Retained earnings | 182 | (15) | 20 | (1) | | 50 | 212 |
| | 604 | | | | | | 743 |

**X** Noncash investing and financing activity

*Intermediate Accounting, 4e*

# Problem 21-14 (continued)

## Spreadsheet for the Statement of Cash Flows
### (continued)

| | Dec.31 2005 | Debits | Credits | Dec. 31 2006 |
|---|---|---|---|---|
| **Statement of Cash Flows** | | | | / |
| *Operating activities:* | | | | |
| Net income | | (1) 50 | | |
| *Adjustments for noncash effects:* | | | | |
| Depreciation expense | | (2) 22 | | |
| Bad debt expense | | (3) 8 | | |
| Patent amortization expense | | (4) 1 | | |
| Decrease in accounts receivable | | (5) 4 | | |
| Increase in inventory | | | (6) 15 | |
| Decrease in accounts payable | | | (7) 15 | |
| Increase in prepaid expenses | | | (8) 3 | |
| Decrease in accrued liabilities | | | (9) 12 | |
| **Net cash flows** | | | | 40 |
| *Investing activities:* | | | | |
| Purchase of LT investment | | | (10) 40 | |
| **Net cash flows** | | | | (40) |
| *Financing activities:* | | | | |
| Issuance of note payable | | (12) 35 | | |
| Retirement of bonds payable | | | (13) 60 | |
| Sale of common stock | | (14) 50 | | |
| Payment of cash dividends | | | (15) 20 | |
| **Net cash flows** | | | | 5 |
| *Net increase in cash* | | | (16) 5 | 5 |
| Totals | | 451 | 451 | |

*Problem 21-14 (concluded)*

---

Surmise Company
**Statement of Cash Flows**
For year ended December 31, 2006 ($ in millions)

**Cash flows from operating activities:**

| | | |
|---|---|---|
| *Net income* | $ 50 | |
| Adjustments for noncash effects: | | |
| Depreciation expense | 22 | |
| Bad debt expense | 8 | |
| Patent amortization expense | 1 | |
| Decrease in accounts receivable | 4 | |
| Increase in inventory | (15) | |
| Decrease in accounts payable | (15) | |
| Increase in prepaid expenses | (3) | |
| Decrease in accrued liabilities | (12) | |
| *Net cash flows from operating activities* | | $40 |

**Cash flows from investing activities:**

| | | |
|---|---|---|
| Purchase of long-term investment | (40) | |
| *Net cash flows from investing activities* | | (40) |

**Cash flows from financing activities:**

| | | |
|---|---|---|
| Issuance of note payable | 35 | |
| Retirement of bonds payable | (60) | |
| Sale of common stock | 50 | |
| Payment of cash dividends | (20) | |
| *Net cash flows from financing activities* | | 5 |

| | | |
|---|---|---|
| **Net increase in cash** | | 5 |
| Cash balance, January 1 | | 40 |
| Cash balance, December 31 | | $45 |

**Noncash investing and financing activities:**

| | | |
|---|---|---|
| Acquired buildings by capital lease | | $111 |

# Problem 21-15

**Dux Company**
**Spreadsheet for the Statement of Cash Flows**

| | Dec.31 2005 | Changes Debits | | | Changes Credits | | Dec. 31 2006 |
|---|---|---|---|---|---|---|---|
| **Balance Sheet** | | | | | | | |
| *Assets:* | | | | | | | |
| Cash | 20 | (20) | 13 | | | | 33 |
| Accounts receivable | 50 | | | (5) | | 2 | 48 |
| Less: Allowance | (3) | | | (6) | | 1 | (4) |
| Dividends receivable | 2 | (7) | 1 | | | | 3 |
| Inventory | 50 | (8) | 5 | | | | 55 |
| Long-term investment | 10 | (13) | 5 | | | | 15 |
| Land | 40 | (14) | 30 X | | | | 70 |
| Buildings and equipment | 250 | (15) | 15 | (4) | | 40 | 225 |
| Less: Acc. depreciation | (50) | (4) | 30 | (2) | | 5 | (25) |
| | 369 | | | | | | 420 |
| **Liabilities:** | | | | | | | |
| Accounts payable | 20 | (9) | 7 | | | | 13 |
| Salaries payable | 5 | (10) | 3 | | | | 2 |
| Interest payable | 2 | | | (11) | | 2 | 4 |
| Income tax payable | 8 | (12) | 1 | | | | 7 |
| Notes payable | 0 | | | X (14) | | 30 | 30 |
| Bonds payable | 70 | | | (16) | | 25 | 95 |
| Less: Discount on bonds | (3) | | | (3) | | 1 | (2) |
| | | | | | | | |
| **Shareholders' Equity:** | | | | | | | |
| Common stock | 200 | | | (17) | | 10 | 210 |
| Paid-in capital-ex. of par | 20 | | | (17) | | 4 | 24 |
| Retained earnings | 47 | (17) | 14 | | | | |
| | | (18) | 13 | (1) | | 25 | 45 |
| Less: Treasury stock | 0 | (19) | 8 | | | | (8) |
| | 369 | | | | | | 420 |

X Noncash investing and financing activity

# Problem 21-15 (continued)

| | Dec.31 2005 | Changes Debits | | Changes Credits | | Dec. 31 2006 |
|---|---|---|---|---|---|---|
| **Statement of Cash Flows** | | | | | | |
| Net income | | (1) | 25 | | | |
| *Adjustments for noncash effects:* | | | | | | |
| Depreciation expense | | (2) | 5 | | | |
| Amortization of discount | | (3) | 1 | | | |
| Loss on sale of building | | (4) | 3 | | | |
| Decrease in accounts receivable | | (5) | 2 | | | |
| Increase in allowance | | (6) | 1 | | | |
| Increase in dividends receivable | | | | (7) | 1 | |
| Increase in inventory | | | | (8) | 5 | |
| Decrease in accounts payable | | | | (9) | 7 | |
| Decrease in salaries payable | | | | (10) | 3 | |
| Increase in interest payable | | (11) | 2 | | | |
| Decrease in income tax payable | | | | (12) | 1 | |
| **Net cash flows** | | | | | | 22 |
| | | | | | | |
| *Investing activities:* | | | | | | |
| Sale of building | | (4) | 7 | | | |
| Purchase of LT investment | | | | (13) | 5 | |
| Purchase of equipment | | | | (15) | 15 | |
| **Net cash flows** | | | | | | (13) |
| | | | | | | |
| *Financing activities:* | | | | | | |
| Sale of bonds payable | | (16) | 25 | | | |
| Payment of cash dividends | | | | (18) | 13 | |
| Purchase of treasury stock | | | | (19) | 8 | |
| **Net cash flows** | | | | | | 4 |
| | | | | | | |
| *Net increase in cash* | | | | (20) | 13 | 13 |
| | | | | | | |
| Totals | | | 216 | | 216 | |

**Spreadsheet for the Statement of Cash Flows** (continued)

Dux Company
**Statement of Cash Flows**
For year ended December 31, 2006 ($ in 000s)

**Cash flows from operating activities:**

| | | |
|---|---|---|
| Net income | $25 | |
| *Adjustments for noncash effects:* | | |
| Depreciation expense | 5 | |
| Amortization of discount | 1 | |
| Loss on sale of building | 3 | |
| Decrease in accounts receivable | 2 | |
| Increase in allowance for uncollectibles | 1 | |
| Increase in dividends receivable | (1) | |
| Increase in inventory | (5) | |
| Decrease in accounts payable | (7) | |
| Decrease in salaries payable | (3) | |
| Increase in interest payable | 2 | |
| Decrease in income tax payable | (1) | |
| *Net cash flows from operating activities* | | $22 |

**Cash flows from investing activities:**

| | | |
|---|---|---|
| Sale of building | 7 | |
| Purchase of long-term investment | (5) | |
| Purchase of equipment | (15) | |
| *Net cash flows from investing activities* | | (13) |

**Cash flows from financing activities:**

| | | |
|---|---|---|
| Sale of bonds payable | 25 | |
| Payment of cash dividends | (13) | |
| Purchase of treasury stock | (8) | |
| *Net cash flows from financing activities* | | 4 |

| | | |
|---|---|---|
| **Net increase in cash** | | 13 |
| Cash balance, January 1 | | 20 |
| Cash balance, December 31 | | $33 |

**Noncash investing and financing activities:**

Acquired $30,000 of land by issuing a 13%, 7-year note.    $30

# Problem 21-16

| | Dec.31 2005 | Changes Debits | | Changes Credits | | Dec. 31 2006 |
|---|---|---|---|---|---|---|
| **Balance Sheet** | | | | | | |
| *Assets:* | | | | | | |
| Cash | 375 | (15) 225 | | | | 600 |
| Accounts receivable | 450 | (7) 150 | | | | 600 |
| Inventory | 525 | (8) 375 | | | | 900 |
| Land | 600 | (11) 150 | X | (2) | 75 | 675 |
| Building | 900 | | | | | 900 |
| Less: Acc. depreciation | (270) | | | (3) | 30 | (300) |
| Equipment | 2,250 | (12) 900 | | (5) | 300 | 2,850 |
| Less: Acc. depreciation | (480) | (5) 270 | | (4) | 315 | (525) |
| Patent | 1,500 | | | (6) | 300 | 1,200 |
| | 5,850 | | | | | 6,900 |
| **Liabilities:** | | | | | | |
| Accounts payable | 450 | | | (9) | 300 | 750 |
| Accrued expenses | 225 | | | (10) | 75 | 300 |
| Lease liability–land | 0 | | X | (11) | 150 | 150 |
| **Shareholders' Equity:** | | | | | | |
| Common stock | 3,000 | | | (13) | 150 | 3,150 |
| Paid-in capital-ex. of par | 675 | | | (13) | 75 | 750 |
| Retained earnings | 1,500 | (13) 225 | | (1) | 975 | |
| | | (14) 450 | | | | 1,800 |
| | 5,850 | | | | | 6,900 |

X Noncash investing and financing activity

# Problem 21-16 (continued)

## Spreadsheet for the Statement of Cash Flows
### (continued)

| | Dec.31 2005 | Changes Debits | Changes Credits | Dec. 31 2006 |
|---|---|---|---|---|
| **Statement of Cash Flows** | | | | |
| ***Operating activities:*** | | | | |
| Net income | | (1) 975 | | |
| *Adjustments for noncash effects:* | | | | |
| Gain on sale of land | | | (2) 90 | |
| Depreciation expense-build | | (3) 30 | | |
| Depreciation expense-equip | | (4) 315 | | |
| Loss on sale of equipment | | (5) 15 | | |
| Amortization of patent | | (6) 300 | | |
| Increase in accounts receivable | | | (7) 150 | |
| Increase in inventory | | | (8) 375 | |
| Increase in accounts payable | | (9) 300 | | |
| Increase in accrued expenses | | (10) 75 | | |
| **Net cash flows** | | | | 1,395 |
| ***Investing activities:*** | | | | |
| Purchase of equipment | | | (12) 900 | |
| Sale of land | | (2) 165 | | |
| Sale of equipment | | (5) 15 | | |
| **Net cash flows** | | | | (720) |
| | | | | |
| ***Financing activities:*** | | | | |
| Payment of cash dividends | | | (14) 450 | |
| **Net cash flows** | | | | (450) |
| *Net increase in cash* | | | (15) 225 | 225 |
| Totals | | 4,935 | 4,935 | |

*Problem 21-16 (concluded)*

---

Metagrobolize Industries
**Statement of Cash Flows**
For year ended December 31, 2006 ($ in 000s)

**Cash flows from operating activities:**

| | | |
|---|---:|---:|
| Net income | $ 975 | |
| *Adjustments for noncash effects:* | | |
| Gain on sale of land | (90) | |
| Depreciation expense – building | 30 | |
| Depreciation expense – equipment | 315 | |
| Loss on sale of equipment | 15 | |
| Amortization of patent | 300 | |
| Increase in accounts receivable | (150) | |
| Increase in inventory | (375) | |
| Increase in accounts payable | 300 | |
| Increase in accrued expenses | 75 | |
| *Net cash flows from operating activities* | | $1,395 |

**Cash flows from investing activities:**

| | | |
|---|---:|---:|
| Purchase of equipment | (900) | |
| Sale of land | 165 | |
| Sale of equipment | 15 | |
| *Net cash flows from investing activities* | | (720) |

**Cash flows from financing activities:**

| | | |
|---|---:|---:|
| Payment of cash dividends | (450) | |
| *Net cash flows from financing activities* | | (450) |

| | | |
|---|---:|---:|
| **Net increase in cash** | | 225 |
| Cash balance, January 1 | | 375 |
| Cash balance, December 31 | | $   600 |

**Noncash investing and financing activities:**

| | |
|---|---:|
| Land acquired by capital lease | $150 |

# Problem 21-17

## Arduous Company
### Spreadsheet for the Statement of Cash Flows

| | Dec.31 2005 | Debits | | | Credits | | Dec. 31 2006 |
|---|---|---|---|---|---|---|---|
| | | | **Changes** | | | | |
| **Balance Sheet** | | | | | | | |
| *Assets:* | | | | | | | |
| Cash | 81 | (25) | 35 | | | | 116 |
| Accounts receivable | 202 | | | (5) | | 2 | 200 |
| Less: Allowance | (8) | | | (6) | | 2 | (10) |
| Investment rev. receivable | 4 | (7) | 2 | | | | 6 |
| Inventory | 200 | (10) | 5 | | | | 205 |
| Prepaid insurance | 8 | | | (9) | | 4 | 4 |
| Long-term investment | 125 | (8) | 6 | | | | |
| | | (17) | 25 | | | | 156 |
| Land | 150 | (18) | 46 X | | | | 196 |
| Buildings and equipment | 400 | (19) | 82 X | (16) | | 70 | 412 |
| Less: Acc. depreciation | (120) | (16) | 35 | (2) | | 12 | (97) |
| Patent | 32 | | | (3) | | 2 | 30 |
| | 1,074 | | | | | | 1,218 |
| **Liabilities:** | | | | | | | |
| Accounts payable | 65 | (11) | 15 | | | | 50 |
| Salaries payable | 11 | (12) | 5 | | | | 6 |
| Bond interest payable | 4 | | | (13) | | 4 | 8 |
| Income tax payable | 14 | (14) | 2 | | | | 12 |
| Deferred tax liability | 8 | | | (15) | | 3 | 11 |
| Notes payable | 0 | | | X (18) | | 23 | 23 |
| Lease liability | 0 | | | X (19) | | 82 | 82 |
| Bonds payable | 275 | (20) | 60 | | | | 215 |
| Less: Discount | (25) | | | (4) | | 3 | (22) |
| **Shareholders' Equity:** | | | | | | | |
| Common stock | 410 | | | (21) | | 20 | 430 |
| Paid-in capital-ex. of par | 85 | | | (21) | | 10 | 95 |
| Preferred stock | 0 | | | (22) | | 75 | 75 |
| Retained earnings | 227 | (21) | 30 | | | | |
| | | (23) | 22 | (1) | | 67 | 242 |
| Less: Treasury stock | 0 | (24) | 9 | | | | (9) |
| | 1,074 | | | | | | 1,218 |

## Problem 21-17 (continued)

| | Dec.31 2005 | Changes | | Dec. 31 2006 |
| --- | --- | --- | --- | --- |
| | | *Debits* | *Credits* | |
| **Statement of Cash Flows** | | | | |
| ***Operating activities:*** | | | | |
| Net income | (1) | 67 | | |
| *Adjustments for noncash effects:* | | | | |
| Depreciation expense | (2) | 12 | | |
| Patent amortization expense | (3) | 2 | | |
| Amortization of discount | (4) | 3 | | |
| Decrease in accounts receivable | (5) | 2 | | |
| Increase in allowance | (6) | 2 | | |
| Increase in investment rev. rec. | | | (7) 2 | |
| Equity method income | | | (8) 6 | |
| Decrease in prepaid insurance | (9) | 4 | | |
| Increase in inventory | | | (10) 5 | |
| Decrease in accounts payable | | | (11) 15 | |
| Decrease in salaries payable | | | (12) 5 | |
| Increase in interest payable | (13) | 4 | | |
| Decrease in tax payable | | | (14) 2 | |
| Increase in deferred tax liability | (15) | 3 | | |
| Loss on flood (extraordinary) | (16) | 18 | | |
| **Net cash flows** | | | | 82 |
| | | | | |
| ***Investing activities:*** | | | | |
| Sale of machine components | (16) | 17 | | |
| Purchase of LT investment | | | (17) 25 | |
| Purchase of land | | | (18) 23 | |
| **Net cash flows** | | | | (31) |
| | | | | |
| ***Financing activities:*** | | | | |
| Retirement of bonds payable | | | (20) 60 | |
| Sale of preferred stock | (22) | 75 | | |
| Payment of cash dividends | | | (23) 22 | |
| Purchase of treasury stock | | | (24) 9 | |
| **Net cash flows** | | | | (16) |
| | | | | |
| ***Net increase in cash*** | | | (25) 35 | 35 |
| Totals | | 588 | 588 | |

Spreadsheet for the Statement of Cash Flows (continued)

---

Arduous Company
**Statement of Cash Flows**
For year ended December 31, 2006 ($ in millions)

**Cash flows from operating activities:**

| | |
|---|---:|
| Net income | $67 |
| *Adjustments for noncash effects:* | |
| Depreciation expense | 12 |
| Patent amortization expense | 2 |
| Amortization of discount | 3 |
| Decrease in accounts receivable | 2 |
| Increase in allowance for uncollectible accounts | 2 |
| Increase in investment revenue receivable | (2) |
| Increase in investment due to equity method income | (6) |
| Decrease in prepaid insurance | 4 |
| Increase in inventory | (5) |
| Decrease in accounts payable | (15) |
| Decrease in salaries payable | (5) |
| Increase in interest payable | 4 |
| Decrease in income tax payable | (2) |
| Increase in deferred tax liability | 3 |
| Loss on flood (extraordinary) | 18 |
| *Net cash flows from operating activities* | $ 82 |
| **Cash flows from investing activities:** | |
| Sale of machine components | 17 |
| Purchase of long-term investment | (25) |
| Purchase of land | (23) |
| *Net cash flows from investing activities* | (31) |
| **Cash flows from financing activities:** | |
| Retirement of bonds payable | (60) |
| Sale of preferred stock | 75 |
| Payment of cash dividends | (22) |
| Purchase of treasury stock | (9) |
| *Net cash flows from financing activities* | (16) |
| **Net increase in cash** | 35 |
| Cash balance, January 1 | 81 |
| Cash balance, December 31 | $116 |

*Problem 21-17 (concluded)*

**Noncash investing and financing activities:**

Acquired $82 million building by 15-year capital lease.

Acquired $46 million of land by issuing cash and a 15%, 4-year note as follows:

| | |
|---|---|
| Cost of land | $46 |
| Cash paid | 23 |
| Note issued | $23 |

X Noncash investing and financing activity

**The following problems use the technique learned in Appendix 21-B.**

# Problem 21-18

## *BALANCE SHEET ACCOUNTS*

### Cash (Statement of Cash Flows )

|  | 13 |  |  |  |
|---|---|---|---|---|
| **Operating Activities:** | | | | |
| From customers | (1) 202 | 132 | (3) | To suppliers of goods |
| From dividends received | (2) 2 | 28 | (4) | To employees |
| | | 5 | (6) | For interest |
| | | 17 | (8) | For income taxes |
| | | | | |
| **Investing Activities:** | | | | |
| Sale of building | (7) 7 | 5 | (10) | Purchase of LT investment |
| | | 15 | (12) | Purchase of equipment |
| | | | | |
| **Financing Activities:** | | | | |
| Sale of bonds payable | (13) 25 | 13 | (15) | Payment of dividends |
| | | 8 | (16) | Purchase of treasury stock |

| **Accounts Receivable** | | **Allowance for Uncollectibles** | |
|---|---|---|---|
| 2 | | | 1 |
| | 2 (1) | | 1 (1) |

| **Inventory** | | **Dividends Receivable** | |
|---|---|---|---|
| 5 | | 1 | |
| (3) 5 | | (2) 1 | |

## Problem 21-18 (continued)

### Long-term Investments

| | |
|---|---|
| 5 | |
| (10)  5 | |

### Land

| | |
|---|---|
| 30 | |
| X (11)  30 | |

### Buildings and Equipment

| | |
|---|---|
| | 25 |
| (12)  15 | 40  (7) |

### Accumulated Depreciation

| | |
|---|---|
| | 25 |
| (7)  30 | 5  (5) |

### Accounts Payable

| | |
|---|---|
| 7 | |
| (3)  7 | |

### Salaries Payable

| | |
|---|---|
| 3 | |
| (4)  3 | |

### Interest Payable

| | |
|---|---|
| | 2 |
| | 2  (6) |

### Income Tax Payable

| | |
|---|---|
| | 1 |
| (8)  1 | |

### Notes Payable

| | |
|---|---|
| | 30 |
| | 30  (11) X |

### Bonds Payable

| | |
|---|---|
| | 25 |
| | 25  (13) |

### Discount on Bonds

| | |
|---|---|
| | 1 |
| | 1  (6) |

### Common Stock

| | |
|---|---|
| | 10 |
| | 10  (14) |

*Problem 21-18 (continued)*

| Paid-in Capital | | | Retained Earnings | | |
|---|---|---|---|---|---|
| | 4 | | | 2 | |
| | 4 | (14) | (14) 14 | 25 | (9) |
| | | | (15) 13 | | |

**Treasury Stock**

| | 8 | |
|---|---|---|
| (16) | 8 | |

X Noncash investing and financing activity

## *INCOME STATEMENT ACCOUNTS*

| Sales | | Dividend Revenue | |
|---|---|---|---|
| | 200 | | 3 |
| | 200   (1) | | 3   (2) |

| Cost of Goods Sold | | Salaries Expense | |
|---|---|---|---|
| 120 | | 25 | |
| (3)  120 | | (4)  25 | |

| Depreciation Expense | | Bad Debts Expense | |
|---|---|---|---|
| 5 | | 1 | |
| (5)  5 | | (1)  1 | |

| Interest Expense | | Loss on Sale of Building | |
|---|---|---|---|
| 8 | | 3 | |
| (6)  8 | | (7)  3 | |

| Income Tax Expense | | Net Income (Income Summary) | |
|---|---|---|---|
| 16 | | 25 | |
| (8)  16 | | (9)  25 | |

**Problem 21-18 (concluded)**

---

Dux Company
**Statement of Cash Flows**
For year ended December 31, 2006 ($ in 000s)

**Cash flows from operating activities:**
*Cash inflows:*

| | | |
|---|---:|---:|
| From customers | $202 | |
| From dividends received | 2 | |
| *Cash outflows:* | | |
| To suppliers of goods | (132) | |
| To employees | (28) | |
| For interest expense | (5) | |
| For income taxes | (17) | |
| *Net cash flows from operating activities* | | $22 |

**Cash flows from investing activities:**

| | | |
|---|---:|---:|
| Sale of building | 7 | |
| Purchase of long-term investment | (5) | |
| Purchase of equipment | (15) | |
| *Net cash flows from investing activities* | | (13) |

**Cash flows from financing activities:**

| | | |
|---|---:|---:|
| Sale of bonds payable | 25 | |
| Payment of cash dividends | (13) | |
| Purchase of treasury stock | (8) | |
| *Net cash flows from financing activities* | | 4 |
| **Net increase in cash** | | 13 |
| Cash balance, January 1 | | 20 |
| Cash balance, December 31 | | $33 |

**Noncash investing and financing activities:**

Acquired $30,000 of land by issuing a 13%, 7-year note.   $30

---

# Problem 21-19

## BALANCE SHEET ACCOUNTS

### Cash (Statement of Cash Flows)

| | | | |
|---|---|---|---|
| | 225 | | |

**Operating Activities:**

| | | | | |
|---|---|---|---|---|
| From customers | (1) 2,495 | 675 | (4) | To suppliers |
| | | 425 | (9) | For expenses |

**Investing Activities:**

| | | | | |
|---|---|---|---|---|
| Sale of land | (3) 165 | 900 | (11) | Purchase of equipment |
| Sale of equipment | (7) 15 | | | |

**Financing Activities:**

| | | | |
|---|---|---|---|
| | 450 | (13) | Payment of div. |

| Accounts Receivable | | Inventory | |
|---|---|---|---|
| 150 | | 375 | |
| (1) 150 | | (4) 375 | |

| Land | | Accumulated Depr.-Buildings | |
|---|---|---|---|
| 75 | | | 30 |
| X (2) 150 | 75 (3) | | 30 (5) |

| Equipment | | Accumulated Depr.-Equipment | |
|---|---|---|---|
| 600 | | | 45 |
| (11) 900 | 300 (7) | (7) 270 | 315 (6) |

## Problem 21-19 (continued)

### Patent

|  |  |  |
|---|---|---|
| 300 |  |  |
| 300 | (8) |  |

### Accounts Payable

|  |  |  |
|---|---|---|
| 300 |  |  |
| 300 | (4) |  |

### Accrued Expenses Payable

|  |  |  |
|---|---|---|
| 75 |  |  |
| 75 | (9) |  |

### Lease Liability-Land

|  |  |  |
|---|---|---|
| 150 |  |  |
| 150 | (2) X |  |

### Common Stock

|  |  |  |
|---|---|---|
| 150 |  |  |
| 150 | (12) |  |

### Paid-in Capital

|  |  |  |
|---|---|---|
| 75 |  |  |
| 75 | (12) |  |

### Retained Earnings

|  |  |  |  |
|---|---|---|---|
|  | 300 |  |  |
| (12) 225 | 975 | (10) |  |
| (13) 450 |  |  |  |

X Noncash investing and financing activity

*Problem 21-19 (continued)*

## INCOME STATEMENT ACCOUNTS

### Sales

| | 2,645 |
|---|---|
| | 2,645  (1) |

### Gain on Sale of Land

| | 90 |
|---|---|
| | 90    (3) |

### Cost of Goods Sold

| 600 | |
|---|---|
| (4)  600 | |

### Depreciation Expense-Build.

| 30 | |
|---|---|
| (5)   30 | |

### Depreciation Expense-Equip.

| 315 | |
|---|---|
| (6)  315 | |

### Loss on Sale of Equipment

| 15 | |
|---|---|
| (7)   15 | |

### Amortization of Patent

| 300 | |
|---|---|
| (8)  300 | |

### Operating Expenses

| 500 | |
|---|---|
| (9) 500 | |

### Net Income (Income Summary)

| 975 | |
|---|---|
| (10)  975 | |

*Problem 21-19 (concluded)*

Metagrobolize Industries
**Statement of Cash Flows**
For year ended December 31, 2006 ($ in 000s)

**Cash flows from operating activities:**
*Cash inflows:*
From customers ............................................ $2,495
*Cash outflows:*
  To suppliers of goods ................................. (675)
  For operating expenses ............................... (425)
*Net cash flows from operating activities* .......... $1,395

**Cash flows from investing activities:**
  Purchase of equipment ............................... (900)
  Sale of land ............................................ 165
  Sale of equipment .................................... 15
*Net cash flows from investing activities* ......... (720)

**Cash flows from financing activities:**
  Payment of cash dividends ......................... (450)
*Net cash flows from financing activities* ......... (450)

  **Net increase in cash** ............................. 225

Cash balance, January 1 ............................... 375
Cash balance, December 31 ........................... $ 600

**Noncash investing and financing activities:**

Land acquired by capital lease ....................... $150

# Problem 21-20

## BALANCE SHEET ACCOUNTS

### Cash (Statement of Cash Flows )

|  |  | 35 |  |  |
|---|---|---|---|---|

**Operating Activities:**

| From customers | (1) | 406 | 200 | (4) | To suppliers of goods |
|---|---|---|---|---|---|
| From investment revenue | (2) | 3 | 70 | (5) | To employees |
| From sale of cash equivalents | (3) | 2 | 3 | (8) | For insurance |
|  |  |  | 21 | (9) | For bond interest |
|  |  |  | 35 | (10) | For income taxes |

**Investing Activities:**

| Sale of machine components | (11) | 17 | 25 | (13) | Purchase of LT invest. |
|---|---|---|---|---|---|
|  |  |  | 23 | (14) | Purchase of land |

**Financing Activities:**

| Sale of preferred stock | (18) | 75 | 60 | (16) | Retirement of bonds |
|---|---|---|---|---|---|
|  |  |  | 22 | (19) | Payment of dividends |
|  |  |  | 9 | (20) | Purch. of treas. stock |

### Accounts Receivable

|  |  |
|---|---|
| 2 |  |
| 2 (1) |  |

### Allowance for Uncollectibles

|  |  |
|---|---|
|  | 2 |
|  | 2 (1) |

### Prepaid Insurance

|  |  |
|---|---|
| 4 |  |
| 4 (8) |  |

### Inventory

|  |  |
|---|---|
| 5 |  |
| (4) 5 |  |

# Problem 21-20 (continued)

## Investment Revenue Receivable

| | |
|---|---|
| 2 | |
| (2) 2 | |

## Long-term Investments

| | |
|---|---|
| 31 | |
| (2) 6 | |
| (13) 25 | |

## Land

| | |
|---|---|
| 46 | |
| X (14) 46 | |

## Buildings and Equipment

| | |
|---|---|
| 12 | |
| X (15) 82 | 70 (11) |

## Accumulated Depreciation

| | |
|---|---|
| 23 | |
| (11) 35 | 12 (6) |

## Patent

| | |
|---|---|
| | 2 |
| | 2 (7) |

## Accounts Payable

| | |
|---|---|
| 15 | |
| (4) 15 | |

## Salaries Payable

| | |
|---|---|
| 5 | |
| (5) 5 | |

## Bond Interest Payable

| | |
|---|---|
| | 4 |
| | 4 (9) |

## Income Tax Payable

| | |
|---|---|
| | 2 |
| (10) 2 | |

X Noncash investing and financing activity

# Problem 21-20 (continued)

### Deferred Tax Payable

| | |
|---|---|
| | 3 |
| | 3 (10) |

### Notes Payable

| | |
|---|---|
| | 23 |
| | 23 (14) X |

### Lease Liability

| | |
|---|---|
| | 82 |
| | 82 (15) X |

### Bonds Payable

| | |
|---|---|
| 60 | |
| (16) 60 | |

### Discount on Bonds

| | |
|---|---|
| | 3 |
| | 3 (9) |

### Common Stock

| | |
|---|---|
| | 20 |
| | 20 (17) |

### Paid-in Capital

| | |
|---|---|
| | 10 |
| | 10 (17) |

### Preferred Stock

| | |
|---|---|
| | 75 |
| | 75 (18) |

### Retained Earnings

| | |
|---|---|
| | 15 |
| (17) 30 | 67 (12) |
| (19) 22 | |

### Treasury Stock

| | |
|---|---|
| 9 | |
| (20) 9 | |

X Noncash investing and financing activity

## INCOME STATEMENT ACCOUNTS

### Sales

|        | 410     |
|--------|---------|
|        | 410 (1) |

### Investment Revenue

|        | 11     |
|--------|--------|
|        | 11 (2) |

### Gain on Sale of Treasury Bills

|        | 2     |
|--------|-------|
|        | 2 (3) |

### Cost of Goods Sold

| 180     |        |
|---------|--------|
| (4) 180 |        |

### Salaries Expense

| 65     |        |
|--------|--------|
| (5) 65 |        |

### Depreciation Expense

| 12     |        |
|--------|--------|
| (6) 12 |        |

### Patent Amortization Expense

|  | 2 |  |
| --- | --- | --- |
| (7) | 2 |  |

### Bad Debts Expense

|  | 8 |  |
| --- | --- | --- |
| (1) | 8 |  |

### Insurance Expense

|  | 7 |  |
| --- | --- | --- |
| (8) | 7 |  |

### Bond Interest Expense

|  | 28 |  |
| --- | --- | --- |
| (9) | 28 |  |

### Income Tax Expense

|  | 45 |  |
| --- | --- | --- |
| (10) | 45 |  |

### Extraordinary Loss (Flood)

|  | 18 |  |
| --- | --- | --- |
| (11) | 18 |  |

### Tax Savings

|  |  | 9 |  |
| --- | --- | --- | --- |
|  |  | 9 | (10) |

### Net Income (Income Summary)

|  |  | 67 |  |
| --- | --- | --- | --- |
| (12) | 67 |  |  |

*Problem 21-20 (concluded)*

---

**Arduous Company**
**Statement of Cash Flows**
For year ended December 31, 2006 ($ in millions)

**Cash flows from operating activities:**
*Cash inflows:*

| | | |
|---|---:|---:|
| From customers | $406 | |
| From investment revenue | 3 | |
| From sale of cash equivalents | 2 | |
| *Cash outflows:* | | |
| To suppliers of goods | (200) | |
| To employees | (70) | |
| For insurance expense | (3) | |
| For bond interest expense | (21) | |
| For income taxes | (35) | |
| *Net cash flows from operating activities* | | $ 82 |
| | | |
| **Cash flows from investing activities:** | | |
| Sale of machine components | 17 | |
| Purchase of long-term investment | (25) | |
| Purchase of land | (23) | |
| *Net cash flows from investing activities* | | (31) |
| | | |
| **Cash flows from financing activities:** | | |
| Retirement of bonds payable | (60) | |
| Sale of preferred stock | 75 | |
| Payment of cash dividends | (22) | |
| Purchase of treasury stock | (9) | |
| *Net cash flows from financing activities* | | (16) |
| | | |
| **Net increase in cash** | | 35 |
| | | |
| Cash balance, January 1 | | 81 |
| Cash balance, December 31 | | $116 |

**Noncash investing and financing activities:**

Acquired $82 million building by 15-year capital lease.
Acquired $46 million of land by issuing cash and a 15%, 4-year note as follows:

| | |
|---|---:|
| Cost of land | $46 |
| Cash paid | 23 |
| Note issued | $23 |

# CASES

## Communication Case 21-1

# Memorandum

*To:*   Mr. Robert James
*From:* Your Name
*Date:* Current Date
*RE:*   Discrepancy between profitability and cash flows

Our operating results for the first half of the year demonstrate that it is possible for operating activities to simultaneously produce a positive net income and negative net cash flows.  Net income was $5 million.  Cash flow from operating activities for the period was negative $16 million.

Generally accepted accounting principles permit us to report cash flows by either of two methods – the direct or the indirect approach as follows:

($ in millions)

[Direct Method]

**Cash flows from operating activities:**

*Cash inflows:*

| | |
|---|---|
| From customers ($75 - 20) | $55 |

*Cash outflows:*

| | | |
|---|---|---|
| To suppliers of goods ($30 + 15 – 2) | (43) | |
| For other expenses ($35 - 7) | (28) | |
| *Net cash flows from operating activities* | | $(16) |

## Case 21-1 (concluded)

| [Indirect Method] | | |
|---|---|---|
| **Cash flows from operating activities:** | | |
| Net income | $ 5 | |
| *Adjustments for noncash effects:* | | |
| Depreciation expense | 5 | |
| Increase in accounts receivable | (20) | |
| Increase in inventory | (15) | |
| Increase in accounts payable | 2 | |
| Increase in accrued expenses payable | 7 | |
| *Net cash flows from operating activities* | | $(16) |

The reason for the apparent discrepancy between cash flows and net income is due to the way the two items are measured. Net income (or loss) is the result of combining the revenues earned during the reporting period, *regardless of when cash is received*, and the expenses incurred in generating those revenues, *regardless of when cash is paid*. We refer to this as the "accrual concept" of accounting. On the other hand, "cash flows from operating activities" are both inflows and outflows of cash that result from the same activities that are reported on the income statement. In other words, this classification of cash flows includes the elements of net income, but reported on a cash basis.

Let me know if I can provide you additional details.

# Judgment Case 21-2

```
                          Daring Company
                      Statement of Cash Flows
            For year ended December 31, 2006 ($ in 000s)


  Cash flows from operating activities:
  Cash inflows:
    From customers ($100 - 25)                              $75
  Cash outflows:
    To suppliers of goods ($50 + 20 - 10)                  (60)
    For remaining expenses ($25 - 5)                       (20)
  Net cash flows from operating activities                        $ (5)


  Cash flows from investing activities:
    Purchase of operational assets (given)                        (55)


  Cash flows from financing activities:
    Issuance of note payable                               $ 45
    Issuance of common stock                                 20
  Net cash flows from financing activities                          65

    Net increase in cash                                          $ 5
  Cash balance, January 1                                           0
  Cash balance, December 31                                        $5
```

Your concerns are justified in the sense that cash flows are insufficient to cover existing interest charges, not to mention additional charges from new debt. In fact, the principal on the debt of $45,000 will come due shortly in addition to additional interest. Although net income is positive, cash flows from operating activities are negative. A difference between cash flows and net income can exist due to the way the two items are measured. Net income, measured on an accrual basis, is the difference between the revenues earned during the reporting period, *regardless of when cash is received*, and the expenses incurred in generating those revenues, *regardless of when cash is paid*. Cash flows from operating activities are inflows and outflows of cash resulting from the same activities that are reported on the income statement.

# Case 21-2 (concluded)

On the other hand, the negative cash flow from operations is not reason, in and of itself, for rejecting the application. Profit is positive. The reason net income is measured on an accrual basis rather than a cash basis is that very often, net income is a better indication of performance, particularly long-term performance, than cash flow. However, many promising companies that have reported profits have failed due to cash shortages. Good business managers understand that bottom line net income has little to do with maintaining solvency. By being able to accurately predict the timing and amounts of cash flows, companies can remain afloat and also avoid financing charges caused by having to undertake emergency borrowing, as is the case here.

The bottom line is that additional information is needed. One cause of the negative operating cash flows is the acquisition of a large amount of inventory that is unsold. If product demand is strong, this is favorable. Why are those inventories unsold? What is the projected growth rate in revenues? Another concern may be the rather high balance in accounts receivable. Cash collected from customers was only 75% of sales for the year. Is credit policy too lax? On the other hand, if the uncollected receivables arose primarily as a result of heavy year-end sales and are eminently collectible, the cash flow situation will benefit. Another practical consideration is the fact that the bank already has a $45,000 investment in this new company, an investment that likely will be lost if the company is denied the new funds it seeks.

# Integrating Case 21-3

## Requirement 1

### Calculation of the present value of lease payments

$$\$391,548 \times 15.32380^{\Phi} \quad = \quad \$6,000,000$$
(rounded)

$\Phi$ present value of an annuity due of $1: n=20, i=3%

Richards would report the $6,000,000* investment in the protein analyzer and its financing with a capital lease as a significant noncash investing and financing activity in the disclosure notes to the financial statements.

The $783,096 ($391,548 x 2) cash lease payments *, ** are divided into the interest portion and the principal portion. The interest portion, $168,254, is reported as cash outflows from operating activities. The principal portion, $391,548 + 223,294, is reported as cash outflows from financing activities.

Note: By the indirect method of reporting cash flows from operating activities, we would add back to net income the $300,000 depreciation expense since it didn't actually reduce cash. The $168,254 interest expense that reduced net income actually did reduce cash [the interest portion of the $783,096 ($391,548 x 2) cash lease payments], so for it, no adjustment to net income is necessary.

### Calculations:

**September 30, 2006***

| | | |
|---|---|---|
| Leased equipment (calculated in req. 1)............................ | 6,000,000 | |
| Lease payable (calculated in req. 1) .............................. | | 6,000,000 |
| | | |
| Lease payable ................................................................ | 391,548 | |
| Cash (rental payment)................................................ | | 391,548 |

**December 31, 2006****

| | | |
|---|---|---|
| Interest expense (3% x [$6 million – 391,548]) ................ | 168,254 | |
| Lease payable (difference)............................................. | 223,294 | |
| Cash (rental payment)................................................ | | 391,548 |
| | | |
| Depreciation expense ($6 million / 5 years x ¼ year) ....... | 300,000 | |
| Accumulated depreciation............................................ | | 300,000 |

# Case 21-3 (continued)

## Requirement 2

Advanced would report the $6,000,000* direct financing lease of the protein analyzer as a significant noncash investing activity (acquiring one asset and disposing of another) in the disclosure notes to the financial statements.

The $783,096 ($391,548 x 2) cash lease payments [*], [**] are divided into the interest portion and the principal portion. The interest portion, $168,254, is reported as cash inflows from operating activities. The principal portion, $391,548 + 223,294, is reported as cash inflows from investing activities.

Note: By the indirect method of reporting cash flows from operating activities, the $168,254 interest revenue that increased net income actually did increase cash [the interest portion of the $783,096 ($391,548 x 2) cash lease payments], so for it, no adjustment to net income is necessary.

## Calculations:
### September 30, 2006*

| | | |
|---|---|---|
| Lease receivable ($391,548 x 20)............................... | 7,830,960 | |
| Unearned interest revenue ($7,830,960 – 6,000,000) ... | | 1,830,960 |
| Inventory of equipment (lessor's cost)........................ | | 6,000,000 |
| | | |
| Cash (rental payment) ......................................... | 391,548 | |
| Lease receivable................................................ | | 391,548 |

### December 31, 2006**

| | | |
|---|---|---|
| Cash (rental payment) ......................................... | 391,548 | |
| Lease receivable................................................ | | 391,548 |
| | | |
| Unearned interest revenue ............................... | 168,254 | |
| Interest revenue (3% x [$6,000,000 – 391,548]) ........... | | 168,254 |

*Case 21-3 (continued)*

### Requirement 3

Makers would report the $6,000,000* sales-type lease of the protein analyzer as a significant noncash activity in the disclosure notes to the financial statements.

The $783,096 ($391,548 x 2) cash lease payments[*],[**] are considered to be cash flows from operating activities. A sales-type lease differs from a direct financing lease in that we assume the lessor is actually selling its product, an operating activity. Thus, both the interest portion, $168,254, and the principal portion, $391,548 + 223,294, are reported as cash inflows from operating activities.

Note: By the indirect method of reporting cash flows from operating activities, the $1,000,000 (Sales revenue: $6,000,000 – Cost of goods sold: $5,000,000) dealer's profit must be deducted from net income because it is included in net income but won't increase cash flows until the lease payments are collected over the next five years. This addition, however, occurs automatically as we make the usual adjustments for the change in receivables (to adjust sales to cash received from customers) and for the change in inventory (to adjust cost of goods sold to cash paid to suppliers).

The $168,254 interest revenue that increased net income actually did increase cash [the interest portion of the $783,096 ($391,548 x 2) cash lease payments], so for it, no adjustment to net income is necessary. The principal portion, $391,548 + 223,294, must be added because it is not otherwise included in net income. This, too, though, occurs automatically as we make the usual adjustments for the change in receivables (to adjust sales to cash received from customers).

***Noncash adjustments to convert net income to cash flows from operating activities:***

| | |
|---|---:|
| Increase in lease receivable............................ | ($7,830,960) |
| Increase in unearned interest (contra lease receivable) | 1,830,960 |
| Decrease in inventory of equipment.............. | 5,000,000 |
| Decrease in lease receivable, Sept. 30........... | 391,548 |
| Decrease in lease receivable, Dec. 31............. | 391,548 |
| Decrease in unearned interest (contra lease receivable), Dec. 31 | (168,254) |

*Case 21-3 (concluded)*

**Calculations:**

**September 30, 2006***

| | | |
|---|---|---|
| Lease receivable ($391,548 x 20)..................................... | 7,830,960 | |
| Cost of goods sold (lessor's cost)..................................... | 5,000,000 | |
|    Sales revenue (present value) ........................................ | | 6,000,000 |
|    Unearned interest revenue ($7,830,960 – 6,000,000) ... | | 1,830,960 |
|    Inventory of equipment (lessor's cost)......................... | | 5,000,000 |
| | | |
| Cash (rental payment)......................................................... | 391,548 | |
|    Lease receivable................................................................ | | 391,548 |

**December 31, 2006****

| | | |
|---|---|---|
| Cash (rental payment)......................................................... | 391,548 | |
|    Lease receivable................................................................ | | 391,548 |
| | | |
| Unearned interest revenue ............................................. | 168,254 | |
|    Interest revenue (3% x [$6,000,000 – 391,548]) ........... | | 168,254 |

# Research Case 21-4

## Requirement 1

From Microsoft's disclosure note regarding unearned revenue:

---

### Unearned Revenue

.... The percentage of revenue recorded as unearned due to undelivered elements ranges from approximately 15% to 25% of the sales price for Windows XP Home, approximately 5% to 15% of the sales price for Windows XP Professional, and approximately 1% to 15% of the sales price for desktop applications. .......

So, 5% to 15% of the sales price for Windows XP Professional is initially recorded as unearned revenue.

## Requirement 2

The statement of cash flows includes "unearned revenue" as an addition to net income in the operations section because this is the amount of revenue collected in cash but not included in the income statement. Conversely, "recognition of unearned revenue" is included as a deduction from net income because this amount previously recorded as unearned revenue when collected, now is being recognized – included in revenue. The recognition now does not increase cash, so subtracting this amount serves to convert net income to a cash basis. Microsoft reported these two items separately rather than just adjusting net income for the change in the unearned revenue account balance because, even though adjusting for the net change would produce the same net result, the dollar amounts are sufficiently large that separate reporting is deemed more informative.

## Requirement 3

Stock-based compensation is recorded as a fraction of the fair value of such compensation (restricted stock, stock options, SARs) on the date of grant. There is no cash flow associated with such compensation, so the expense is added back to net income to remove this noncash item from the determination of cash from operating activities.

# Analysis Case 21-5

## Requirement 1

(a)

### Cash

| | | |
|---|---|---|
| Beginning balance | **?** | |
| Net increase (from SCF) | 183 | |
| | | |
| Ending balance | 360 | |

Beginning Cash + Net increase in cash = Ending Cash

Beginning Cash + 183 = 360
Beginning Cash = 360 - 183

Beginning Cash = $\boxed{177}$

(b)

### Accounts Receivable

| | | | |
|---|---|---|---|
| Beginning balance | 252 | | |
| Sales (from IS) | 240 | | |
| | | 213 | Collected from customers (from SCF) |
| | | | |
| Ending balance | **?** | | |

Ending Accounts Receivable =
Beginning Accounts Receivable + Sales – Cash collections =
  252         + 240      – 213      = $\boxed{279}$

*Case 21-5 (continued)*

(c)

## Accounts Payable

|  |  | 90 | Beginning balance |
|  |  | ? | Purchases |
| Cash paid to suppliers | 90 |  |  |
|  |  | 120 | Ending balance |

Beginning A/P + Purchases − Cash Paid = Ending A/P

| 90 | + Purchases | − 90 | = 120. |
| 90 | + Purchases | − 90 | = 120. |

Therefore, Purchases = $\boxed{120}$

## Inventory

| Beginning balance | ? |  |  |
| Purchases (from above) | 120 |  |  |
|  |  | 96 | Cost of goods sold (from IS) |
| Ending balance | 180 |  |  |

Beginning Inventory + Purchases − Ending Inventory = Cost of goods sold

| Beginning Inventory | + 120 | − 180 | = 96 |
| Beginning Inventory | = 96 | − 120 + 180 |
| Beginning Inventory | = $\boxed{156}$ |

*Case 21-5 (continued)*

(d)

Gain on sale of equipment was 45; Cash received was 120; therefore, book value of equipment was 75. Since the cost of equipment sold was 150 (600 - 450), accumulated depreciation must have been 75.

**Summary Entry**

| | | |
|---|---|---|
| Cash (from SCF) | 120 | |
| Accumulated depreciation (to balance) | 75 | |
| P, P, & E (450 - 600) | | 150 |
| Gain on sale of equipment (from IS) | | 45 |

**Accumulated Depreciation**

| | |
|---|---|
| | **?**  Beginning balance |
| | 30  Depreciation expense |
| Equipment sold (from above) 75 | |
| | 120  Ending balance |

Beginning Accumulated depreciation + Depreciation expense – Accumulated depreciation on equipment sold = Ending Accumulated depreciation
Beginning Accumulated depreciation + 30 – 75 = 120
Beginning Accumulated depreciation = 120 – 30 + 75 = $\boxed{165}$

(e)

**Income Taxes Payable**

| | |
|---|---|
| | **?**  Beginning balance |
| | 21  Income tax expense |
| Cash paid (from SCF)  27 | |
| | 66  Ending balance |

Beg. Inc. taxes payable + Inc. tax expense – Inc. taxes paid = Ending Inc. taxes payabl
Beg. Inc. taxes payable = Ending Inc. taxes payable + Taxes paid - Inc. tax expense
Beg. Inc. taxes payable =          66          + 27          – 21   = $\boxed{72}$

## Case 21-5 (continued)

(f)

### Retained Earnings

|  |  | 141 | Beginning balance |
|---|---|---|---|
|  |  | 84 | Net income |
| Dividends declared | 9 |  |  |
|  |  | ? | Ending balance |

Ending R/E = Beginning R/E + Net income − Dividends

$$= \quad 141 \quad + 84 \quad - 9 \quad = \boxed{216}$$

### Distinctive Industries
### Comparative Balance Sheets
### At December 31

|  | 2006 | 2005 |
|---|---|---|
| **Assets:** |  |  |
| Cash | $ 360 | $ 177 |
| Accounts receivable (net) | 279 | 252 |
| Inventory | 180 | 156 |
| Property, plant & equipment | 450 | 600 |
| Less: Accumulated depreciation | (120) | (165) |
| Total assets | $1,149 | $1,020 |
|  |  |  |
| **Liabilities and shareholders' equity:** |  |  |
| Accounts payable | $ 120 | $ 90 |
| General and administrative expenses payable | 27 | 27 |
| Income taxes payable | 66 | 72 |
| Common stock | 720 | 690 |
| Retained earnings | 216 | 141 |
| Total liabilities and shareholders' equity | $1,149 | $1,020 |

*Case 21-5 (concluded)*

**Requirement 2**

**Distinctive Industries**
Statement of Cash Flows
For the Year Ended December 31, 2006
($ in millions)

*Cash flows from operating activities:*
| | | |
|---|---|---|
| Net income | $ 84 | |
| *Adjustments to net income:* | | |
| Depreciation expense | 30 | |
| Gain on sale of equipment | (45) | |
| Increase in accounts receivable (net) * | (27) | |
| Increase in inventory ** | (24) | |
| Increase in accounts payable *** | 30 | |
| Decrease in income taxes payable **** | (6) | |
| Net cash inflows from operating activities | | $42 |

| | |
|---|---|
| * | $279 – 252 = $27 |
| ** | $180 – 156 = $24 |
| *** | $120 – 90 = $30 |
| **** | $66 – 72 = $(6) |

# Real World Case 21-6

## Requirement 1

In the three years, Cingular's largest investing activity was construction and capital expenditures. Investments used a large amount of cash as well. In fact, the single largest expenditure was for the acquisition of AT&T in 2004. A look at financing activities reveals that funds from external financing were insufficient to fund these and other investments. In fact, in 2003, financing activities produced a decrease, not an increase, in cash. The bulk of the funds for investments came from cash provided by operations (internal financing) in each year.

## Requirement 2

Transactions that involve merely transfers from cash to "cash equivalents" such as the purchase of a CD should not be reported in the statement of cash flows. A dollar amount is simply transferred from one "cash" account to another "cash" account so that the *total* of cash and cash equivalents is not altered by such transactions. An exception is the sale of a cash equivalent at a gain or loss. In this case, the *total* of cash and cash equivalents actually increases or decreases. The increase or decrease is reported as a cash flow from operating activities.

## Requirement 3

The sale of debt and the sale of stock are reported as financing activities.

## Requirement 4

The payment of cash dividends to shareholders is classified as a financing activity, but paying *interest* to creditors is classified as an *operating activity*. This is because "cash flows from operating activities" should reflect the cash effects of items that enter into the determination of net income. Interest expense is a determinant of net income. A dividend, on the other hand, is a *distribution of net income* and *not an expense*.

*Case 21-6 (concluded)*
**Requirement 5**

A statement of cash flows reports transactions that cause an increase or a decrease in cash. However, some transactions that do not increase or decrease cash, but which result in significant investing and financing activities, must be reported in related disclosures. Entering a significant investing activity and a significant financing activity as two parts of a single transaction does not limit the value of reporting these activities. Examples of noncash transactions that would be reported:

- Acquiring an asset by incurring a debt payable to the seller.

- Acquiring an asset by entering into a capital lease.

- Converting debt into common stock or other equity securities.

- Exchanging noncash assets or liabilities for other noncash assets or liabilities.

# Ethics Case 21-7

Discussion should include these elements.

## The apparent situation:

There seems to be at least superficial evidence that income is being artificially propped up by management practices that might not be healthy for the company in the long run. Ben apparently suspects the motivation may be partly due to management compensation tied to reported profits.

## Ethical Dilemma:

Does Ben have an obligation to challenge the questionable practices? If his suspicions are confirmed, what action, if any, should he take?

## Who is affected?:
Ben
President, controller, and other managers
Shareholders
Potential shareholders
The employees
The creditors
The company's auditors

# Real World Case 21-8

## Requirement 1

Cash flows from operating activities are both inflows and outflows of cash that result from the same activities that are reported on the income statement. The income statement, however, reports the activities on an accrual basis. This means that the income statement reports revenues earned during the reporting period, *regardless of when cash is received*, and the expenses incurred in generating those revenues, *regardless of when cash is paid*. Cash flows from operating activities, on the other hand, report those activities when the cash is exchanged (i. e., on a cash basis).

## Requirement 2

Depreciation is the major contributor to the Northwest having positive cash flows from operating activities despite a net loss. When using the indirect method, the net cash increase or decrease from operating activities is derived indirectly by starting with reported net income, or net loss in this case, and "working backwards" to convert that amount to a cash basis. Amounts that were subtracted in determining net income or loss, but which did not reduce cash, are added back to net income to reverse the effect of the amounts having been subtracted. Depreciation and amortization expense is one example. In 2004, that was $731 million for Northwest.

## Requirement 3

When assets are sold at a gain, the gain is not reported as a cash inflow from operating activities. A gain (or loss) is simply the difference between cash received in the sale of an asset and the book value of the asset; it's not a cash flow. The cash effect of the transaction is reported as an investing activity. To report the gain as a cash flow from operating activities, in addition to reporting the entire cash flow from investing activities, would be to report the gain twice.

# Research Case 21-9

The results students report will vary depending on the companies chosen. It can be interesting to have students compare in class their findings with those of their classmates.

Most companies use the indirect method to report operating activities. Adjustments to net income in reconciling net income and cash flows from operations are reported on the face of the statement of cash flows when the indirect method is used and in a separate reconciliation schedule when the direct method is used.

The cash payments for interest and for taxes are reported on the face of the statement of cash flows when the direct method is used and in a separate disclosure note when the indirect method is used.

Significant investing activities can point to new directions in which the company may be moving or perhaps may indicate that investment funds are being invested in passive peripheral activities for lack of profitable opportunities in mainstream operations.

What combination of debt and equity does a company use to finance its activities? Significant financing activities in recent years can point to shifts in that combination.

# Analysis Case 21-10

1. FedEx is expanding its business as evidenced by the investing activities. External financing need not be sufficient to fund those investments because of the substantial internal financing provided by operating activities. Notice that dividends to shareholders are relatively small, so most funds from operating activities are being reinvested in the business.

2. The six activities listed under financing activities for the 2004 fiscal year are ($ in millions):

| Financing Activities | 2004 | 2003 | 2002 |
|---|---|---|---|
| Principal payments on debt | (319) | (10) | (320) |
| Proceeds from debt issuances | 1,599 | -- | -- |
| Proceeds from stock issuances | 115 | 81 | 88 |
| Dividends paid | (66) | (60) | -- |
| Purchase of treasury stock | (179) | (186) | (177) |
| Other, net | -- | 1 | 3 |
| | --------- | --------- | --------- |
| Cash from financing activities | 1,150 | (174) | (406) |

The statement tells us that FedEx borrowed much more cash in 2004 than it paid to retire debt after not borrowing any the two previous years. Also noteworthy is that FedEx paid no dividends prior to 2003. A relatively small amount of cash also was received from sale of stock. [Reference to FedEx's Statement of Changes in Common Stockholders' Investment tells us that stock was sold or granted under employee benefit plans rather than being sold to the public.]

3. Companies are required to separately disclose cash payments for both interest and income taxes. When the direct method is used to report operating activities, those amounts automatically are shown. But when a company uses the indirect method as FedEx does, supplemental disclosure is needed. Note 14 in the disclosure notes serves this purpose:

---

**Note 14: Supplemental Cash Flow Information**
Cash paid for interest expense and income taxes for the years ended May 31 was as follows:

| In thousands | 2004 | 2003 | 2002 |
|---|---|---|---|
| Interest (net of capitalized interest) | $151 | $125 | $146 |
| Income taxes | 364 | 53 | 312 |

---

# Appendix A  Derivatives

## QUESTIONS FOR REVIEW OF KEY TOPICS

### Question A-1
These instruments "derive" their values or contractually required cash flows from some other security or index.

### Question A-2
The FASB has taken the position that the income effects of the hedge instrument and the income effects of the item being hedged should be recognized at the same time.

### Question A-3
If interest rates change, the change in the debt's fair value will be less than the change in the swap's fair value. The gain or loss on the $500,000 notional difference will not be offset by a corresponding loss or gain on debt. Any increase or decrease in income resulting from a hedging arrangement would be a result of hedge ineffectiveness such as this.

### Question A-4
A futures contract is an agreement between a seller and a buyer that calls for the seller to deliver a certain commodity (such as wheat, silver, or treasury bond) at a specific future date, at a *predetermined* price. Such contracts are actively traded on regulated futures exchanges. If the "commodity" is a *financial instrument*, such as a Treasury bill, commercial paper, or a CD, the contract is called a financial futures agreement.

### Question A-5
An interest rate swap exchanges fixed interest payments for floating rate payments, or vice versa, without exchanging the underlying notional amount.

### Question A-6
All derivatives without exception are reported on the balance sheet as either assets or liabilities at fair (or market) value. The rationale is that (a) derivatives create either rights or obligations that meet the FASB's definition of assets or liabilities and (b) fair value is the most meaningful measurement.

### Question A-7
A gain or loss from a cash flow hedge is deferred as other comprehensive income until it can be recognized in earnings along with the earnings effect of the item being hedged.

# EXERCISES

## Exercise A-1

Indicate (by abbreviation) the type of hedge each activity described below would represent.

### Hedge Type
FV.   Fair value hedge
CF.   Cash flow hedge
FC.   Foreign currency hedge
N.    Would not qualify as a hedge

### Activity
_FV_ 1.   An options contract to hedge possible future price changes of inventory.
_CF_ 2.   A futures contract to hedge exposure to interest rate changes prior to replacing bank notes when they mature.
_CF_ 3.   An interest rate swap to synthetically convert floating rate debt into fixed rate debt.
_FV_ 4.   An interest rate swap to synthetically convert fixed rate debt into floating rate debt.
_FV_ 5.   A futures contract to hedge possible future price changes of timber covered by a firm commitment to sell.
_CF_ 6.   A futures contract to hedge possible future price changes of a forecasted sale of tin.
_FC_ 7.   ExxonMobil's net investment in a Kuwait oil field.
_CF_ 8.   An interest rate swap to synthetically convert floating rate interest on a stock investment into fixed rate interest.
_N_ 9.   An interest rate swap to synthetically convert fixed rate interest on a held-to-maturity debt investment into floating rate interest.
_CF_ 10. An interest rate swap to synthetically convert floating rate interest on a held-to-maturity debt investment into fixed rate interest.
_FV_ 11. An interest rate swap to synthetically convert fixed rate interest on a stock investment into floating rate interest.

# Exercise A-2
## Requirement 1

|  | January 1 | March 31 | June 30 |
|---|---|---|---|
| Fair value of interest rate swap | 0 | $6,472 | $11,394 |
| Fair value of note payable | $200,000 | $206,472 | $211,394 |
| Fixed rate | 10% | 10% | 10% |
| Floating rate | 10% | 8% | 6% |
| Fixed interest receipts |  | $5,000 | $5,000 |
| Floating payments |  | 4,000 | 3,000 |
| Net interest receipts (payments) |  | $1,000 | $2,000 |

*Exercise A-2 (concluded)*

**Requirement 2**
**January 1**

| | | |
|---|---|---|
| Cash | 200,000 | |
|    Notes payable | | 200,000 |
| *To record the issuance of the note* | | |

**March 31**

| | | |
|---|---|---|
| Interest expense ([10% x ¼] x $200,000) | 5,000 | |
|    Cash | | 5,000 |
| *To record interest* | | |
| | | |
| Cash ($5,000 – ([8% x ¼] x $200,000)) | 1,000 | |
|    Interest expense | | 1,000 |
| *To record the net cash settlement* | | |
| | | |
| Interest rate swap [asset] ($6,472 - 0) | 6,472 | |
|    Holding gain – interest rate swap | | 6,472 |
| *To record change in fair value of the derivative* | | |
| | | |
| Holding loss - hedged note | 6,472 | |
|    Note payable ($206,472, – 200,000) | | 6,472 |
| *To record change in fair value of the note* | | |

**June 30**

| | | |
|---|---|---|
| Interest expense ([10% x ¼] x $200,000) | 5,000 | |
|    Cash | | 5,000 |
| *To record interest* | | |
| | | |
| Cash ($5,000 – ([6% x ¼] x $200,000)) | 2,000 | |
|    Interest expense | | 2,000 |
| *To record the net cash settlement* | | |
| | | |
| Interest rate swap [asset] ($11,394 - 6,472) | 4,922 | |
|    Holding gain – interest rate swap | | 4,922 |
| *To record change in fair value of the derivative* | | |
| | | |
| Holding loss - hedged note | 4,922 | |
|    Note payable ($211,394 – 206,472 ) | | 4,922 |
| *To record change in fair value of the note* | | |

# Exercise A-3
## Requirement 1

|  | January 1 | March 31 | June 30 |
|---|---|---|---|
| Fair value of interest rate swap | 0 | $6,472 | $11,394 |
| Fair value of investment | $200,000 | $206,472 | $211,394 |
| Fixed rate | 10% | 10% | 10% |
| Floating rate | 10% | 8% | 6% |
| Fixed interest payments |  | $5,000 | $5,000 |
| Floating interest receipts |  | (4,000) | (3,000) |
| Net interest payments |  | $1,000 | $2,000 |

*Exercise A-3 (concluded)*

**Requirement 2**

**January 1**

| | | |
|---|---|---|
| Investment in notes | 200,000 | |
|    Cash | | 200,000 |

*To record the investment of the note*

**March 31**

| | | |
|---|---|---|
| Cash | 5,000 | |
|    Interest revenue ([10% x ¼] x $200,000) | | 5,000 |

*To record interest*

| | | |
|---|---|---|
| Interest revenue | 1,000 | |
|    Cash ($5,000 – ([8% x ¼] x $200,000)) | | 1,000 |

*To record the net cash settlement*

| | | |
|---|---|---|
| Holding loss – interest rate swap | 6,472 | |
|    Interest rate swap [liability] ($6,472 - 0) | | 6,472 |

*To record change in fair value of the derivative*

| | | |
|---|---|---|
| Investment in notes ($206,472, – 200,000) | 6,472 | |
|    Holding gain - hedged investment | | 6,472 |

*To record change in fair value of the investment*

**June 30**

| | | |
|---|---|---|
| Cash | 5,000 | |
|    Interest revenue ([10% x ¼] x $200,000) | | 5,000 |

*To record interest*

| | | |
|---|---|---|
| Interest revenue | 2,000 | |
|    Cash ($5,000 – ([6% x ¼] x $200,000)) | | 2,000 |

*To record the net cash settlement*

| | | |
|---|---|---|
| Holding loss – interest rate swap | 4,922 | |
|    Interest rate swap [liability] ($11,394 – $6,472) | | 4,922 |

*To record change in fair value of the derivative*

| | | |
|---|---|---|
| Investment in notes ($211,394 – 206,472) | 4,922 | |
|    Holding gain - hedged investment | | 4,922 |

*To record change in fair value of the investment*

# Exercise A-4
**Requirement 1**

|  | **June 30** |  |
|---|---|---|
| Fair value of interest rate swap | $11,394 | |
| Fair value of note payable | $220,000 | |
| Fixed rate | 10% | |
| Floating rate | 6% | |
| Fixed receipts | $5,000 | ([10% x ¼ ] x $200,000) |
| Floating payments | (3,000) | ([6% x ¼ ] x $200,000) |
| Net interest receipts (payments) | $ 2,000 | |

*Exercise A-4 (concluded)*

**Requirement 2**

Your entries would be the same whether there was or was not an additional rise in the fair value of the note (higher than that of the swap) on June 30 due to investors' perceptions that the creditworthiness of LLB was improving. When a note's fair value changes by an amount different from that of a designated hedge instrument for reasons unrelated to interest rates, we ignore those changes. We recognize only the fair value changes in the hedged item that we can attribute to the risk being hedged (interest rate risk in this case). The entries would be:

**June 30**

| | | |
|---|---|---|
| Interest expense ([10% x ¼] x $200,000) | 5,000 | |
|    Cash | | 5,000 |
| *To record interest* | | |
| | | |
| Cash ($5,000 – ([6% x ¼] x $200,000)) | 2,000 | |
|    Interest expense | | 2,000 |
| *To record the net cash settlement* | | |
| | | |
| Interest rate swap [asset] ($11,394 - 6,472) | 4,922 | |
|    Holding gain – interest rate swap | | 4,922 |
| *To record change in fair value of the derivative* | | |
| | | |
| Holding loss - hedged note | 4,922 | |
|    Note payable ($211,394 – 206,472 ) | | 4,922 |
| *To record change in fair value of the note due to interest* | | |

# Exercise A-5

**January 1**

| | | |
|---|---|---|
| Cash | 200,000 | |
|    Notes payable | | 200,000 |

*To record the issuance of the note*


**March 31**

| | | |
|---|---|---|
| Interest expense ([10% x ¼] x $200,000) | 5,000 | |
|    Cash | | 5,000 |

*To record interest*


| | | |
|---|---|---|
| Cash ($5,000 – ([8% x ¼] x $200,000)) | 1,000 | |
| Interest rate swap ($6,472 - 0) | 6,472 | |
|    Interest revenue ([10% x ¼] x $0) | | 0 |
|    Holding gain - interest rate swap (to balance) | | 7,472 |

*To record the net cash settlement, accrued interest on the*
*swap, and change in fair value of the derivative*


| | | |
|---|---|---|
| Holding loss - hedged note | 6,472 | |
|    Notes payable ($206,472 – 200,000) | | 6,472 |

*To record change in fair value of the note due to interest*


**June 30**

| | | |
|---|---|---|
| Interest expense ([8% x ¼] x $206,472) | 4,129 | |
| Notes payable (difference) | | 871 |
|    Cash ([10% x ¼] x $200,000) | | 5,000 |

*To record interest*


| | | |
|---|---|---|
| Cash ($5,000 – ([6% x ¼] x $200,000)) | 2,000 | |
| Interest rate swap ($11,394 – 6,472) | 4,922 | |
|    Interest revenue ([8% x ¼] x $6,472) | | 129 |
|    Holding gain - interest rate swap (to balance) | | 6,793 |

*To record the net cash settlement, accrued interest on the*
*swap, and change in fair value of the derivative*


| | | |
|---|---|---|
| Holding loss - hedged note | 5,793 | |
|    Notes payable ($211,394 – 206,472 + 871) | | 5,793 |

*To record change in fair value of the note due to interest*

# Exercise A-6
**Requirement 1**

|  | June 30 |
|---|---|
| Fair value of interest rate swap | $11,394 |
| Fair value of note payable | $220,000 |
| Fixed rate | 10% |
| Floating rate | 6% |
| Fixed receipts | $5,000   ([10% x ¼ ] x 200,000) |
| Floating payments | (3,000)  ([6% x ¼ ] x 200,000) |
| Net interest receipts (payments) | $2,000 |

*Exercise A-6 (concluded)*

**Requirement 2**

Your entries would be the same whether there was or was not an additional rise in the fair value of the note (higher than that of the swap) on June 30 due to investors' perceptions that the creditworthiness of LLB was improving. When a note's fair value changes by an amount different from that of a designated hedge instrument for reasons unrelated to interest rates, we ignore those changes. We recognize only the fair value changes in the hedged item that we can attribute to the risk being hedged (interest rate risk in this case). The entries would be:

**June 30**

| | | |
|---|---|---|
| Interest expense ([8% x ¼] x $206,472) | 4,129 | |
| Notes payable (difference) | | 871 |
| Cash ([10% x ¼] x $200,000) | | 5,000 |
| *To record interest* | | |

| | | |
|---|---|---|
| Cash ($5,000 – ([6% x ¼] x $200,000)) | 2,000 | |
| Interest rate swap ($11,394 – 6,472) | 4,922 | |
| Interest revenue ([8% x ¼] x $6,472) | | 129 |
| Holding gain - interest rate swap (to balance) | | 6,793 |
| *To record the net cash settlement, accrued interest on the* | | |
| *swap, and change in fair value of the derivative* | | |

| | | |
|---|---|---|
| Holding loss - hedged note | 5,793 | |
| Notes payable ($211,394 – 206,472 + 871) | | 5,793 |
| *To record change in fair value of the note due to interest* | | |

# PROBLEMS

## Problem A-1

### Requirement 1

|  | January 1 | December 31 | | |
|---|---|---|---|---|
|  | 2006 | 2006 | 2007 | 2008 |
| Fixed rate | 8% | 8% | 8% | 8% |
| Floating rate | 8% | 9% | 7% | 7% |
| Fixed receipts |  | $ 8,000 | $8,000 | $8,000 |
| Floating payments |  | 9,000 | 7,000 | 7,000 |
|   Net interest receipts (payments) |  | $(1,000) | $1,000 | $ 1,000 |

### Requirement 2

**January 1, 2006**

| | | |
|---|---|---|
| Cash | 100,000 | |
|   Notes payable | | 100,000 |

*To record the issuance of the note*

**December 31, 2006**

| | | |
|---|---|---|
| Interest expense (8% x $100,000) | 8,000 | |
|   Cash | | 8,000 |

*To record interest*

| | | |
|---|---|---|
| Interest expense | 1,000 | |
|   Cash  ($8,000 – [9% x $100,000]) | | 1,000 |

*To record the net cash settlement*

| | | |
|---|---|---|
| Holding loss - interest rate swap (to balance) | 1,783 | |
|   Interest rate swap (0 - $1,783) | | 1,783 |

*To record the change in fair value of the derivative*

| | | |
|---|---|---|
| Notes payable ($98,217 – 100,000) | 1,783 | |
|   Holding gain - hedged note | | 1,783 |

*To record change in fair value of the note*

# Problem A-1 (continued)

## Requirement 3

**December 31, 2007**

| | | |
|---|---|---|
| Interest expense (8% x $100,000) | 8,000 | |
|     Cash | | 8,000 |

*To record interest*

| | | |
|---|---|---|
| Cash  ($8,000 – [7% x $100,000]) | 1,000 | |
|     Interest expense | | 1,000 |

*To record the net cash settlement*

| | | |
|---|---|---|
| Interest rate swap ($935 – [1,783]) | 2,718 | |
|     Holding gain - interest rate swap (to balance) | | 2,718 |

*To record the change in fair value of the derivative*

| | | |
|---|---|---|
| Holding loss - hedged note ($100,935 – 98,217) | 2,718 | |
|     Notes payable (to balance) | | 2,718 |

*To record change in fair value of the note due to interest*

## Problem A-1 (continued)

### Requirement 4

**December 31, 2008**

| | | |
|---|---|---|
| Interest expense (8% x $100,000) | 8,000 | |
| Cash | | 8,000 |

*To record interest*

| | | |
|---|---|---|
| Cash  ($8,000 – [7% x $100,000]) | 1,000 | |
| Interest expense | | 1,000 |

*To record the net cash settlement*

| | | |
|---|---|---|
| Holding loss - interest rate swap (to balance) | 935 | |
| Interest rate swap (0 - $935) | | 935 |

*To record the change in fair value of the derivative*

| | | |
|---|---|---|
| Notes payable ($100,000 – 100,935) | 935 | |
| Holding gain - hedged note | | 935 |

*To record change in fair value of the note due to interest*

| | | |
|---|---|---|
| Note payable | 100,000 | |
| Cash | | 100,000 |

*To repay the loan*

## Problem A-1 (continued)

### Requirement 5

|  | Swap | | | Note | | |
|---|---|---|---|---|---|---|
| Jan. 1, 2006 | | | | | | 100,000 |
| Dec. 31, 2006 | | | 1,783 | | 1,783 | |
| Balance | | | 1,783 | | | 98,217 |
| | | | | | | |
| Dec. 31, 2007 | 2,718 | | | | | |
| | | | | | | 2,718 |
| Balance | 935 | | | | | 100,935 |
| | | | | | | |
| Dec. 31, 2008 | | | 935 | | 935 | |
| | | | | | 100,000 | |
| Balance | 0 | | | | | 0 |

# Problem A-1 *(continued)*

## Requirement 6

### Income Statement + (−)

| 2006 | (8,000) | Interest expense |
| | (1,000) | Interest expense |
| | (1,783) | Holding loss – interest rate swap |
| | 1,783 | Holding gain – hedged note |
| | (9,000) | Net effect – same as floating interest payment on swap |
| | | |
| 2007 | (8,000) | Interest expense |
| | 1,000 | Interest expense |
| | 2,718 | Holding gain – interest rate swap |
| | (2,718) | Holding loss – hedged note |
| | (7,000) | Net effect – same as floating interest payment on swap |
| | | |
| 2008 | (8,000) | Interest expense |
| | 1,000 | Interest expense |
| | (935) | Holding loss – interest rate swap |
| | 935 | Holding gain – hedged note |
| | (7,000) | Net effect – same as floating interest payment on swap |

# Problem A-1 (concluded)

## Requirement 7

Your entries would not be affected. When a note's fair value changes by an amount different from that of a designated hedge instrument for reasons unrelated to interest rates, we ignore those changes. We recognize only the fair value changes in the hedged item that we can attribute to the risk being hedged (interest rate risk in this case). The entries still would be:

| | | |
|---|---|---|
| Interest expense (8% x $100,000) | 8,000 | |
|    Cash | | 8,000 |
| *To record interest* | | |
| | | |
| Interest expense | 1,000 | |
|    Cash ($8,000 – [9% x $100,000]) | | 1,000 |
| *To record the net cash settlement* | | |
| | | |
| Holding loss - interest rate swap (to balance) | 1,783 | |
|    Interest rate swap (0 - $1,783) | | 1,783 |
| *To record the change in fair value of the derivative* | | |
| | | |
| Notes payable ($98,217 – 100,000) | 1,783 | |
|    Holding gain - hedged note | | 1,783 |
| *To record change in fair value of the note* | | |

# Problem A-2

## Requirement 1

CMOS has an unrealized gain due to the increase in the value of the derivative (not necessarily the same amount). Because interest rates declined, the swap will enable CMOS to pay the lower floating rate (receive cash on the net settlement of interest). The value of the swap (an asset) represents the present value of expected future net cash receipts. That amount has increased, as has the swap's fair value, creating the unrealized gain. There is an offsetting loss on the bonds (a liability) because the fair value of the company's debt has increased. Because the loss on the bonds exactly offsets the gain on the swap, earnings will neither increase nor decrease due to the hedging arrangement.

## Requirement 2

CMOS would have an unrealized *loss* due to the decrease in the value of the derivative. Because interest rates increased, the swap will cause CMOS to pay the higher floating rate (pay cash on the net settlement of interest). The value of the swap (an asset) represents the present value of expected future net cash receipts. That amount has decreased, as has the swap's fair value, creating the unrealized loss. There is an offsetting gain on the bonds (a liability) because the fair value of the company's debt has decreased. Because the gain on the bonds exactly offsets the loss on the swap, earnings will neither increase nor decrease due to the hedging arrangement.

## Problem A-2 (continued)

### Requirement 3

The unrealized gain on the swap and loss on the bonds would not be affected. When a hedged debt's fair value changes by an amount different from that of a designated hedge instrument for reasons unrelated to interest rates, we ignore those changes. We recognize only the fair value changes in the hedged item that we can attribute to the risk being hedged (due to interest rate risk in this case). Because the loss on the bonds exactly offsets the gain on the swap, earnings will neither increase nor decrease due to the hedging arrangement.

### Requirement 4

There would be an unrealized gain due to the increase in the value of the derivative. There is an unrealized loss on the bonds (a liability). However, the gain on the derivative would be $20,000 more than the loss on the bonds. Because the loss on the bonds is less than the gain on the swap, earnings will increase by $20,000 (ignoring taxes) due to the hedging arrangement, an effect resulting from hedge ineffectiveness. This is an intended effect of hedge accounting. To the extent that a hedge is effective, the earnings effect of a derivative cancels out the earnings effect of the item being hedged. All ineffectiveness of a hedge is recognized currently in earnings.

## Problem A-2 (concluded)

## Requirement 5

There would be an unrealized loss due to a decrease in the value of the derivative, a liability to BIOS. Because interest rates declined, the swap would cause BIOS to receive the lower floating rate (pay cash on the net settlement of interest). The value of the swap represents the present value of expected future net cash payments. That amount has increased, as has the swap's fair value, creating the unrealized loss. There would be an offsetting gain, though, on the bond investment because the fair value of the company's investment has increased. Because the gain on the bonds exactly offsets the loss on the swap (a liability), earnings will neither increase nor decrease due to the hedging arrangement.

# Problem A-3

## Requirement 1

|  | January 1 | December 31 | | |
|---|---|---|---|---|
|  | **2006** | **2006** | **2007** | **2008** |
| Fixed rate | 8% | 8% | 8% | 8% |
| Floating rate | 8% | 9% | 7% | 7% |
| Fixed payments | | $ 8,000 | $8,000 | $8,000 |
| Floating payments | | 9,000 | 7,000 | 7,000 |
| Net interest receipts (payments) | | $(1,000) | $1,000 | $ 1,000 |

## Requirement 2

**January 1, 2006**

| | | |
|---|---|---|
| Cash | 100,000 | |
| Notes payable | | 100,000 |

*To record the issuance of the note*

**December 31, 2006**

| | | |
|---|---|---|
| Interest expense (8% x  $100,000) | 8,000 | |
| Cash | | 8,000 |

*To record interest*

| | | |
|---|---|---|
| Interest expense (8% x $0) | 0 | |
| Holding loss - interest rate swap (to balance) | 2,783 | |
| Interest rate swap (0 - $1,783) | | 1,783 |
| Cash  ($8,000 – [9% x $100,000]) | | 1,000 |

*To record the net cash settlement, accrued interest on the
 swap, and change in fair value of the derivative*

| | | |
|---|---|---|
| Notes payable ($98,217 – 100,000) | 1,783 | |
| Holding gain - hedged note | | 1,783 |

*To record change in fair value of the note due to interest*

## Problem A-3 (continued)

### Requirement 3

**December 31, 2007**

| | | |
|---|---:|---:|
| Interest expense (9% x $98,217) | 8,840 | |
|    Notes payable (difference) | | 840 |
|    Cash (8% x $100,000) | | 8,000 |

*To record interest*

| | | |
|---|---:|---:|
| Cash ($8,000 – [7% x $100,000]) | 1,000 | |
| Interest rate swap ($935 – [1,783]) | 2,718 | |
| Interest expense (9% x $1,783) | 160 | |
|    Holding gain - interest rate swap (to balance) | | 3,878 |

*To record the net cash settlement, accrued interest on the*
*swap, and change in fair value of the derivative*

| | | |
|---|---:|---:|
| Holding loss - hedged note ($100,935 – 98,217 – 840) | 1,878 | |
|    Notes payable (to balance) | | 1,878 |

*To record change in fair value of the note due to interest*

*Problem A-3 (continued)*

**Requirement 4**

**December 31, 2008**

| | | |
|---|---|---|
| Interest expense (7% x  $100,935) | 7,065 | |
| Notes payable (difference) | 935 | |
| Cash  (8% x $100,000) | | 8,000 |

*To record interest*

| | | |
|---|---|---|
| Cash  ($8,000 – [7% x $100,000]) | 1,000 | |
| Holding loss - interest rate swap (to balance) | 0 | |
| Interest rate swap (0 - $935) | | 935 |
| Interest revenue (7% x $935) | | 65 |

*To record the net cash settlement, accrued interest on the swap,*
 *and change in fair value of the derivative*

| | | |
|---|---|---|
| Notes payable ($100,000 – 100,935 + 935) | 0 | |
| Holding gain - hedged note | | 0 |

*To record change in fair value of the note due to interest*

| | | |
|---|---|---|
| Note payable | 100,000 | |
| Cash | | 100,000 |

*To repay the loan*

## Problem A-3 (continued)

### Requirement 5

| | Swap | | | Note | |
|---|---|---|---|---|---|
| *Jan. 1, 2006* | | | | | 100,000 |
| *Dec. 31, 2006* | | 1,783 | | 1,783 | |
| *Balance* | | 1,783 | | | 98,217 |
| | | | | | |
| *Dec. 31, 2007* | 2,718 | | | | 840 |
| | | | | | 1,878 |
| *Balance* | 935 | | | | 100,935 |
| | | | | | |
| *Dec. 31, 2008* | | 935 | | 935 | |
| | | | | 100,000 | |
| *Balance* | 0 | | | | 0 |

## Problem A-3 (continued)

### Requirement 6

**Income Statement + (–)**

| 2006 | (8,000) | Interest expense |
| | (2,783) | Holding loss – interest rate swap |
| | 1,783 | Holding gain – hedged note |
| | (9,000) | Net effect – same as floating interest payment on swap |

| 2007 | (8,840) | Interest expense |
| | (160) | Interest expense |
| | 3,878 | Holding gain – interest rate swap |
| | (1,878) | Holding loss – hedged note |
| | (7,000) | Net effect – same as floating interest payment on swap |

| 2008 | (7,065) | Interest expense |
| | 65 | Interest revenue |
| | (0) | Holding loss – interest rate swap |
| | 0 | Holding gain – hedged note |
| | (7,000) | Net effect – same as floating interest payment on swap |

## Problem A-3 (concluded)

### Requirement 7

Your entries would not be affected. When a note's fair value changes by an amount different from that of a designated hedge instrument for reasons unrelated to interest rates, we ignore those changes. We recognize only the fair value changes in the hedged item that we can attribute to the risk being hedged (interest rate risk in this case). The entries still would be:

| | | |
|---|---|---|
| Interest expense (8% x  $100,000) | 8,000 | |
|    Cash | | 8,000 |
| *To record interest* | | |
| | | |
| Interest expense (8% x $0) | 0 | |
| Holding loss - interest rate swap (to balance) | 2,783 | |
|    Interest rate swap (0 - $1,783) | | 1,783 |
|    Cash  ($8,000 – [9% x $100,000]) | | 1,000 |
| *To record the net cash settlement, accrued interest on the* | | |
| * swap, and change in fair value of the derivative* | | |
| | | |
| Notes payable ($98,217 – 100,000) | 1,783 | |
|    Holding gain - hedged note | | 1,783 |

# CASES

## Real World Case A-1

### Requirement 1

When Johnson & Johnson indicates that it expects that substantially all of the balance of deferred net losses on derivatives will be reclassified into earnings over the next 12 months as a result of transactions that are expected to occur over that period, it is saying that these as-yet-unrecognized net losses will be included in net income. A gain or loss from certain hedges is deferred as other comprehensive income until it can be recognized in earnings along with the earnings effect of the item being hedged.

### Requirement 2

A gain or loss from a "fair value" hedge is recognized immediately in earnings along with the loss or gain from the item being hedged. On the other hand, a gain or loss from a "cash flow" hedge is deferred in the manner described by Johnson & Johnson until it can be recognized in earnings along with the earnings effect of the item being hedged. The hedging transactions referred to by Johnson & Johnson might also include foreign currency hedges used to hedge foreign currency exposure to a forecasted transaction because they are treated as a cash flow hedge.

# Communication Case A-2

Depending on the assumptions made, different views can be convincingly defended. The process of developing and synthesizing the arguments will likely be more beneficial than any single solution. Each student should benefit from participating in the process, interacting first with his or her partner, then with the class as a whole. It is important that each student actively participate in the process. Domination by one or two individuals should be discouraged.

Hedging means taking an action that is expected to produce exposure to a particular type of risk that's precisely the *opposite* of an actual risk to which the company already is exposed. Under existing hedge accounting, if the contract meets specified hedging criteria, the income effects of the hedge instrument and the income effects of the item being hedged should be recognized at the same time.

Arguments raised may focus on a variety of issues including:

- Which hedges should qualify for special accounting? Hedges of risk of loss? Hedges that reduce the variability of outcomes?

- Should treatment be different for fair value hedges and cash flow hedges?

- Should only risk exposures arising from existing assets or liabilities qualify for special accounting? Should anticipated transactions be included also?

- To what extent if any must there be correlation between the gains and losses on the hedge instrument and the item being hedged?

- How should any deferred gain or loss be classified prior to recognition?

# Real World Case A-3

The following is a copy of the 13-Week U.S. Treasury Bill Futures: Settlement Prices as of March 2005:

Listed 13 Week US T-Bill Futures Contracts

| | | |
|---|---|---|
| Months Traded | All Calendar Months | Month Key Code |
| Eligible Months | 6 | |
| Currently Listed | 6 | |
| Last Day of Trading Rule | Futures trading shall terminate at 12:00 noon Chicago time on the business day of the 91 Day U.S. Treasury Bill auction in the week of the third Wednesday of the contract month. | |
| New Contract Listing Rule | The day after the front month expires. | |
| Special Notes | None | |
| CME Rule Book Chapter | 451 | |
| Settlement Type | Cash Settled | |

| Seq. No. | Contract Month | Product Code | First Trade Date | Last Trade Date | Cash Settlement Date | Delete Date |
|---|---|---|---|---|---|---|
| 1 | Mar 2005 | TBH5 | 03/16/04 | 03/14/05 | 03/14/05 | 03/18/05 |
| 2 | Apr 2005 | TBJ5 | 01/19/05 | 04/18/05 | 04/18/05 | 04/22/05 |
| 3 | May 2005 | TBK5 | 02/15/05 | 05/16/05 | 05/16/05 | 05/20/05 |
| 4 | Jun 2005 | TBM5 | 06/15/04 | 06/13/05 | 06/13/05 | 06/17/05 |
| 5 | Sep 2005 | TBU5 | 09/14/04 | 09/19/05 | 09/19/05 | 09/23/05 |
| 6 | Dec 2005 | TBZ5 | 12/14/04 | 12/19/05 | 12/19/05 | 12/23/05 |

**New 13 Week US T-Bill futures contracts to be added on Mar 15, 2005:**

| | | | | | | |
|---|---|---|---|---|---|---|
| | Mar 2006 | TBH6 | | 03/13/06 | 03/13/06 | 03/17/06 |

# Research Case A-4

**[Note: This case requires the student to reference a journal article.]**

## Requirement 1

According to the authors, the primary problems or issues the FASB is attempting to address with the new standard are the following:

- Previous accounting guidance for derivatives and hedging was incomplete. Only a few types of derivatives used today were specifically addressed in accounting standards. SFAS No. 52, Foreign Currency Translation, addresses forward foreign exchange contracts, and SFAS No. 80, Accounting for Futures Contracts, addresses exchange-traded futures contracts. Similarly, those two standards were the only ones that specifically provided for hedge accounting. The Emerging Issues Task Force (EITF) addressed the accounting for some derivatives and for some hedging activities not covered in Statements 52 or 80; however, that effort was on an ad hoc basis. Large gaps remained in the authoritative accounting guidance. Accounting practice had filled some of those gaps on issues such as "synthetic instrument accounting" without any commonly understood limitations on their appropriate use. The result of this accounting hodgepodge was that a) many derivative instruments were carried "off balance sheet" regardless of whether they are part of a hedging strategy, b) practices were inconsistent among entities and for similar instruments held by the same entity, and c) users of financial reports were confused or even misled.

- Previous accounting guidance for derivatives and hedging was inconsistent. Under the previous accounting guidance (FASB standards and EITF consensuses), the required accounting treatment may have differed depending on the type of instrument used in hedging and the type of risk being hedged. For example, an anticipated transaction could qualify as a hedged item only if the hedging instrument was a nonforeign currency futures contract or a nonforeign currency purchased option. Additionally, derivatives were measured differently under the previous accounting standards--futures contracts were reported at fair value, foreign currency forward contracts at amounts that reflect changes in foreign exchange rates but not other value changes, and other derivatives unrecognized or reported at nominal amounts that were a small fraction of the value of their potential cash flows. Other hedge accounting inconsistencies related to level of risk assessment (transaction-based versus entity-wide) and measurement of hedge effectiveness.

## Case A-4 (concluded)

- Previous accounting guidance for derivatives and hedging was complex. The lack of a single, comprehensive approach to accounting for derivatives and hedging made the accounting guidance very complex. The incompleteness of the FASB statements on derivatives and hedging forced entities to look to a variety of different sources, including the numerous EITF issues and nonauthoritative literature, to determine how to account for specific instruments or transactions. Because there was often nothing directly on point, entities were forced to analogize to existing guidance. Because different sources of analogy often conflict, a wide range of answers could often be supported, and no answer was safe from later challenge.

- Effects of derivatives were not apparent. Under the previous varied practices, derivatives may or may not have been recognized in the financial statements. If recognized in the financial statements, realized and unrealized gains and losses on derivatives may have been deferred from earnings recognition and reported as part of the carrying amount (or basis) of a related item or as if they are freestanding assets or liabilities. As a result, users of financial statements found it difficult to determine what an entity has or has not done with derivatives and what the related effects were. It was difficult to understand how financial statements could purport to present financial position without reporting the material benefits and obligations associated with derivative instruments.

## Requirement 2

In considering the issues, the FASB made four fundamental decisions that became the cornerstones of the proposed statement. According to the article, those fundamental decisions were:

- Derivatives are assets or liabilities and should be reported in the financial statements.

- Fair value is the most relevant measure for financial instruments and the only relevant measure for derivatives.

- Only items that are assets or liabilities should be reported as such in the financial statements. A derivative loss should not be reported as an asset because it has no future economic benefit associated with it.

- Hedge accounting should be provided for only qualifying transactions, and one aspect of qualification should be an assessment of offsetting changes in fair values or cash flows.

# Trueblood Accounting Case A-5

A solution and extensive discussion materials accompany each case in the Deloitte & Touche Trueblood Case Study Series. These are available to instructors at: https://secure.deloitte.com/rmtbcs00/casesolutions.asp.